Comparative Learning and Cognition

Comparative Learning and Cognition offers a comprehensive analysis of experimental and field research on learning, cognition, and behavior in nonhuman animals.

Over the past two decades, the field has advanced significantly. While still firmly rooted in the study of behavior, contemporary research now interweaves principles from neuroscience and human cognition. This book emphasizes behavioral plasticity and integrates evolutionary, neuroscientific, and comparative perspectives in examining topics such as associative and nonassociative learning, social learning, tool use, navigation, and communication in nonhuman animals.

With its integrative approach, this is an essential text for core psychology courses on comparative learning and cognition.

Mauricio R. Papini is Professor of Psychology at Texas Christian University, Fort Worth, TX, USA

Kenneth J. Leising is Professor of Psychology at Texas Christian University, Fort Worth, TX, USA

"The book by Papini and Leising constitutes a valuable and comprehensive contribution to the study of the relationship between evolution and behavior across different species. It presents an updated and thorough view of comparative psychology, addressing evolutionary perspectives on learning processes and animal cognition. I highly recommend this book for researchers and students seeking to deepen their understanding of the evolution of biological, psychological, and social aspects related to animal behavior."

Luis Gonzalo de la Casa, *professor at Universidad de Sevilla, Seville, Spain*

"This book offers a fresh and insightful perspective on comparative learning and cognition, grounding current research within a robust evolutionary framework. Clearly written and highly engaging, it will be an invaluable resource for both graduate seminars and advanced undergraduate courses. I look forward to incorporating it into my teaching."

Suzanne E. MacDonald, *professor at York University, Toronto, Canada*

"This textbook offers a precise and balanced introduction to learning and cognition across species. By focusing on behavioral mechanisms—such as association, reinforcement, timing, categorization, and communication—and grounding them in neurobiological evidence, it serves as a reliable resource for both students and experts in comparative cognition."

Tetsuro Matsuzawa, *primatologist and former director of the Kyoto University Primate Research Institute, Kyoto, Japan*

"Papini and Leising integrate evolution thoroughly into their updated discussion of animal learning, scaffolding the reader's understanding much like evolutionary processes scaffolded cognition from simple building blocks to more complex processes. This book presents a much-needed integrative approach to comparative cognition and is a welcome addition to a sparse selection of comparative texts."

Jennifer Vonk, *Professor of Psychology at Oakland University, Rochester, MI, USA*

"This is a remarkable book, remarkable for its solid grounding in evolutionary theory, for the breadth of its coverage (from behavioral plasticity in bacteria to language learning in primates), and for the depth of its scholarship, integrating behavioral and neural levels of analysis."

Michael Domjan, *The University of Texas at Austin, TX, USA, and Doctorem Honoris Causa, Konrad Lorenz University, Bogotá, Colombia*

Comparative Learning and Cognition

Mauricio R. Papini and
Kenneth J. Leising

Routledge
Taylor & Francis Group
NEW YORK AND LONDON

Designed cover image: Mauricio R. Papini and Kenneth J. Leising

First published 2026
by Routledge
605 Third Avenue, New York, NY 10158

and by Routledge
4 Park Square, Milton Park, Abingdon, Oxon, OX14 4RN

Routledge is an imprint of the Taylor & Francis Group, an informa business

ISBN: 978-1-032-51383-6 (hbk)
ISBN: 978-1-032-51381-2 (pbk)
ISBN: 978-1-003-40195-7 (ebk)

DOI: 10.4324/9781003401957

Typeset in ITC Galliard Pro
by Apex CoVantage, LLC

Contents

About the authors

Mauricio R. Papini is Professor of Psychology at Texas Christian University. He received his Ph.D. in psychology from the University of San Luis, Argentina (1987). He was the 2023 recipient of the D. O. Hebb Distinguished Scientific Contributions Award (American Psychological Association, Division 6) and former editor of the *International Journal of Comparative Psychology* (2000–2006). He was twice recipient of the TCU College of Science and Engineering Award for Distinguished Achievement as a Creative Teacher and Scholar (2014, 2015) and recipient of a Fulbright US Scholar Award (2015). He is author of *Comparative Psychology: Evolution and Development of Brain and Behavior* (3rd Edition, 2021, Taylor & Francis) and co-editor of *Evolution of Learning and Memory Mechanisms* together with Mark Krause and Karen Hollis (2022, Cambridge University Press). He is author of about 150 empirical articles reporting research on learning and emotion and numerous theoretical and review articles. His research has focused on the behavioral and neurobiological mechanisms underlying frustration.

Kenneth J. Leising is Professor of Psychology at Texas Christian University. He received his Ph.D. from the University of California, Los Angeles, and completed postdoctoral research at the University of Texas Health Science Center in Houston. He has served as President of the Comparative Cognition Society, Chair of the Committee on Animal Research Ethics (CARE) for the American Psychological Association (APA), and Chair of the Membership and Growth Committee for APA's Division 6 (Behavioral Neuroscience & Comparative Psychology). He was co-editor of a special issue on occasion setting published by *Behavioural Processes* and section editor for the *Encyclopedia of Animal Cognition and Behavior*. He received the Psi Chi Faculty Impact Award from the TCU Chapter of Psi Chi. He is the author of more than 30 empirical articles on learning and cognition, as well as several chapters and review articles. He is the director of the TCU Comparative Cognition Laboratory, which examines how temporal and spatial variables influence visual working memory, discrimination learning, higher-order learning, and cue competition.

Part I

Foundations

1 Evolution

A context for comparative learning and cognition

1.1 Evolution

Evolutionary processes have shaped the genotype of every organism, from the oldest evidence of life on earth (approximately 3.6 billion years ago) to all those alive today. Despite its pervasiveness and enduring influence, the concept of evolution is relatively modern. Although ancient philosophers (e.g., Lucretius, ca. 99–55 BCE) entertained ideas consistent with some key evolutionary concepts, no surviving texts provide a detailed account of evolutionary change. This is due, in part, to the complexity of evolution, a phenomenon resulting from the interplay of evolutionary processes, such as natural selection and genetic drift, and evolutionary patterns, such as the constraints imposed by phylogenetic history and existing variations. ***Evolutionary processes*** can be viewed as innovative forces, whereas ***evolutionary patterns*** can be viewed as forces providing limits for change. For example, ***tetrapods*** (amphibians, reptiles, birds, and mammals) include species adapted for running, swimming, climbing, jumping, or flying (illustrating evolutionary processes), but they share a body plan involving four limbs (illustrating evolutionary patterns).

Species exhibit a mixture of unique and common traits. Unique traits illustrate the role of evolutionary processes resulting in the ***adaptation*** of the organism's morphology and function to its environment. For example, human verbal behavior suggests adaptation to social environments. Common traits illustrate evolutionary patterns and characterize a ***phylogeny***—a lineage of ancestors and descendants. The five-digit hand is an example of a basal, or primitive, trait common to many land vertebrates. Evidence for evolution is found in unique and shared traits across species.

Understanding the evidence for the evolution of animals in different lineages is relevant to the comparative study of ***learning*** and ***cognition***. A once-conventional approach to comparative psychology was to ask whether an organism exhibited a particular trait or not, such as tree climbing. This approach is often referred to as a forced dichotomy—it must either be present or not and assumes organisms evolved in a so-called ladder of life. Full appreciation for evolution changes the approach to the question in two ways. First, any evaluation of the trait must take into consideration whether tree climbing would require different claws, muscles, etc. to be effective in the organism's environment (e.g., characteristics of the bark and wood of the trees that would be climbed). This leads logically to the second, that tree climbing need not appear in only one form. By studying many species across diverse environments, we may isolate what features best represent tree climbing. Using this list of features, a continuum is likely to emerge in which some species demonstrate more of the features than others. This same approach can be applied to learning and cognition (see Figure 1.1).

Evidence for evolution can be found at many levels of analysis, from the set of genes making up the ***deoxyribonucleic acid*** (***DNA***) molecule (genotype) an organism carries to the

DOI: 10.4324/9781003401957-2

Figure 1.1 **Species comparisons.** Comparing the ability of animals using the same test fails to recognize that evolutionary processes resulted in abilities that were successful in the environments in which they evolved. Superior performance by the rat does not necessarily reflect general superiority. (Cartoon by Brianna Bella Vaughan; reproduced with permission from the author.)

observable characteristics (phenotype) of the organism. Given that genotype influences phenotype, it should not be surprising that evidence for evolution is present at all levels.

1.1.1 Evidence

1.1.1.1 Molecular evidence

Evidence for evolutionary processes and patterns can be found in the DNA molecule. An organism's traits (e.g., size, shape, and even learning rate) are determined by an interaction between the expression of sections of DNA (*genes*) as proteins and the environment, both external and internal to the organism. The genetic instruction for proteins is encoded in the sequence of nucleotides (adenine, thymine, guanine, and cytosine) within each gene that, together, make up the DNA molecule. DNA is located inside the cell, either in the cytoplasm as in bacteria or surrounded by a nuclear membrane as in animals. DNA must first undergo transcription into RNA and then translation of RNA into amino acids before a functional protein is manufactured. Importantly, as far as we know, this sequence of events resulting in gene expression is common to all animals. Because it is so detailed a process, it is difficult to argue that the similarity arose by chance. Rather, such similarities point to inheritance from a common ancestor. These steps are illustrated in Figure 1.2.

- *DNA replication.* Duplicates of the DNA molecule are formed during cell division.
- *Transcription.* Conversion of DNA into *RNA* (*ribonucleic acid*).
- *Splicing.* Removal of noncoding sections of RNA (called introns) and fusion of coding sections of RNA (called exons) to form messenger RNA (mRNA).
- *Translation.* mRNA is used as a template to synthesize proteins.

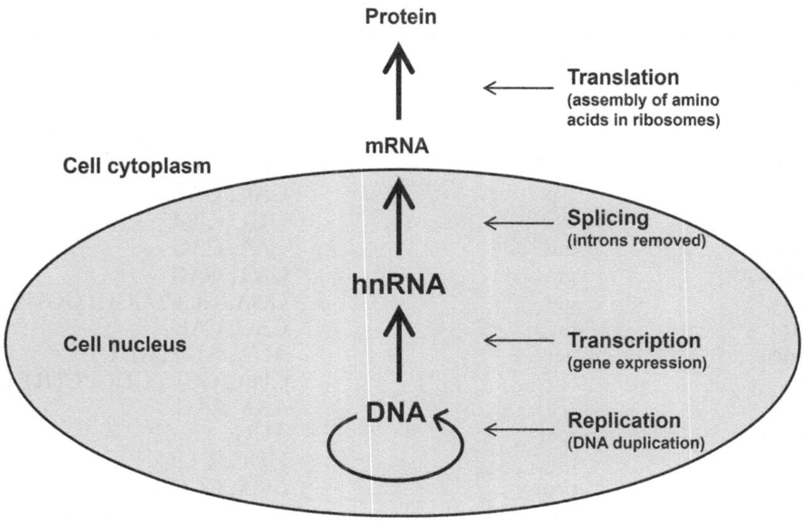

Figure 1.2 **Major steps in the transition from genotype (DNA) to phenotype (the organism).** DNA is replicated during cell division. Portions of DNA are also transcribed within the cell nucleus to form heterogeneous nuclear RNA (hnRNA). Introns are then removed, and exons are spliced together. The edited molecule, messenger RNA (mRNA), is used as a template to synthesize a protein in ribosomes. (Modified from Papini, 2021, with permission from Taylor & Francis.)

During transcription, mRNA mirrors the sequence of nucleotides in the DNA molecule except that thymine is replaced by uracil. Triplets of nucleotides (called *codons*) arranged in a specific order are translated into one of the 20 known *amino acids*, the building blocks of proteins. Translation occurs according to the code described in Table 1.1. Some amino acids are coded by more than one codon. Most codons add amino acids to the building of a protein, but some codons (STOP) terminate the process. The information in this table is not provided to memorize the specific codons corresponding to an amino acid. Rather, it is meant to provide a clear view of the intricacy of this *genetic code*. As was the case for the process of gene expression, it is extremely unlikely that such a code would be common to all animals just by chance, a fact providing a compelling argument for the evolution of animal diversity from a common ancestor (Bacher et al., 2004).

Sequential information in DNA nucleotides and protein amino acids can be compared across species to determine their similarity. When sequences from different species are very similar, the DNA or proteins are said to be homologous. *Homology* reflects inheritance from a common ancestor. Assuming that sequential similarity among species relates to the time since divergence from the common ancestor, the evolutionary history can be represented in a *phylogenetic tree*.

Some proteins are so common to living organisms that it is possible to build a phylogenetic tree that includes a wide array of species, such as plants, fungi, and animals. One such protein, cytochrome-c, participates in the respiratory cycle as part of the electron transport chain and is common to many living organisms (Fitch & Margoliash, 1967). Such a tree shows that animals are more closely related to each other than they are to plants, and mammals are more closely related to each other than they are to birds, reptiles, and fish.

Table 1.1 Genetic code

Amino acid	*Abbreviation*	*mRNA codons*
1. Alanine	ala	GCA, GCC, GCG, GCU
2. Arginine	arg	AGA, AGG, CGA, CGC, CGG, CGU
3. Asparagine	asn	AAC, AAU
4. Aspartic acid	asp	GAC, GAU
5. Cysteine	cys	UGC, UGU
6. Glutamine	gln	CAA, CAG
7. Glutamic acid	glu	GAA, GAG
8. Glycine	gly	GGA, GGC, GGG, GGU
9. Histidine	his	CAC, CAU
10. Isoleucine	ile	AUA, AUC, AUU
11. Leucine	leu	CUA, CUC, CUG, CUU, UUA, UUG,
12. Lysine	lys	AAA, AAG
13. Methionine	met	AUG
14. Phenylalanine	phe	UUC, UUU
15. Proline	pro	CCA, CCC, CCG, CCU
16. Serine	ser	AGC, AGU, UCA, UCC, UCG, UCU
17. Threonine	thr	ACA, ACC, ACG, ACU
18. Tryptophan	trp	UGG
19. Tyrosine	tyr	UAC, UAU
20. Valine	val	GUA, GUC, GUG, GUU
Stop		UAA, UGA, UAG

Note. A: adenine. C: cytosine. G: guanine. U: uracil. Uracil replaces thymine in RNA.

1.1.1.2 Embryology

Basal vertebrate traits such as the notochord (precursor of the vertebrate column), pharynx, and dorsal neural tube appear earlier than derived traits typical of specific groups, such as gill pouches in fish and limbs in tetrapods (Figure 1.3). The phase in which the traits typical of a particular phylum (e.g., vertebrates) appear is called the *phylotypic stage*. The phylotypic stage remains stable across species that show large variation in adult morphology. This observation was first made by Karl von Baer in 1828. Substantial species variation in development may occur before and after the phylotypic stage. Phylotypic stages also suggest common ancestry.

1.1.1.3 Anatomy

Trait similarity is the most important criterion for taxonomic classification. When similarity is observed in details of structure or function, as in the tetrapod limb, it is interpreted as evidence of homology. Limb bones differ in shape and size because they have evolved for different functions (adaptive process) but are recognizable as homologous because of their common relative position (phylogenetic pattern; Figure 1.4). Such commonality points to shared ancestry.

1.1.1.4 Biogeography

Darwin was impressed by the resemblance in the armors of South American fossil glyptodonts and living armadillos (Figure 1.5). There are many examples of faunas limited to

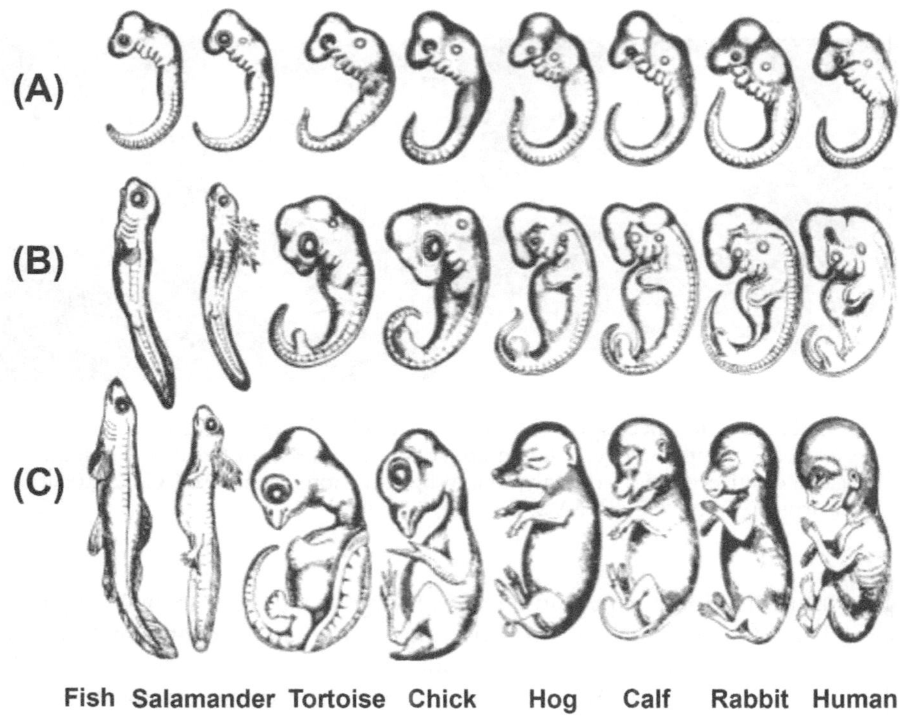

Figure 1.3 **Vertebrate development.** Stages of vertebrate development **(A–C)** as visualized by Haeckel (1879). The phylotypic stage **(A)** is quite advanced relative to fertilization, but it varies little within a particular phylum (e.g., chordates). (From Haeckel, 1879; public domain.)

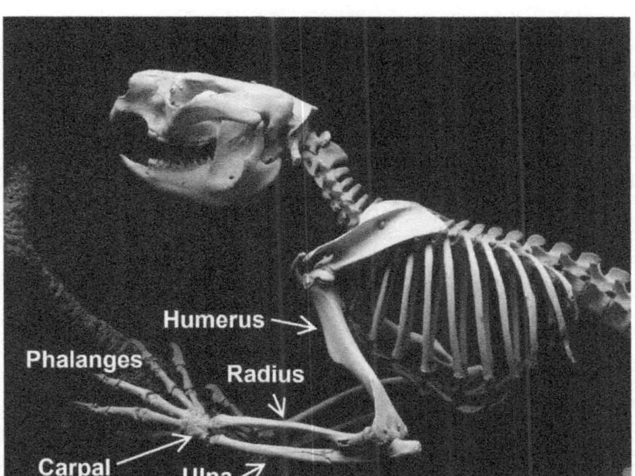

Figure 1.4 **Homology in the arms of tetrapods.** The bones in the arms of all tetrapods contain the same bones in the same sequence. Some bones are missing, enlarged, or reduced in some species, but their relative position is conserved. (Photo from Creative Commons https://search.creativecommons.org; by A. Galassi, license CC BY-ND 2.0.)

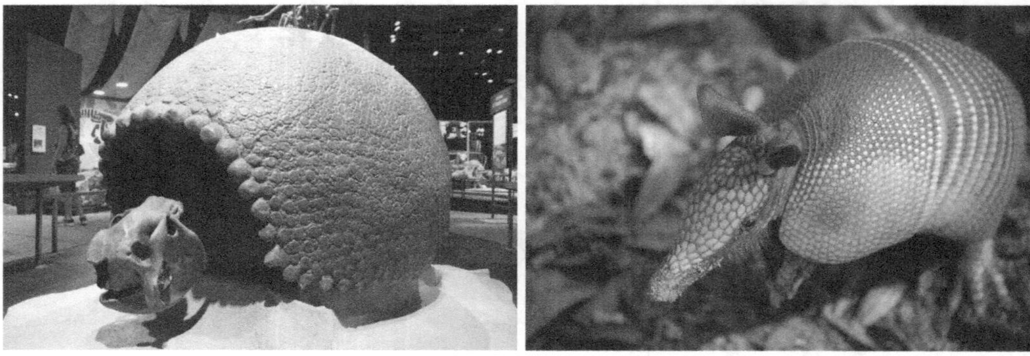

Figure 1.5 **Fossil and living species from the same area.** A fossil glyptodont, an extinct mammal from North and South America, and an armadillo. (Photos from Creative Commons https://search.creativecommons.org; glyptodont by Ryan Somma, license CC BY 2.0; armadillo by mbarrison, license CC BY-SA 2.0.)

particular continents (South American monkeys), large islands (lemurs in Madagascar), and lakes (cichlid fish of African lakes). Biogeography also points to continental drift. For example, all living species of lung fish and flightless birds (rheas, ostriches, cassowaries) live in southern continents (South America, Southern Africa, Australia), a consequence of the proximity of these land masses during the Mesozoic. Galapagos finches, for example, exhibit variation in beak size and shape depending on the food resources available in the islands in which they evolved. Seed eaters have short and strong beaks, whereas finches that feed on cactus flowers have long beaks. These differences represent variations on a basic beak pattern inherited from the common ancestor, probably a species that migrated from South America.

1.1.1.5 Paleontology

Fossil evidence consistent with evolution is found in the sequential appearance of animal groups. Among vertebrates, the oldest known fossil fish appeared in Silurian rocks from China, dated 419 million years ago (Ma) (Zhu et al., 2013). Rocks from that period yield no evidence of tetrapods, which appeared about 300 Ma, during the Devonian, while birds and mammals appeared during the Triassic and Jurassic, some 200 Ma. *Transitional forms* are fossils that provide evidence of the link among different groups of animals. *Archaeopteryx lithographica* (Figure 1.6), a fossil bird from the Jurassic, exhibits a mixture of reptilian (bony tail, teeth) and avian traits (wings).

1.1.1.6 Contemporary evidence

During the European invasion of the Americas beginning in the 15th century, human populations separated for many generations met. Having been exposed to a greater diversity of pathogens because of trade with Asian and African populations, the Europeans had an advantage over native inhabitants, who were decimated in large numbers by common diseases like smallpox, typhus, cholera, and measles brought from Europe by the conquerors (Diamond, 2005). Similarly, the excessive prescription and misuse of antibiotics has recently produced the evolution of antibiotic-resistant bacteria. Mutants that repress the uptake of antibiotics,

Figure 1.6 ***Archaeopterix lithographica.*** A fossil bird from the Jurassic of Germany that displays reptilian and avian traits. Like reptiles, and unlike any living bird, *Archaeopterix* had a bony tail and teeth. Like living birds, *Archaeopterix* had feathers and anterior limbs modified as wings. (Photo reproduced with permission from the Museum für Naturkunde, Berlin, Germany.)

activate their efflux from the bacterium, or simply inactivate the antibiotic had a higher success rate than their nonresistant competitors (Andersson, 2003).

1.1.1.7 Domestication

The ***domestication*** (also known as ***selective breeding*** when implemented in the lab) of animals and plants provides clear examples of evolution. Dogs, cats, cattle, goldfish, and canaries are common domesticated species. Domestication led to varieties with traits that rarely evolve in the animal's typical ecological niche but are useful in terms of companionship, ornamentation, or food production. Domestication inspired Darwin's (1868/1998) notion of ***natural selection.*** Evolutionary processes are natural, irrespective of the environment they operate in or the source of the selective pressure; in "domestication" the selective process is driven by human intervention.

Selective breeding is surprisingly powerful (Figure 1.7). First, a trait is selected in a parental population of randomly bred animals. Second, individuals scoring high (H) in that trait are bred with each other and individuals scoring low (L) are bred with each other to produce the first filial generation. Third, H and L phenotypes continue to be selectively bred in successive generations. A random-mating control (C) assesses the contribution of factors other than selective breeding to the evolution of H and L strains. There are many cases of rapid response of behavioral phenotypes to selective breeding. For example, male guppy fish (***Poecilia reticulata***) selected for the frequency of the sigmoid response (part of the male's courtship

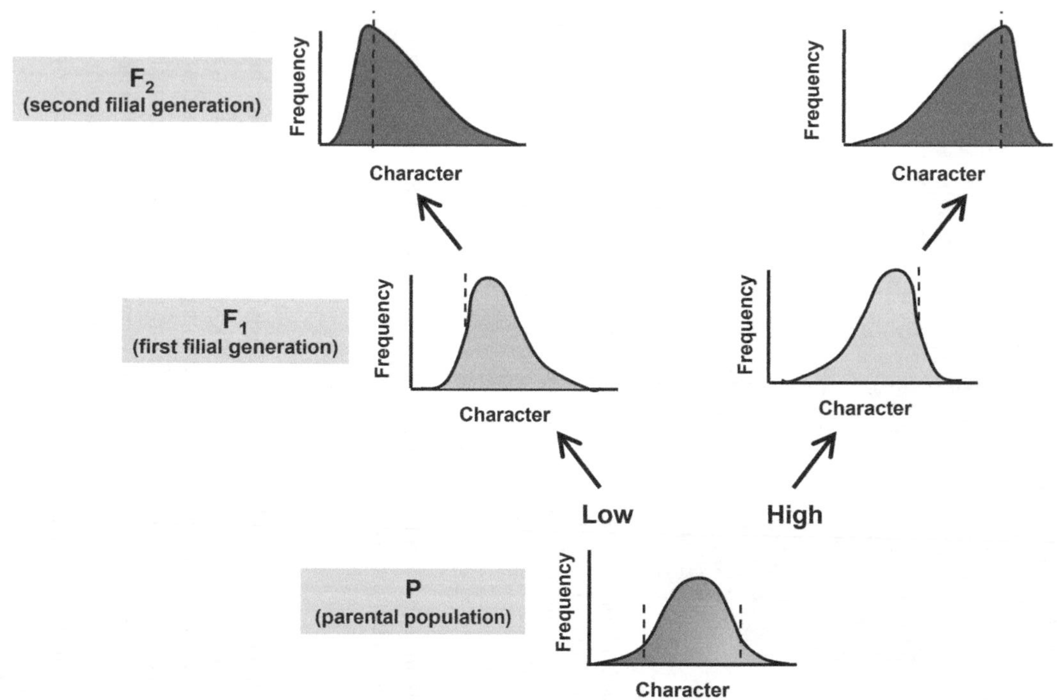

Figure 1.7 **The selective breeding procedure.** Animals scoring high or low on a given trait are paired for mating, thus resulting in the evolution of High and Low strains. A line generated by random mating (omitted in figure) controls for general effects of the procedure. (Modified from Papini, 2021; reproduced with permission from Taylor & Francis.)

display) evolved H and L lines within three generations, whereas a control line exhibited little change (Roubertoux, 1992).

Selective breeding has limitations. First, some behaviors do not respond to selective breeding. Selective breeding modified the sigmoid response of male guppies but did not affect another courtship component involving the spread of fins (Roubertoux, 1992).

Second, in some cases, selective breeding affects only one of the lines. This provides clues about the natural history of the behavior. Aversive olfactory conditioning involves pairing a particular scent with painful or threatening outcomes (e.g., shock). Learning about the relationship is measured by avoidance of the conditioned scent compared to odors not paired with an aversive outcome. Selection for aversive olfactory conditioning in fruit flies (*Drosophila melanogaster*) was successful in the L line but not in the H line (Hewitt et al., 1983). Such selective effect reflects minimal genetic variation for higher levels of olfactory conditioning, a kind of ceiling effect, suggesting that this behavior has been under strong natural selection.

Third, selective breeding on one trait can change other traits. Tryon (1934) selected rats based on the number of errors in a food-reinforced maze-learning task, evolving H ("bright") and L ("dull") lines. Even though selection was successful in both lines, "dull" rats were better than "bright" rats in aversive learning tasks (Searle, 1949). The "bright" rats were successful due to differences in emotionality (e.g., reactivity to stimuli) rather than learning ability. Increased emotionality in "dull" rats impaired food-reinforced learning but enhanced aversive learning.

Fourth, in most cases, relaxing selective pressures after several generations (i.e., letting H and L animals interbreed freely) leads to a regression to the parental trait, implying that selective breeding did not result in stable new phenotypes. One possibility is that alleles present in any population are coadapted because of the past action of natural selection, and selective breeding is only partially disrupting this equilibrium (Dobzhansky, 1970). As shown next, extending selective breeding to a much higher number of generations can result in stable changes.

Selective breeding over a substantial number of generations can induce a novel coadaptation of genes. One example involves H and L lines for geotaxis in *Drosophila melanogaster* (Ricker & Hirsch, 1985). *Geotaxis* is the tendency to move in the direction of the ground (positive geotaxis) or away from the ground (negative geotaxis). Selective breeding for geotaxis started in 1957, and by 1983, after 550 generations, H and L lines had diverged extensively. Starting in generation 415 and for the next 30 generations, selective pressures were occasionally relaxed, but, surprisingly, no regression to the original geotaxis scores was observed in either line. A stable geotaxis suggests that the underlying genes had become associated in coadapted clusters, a process likely to correlate with *speciation*—the evolution of new species. To test whether H and L lines had achieved new stable phenotypes, they were subjected to counterselection and relaxation (Ricker & Hirsch, 1988). If H and L lines were now selected for intermediate scores and the filial populations obtained were relaxed, would the resulting animals regress toward middle geotactic scores or toward their new H and L levels? As shown in Figure 1.8, relaxation produced mixed results for the H line, but regression toward the new phenotypic level was clear in the L line, indicating that L flies had achieved a new homeostatic level. There was also evidence of partial *reproductive isolation*, that is, reduced interbreeding between H and L animals relative to breeding among H or among L animals (Lofdahl et al., 1992). Consistent with incipient speciation, several genes were differentially expressed in H and L animals (Toma et al., 2002). These demonstrations indicate

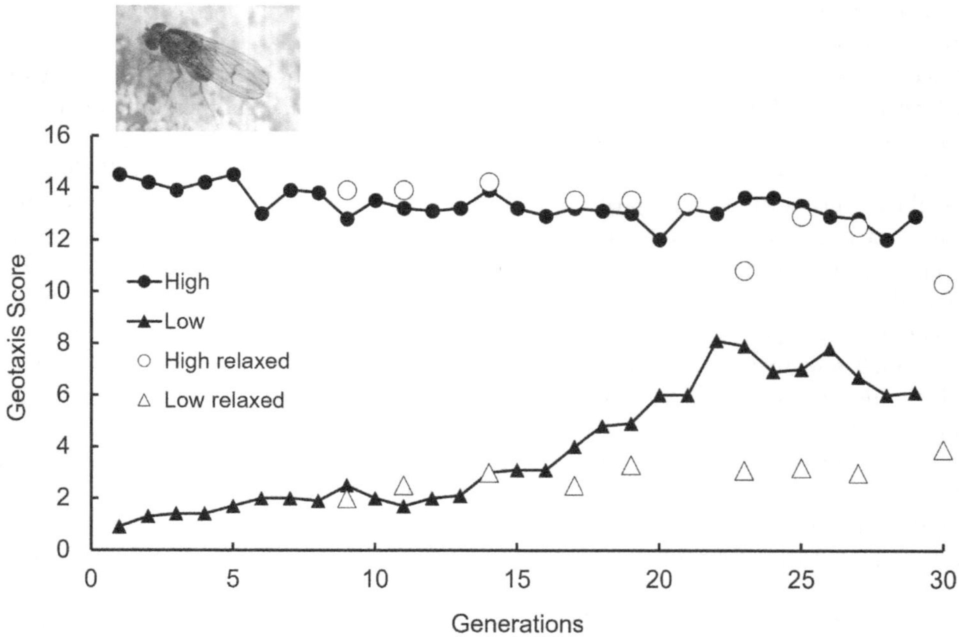

Figure 1.8 **Extensive selective breeding for geotaxis.** H and L lines of fruit flies *Drosophila melanogaster* were selected as a function of their tendency to go against the ground (negative geotaxis, high scores) or toward the ground (positive geotaxis) in a vertical maze of interconnected tubes. Flies were collected at the end of each tube. Flies at the top and bottom tubes were selectively bred to evolve the H and L lines, respectively. This figure shows the results of counterselection, that is, animals in the H line (negative geotaxis) selected for negative geotaxis and animals in the L line (positive geotaxis) selected for negative geotaxis. Occasional relaxation of selective breeding is represented by open circles and open triangles. (From Ricker & Hirsch, 1988; reproduced with permission from the American Psychological Association. *Drosophila* photo from Creative Commons https://search.creativecommons.org, by treegrow, license CC BY 2.0.)

that selective breeding can influence the subsequent distribution of a particular phenotype and, in some conditions, induce long-term changes in genotype.

1.2 Natural selection and adaptation

1.2.1 Logic of natural selection

Darwin argued that if male and female elephants were to procreate freely, and their offspring were to survive and procreate freely, and so on, the Earth would be covered with elephants in a few generations. Despite the potential for exponential growth, populations remain relatively constant over long periods of time because of natural selection. The following three properties are necessary and sufficient for natural selection to operate in a population across generations:

- Phenotypic variation—individual male deer vary in their ability to defend a group of females from other males.

- Differential reproductive success—large male deer can defend female groups more successfully than small males, so they tend to produce more offspring.
- Inheritance—large male deer tend to produce large male offspring.

1.2.2 Natural selection

Natural selection is usually identified with ***reproductive success*** (*RS*), that is, the ability of organisms to pass their genes on to the next generation via offspring. This is referred to as ***direct fitness***. Survival is generally regarded as secondary in importance to RS (Darwin, 1871/1981; Stahlman & Leising, 2018). However, within a given species, animals that live longer tend to bear more offspring than animals that live shorter lives (Stearns, 1992).

In addition to bearing offspring, helping behavior that increases the RS of relatives (genetically related organisms) can lead to the spread of the helper's genes, even if the helper's own direct fitness is reduced (Hamilton, 1964). This is known as ***indirect fitness***, an important factor in the evolution of social behavior. There is evidence for indirect fitness in natural populations that include helpers. In some monogamic birds, such as Florida scrub jays (*Aphelocoma coerulescens coerulescens*), helpers provide infant care and protection against predators for genetically related breeding pairs (Figure 1.9). By contributing to the rearing of siblings (sharing 50% of the genes) and half siblings (sharing 25% of the genes), helper jays could gain sufficient indirect fitness to compensate for the cost of delaying direct reproduction while simultaneously increasing their direct fitness by acquiring a good breeding territory in the future (Woolfenden & Fitzpatrick, 1997).

An organism's ***inclusive fitness*** is equal to the sum of its direct fitness (offspring) plus its indirect fitness (offspring of relatives surviving because of the organism's helping behavior

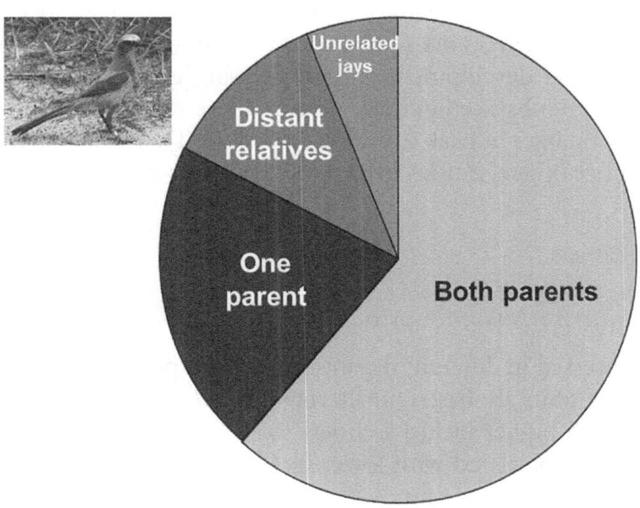

Figure 1.9 **Helpers at the nest.** Scrub jay helpers in the Florida population (*Aphelocoma coerulescens coerulescens*) provide extensive help to young even though this postpones their own reproduction. Helpers tend to support relatives, thus increasing their indirect fitness. (Source: Woolfenden & Fitzpatrick, 1997; photo from Creative Commons https://search.creativecommons.org, by leppyone, license CC BY 2.0.)

weighed by the degree of genetic relatedness). Thus, traits that maximize inclusive fitness evolve by natural selection.

1.2.2.1 *Field observations and experiments*

Evidence suggests that natural selection can lead to surprisingly rapid phenotypic changes. A population of *Geospiza fortis*, a Galapagos finch species, exhibited rapid change across generations in beak and body size correlated with changes in weather (Grant, 1986). After several annual droughts during 1977, 1980, and 1982, large seeds became more abundant than small seeds, and the finch population declined during these years, but survivors tended to have large beaks and body size. Small birds had trouble opening large seeds and thus were more likely to die of starvation. Beak size depends on the expression of a gene known as HMGA2, which varies in finch populations that differ in beak size (Lamichhaney et al., 2016). Thus, selection for variants of a single gene determined whether this population evolved larger or smaller beaks.

At Trinidad Island in the Caribbean, populations of guppies (*Poecilia reticulata*) were transferred to river sections above waterfalls where these fish did not occur (Reznick et al., 1997). Guppies living downstream in the same currents are exposed to a variety of predators, including several cichlid fish that prey preferentially on large guppies. By contrast, guppies introduced into upstream currents were exposed to a single predator, the killifish *Rivulus hartii*, an omnivore that occasionally attacks guppies. After 11 years (about 18 generations), transferred guppies had evolved larger body size, exhibited delayed onset of reproduction, and produced a lower number of fries per spawn.

Two cautionary notes about these results. First, the observed changes in morphology in finches and guppies cannot be unambiguously interpreted as resulting from natural selection. Not only did seed size or predatory pressures differ across years or locations, but other correlated factors might account for phenotypic changes. In the case of guppies, for example, the upstream environment could offer different types of food, in addition to predatory pressures, that could induce changes via *phenotypic plasticity*—environmental factors that influence gene expression and development without causing genetic changes. Second, whereas phenotypic changes were observed in these studies, there was no evidence of speciation—for example, population changes in beak size were reversible. This could be a consequence of the relatively small number of generations involved in these cases.

1.2.3 *Types of direct fitness*

1.2.3.1 *Measuring lifetime reproductive success (LRS)*

Alternative traits expressed in different organisms within a population can convey differential fitness. Provided these traits are based on alternative *alleles* (versions of the same gene), then the trait correlated with higher inclusive fitness would spread in the population across generations, while the one correlated with lower inclusive fitness would decrease in frequency. An accurate assessment of inclusive fitness needs to include the entire reproductive life of an individual—*LRS*.

It is difficult to obtain information on LRS in species with a long reproductive life, as is the case for many mammals. Relevant data were reported on the social behavior of lions, *Panthera leo* (Bygott et al., 1979). Lions are the only large cats that live in stable social groups. In lions, males form coalitions, take over female prides, and tend to kill 6-month-old or younger

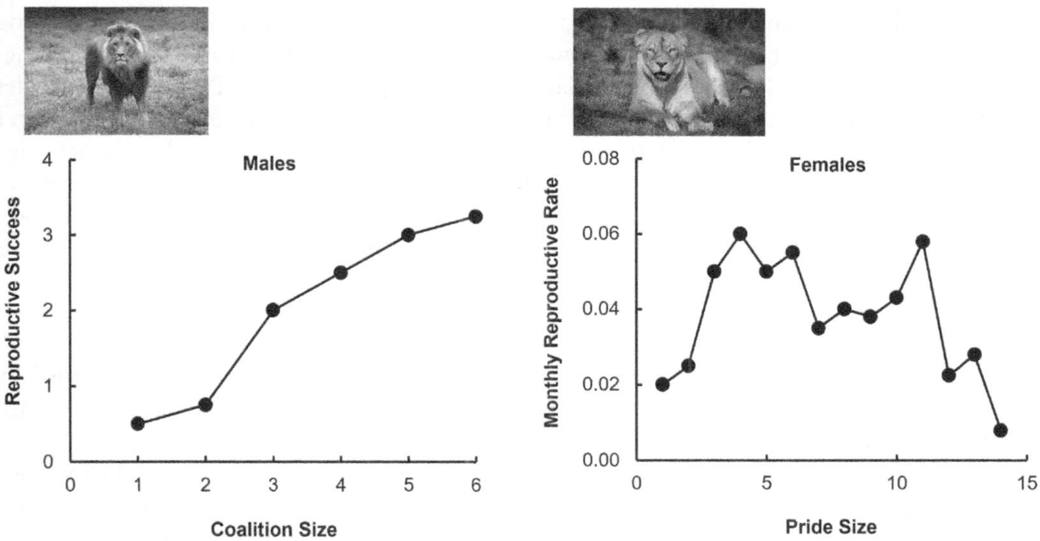

Figure 1.10 **LRS in lions (*Pantera leo*).** Data were obtained in the Serengeti and Ngorongoro areas of Tanzania. (From Packer et al., 1988; reproduced with permission from University of Chicago Press). (Photos from Creative Commons, https://search.creativecommons.org; male: whippets.chrichri, license CC BY-ND 2.0; female: Mathias Appel, license CC0 1.0.)

cubs—about 27% of all cubs die because of infanticide. Infanticide speeds up the females' return to sexual receptivity by an average of 8 months, thus increasing the males' direct fitness, but it reduces the females' direct fitness after a considerable investment in pregnancy, lactation, and infant care. Thus, the contribution of LRS to social grouping must be assessed separately for males and females. In one study (Packer et al., 1988), LRS was defined as the numbers of offspring reaching 12 months of age. In males, LRS increased with the size of the coalition (Figure 1.10). Most solitary males never reproduce, whereas males forming coalitions of up to six animals have increasingly higher LRS. In females, the relationship between grouping and LRS is more complex. Small (1–2 individuals) or large (more than 10) groups of females are correlated with low LRS, but an intermediate group size (3–10 females) is correlated with the highest levels of LRS. Middle-size groups experience fewer takeovers by males and, therefore, low levels of infanticide.

1.2.4 Natural selection and diversity

Male and female lions are exposed to different selective pressures. In males, the larger the group, the higher the LRS. When LRS increases toward one end of the scale, and assuming there is genetic variability in the population, the population mean for that trait will gradually increase (or decrease) over generations. This is *directional selection*. It is possible that the size of male coalitions has been increasing in the recent evolution of social behavior in lions. In evolutionary terms, an increase in coalition size may be limited by excessive in-group conflicts or any consequence that would trigger negative selective pressures.

This could be the case for females, for which either small or large groups were correlated with lower LRS than intermediate group sizes. This is *stabilizing selection*, which tends to reduce trait variability over generations as natural selection favors intermediate phenotypes over extreme phenotypes. Stabilizing selection illustrates opposing selective pressures.

Polymorphisms, or the coexistence of discretely different phenotypes in an interbreeding population, illustrate the action of ***disruptive selection***. In disruptive selection, extreme phenotypes have greater LRS than intermediate ones. For example, North Pacific salmon males migrating from the ocean into rivers for reproduction can be either 2 or 3 years old. Younger males are about one third the size of older males and exhibit different reproductive behavior (Gross, 1985). Older males compete for access to spawning females, whereas younger males remain quiet until an opportunity to fertilize eggs arises (fertilization is external in salmon). These reproductive strategies have evolved as a result of disruptive selection.

1.2.4.1 Traits contributing to survival

Three contributions to direct fitness are recognized: (1) traits that contribute to LRS by improving survival; (2) traits that may not contribute directly to LRS but are correlated with traits that enhance LRS; and (3) traits that evolved through ***sexual selection***.

Many animals must grow and survive from a fertilized egg to sexual maturity before they can reproduce. Genes expressed early in ***development*** can be eliminated if they lead to premature death, which leads to the evolution of developmental programs involving the coordinated action of thousands of genes and intricate gene–environment interactions that produce viable individuals. Survival is important to the extent that it increases individual LRS. A classic example involves changes in protective coloration of peppered moths, *Biston betularia* (Bishop & Cook, 1980). In England, light-colored individuals were common until tree trunks were darkened by industrial pollution. As light-colored individuals settled on dark trunks, they were easily caught by birds, thus leading to an increase of dark-colored moths in industrial areas. When air pollution was reduced by legislation, trees recovered their original coloration, and light-colored individuals again spread in the population.

1.2.4.2 Correlated traits

A gene can exert its effects on several traits during development; this is called ***pleiotropy***. If a trait dependent on this gene contributes significantly to LRS, ***correlated traits*** will likely also increase in frequency even if they do not have adaptive significance. In Galapagos finches, changes in beak size and shape are examples of correlated traits. Therefore, not every trait evolves by natural selection.

Evolution can alter entire sets of traits rather than working trait by trait. Correlated traits may provide a reproductive advantage when environmental conditions change if they can be co-opted into playing new functions. The accumulation of the pigment melanin could result from strong selection of an enzyme that regulates some metabolic process. If external coloration later contributes to LRS, as in the case of peppered moths, then coloration itself would be selected. Traits that are available for selection in this manner are referred to as ***exaptations*** (Gould & Vbra, 1982).

Changes in entire patterns of traits can have important behavioral implications. Consider the case in which natural selection favors the evolution of increased body size in a mammalian lineage because of reduced predation. Since it would take longer to develop a larger body size, a longer lifespan could change parental care, social interactions, and the relative importance of experience. The coordinated evolution of an entire adaptive pattern is called a ***life-history strategy***. In mammals, increased body size is positively correlated with longevity and brain size and negatively correlated with the number of offspring per birth (Eisenberg, 1981).

1.2.4.3 Direct fitness and adaptation

According to the ***adaptationist paradigm***, the environment poses problems and adaptations represent solutions that increase LRS. There are several problems with this view of evolution (Williams, 1966). As an evolutionary process, natural selection goes beyond the physics and chemistry of nature and should be invoked only when simpler processes cannot explain the facts. Flying fish cannot survive outside water, so returning to water after an aerial glide could be seen as adaptive. However, this hypothesis is unnecessary, for the return to water is caused by gravity.

A benefit conferred by an adaptation could be secondary to the trait's function. For example, a fox may take the same path to a foraging site after a heavy snowfall because once the path is opened, it is easier to travel through the snow. However, the fox's paws are adapted for walking and running; opening a path through the snow is a by-product of their morphology.

A trait is not necessarily the best possible solution to a problem. Solutions must be worked out from the available genetic variation and within the constraints imposed by the evolutionary history of the species. Pandas are herbivorous mammals that evolved from carnivorous ancestors. As in most carnivores, the panda's ancestors used the thumb for running, so that this digit is not mobile. But pandas have evolved a bone in the wrist that functions as a thumb, allowing the animal to strip the leaves of bamboo shoots (Gould & Lewontin, 1979). False thumbs have evolved independently in two distantly related panda species (giant panda, *Ailuropoda melanoleuca*, and red panda, *Ailurus fulgens*). Molecular studies show that these two species share two genes that affect limb development and may be responsible for the false thumb (Hu et al., 2017). It is likely that developmental constraints restrict change in the digits because the arm evolved a running function, whereas wrist bones may be less constrained to change.

Historical factors can also restrict the evolutionary pathway taken by a population of animals. For example, the Indian rhinoceros has one horn whereas the African rhinoceros has two horns. It is unlikely that the one horn is more adaptive in India than in Africa and vice versa for two horns (Lewontin, 1978). It is simpler to assume that the founder populations of these two species differed in the genetic diversity underlying this trait, such that different phenotypes prevailed in each population (Liu et al., 2021).

The notion that all behaviors are adaptations that evolved as solutions to environmental problems is probably too simplistic. Evolution is an opportunistic process that draws from available variations to favor the best possible solution (Jacob, 1977). Unlike an engineer, a new species is not designed by evolutionary processes from scratch as if using a blank sheet of paper, but transformed from an old design. A lineage may become extinct when this transformation is not possible.

1.2.5 From morphology to behavior

The same evolutionary logic applied to behavior and morphology can be extended to learning. Behaviors that occur before a biologically relevant event have the advantage of preparing the organism for the event's arrival (Hollis, 1982). The behaviors that support effective territorial defense are different from those that support effective mating with a receptive female, and consequently, both defense and mating would be more effective if the identity (male or female) of an approaching animal was reliably preceded by a stimulus in the environment. In blue gourami fish (*Trichogaster trichopterus*) and Japanese quail (*Coturnix japonica*), males defend small territories against intruders, and females rarely mate with males lacking a territory. Failure to discriminate between an intruder male and a receptive female can lead to maladaptive behavior (e.g., courting a male intruder, attacking a female). Experiments described in detail in Chapter 7 (see Figure 7.3) show that in both species males gain a reproductive advantage when the arrival of a male or female is signaled (Gutiérrez & Domjan, 1996; Hollis et al., 1995). That advantage translated into greater reproductive success, as measured in the blue gourami by number of offspring produced and in Japanese quail by number of sperm released.

1.2.6 Sexual selection and the brain

The connections between ***mating systems*** (ecology, parental care, etc.), spatial behavior, and the brain are illustrated by some of the 65 rodent species of the genus *Microtus*. These species are closely related and similar in body size, diet, and ecology but exhibit different mating systems. Table 1.2 illustrates these characteristics for three species: meadow voles (*M. pennsylvanicus*), montane voles (*M. montanus*), and prairie voles (*M. ochrogaster*).

Consider the connection between polygyny (i.e., males mating with more than one female) and hippocampal size. In polygynous meadow voles, male territories can be 4 to 7 times larger than those of females. The size of male territories varies as a function of season—males defend greater territory during the breeding season. Reproductive success is thus more dependent on spatial navigation for males than for females. Comparative studies show that polygynous males exhibit greater spatial learning abilities and larger hippocampal size (relative to brain size) than female meadow voles. No such sex differences are found in monogamous pine voles, which defend small territories (Jacobs et al., 1990).

Table 1.2 A comparison of three vole species

Microtus	*Common name*	*Mating system*	*Behavior*
ochrogaster	Prairie vole	Monogamy	Grasslands of central North America Burrowing Mainly nocturnal Diet: grass, fruit, seeds, insects Ms and Fs have overlapping territories Ms contribute to infant care Pair bonding Mate preference Aggressive to unfamiliar animals
pennsylvanicus	Meadow vole	Polygyny	North America, from coast to coast Burrowing Active day and night Diet: grass, fruit, fungi, insects Ms defend larger territories than Fs No pair bonding
montanus	Montane vole	Promiscuity	Western North America Burrowing Nocturnal (summer) or diurnal (winter) Ms are territorial No pair bonding

Note. Ms: males. Fs: females. The mating system characterization must be taken with caution because some animals can deviate from the stated system. The behavioral characterization given here describes only general tendencies.

Vole species exhibit diversity in the brain distribution of neurotransmitter receptors involved in social behavior, including vasopressin, oxytocin, and dopamine. Dopamine receptors in the nucleus accumbens, a key area in the reward system, are highly expressed in nonmonogamous species relative to monogamous voles. Interestingly, a single mating event triggers some of these differences. Sexually naïve prairie voles (monogamous) show densities of vasopressin and oxytocin receptors similar to those of nonmonogamous species, but higher densities are observed after pair bonding is established (Gobrogge & Wang, 2016).

Evolution was defined as an interplay between evolutionary processes and evolutionary patterns. Thus far, this chapter has focused on general principles underlying evolutionary processes. These principles can also be applied to evolutionary patterns, that is, to the history of life on Earth. Understanding the phylogenetic connections between animals from different lineages is relevant to the comparative study of learning and cognition.

1.3 Diversity of life

1.3.1 Taxonomy of life

More than 2 million species have been scientifically described (Hannah, 2022), but there may be more than 8 million living species on Earth. Attempting to understand biodiversity begins by putting together organisms that resemble each other. This gave rise to taxonomy, the classification of living organisms.

Each species is scientifically identified by two names, the genus (italicized and capitalized) and the species (italicized but not capitalized). Thus, *Homo sapiens* is the scientific name of humans, "*Homo*" indicating the genus and "*sapiens*" the species. Whereas common names can be vague (e.g., "sparrow" refers to several bird species), scientific names are assigned after rigorous description of the species. Taxonomic classification has a hierarchical structure. Only one species bears the name "*sapiens*," but several species share the same genus based on character similarity (e.g., *H. sapiens, H. habilis, H. erectus*). Species can be grouped into higher-order units called *taxa* (*taxon* in singular), as shown in Figure 1.11, from general (bottom) to specific (top). Similarities in morphology, embryology, behavior, protein structure, and DNA sequence are the main criteria for assigning a particular species to a taxon.

Living organisms are grouped into three domains: Bacteria, Archaea, and Eukarya (Woese et al., 1990). Bacteria are *prokaryotes*, single-celled organisms lacking a membrane-bound nucleus, mitosis, and meiosis. Archaea are also single-cell prokaryotes, notable by their high tolerance of salts and heat. Bacteria and archaea are sufficiently different in their genetics that they seem to have had a long history of divergent evolution, enough to warrant inclusion in different life domains. There are no known multicellular prokaryotes, although some bacteria form colonies. Eukarya is a domain that includes multicellular kingdoms (plants, fungi, and animals) and protists (unicellular organisms). All *eukaryote* cells possess a nuclear membrane surrounding several chromosomes, many cytoplasmatic organelles (ribosomes, mitochondria, chloroplasts, etc.), and a large size (10–100 μm) relative to bacteria and archaea. The amoeba, paramecium, and vorticella are among the most common protists. Multicellular eukaryotes are formed by a mass of cells with various degrees of differentiation, many reproducing sexually and exhibiting true development from a fertilized egg to sexual maturity.

Living bacteria are thought to be direct descendants from the most primitive organisms; protists evolved from bacteria; and plants, fungi, and animals evolved independently from different protist ancestors. Viruses are not included because their status as living organisms

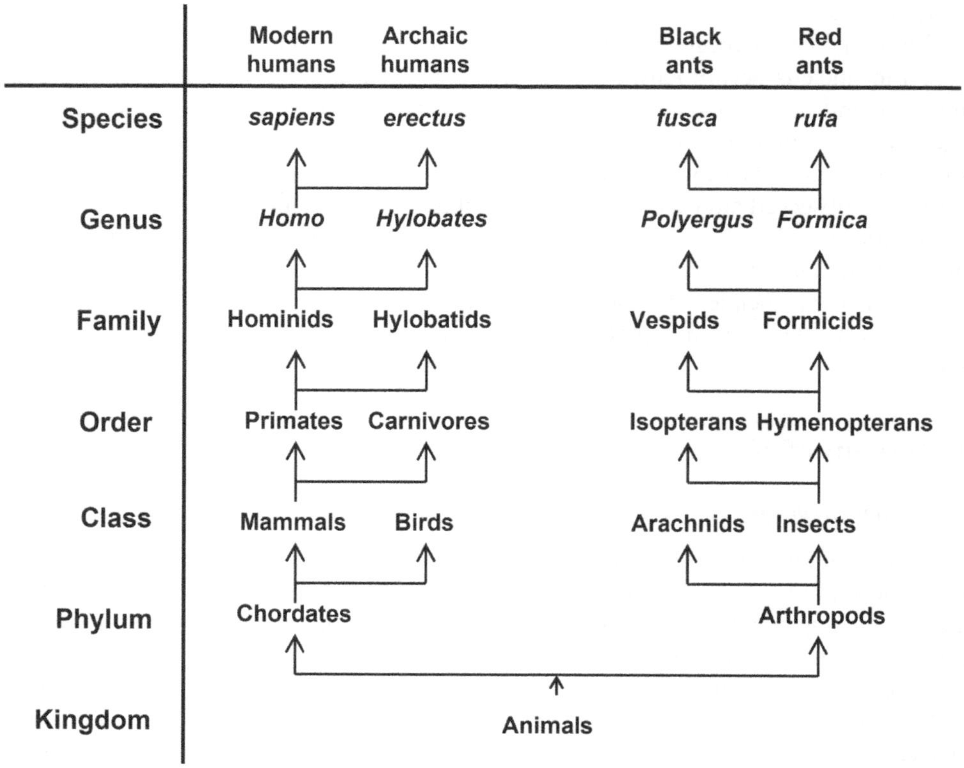

Figure 1.11 **Common taxonomic categories arranged hierarchically.** Two examples are given, humans and ants. Two instances of each particular category are typically included in the immediately higher category. Common names are used for examples in all categories, except for Genus and Species, in which the scientific names are given (e.g., *Homo sapiens*).

depends on the definition of life (Harris & Hill, 2021). Viruses use the familiar genetic code (see Table 1.1), but, lacking ribosomes, they can only proliferate by using another cell's cytoplasmatic machinery.

1.3.2 Animal phyla

By and large, the comparative study of learning and cognition concentrates on animals (but see **Aneural organisms**, Chapter 3). Animals are assigned to 30-something phyla—the exact number is still in dispute. Each animal phylum represents a distinct *body plan*, a set of traits common to all species assigned to that phylum. For example, chordates (including cephalochordates, fish, humans) are characterized by a ventral digestive system and a dorsal nervous system. Figure 1.12 presents several animal phyla and illustrates several points. First, connected lines are hypotheses of relatedness. The graph is called a *phylogenetic tree* because the evolutionary relationships among animal phyla are captured by the tree metaphor. The common ancestor is represented by the trunk of the tree, and the lineages are the branches stemming off by evolutionary *divergence*.

Second, some aspects of animal evolution are well established. For example, flagellate protists (a flagellum allows for movement in water) are hypothesized to be ancestors to all

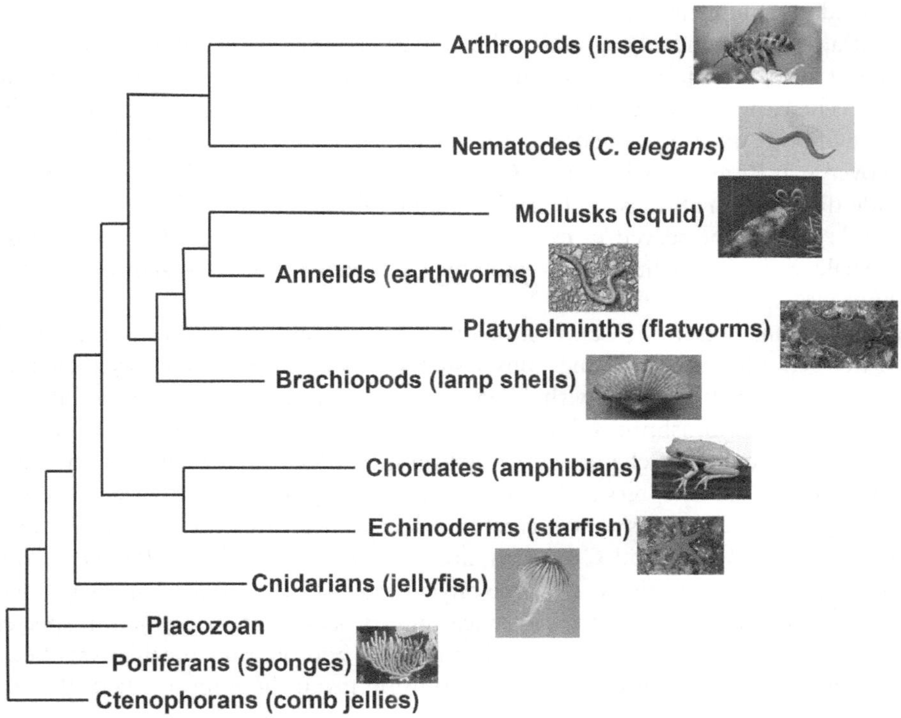

Figure 1.12 **Phylogenetic relationships among some animal phyla based on molecular data.** (Modified from Knoll & Carroll, 1999; photo of *C. elegans* by Ryla Cantergiani, courtesy of Mark A. McCormick; other photos from Creative Commons https://search.creativecommons.org: sponge by Velo Steve, license CC BY-SA 2.0; jellyfish by Fool4myCanon, license CC BY 2.0; starfish by stupidhead, license CC BY-SA 2.0; frog by watts_photos, license CC BY 2.0; brachiopod by GorissM, licensed CC BY-SA 2.0; flatworm by stupidhead, licensed CC BY-SA 2.0; earthworm by Smabs Sputzer (1956–2017), licensed CC BY 2.0; squid by Tracy Candish, licensed CC PDM 1.0; honeybee by tracie7779, license CC BY-SA 2.0.)

animals. Sponges (Porifera), placozoans (Placozoa), and comb jellies (Ctenophora) are basal animal phyla (i.e., morphologically conservative). Sponges and placozoans have different cell types but lack internal organs and neurons. Comb jellies (Ctenophora) and cnidarians (Cnidaria; sea anemones, jellyfish, coral) are characterized by *radial symmetry*—a body organized around one (or more) central axis—and have the simplest nervous systems consisting of diffuse nerve nets. They are diploblastic, that is, a body plan containing two layers of cells: an external layer with skin, muscle, and neuron cells (ectoderm) and an internal layer that functions as a gut (endoderm). Nutrients enter and exit the body through a single opening. All the other animal phyla possess *bilateral symmetry* at some point in their development—an anterior–posterior axis and paired body parts. Bilaterials are triploblastic and thus have three cell layers: ectoderm, mesoderm, and endoderm. The intermediate cell layer (mesoderm) is related to the evolution of larger and more complex organs.

1.3.3 Ediacaran and Cambrian faunas

Fossil animals discovered in pre-Cambrian rocks in the Ediacara Hills, Australia, and subsequently around the world, were formed about 555 Ma (Martin et al., 2000). This *Ediacaran fauna* includes some forms difficult to classify because they show few affinities with known phyla, but a few are generally agreed to be cnidarians similar to jellyfish or sea pens. ***Fossil traces*** as old as 1,000 Ma provide evidence of pre-Cambrian bilateral animals (Seilacher et al., 1998). The early Cambrian (544–520 Ma) is marked by an ***adaptive radiation***, the rapid divergence of body plans, in a phenomenon called the ***Cambrian explosion***. These fossils were first discovered at Burgess Shale, British Columbia, Canada, but this ***Burgess Shale fauna*** has a worldwide distribution (Briggs et al., 1994). Some of these fossils include soft tissue, larvae, and juvenile animals preserved in extraordinary detail (Fu et al., 2019). Specimens in the Burgess Shale fauna can be linked to living phyla, including chordates, arthropods, mollusks, and echinoderms.

Key innovations present in Cambrian animals include an exoskeleton, predatory behavior, and the evolution of central nervous systems (CNSs) in bilaterally organized animals. Associative learning in animals with CNSs may be responsible for the evolution of the Burgess Shale fauna (Ginsburg & Jablonka, 2019). Associative learning is a broad category that encompasses behavior change as a function of the observed relation between stimuli and/or responses (see Chapters 3–4). Associative learning was relevant after the emergence of predator–prey interactions that increased selective pressures for efficient foraging and defensive learning. By the mid-Cambrian, about 520 Ma, chordates (*Pikaia*), arthropods (trilobites), and mollusks (bivalves), three phyla targeted by behavioral studies of learning, had already diverged. Thus, when similar learning processes are identified in species from these phyla, caution should be exercised in inferring homologous mechanisms because of the extensive opportunity for independent evolution given the remoteness of the common ancestor.

1.3.4 Evolution of chordates

Chordates include three major groups: urochordates (tunicates), cephalochordates (lancelets, like *Brachiostoma*), and vertebrates. It is widely accepted that this group is ***monophyletic***, that is, derived from a common ancestor. Urochordates (about 1,300 species) and cephalochordates (about 28 species) are all marine animals. Virtually nothing is known about their learning abilities.

The major vertebrate innovations relate to an active lifestyle: complex sense organs, motor ganglia, and a well-defined brain. Eight or nine classes of vertebrates are usually recognized in the literature, each with basal and derived lineages. Each class represents a tree of radiating branches, of which only one gave rise to another class. Therefore, it is inappropriate to consider a living species from one class as the ancestor of living species from another class. For example, mammals evolved from a group of extinct reptiles known as the cynodonts; therefore, living reptiles (turtles, lizards, crocodiles) cannot be considered as mammalian ancestors because they represent other diverging branches of the reptilian tree. Figure 1.13 shows the appearance of the various vertebrate groups in the fossil record.

There are two major groups of living birds (about 9,000 species), Palaeognathae (including tinamous birds, rheas, ostriches, cassowaries, emus, and kiwis) and Neognathae (including chickens, ducks, quail, penguins, parrots, pigeons, and songbirds). Comparative studies of learning and cognition in Neognathae species is covered extensively in this book. Mammals (Class Mammalia) are by far the most typical species used in comparative research on learning and cognition. Mammals were preceded by cynodonts, a group of reptiles with some mammalian characteristics, including the jaw joint and tooth

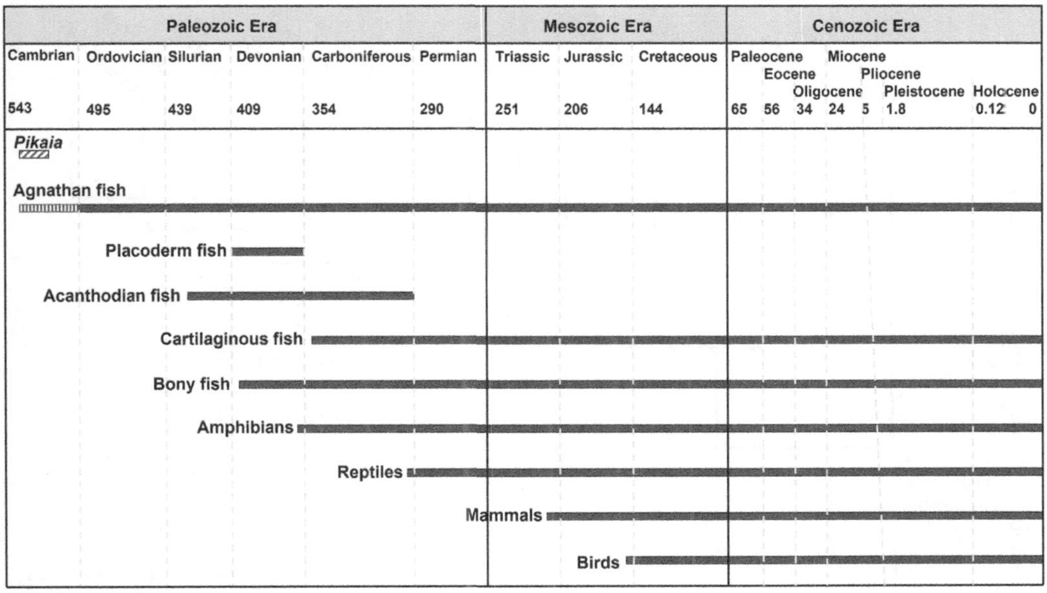

Figure 1.13 **The fossil record of the various classes of vertebrates.** *Pikaia* and similar species from the Cambrian are presumed to be chordates. Placoderms and acanthodians are extinct. (From Papini, 2021; reproduced with permission from Taylor & Francis.)

specialization (incisors, canines, molars), suggesting major changes in feeding behavior (e.g., chewing). *Tooth replacement* in cynodonts was as in living mammals: one replacement from milk teeth to adult teeth. By contrast, teeth are replaced continuously in living reptiles.

Morganucodon, from the late Triassic (about 200 Ma), and related forms are the oldest known mammals. With a body size estimated to vary between 20 and 30 g, these early mammals were ten times smaller than the smallest cynodonts of the same period. Some cynodonts have small cavities in the snout suggesting the presence of whiskers (hair), which, in turn, suggest *endothermy*—the ability to maintain a constant internal temperature (as opposed to *ectothermy*, when internal temperature fluctuates with external temperature). *Morganucodon* shows a brain enlargement in olfactory and auditory areas, two sensory systems suggesting nocturnal habits, that could also explain the increase in relative brain size (see *Principles of brain size* in what follows). Some Jurassic mammals, such as *Hadrocodium* (about 195 Ma), exhibit a degree of brain enlargement similar to that of living basal mammals (Luo et al., 2001). Mesozoic mammals remained relatively unchanged during approximately 140 Ma of evolution, but an adaptive mammalian radiation occurred during the early Paleocene, after the mass extinction of reptiles at the end of the Cretaceous (Figure 1.14). Newly opened ecological niches were readily occupied by new orders of mammals with new body plans and behavioral capacities.

There are three groups of living mammals (about 4,500 species). *Egg-laying mammals* (monotremes) include three species from Australia and New Guinea: the platypus and two species of echidnas. These mammals may represent what remains of Jurassic species (Rauhut et al., 2002). After hatching from an egg, monotreme infants move into a pouch and feed on milk secreted by glands distributed on the ventral skin of the mother. A number

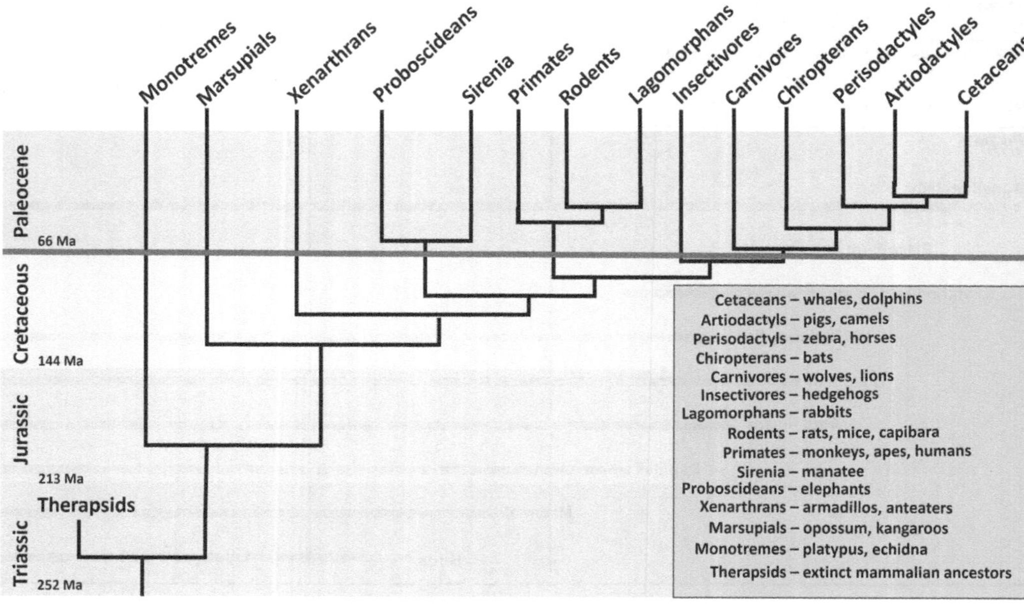

Figure 1.14 **Adaptive radiation of mammals.** A tree representing the adaptive radiation of mammals during the early Cenozoic (Paleocene) era. A lineage of extinct mammal-like reptiles, therapsids, is also included. Some examples of species from each mammalian order are mentioned in the inset. The thick horizontal line between the Cretaceous and Paleocene marks a mass extinction event that led to the extinction of many large reptiles (e.g., dinosaurs) and marine invertebrates (e.g., ammonites).

of experiments on learning and cognition have been reported using echidnas (Russell & Burke, 2016).

Marsupials (about 260 species) live in the Americas (opossums) and Australia (kangaroos, koalas, etc.). In marsupials, the embryo emerges from the uterus at an early stage and continues its development in a pouch, where it attaches itself to a teat and extracts milk. Marsupial learning and cognition have been subject to extensive research (Todorov, 2020).

Placentals (about 4,250 species) are distributed all over the world and in a variety of ecological niches: bats, dolphins, apes, and cats, among many others. Marsupials and placentals are characterized by a *tribosphenic molar* with three main cusps, a variable number of small cusps, and the presence of several crests with sharp edges and valleys, all of which improves chewing and reduces the wearing of the enamel. The earliest placentals appeared in the early Cretaceous of China (Ji et al., 2002). Most species were relatively small insectivores, wolf-size carnivores, and a cow-size herbivore. In about 10 million years, from the late Cretaceous to the early Eocene, the number of placental families increased from 15 to 78 and the number of genera from 40 to about 200. Factors contributing to this adaptive radiation include improved dentition, efficient feeding behavior, extensive parental care, and increased brain size.

Most of the modern placental orders were differentiated in the Paleocene, about 55 to 65 Ma, and therefore, the subsequent evolution has occurred in parallel. Behavioral and neural traits that changed substantially since the Paleocene, such as social behavior and the neocortex, have evolved largely in parallel. Parallel evolution can be appreciated by comparing marsupials and placentals that have evolved striking similarities independently, including adaptations for a subterranean mode of life (marsupial and placental moles), similar gliding structures (arboreal marsupials and placentals), and analogous saber-toothed carnivore species in South America (the extinct marsupial *Thylacosmilus* and the placental *Smilodon*). Because of extensive parallel evolution, caution must be exercised when comparing learning and cognition across mammalian species.

1.3.4.1 Primates

A special order of placental mammals includes the approximately 200 species of living primates, including humans. Primates are characterized by adaptations for arboreal life (e.g., grasping hands and feet, flat nails, sensitive tactile pads in each digit, highly movable arms), a complex visual system (e.g., binocular vision, depth perception, color vision), and a reproductive biology characterized by giving birth to a single offspring (twins in some species) and extensive parental care. Living primates include the following groups:

- Lemurs. Found only in Madagascar, most lemurs are nocturnal and herbivorous and live almost continuously on trees.
- Galagos or bushbabies. These African primates are all nocturnal and arboreal. They tend to have long hind legs used to leap from branch to branch.
- Lorises. These species inhabit the rainforests of Africa and South East Asia and are also nocturnal, arboreal, and generally sluggish in their movements.
- Tarsiers. The single living species, *Tarsius bancanus*, is a nocturnal carnivore feeding on small vertebrates and insects, which it catches by leaping. Leaping involves visuomotor coordination achieved by enlarged eyes and long ankle bones. Tarsiers inhabit the rainforests of Borneo, Sumatra, Sulawesi, and the Philippines.
- New World monkeys. These species have a broad nose and prehensile tail and live exclusively in the forests of South and Central America. With a few exceptions, they are diurnal.
- Old World monkeys. These monkeys have a narrow nose and teeth specialized for leaf eating and live in Africa and Asia. Most species are arboreal, although some are predominantly terrestrial, like baboons and vervets.
- Apes. Apes are characterized by elongated arms and wide chests. Asian apes (gibbons, siamangs, and orangutans) are predominantly arboreal and vegetarian. African apes (gorillas, chimpanzees, and bonobos) live both on the ground and in trees. Chimpanzees and bonobos display substantial variation in social behavior. Gorillas, the largest living primates, live in small groups and are polygynous.
- Humans. Humans have lost many anatomical features associated with an arboreal lifestyle (e.g., curved fingers, opposable big toe, elongated arms) and evolved adaptations for bipedality (e.g., flat feet). The evolution of language, social communities, culture, and technology has allowed humans a worldwide distribution.

Primates appeared during the Eocene (54–38 Ma) of North America, Europe, and Asia (Kay, 2018). These primates had grasping hands and feet, stereoscopic vision, a diet based on insects and fruits, relatively large brains and long tails and were nocturnal. Primates from the late Eocene-early Oligocene (about 30–37 Ma) of North Africa and Arabia exhibited sexual dimorphism in canine size, a trait associated with polygynous mating systems in primates. Thus, basal monkeys were small, nocturnal animals with some degree of sociality. Little is known about the divergence between New World monkeys and Old World monkeys, which probably occurred in the late Eocene of Africa (Kay, 2015). *Aegyptopithecus* (early Oligocene, about 33 Ma), exhibits intermediate characters between the earliest monkeys and living Old World monkeys and apes.

As many as 100 species of apes may have lived in rainforests of the Old World (Africa, Europe, and Asia) during the Miocene and Pleistocene (5–16 Ma), with estimated body sizes ranging between 10 kg and 270 kg (Kelley, 1992). *Proconsul* (early Miocene, Eastern Africa) is considered a possible ancestral ape. Whereas Old World monkeys expanded and tended to occupy a wide range of habitats, apes diminished in diversity toward the end of the Miocene and remained isolated until the present day in rainforests of Southeast Asia and Western Africa. It is unclear whether monkeys displaced apes or ape diversity decreased because of a reduction in rainforest habitats for which they are highly specialized.

1.3.5 Hominins

1.3.5.1 Early hominins

Molecular evidence suggests that chimpanzees and bonobos are the closest living primates to humans (Kuhlwilm, de Manuel, et al., 2016). Chimpanzees and humans share anywhere

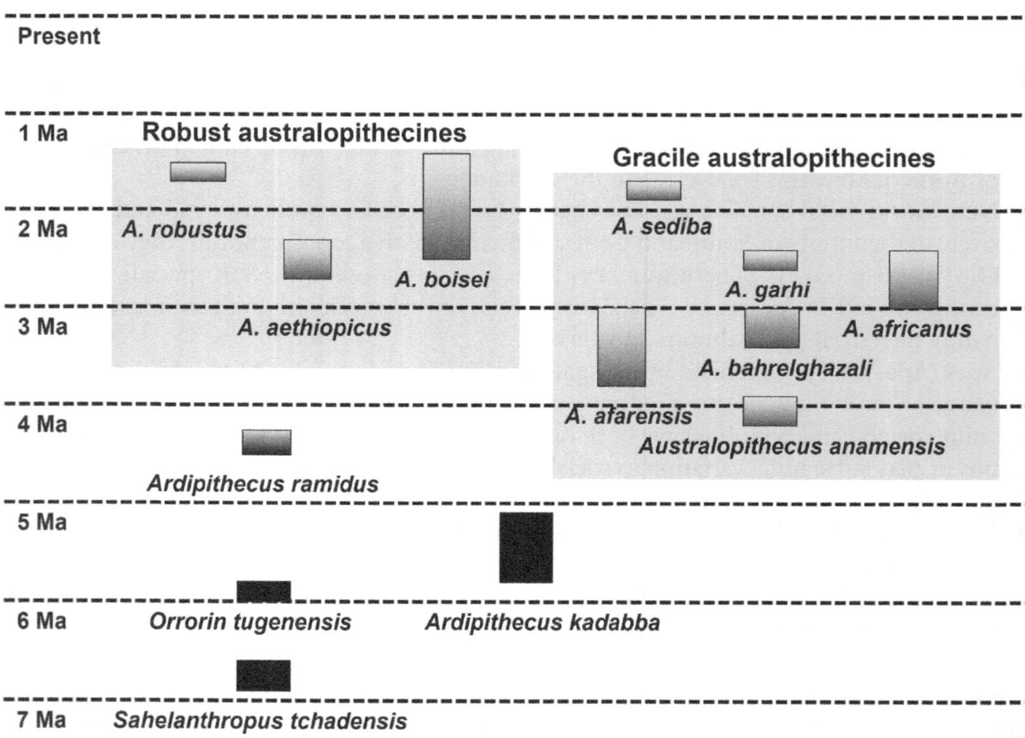

Figure 1.15 **The age of early hominin remains.** Some specimens were assigned tentatively to the hominin tribe because the evidence for bipedalism is either absent or ambiguous (black bars). Grey boxes distinguish between the gracile (starting with *A. anamensis*) and robust australopithecines (starting with *A. aethiopicus*). Some experts assign robust australopithecines to a different genus, *Paranthropus*. (From Papini, 2021; reproduced with permission from Taylor & Francis.)

between 98% and 99% of their genes. The estimated divergence time is still debated, and it ranges between 5 Ma and 13 Ma depending on the source of the evidence. Living humans, *Homo sapiens*, are classified as ***hominins*** together with several fossil specimens grouped by their shared adaptations for bipedal posture. ***Bipedalism*** is consistent with several anatomical traits that are unique to the hominin lineage.

Evidence of bipedalism was found in fossil specimens from Eastern Africa, a region covered with rainforests that gradually receded during the last 5 million years to become a grassland savanna. The origin of hominins could be related to these habitat changes (i.e., ***allopatric speciation***). About 4 Ma, a new group known as the ***australopithecines*** emerged in Eastern Africa. Seemingly small differences in bone anatomy could determine whether specimens are assigned to different species, as opposed to representing individual variability or sexual dimorphism within a single species. Therefore, the number of species is kept to a minimum here; the genus *Australopithecus* is applied to all of them. Figure 1.15 shows the estimated dates of these species. All australopithecines were bipedal and had small canines, and their brain size was above that estimated for *Ardipithecus* and African apes but lower than those obtained for species of the genus *Homo* that appeared later in the fossil record (Table 1.3). Australopithecines were eventually replaced by *Homo* species about 2 Ma.

Two groups of australopithecines are distinguished based on their body type: robust and gracile. There were periods and locations when some of these species coexisted and perhaps competed for resources. It is widely believed that species from the genus *Homo* evolved from a gracile australopithecine.

Table 1.3 Estimated body size, brain size, and EQ for apes and hominins

Species	*Age (Ma)* (*)	*Body weight (kg)*		*Brain*		*EQs* (*)
		Males (*)	*Females* (*)	*volume (cm³)* (*)	(^)	
Living apes						
Gorilla gorilla	Living	140	70	05	505	1.7
Pan paniscus	Living	38	32	343	344	2.0
P. troglodytes	Living	49	41	395	383	2.0
Australopithecus						
A. anamensis (+)	3.8			365		
A. afarensis	3.6–2.9	45	29	384	414	2.2
A. africanus	3.0–2.4	41	30	420	440	2.5
A. aethiopicus	2.7–2.2	?	?	399	?	?
A. boisei	2.3–1.4		49	34	488	463
A. robustus	1.9–1.4		40	32	502	530
A. sediba (#)	2.0	?	?	420	?	?
Homo						
H. habilis	1.9–1.6	37	32	579	640	3.5
H. rudolfensis	2.4–1.6	60	51	709	?	3.0
H. sapiens	Living	58	49	1350	1350	5.8

Note. Age data from Hartwig (2002). *: Data from McHenry (1995). ^: Data from Tobias (1995). +: Data from *A. anamensis* in Haile-Selassie et al. (2019); no estimates of the sex, body weight, and height are available for this specimen. #: Data from *A. sediba* in Berger et al. (2010). EQ: encephalization quotient; EQ parameters: $E = 0.0589(S)^{0.76}$ (Martin, 1981).

1.3.5.2 *Homo*

Species of this genus (Figure 1.16) were once associated with *stone tools* known as *Oldowan technology* (2.5 Ma, Tanzania). However, older stone tools were discovered in other locations (3.3 Ma, Kenya). It is possible that these tools were made by australopithecines (Harmand et al., 2015). Moreover, long-tailed macaques (*Macaca fascicularis*) from Thailand have been observed to make stone tools practically indistinguishable from those produced by hominins (Proffitt et al., 2023). So the status of stone technology in human evolution is uncertain.

The data presented in Table 1.3 provide evidence for hominin encephalization in three steps. First, the *encephalization quotients* (*EQs*) for australopithecines are consistently above those for African apes. (The EQ is a measure of relative brain size obtained by calculating the ratio of brain size divided by the expected brain size given by the allometric equation for mammals; see ***Relative brain size*** in what follows.) This increase in EQ from apes to australopithecines may be related to the evolution of the bipedal posture. Second, early *Homo* species are also above australopithecines in cranial capacity, an increase that could be related to a change in diet (incorporating meat) and foraging patterns (scavenging?). Finally, the increase in EQ for *Homo sapiens* may be a consequence of the evolution of language (see also Chapter 11).

H. erectus is important because of the extensive period of time and the locations in which its remains have been found (1.9 Ma–0.2 Ma, Georgia, China, Java). Key evidence for *H. erectus* comes from several skulls and postcranial bones found in association with stone tools (1.85 Ma–1.77 Ma, Georgia, Asia; Lordkipanidze et al., 2013). For one individual, the cranial

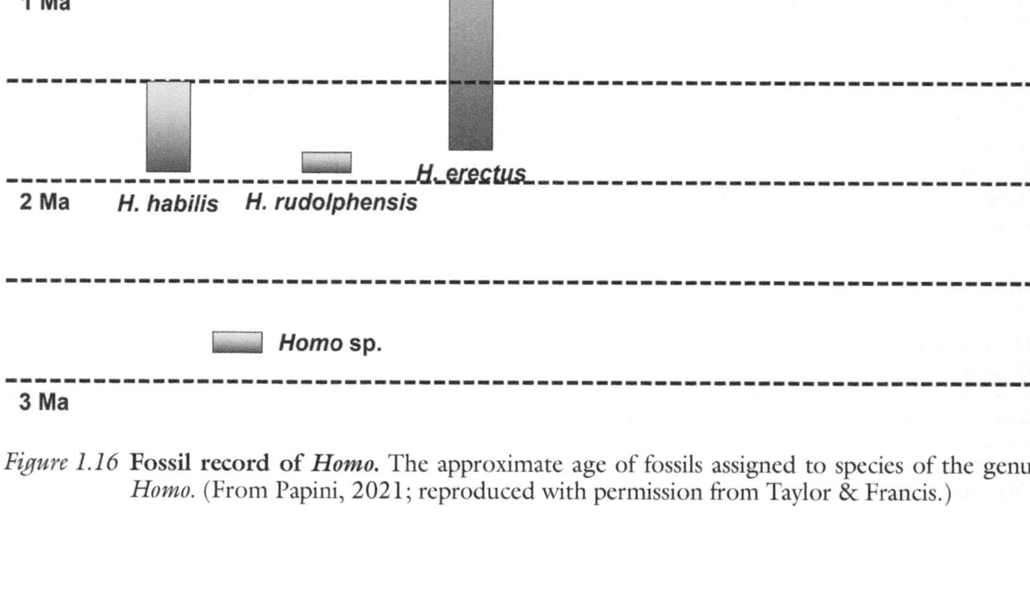

Figure 1.16 **Fossil record of *Homo*.** The approximate age of fossils assigned to species of the genus *Homo*. (From Papini, 2021; reproduced with permission from Taylor & Francis.)

capacity was estimated at 546 cm^3, a height of 1.46 m to 1.66 m, a weight of 47 kg to 50 kg, and an EQ = 2.4, within the range of *Australopithecus*. The morphological and neurocranial size variation in the skulls from Georgia overlapped with early *Homo* from Africa and with a single skull of *H. erectus* from Java and was similar to that of living chimpanzees and bonobos and to modern humans from Africa, Australia, and America (*H. sapiens*). Although these skulls are at the extremes of neurocranial size (lowest for apes and highest for *H. sapiens*), variation in this trait is similar.

The hypothesis that these specimens from East Africa, Southern Caucasus in Georgia, and the island of Java in Southeast Asia belong to a single species, *H. erectus*, implies extraordinary morphological stability despite significant ecological differences among these regions. Hominin stability contrasts with the morphological discontinuity of the mammalian faunas of these regions during the same period (Agustí & Lordkipanidze, 2011). Dispersal over long distances presupposes large population numbers, implying that these hominins used their stone tool technology to exploit new food resources and displayed high levels of intragroup cooperation. *H. erectus* remains are also associated with evidence for the controlled use of fire, including burned bones and ashes of plant material dated 1 Ma, from South Africa (Berna et al., 2012). Fire provided warmth, light, protection against predators, processing of meat that could be stored before consumption, and opportunities for social interactions.

Early migratory waves out of Africa must have occurred about 2.0 Ma to 1.8 Ma, before the significant increase in cranial capacity observed in later hominins (Lordkipanidze et al., 2013). *H. erectus* survived in some isolated environments, such as the island of Java, until about 200 Ka (thousand years ago), after they had disappeared from the fossil record in continental populations. An analysis of 18 adult crania from different localities in Java and from a time span between 500 Ka to 200 Ka shows a modest degree of expansion in cranial capacity during this period (Kaifu et al., 2008).

1.3.5.3 Archaic humans

A variety of new names have been proposed for specimens found in Africa and Eurasia and dated between 1 Ma and 110 Ka, including *H. heidelbergensis*, *H. rhodesiensis*, *H. luzonensis*, *H. antecessor*, *H. naledi*, *H. floresiensis*, Neanderthals, and Denisovans, among others. The discovery of hybrids and of DNA fragments from Neanderthals and Denisovans in the genome of *H. sapiens* confirms that there was interbreeding among some of these populations. What do we know about these archaic humans?

The oldest evidence of Neanderthals was discovered in the United Kingdom and dated 400 Ka. More recent remains are spread all over Europe, Israel, Iraq, and Siberia. The youngest remains are dated to about 40 Ka, and they tend to come from Western Europe, but they disappeared from the record more or less abruptly. Neanderthals were generally more robust than modern humans in their rib cage, with shorter limbs, a large nose, and a reduced chin. Some of these traits could be adaptations for the cold climate of glacial periods. They were comparable to modern humans in height, weight, reduced sexual dimorphism in body size, and range of cranial capacity (1,200–1,750 cm^3). DNA samples from several localities show diversity. For example, specimens from Spain show an allele of the melanocortin 1 receptor associated with reduced expression, which would lead to a light skin pigmentation (Lalueza-Fox et al., 2007). DNA from a specimen found in Croatia did not show the same allele, suggesting a degree of variation in skin pigmentation similar to that in modern humans. There is also evidence of familiar cultural practices, including intentional burials, use of clothing and fire, caring for the injured, and hunting.

Neanderthals and modern humans coexisted during a period of approximately 50 Ka in Israel. A long coexistence and interbreeding suggest that the replacement was not violent. Mitochondrial DNA (mtDNA) from Neanderthals is absent in modern humans. Because mtDNA is carried only by females, interbreeding may have occurred mainly between Neanderthal males and modern females (Krings et al., 1997). Mapping of the genome of a few Neanderthal individuals suggest an initial episode of interbreeding with modern humans about 100 Ka as detected in Neanderthal DNA from Siberia (Kuhlwilm, Gronau, et al., 2016). Interbreeding episodes that occurred later, around 65 Ka to 47 Ka, have also been detected. An analysis of chromosome 21 suggests greater similarity between modern humans and Neanderthals from specimens found in Spain and Croatia than with the Siberian population (Kuhlwilm, Gronau, et al., 2016). Moreover, among African populations, only those in the northern region show evidence of interbreeding; sub-Saharan Africans apparently did not interbreed with Neanderthals (Sánchez-Quinto et al., 2012).

There is also evidence of negative selection for Neanderthal genes. For example, modern human remains from China dated to 40 Ka carry a higher percentage of Neanderthal genes than contemporary humans: 4% to 5% vs. 1% to 2% (Yang et al., 2017). Genes that are expressed in reproductive organs, such as the testis, exhibit reduced frequency of Neanderthal alleles compared to other genome regions, suggesting negative selection perhaps related to decreased fertility of hybrids (Sankararaman et al., 2014). This study also showed that a variety of genes linked to various diseases, including lupus, cirrhosis, and even smoking behavior, are of Neanderthal origin. Interestingly, DNA sections involved in the formation of keratin filaments that play a role in skin and hair are especially rich in Neanderthal genes. This suggests that interbreeding may have helped modern humans cope with colder climates. Morphological signs of interbreeding have also been found in an almost complete skeleton of a 4-year-old infant (25 Ka, Portugal; Duarte et al., 1999). This child's cranium has a mixture of early modern human (e.g., size and proportion of teeth) and Neanderthal features (e.g., a receding chin). Similar findings from several European locations suggest this was not an isolated case of hybridization but a common occurrence.

Coexisting populations of Neanderthals and *H. sapiens* almost certainly exploited similar resources, including food, shelter, and raw materials for tools. As a result, even a small advantage of one population over the other in the ability to exploit these resources could lead to a replacement. Neanderthal camps tend to be located in valleys and reflect the use of local materials in tool making; conversely, *sapiens* camps tend to be on top of hills, which could have been better for surveillance and hunting, and the use of materials from diverse locations suggests extensive trade. The division of labor across sex lines for hunting (men) and gathering (women) may have given *H. sapiens* groups an advantage over the more homogeneous Neanderthal groups (Kuhn & Stiner, 2006). Modern *H. sapiens* appeared in Europe about 45 Ka, and they replaced Neanderthals in an east-to-west direction.

Denisovans were found in the Altai Mountains of Siberia, Russia, which also yielded remains of Neanderthals and modern humans (Krause et al., 2010), and in Tibet, China (Chen et al., 2019). Molecular analyses (DNA and protein fragments) suggest Denisovans interbred with *H. sapiens* and Neanderthals, from which they diverged about 1 Ma, according to Denisovan mtDNA sequencing. These populations of archaic and modern humans apparently interbred extensively, as summarized in Figure 1.17 (Kuhlwilm, Gronau, et al., 2016). Two features of these interbreeding episodes merit emphasis. First, neither Denisovan nor Neanderthal genes have been identified in sub-Saharan African populations. Second, Denisovan genes (and, to a lesser extent, Neanderthal genes) are especially prominent in populations from Papua New Guinea (Browning et al., 2018).

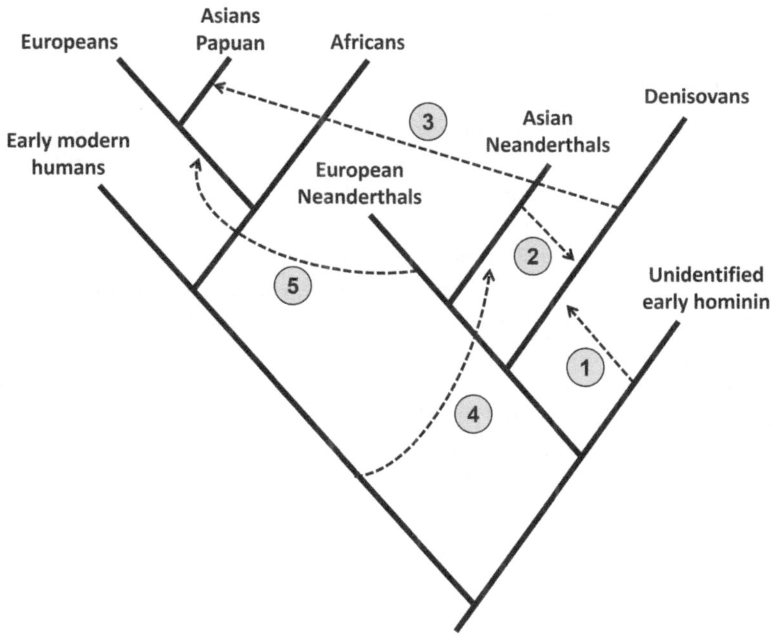

Figure 1.17 **Admixture events in human populations.** Admixture events suggested by molecular evidence extracted from several locations (based on data from Kuhlwilm, Gronau, et al., 2016). Five admixtures between different populations are represented in this figure. Extensive interbreeding seems to have occurred among human populations. (From Papini, 2021; reproduced with permission from Taylor & Francis.)

1.3.5.4 Early and recent modern humans

Paleoanthropologists distinguish between *early modern humans* (*EMH*) and *recent modern humans* (*RMH*) based on cranial morphology. Both types have a flat, short face retracted under the brain case, but EMH have more prominent brow ridges than RMH and an elongated brain case rather than a globular one as in RMH. The oldest cranial specimens attributed to *H. sapiens* (315 Ka, Morocco) are closer to the EMH pattern than the RMH pattern in cranial morphology (Hublin et al., 2017). Not only was brain size a later expansion in the hominin line relative to bipedality (as in *Australopithecus*), but brain size also evolved after a retracted face.

Evidence of early human remains in the Americas are not older than 23 Ka and involve some stone tools and remains of butchered mammoths (new discoveries may challenge this date). The archeological artifacts originally found near Clovis, in New Mexico, have also been retrieved from a variety of locations (11–10 Ka, from Alaska to Tierra del Fuego). This extensive dispersal of the tool kit suggests that populations were already spread over the Americas before Clovis (Waters & Stafford, 2007).

Hominin populations yield progressively more evidence of culture, a fact that highlights the increasing role of learning and cognition. The next section provides a general overview of the vertebrate brain (invertebrate nervous systems will be described in Chapter 3). Without minimizing the importance of the size and complexity of the human brain, the fact remains that the same basic organization can be recognized in the brains of all vertebrates.

1.4 Evolution of the vertebrate brain and behavior

1.4.1 Key innovations of vertebrates

All vertebrates exhibit a brain. The vertebrate head contains well-developed sensory organs (e.g., eyes, ears, gustatory papillae) and sensory/motor nerves with peripheral ganglia. The organization of the vertebrate brain is quite stable and, despite variations, broad sections of the CNS are easily identifiable across species (Figure 1.18).

Living cephalochordates and Cambrian chordates have provided clues about the origin of the vertebrate CNS. The chordate *Brachiostoma floridae* has a brain that corresponds to the more posterior portions of the vertebrate brain (diencephalon, rhombencephalon), with similar genes to those of vertebrates expressed in these regions. Extensive gene duplication in the transition from early chordates to vertebrates could be responsible for the evolution of the vertebrate brain (Holland, 2015). Moreover, the fossil chordate *Haikouella lanceolata* (530 Ma, China) revealed a rudimentary brain that appears to correspond to the posterior sections of the vertebrate brain. A phylogenetic analysis including a wide range of characters places *Haikouella* as a close ancestor to vertebrates (Mallatt & Chen, 2003). Thus, the vertebrate brain may have evolved as an enlargement of the CNS of early chordates.

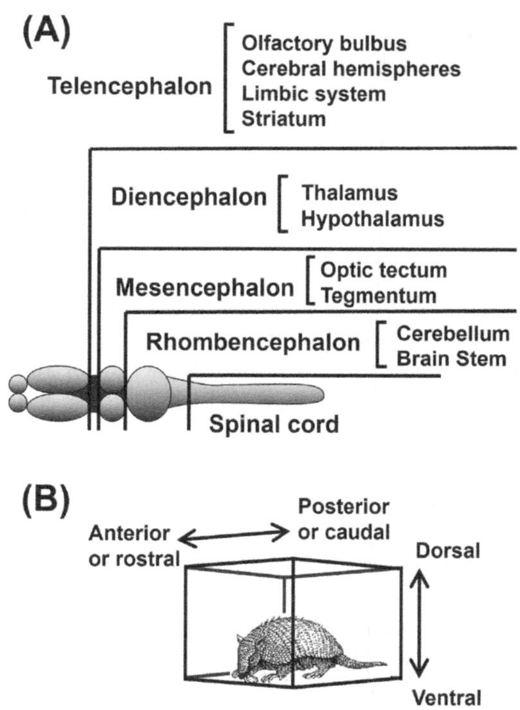

Figure 1.18 **The vertebrate brain. (A)** Dorsal view of a prototypical vertebrate brain. Some brain areas found in each segment are listed. **(B)** Planes of reference. Most vertebrates are disposed as illustrated by the armadillo. In some species, the animal is erect such that dorsal corresponds to the back and ventral to the front (e.g., humans, kangaroos, seahorses). (From Papini, 2021, reproduced with permission from Taylor & Francis.)

1.4.2 *Agnathan brains*

Agnathan fish have a circular mouth with teeth but lack true bone. A phylogenetic analysis of living (hagfish, lampreys) and extinct agnathans suggests that these are the most primitive vertebrates (Janvier, 2008). Extinct and living agnathans are marine animals, suggesting that vertebrates evolved in the sea and only later entered freshwater habitats. Early vertebrates are characterized by the evolution of sensory systems that required changes in associated brain structures (Forey & Janvier, 1994). The lens of the eye, for example, focuses an image in the retina and is present in lampreys and most vertebrates. Hagfish, though, have eyes without lenses. The lensless eyes of hagfish are correlated with the absence of optic tecti, a mesencephalic structure receiving projections from both retinas, and with a rudimentary cerebellum, which controls the muscles that accommodate the lenses.

There is limited information on conditioning phenomena in agnathans (Suzuki, 2021). Hagfish can be trained to respond using operant procedures and various types of stimuli, including odor, taste, and tactile stimuli. In one study (Glover et al., 2019), a single group of hagfish (*Eptatretus stoutii*) exposed to a T-maze tended to spend more time in the appetitive arm (marked with an olfactory cue for food) than in the empty arm but also tended to stay away from the arm baited with an aversive chemical. Additional controls would be necessary to demonstrate that these approach-avoidance responses are controlled by the appetitive and aversive outcomes used with these basal vertebrates.

1.4.3 *Regions of the vertebrate brain*

1.4.3.1 *Spinal cord*

The spinal cord can be viewed as a cylinder of nerve tissue enclosed in the core of the vertebrate column made of cartilage or bone. Between successive vertebrae, the spinal cord has dorsal and ventral roots connecting the CNS with the periphery. The dorsal roots convey afferent sensory information (skin, internal organs, muscles, tendons) into the CNS. The somas of sensory neurons are in a chain of dorsal root ganglia adjacent to the spinal cord. The axons of these sensory neurons establish synaptic connections with neurons that send information either back to the periphery through the ventral roots or to anterior CNS regions. Motoneurons in the ventral horns send axons to peripheral structures (muscles, glands).

Associated with the ventral roots are a series of ganglia that form the ***autonomic nervous system*** (***ANS***), which includes regulation of digestive processes, heart rate, respiratory rate, and tear and salivary glands. The study of spinal cord morphology is responsible for the ***neuron doctrine***, according to which neurons communicate through tiny gaps, proposed by Santiago Ramón y Cajal [1852–1934]; and for the concept of ***synapse***, coined by Charles S. Sherrington [1857–1952] in reference to the gaps through which adjacent neurons interchange information. The spinal cord contains circuitry that controls reflexes, escape behavior, and learning (Grau, 2014).

1.4.3.2 *Rhombencephalon and mesencephalon*

The anterior portion of the spinal cord leads to the medulla, pons, and tegmentum (collectively called the ***brainstem***). Dorsal to the medulla and pons is the ***cerebellum***, and dorsal to the tegmentum is the ***optic tectum***. An imaginary line between the pons and tegmentum (leaving the cerebellum and optic tectum at each side, respectively) establishes the boundary between rhombencephalon (medulla, pons, and cerebellum) and mesencephalon (optic tectum and various tegmental nuclei).

The rhombencephalon contains a variety of behaviorally relevant areas that have been studied mainly in mammals. These include the *reticular formation* (muscle tone, sleep–wakefulness cycle, arousal, attention), *locus coeruleus* (noradrenergic axons, emotional stress), and *raphe nuclei* (serotoninergic neurons, mood). Two other regions are relevant to learning. The *periaqueductal gray* links anterior structures involved in memory, motivation, and perception with behavior served by spinal motoneurons. Many of its neurons respond to endogenous opioids and can block the activity of ascending pathways carrying nociceptive information from the spinal cord, thus leading to hypoalgesia (Reichling et al., 1988). Periaqueductal neurons also are necessary for freezing responses induced during fear conditioning. The cerebellum, with its own cortex and subcortical nuclei, receives sensory inputs, controls motor coordination, and also exhibits plasticity. The cerebellum is critical for motor learning, as in the conditioning of the rabbit's (*Oryctolagus cuniculus*) nictitating membrane response. Stimulation of the eye with an air puff to the cornea elicits a protective reflex involving eyelid closure, eyeball retraction, and the closure of the nictitating membrane. A signal for the air puff can trigger an anticipatory closure of the nictitating membrane; this learned behavior depends on the dentate and interpositus nuclei (Christian & Thompson, 2005).

1.4.3.3 *Diencephalon*

The main regions of the diencephalon are common to all vertebrates and participate in a variety of behavioral functions, both directly and through their connections with the pineal and pituitary glands. The *lateral habenula* inhibits the reward system, therefore playing a central role in aversive learning. The *thalamus* is a cluster of nuclei with several functions, from sensory-motor control to cognition. The *hypothalamus* controls the pituitary gland via neural and neuroendocrine signals, thus regulating a variety of functions via hormones rather than neural impulses. It also participates in motivational processes: hunger and satiety, temperature regulation, thirst, and sex drive.

1.4.4 *Telencephalon*

1.4.4.1 *Subdivisions*

The telencephalon of all vertebrates can be subdivided into pallium and subpallium. The *pallium* corresponds to all the structures located in the medial, dorsal, and lateral portions and is predominantly formed by glutamatergic excitatory neurons. The *subpallium* corresponds to the ventral portions of the telencephalon and is predominantly populated by GABAergic inhibitory neurons, which also migrate to the pallium as inhibitory interneurons (Briscoe & Ragsdale, 2019).

1.4.4.2 *Fish telencephalon*

For all its size and complexity, it is somewhat surprising that the ablation of the entire fish telencephalon often produces no obvious changes in behavior. Detecting behavioral deficits after lesions required refined behavioral procedures, especially in relation to learning. Goldfish (*Carassius auratus*) with complete ablation of the telencephalon exhibit normal escape conditioning but show deficits in avoidance conditioning (Hainsworth et al., 1967). Escape learning involves responding to the presentation of aversive electric shocks, whereas avoidance involves preventing the shock by responding during the presentation of a signal for shock. Ablated fish eventually do avoid the signal for shock, especially when the shock is intense, suggesting that the telencephalon modulates a process that is instantiated by other crucial neural mechanisms (Overmier & Papini, 1986). Partial telencephalic ablations provide evidence of the functional correspondence between the everted telencephalon of teleost fish and the evaginated telencephalon of mammals. *Spatial learning*, which is sensitive to hippocampal damage in mammals, is disrupted by lateral lesions of the telencephalon in goldfish (homologous to hippocampus) but remains unimpaired by medial lesions (Gómez et al., 2022). By contrast, *avoidance learning*, which is sensitive to amygdala damage in mammals, is disrupted by medial lesions in goldfish (homologous to amygdala) but not by lateral lesions (Portavella et al., 2004). Thus, the evolution of some learning mechanisms in vertebrates appears to be highly conserved because homologous telencephalic areas play similar functions in teleost fish and mammals despite their dissimilar development.

1.4.4.3 Striatum

The striatum has traditionally been conceptualized as a motor area via dopaminergic inputs from diencephalic areas. The dorsal portion is highly differentiated in mammals, especially in primates, into the caudate nucleus, putamen, and globus pallidus. The ventral striatum includes the nucleus accumbens and olfactory tubercle. The striatum is also implicated in the acquisition of *stimulus–response habits* (Mishkin et al., 1984; see stimulus–response associations in Chapter 4).

1.4.4.4 Limbic system

Most experts include the hippocampus, amygdala, septum, entorhinal cortex, cingulate cortex, and olfactory bulbs as components of the *limbic system*. Limbic structures, such as the amygdala, control vertebrate learning and behavior. The hippocampus also produces new neurons (*neurogenesis*) in adult vertebrates (Bond et al., 2015). Consider these two areas in greater detail.

Lesions of the *amygdala* impair *fear conditioning* in mammals (Pessoa, 2023). Fear conditioning involves anticipating pain typically induced by electric shocks. *Frustration* activated by unexpected reward omissions and leading to reward rejection is also regulated by the mammalian amygdala (Guarino et al., 2020). Amygdala homologues are also important for aversive conditioning in ray-finned fish and amphibians (Puddington et al., 2016), suggesting conservation of function.

The *hippocampus* (Figure 1.19) is especially important for spatial learning. In birds that store and retrieve food during the fall, winter, and early spring, locating the caches accurately depends on spatial learning. In these species, the hippocampus is enlarged relative to nonstoring species and it also tends to increase in size during the storing period (Sherry & Hoshooley, 2010). The hippocampus is also implicated in spatial learning in fish (see earlier), toads (Muzio & Bingman, 2022), pigeons (Bingman et al., 2003), and rats (Morris et al., 1982). Polygynous meadow vole males patrol a large breeding territory and display enlarged hippocampal size relative to females or to monogamous pine vole males that exhibit more restrictive spatial movements (see **Sexual selection and the brain** earlier).

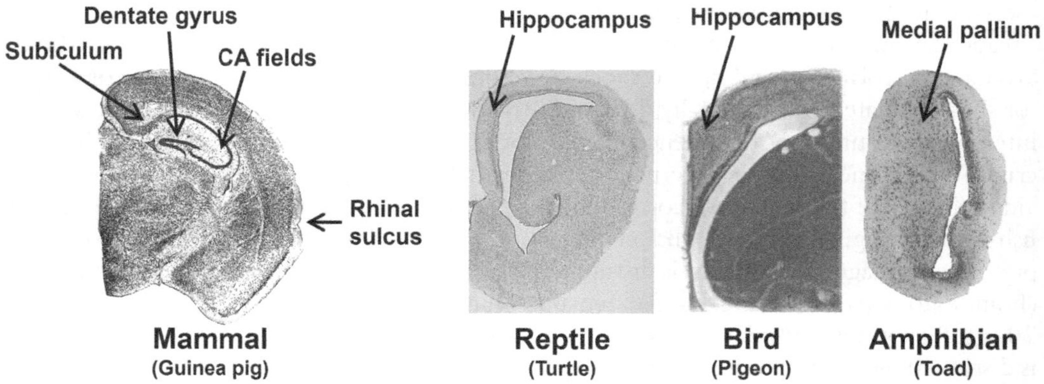

Figure 1.19 **The hippocampus of tetrapods.** Homologies with respect to the mammalian dentate gyrus, CA fields, and subiculum are not yet fully established. The middle line is to the left. The rhinal sulcus is visible as an indentation in the cortex of mammals. (Mammal: Guinea pig, *Cavia aperea*, from Jacob & Onelli, 1913, public domain. Bird: homing pigeon, *Columba livia*, photo courtesy of Vern Bingman. Reptile: turtle, *Pseudemys scripta*, photo courtesy of Cosme Salas. Amphibian: toad, *Rhinella arenarum*, photo courtesy of Rubén Muzio.)

1.4.4.5 Origin and evolution of the cortex

The pallium of amniotes (reptiles, birds, and mammals) is characterized by the migration of cell somas to the outer surface to form layers of ***cerebral cortex***. Precursors of cortical cells have been found in all vertebrates, but the cortical organization is restricted to amniotes. Three types of cortices have been recognized: archicortex, paleocortex, and neocortex. The archicortex refers to the hippocampal formation of mammals: dentate gyrus, CA fields, and subiculum. The interlacing architecture of the dentate gyrus and CA fields is peculiar to mammals (see Figure 1.19). In mammals, the paleocortex lies ventral to the lateral rhinal sulcus, whereas the neocortex lies dorsal to the rhinal sulcus. The neocortex includes up to six cell layers, whereas the paleocortex has up to three layers. The precursor of the amniote paleocortex and neocortex is the amphibian dorsal pallium, which develops in connection with the dorsal thalamus (Butler, 1994).

Large brains evolved independently in several mammalian orders since the Paleocene (about 66–56 Ma), including primates (apes and humans), cetaceans (dolphins), perissodactyls (rhinoceros), carnivores (lions), and proboscideans (elephants). Despite this independent evolution, primary sensory (visual, auditory, and somatosensory) and motor areas appear to be homologous among distantly related rodents and primates. These areas have topographic representations of sensory organs (e.g., the retina for vision) and motor outputs (e.g., the skeletal muscles). Primates have between 20 and 40 supplementary visual areas, depending on the species, at least 4 times as many as in rodents. Therefore, some secondary visual areas in primates have no homologous counterparts in rodents (Northcutt & Kaas, 1995).

In addition to sensory and motor areas, the mammalian neocortex has integrative areas called ***association cortex*** that relate to behavior in subtle ways. For example, experimental removal of the mammalian neocortex does not prevent conditioning, but noninvasive techniques show substantial neural plasticity during learning (McGann, 2015). Prefrontal, parietal, and temporal association cortices control complex cognitive functions, including planning, working memory, social behavior, spatial orientation, attention, and language comprehension in humans (Striedter, 2005).

1.4.5 Principles of brain size

Vertebrate brains are among the most complex natural systems known to science. Some neocortical regions are primarily concerned with a small number of functions, such as the primary sensory and motor areas. Little would be gained by studying overall brain size if such *functional localization* were extreme, but many brain functions are distributed over several regions. Therefore, brain size provides a useful approach to brain function (Jerison, 1973). Functional localization suggests the *principle of proper mass*: There is a positive correlation between the size of a brain area and the amount of information processed by that area. For example, primates tend to be diurnal, use vision in their foraging and social behavior, and unsurprisingly have many brain areas devoted to visual perception. When functions are extremely localized, the loss of neurons in a particular area may cause permanent deficits. However, when functions are controlled by several areas, the extent of the deficit may depend on the magnitude of the damage rather than its localization. This is the *principle of mass action*, revealed by the observation that deficits in visual discrimination learning were proportional to the size of neocortical lesions rather than their location (Eichenbaum, 2016). Mass action suggests that absolute brain size would be related to general capacities for processing information and, therefore, it could be treated as any other trait that evolved by natural selection.

1.4.5.1 Selective breeding for brain size

Traits that evolved by natural selection should also respond to selective breeding, that is, by selectively breeding individuals with large or small brains for several generations to determine whether high (H) and low (L) strains can be obtained. In one study with guppies (*Poecilia reticulata*), the brain size of parents was assessed after reproduction on the assumption that parents and offspring would tend to share a similar brain size (Kotrschal et al., 2013). Then offspring from parents with large brains were bred for two generations with each other, and the same was done with offspring from parents with small brains, avoiding sibling mating. The average relative brain size (brain size corrected for body weight) increased in the H line and decreased in the L line within two generations of selective breeding. To assess the consequences of selective breeding, offspring were tested in a visual discrimination task in which approaching one stimulus was reinforced with food, but approaching a second stimulus was not rewarded. Large-brain females performed better than small-brain females in this discrimination task, but this difference was not observed in males. However, a count of the number of offspring produced indicated that large-brain animals, both males and females, produced 19% fewer offspring than small-brain fish. These results show that evolving a large brain may have cognitive benefits but at a potential reproductive cost. Interestingly, mammals with relatively large brains (e.g., whales, monkeys) tend to have a low reproductive output.

1.4.5.2 Relative brain size

It makes sense for brain and body size to be positively correlated. The brain contains cells sensitive to sensory afferents from the body and produces effects at muscles and organs. The larger the body of an animal, the greater the number of neurons needed to perform these functions. An elephant's brain should be larger than a mouse's brain simply because elephants are larger.

That body size and brain size are positively correlated could be explained by common genes controlling their growth (e.g., genes for growth hormones). However, the size of the brain can increase beyond the size of the body, a process called ***encephalization***, to be discussed in the next section. The ***allometric equation*** relates variation in the size of one organ, body part, or function to variations in body size across species according to a power function:

$$\mathbf{E} = \mathbf{a} * \mathbf{S}^{\mathbf{b}}$$

where *E* is brain size or weight (from the French "poids encephalique"), *S* is body size or weight ("poids somatique"), and *a* and *b* are empirical constants for the point of origin and slope, respectively, of the function relating brain and body size. Allometric functions represented in double logarithmic coordinates yield a straight line:

$$\log(\mathbf{E}) = \log(\mathbf{a}) + \mathbf{b} * \log(\mathbf{S})$$

The allometric equation can be used to generate the EQ, which weighs E for a particular species against the allometric equation with the parameters appropriate for the class to which that species belongs, according to the following equation:

$$\mathbf{EQ} = \frac{\mathbf{E}}{\mathbf{a} * \mathbf{S}^{\mathbf{b}}}$$

If the brain size of a species falls on top of the regression line, the obtained and expected brain sizes are equal and EQ = 1. An EQ > 1 implies that the brain of a given species is larger than expected for that class (encephalization), whereas an EQ < 1 implies a smaller brain than expected for that class (decephalization). Table 1.4 presents a list of EQs for various mammals that provides a general idea of the variation within taxa.

Is the size of neurons related to brain size across species? To determine the size of neurons and nonneural cells, brains can be processed with a method that preserves cell nuclei. Then, nuclei are sampled and stained with a fluorescent marker, and the size and number of neurons and other cells in the CNS are estimated. In rodents, from the small mouse to the large capybara, neuron size increases with brain size, whereas the size of nonneural cells remains constant (Herculano-Houzel, Mota, et al., 2006). Therefore, neuronal density decreases as brain size increases across rodent species. However, neuron size remains constant with changes in brain size in primates (Herculano-Houzel, Collins, et al., 2006) and birds (Olkowicz et al., 2016). In corvids and parrots, neuronal density in the telencephalon is even higher than in primates. Thus, for a given brain size, neuronal density is higher in primates and birds than in rodents.

Plotting brain and body size from a sample of vertebrates in double logarithmic scales results in linear functions that follow the allometric equation. The slopes of these polygons (*b* in the allometric equation) are lower than 1. When $b = 1$, then for every unit of increase in body size, there is a unit of increase in brain size; this is called isometric growth. But when $b < 1$, increases in brain size across species do not match increases in body size. This is called negative allometry (then, $b > 1$ is called positive allometry). Table 1.5 summarizes the slope

Table 1.4 EQs for selected species of mammals

Taxon	*Species*	*Common name*	*EQs*
Monotremes	*Ornithorhynchus anatinus*	Plathypus	0.94
	Tachyglossus aculeatus	Echidna	0.72
Marsupials	*Dasyurus quoll*	Marsupial cat	1.05
	Macropus giganteus	Kangaroo	0.47
	Didelphis marsupialis	Opossum	0.46
Insectivors	*Suncus murinus*	Shrew	0.48
	Setifer setosus	Greater hedgehog	0.45
	Neomys fodiens	Mole	0.75
Edentates	*Choloepus hoffmanni*	Tree sloth	1.09
	Myrmecophaga tridactyla	Ant eater	0.81
	Dasypus novemcinctus	Armadillo	0.37
Chiropterans	*Desmodus rotundus*	Vampire bat	1.23
	Pteropus geddeiri	Fruit-eating bat	0.95
	Myotis lucifugus	Little brown bat	0.52
Rodents	*Atherurus africanus*	Porcupine	1.19
	Rattus norvegicus	Albino rat	0.79
	Hydrochoerus hydrochoeris	Capibara	0.68
Primates	*Homo sapiens*	Human	7.33
	Cebus capuchinus	Cebus monkey	3.40
	Lemur catta	Lemur	1.45
Carnivores	*Vulpes vulpes*	Wild fox	1.89
	Ursus arctos	Bear	0.91
	Panthera leo	Lion	0.70
Cetaceans	*Phocaena phocaena*	Porpoise	4.90
	Tursiops tursia	Dolphin	3.23
	Globicephala melaena	Porpoise	1.70
Perissodactyls	*Equus zebra*	Zebra	1.70
	E. caballus	Horse	1.07
	Tapirus bairdi	Tapir	0.87
Artiodactyls	*Bison bison*	Bison	0.35
	Hippopotamus amphibius	Hippopotamus	0.33
	Sus scrofa	Wild pig	0.27

Note. EQ values from Eisenberg (1981; $a = 0.05$, $b = 0.74$).

Table 1.5 Allometric equation parameters obtained for vertebrate classes

Class	*Number of species*	a	b	r^2
Mammals	1174	0.06	0.74	0.96
Birds	221	0.12	0.59	0.89
Reptiles	74	0.02	0.53	0.91
Amphibians	118	0.01	0.55	0.81
Bony fish	878	0.01	0.64	0.85
Cartilaginous fish	61	0.05	0.56	0.74
Jawless fish	5	0.01	0.21	0.35

Note. Data from van Dongen (1998). *a*: the point of origin of the regression line. *b*: the slope of the regression line. r^2: coefficient of determination assessing the strength of the brain:body correlation.

values (*b*) and point of origin (*a*) for various classes of vertebrates. Notice that all exponents show negative allometry and variability, suggesting that the evolution of relative brain size was driven by different factors in different vertebrate classes.

1.4.5.3 Comparative and developmental aspects of encephalization

Encephalization could be the result of different factors. The relatively large hippocampal formation of food-storing birds contains neurons with larger somas than homologous hippocampal neurons from nonstoring species with average hippocampal size (Montagnese et al., 1993). In cetaceans, relatively larger brains involve an expansion in the number of basic components in the columnar architecture of the cortex (Marino, 2004). In primates, relatively larger brains display greater morphological differentiation and a more complex architecture in the neocortex than relatively smaller brains (Kaas, 2004). Clearly, encephalization has evolved independently in several vertebrate lineages.

A selective breeding experiment with mice suggests the developmental trajectory leading to a large brain size. High (H), low (L), and control (C; mice were paired randomly) lines for relative brain size were selectively bred, and brain–body weights of fetuses were measured after a few generations to determine the developmental profile of each strain. In mammals, brain and body grow at similar rates during prenatal development, but whereas brain growth stops sometime after birth, body growth continues during an additional period. Whereas L and C lines were not different from each other, H mice had larger relative brain size in late prenatal age. Thus, large brains in these mice were the product of increased growth rate during the same period in which the brain grows in control animals (Fuller & Geils, 1972).

Among songbirds and parrots, the large telencephalon is the result of delayed neurogenesis. In zebra finches (*Taeniopygia guttata*), neurogenesis occurs during the first week after hatching, but new neurons are produced on a more limited basis in adults (Kirn, 2010). By contrast, the enlarged telencephalon of ducks and geese is achieved by expanding the precursor regions, before neurogenesis starts (Charvet & Striedter, 2009). Because songbird species that exhibit vocal learning show delayed neurogenesis, it is tempting to speculate that the assembly of the brain circuits devoted to this function is facilitated by the late occurrence of neurogenesis. Ducks and geese exhibit stereotypical vocal behavior, and neurogenesis in these animals is complete by hatching. Thus, different developmental programs may promote encephalization.

1.4.5.4 Brain size and intelligence

A provocative hypothesis suggests that brain size relates to ***biological intelligence***, "the capacity to construct a perceptual world" (Jerison, 1973, p. 17). This is based on the fact that the size of sensory nuclei is proportional to the importance of that sensory modality in the natural behavior of the animal—the principle of proper mass. Biological intelligence might be a factor in the world-wide extinction of large mammals during a period ranging between 100 Ka to 10 Ka. Many extinctions have been related to human hunting, climate change, invading species, and similar factors. Large species that became extinct include artiodactyls (camels, hippopotami), perissodactyls (horses), primates (monkeys, lemurs), carnivores (wolves, lions, sabertooth tigers, bears), edentates (glyptodons, ground sloths), marsupials (*Diprotodon*, kangaroos), notungulates (*Toxodon*), proboscideans (mammoths), and monotremes (giant echidna). A study comparing hundreds of recently extinct and living species of the same genera revealed that extinct species had consistently lower relative brain size (Dembitzer et al., 2022). The authors concluded that relatively small brains may limit behavioral flexibility needed to cope with changing environments.

There is evidence for a connection between brain size and behavioral flexibility. The index of extra cortical neurons, which estimates the number of cortical neurons above that required for sensory-motor functions (Jerison, 1973), predicts performance in the *learning set* task. In this task, animals are reinforced with food for choosing one of two stimuli; once the first discrimination is learned, a similar discrimination with two new stimuli is introduced; when this is learned, a third one is introduced; and so on. Because all discrimination problems are of the same format (one positive stimulus vs. one negative stimulus), animals show progressive improvement in solving new discriminations, a phenomenon suggesting the acquisition of a *win-stay/lose-shift strategy*. Thus, the animal can be said to have "learned to learn" new problems (Harlow, 1949). Slope estimates of learning set performance showed a high correlation ($r = 0.98$) with the index of extra cortical neurons in several mammalian species (Riddell & Corl, 1977).

Is this behavioral flexibility the result of more efficient learning or sensory-motor biases? A low learning set performance in rats solving visual discriminations could result from their limited visual capacity. However, faster learning set acquisition, as fast as that exhibited by some primates in similar tasks, was reported in rats when three-dimensional objects (Kay & Oldfield-Box, 1965), spatial cues (Zeldin & Olton, 1986), or odors (Slotnick & Katz, 1974) were used as discriminative stimuli. Mice selected for large brain size exhibited faster acquisition of brightness discriminations, spatial reversals, and active avoidance tasks, all tasks requiring active responses (Elias, 1969, 1970). However, these mice were poor at tasks requiring response inhibition, such as passive avoidance (avoiding entering a dark compartment previously associated with shock; Wimer et al., 1969). Increased behavioral flexibility in these mice selected for large brains was thus attributable to high levels of exploratory behavior.

1.4.5.5 Behavioral specializations and the brain

Several examples of correlations between behavior and either brain size, EQ, or the size of particular brain areas have been discovered in mammals and birds. These are some examples:

- The EQ of bat species that forage for fruits tends to be higher than that of species that forage for insects (Eisenberg & Wilson, 1978).
- Frugivorous primates tend to have a larger brain size than primates that have different diets (Mace et al., 1980).
- In bats that echolocate animal prey, species that concentrate in either ground gleaning or aerial hawking during foraging exhibit smaller relative brain size than species that switch between these foraging strategies (Ratcliffe et al., 2006).
- Mammalian species that move both on the ground and in trees or water (3D lifestyle) tend to have larger brains than species that live predominantly on the ground (2D life-style; Eisenberg, 1981).
- Among conservative mammals of the same orders, an active antipredator strategy is associated with larger EQs than a passive antipredator strategy (Eisenberg, 1981).
- Hippocampal size is larger in food-hoarding bird species than in nonstoring species (Sherry et al., 1989).
- In birds, brain size correlates positively with behavioral innovations assessed by field observations (Overington et al., 2009).

Results such as these confirm the connection between brain and behavior, whether in terms of diet, movement in space, antipredator strategies, or cognitive skills. Brain–behavior comparisons among larger arrays of species are also informative. A large study of *self-control* with a total of 36 species of mammals and birds assessed performance in two tasks and correlated the results with three indices of brain size—absolute brain size, relative brain size, and EQ (MacLean et al., 2014). In the A-Not-B task (Figure 1.20-A), subjects watched the experimenter placing food in one of three containers and then searched for and ate the food in three trials. The test involved watching the experimenter place food in the same container as during training but then moving the food to a different container. Would the first search attempt be directed at the previously positive container (an A-Not-B error) or at the new container? A-Not-B errors reflect perseverative behavior. In the cylinder task (Figure 1.20-B), subjects watched the experimenter placing food inside an opaque cylinder and could then retrieve the food through one end of the cylinder until they scored four trials with a correct first attempt at retrieving the food. The test involved subjects having to retrieve the food from a transparent cylinder. Would their first attempt be directed at the visible but inaccessible food (impulsive choice) or to the open end of the cylinder as learned during training?

Correlational assessment of brain–behavior data yielded a surprising result: The strongest predictor of correct performance was absolute brain size. This was true for all species, for nonprimates and for primates. The exception was the A-Not-B task, which showed weak correlations for all species combined, a result due to low scores by elephants. When elephants were excluded, absolute brain size was also the strongest predictor of performance in the A-Not-B task. Population group size, foraging group size, and percentage fruit in the diet

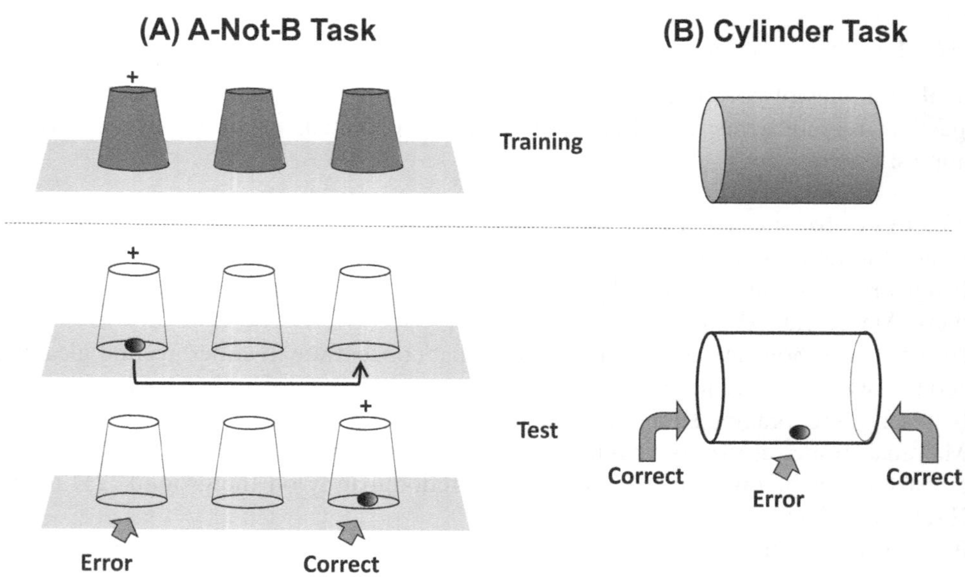

Figure 1.20 **Comparative analysis of self-control.** Tasks used by MacLean et al. (2014) to test self-control in mammals and birds. **(A)** The A-Not-B task assessed perseverative errors. **(B)** The cylinder task evaluated impulsivity.

were weak predictors of self-control behavior. However, they found that several additional factors achieved significant status, including:

- Dietary breadth: the number of dietary categories consumed by each species.
- Social learning: acquiring information from group members.
- Innovation: developing novel strategies to exploit resources.
- Extractive foraging: exploiting hidden sources of food (roots, nuts).
- Tool use: the use of an object to access a resource.
- Tactical deception: a misrepresentation of a situation to another group member.
- General intelligence: ability to solve an array of problems.

The evolutionary reason for the observed relationship between performance in these self-control tasks and absolute brain size is unclear. Self-control and response inhibition are related to the prefrontal cortex, an extensive cortical area in primates (Passingham & Wise, 2012). Thus, it is not surprising that primates performed well in these tasks. Primates show impressive behavioral flexibility in discrimination tasks, as in the learning set task described previously. It is plausible that encephalization in primates was driven, to a large extent, by the absolute increase of the prefrontal cortex.

Glossary

Adaptation Traits (whether morphological or functional) are shaped by natural selection to fit a specific environmental demand.

Adaptationist paradigm The view that organisms are collections of traits that evolved by natural selection.

Adaptive radiation The divergence of body plans during a geologically short period.

Alleles Different versions of homologous genes (genes located in the same locus in homologous chromosomes) are present in different animals within a population. A locus (loci in plural) refers to a specific position of a gene in a chromosome.

Allometric equation This equation describes the relationship between an organ and body size. Applied to the brain, the equation is expressed as $E = aS^b$, where E = brain weight or volume, S = body weight or volume, a = the point of origin of the regression line, and b = the slope of the regression line.

Amino acids Components of a protein. There are 20 amino acids.

Amygdala A ventral region of the vertebrate brain involved in various functions, including positive and negative emotions and aggressive behavior.

Association cortex Areas of the mammalian neocortex not strictly involved in sensory or motor processing.

Autonomic nervous system (ANS) Branches of the nervous system that connect the central nervous system with peripheral organs. Three branches are recognized: the enteric, parasympathetic, and sympathetic systems.

Avoidance learning Acquiring a response (or the inhibition of a response) that prevents the delivery of an aversive outcome.

Bilateral symmetry An animal body plan involving pairs of appendages and an anterior–posterior axis.

Biological intelligence The ability to develop a perceptual representation of the environment.

Bipedalism In primates, a set of skeletal adaptations to use only the hind legs for locomotion.

Body plan A set of morphological traits unique to a particular group of animals.

Brainstem A section of the central nervous system of vertebrates that includes (anterior to posterior) the tegmentum, pons, and medulla. Nuclei for many of the cranial nerves and for the control of vital functions are located in the brainstem.

Burgess Shale fauna A set of fossil animals from the Cambrian period discovered in several locations around the world that includes species from a variety of phyla.

Cambrian explosion The geologically fast emergence in the fossil record of animals from a variety of phyla during the Cambrian period. These species are also known as the Burgess Shale fauna.

Cerebellum A structure of the vertebrate central nervous system located in the rhombencephalon, dorsal relative to the brainstem. The cerebellum includes a cortex and up to three subcortical nuclei. It is involved in a wide variety of functions, including electroreception, motor coordination, and motor learning.

Cerebral cortex A layered structure in the telencephalon of amniotes, with up to six layers, devoted to sensory, motor, learning, and cognitive functions.

Codons Sets of three bases in the DNA molecule coding for an amino acid.

Correlated traits Selection favoring one trait usually leads to changes in other traits not specifically selected for because of a common genetic basis.

Deoxyribonucleic acid (DNA) A molecule with a double-helix structure containing a sequence of four bases (adenine, thymine, cytosine, and guanine) that codes for the synthesis of proteins. A gene is defined as a section of the DNA molecule. DNA is enclosed inside the cell nucleus in eukaryotes, but it is in the cytoplasm of prokaryote bacteria.

Direct fitness The production of offspring by an individual organism.

Directional selection Positive selection for higher or more intense versions of a trait at the expense of lower or less intense versions.

Disruptive selection Positive selection for extreme versions of a trait at the expense of intermediate versions.

Divergence An evolutionary outcome leading to the split of a population into two or more populations across generations based on the evolution of traits adapted to different environmental demands. Divergence can lead to speciation events if interbreeding in the descendant populations is no longer capable of producing viable offspring.

DNA replication The duplication of the DNA molecule during the process of cell division.

Domestication The selective breeding of organisms based on traits useful to humans.

Early modern humans (EMH), recent modern humans (RMH) EMH are distinguished from RMH because of their more prominent eye ridges and an elongated cranium. These remains are considered *Homo sapiens.*

Ectothermy Ability to regulate internal temperature via behavior. Ectothermic animals are more vulnerable to environmental fluctuations in temperature.

Ediacaran fauna Vendian (pre-Cambrian) fossils of possible animals such as jellyfish and superficial traces of bilaterally organized animals. Some of these "fossils" may be mineral formations rather than true animals.

Encephalization A brain size above what is expected for an animal in a specific vertebrate class. Encephalization suggests positive natural selection for an increase in relative brain size (i.e., an increase independent of body size).

Encephalization quotient (EQ) Ratio of brain size of a particular species and the allometric equation with parameters derived from the vertebrate class of that species. EQs provide information about relative brain size independent of body size.

Endothermy Ability to regulate internal temperature via physiological and behavioral adjustments. Endothermic animals are less affected by environmental fluctuations in temperature than ectothermic organisms.

Eukaryote Cells with a true nucleus that encloses the chromosomes (DNA) inside a nuclear membrane. Protists, fungi, plants, and animals are eukaryote organisms.

Evolutionary patterns and processes Patterns refer to the stability of traits in evolution, whereas processes refer to the evolution of novel traits. For example, the relative positions of arm bones are the same in all vertebrates (pattern), but the limbs evolved different functions for flying, swimming, grasping, etc. (process).

Exaptation (preadaptation) Traits that evolve for one function may eventually be coopted into acquiring new functions. For example, the feathers of birds may have evolved as temperature-regulating structures and later become important in courtship displays.

Fear conditioning A classical conditioning situation in which organisms receive pairings of a signal (e.g., a tone) and a painful event (e.g., electric shock). Fear conditioning is usually measured in terms of freezing responses.

Fossil traces The fossilized remains of animal tracks. Fossil traces allow for inferences regarding morphological and behavioral features of the animals that made them.

Frustration A negative emotional state induced by the unexpected omission or reduction of an appetitive outcome or by the anticipation of that negative emotional state.

Functional localization Allocation of a brain area to a relatively specific function.

Genetic code A sequence of three bases in the DNA molecule that results in the transcription of a specific amino acid. The triplet of bases is called a codon. Amino acids, in turn, are the building blocks of proteins. As far as it is known, all animals use the same genetic code.

Geotaxis Tendency to move toward the ground (positive geotaxis) or away from the ground (negative geotaxis).

Helpers Sexually mature individuals that postpone their own reproduction and allocate their time to provide care for the chicks of other animals. Helpers usually contribute to the raising of genetically related animals.

Hippocampus A region in the limbic system of mammals, with homologous areas in other vertebrates, implicated in spatial learning, memory formation, response inhibition, and timing, among other functions.

Hominin A primate exhibiting skeletal adaptations for bipedal posture.

Homology Similarity in genotype (DNA sequence) or phenotype (morphology or function) based on inheritance from a common ancestor.

Inclusive fitness The sum of direct (or Darwinian) and indirect fitness.

Indirect fitness Traits that contribute to the fitness of genetically related organisms at the expense of generating offspring are said to confer high indirect fitness.

Learning sets The successive acquisition of discriminations (e.g., A→Food/B-only, followed by C→Food/D-only, E→Food/F-only, etc., where letters represent stimuli).

Life-history strategy Evolutionary changes in sets of traits. For example, selection for increased body size may also result in a variety of changes in reproductive biology and behavior, longevity, and social behavior.

Lifetime reproductive success (LRS) Direct (or Darwinian) fitness measured across the organism's entire lifespan.

Limbic system A set of nuclei and areas located in the core of the telencephalon known to be involved in many functions relevant for an understanding of behavior (e.g., learning, memory, emotion, motivation, etc.).

Locus coeruleus A nucleus in the brainstem that participates in the control of arousal cycles of sleep and wakefulness.

Mating systems Reproductive arrangements of males and females in a given species or population.

Monophyletic group A group of lineages stemming from a common ancestor.

Natural selection Natural selection occurs when individuals within a population exhibit phenotypic variation in some trait, when alternative traits possess differential reproductive success, and when the traits under selection have a genetic basis.

Neurogenesis Production of new neurons.

Neuron doctrine The theory according to which neural networks are formed by discrete cells, called neurons, that communicate with each other through tiny gaps called synapses.

Oldowan technology The tool kit characteristic of early *Homo* spp., including hammer stones, choppers, and scrapers.

Optic tectum A dorsal structure of the mesencephalon that plays a key role in vision.

Pallium Structures located in the medial, dorsal, and lateral portions of the telencephalon of vertebrates.

Periaqueductal gray (PAG) An area located in the brainstem that controls a variety of motor responses (e.g., freezing in fear conditioning).

Phenotypic plasticity Changes in developing traits that result from environmental factors influencing gene expression.

Phylogenetic tree A graphical representation of genealogical relationships among taxa.

Phylogeny The evolutionary history of lineages.

Phylotypic stage. The stage at which characters unique to a particular phylum first appear during development.

Pleiotropy The effect of a single gene on the development of several traits.

Polymorphism The stable coexistence of alternative phenotypes in a population.

Principle of mass action The extent to which brain damage affects a specific function depends on the size of the damage rather than on its location.

Principle of proper mass The relationship between the size of a brain area and the functional importance of that area.
Prokaryotes Unicellular (bacteria, archaea) organisms characterized by the lack of a nuclear membrane and a relatively small size (less than 10 μm).
Radial symmetry A body organized around one (or more) central axis (e.g., jellyfish).
Raphe nuclei Located in the brainstem, these nuclei control several functions, including levels of arousal.
Reproductive isolation Two populations of descendants that do not interbreed or that produce non-viable offspring that evolved from an ancestral population of interbreeding individuals.
Reproductive success (RS) Ability to reproduce and pass genes onto the next generation via offspring.
Reticular formation An area of the brainstem of vertebrates involved in the regulation of activity cycles. Neurons located in various nuclei of the reticular formation give rise to some of the most important neurochemical systems.
Ribonucleic acid (RNA) DNA information is transcribed into RNA in the cell nucleus. The RNA molecule, called messenger RNA, leaves the nucleus and enters the cell cytoplasm where it is used as a template to produce a protein. The RNA molecule is a sequence of four bases: adenine, cytosine, guanine, and uracil.
Selective breeding The mating organisms based on a specific trait aimed at evolving descendants with enhanced or diminished versions of that trait.
Self-control Ability to inhibit a dominant response. Animals exhibit self-control when they favor a detour leading to a reward over an apparently direct path that fails to reach the reward.
Sexual selection Evolution of traits that enhance fitness by improving intrasexual competition (e.g., male–male competition for access to females) or by affecting the choice of sexual partner.
Spatial learning Acquisition of information about the features (e.g., landmarks) that characterize a particular environment.
Speciation, allopatric and sympatric Evolution of a new species. There are two major speciation scenarios. Allopatric speciation involves the geographic isolation of previously interbreeding populations for a number of generations sufficient to result in reproductive isolation. Islands, lakes, a mountain range, and changes in continental land masses are some of the possible geographical barriers that lead to allopatric speciation. Sympatric speciation involves the emergence of reproductive isolation within subpopulations of animals occupying the same habitat. Mutations affecting species recognition, changes in resource exploitation, and similar factors may induce sympatric speciation.
Splicing Removal of noncoding sections of RNA (called introns) and fusion of coding sections of RNA (called exons) to form messenger RNA (mRNA).
Stabilizing selection Selection against extreme versions of a particular trait.
Stimulus–response (S–R) habits An acquired tendency to respond in a certain way when confronted with a particular stimulus or situation.
Stone tools Lithic technology dated to at least 2.5 Ma.
Subpallium Structures located in the ventral portions of the telencephalon of vertebrates.
Synapse Gap through which contiguous neurons communicate either by the release of neurotransmitters or by the passage of electrical potentials.
Taxon (plural: taxa) A unit of taxonomic analysis.
Tetrapods A vertebrate taxon characterized by four limbs and including amphibians, reptiles, birds, and mammals.
Tooth replacement In reptiles, tooth replacement is a continuous process. By contrast, mammalian teeth are replaced only once (milk teeth to adult teeth). These differences provide clues as to the identity of fossils in the therapsid-mammal lineage.
Trait similarity The sharing of traits across species.
Transcription Conversion of DNA into RNA.
Transitional forms Species that contain a combination of traits from different taxonomic groups.
Translation Protein synthesis from a mRNA template.
Tribosphenic molar A molar characterized by the presence of three main cusps, a variable number of accessory cusps, and crests with sharp edges. It first appeared in therian mammals (the ancestors of living marsupials and placentals).
Win-stay/lose-shift strategy A response strategy useful to resolve simple discriminations, as observed in some experiments on learning sets.

References

Agustí, J., & Lordkipanidze, D. (2011). How "African" was the early human dispersal out of Africa? *Quaternary Science Reviews*, *30*, 1338–1342. https://doi.org/10.1016/j.quascirev.2010.04.012

Andersson, D. I. (2003). Persistence of antibiotic resistant bacteria. *Current Opinion in Microbiology*, *6*, 452–456. https://doi.org/10.1016/j.mib.2003.09.001

Bacher, J. M., Hughes, R. A., Wong, J. T. F., & Ellington, A. D. (2004). Evolving new genetic codes. *Trends in Ecology and Evolution*, *19*, 69–75. https://doi.org/10.1016/j.tree.2003.11.007

Berger, L. R., de Ruiter, D. J., Churchill, S. E., Schmid, P., Carlson, K. J., Dirks, P. H. G. M., & Kibii, J. M. (2010). *Australopithecus sediba*: A new species of *Homo*-like australopith from South Africa. *Science*, *328*, 195–204. https://doi.org/10.1126/science.1184944

Berna, F., Goldberg, P., Horwitz, L. K., Brink, J., Holt, S., Bamford, M., & Chazan, M. (2012). Microstratigraphic evidence of in situ fire in the Acheulean strata of Wonderwerk Cave, Northern Cape province, South Africa. *Proceedings of the National Academy of Sciences USA*, *109*, E1215–E1220. https://doi.org/10.1073/pnas.1117620109

Bingman, V. P., Hough, G. E. II, Kahn, M. C., & Siegel, J. J. (2003). The homing pigeon hippocampus and space: In search of adaptive specialization. *Brain, Behavior and Evolution*, *62*, 117–127. https://doi.org/10.1159/000072442

Bishop, J. A., & Cook, L. M. (1980). Industrial melanism and the urban environment. *Advances in Ecological Research*, *11*, 373–404. https://doi.org/10.1016/S0065-2504(08)60270-6

Bond, A. M., Ming, G., & Song, H. (2015). Adult mammalian neural stem cells and neurogenesis: Five decades later. *Cell Stem Cell*, *17*, 385–395. https://doi.org/10.1016/j.stem.2015.09.003

Briggs, D. E. G., Erwin, D. H., & Collier, F. J. (1994). *The fossils of the Burgess Shale*. Smithsonian Institution Press.

Briscoe, S. D., & Ragsdale, C. W. (2019). Evolution of the chordate telencephalon. *Current Biology*, *29*, R647–R662. https://doi.org/10.1016/j.cub.2019.05.026

Browning, S. R., Browning, B. L., Zhou, Y., Tucci, S., & Akey, J. M. (2018). Analysis of human sequence data reveals two pulses of archaic Denisovan admixture. *Cell*, *173*, 53–61. https://doi.org/10.1016/j.cell.2018.02.031

Butler, A. B. (1994). The evolution of the dorsal pallium in the telencephalon of amniotes: Cladistic analysis and a new hypothesis. *Brain Research Reviews*, *19*, 66–101. https://doi.org/10.1016/0165-0173(94)90004-3

Bygott, J. D., Bertram, B. C. R., & Hanby, C. R. (1979). Male lions in large coalitions gain reproductive advantages. *Nature*, *282*, 839–841. https://doi.org/10.1038/282839a0

Charvet, C. J., & Striedter, G. F. (2009). Developmental basis for telencephalon expansion in waterfowls: Enlargement prior to neurogenesis. *Proceedings of the Royal Society: Biological Sciences*, *276*, 3421–3427. https://doi.org/10.1098/rspb.2009.0888

Chen, F., Welker, F., Shen, C. C., Bailey, S. E., Bergmann, I., Davis, S., Xia, H., Wang, H., Fischer, R., Freidline, S. E., Yu, T. L., Skinner, M. M., Stelzer, S., Dong, G., Fu, Q., Dong, G., Wang, J., Zhang, D., & Hublin, J. J. (2019). A late middle Pleistocene Denisovan mandible from the Tibetan plateau. *Nature*, *569*, 409–412. https://doi.org/10.1038/s41586-019-1139-x

Christian, K. M., & Thompson, R. F. (2005). Long-term storage of an associative memory trace in the cerebellum. *Behavioral Neuroscience*, *119*, 526–537. https://doi.org/10.1037/0735-7044.119.2.526

Darwin, C. (1871/1981). *The descent of man, and selection in relation to sex*. Princeton University Press.

Dembitzer, J., Castiglione, S., Raia, P., & Mairi, S. (2022). Small brains predisposed Late Quaternary mammals to extinction. *Science Reports*, *12*, 3453. https://doi.org/10.1038/s41598-022-07327-9

Diamond, J. M. (2005). *Guns, germs, and steel: The fates of human societies*. Norton.

Dobzhansky, T. (1970). *Genetics of the evolutionary process*. Columbia University Press.

Duarte, C., Maurício, J., Pettitt, P. B., Souto, P., Trinkaus, E., van der Plicht, H., & Zilhão, J. (1999). The early Upper Paleolithic human skeleton from the Abrigo do Lagar Velho (Portugal) and modern human emergence in Iberia. *Proceedings of the National Academy of Sciences USA*, *96*, 7604–7609. https://doi.org/10.1073/pnas.96.13.7604

Eichenbaum, H. (2016). Still searching for the engram. *Learning & Behavior*, *44*, 209–222. https://doi.org/10.3758/s13420-016-0218-1

Eisenberg, J. F. (1981). *The mammalian radiations*. Chicago University Press.

Eisenberg, J. F., & Wilson, D. E. (1978). Relative brain size and feeding strategies in the Chiroptera. *Evolution*, *32*, 740–751. https://doi.org/10.1111/j.1558-5646.1978.tb04627.x

Elias, M. F. (1969). Differences in spatial discrimination reversal learning for mice genetically selected for high brain weight and unselected controls. *Perceptual and Motor Skills*, *28*, 707–712. https://doi.org/10.2466/pms.1969.28.3.707
Elias, M. F. (1970). Spatial discrimination reversal learning for mice genetically selected for differing brain size: A supplementary report. *Perceptual and Motor Skills*, *30*, 239–245. https://doi.org/10.2466/pms.1970.30.1.239
Fitch, W. M., & Margoliash, E. (1967). Construction of phylogenetic trees. *Science*, *155*, 279–284. https://doi.org/10.1126/science.155.3760.279
Forey, P., & Janvier, P. (1994). Evolution of early vertebrates. *American Scientist*, *82*, 554–565.
Fu, D., Tong, G., Dai, T., Liu, W., Yang, Y., Zhang, Y., Cui, L., Li, L., Yun, H., Wu, Y., Sun, A., Liu, C., Pei, W., Gaines, R. R., & Zhang, X. (2019). The Qingjiang biota—A Burgess Shale–type fossil Lagerstätte from the early Cambrian of South China. *Science*, *363*, 1338–1342. https://doi.org/10.1126/science.aau8800
Fuller, J. L., & Geils, H. D. (1972). Brain growth in mice selected for high and low brain weight. *Developmental Psychobiology*, *5*, 307–318. https://doi.org/10.1002/dev.420050404
Ginsburg, S., & Jablonka, E. (2019). *The evolution of the sensitive soul: Learning and the origins of consciousness*. MIT Press.
Glover, C. N., Newton, D., Bajwa, J., Goss, G. G., & Hamilton, T. J. (2019). Behavioural responses of the hagfish *Eptatretus stoutii* to nutrient and noxious stimuli. *Science Reports*, *9*, 13369. https://doi.org/10.1038/s41598-019-49863-x
Gobrogge, K., & Wang, Z. (2016). The ties that bond: Neurochemistry of attachment in voles. *Current Opinion in Neurobiology*, *38*, 80–88. https://doi.org/10.1016/j.conb.2016.04.011
Gómez, A., Ocaña, F. M., del Águila, T., Rodríguez, F., & Salas, C. (2022). Relational memory functions of the hippocampal pallium in teleost fish. In M. Krause, K. L. Hollis, & M. R. Papini (Eds.), *Evolution of learning and memory mechanisms* (pp. 159–175). Cambridge University Press.
Gould, S. J., & Lewontin, R. C. (1979). The spandrels of San Marco and the Panglossian paradigm: A critique of the adaptationist programme. *Proceedings of the Royal Society London*, *B205*, 581–598. https://doi.org/10.1098/rspb.1979.0086
Gould, S. J., & Vbra, E. (1982). Exaptation—A missing term in the science of form. *Paleobiology*, *8*, 4–15.
Grant, P. R. (1986). *Ecology and evolution of Darwin's finches*. Princeton University Press.
Grau, J. W. (2014). Learning from the spinal cord: How the study of spinal cord plasticity informs our view of learning. *Neurobiology of Learning and Memory*, *108*, 155–171. https://doi.org/10.1016/j.nlm.2013.08.003
Gross, M. R. (1985). Disruptive selection for alternative life histories in salmon. *Nature*, *313*, 47–48. https://doi.org/10.1038/313047a0
Guarino, S., Conrad, S. E., & Papini, M. R. (2020). Frustrative nonreward: Chemogenetic inactivation of the central amygdala abolishes the effect of reward downshift without affecting alcohol intake. *Neurobiology of Learning & Memory*, *169*, 107173. https://doi.org/10.1016/j.nlm.2020.107173
Gutiérrez, G., & Domjan, M. (1996). Learning and male-male sexual competition in Japanese quail (*Coturnix japonica*). *Journal of Comparative Psychology*, *110*, 170–175. https://doi.org/10.1037/0735-7036.110.2.170
Haeckel, E. (1879). *The evolution of man: A popular exposition of the principal points of human ontogeny and phylogeny*. Appleton & Century.
Haile-Selassie, Y., Melillo, S. M., Vazzana, A., Benazzi, S., & Ryan, T. M. (2019). A 3.8-million-year-old hominin cranium from Woranso-Mille, Ethiopia. *Nature*, *573*, 214–219. https://doi.org/10.1038/s41586-019-1513-8
Hainsworth, F. R., Overmier, J. B., & Snowden, C. T. (1967). Specific and permanent deficits in instrumental avoidance responding following forebrain ablation in the goldfish. *Journal of Comparative and Physiological Psychology*, *63*, 111–116. https://doi.org/10.1037/h0024143
Hamilton, W. D. (1964). The genetical evolution of social behavior, I and II. *Journal of Theoretical Biology*, *7*, 1–52. https://doi.org/10.1016/0022-5193(64)90038-4
Hannah, R. (2022). How many species are there? *OurWorldInData.org*. https://ourworldindata.org/how-many-species-are-there
Harlow, H. (1949). The formation of learning sets. *Psychological Review*, *56*, 51–65. https://doi.org/10.1037/h0062474
Harmand, S., Lewis, J. E., Feibel, C. S., Lepre, C. J., Prat, S., Lenoble, A., Boës, X., Quinn, R., Brenet, M., Arroyo, A., Taylor, N., Clément, S., Daver, G., Brugal, J. P., Leakey, L., Mortlock, R. A., Wright,

J. D., Lokorodi, S., Kirwa, C., . . . Roche, H. (2015). 3.3-million-year-old stone tools from Lomekwi 3, West Turkana, Kenya. *Nature*, *521*, 310–315. https://doi.org/10.1038/nature14464

Harris, H. M. B., & Hill, C. (2021). A place for viruses on the tree of life. *Frontiers in Microbiology*, *11*. https://doi.org/10.3389/fmicb.2020.604048

Hartwig, W. C. (Ed.). (2002). *The primate fossil record*. Cambridge University Press.

Herculano-Houzel, S., Collins, C. E., Wong, P., & Kaas, J. H. (2006). Cellular scaling rules for primate brains. *Proceedings of the National Academy of Sciences USA*, *104*, 3562–3567. https://doi.org/10.1073/pnas.0611396104

Herculano-Houzel, S., Mota, B., & Lent, R. (2006). Cellular scaling rules for rodent brains. *Proceedings of the National Academy of Sciences USA*, *103*, 12138–12143. https://doi.org/10.1073/pnas.0604911103

Hewitt, J. K., Fulker, D. W., & Hewitt, C. A. (1983). Genetic architecture of olfactory discriminative avoidance conditioning in *Drosophila melanogaster*. *Journal of Comparative Psychology*, *97*, 52–58. https://doi.org/10.1037/0735-7036.97.1.52

Holland, L. Z. (2015). The origin and evolution of chordate nervous systems. *Philosophical Transactions of the Royal Society London, B Biological Sciences*, *370*, 20150048. https://doi.org/10.1098/rstb.2015.0048

Hollis, K. L. (1982). Pavlovian conditioning of signal-centered action patterns and autonomic behavior: A biological analysis of function. *Advances in the Study of Behavior*, *12*, 1–64. https://doi.org/10.1016/S0065-3454(08)60045-5

Hollis, K. L., Dumas, M. J., Singh, P., & Fackelman, P. (1995). Pavlovian conditioning of aggressive behavior in blue gourami fish (*Trichogaster trichopterus*): Winners become winners and losers stay losers. *Journal of Comparative Psychology*, *109*, 123–133. https://doi.org/10.1037/0735-7036.109.2.123

Hu, Y., Wu, Q., Ma, S., Ma, T., Shan, L., Wang, X., Nie, Y., Ning, Z., Yan, L., Xiu, Y., & Wei, F. (2017). Comparative genomics reveals convergent evolution between the bamboo-eating giant and red pandas. *Proceedings of the National Academy of Sciences USA*, *114*, 1081–1086. https://doi.org/10.1073/pnas.1613870114

Hublin, J-J., Ben-Ncer, A., Bailey, S. E., Freidline, S. E., Neubauer, S., Skinner, M. M., Bergmann, I., Le Cabec, A., Benazzi, S., Harvati, K., & Gunz, P. (2017). New fossils from Jebel Irhoud, Morocco and the pan-African origin of *Homo sapiens*. *Nature*, *546*, 289–292. https://doi.org/10.1038/nature22336

Jacob, C., & Onelli, C. (1913). *Atlas del cerebro de los mamíferos de la República Argentina*. Kraft.

Jacob, F. (1977). Evolution and tinkering. *Science*, *196*, 1161. https://doi.org/10.1126/science.860134

Jacobs, L. F., Gaulin, S. J. C., Sherry, D. F., & Hoffman, G. E. (1990). Evolution of spatial cognition: Sex-specific patterns of spatial behavior predict hippocampal size. *Proceedings of the National Academy of Sciences USA*, *87*, 6349–6352. https://doi.org/10.1073/pnas.87.16.6349

Janvier, P. (2008). Early jawless vertebrates and cyclostome origins. *Zoological Science*, *25*, 1045–1056. https://doi.org/10.2108/zsj.25.1045

Jerison, H. J. (1973). *Evolution of the brain and intelligence*. Academic Press.

Ji, Q., Luo, Z. X., Yuan, C. X., Wible, J. R., Zhang, J. P., Georgi, J. A. (2002). The earliest known eutherian mammal. *Nature*, *416*, 816–822. https://doi.org/10.1038/416816a

Kaas, J. H. (2004). Evolution of the large, complex sensorimotor systems of anthropoid primates. *International Journal of Comparative Psychology*, *17*, 34–52. https://doi.org/10.46867/ijcp.2004.17.01.04

Kaifu, Y., Aziz, F., Indriati, E., Jacob, T., Kurniawan, I., & Baba, H. (2008). Cranial morphology of Javanese *Homo erectus*: New evidence for continuous evolution, specialization, and terminal extinction. *Journal of Human Evolution*, *55*, 551–580. https://doi.org/10.1016/j.jhevol.2008.05.002

Kay, H., & Oldfield-Box, H. (1965). A study of learning-sets in rats with an apparatus using 3-dimensional shapes. *Animal Behaviour*, *13*, 19–24. https://doi.org/10.1016/0003-3472(65)90066-7

Kay, R. F. (2015). Biogeography in deep time–What do phylogenetics, geology, and paleoclimate tell us about early platyrrhine evolution? *Molecular Phylogenetics and Evolution*, *82*, 358–374. https://doi.org/10.1016/j.ympev.2013.12.002

Kay, R. F. (2018). 100 years of primate paleontology. *Journal of Physical Anthropology*, *165*, 652–676. https://doi.org/10.1002/ajpa.23429

Kelley, J. (1992). Evolution of apes. In S. Jones, R. Martin, & D. Pilbeam (Eds.), *Cambridge encyclopedia of human evolution* (pp. 223–230). Cambridge University Press.

Kirn, J. R. (2010). The relationship of neurogenesis and growth of brain regions to song learning. *Brain and Language*, *115*, 29–44. https://doi.org/10.1016/j.bandl.2009.09.006

Knoll, A. H., & Carroll, S. B. (1999). Early animal evolution: Emerging views from comparative biology and geology. *Science*, *284*, 2129–2137. https://doi.org/10.1126/science.284.5423.2129

Kotrschal, A., Rogell, B., Bundsen, A., Svensson, B., Zajitschek, S., Brännström, I., Immler, S., Maklakov, A. A., & Kolm, N. (2013). Artificial selection on relative brain size in the guppy reveals costs and benefits of evolving a larger brain. *Current Biology*, *23*, 168–171. https://doi.org/10.1016/j.cub.2012.11.058

Krause, J., Fu, Q., Good, J. M., Viola, B., Shunkov, M., Derevianko, A. P., & Pääbo, S. (2010). The complete mitochondrial DNA genome of an unknown hominin from southern Siberia. *Nature*, *464*, 894–897. https://doi.org/10.1038/nature08976

Krings, M., Stone, A., Schmitz, R. W., Krainitzki, H., Stoneking, M., & Pääbo, S. (1997). Neanderthal DNA sequences and the origin of modern humans. *Cell*, *90*, 19–30. https://doi.org/10.1016/s0092-8674(00)80310-4

Kuhlwilm, M., de Manuel, M., Nater, A., Greminger, M. P., Krützen, M., & Marques-Bonet, T. (2016). Evolution and demography of the great apes. *Current Opinion in Genetics and Development*, *41*, 124–129. https://doi.org/10.1016/j.gde.2016.09.005

Kuhlwilm, M., Gronau, I., Hubisz, M. J., de Filippo, D., Prado-Martinez, J., Kircher, M., Fu, Q., Burbano, H. A., Lalueza-Fox, C., de la Rasilla, M., Rosas, A., Rudan, P., Brajkovic, D., Kucan, Ž., Gušic, I., Marques-Bonet, T., Andrés, A. M., Viola, B., Pääbo, S., . . . Castellano, S. (2016). Ancient gene flow from early modern humans into Eastern Neanderthals. *Nature*, *530*, 429–433. https://doi.org/10.1038/nature16544

Kuhn, S. L., & Stiner, M. C. (2006). What's a mother to do? The division of labor among Neandertals and modern humans in Eurasia. *Current Anthropology*, *47*(6), 953–980. https://doi.org/10.1086/507197

Lalueza-Fox, C., Römpler, H., Caramelli, D., Stäubert, C., Catalano, G., Hughes, D., Rohland, N., Pilli, E., Longo, L., Condemi, S., de la Rasilla, M., Fortea, J., Rosas, A., Stoneking, M., Schöneberg, T., Bertranpetit, J., & Hofreiter, M. (2007). A melanocortin 1 receptor allele suggests varying pigmentation among Neanderthals. *Science*, *318*, 1453–1455. https://doi.org/10.1126/science.1147417

Lamichhaney, S., Han, F., Berglund, J., Wang, C., Almén, M. S., Webster, M. T., Grant, B. R., Grant, P. R., & Andersson, L. (2016). A beak size locus in Darwin's finches facilitated character displacement during a drought. *Science*, *352*, 470–474. https://doi.org/10.1126/science.aad8786

Lewontin, R. C. (1978). Adaptation. *Scientific American*, *239*, 156–169. https://doi.org/10.1038/scientificamerican0978-212

Liu, S. et al. (2021). Ancient and modern genomes unravel the evolutionary history of the rhinoceros family. *Cell*, *184*, 1–12. https://doi.org/10.1016/j.cell.2021.07.032

Lofdahl, K. L., Hu, D., Ehrman, L., Hirsch, J., & Skoog, L. (1992). Incipient reproductive isolation and evolution in laboratory *Drosophila melanogaster* selected for geotaxis. *Animal Behaviour*, *44*, 783–786. https://doi.org/10.1016/S0003-3472(05)80307-0

Lordkipanidze, D., Ponce de León, M. S., Margvelashvili, A., Rak, Y., Rightmire, G. P., Vekua, A., & Zollikofer, C. P. E. (2013). A complete skull from Dmanisi, Georgia, and the evolutionary biology of early *Homo*. *Science*, *342*, 326–331. https://doi.org/10.1126/science.1238484

Luo, Z.-X., Crompton, A. W., & Sun, A.-L. (2001). A new mammaliaform from the early Jurassic and evolution of mammalian characteristics. *Science*, *292*, 1535–1540. https://doi.org/10.1126/science.1058476

Mace, G. M., Harvey, P. H., & Clutton-Brock, T. H. (1980). Is brain size an ecological variable? *Trends in Neuroscience*, *3*, 193–196.

MacLean, E. L., Hare, B., Nunn, C. L., Addessi, E., Amici, F., Anderson, R. C., Aureli, F., Baker, J. M., Bania, A. E., Barnard, A. M., Boogert, N. J., Brannon, E. M., Bray, E. E., Bray, J., Brent, L. J. N., Burkart, J. M., Call, J., Cantlon, J. F., Cheke, L. G., . . . Zhao, Y. (2014). The evolution of self-control. *Proceedings of the National Academy of Sciences USA*, *111*, E2140–2148. https://doi.org/10.1073/pnas.1323533111

Mallatt, J., & Chen, J. Y. (2003). Fossil sister group of craniates: Predicted and found. *Journal of Morphology*, *258*, 1–31. https://doi.org/10.1002/jmor.10081

Marino, L. (2004). Cetacean brain evolution: Multiplication generates complexity. *International Journal of Comparative Psychology*, *17*, 1–16.

Martin, M. W., Grazhdankin, D. V., Bowring, S. A., Evans, D. A. D., Fedonkin, M. A., & Kirschvink, J. L. (2000). Age of neoproterozoic bilaterian body and trace fossils, White Sea, Russia: Implications for metazoan evolution. *Science*, *288*, 841–845. https://doi.org/10.1126/science.288.5467.841

Martin, R. D. (1981). Relative brain size and basal metabolic rate in terrestrial vertebrates. *Nature*, *293*, 57–60. https://doi.org/10.1038/293057a0

McGann, J. P. (2015). Associative learning and sensory neuroplasticity: How does it happen and what is it good for? *Learning and Memory*, *22*, 567–576. https://doi.org/10.1101/lm.039636.115

McHenry, H. M. (1995). Tempo and mode in human evolution. In W. M. Fitch & F. J. Ayala (Eds.), *Tempo and mode in evolution* (pp. 169–186). National Academy Press.

Mishkin, M., Malamut, B., & Bachevalier, J. (1984). Memories and habits: Two neural systems. In J. L. McGaugh & N. M. Weinberger (Eds.), *Neurobiology of learning and memory* (pp. 68–88). Guilford.

Montagnese, C. M., Krebs, J. R., Székely, A. D., & Csillag, A. (1993). A subpopulation of large calbindin-like immunopositive neurones is present in the hippocampal formation in food-storing but not in non-storing species of bird. *Brain Research*, *614*, 291–300. https://doi.org/10.1016/0006-8993(93)91047-v

Morris, R. G., Garrud, M., Rawlins, J. N. P., & O'Keefe, J. (1982). Place navigation impaired in rats with hippocampal lesions. *Nature*, *297*, 681–683. https://doi.org/10.1038/297681a0

Muzio, R. N., & Bingman, V. P. (2022). Brain and spatial cognition in amphibians: Stem adaptations in the evolution of tetrapod cognition. In M. Krause, K. L. Hollis, & M. R. Papini (Eds.), *Evolution of learning and memory mechanisms* (pp. 105–124). Cambridge University Press.

Northcutt, R. G., & Kaas, J. H. (1995). The emergence and evolution of mammalian neocortex. *Trends in Neuroscience*, *18*, 373–379. https://doi.org/10.1016/0166-2236(95)93932-n

Olkowicz, S., Kocourek, M., Lucan, R. K., Portes, M., Fitch, W. T., Herculano-Houzel, S., & Nemec, P. (2016). Birds have primate-like numbers of neurons in the forebrain. *Proceedings of the National Academy of Sciences USA*, *113*, 7255–7260. https://doi.org/10.1073/pnas.1517131113

Overington, S. E., Morand-Ferron, J., Boogert, N. J., & Lefebvre, L. (2009). Technical innovations drive the relationship between innovativeness and residual brain size in birds. *Animal Behaviour*, *78*, 1001–1010. https://doi.org/10.1016/j.anbehav.2009.06.033

Overmier, J. B., & Papini, M. R. (1986). Factors modulating the effects of teleost telencephalon ablation on retention, relearning, and extinction of instrumental avoidance behavior. *Behavioral Neuroscience*, *100*, 190–199. https://doi.org/10.1037//0735-7044.100.2.190

Packer, C., Herbst, L., Pusey, A. E., Bygott, J. D., Hanby, J. P., Cairns, S. J., & Mulder, M. B. (1988). Reproductive success of lions. In T. H. Clutton-Brock (Ed.), *Reproductive success* (pp. 363–383). University of Chicago Press.

Papini, M. R. (2021). *Comparative psychology. Evolution and development of brain and behavior*. Taylor and Francis.

Passingham, R. E., & Wise, S. P. (2012). *The neurobiology of the prefrontal cortex: Anatomy, evolution, and the origin of insight*. Oxford University Press.

Pessoa, L. (2023). How many brain regions are needed to elucidate the neural bases of fear and anxiety? *Neuroscience and Biobehavioral Reviews*, *146*, 105039. https://doi.org/10.1016/j.neubiorev.2023.105039

Portavella, M., Salas, C., Vargas, J. P., & Papini, M. R. (2003). Involvement of the telencephalon in spaced-trial avoidance learning in the goldfish (*Carassius auratus*). *Physiology and Behavior*, *80*(1), 49–56. https://doi.org/10.1016/s0031-9384(03)00208-7

Portavella, M., Torres, B., Salas, C., & Papini, M. R. (2004). Lesions of the medial pallium, but not of the lateral pallium, disrupt spaced-trial avoidance learning in goldfish (*Carassius auratus*). *Neuroscience Letters*, *362*, 75–78. https://doi.org/10.1016/j.neulet.2004.01.083

Proffitt, T., Reeves, J. S., Braun, D. R., Malaivijitnond, S., & Luncz, L. V. (2023). Wild macaques challenge the origin of intentional tool production. *Science Advances*, *9*, 10. https://doi.org/10.1126/sciadv.ade8159

Puddington, M. M., Daneri, M. F., Papini, M. R., & Muzio, R. M. (2016). Telencephalic neural activation following passive avoidance learning in a terrestrial toad. *Behavioural Brain Research*, *315*, 75–82. https://doi.org/10.1016/j.bbr.2016.08.003

Ratcliffe, J. M., Fenton, M. B., & Shettleworth, S. J. (2006). Behavioral flexibility positively correlated with relative brain volume in predatory bats. *Brain, Behavior and Evolution*, *67*, 165–176. https://doi.org/10.1159/000090980

Rauhut, O. W. M., Martin, T., Ortiz-Juareguizar, E., & Puerta, P. (2002). A Jurassic mammal from South America. *Nature*, *416*, 165–167. https://doi.org/10.1038/416165a
Reichling, D. B., Kwiat, G. C., & Basbaum, A. I. (1988). Anatomy, physiology, and pharmacology of the periaqueductal gray contribution to antinociceptive controls. In H. L. Fields & J. M. Besson (Eds.), *Progress in brain research* (Vol. 77, pp. 31–46). Elsevier.
Reznick, D. N., Shaw, F. H., Rodd, F. H., & Shaw, R. G. (1997). Evaluation of the rate of evolution in natural populations of guppies (*Poecilia reticulata*). *Science*, *275*, 1934–1937. https://doi.org/10.1126/science.275.5308.1934
Ricker, J. P., & Hirsch, J. (1985). Evolution of an instinct under long-term divergent selection for geotaxis in domesticated populations of *Drosophila melanogaster*. *Journal of Comparative Psychology*, *99*, 380–390. https://doi.org/10.1037/0735-7036.99.4.380
Ricker, J. P., & Hirsch, J. (1988). Reversal of genetic homeostasis in laboratory populations of *Drosophila melanogaster* under long-term selection for geotaxis and estimates of gene correlates: Evolution of behavior-genetic systems. *Journal of Comparative Psychology*, *102*, 203–214. https://doi.org/10.1037/0735-7036.102.3.203
Riddell, W. I., & Corl, K. G. (1977). Comparative investigation of the relationship between cerebral indices and learning abilities. *Brain, Behavior and Evolution*, *14*, 385–398. https://doi.org/10.1159/000125804
Roubertoux, P. L. (1992). Courtship behavior in the male guppy (*Poecilia reticulata*): A genetic analysis. *International Journal of Comparative Psychology*, *5*, 145–163.
Russell, F., & Burke, D. (2016). Conditional same/different concept learning in the short-beaked echidna (*Tachyglossus aculeatus*). *Journal of the Experimental Analysis of Behavior*, *105*, 133–154. https://doi.org/10.1002/jeab.185
Sánchez-Quinto, F., Botigué, L. R., Civit, S., Arenas, C., Ávila-Arcos, M. C., Bustamante, C. D., Comas, D., Lalueza-Fox, C. (2012). North African populations carry the signature of admixture with Neandertals. *PLoS ONE*, *7*, e47765. https://doi.org/10.1371/journal.pone.0047765
Sankararaman, S., Mallick, S., Damnemann, M., Prüfer, K., Kelso, J., Pääbo, S., Patterson, N., & Reich, D. (2014). The genomic landscape of Neanderthal ancestry in present-day humans. *Nature*, *507*, 354–357. https://doi.org/10.1038/nature12961
Searle, L. V. (1949). The organization of hereditary maze-brightness and maze-dullness. *Genetic Psychology Monographs*, *39*, 279–325.
Seilacher, A., Bose, P. K., & Pfluger, F. (1998). Triploblastic animals more than 1 billion years ago: Trace fossil evidence from India. *Science*, *282*, 80–83. https://doi.org/10.1126/science.282.5386.80
Sherry, D. F., & Hoshooley, J. S. (2010). Seasonal hippocampal plasticity in food-storing birds. *Philosophical Transactions of the Royal Society, London, B Biological Sciences*, *365*, 933–943. https://doi.org/10.1098/rstb.2009.0220
Sherry, D. F., Vaccarino, A. L., Buckenham, K., & Herz, R. S. (1989). The hippocampal complex of food-storing birds. *Brain, Behavior and Evolution*, *34*, 308–317. https://doi.org/10.1159/000116516
Slotnick, B. M., & Katz, H. M. (1974). Olfactory learning-set formation in rats. *Science*, *185*, 796–798. https://doi.org/10.1126/science.185.4153.796
Stahlman, W. D., & Leising, K. J. (2018). The coelacanth still lives: Bringing selection back to the fore in a science of behavior. *American Psychologist*, *73*, 918–929. https://doi.org/10.1037/amp0000261
Stearns, S. C. (1992). *The evolution of life histories*. Oxford University Press.
Striedter, G. F. (2005). *Principles of brain evolution*. Sinauer.
Suzuki, D. G. (2021). Consciousness in jawless fishes. *Frontiers in Systems Neuroscience*, *15*. https://doi.org/10.3389/fnsys.2021.751876
Tobias, P. V. (1995). The brain of the first hominids. In J.-P. Changeux & J. Chavaillon (Eds.), *Origins of the human brain* (pp. 61–81). Clarendon Press.
Todorov, O. S. (2020). Marsupial cognition. In J. Vonk, & T. Shackelford (Eds.), *Encyclopedia of animal cognition and behavior* (pp. 1–8). Springer Nature. https://doi.org/10.1007/978-3-319-47829-6_1167-1
Toma, D. P., White, K. P., Hirsch, J., & Greenspan, R. J. (2002). Identification of genes involved in *Drosophila melanogaster* geotaxis, a complex behavioral trait. *Nature Genetics*, *31*, 349–353. https://doi.org/10.1038/ng893
Tryon, R. C. (1934). Individual differences. In F. A. Moss (Ed.), *Comparative psychology* (pp. 409–445). Prentice-Hall.

van Dongen, P. A. M. (1998). Brain size in vertebrates. In R. Nieuwenhuys, H. J. ten Donkelaar, & C. Nicholson (Eds.), *The central nervous system of vertebrates* (pp. 2099–2134). Springer.
Waters, M. R., & Stafford, T. W. Jr. (2007). Redefining the age of Clovis: Implications for the peopling of the Americas. *Science*, *315*, 1122–1126. https://doi.org/10.1126/science.1137166
Williams, G. C. (1966). *Adaptation and natural selection*. Princeton University Press.
Wimer, C., Roderick, T. H., & Wimer, R. E. (1969). Supplementary report: Behavioral differences in mice genetically selected for brain weight. *Psychological Reports*, *25*, 363–368. https://doi.org/10.2466/pr0.1969.25.2.363
Woese, C. R., Kandler, O., & Wheelis, M. L. (1990). Towards a natural system of organisms: Proposal for the domains Archaea, Bacteria, and Eucarya. *Proceedings of the National Academy of Sciences USA*, *87*, 4576–4579. https://doi.org/10.1073/pnas.87.12.4576
Woolfenden, G. E., & Fitzpatrick, J. W. (1997). Florida scrub jays: A synopsis after 18 years of study. In P. B. Stacy & W. D. Koenig (Eds.), *Cooperative breeding in birds: Long-term studies of ecology and behavior* (pp. 241–266). Cambridge University Press.
Yang, M. A., Gao, X., Theunert, C., Tong, H., Aximu-Petri, A., Nickel, B., Slatkin, M., Meyer, M., Pääbo, S., Kelso, J., & Fu, Q. (2017). 40,000-year-old individual from Asia provides insight into early population structure in Eurasia. *Current Biology*, *27*, 3202–3208. https://doi.org/10.1016/j.cub.2017.09.030
Zeldin, R. K., & Olton, D. S. (1986). Rats acquire spatial learning sets. *Journal of Experimental Psychology: Animal Behavior Processes*, *12*, 412–419. https://doi.org/10.1037/0097-7403.12.4.412
Zhu, M., Yu, X., Ahlberg, P., Choo, B., Lu, J., Qiao, T., Zhao, W., Jia, L., Blom, H., & Zhu, Y. (2013). A Silurian placoderm with osteichthyan-like marginal jaw bones. *Nature*, *502*, 188–193. https://doi.org/10.1038/nature12617

2 Fundamentals of stimulus control

2.1 Properties of a stimulus

Behavior has been described as anything a dead person cannot do (Lindsley, 1991). Thus, we can conclude that all animals behave. *Stimulus control*, or the degree to which the probability of a behavior varies with the presence or absence of stimuli, has important implications for *direct fitness*. Elicited behavior exhibits the highest degree of stimulus control and consists of an eliciting stimulus or *unconditioned stimulus* (US), and a corresponding response, or *unconditioned response* (UR, Figure 2.1). Elicited behavior is most consistent with the original Latin for *stimulus*, which means to goad, prick, or incite. Staddon (2016) identified a stimulus as having the properties of intensity, quality, duration, and location. All of these properties affect dimensions of the incited response (e.g., its magnitude). The sheer quantity of potential stimuli in the world is intimidating, but fortunately, the specification of an animal (and not, e.g., an electron or a planet) as the reacting agent imposes certain limitations. Take a moment to look around and count how many stimuli have the potential to incite action. You may have noticed obvious stimuli, such as the light coming through your window, the clock on the wall, or the phone on the desk. You may have also tried to make a distinction between stimuli that elicit a response automatically (e.g., pupil dilation in response to light) compared to those that merely influence voluntary actions (e.g., going to class based on the clock). However, you may not have counted other stimuli, such as your bed, water bottle, or roommate. Each of those stimuli could be further broken down (e.g., your pillow, the straw of your water bottle, and the clothes your roommate is wearing). Even if all of these discrete stimuli were removed, you would still be in a particular space and time, both of which can influence your behavior. Behavior never occurs in a stimulus vacuum.

Identifying a stimulus involves, at a minimum, a test with the presence and absence of that stimulus (independent variable) and a measure of behavior (dependent variable). The scientific method necessitates that the relationship between a stimulus and the changing probability of a response be observable and replicable. The history of psychology has encouraged humility in concluding what is a stimulus. For example, rabbits given several pairings of a brief 0.75-s Tone (*conditioned stimulus*, CS) that terminated in a Shock (US) to its cheek exhibited eyelid blinking (*conditioned response*, CR) during subsequent presentations of the CS (Vandercar & Schneiderman, 1967). If the Tone was extended to 6.75 s, then the CR was not observed. We could conclude that a Tone presented at this duration and paired with Shock is not a stimulus for rabbits because a CR was not observed, but we would be mistaken. Rabbits exhibited an increase in heart rate (a second dependent measure) in both groups. It is difficult to prove that something is not a stimulus for some not-yet-measured response. Similarly, the molecular and cellular physiology of organisms is certainly observable, replicable, and constantly reacting to the sensory world; however, we limit this chapter

DOI: 10.4324/9781003401957-3

Figure 2.1 **Startle reflex to a loud noise.** The loud noise (US) from fireworks elicits an unconditioned, or reflexive, startle response with a high probability in many animals as well as a UR to orient toward the origin of the sound. (Photo by K. J. Leising.)

to stimuli whose reactions at the molecular and cellular level manifest as a change in overt behavior either at the time of their presentation or subsequently under similar conditions. These considerations are among the reasons why defining a stimulus is not a simple matter. As Gibson (1960, p. 701) wrote:

> In short, whether or not a potential stimulus becomes effective depends on the individual. It depends on the species to which he belongs, on the anatomy of the sense organs, the stage of maturation, the capacities for sense organ adjustment, the habits of attention, the activity in progress, and the possibilities of educating the attention of the individual. Such facts make up the field of perceptual development and perceptual learning. At the lower levels they are called facts of sensory physiology; at the higher levels, facts of attention or exploration, but they are all one problem.

As psychological scientists interested in behavior, we must seek to account for all that we do, from the most banal muscle twitch to the most impressive guitar solo to the enormous complexity of our verbal behavior—this all happens for discoverable reasons, and these reasons are to be found in the environments in which you and your ancestors have lived (see Chapter 1). A helpful way to introduce students to learning and cognition is with reference to the popular-culture movie *The Matrix*. What at first will seem to you like a world (and course) full of a constant stream of uninterpretable symbols, over time, the symbols come to represent stimuli and relations among them that are important causes of behavior; and you, like Neo in the movie, will be able to interpret and manipulate them (Figure 2.2). An understanding of comparative learning and cognition must start with a discussion of stimuli and the stimulus control of behavior.

Figure 2.2 **An image in the style of** ***The Matrix*****.** The image can be seen as a random matrix of symbols, or one can see the outline of two stimuli important to the history of psychology, that of a bell and a dog (Image created by K. J. Leising.)

2.1.1 Evolutionary framework

Stimuli must have physical properties, but not everything with physical properties can be said to be a stimulus. For something to be called a stimulus, it must have a measurable impact on the behavior of the organism in question. Individual differences and species differences mean that physical events cannot necessarily be defined as stimuli for all organisms. Every organism has evolved within a unique sensory and perceptual world, or *umwelt* (von Uexküll, 1957). The umwelt encompasses the subset of environmental stimuli that are biologically relevant and accessible to that organism, many of which function as USs and CSs in conditioning procedures.

Take, for example, the blinking of a strobe light. This would typically be called a stimulus—but this is not quite right! It is true for most human beings and most standard laboratory animals. The flashing of such a light will often have measurable impacts on behavior: a person might, for example, shield their eyes or look away; they may complain about it; physiological measures of stress may spike; etc. But this light would not be a stimulus for someone who is not sighted nor in any animal that does not detect this form of energy. Take, for example, the Mexican cave tetra (*Astyanax mexicanus*). This is a species of fish whose ancestors could see but were then reproductively isolated in caves in which visible light does not penetrate. Eyes are biologically costly to maintain and, in this case, useless. Thus, over generations, the eyes of these fish were lost (Protas et al., 2007). A blinking light is nothing to the Mexican cave tetra, much like the myriad of radio waves currently penetrating your body are nothing to you (unless this energy is transduced into another form, e.g., vibrational energy).

Biological evolution is a function of differential reproduction over generations (see Chapter 1). Reproduction is dependent on what organisms can do. What organisms can do depends on their personal and ancestral environments (Figure 2.3). The problems of finding food and water, finding sexual partners, and avoiding threats are ubiquitous, but their solutions are selective and varied. The Mexican cave tetra solves problems using different specific means than its sighted counterparts.

"Why is the sky blue?" When students are asked this question, the typical answers refer to the physical properties of the atmosphere or sky itself (e.g., wavelengths of light). Though these answers are technically correct, they overlook that the ability to detect wavelengths of blue light (i.e., to see a blue sky) is not shared by all species. In other words, although the wavelengths of light radiating from the sky may be in the portion of the spectrum we categorize as blue, a Mexican tetra would not see a blue sky. Another correct answer reflects an evolutionary perspective on adaptive behavior and on the nature of stimuli: "Because we eat fruit" (Figure 2.4).

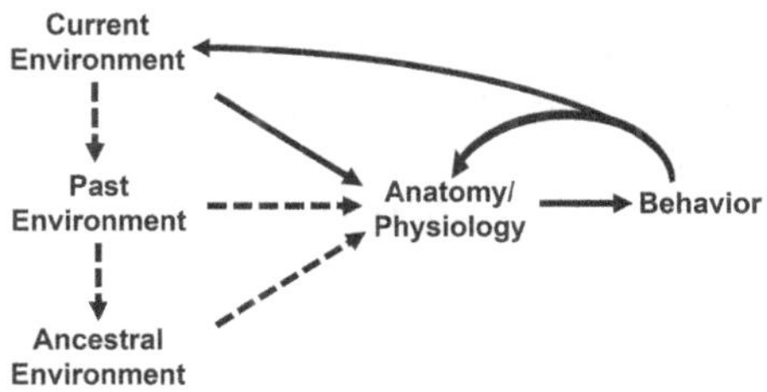

Figure 2.3 **Interactions between an animal and its environment.** The current environment becomes the past environment with every passing moment, the sum of which constitutes the ancestral environment. These influence the anatomy and physiology of an organism, from which behavior emerges. Behavior is capable of directly altering the anatomy and physiology but can also influence it indirectly by altering the environment. The solid arrows indicate connections that are observable, whereas dashed lines indicate connections or transitions that occurred in the past.

Figure 2.4 **A blue sky and fruit.** One explanation of the reason why we see the colors in these pictures is because our primate ancestors depended on identifying fruits in the dense canopy of rainforests, as in this tree branch with ripe (edible) and unripe (not ready to be eaten) figs, as a significant portion of their daily diet. (Photo of sky by K. J. Leising; fig tree photo from https://creative.commons.org, by Fir0002, licensed under CC BY-SA 3.0.)

When multiple stimuli are present, an organism's umwelt may bias stimulus control in favor of a stimulus that is more biologically relevant to that organism. The *salience*, or noticeability, of a stimulus is often used interchangeably with its intensity but applies equally to a stimulus high in biological relevance. A researcher may present experimental trials in which the amplitude (in decibels) is varied for some auditory stimulus. All else being equal, the loudness of a sound is correlated with its salience—louder sounds and brighter lights are more salient, more noticeable, than are quieter sounds and dimmer lights. Hence, the salience of stimuli bears a close correspondence to variance in a physical dimension. This correspondence is not absolute, however. Remember that a stimulus, by definition, must be perceptible. Evolution has built organisms that are only sensitive to a small subset of possible physical events, with variance between species and between individuals reflecting this phylogenic history. A sound frequency above 20,000 Hz will not be heard by most human beings, no matter its amplitude. Such sounds may, of course, be heard by other animals. Blowing a dog whistle will not directly cause behavioral changes in nearby humans but may cause an intense reaction in nearby dogs.

Salience does not just refer to a physical property such as intensity. It is also a concept that can be measured in relative terms, empirically, by virtue of comparisons of behaviors influenced by multiple stimuli in controlled circumstances. All else being equal, one would expect that a rat will learn about a loud sound more quickly than about a quiet one or about a bright light more quickly than about a dim one. But other factors need to be considered in establishing the nature of stimuli.

2.2 Stimulus control

2.2.1 Response probability

For behavior to be adaptive, the crucial element is its outwardness—no matter the complexity of any interior, covert world, only overt action that modifies the interaction between the animal and its environment can produce changes in direct fitness. In this way, thinking and feeling are like genes, only indirectly influenced by evolution. To investigate factors that influence behavior change, the selection of a behavior elicited under well-known conditions is ideal. One of the earliest reports of this method in a psychological investigation was Galen's (circa 168 BCE) attempt to diagnose love sickness in a subject by having his assistant read the names of people of interest while Galen measured the subject's pulse (Veith, 1961).

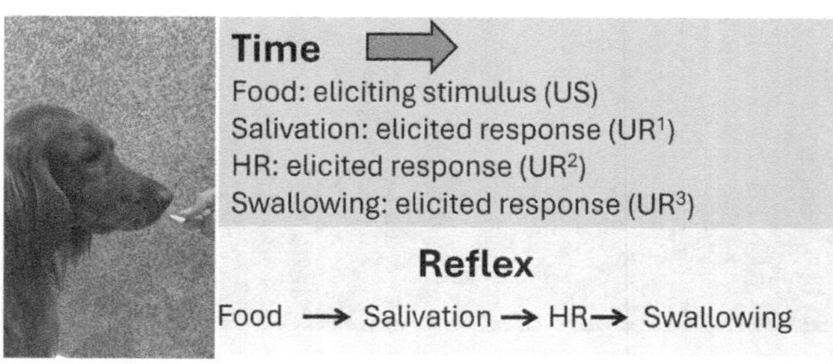

Figure 2.5 **An example of some components of a reflex.** A reflex involves an eliciting, or unconditioned stimulus (US), and one or more elicited, or unconditioned responses (UR). When food (US) is placed in a dog's mouth, it will tend to elicit a variety of responses (URs), including salivation (UR^1), changes in heart rate (HR; UR^2), and swallowing (UR^3).

He assumed that an encounter with the target (US) of the subject's attraction would automatically elicit an increase in their pulse (UR), and by association, so would the target's name (CS). Descartes (1985/1662) formalized the notion of a *reflex* (US-UR connection, Figure 2.5) as behavior that appeared to be tightly controlled by "external objects presented to the senses" (Descartes, 1985/1662, p. 202), including blinking in response to an object moving toward the eye. He posited that some responses were not initiated by the mind, but followed from "the mere arrangement of the machine's organs every bit as naturally as the movements of a clock" (p. 202). A few years later, Jan Swammerdam confirmed the mechanistic nature of reflexes by demonstrating that a thigh muscle that had been surgically removed from the body of a frog could be stimulated with near-perfect probability by the touch of a scalpel to an exposed nerve (Pubols, 1959).

2.2.1.1 Reflexes

Replicability is a key attribute of a successful science. Astronomy, physics, and chemistry have ancient origins in part because they each deal with stable phenomena that were important to our ancestors. Understanding the night sky allowed for reliable navigation to far-flung areas; understanding the regularities by which certain compounds interacted allowed for improvements in industrialization. The earliest scientific investigations of behavior focused on the eliciting characteristics of stimuli.

A reflex is a relation between a stimulus and a response—it is not a response itself (Skinner, 1935). Imagine a continuum of stimulus control, with a low probability of a response in the presence of a stimulus at one extreme and a high probability at the other. Reflexes exhibit strong stimulus control with little-to-no prior experience. A reflex, or what is commonly referred to as a reflex arc, involves three main components: (1) detection and transduction of the stimulus by sensory receptors, (2) transmission between neurons across at least one synapse, and (3) a movement elicited as a result of the transmission. Strong stimulus control is accomplished by a dependence on relatively few connections from detection to movement. The human *patellar reflex*, for example, is one in which sensory receptors in a tendon are stimulated by a tap to the knee and transduce the stimulation into action potentials in afferent neurons that carry the signal into the dorsal horn of the spinal cord. These sensory neurons make synaptic connection with efferent motor neurons that carry the signal out of the ventral horn of the spinal cord to stimulate the quadriceps muscle and relax the antagonistic hamstring muscle. It is this combination of contraction and relaxation of these muscles that produces the small kick. The probability of this response is so high that it is routinely stimulated in medical evaluations to test the integrity of the central nervous system. This reflex plays a critical role in walking and running by raising the foot forward after stimulation of the muscle tissue when a foot contacts the ground. Most USs activate multiple URs. For example, the *withdrawal-flexion reflex* is elicited by stepping on a sharp object, and it results in the flexion of the affected leg (i.e., raising it away from the painful stimulus) as well as a weight shift to and extension of the other leg. The overall result: A person pulls their foot away from something causing tissue damage and balances on their other, uninjured foot. This latter component is critical—failure to adjust the posture could cause a fall, potentially adding injury. In other examples, a stimulus elicits a *behavioral system*—a temporally organized collection of responses that accomplish critical biological functions, such as feeding, mating, and defense (Timberlake, 1994). Activation of a behavioral system by a US increases the probability of observing URs associated with that system (Domjan & Fanselow, 2024). In Figure 2.5, the placement of food (US) in a dog's mouth leads to salivation (UR), an increase in heart rate (UR), and swallowing (UR), among other behaviors.

The given examples occur automatically when the appropriate form of stimulation is applied (e.g., a tap to the patellar tendon, sharp pain on the underside of the foot, or the delivery of food). But why do they occur, and why is the probability of their occurrence so high? Such reflexes are largely the product of an evolutionary history, and when you look at the relations between the events in question, it is easy to see why they have been selected for. A terrestrial organism, moving through space, ought to recoil from stimuli that produce tissue damage. Such damage (and its avoidance) is biologically meaningful. Injuries increase vulnerability to predation and infection and thus reduce future reproductive success. If we assume that the three ingredients of ***natural selection*** reviewed in Chapter 1 are present, such that (1) there is variability in the population in the probability of recoiling to a stimulus that produces damage, (2) there is a reproductive advantage associated with a strong response, and (3) strong responders are likely to produce offspring that respond strongly, then positive natural selection should occur for fast, automatic, and strong responders. Indeed, this relationship has been so consistently adaptive for so many millions of years that differential reproduction comprising evolutionary history has resulted in most organisms having this automatic and largely "correct" response to stimuli that cause tissue damage. We say "largely" because the correct response may depend on other outcomes associated with the US that conflict with the UR. For example, inhibiting the tendency to recoil (UR) from the pain in your mouth (US) caused by a dentist is adaptive, provided that the costs to survival and reproduction of tissue damage outweigh the costs of a continued cavity.

The temporally extended biological consequences of reflexive behavior have ensured that substantial behavioral variations in URs to USs are now rare, and the probability of observing the response to the stimulus is high. A similar story holds for all other reflexes, including those that allow for efficient feeding of newborns (i.e., the rooting reflex) and for clearing of the airway (i.e., sneezing). The absence of usual reflexive behavior (e.g., as revealed in abnormal or absent action when a US is applied) potentially reflects serious neuropathies that interfere with typical behavior. This conclusion can be generalized more broadly to all stimulus control. It is expected that any animal's behavior, including humans, will be a function of the stimuli present. ***Ethograms*** are systematic observations of behavior that quantify instances of typical behavior during a given time period. A comparative psychologist would predict a chimpanzee to groom, inspect observers, and interact with conspecifics at a similar rate every day, provided the conditions are unchanged. If the rate of these behaviors changes, then further investigation of the health of the animal is undertaken. The same may be true of a parent that notices their child is not playing outside as much, spending time with peers, or consuming the same amount of food at meals.

Much of behavior can be categorized into those that facilitate contact (i.e., approach) with those USs that support direct fitness (e.g., food), and reduce contact (i.e., withdrawal) with those that threaten survival (e.g., tissue damage). These behaviors are referred to as ***taxes*** or ***tropisms***. In humans, the withdrawal-flexion reflex moves the foot away from a painful threat that could cause damage to it, whereas the rooting reflex moves an infant's mouth toward a food source. An example in invertebrates involves movement along a gradient of light. ***Negative phototaxis*** describes an organism's moving away from light, whereas ***positive phototaxis*** describes movement toward light. These are ancient behaviors that have likely evolved independently many times (Jékely, 2021). For example, it is crucial for marine cyanobacteria and phototactic green algae, each of which depend on photosynthesis, to be able to move or grow toward sunlight. In some moths that evolved to navigate by moonlight—aside from the sun, the most prominent and consistent light for billions of years of evolution—human-made lights result in the maladaptive action of approach to bug zappers and flames. In addition to phototaxis, organisms exhibit chemotaxis, geotaxis, and hydrotaxis among others. It would seem that stimulus control of the probability of elicited approach to or avoidance of a source of stimulation form the bedrock of reproductive success in a wide range of organisms. Thinking about your own behavior, you are more likely to approach friends that bring you joy (and food), take jobs that pay well or provide security, and attend a university that offers resources—all providing support for your survival. You are likely to stay away from friends, jobs, or schools that threaten your survival.

The importance of organisms with preorganized "intelligent" responses to common kinds of biologically relevant stimuli cannot be overstated. That we take them for granted is part of the point: We can behave adaptively, quickly, without having to learn something or deliberate over our options. One implication of the foregoing argument is that reflexive behavior did not always exist but was selected for and shaped by natural selection. In a distant past, there may have been far more behavioral variability in response to certain kinds of physical events. Inflexible, reflexive behavior may have thus derived from flexible and variable behavior (Robinson & Barron, 2017; Stahlman & Leising, 2024). Still, the probability that a US will produce a UR is modifiable by experience, and even under constant conditions, the elicited response in a whole-behaving animal cannot be perfectly predicted (Brembs, 2011).

2.2.2 Response strength

Learning processes are typically divided into two major categories: ***associative learning***, encompassing classical and operant conditioning, and ***nonassociative learning***, which includes habituation, dishabituation, pseudoconditioning, and sensitization. In associative learning, the relationships (e.g., timing) between different kinds of stimuli, responses, and outcomes in the environment are the critical factors driving behavioral change, whereas behavior changed nonassociatively is solely a function of direct contact with a US. Nonassociative learning is considered the most fundamental and evolutionarily conserved form of behavioral plasticity (Harris, 1943). ***Habituation*** occurs when the UR to a US is reduced during repeated presentations of the US (Figure 2.6). URs, such as orienting movements or protective reactions, typically enhance direct fitness. However, in naturalistic contexts, repeated URs may interfere with other important behaviors, such as foraging or courtship. Habituation serves to attenuate the UR when the US is low in intensity (e.g., the low-sugar solution in Figure 2.6). In mammals, activation of a reflex by a US is modulated by a dynamic threshold (i.e., gate) in the connection between the afferent and efferent neurons. The level of this sensory-response threshold is influenced by motivation, arousal, and prior exposure (Staddon, 2016). For example, if you are trying to study and your roommate's fan is blowing air into your eyes and causing blinking, then blinking may be reduced via changes in the level of receptor activity (nociceptor in the cornea). This change in the sensory receptor is called ***sensory adaptation***. Alternatively, reductions in glucose and oxygen in the muscle controlling blinking would reduce its strength. This is referred to as ***muscular fatigue***. However, a reduction in a response to a repetitive stimulus may be the result of a change in transmission of the stimulus signal across the synapse between the afferent and efferent neuron. Habituation refers to a reduction of behavior caused by changes in synaptic transmission (more on habituation in Chapter 3).

Four of the 10 properties that characterize habituation are most relevant to a discussion of stimulus control of the strength of a UR (see Figure 3.5). First, the response decrement during repeated stimulation is usually a negative exponential function of the number of stimulus presentations. This best represents what is referred to as ***short-term habituation***, or a temporary increase in the sensory-response threshold. A marine slug, *Aplysia californica*,

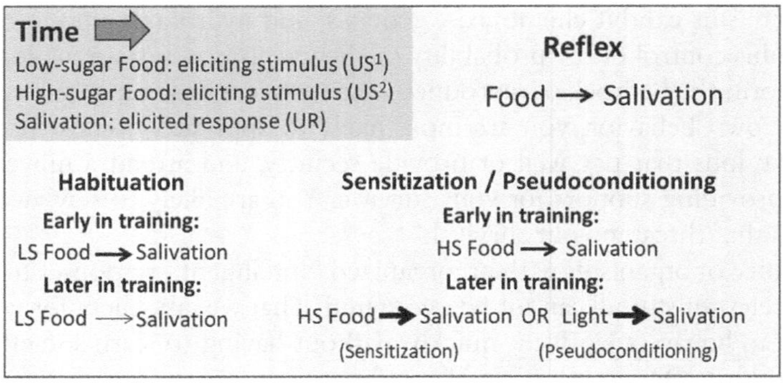

Figure 2.6 **Nonassociative learning.** Terminology to represent three nonassociative learning phenomena: habituation, sensitization, and pseudoconditioning. Because these effects involve learning, they are represented early (before changes occur) and later in training (when changes have occurred). Notice the thickness of the arrows representing response decrements (arrows become thinner after training in habituation) after repeated presentation of a low-sugar (LS) food or response increments (arrows become thicker after training in sensitization and pseudoconditioning) after presentation of a high-sugar (HS) food.

exhibits habituation of defensive response, the gill-withdrawal reflex (Carew et al., 1972). *Aplysia* breathes by circulating water through its gill, a vulnerable and vital organ which is retracted and protected by a harder outer membrane (mantle shelf) in response to a tactile stimulus (e.g., a water jet) applied at any one of several areas of its body (e.g., siphon). The response is typically measured as the intensity or duration of the contraction. Carew et al. reported evidence for habituation of the intensity of the gill-withdrawal reflex when a water jet stimulated the area around the siphon every 30 s in a single session. Second, after a period of rest without stimulation, the strength of a habituated response spontaneously recovered during the next presentation of the habituation stimulus. Carew et al. reported that 75% to 85% of the intensity of the reflex recovered within 10 to 20 min after habituation training. Third, successive episodes of spontaneous recovery result in progressively less recovery of the habituated response, suggesting a long-term adjustment in the threshold that persists across the resting period, or ***long-term habituation***. Last, the reduction in the response is stimulus specific. A change to the habituation stimulus results in a recovery of the reflexive response. More details, along with the neurobiological changes that alter the threshold, are discussed in Chapter 3.

Stimuli that are intense and presented at a low rate are likely to result in ***sensitization***: an increase in the strength of the UR to the US with its repeated presentation (Figure 2.6). The stronger the stimulus, the less likely it is that the UR will habituate and more likely that it will be sensitized. Marcus et al. (1988) stimulated the siphon of *Aplysia* with varying degrees of intensity (from a touch to four tail shocks) two times with a 10-min interstimulus interval. They reported that sensitization only occurred with stronger stimulation. Sensitization typically occurs over short time frames; in such cases, the heightened response of this short-term sensitization diminishes within a few hours poststimulation. In contrast to the stimulus specificity of habituation, sensitization results in an increased response strength to stimuli in general. A loud noise results in a startle response in many animals, including humans (Landis & Hunt, 1939). The startle response consists of closing of the eyelids and contraction of facial and shoulder muscles. The stimulus intensity required to generate startle varies across and within individuals (Plappert et al., 1993). Interestingly, repeated loud noises do not result in sensitization of the strength of the startle response (though a measure of latency to startle does). However, if rodents are given a preexposure to single foot shock, a bright light, or a predator odor (e.g., fox odor) before a loud noise (transfer stimulus), then they will exhibit sensitization of the startle response (Davis, 1989; Hebb et al., 2003; Walker & Davis, 1997). The strength of startle increased despite the different modalities of the sensitization and transfer stimulus (Figure 2.6).

In *pseudoconditioning*, the UR to a US may be triggered by a neutral stimulus, even if it is novel (Figure 2.6). This would be equivalent to salivating when a friend asks about the weather while I am waiting for my pizza to arrive. Conditions cannot be properly controlled in this example, but in an experiment, repeated presentations of Food could make the animal salivate to the presentation of a Light, although the Light has never been paired with Food and salivation is usually not an unconditioned response to a Light (Figure 2.6). Sensitization and pseudoconditioning mimic Pavlovian conditioning (see next section), except that the relevant experience with the CS→US pairing has never occurred in either case. This is the main reason to incorporate controls for these nonassociative effects in Pavlovian conditioning experiments, such as the explicitly unpaired control (experiencing both CS and US but not closely paired) or differential conditioning that leads to differential responding to two CSs (sensitization and pseudoconditioning would induce generalized responding to stimuli present in the situation where USs had been presented).

The organization of the presynaptic and postsynaptic neurons involved in a reflex is the product of an evolutionary history of natural selection for organisms with specific genetic instructions for this sensory-motor connection. In a real sense, evolutionary history is "stored" in DNA, which gets expressed in the molecular and cellular structure of the organism. These ancestral memories are sufficient to enable the animal to respond with a high probability to many biologically relevant stimuli. Habituation and sensitization require modification of signal processing within one or more synapses. These modifications allow for the organism to adjust the strength of a UR to a repeated US.

2.2.3 *Associative learning*

2.2.3.1 *Classical (or Pavlovian) conditioning*

One would expect characteristic reflexes to evolve only when the relationship between a US and UR has been consistently adaptive for many generations of a species' evolutionary history. Some stimuli, such as the visual properties of a cliff, are reliable and stable over time, but selection pressures and natural events (e.g., a volcanic eruption) can alter the features and resources of a landscape relatively quickly. A reflex is useful only to the extent that the current environment resembles the ancestral environments in which it evolved. If the environment did change quickly and dramatically from a recognizable ancestral state, then an organism capable of taking advantage of new regularities within its environment would have a direct fitness advantage over an organism capable of responding only via reflexes. In this scenario, reflex-only animals may be replaced by organisms capable of detecting novel regularities.

Stimulus control of the probability and strength of an elicited response can be extended to a new stimulus through a process called *classical* or *Pavlovian conditioning* (named after Nobel-laureate Russian physiologist Ivan Pavlov). Pavlov was investigating salivation, an unconditioned response (UR), as part of a reflex elicited by food, an unconditioned stimulus (US) placed in a dog's mouth (Figure 2.7). However, Pavlov and his students noticed that

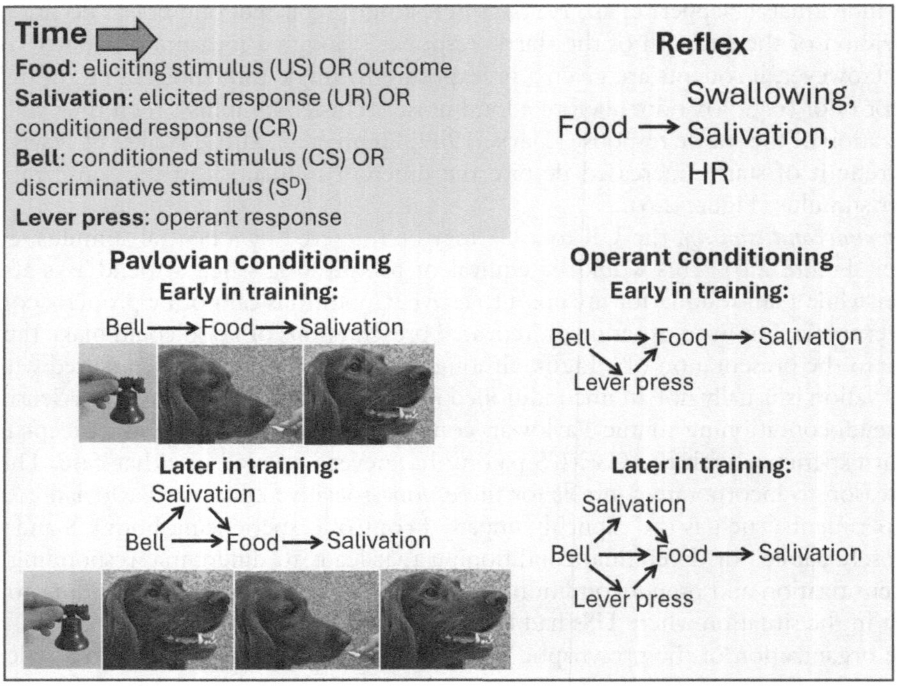

Figure 2.7 **Associative learning.** Terminology to represent two associative learning phenomena: classical or Pavlovian conditioning and operant or instrumental conditioning. The terminology used here is consistent with that used for nonassociative phenomena (see Figure 2.6). Learning is represented by distinguishing the early (before changes occur) and later training (when changes have occurred). Notice that the responses (salivation and lever press) are anticipatory, that is, they occur before the delivery of the Food. The area of the figure illustrating operant conditioning integrates Pavlovian conditioning. The two types of conditioning, often discussed separately, can occur anytime a US is present. One stimulus missing from the figure is the context, which is always present and, in many cases (e.g., explicitly unpaired control groups), may act as a CS or S^D.

after many deliveries of food, even preparing the animal for the experiment tended to elicit salivation in the absence of food.

This was a problem for Pavlov, so he introduced a neutral stimulus, such as the sound of a bell, to distract the animal and prevent salivation. However, soon, the dog started to salivate to the sound of the bell. Pavlov decided that there was something interesting in this anticipatory behavior. He then placed the sound of the bell purposely before presenting the food, and after a few such Bell→Food pairings, the dog was salivating reliably to the Bell. He called this bell–salivation relation a conditioned reflex because of the power of the bell, a conditioned stimulus (CS), to control salivation, now a conditioned response (CR).

The UR (salivation) to the US (food) in this situation was part of a reflex resulting from natural selection (US-UR), whereas the CR (salivation) to the CS (bell) was the result of a conditioning procedure that bears his name (Pavlovian). CRs are acquired as a result of Pavlovian (or classical) conditioning of a CS and US, which we will represent as CS→US pairings. This can be shown by including control groups that receive the CS and US but presented in an unpaired arrangement (CS/US) with respect to one another such that the US is not likely to occur immediately after the CS (nonassociative controls are mentioned again in Chapters 3 and 4).

We like to think of laboratory experiments as creating new worlds for animals to adapt to. Adaptation, or the fit of an organism to its environment, can be assessed in many different ways. In studies involving selective breeding in a laboratory environment, adaptation may involve many phenotypic changes that support reproduction. In conditioning, behavioral adaptation is assessed. Despite not being a regularity in the evolutionary history of dogs, in Pavlov's laboratory, the sound of a bell preceded the delivery of food. Behavioral adaptation can be assessed by the degree to which a dog learns about the novel regularity. If control of the probability of salivation (UR) by food in the mouth (US) is adaptive, then all other things being equal, the control of the probability of salivation (CR) by a stimulus (CS) that immediately precedes the delivery of food should also be adaptive. Indeed, salivation before and during food supports digestion, and salivation conditioned to the sight or smell (CSs) of food depends on previous pairings of those stimuli with food (Mattes, 2000). Not surprisingly, the magnitude of salivation (CR) to a picture (CS) paired with food was proportional to the magnitude of salivation (UR) caused by placing the food (US) directly in the mouth (Blumberger & Glatzel, 1968).

The absence of sensory resemblance between the CS and any extant US is frequently cited as a necessary condition of a CS. Though there are certain limitations imposed by an animal's evolutionary history, there is surprising flexibility in what can become a CS. Krause and Domjan (2017) identified that few CSs used in laboratory experiments resemble anything an organism would encounter in its natural habitat. The ringing of bells does not generally, automatically, cause salivation in dogs; but if the ringing of a Bell reliably precedes the availability of Food, then the Bell will come to elicit a ***salivary response***.

However, a CS can resemble a US that already controls a response, and it can even elicit its own UR (i.e., technically, the CS would then also be a US). This raises the question of what it means for a CS to be initially neutral (see Figure 2.7). The obvious answer is that a CS is neutral because it does not elicit a UR. However, that would mean that stimuli frequently used as "neutral" CSs, like sounds, lights, and tastes cannot elicit any URs; but in fact, sounds and lights elicit URs of orientation and startle, and tastes (e.g., sweet vs. bitter) elicit URs in the form of mouth movements that facilitate or attenuate consumption.

A simple modification may be all that is needed to allow for these exceptions; a CS cannot already elicit the UR that is being conditioned (Pear, 2016). A Bell paired with Food may elicit a UR of orientation, but the Bell should not elicit salivation. Support for this notion goes back to Pavlov (1927), who conditioned dogs to salivate (CR) to a mild electric shock (a US and a CS) paired with food (US) after several Shock→Food pairings. The shock elicits its own URs, but salivation is not one of them, although it could be conditioned to elicit salivation by pairing it with food.

Another perspective posits that a CS can be a US that elicits the same UR as the US it will be conditioned with, but specifies that the UR should wane (i.e., habituate) with repeated presentations faster than it does to the conditioning US, which should exhibit resistance to habituation (Silva, 2018). Consequently, we could say that a US to be conditioned as a CS must be weaker than the US with which it is paired. Bolles (1979, p. 27) summarized the issues surrounding a "neutral" CS with the following:

> First of all, there may not be any really neutral stimuli. Any stimulus that is detectable at all is likely to invoke at least an investigatory reflex. Indeed, there is reason to think that, in the absence of such a response, conditioning will not occur. It is not even true that

the CS must be emotionally neutral, in the sense that it evokes no appetitive or defensive behavior. It is only necessary that the CS be weaker or more neutral than the US itself.

Silva (2018) reviewed one particularly striking example of a US conditioned to another US. Cats were trained that a shock (itself a US) delivered to one forepaw preceded a shock to the other forepaw (US). During conditioning, the shock to the first forepaw came to produce a limb flexion response (CR) in the *other* forepaw (Tuber, 1986)!

Even when the CS is not an obvious US, the nature of the CS can have clear effects on the probability and intensity of the CR. Davey et al. (1989) trained rats in a cold conditioning chamber with a CS that was either an aluminum lever (aluminum CS) or a furry lever (furry CS) inserted into the chamber and followed by the activation of a heat lamp (US). Rats exposed to the furry CS exhibited more CRs characteristic of rats huddling together (e.g., sniffing and snuggling for warmth) than those exposed to the aluminum lever. We can conclude that a "neutral" CS may already control the probability and strength of some URs at the start of conditioning, but it should also acquire the ability to control CRs as a function of CS→US pairings. Additionally, the form of the CRs is influenced by the nature of the CS.

A frequent question among learning students is whether the response controlled by the CS must be the same as the response controlled by the US (i.e., CR = UR?). It is often the case that the CR and UR match, but the short answer is that they will not always match. The long answer is that the CR must match one of the URs that is elicited by the behavioral system associated with the US, though it may not be the UR you are measuring when the US is presented.

Let us start with a case of matching responses. The similarity between CR and UR was demonstrated by Jenkins and Moore (1973) with pigeons trained with pairings of a small, localized Light (CS) presented for a few seconds prior to the delivery of either Food or Water (US). When the US was Food, pigeons exhibited conditioned pecking responses (CR) directed toward the Light (CS) characteristic of pecking at seed on the ground (e.g., an open beak). However, when the US was Water, pigeons exhibited conditioned pecks toward the Light characteristic of drinking (e.g., a closed beak and slow, shallow movements).

However, the form of the CR can be dependent on which aspects of the US are conditioned to the CS. Konorski (1967) proposed that animals learn about different properties of the US during conditioning depending on the timing of the CS relative to the US, which results in stimulus control of different aspects of behavior. The delivery of a food US activates a behavioral feeding system, which includes two types of responses. First, ***preparatory responses*** (e.g., searching for food, an increase in heart rate while foraging) elicited by the affective features of the US (e.g., pleasure) support food procurement. Second, discrete ***consummatory responses*** (e.g., salivation) elicited by the sensory properties of the US (e.g., taste) support immediate contact with the US. A CS paired with a US can condition to one or both components.

Konorski's (1967) perspective predicts the results described previously by Vandercar and Schneiderman (1967) from rabbits conditioned with a CS that was either immediately (0.75 s, Group Short) followed by shock (US) or followed several seconds later by shock (6.75 s, Group Long). Rabbits in Group Short conditioned to the affective (i.e., an increase in heart rate to prepare for something aversive) and sensory (i.e., an increase in blinking to prepare for potential damage to the eye) properties of the US, whereas rabbits in Group Long conditioned only to the affective properties. It is as if the rabbits in Group Long associated the Tone with something aversive, resulting in preparation for the outcome, but they did not learn about the specifics of what outcome was coming (shock).

Behavior systems theory further expands this idea by allowing for multiple response modes elicited by a US, thereby allowing for more flexibility in what CRs get conditioned (Timberlake, 1994). Shock (US) elicits a variety of URs that include an activity burst and escape behavior. Rats display conditioned activity to a CS paired simultaneously with shock but conditioned freezing to a CS that precedes shock.

In contrast to that of a reflex, the picture of stimulus control that is emerging during Pavlovian conditioning is one of complexity. *That is, predicting the probability and intensity of stimulus control by a CS requires a consideration of the nature of the CS and the nature of the US as well as the timing of the CS relative to the US.* By doing so, we can also explain one of the most interesting results in Pavlovian conditioning, namely, the findings that the CR and UR are not always the same. The rabbits in Vandercar and Schneiderman's (1967) study all blinked in response to the shock, but only the rabbits in Group Short acquired conditioned blinking to the CS.

It is worth noting that the *consequences* of a conditioned response do not matter with respect to its future expression—a dog does not salivate during a bell to bring about food but only because the bell has reliably preceded the food. CRs are adaptive in the sense that ancestral organisms that behaved thusly were more likely to reproduce. This, at bottom, is why a dog salivates to a bell that reliably precedes nutritive food. In other words, the enhanced reproductive success afforded by Pavlovian conditioning is dependent on the probability of the CR being influenced by whether food follows the bell (CS→US), not whether or not food follows salivation (CR→US).

Pavlovian conditioning can shift the control of elicited behavior to an arbitrary stimulus that has not been encountered by an organism's ancestors (e.g., a bell acting as a CS). However, the behaviors controlled by the CS are constrained by the nature of the US and the adaptations that evolved to deal with that US (i.e., the corresponding behavior system). An organism that only has reflex action and classical conditioning has no mechanism for changing the probability or intensity of behaviors outside of its evolutionary behavioral toolkit. Greater behavioral flexibility could emerge if the future probability of a behavior were a function of its consequences.

2.2.3.2 *Operant (or instrumental) conditioning*

Another form of associative learning is known as *operant* or *instrumental conditioning* (see Figure 2.7). Unlike reflex action and classically conditioned responses (each under the control of antecedent stimuli), the probability of an operant behavior is substantially a function of its past consequences. "Operant" can refer to a conditioning procedure, an individual response, or a class of responses. As a procedure, delivery of the US (e.g., food), or outcome, is contingent on a particular response, or operant. Contingencies can be positive, such that an operant response initiates the delivery of the outcome, or negative, such that the operant initiates the termination of an outcome. For example, a rat may receive a food pellet based on a positive contingency between a press on an aluminum lever inserted into a conditioning box and food delivery. *Contingency* here will refer to the conditional (i.e., if–then) relationship between events. Importantly, the delivery of food is not controlled by any other aspect of the rat's environment. An operant class of lever pressing contains all of the various behaviors (e.g., left paw, right paw, nose, biting, jumping, etc.) that result in the lever being depressed to the extent that it will result in the delivery of the outcome (Neuringer, 2014). The delivery of an outcome for one behavior in an operant class tends to result in a temporary increase in the probability of other behaviors in that class.

Many of our behaviors reflect a personal history with outcomes. We open jars, pull doorknobs, and type on keyboards primarily because of the rewarding consequences of doing so in the past. A golfer finds that a more upright stance produces less variability in the path of her shots, a desirable consequence in a game that rewards precision; she then tends to swing in this new, improved fashion. A baseball pitcher finds that a different grip produces greater lateral movement on his fastball. Consequently, hitters are more likely to swing and miss; the pitcher then moves to more often grip the baseball in this new, improved way.

Operant behavior is ubiquitous. You likely already noticed some major differences between classically conditioned responses and operant behavior. All of the examples of behavior in the preceding paragraph have a striking arbitrariness about them. Jars typically open by turning their lids in a counterclockwise fashion—"righty-tightly, lefty loosely"—but there is little reason to suspect that there is anything evolutionarily special about turning to the left rather than the right. We type efficiently on keyboards, resulting in words appearing on the screen—but keyboards are different in other countries, and people performed equally well with those keyboards. Sports, in general, are sets of largely arbitrary contingencies. A deep evolutionary history seems to be less important in these cases.

Operant behavior is variable, flexible, and tuned to its consequences—based on what follows rather than only on what precedes it. Skinner (1981, p. 502) described it this way: "Operant conditioning is selection in progress. It resembles a hundred million years of natural selection or a thousand years of the evolution of culture compressed into a very short period of time." A trait that is selected via reproductive success will become likely in the next generation of the population, and an operant or CR will become more likely across conditioning (Figure 2.8). Of course, there are limits to this: An organism must be physically capable of performing an action if it is to be reinforced, and whether it is so depends on an evolutionary history (see Figure 1.1). However, what may appear at first a physical impossibility for a species may, in some cases, be accomplished via shaping by successive approximations (more on shaping in Chapter 4)—for example, the finger speed and dexterity demonstrated by a professional pianist, the strength of an Olympian shot-putter, or the vocal control of an opera singer. The natural occurrence of such behaviors is unlikely. The constituent parts of the actions do exist in the natural repertoire of the animal, but require discrimination training to refine and merge them into the observed behavior.

It is worth describing a pair of laboratory preparations that will serve to further illuminate the difference between elicited, automatic behavior (e.g., reflex action and Pavlovian responses) and operant behavior. The psychological scientist again creates a new world in which the animal demonstrates what aspects of the environment are able to influence the probability and strength of its subsequent responses.

The first example involves a naïve rat placed in a chamber in which there is a single lever extending from the wall (Figure 2.9-A). The rat may explore the space, sniff, groom, and do the things rats often do. Eventually, the rat is likely to depress the lever, at which point a sugar pellet falls into a food cup in the side wall. The rat eats. Following this, the rat presses the lever more and more, receiving sugar pellets along the way. Can we distinguish this behavior from the stimulus-elicited responding in classical conditioning?

Let us suppose this rat is now pressing the lever with regularity. We now will only deliver a sugar pellet freely every 10 s as long as the rat does not press the lever. If the rat presses during the 10-s interval, this sugar-pellet delivery is cancelled. We have reversed the contingency between a behavior and its consequence. The rat quickly ceases its lever-pressing behavior (Locurto et al., 1981). This demonstrates that lever pressing was being controlled by its consequences (i.e., the sugar pellet). When the consequences change—when the environmental

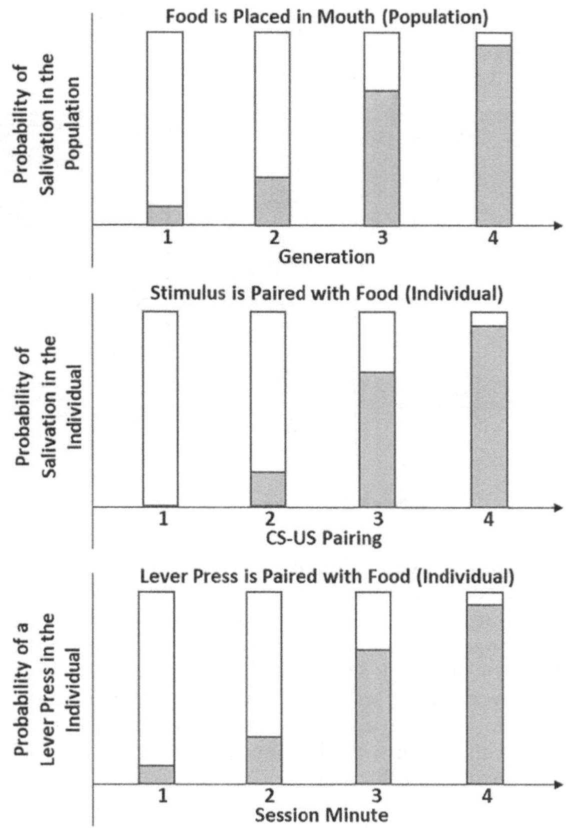

Figure 2.8 **Three hypothetical timelines.** These timelines illustrate the parallel between the evolution of a reflex by natural selection across generations and the development of a CR or operant over the course of conditioning. The highlighted area indicates the probability of observing the evolution of a reflex across generations in a hypothetical population (top) or the probability of observing the learned response during the CS (middle) or during an operant conditioning session (bottom) in an individual animal.

contingencies dynamically shift—at least some forms of behavior change with them (see Table 4.8, Chapter 4, for a complete description of operant contingencies).

The second example involves a dog salivating to the presentation of a bell that has preceded food delivery in past trials. The bell elicits the salivary CR, but is there any reason to suspect that the dog salivates because doing so is followed by food? Imagine now that we set up an experiment such that conditioned salivation produces the absence of food—that the dog will only receive food after the bell if it does not salivate when the bell sounds. If the dog continues to salivate during the bell, it cannot be because of the consequences of doing so; food is never delivered after salivating. Note the similarity in the contingencies in these two examples. However, unlike the case of the rat pressing a lever for pellets, in this instance, the salivary response continues (Patten & Rudy, 1967).

Similar results were obtained with pigeons pecking at a key for access to food (Figure 2.9B; Picker et al., 1984). Persistence of conditioned salivation in dogs and key pecking in pigeons would indicate that these responses are a function of the relationship between the CS and US

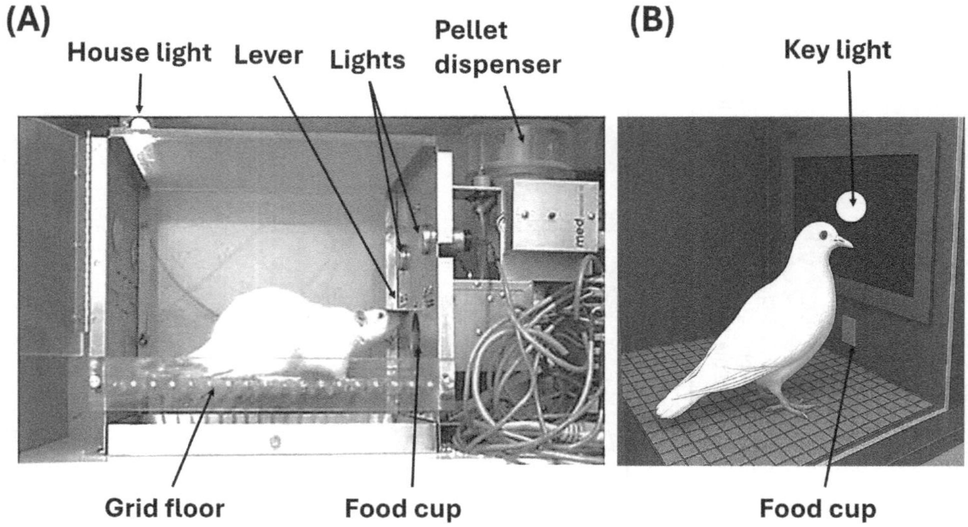

Figure 2.9 **Two typical operant conditioning boxes.** **(A)** A conditioning box for rats and **(B)** an analogous touchscreen-equipped box for pigeons. The main components involve a manipulandum (lever for rats, localized key light for pigeons), a device to deliver rewards (pellets for rats, grain for pigeons), and a system for recording a response (lever pressing for rats, key-light pecking for pigeons). Discriminative stimuli can be added to these boxes. White noise is usually played during sessions to mask unsystematic noises than might disrupt behavior. All the events during training sessions are controlled by a computer so that the animals are not handled or disturbed in any explicit way. (Photo of rat box by M. R. Papini; photo of pigeon box by K. J. Leising.)

rather than between the response and food. The dogs and pigeons continued to respond at a high rate even when doing so was met with a lack of food. This illustrates that the consequences of salivation in dogs or key pecking in pigeons are largely irrelevant to their expression. Hence, these responses are automatically elicited by the antecedent CS.

The procedure implemented in these two examples is known as *omission training* (Sheffield, 1965). To establish the conclusions about salivation and lever pressing drawn for these examples on a firm basis, one would need a control condition in which the environments are matched, but the response-outcome contingency operates only in animals exposed to omission training. This is known as the *master-yoked design* (read more about omission training and the master-yoked design in Chapter 4).

2.2.3.3 Motivational control of operant behavior

The future probability and strength of a lever press in a rat are largely controlled by the past consequences of lever pressing. However, behavior is produced by living organisms that vary in the degree to which their needs are currently being met. Another area of stimulus control has investigated how the level of deprivation of biological needs (i.e., drives) in an organism can change the value of the consequences of a behavior (i.e., motivating operations). For example, the consequences of pressing a lever for food are biologically relevant (value) for any rat, even one that has regular access to food in a laboratory. The value of food could be enhanced by restricting access to food to a level comparable to that of the average wild rat.

Table 2.1 Stimulus control under different levels of food deprivation and preexposure

Group	*Preexposure*	*Training* *LP→Pellet*	*Test*	*Results* *LP*	*Reacquisition* *LP→Pellet*
None-Full	Full-*No Pellets*	Hungry	*Full*	No change	Decrease
Full-Full	*Full*-Pellets	Hungry	*Full*	Decrease	Decrease
None-Hungry	Hungry-*No Pellets*	Full	*Hungry*	No change	Increase
Hungry-Hungry	*Hungry*-Pellets	Full	*Hungry*	Increase	Increase

Note. Full refers to rats with free access to food, while hungry refers to rats only given access to food for 1.5 h per day. The results of groups that were preexposed to pellets are relative to the group that did not receive preexposure, which are relative to control animals (not shown). Italics were added to indicated the parts of the procedure contributing to the group name. The experimental design comes from Balleine (1992).

This manipulation should result in a higher rate of lever pressing, which, under most circumstances, would lead to greater access to food.

To test this, what if, in the laboratory, we created a world in which the rat never experienced the value of the food that follows lever pressing while hungry? If food was then restricted in those rats, a procedure that should enhance the value of food, would they press the lever more when given access to it (Table 2.1)? Balleine (1992) tested this prediction and found that rats increase lever pressing when made hungry *only* if they learned the value of food while hungry during preexposure (Group Hungry-Hungry). The reverse was also true; rats trained to lever press for food while hungry only decreased lever pressing at test while full if they had learned the value of food when full during preexposure (Group Full-Full). Importantly, when the pellets were delivered for lever pressing during a subsequent reacquisition phase, the animals that lacked the necessary preexposure could now detect the value of food, and lever pressing adjusted accordingly.

These data underscore a point of broad significance for comparing the acquisition of stimulus control across studies of comparative learning and cognition. Comparisons across species must acknowledge the role of motivating operations. Thinking back to the comic in Figure 1.1, there are many contextual variables that differ between the species (e.g., the honeybee, rat, and fish). One of them will be the biological relevance of the pellet *reinforcer*. Even in groups of the same species, animals must be trained and tested under comparable levels of motivation.

2.2.3.4 Stimulus control of operant behavior

Does the foregoing indicate no role for antecedent stimuli? Clearly not. Behavior always occurs somewhere, and its consequences are largely dependent on where and when it happens. Driving through an intersection is usually a good idea only when the traffic light is green and not red. Children who say curse words among their friends at recess may get a laugh, but if they do so in the presence of their strict mother, they may be reprimanded. Standing and cheering may be met with approval at a wedding reception and reprobation at a funeral. Thus, an organism would do well to learn not only about the consequences of behaviors in general but also about the subtle distinctions in the settings that indicate what consequences follow those behaviors. It may not always be obvious what stimuli are most important. Environments are complex and dynamic, with many sensory features that may enter into important behavioral contingencies.

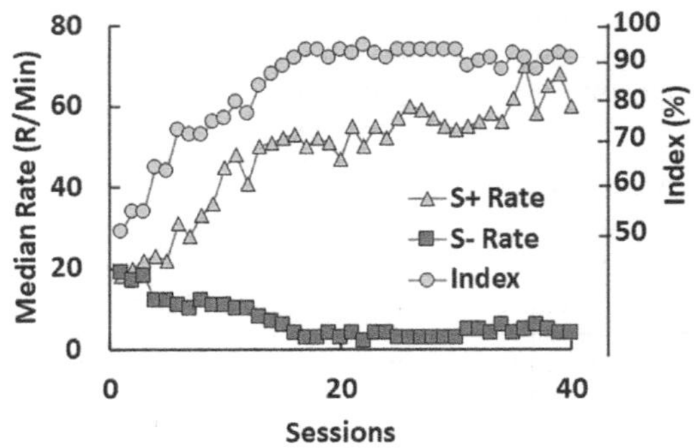

Figure 2.10 **Discrimination learning.** Mean rate of responding in the presence of a discriminative stimulus (S+) signaling the opportunity for a reinforcer and another stimulus signaling its absence (S-). Index (i.e., percent of responding to the S^D) is calculated from the rate of responding in the S+ relative to all responses recorded (S+ + S-). (From Herrick et al., 1959; reproduced with permission from the American Psychological Association.)

A simple experiment will illustrate a typical example of the development of stimulus control (Herrick et al., 1959). Rats were placed in a chamber in which there was a small Light that slowly alternated between being turned on and off (Figure 2.10). Lever presses in the presence of the Light were occasionally reinforced with Food; lever presses in the absence of the Light were never reinforced. Over sessions, lever pressing steadily increased when the Light was on and decreased when the Light was off. In this case, the Light served as a ***discriminative stimulus*** (*S^D* or *S+*) for the reinforcement of lever pressing. Lever pressing was under stimulus control by the Light. Even when a specific stimulus is not present (S-), behavior does not occur in a stimulus vacuum. The probability of an operant behavior can be influenced by the physical (e.g., visual features), spatial (e.g., location), and temporal context (e.g., time of day or time relative to some other event) in which it is conditioned.

2.2.4 Stimulus generalization and discrimination

Thus far, we have discussed stimulus control that develops as a result of interactions with a stimulus throughout an organism's evolutionary (phylogenetic) or developmental (ontogenetic) history. However, there are conditions in which the probability and strength of an adaptive or learned response may be controlled by stimuli not present in either history (i.e., a novel stimulus). ***Generalization*** is behaving similarly in response to each of two (or more) stimulus circumstances. The degree of stimulus similarity between circumstances, which most often refers to the degree of physical resemblance, predicts well the degree of generalization. If you train a dog that a certain Bell reliably precedes Food delivery, then subsequent introduction of a new, slightly different Bell will probably not completely disrupt conditioned salivation. By virtue of the dog's auditory sensory system, there will be some overlap in the receptors activated by both Bells and, consequently, overlap in the activation of downstream brain areas. This is ***primary generalization***. The dog has not learned to treat the two sounds similarly. The dog probably can discriminate the new sound from the trained sound, but it lacks the training necessary to respond differently to it. You are likely to successfully open doors to shops in a new city you are visiting despite never having opened these specific doors before—but you have had lots of practice with similar doors, providing the foundation for secondary generalization, or ***acquired equivalence***, that occurs when two somewhat dissimilar stimuli have been trained with the same response (e.g., peck both stimuli), the same outcome (e.g., food is delivered following both), or both.

Is a failure to generalize the same as successful discrimination? Technically, yes, generalization and discrimination are two sides of the same coin. However, when the sensory properties between two stimuli are dissimilar enough to reduce or eliminate generalization, it is more commonly referred to as ***generalization decrement***. If you train a dog that the sound of a Bell alone (i.e., no view of the bell) reliably precedes Food delivery, it will not salivate to a picture of a bell (i.e., no sound).

Discrimination is typically reserved for explicit training with different response contingencies or outcomes with the goal of establishing differences in the probability of making a response in the presence of two stimuli. In a demonstration of the importance of discrimination training (Jenkins & Harrison, 1960), researchers compared two procedures with pigeons in which a Tone was presented as part of the context in which pecking was reinforced with Grain (Figure 2.11). In the first—Group No-Discrimination—the 1000-Hz Tone was continuously on and pecks were reinforced throughout the session; in the second—Group Discrimination—pecks were reinforced in the presence of the 1000-Hz Tone, but nonreinforced in its absence. Following this, test trials were administered with Tones of different frequencies (300–3500 Hz). There were two questions: To what extent would the birds peck at these new, different sounds? Would differences in discrimination training alter their responses to the new sounds?

Pecking was more robust when the sound frequency was closer to the frequency of the original training stimulus (i.e., primary generalization) in both groups. Testing a variety of stimuli that varied along a single stimulus dimension (e.g., frequency of sound) resulted in construction of a ***generalization gradient***, which refers to changes in the probability or rate of behavior as a function of stimulus similarity. When looking at these gradients, pigeons in Group Discrimination (Tone S+) responded to most of the frequencies tested, revealing a generalization gradient that was quite flat. Indeed, the percentage of pecking on trials with No Tone was comparable to trials with novel frequencies. Pigeons in Group Discrimination

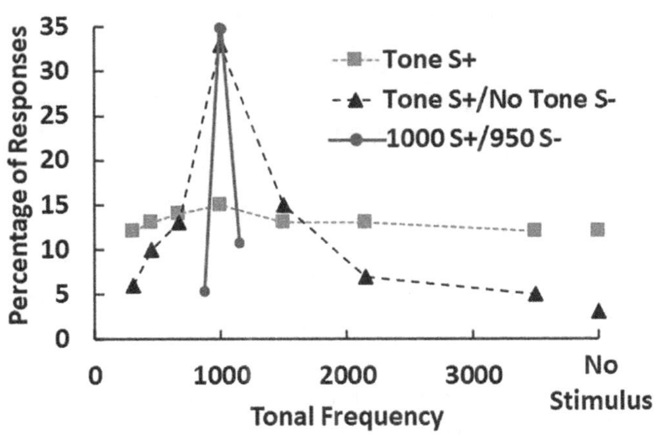

Figure 2.11 **Generalization gradients.** Data based on the means of individual pigeons from Jenkins and Harrison (1960, 1962) for discrimination training conditions of Tone S+ only (n = 3; Group No-discrimination), Tone S+ and No Tone S- (n = 5; Group Discrimination), and 1000 Hz Tone S+ and 950 Hz Tone S- (n = 2).

(Tone S+/No Tone S-), however, pecked most frequently in the presence of the training Tone (1000 Hz) and pecked markedly less with No Tone or with Tone frequencies differing from the training Tone.

These generalization gradients demonstrate the efficacy of discrimination training, that is, of establishing contingencies in which responses to some stimuli are reinforced, but responses in the absence of that stimulus are not reinforced. The pigeons in Group No-Discrimination were likely discriminating between their colony cage, in which no pecks were reinforced, and the training cage. The Tone was simply one feature of a rich context of features that defined the training cage. However, pecks for Group Discrimination were reinforced and nonreinforced in the training cage and thus these pigeons had to learn to discriminate the presence from the absence of the Tone. Even better discrimination was observed in pigeons trained to peck for a reinforcer in the presence of a 1000-Hz but not a 950-Hz Tone (Jenkins & Harrison, 1962). A similar finding was reported with visual stimuli presented to pigeons (Guttman & Kalish, 1956).

Organisms that have the requisite genetic makeup to discriminate between subtle differences in stimuli may not automatically do so. It is clear some discriminations are simpler than others—early childhood is characterized by learning words that correspond to shape, color, and number, the physical differences within each category being generally large. Should a child be biologically able to distinguish red and green, it is not very difficult to teach them to call objects of certain wavelengths red or green. Similarly, it is usually not difficult to teach a child the differences between squares, circles, and triangles. But the verbal label—saying "square" in the presence of a square, for instance—requires more extensive training.

Over the course of a lifetime, discrimination training enables ever-sharper stimulus distinctions. Discrimination training is the foundation of expertise. A medical doctor, a composer, and a computer programmer share a long history of discrimination training to achieve a level of sensory discrimination that eludes an amateur. Even discriminations that we take for granted, children saying "square" in the presence of a square and "blue" in the presence of a blue object, require the proper experience and education.

2.3 Stimulus control over other properties of behavior

Both stimuli and behaviors are composed of multiple dimensions. We have discussed the relationship between the physical properties of events and their status as stimuli. We can turn now to behavior: What are its physical properties, broadly construed? Are these properties individually manipulable? The physical properties of a single instance of behavior are captured by three questions (Figure 2.12):

1. What does the behavior look like? This is a question about its form;
2. When does the behavior occur? This is about its probability as a function of time; and
3. Where does the behavior occur? This is about its broader context.

Questions of "who" and "why" are about the organism under study and largely regard its ancestral and personal histories. Answers to these questions are also important to predict and explain behavior. We will address these questions, too, throughout this book.

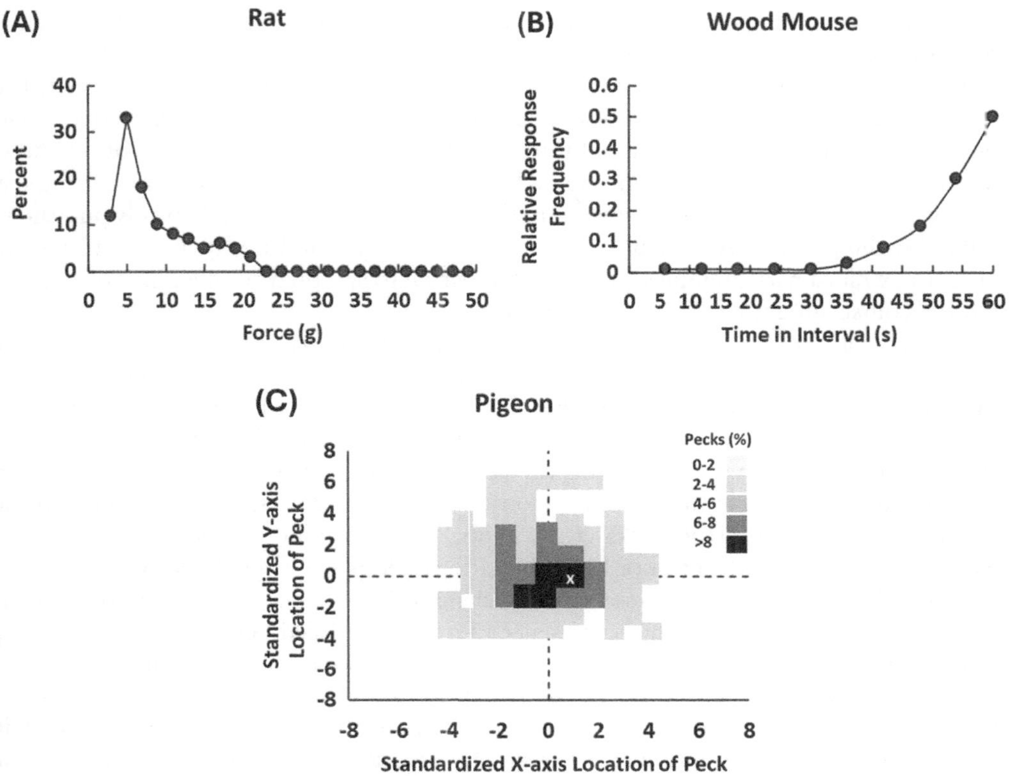

Figure 2.12 **Stimulus control of response form, timing, and location. (A)** Distribution of the force of a lever press maintained on a continuous reinforcement schedule and a force requirement of at least 5 g. (From Notterman, 1959; reproduced with permission from the American Psychological Association.) **(B)** Lever press data from mice reinforced 60 s after the onset of a stimulus. (From Lejeune & Wearden, 1991; reproduced with permission from Elsevier.) **(C)** Spatial distribution of pecks during a trial with a landmark, X, which predicted a reinforced target location one unit to the left within an 8 × 7 grid of response locations. (From Sawa et al., 2005; reproduced with permission from the American Psychological Association.)

2.3.1 *What does the behavior look like?*

Is the animal pressing a button, pulling a lever, turning in a circle, flying a plane, speaking at a conference? It should be obvious, though, that things are never as simple as they seem. The physical properties of any of these examples or any others one may consider may vary along many dimensions. Variance along some of these dimensions may not be important—a golfer might just hit her ball into a pond and move on to the next hole with little regret. It may, in other cases, be a matter of life and death—a pilot may err and crash her plane. Knowing how stimuli may come to control specific behaviors is important.

The kinds of behavior in which an organism engages are specified by the conditions. Lever pressing can only be reinforced if a pressable lever is present. You will have a tough time typing when there is no keyboard about and a tough time catching a ball in a full-body cast. The structure of behavior—what it looks like—is thus a direct function of what the environment affords. Assuming the environment does not prohibit certain forms of behavior, then control is exerted by relevant histories of the organism in question. An extroverted person who speaks often and boisterously will usually learn to not do so if on a golf course and especially so when another player is in the middle of their swing. Talking and not talking have come under the control of contingencies. In this context, loud talking is robustly punished—a talker on the golf course may be reprimanded, ostracized, and not invited to play in the future. In extraordinary examples, golfers not adhering to accepted conduct may be banished from the course altogether. More on punishment later.

The form of behavior is substantially determined by the nature of training stimuli. In Pavlovian appetitive conditioning with rats, the use of Light as a CS tends to itself produce a great deal of open rearing, to the exclusion of other behaviors; however, in a structurally identical experiment, the use of Tone as a CS tends to produce head jerking rather than rearing (Holland, 1977). These kinds of effects underscore the fact that stimuli have behavioral effects. In another example, an operant response was reinforced in the presence of one of two acoustic stimuli in dogs (Dobrzecka et al., 1966). These stimuli differed in their nature as well as their location (in front of or behind the dog). Dogs in Group A received food when they raised their right leg in the presence of a ticking Metronome placed in front of them and when they raised their left leg in the presence of a Buzzer placed behind them. Other dogs (Group B) received food when they raised their right leg when the Buzzer sounded and when they did not raise their leg during the Metronome. Hence, Group A dogs were subject to contingencies in which the directionality of their behavior (i.e., left vs. right) mattered with respect to stimulation, but Group B dogs simply responded or did not (this is called a *go/no-go task* and will be discussed more later).

Following this training, the positions of the two acoustic cues were reversed, and both groups were tested in trials with each stimulus. The behavior of dogs in Group A was largely a function of the directionality of the stimulus. When the test stimulus came from the front, the animals tended to raise their right leg, and when the stimulus came from behind, they tended to raise their left leg, independently of the identity of the stimulus (Buzzer or Metronome). This demonstrates that the location of stimulation mattered more than the nature of the acoustic stimulus itself. These results were reversed for Group B: They raised their right legs when the buzzer was sounded no matter its point of origin and did not raise their leg when the metronome was played. Hence, the form of behavior observed—whether a dog raises a leg and which leg it is—is a function of the training conditions.

2.3.2 When does the behavior occur?

Here, we want to know about both the temporal placement and the frequency of performance. It should not surprise you that this dimension of behavior is also controllable by stimuli. In a conditioning experiment, we might deliver food to a pigeon upon the first peck to a key light that happens after the termination of a 40-s Tone. The Tone is a discriminative stimulus for pecking to the Light but only after the Tone has been playing continuously for 40 s (Figure 2.13). Pecks prior to the 40-s threshold are nonreinforced. Initially, the pigeon will come to peck during the Tone at its onset and periodically throughout, but over time, pecks will occur preferentially late in the presentation of the Tone—more responses will happen close to the 40-s mark than at the start of the trial.

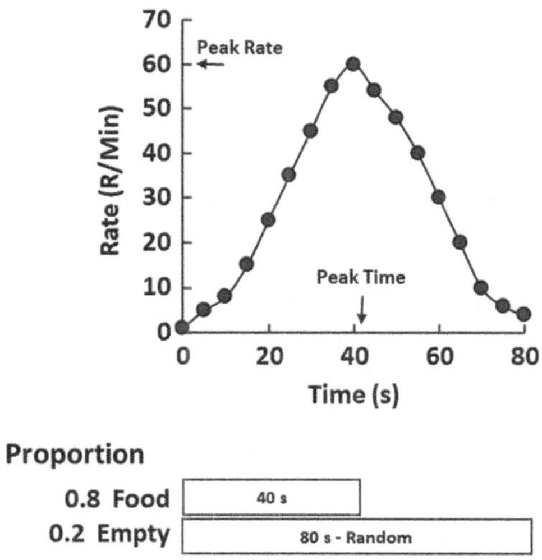

Figure 2.13 **Timing behavior.** Timing behavior can be observed as a gradual increase in response rate up until the time when the reinforcer was delivered during training (40 s). (From Roberts, 1981; reproduced with permission from the American Psychological Association.)

On occasional probe trials in which the Tone is temporally extended and reinforcement withheld, we can track the frequency of pecks to the key as a function of time. Pecking becomes more probable as the Tone approaches 40 s in duration and then tapers off gradually after the 40-s mark is passed and no reinforcer is delivered (e.g., Roberts, 1981). This suggests ***timing***—stimuli have temporal properties that can control behavior just as they have spatial and visual properties. The sharpness of the resultant function tells us something about the temporal control of Pavlovian or operant behavior—steeper curves indicate greater temporal control than do more gradual curves.

We can identify generalization and discrimination both over time during training as well as in the distribution of responses during probe trials. Early in training, peck timing indicates mostly generalization across the duration of the stimulus. Over training, the later portion of the Tone comes to control the probability of pecking better (i.e., is discriminated from) than the early portion of the Tone. More generalization is expected among the seconds that occur in the later portion of the stimulus than with those occurring earlier (more about timing behavior in Chapter 8).

2.3.3 Where does the behavior occur?

Here, we want to know about the spatial location, or context, in which the action occurs. A difference in the probability of behavior occurring at one location over another location may result from the fact that some locations afford certain kinds of actions that others do not. Organisms learn about the contexts in which behavior and its consequences occur. A seasoned baseball player may laugh when a friend misspeaks and calls a ball hit over the outfield fence a "touchdown," a term reserved for an American football field. For animals, a particular food source may only grow in one area within its territory, thus its foraging responses are more likely to be reinforced only when they occur in this area.

Animals learn about the spatial dimensions (e.g., distance and direction) between objects in areas they repeatedly visit. Pigeons and humans trained to peck or click a visual stimulus (a small white circle) displayed at one location (S+) on a touchscreen-equipped monitor demonstrate a spatial generalization gradient when the white circle is displayed at other locations (Cheng et al., 1997; Cheng & Spetch, 2002). The location of the white circle during training must have been learned about relative to other features of the training situation (e.g., the frame of the monitor). Strong generalization occurred between locations nearest to the training location (S+), and generalization decreased as the distance from the training location increased. Just as a discriminative stimulus may signal the opportunity for a reinforced response 40 s after its onset, a discriminative stimulus may signal a reinforced response 40 cm from its location. These kinds of stimuli are called *landmarks*. Similar to the development of timing, stimulus control of the spatial location of responses is evident early in training but increases over time (more about spatial behavior in Chapter 9).

2.4 The nature of the reinforcer

USs elicit URs, each of which is primarily a function of an evolutionary history. During development, the consequences of behavior can serve to change the future likelihood of behavior. We may call them *reinforcers* or *punishers* depending on whether they increase the probability the behavior or decrease it, respectively.

A reinforcer in one scenario is likely to be a reinforcer in others. Sucrose, in both rats and humans, is often a consequence that increases the probability of future behavior. Contingent delivery of sucrose may make many forms of behavior more likely. Spending time with a small child will corroborate this fact—the promise of candy increases the probability that the child will behave appropriately in a variety of circumstances, especially when promises have been honored in the past.

Some reinforcers will be more effective when the animal is under threat in comparison to when it is not. There is substantial evidence to indicate that stimulus control differs as a function of the kind of reinforcers that are available. Consider the following example (Foree & LoLordo, 1973). In two groups of pigeons, pressing a treadle was reinforced only in the simultaneous presence of a Tone and a red Light (Figure 2.14). One group (Appetitive) received food when they pressed the treadle in the presence of the compound stimulus; the other group (Avoidance) avoided shock when they engaged in treadle pressing. Note that in each case, we might expect that pigeons should learn to press the treadle—the consequences of doing support survival for the birds in each case. However, the nature of the reinforcer is different—only in the second group are birds under threat. This illustrates, respectively, a difference between *positive* and *negative reinforcement*, a distinction we will discuss more later in the text (see operant contingencies in Chapter 4).

All birds learned to press the treadle. The action, itself, was thus similar in all cases irrespective of the reinforcer. Subsequent test trials were performed in which one element of the compound (i.e., Tone or Light) was presented to the birds. Pigeons that received food upon pressing during the compound stimulus responded preferentially to test trials in which the Light was presented—in fact, they responded nearly as much to the Light as they did to the original LightTone compound. Pigeons that avoided shocks, however, preferentially pressed during the presentation of the Tone. The Tone had acquired control of the avoidance behavior more than had the Light.

This discrepancy suggests relatively separable roles for visual and auditory stimuli in governing operant behavior. In pigeons, visual stimuli—perhaps related to a lengthy ancestral

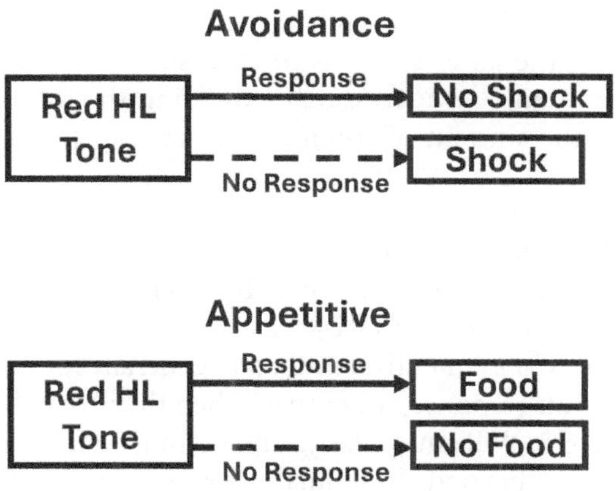

Figure 2.14 **Positive and negative reinforcement.** The stimuli presented and consequences of responses to those stimuli in an avoidance and appetitive operant conditioning preparation. HL: a house light. Solid arrows represent the consequence for a response and dashed arrows for a period of time without a response. Pigeons that received food upon pressing during training responded more during subsequent test trials in which the Light was presented, whereas pigeons that pressed to avoid shocks during training pressed more during the presentation of the Tone. (Based on Foree and LoLordo, 1973.)

history of foraging—appear to preferentially gain control of food-related behavior. Auditory stimuli—perhaps related to a lengthy ancestral history of avoiding predation—appear to preferentially gain control of avoidance behaviors (more on avoidance learning in Chapter 7). The precise location and identity of food is much more likely to be identified based on its visual properties rather than its auditory ones. Similarly, for prey animals, preventing predators from precisely identifying their location and identity may be a key to survival; hence, behaving adaptively (e.g., hiding) before a predator is within sight is useful, and this behavior may preferentially map onto more distal forms of stimuli that can travel further in space, like sounds.

2.5 Contiguity, contingency, and relative validity

As we have seen, the degree to which stimuli control behavior typically corresponds to the degree to which the stimuli relate to direct fitness. An electric shock to the feet of an organism immediately elicits a burst of activity; a bell that has reliably signaled the availability of palatable food elicits the production of saliva; delivery of sucrose for lever pressing only in the presence of a bright light will establish and maintain lever pressing only in the presence of the light and not in its absence.

To say that two events are ***contiguous*** is to identify them as happening close to each other in space and/or time. For instance, we could perform an experiment in which one group (Experimental) of rats receives trials in which Sucrose immediately follows the presentation of a Tone (Tone→Sucrose), while another group (Control) receives the same stimuli but with a long interstimulus interval (ISI, e.g., 2 min) inserted between them (Tone/Sucrose). In this example, the Experimental group would be receiving more contiguous stimuli than the Control group, as measured in terms of the time interval between the Tone and Sucrose. In practice, most empirical demonstrations of learning employ contiguous stimuli, referred to as a ***pairing*** of stimuli. A Pavlovian CS is usually forward-paired with the presentation of the US (i.e., CS→US); the latter stimulus produces a UR by virtue of the animal's evolutionary history. There is ample evidence that extending the interval between the CS and the US typically reduces the amount of conditioned behavior (e.g., Boakes & Costa, 2014; Odling-Smee, 1975).

In operant learning, the context in which a particular response is reinforced may come to control the emission of the response; in these sorts of instances, there is strong contiguity between the context, response, and reinforcer. However, ***delay discounting*** is a ubiquitous finding. That is, the value of a reinforcer is negatively correlated with the duration of the delay required to obtain it. Consequently, reinforcers generally function better when they immediately follow the operant response rather than when they are delayed (e.g., Catania et al., 2015; Dickinson et al., 1992; Williams, 1976). The ubiquity and obvious importance of such findings have been extended beyond the animal laboratory to the study of human behavior. For example, tobacco use accounts for 90% of lung cancers diagnosed worldwide and is the leading cause of cancer-related deaths (Alberg & Samet, 2003). Among many factors, the relatively immediate effects of nicotine compared to the approximately 20-year lag between tobacco use and cancer diagnosis (Heloma et al., 2004) reduce the effectiveness of warnings to prevent or cease the use of tobacco products. In a related finding, children whose operant behavior can come under control by delayed reinforcers have better long-term academic outcomes than do children more strongly controlled by immediate reinforcers; one may call the former behavior ***self-controlled*** and the latter something akin to ***impulsive*** behavior (Duckworth et al., 2016; more on delay discounting in Chapter 5).

This suggests, at first glance, that the mere contiguity of stimuli is the only crucial factor in establishing stimulus control. But of course, the same US that is forward-paired with a CS on many occasions may also occur in the absence of the CS (and the same is true for a reinforcer delivered in the absence of an operant response). This will likely decrease the effectiveness of the CS-US pairings, but thinking about contiguity does not provide an easy formula for predicting the detrimental effects of these US-only occurrences on conditioning. ***Contingency*** here will refer to the conditional (i.e., if–then) relationship between events, and along with contiguity, in a naturalistic science denotes cause and effect (Lattal, 1995).

Let us consider contingency within a reflex before returning to CS-US pairings. If you were testing the possibility of a new reflex (US-UR relation), then you would observe how close in time the UR occurs after the US, but you might also consider occurrences of the same response (e.g., URs not elicited by the US) that are so far removed in time from the stimulus as to be unrelated to the US. You could then calculate the probability of the UR occurring closely after the US and compare that to the probability of the same response (here, not a UR, as it is likely not elicited by the US) occurring when the US was not recently presented. This would give you an indication of whether the US is changing the probability of the UR. If the UR is more likely to occur immediately after the US than in its absence, then there is ***excitatory stimulus control*** of behavior by the US, whereas a UR that is more likely to occur in the absence of the US indicates possible ***inhibitory stimulus control.*** Lastly, if the probability of the UR is the same in the presence and absence of the US, then there is no stimulus control by the US (i.e., the US is irrelevant to predicting the occurrence of the UR). You would likely perform a similar kind of analysis if you were a chemist testing a new reaction or an engineer testing a new product.

For descriptive purposes, Pavlovian contingencies can be expressed in terms of two probabilities. The first is the probability of the US given the occurrence of the CS [denoted as $p(\text{US}|\text{CS})$], and the second is the probability of the US given the absence of the CS [denoted as $p(\text{US}|\overline{\text{CS}})$]. The contingency of two events may bear a strong correlation to the contiguity between them, but they are indeed separable characters.

The effect of the contiguity of paired events has conventionally been best captured by the first probability. For example, how many times have you heard the phrase (on TV or in person), "we need to talk" followed by bad news? It is likely the case these words have been paired a number of times in close proximity to the delivery of bad news, indicating you should brace yourself if you hear them. However, whether we anticipate bad news should also be affected by how often bad news happens in the absence of those words. In a fear-conditioning preparation, a rat could be exposed to 10 Tone→Shock pairings. In the absence of any other information, we are unable to distinguish here the effects of contiguity and contingency in the control of the rat's behavior. The Tone and Shock are highly contiguous, and the conditional relationship between them (i.e., $p(\text{US}|\text{CS})$ is 1.0. If we also know that the rat receives no Shocks in the absence of the Tone, then we can calculate the $p(\text{US}|\overline{\text{CS}})$ as 0.0.

Imagine, now, that we have a second rat that receives all the same 10 Tone→Shock pairings as the first, but also receives many Shock presentations in the absence of the Tone. The contiguity between Tone and Shock is the same here as for the first rat; there are 10 points at which the Tone and the Shock occur in close proximity. However, a rat that receives unsignaled shocks will show less freezing to a stimulus paired with the shock than does a rat which receives only signaled shocks (Rescorla, 1968). Calculating the additional probability of the US occurring in the absence of the CS provides a clear method for predicting their detrimental effects. This is true not only in classical conditioning procedures but also with respect to the contingency between an operant response (R) and reinforcer (outcome) in operant learning (i.e., $p(\text{O}|\text{R})$ compared to the $p(\text{O}|\overline{\text{R}})$).

It is worth noting that the concept of contingency may accurately predict behavior, but in at least some cases, for the wrong reason. Let us return to the idea of testing a new reflex. If we find that a UR occurs equally often in the presence and absence of a stimulus, then we may still have a reflex, but we have not detected the actual (or only) US that is eliciting the UR. Returning to Pavlovian conditioning, when unpaired USs occur, they are paired with the context rather than the CS (Papini & Bitterman, 1990). The need to account for the role of the context as another stimulus that is part of any conditioning procedure was part of the impetus for formalizing the notion of relative validity.

Calculating the contingency between a single CS and a US is not sufficient to predict stimulus control because there are other stimuli that could be conditioned. Especially important are contextual stimuli present during the CS→US trials (pairings). If we represent the CS with a single letter, A, and the context with another letter, X, then every Pavlovian conditioning trial is in fact an AX→US trial in which the CS and the context are both paired with the US. There are important implications of this way of thinking about Pavlovian conditioning (Rescorla & Wagner, 1972). *Relative validity* captures the effect that control of behavior by stimuli will be a function of the best available predictors of important events. The isolated value of a given predictor is often of less importance than is its value relative to other predictors. In complex environments with many possible predictors, this is crucial—an animal will tend to behave in accordance with those stimuli that are most valid. Let us look at an example described in Table 2.2 (Wagner, 1969; Wagner et al., 1968).

One group of rats (Group A) receives a series of compound trials in which Light and Tone precede the delivery of a Shock (LT+) and an equivalent number of Light-alone trials (L-). (Notice that the plus sign, +, refers to the presentation of the US, whereas the minus sign, –, symbolizes the absence of the US.) Another group of rats (Group B) receives precisely the same compound stimulus trials (LT+) as the first, but it also receives an equivalent number of

Table 2.2 Relative validity design

Group	*Training*	*Test*	*Theoretical predictions*			*Results*
			SC	*Contingency*	*RV*	
Group A	TL+, L–	L?	L:Cr	L: CR	L:cr	L:cr
Group B	TL+, L+	L?	L:CR	L: CR	L:CR	L:CR

Note. T: Tone CS. L: Light CS. +: US presentation. –: US omission. ?: a test trial without US presentation. CR: strong conditioned responding in the presence of a conditioned stimulus. Cr: moderate conditioned responding. cr: weak conditioned responding. SC: simple contiguity (contiguity without reference to other stimuli accompanying the target CS). Contingency: the view that responding to a CS depends on conditional probabilities (see text). RF: relative validity (a prediction based on the conditioning of the target CS and other accompanying stimuli in the situation). The results were consistent with relative validity predictions, that is, a stronger response (CR) to the Tone in Group A and a weaker response (cr) to the Tone in Group B (based on data from Wagner et al., 1968).

L+ trials. We then may test conditioned fear to the elements, the Tone (T) and the Light (L), and to the ToneLight compound (TL). Under these circumstances, the contingency between the Light and Shock is high for both groups, as is the simple contiguity between Light and Shock. In the absence of any other information, the Light would support conditioned fear in both groups. However, as is often the case, all else is not equal. We find here that animals in Group A show a strong CR to the Tone and the TL compound but little to no responding to the Light. Despite the same number of Tone and Light pairings, animals in Group B have a strong CR to the Light and the TL compound but little or no responding to the Tone (cr). How to interpret this?

Stimulus control of behavior is a function not of the raw predictive value of any given CS but of its relative predictive value. In Group A, the Tone was the best predictor of Shock—it was always followed by the US, whereas the Shock followed the Light only half of the time it was presented. Test trials of the Tone thus produced a strong CR, and test trials without the Tone produced weak responding. In Group B, the Light was the best predictor of Shock—it was always followed by the US, whereas the Shock followed the Tone only half of the time it was presented.

Relative validity is a general consideration when investigating animal behavior. Its role extends to both Pavlovian and operant scenarios. A student of behavior would do well to consider all of the stimuli involved in a particular situation, including CSs, contextual cues, and USs, to understand how their relation to one another may affect behavior (for more information on cue validity effects, see Chapters 4 and 5).

2.6 Summing up

This chapter introduced the concept of stimulus control, the notion that environmental stimuli come to determine the nature (i.e., the form and probability in time and location) of behavior. A naturalistic account of animal learning and cognition must necessarily work with measurable and predictable events. We start with two reasonable assumptions—that behavior is lawful and the result of an evolutionary process. From this point, we can seek the measurable events (antecedent and consequent stimuli) that come to control behavior and evaluate them across species.

The origins for some behaviors are deep in an evolutionary history and are no longer directly observable except for their effects (e.g., in extant behavior, in genes, and in the fossil record). Automatic behavior (e.g., unconditioned responses, reflex action, etc.) represents the end point of a lengthy evolutionary history in which behavior enhanced reproductive success and was thus subjected to natural selection forces. Accordingly, some behaviors have evolved into automatic responses (URs) to stimuli (USs) and often require little or no learning. Rats will automatically startle when a loud crashing noise is presented. Grasping a scorching-hot pan will automatically produce release and retreat in humans. In each of these and many other cases, the critical stimulus controls the response directly because of an evolutionary history—one might consider these responses to reflect *ancestral memory* (Robinson & Barron, 2017).

Many behaviors are not as fixed, but instead depend on events that occur within an individual organism's lifetime. Three such examples we discussed were nonassociative effects (e.g., habituation, sensitization, pseudoconditioning, dishabituation), classical (or Pavlovian) conditioning, and operant (or instrumental) conditioning. In each, stimuli come to control behavior. Nonassociative effects reflect changes in behavior resulting from repeated presentations of a single US. In Pavlovian conditioning, the observed relation between events comes to control a repertoire of behaviors tuned to the nature of the biologically relevant event, the US. In operant conditioning, more arbitrary forms of behavior may be constructed by virtue of their biologically relevant consequences. Organisms may learn to behave discriminatively on the basis of antecedent (or contextual) stimuli and on the basis of their behavior's outcomes.

In all of these cases, one might suggest that organisms must *remember* what had happened to them previously. Did this Tone result in Sugar, or was it Shock? Did pressing this Lever do anything good . . . or was it this other Lever? When this Light turned on before, did pressing this Treadle produce Food? All statements regarding *memory* necessarily reflect the degree to which behavior is a predictive function of a personal history of events and consequences. Organisms that learn can behave dynamically within a dynamic environment; organisms that cannot learn are bound to a particular repertoire of behavior that remains useful to the extent that the current environment resembles ancestral environments.

In the next chapter, we will examine learning in simple systems. The examination of basic learning in simple organisms will illustrate the fundamentals on top of which more complexity may be built. Thus, this examination is needed to gain a proper appreciation for the daunting complexity of other organisms (e.g., humans, apes, social insects).

Glossary

Acquired equivalence Generalization established between stimuli after training with the same outcome or response contingency.

Adaptation A feature in an organism or species that increases biological fitness.

Ancestral memory Stimulus control that results from the genotype of an organism.

Associative learning Establishing links between stimuli, responses, and/or outcomes by experience.

Behavioral system A collection of temporally organized unconditioned responses that are activated by an unconditioned stimulus and accomplish critical biological functions.

Classical conditioning Learning process in which organismal behavior changes as a function of the relation between stimuli. Synonymous with Pavlovian conditioning.

Conditioned response A response elicited by a conditioned stimulus.

Conditioned stimulus A stimulus that, by virtue of classical conditioning with an unconditioned stimulus, has come to elicit a specific learned response.

Consequences An unconditioned stimulus, reinforcer, or any other results of an operant response (e.g., food upon a lever press).

Consummatory responses Responses elicited by the sensory properties of the unconditioned stimulus that support immediate contact with it.

Contiguity or contiguous The degree to which events occupy the same space and/or time. Compare with *pairing*.
Contingency The degree to which events have an *if–then* or causal relationship.
Delay discounting The effect of a reinforcer is negatively correlated with the length of the delay required to obtain it.
Direct fitness The production of offspring by an individual organism.
Discrimination Behaving differently under one set of circumstances than another.
Discriminative stimulus (S^D) A stimulus in a discrimination training procedure that signals that a response will be followed by an outcome.
Ethograms An observational technique used to catalog the frequency of distinct behaviors in an individual or species.
Excitatory stimulus control The probability of a behavior (reflexive, Pavlovian, or operant) increases in the presence of a specific external physical event compared to its absence.
Generalization The degree to which an organism responds similarly across two sets of circumstances.
Generalization decrement The failure of an organism to responds similarly to two sets of circumstances that vary in their stimulus properties.
Generalization gradient A function by which behavior changes as it deviates from an established baseline.
Go/no-go task An experimental procedure in which subjects are trained to perform a specific response when presented with one stimulus and to withhold that response when a different stimulus is presented.
Habituation A decrease in the response to a stimulus that results from its repetitive presentation. Short-term habituation is an example of nonassociative learning. Long-term habituation may involve associative learning between the habituation stimulus and context present during training.
Inhibitory stimulus control The probability of a behavior (reflexive, Pavlovian or operant) decreases in the presence of a specific external physical event compared to its absence.
Landmarks A discriminative stimulus with a consistent spatial relationship to a US or reinforcer.
Long-term habituation Habituation persisting beyond the interstimulus interval used during training and likely to involve associative learning between the habituation stimulus and context present during training.
Master-yoked design Pairs of animals are randomly assigned to either the master or the yoked condition. During training, the behavior of the master animal determines the occurrence of events in its own environment and also in the environment of the yoked animal. The behavior of yoked animals is irrelevant as far as the events in their own environment. This design equates environmental conditions across master and yoked animals, but only master animals have operant control over events. Yoked animals are exposed to a Pavlovian procedure.
Memory The neurobiological changes essential for the expression of learned behaviors.
Natural selection A phenomenon that occurs when individuals within a population exhibit phenotypic variation in some trait, when alternative traits possess differential reproductive success, and when the traits under selection have a genetic basis.
Negative phototaxis Behavior that directs an organism away from light.
Negative reinforcement An operant contingency in which a response removes or prevents an aversive reinforcer. The aversive reinforcer occurs in the absence of a response.
Nonassociative learning Learning that occurs when organisms modify their response to a single event after repeated presentations.
Omission training In the presence of a stimulus, a response causes the withdrawal of an appetitive reinforcer that would otherwise occur.
Operant learning Change in behavior characterized by control by its consequences.
Pairing Traditional term in classical conditioning for the relation between stimuli within a procedure, characterized by the contiguity of stimulus events.
Patellar reflex In humans, the relation between stimulation of the patellar tendon and resulting kick of the leg.
Pavlovian conditioning See classical conditioning.
Peak shift Phenomenon in which discrimination training with S+ and S- stimuli along a single dimension finds maximal responding not to the S+ but at a location shifted away from the nonreinforced stimulus.
Phylogeny References the deep evolutionary history of organisms.

Positive phototaxis Behavior that directs an organism toward light.

Positive reinforcement An operant contingency in which a response leads to the presentation of an appetitive reinforcer and the absence of the response is paired with the absence of the reinforcer.

Preparatory responses Responses elicited by the affective features of the unconditioned stimulus that support food procurement.

Primary generalization The degree to which an organism responds similarly across two sets of circumstances due solely to the nature of the sensory systems detecting the circumstances.

Pseudoconditioning After exposure to intense stimuli that cause a particular response, other stimuli may elicit the same response in the absence of specific training.

Punishers A stimulus consequence of a response which has the effect of reducing the future probability of the response.

Reflex A necessary relationship between an unconditioned stimulus and unconditioned response. In phylogeny, is constructed via natural selection under long-standing, stable contingencies.

Reinforcer An unconditioned stimulus that, when delivered upon an operant response, causes that response to become more probable in the future.

Relative validity The control of conditioned behavior as a function of the degree to which individual stimuli are predictive of biologically important events. Control is greatest for stimuli that have greatest validity with respect to outcomes.

Remember The degree to which behavior is a predictive function of a personal history of events and consequences for behavior. Synonymous with recall.

Salience Concept referring to the relative noticeability of stimuli and the rate at which they may feature into learning.

Salivary response Characteristic mammalian response to substances (e.g., food) in the mouth and to the conditioned stimuli predictive of such events.

Sensitization An increase in the strength of a response because of the repeated presentation of a relatively intense stimulus.

Sensory adaptation A reduction in the response of a sensory receptor to a stimulus because of repeated stimulation.

Short-term habituation A decrease in the response to a stimulus that occurs within the interstimulus interval between its repetitive presentation.

Stimulus A physical event that causes a change in an organism's behavior. Plural *stimuli*.

Stimulus control The degree to which the probability of behavior varies in the presence of external physical events.

Taxis An orientation reflex that directs movements toward (positive) or away (negative) from a stimulus.

Timing Behavior that occurs at a time relative to a stimulus or event.

Tropism A growth response, typically in plants, that involves bending or turning part of the body toward a stimulus.

Umwelt The unique sensory and perceptual world experience by each organism.

Unconditioned response Behavior elicited automatically by virtue of the presentation of an unconditioned stimulus. See *reflex*.

Unconditioned stimulus An event that automatically produces a particular form of behavior in the absence of learning.

Withdrawal-flexion reflex The relation between painful stimulation at the bottom of the foot and the resulting withdrawal and weight shift to the uninjured foot.

References

Alberg, A. J., & Samet, J. M. (2003). Epidemiology of lung cancer. *Chest*, *123*(1), 21S–49. https://doi.org/10.1378/chest.123.1_suppl.21s

Balleine, B. (1992). Instrumental performance following a shift in primary motivation depends on incentive learning. *Journal of Experimental Psychology. Animal Behavior Processes*, *18*(3), 236–250. https://doi.org/10.1037/0097-7403.18.3.236

Blumberger, W., & Glatzel, H. (1968). Conditioned salivary response and its significance. *Nutritio et dieta*, *10*(2), 123–132.

Boakes, R. A., Costa, D. S. J. (2014). Temporal contiguity in associative learning: Interference and decay from an historical perspective. *Journal of Experimental Psychology: Animal Learning and Cognition*, *40*(4), 381–400. https://doi.org/10.1037/xan0000040

Bolles, R. C. (1979). *Learning theory* (2nd ed.). Holt, Rinehart and Winston.
Brembs, B. (2011). Towards a scientific concept of free will as a biological trait: Spontaneous actions and decision-making in invertebrates. *Proceedings of the Royal Society. B, Biological Sciences, 278*(1707), 930–939. https://doi.org/10.1098/rspb.2010.2325
Carew, T. J., Pinsker, H. M., & Kandel, E. R. (1972). Long-term habituation of a defensive withdrawal response reflex in *Aplysia*. *Science, 175*, 451–454. https://doi.org/10.1126/science.175.4020.451
Catania, A. C., Reilly, M. P., Hand, D., Kehle, L. K., Valentine, L., & Shimoff, E. (2015). A quantitative analysis of the behavior maintained by delayed reinforcers. *Journal of the Experimental Analysis of Behavior, 103*(2), 288–331. https://doi.org/10.1002/jeab.138
Cheng, K., & Spetch, M. L. (2002). Spatial generalization and peak shift in humans. *Learning and Motivation, 33*(3), 358–389. https://doi.org/10.1016/S0023-9690(02)00003-6
Cheng, K., Spetch, M. L., & Johnston, M. (1997). Spatial peak shift and generalization in pigeons. *Journal of Experimental Psychology. Animal Behavior Processes, 23*(4), 469–481. https://doi.org/10.1037/0097-7403.23.4.469
Davey, G. C. L., Phillips, J. H., & Witty, S. (1989). Signal-directed behavior in the rat: Interactions between the nature of the CS and the nature of the UCS. *Animal Learning & Behavior, 17*(4), 447–456. https://doi.org/10.3758/BF03205225
Davis, M. (1989). Sensitization of the acoustic startle reflex by footshock. *Behavioral Neuroscience, 103*(3), 495–503. https://doi.org/10.1037/0735-7044.103.3.495
Descartes, R. (1985). The world and treatise on man. In *The philosophical writings of Descartes* (Vol. 1) (J. Cottingham, R. Stoothoff & D. Murdoch, Trans.). Cambridge University Press. (Original work published 1662).
Dickinson, A., Watt, A., & Griffiths, W. J. H. (1992). Free-operant acquisition with delayed reinforcement. *Quarterly Journal of Experimental Psychology, 45*(3b), 241–258. https://doi.org/10.1080/14640749208401019
Dobrzecka, C., Szwejkowska, G., & Konorski, J. (1966). Qualitative versus directional cues in two forms of differentiation. *Science, 153*(3731), 87–89. https://doi.org/10.1126/science.153.3731.87
Domjan, M., & Fanselow, M. S. (2024). Pavlovian or associative sensitization and its biological significance. *Neuroscience and Biobehavioral Reviews, 163*, 105790. https://doi.org/10.1016/j.neubiorev.2024.105790
Duckworth, A. L., White, R. E., Matteucci, A. J., Shearer, A., & Gross, J. J. (2016). A stitch in time: Strategic self-control in high school and college students. *Journal of Educational Psychology, 108*(3), 329–341. https://doi.org/10.1037/edu0000062
Foree, D. D., & LoLordo, V. M. (1973). Attention in the pigeon: Differential effects of food-getting versus shock-avoidance procedures. *Journal of Comparative and Physiological Psychology, 85*(3), 551–558. https://psycnet.apa.org/doi/10.1037/h0035300
Gibson, J. J. (1960). The concept of the stimulus in psychology. *American Psychologist, 15*(11), 694–703. https://psycnet.apa.org/doi/10.1037/h0047037
Guttman, N., & Kalish, H. I. (1956). Discriminability and stimulus generalization. *Journal of Experimental Psychology, 51*(1), 79–88. https://psycnet.apa.org/doi/10.1037/h0046219
Harris, J. D. (1943). Habituatory response decrement in the intact organism. *Psychological Bulletin, 40*, 385–422. https://doi.org/10.1037/h0053918
Hebb, A. L. O., Zacharko, R. M., Gauthier, M., & Drolet, G. (2003). Exposure of mice to a predator odor increases acoustic startle but does not disrupt the rewarding properties of VTA intracranial self-stimulation. *Brain Research, 982*(2), 195–210. https://doi.org/10.1016/S0006-8993(03)03008-7
Heloma, A., Nurminen, M., Reijula, K., & Rantanen, J. (2004). Smoking prevalence, smoking-related lung diseases, and national tobacco control legislation. *Chest, 126*(6), 1825–1831. https://doi.org/10.1378/chest.126.6.1825
Herrick, R. M., Myers, J. L., & Korotkin, A. L. (1959). Changes in SD and in SD rates during the development of an operant discrimination. *Journal of Comparative and Physiological Psychology, 52*(3), 359–363. https://psycnet.apa.org/doi/10.1037/h0044283
Holland, P. C. (1977). Conditioned stimulus as a determinant of the form of the Pavlovian conditioned response. *Journal of Experimental Psychology: Animal Behavior Processes, 3*(1), 77–104. https://doi.org/10.1037/0097-7403.3.1.77
Jékely, G. (2021). The chemical brain hypothesis for the origin of nervous systems. *Philosophical Transactions of the Royal Society London, B376*, 20190761. https://doi.org/10.1098/rstb.2019.0761
Jenkins, H. M., & Harrison, R. H. (1960). Effect of discrimination training on auditory generalization. *Journal of Experimental Psychology, 59*(4), 246–253. https://psycnet.apa.org/doi/10.1037/h0041661

Jenkins, H. M., & Harrison, R. H. (1962). Generalization gradients of inhibition following auditory discrimination learning. *Journal of the Experimental Analysis of Behavior*, *5*(4), 435–441. https://doi.org/10.1901/jeab.1962.5-435

Jenkins, H. M., & Moore, B. R. (1973). The form of the auto-shaped response with food or water reinforcers. *Journal of the Experimental Analysis of Behavior*, *20*(2), 163–181. https://doi.org/10.1901/jeab.1973.20-163

Konorski, J. (1967). *Integrative activity of the brain*. University of Chicago Press.

Krause, M. A., & Domjan, M. (2017). Ethological and evolutionary perspectives on Pavlovian conditioning. In J. Call, G. M. Burghardt, I. M. Pepperberg, C. T. Snowdon, & T. Zentall (Eds.), *APA handbook of comparative psychology: Perception, learning, and cognition* (Vol. 2, pp. 247–266). American Psychological Association. https://doi.org/10.1037/0000012-012

Landis, C., & Hunt, W. A. (1939). *The startle pattern*. Farrar & Rinehart.

Lattal, K. A. (1995). Contingency and behavior analysis. *Behavior Analyst, 18*, 209–224. https://doi.org/10.1007/BF03392709

Lejeune, H., & Wearden, J. H. (1991). The comparative psychology of fixed-interval responding: Some quantitative analyses. *Learning and Motivation*, *22*(1–2), 84–111. https://doi.org/10.1016/0023-9690(91)90018-4

Lindsley, O. R. (1991). From technical jargon to plain English for application. *Journal of Applied Behavior Analysis*, *24*, 449–458. https://doi.org/10.1901/jaba.1991.24-449

Locurto, C. M., Tierney, J., & Fitzgerald, S. (1981). Omission training and positive conditioned suppression in the rat. *Animal Learning & Behavior*, *9*, 261–268. https://doi.org/10.3758/BF03197829

Marcus, E., Nolen, T., Rankin, C., & Carew, T. (1988). Behavioral dissociation of dishabituation, sensitization, and inhibition in *Aplysia*. *Science*, *241*(4862), 210–213. https://doi.org/10.1126/science.3388032

Mattes, R. D. (2000). Nutritional implications of the cephalic-phase salivary response. *Appetite*, *34*(2), 177–183.

Neuringer, A. (2014). Operant variability and the evolution of volition. *International Journal of Comparative Psychology*, *27*(2). https://doi.org/10.46867/ijcp.2014.27.02.09

Notterman, J. M. (1959). Force emission during bar pressing. *Journal of Experimental Psychology*, *58*(5), 341–347. https://doi.org/10.1037/h0042801

Odling-Smee, F. J. (1975). Background stimuli and the inter-stimulus interval during Pavlovian conditioning. *Quarterly Journal of Experimental Psychology*, *27*(3), 387–392. https://doi.org/10.1080/14640747508400498

Papini, M. R., & Bitterman, M. E. (1990). The role of contingency in classical conditioning. *Psychological Review*, *97*(3), 396–403. https://doi.org/10.1037/0033-295X.97.3.396

Patten, R. L., & Rudy, J. W. (1967). The Sheffield omission training procedure applied to the conditioning of the licking response in rats. *Psychonomic Science*, *8*(11), 463–464. https://doi.org/10.3758/BF03331699

Pavlov, I. P. (2003/1927). *Conditioned reflexes* (G. V. Anrep, Trans. & Ed.). Dover.

Pear, J. J. (2016). *The science of learning* (2nd ed.). Routledge.

Picker, M., Grossett, D., Thomas, J., & Poling, A. (1984). Negative automaintenance: Performance of pigeons under selective omission training procedures. *Psychological Record, 34*, 297–311. https://doi.org/10.1007/BF03394872

Plappert, C. F., Pilz, P. K. D., & Schnitzler, H.-U. (1993). Acoustic startle response and habituation in freezing and nonfreezing rats. *Behavioral Neuroscience*, *107*(6), 981–987. https://doi.org/10.1037/0735-7044.107.6.981

Protas, M., Conrad, M., Gross, J. B., Tabin, C., & Borowsky, R. (2007). Regressive evolution in the Mexican cave tetra. *Astyanax mexicanus*. *Current Biology*, *17*(5), 452–454. https://doi.org/10.1016/j.cub.2007.01.051

Pubols, B. H. (1959). Jan Swammerdam and the history of reflex action. *American Journal of Psychology*, *72*(1), 131–135. https://doi.org/10.2307/1420225

Rescorla, R. A. (1968). Probability of shock in the presence and absence of CS in fear conditioning. *Journal of Comparative and Physiological Psychology*, *66*(1), 1–5. https://psycnet.apa.org/doi/10.1037/h0025984

Rescorla, R. A., & Wagner, A. R. (1972). A theory of Pavlovian conditioning: Variations in the effectiveness of reinforcement and nonreinforcement. In A. H. Black & W. F. Proktsy (Eds.), *Classical conditioning II: Current research and theory* (pp. 64–99). Appleton-Century-Crofts.

Roberts, S. (1981). Isolation of an internal clock. *Journal of Experimental Psychology: Animal Behavior Processes*, *7*(3), 242–268. https://psycnet.apa.org/doi/10.1037/0097-7403.7.3.242

Robinson, G. E., & Barron, A. B. (2017). Epigenetics and the evolution of instincts. *Science*, *356*(6333), 26–27. https://doi.org/10.1126/science.aam6142
Sawa, K., Leising, K. J., & Blaisdell, A. P. (2005). Sensory preconditioning in spatial learning using a touch screen task in pigeons. *Journal of Experimental Psychology: Animal Behavior Processes*, *31*(3), 368–375. https://doi.org/10.1037/0097-7403.31.3.368
Sheffield, F. D. (1965). Relation between classical and instrumental learning. In W. Prokasy (Ed.), *Classical conditioning: A symposium*. Appleton-Century-Crofts.
Silva, F. J. (2018). The puzzling persistence of "neutral" conditioned stimuli. *Behavioural Processes*, *157*, 80–90. https://doi.org/10.1016/j.beproc.2018.07.004
Skinner, B. F. (1935). The generic nature of the concepts of stimulus and response. *Journal of General Psychology*, *12*(1), 40–65. https://doi.org/10.1080/00221309.1935.9920087
Skinner, B. F. (1981). Selection by consequences. *Science*, *213*(4507), 501–504. https://doi.org/10.1126/science.7244649
Staddon, J. E. R. (2016). *Adaptive behavior and learning*. Cambridge University Press.
Stahlman, W. D., & Leising, K. J. (2024). The behavioral origins of phylogenic responses and ontogenic habits. *Journal of the Experimental Analysis of Behavior*, *121*(1), 27–37. https://doi.org/10.1002/jeab.892
Timberlake, W. (1994). Behavior systems, associationism, and Pavlovian conditioning. *Psychonomic Bulletin & Review*, *1*(4), 405–420. https://doi.org/10.3758/BF03210945
Tuber, D. S. (1986). Dominance, the bidirectional hypothesis, and Pavlovian backward conditioning in the US-US paradigm. *Learning & Behavior*, *14*(4), 421–426.
Vandercar, D. H., & Schneiderman, N. (1967). Interstimulus interval functions in different response systems during classical discrimination conditioning of rabbits. *Psychonomic Science*, *9*(1), 9–10. https://doi.org/10.3758/BF03330733
Veith, I. (1961). Galen's psychology. *Perspectives in Biology and Medicine*, *4*(3), 316–323.
von Uexküll, J. (1957). A stroll through the worlds of animals and men: A picture book of invisible worlds (C. H. Schiller, Trans.). In C. H. Schiller (Ed.), *Instinctive behavior: The development of a modern concept* (pp. 5–80). International Universities Press. (Original work published 1940).
Wagner, A. R. (1969). Stimulus validity and stimulus selection in associative learning. In N. J. Mackintosh & W. K. Honig (Eds.), *Fundamental issues in associative learning* (pp. 90–122). Dalhousie.
Wagner, A. R., Logan, F. A., Haberlandt, K., & Price, T. (1968). Stimulus selection in animal discrimination learning. *Journal of Experimental Psychology*, *76*(2, Pt. 1), 171–180. https://psycnet.apa.org/doi/10.1037/h0025414
Walker, D. L., & Davis, M. (1997). Double dissociation between the involvement of the bed nucleus of the stria terminalis and the central nucleus of the amygdala in startle increases produced by conditioned versus unconditioned fear. *Journal of Neuroscience*, *17*(23), 9375–9383. https://doi.org/10.1523/jneurosci.17-23-09375.1997
Williams, B. A. (1976). The effects of unsignalled delayed reinforcement. *Journal of the Experimental Analysis of Behavior*, *26*(3), 441–449. https://doi.org/10.1901/jeab.1976.26-441

Part II

Learning

3 Learning in simple systems

Inexperienced observers are likely to be willing to attribute human psychological capacities to chimpanzees or dolphins, but they would pause if asked about the psychology of frogs or earthworms. Thinking about the generalization effects reviewed in Chapter 2, this is not surprising. Eddy et al. (1993) reported that ratings of physical similarity to humans predicted the degree to which human participants attributed cognitive capacities to animals. Invertebrates are consistently rated by participants as the least similar to humans. Our own experience with the world also biases the way in which we investigate the cognitive capacities of other species—referred to as ***anthropocentrism***. These factors largely explain why some species differences in learning may appear obvious to the amateur observer. However, when comparative psychologists evaluate species with methods that control for these and other ***contextual variables***, they have found it difficult to demonstrate species differences in learning mechanisms. In fact, some basic forms ***of associative*** and ***nonassociative learning*** are similar across many species, a similarity that could be based on homologous cellular mechanisms. These are remarkable conclusions given the remoteness of the common ancestor of species used in learning experiments.

3.1 Phenomena and mechanisms

3.1.1 What is a learning phenomenon?

Behavioral similarities in learning experiments among animal species could reflect inheritance from a common ancestor (homology) or be the result of independent evolution driven by similar environmental pressures (homoplasy). When homology and homoplasy, two central concepts in evolutionary theory (see Chapter 1), are applied to learning and cognition, a distinction needs to be made between phenomena and mechanisms. ***Learning*** or ***cognition phenomena*** are defined by a behavioral difference between conditions in an experiment. For example, ***dishabituation*** involves the relapse of a habituated response to one stimulus by the presentation of another stimulus ***compared*** to responding in animals that were not exposed to the dishabituation stimulus (see Figure 3.6-B).

The differences in conditions that result in phenomena also change how the environment is processed. Learning and cognitive ***mechanisms*** refer to processes intervening between training conditions and behavior. For example, dishabituation causes a reactivation of a depressed synapse that leads to a relapse of the response. Because they are induced under laboratory conditions and are defined by a comparison, phenomena are not akin to morphological traits, such as the grasping hand of primates. In other words, it is not as if some members of a

DOI: 10.4324/9781003401957-5

species exhibit a dishabituation trait and others do not; all members of a species will exhibit dishabituation to varying degrees, but certain conditions are required to observe it.

They are also not behavioral traits defined in terms of their presence/absence in a given species, such as a specific aggressive display of a territorial fish, which can be directly observed. Differences in evolutionary pressures can change the way in which similar environmental events are processed by two different species (e.g., food-storing vs. nonstoring birds). Behavioral differences across species that are studied at multiple levels are particularly advantageous, as an explanation that cites differences in a learning or cognitive mechanism is of limited utility without an account of why those differences evolved and under what conditions they are observed. Phenomena are a platform to study when (i.e., under what conditions), why, and how experience leads to behavioral change. Therefore, the phrase "the evolution of learning or cognition" really refers to "the evolution of learning or cognitive *mechanisms*."

3.1.2 Levels of mechanistic analysis

A problem with questions of homology vs. homoplasy is that there is more than one level of mechanistic analysis (Papini, 2002). Similarities in learning and cognitive phenomena can be characterized at least at four levels of analysis (Figure 3.1): psychological, neurobiological, neurochemical, and cell-molecular. The *psychological level* was developed specifically to explain learning and cognitive phenomena, and it involves concepts such as stimulus generalization

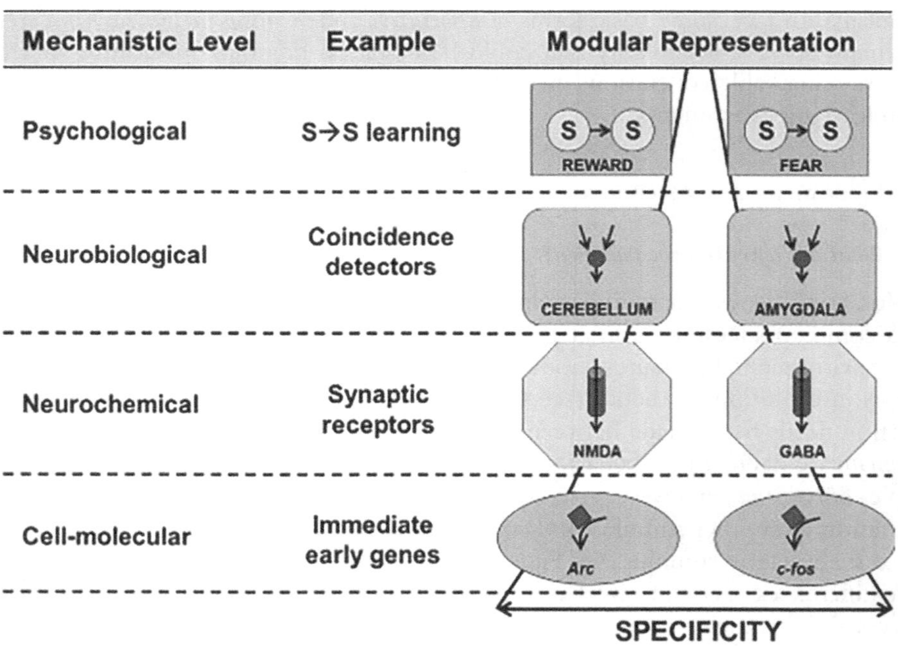

Figure 3.1 **Levels of mechanistic analysis of learning processes.** Components are represented by different geometric figures to emphasize their modular nature at each level of analysis. "Specificity" refers to the extent to which these modules apply exclusively to learning mechanisms. Lower levels of analysis apply to processes other than learning. (From Papini, 2021; reproduced with permission from Taylor & Francis.)

(see Chapter 2) and S→S associations (see Chapter 4), among others. Relevant methodology involves identifying key factors via experimental designs in which different treatments are administered, with attention to control conditions. Well-tested psychological mechanisms offer a guide to interpret the effects on behavior of manipulations at lower levels of analysis (Bitterman & Woodard, 1976).

The *neurobiological level* involves brain circuits, that is, brain areas and pathways. The methodology involves lesions, inhibition/excitation, stimulation and recording of various brain regions using techniques such as excitotoxic lesions (chemicals causing neuronal death by excessive excitation), designer receptors exclusively activated by designer drugs (DREADDs; infusing a viral vector to express an engineered receptor in a brain region which, when activated, causes either the inhibition or excitation of neurons), and optogenetics (infusing a viral vector to express a light-sensitive protein in a specific area that can be stimulated with light to inhibit or excite neural activity or to record neural activity with genetically modified biosensors). The goal of these studies is to identify areas and pathways involved in behavioral plasticity.

The *neurochemical level* refers to synaptic plasticity necessary to detect coincidences, such as those involving pairings between a conditioned stimulus and an unconditioned stimulus (CS→US pairings; see Chapter 2 for conditioning procedures). The methodology includes the administration of drugs (e.g., receptor agonists and antagonists) and genetic manipulations (e.g., gene knock-out and knock-in, transgenic organisms) that affect synaptic transmission. The goal is to identify neurotransmitters and neuromodulators in specific synapses within a circuit relevant for a particular phenomenon.

The *cell-molecular level* includes processes necessary for short- and long-term cellular changes involved in learning and cognition. Such changes include the use of proteins already available in neurons as well as the synthesis of new proteins via gene expression. The methodology includes the administration of drugs or genetic manipulations that affect second-messenger systems (such as cyclic adenosine monophosphate, cAMP), proteins that regulate gene expression (such as the cAMP response element-binding protein, CREB), specific genes (including immediate early genes, such as *Arc* and *c-Fos*), and posttranscriptional factors (such as RNA-binding proteins). The goal is to identify cellular cascades that participate in synaptic plasticity necessary for particular learning or cognitive phenomena.

Figure 3.1 also represents the degree of specificity of these mechanisms. Whereas psychological concepts are postulated to explain learning phenomena, as one moves to lower levels of analysis, mechanisms involved in learning are also involved in other functions. For example, the amygdala is part of the neural circuit involved in fear conditioning, but it is also implicated in appetitive, aggressive, and sexual behaviors.

Cell-molecular mechanisms are the least specific of all. A key component of gene expression involved in synaptic plasticity, cAMP, is also present in bacteria such as *Escherichia coli*. The fact that these proteins are involved in learning but in other functions as well explains their conservation across species. Evolutionary changes affecting one function could result in maladaptive consequences for other functions. In human evolution, a change toward a more omnivorous diet incorporating animal protein and fat is likely one factor facilitating the evolution of a relatively large brain (see Chapter 1). However, this change in diet has led to pathological consequences (e.g., heart disease, hypertension) because of deficient metabolic mechanisms to process meat. Consistent with a high level of conservation, there are deep homologies in learning mechanisms across widely divergent species at the cell-molecular level.

3.1.3 Species similarity in learning phenomena

The mechanistic view illustrated in Figure 3.1 suggests that a hypothesis of homology among learning or cognitive phenomena observed in two species must be consistent with manipulations at each level of analysis producing the same effects on behavior (Papini, 2002). Species similarities in learning or cognitive phenomena can also be caused by homoplasy when common behavioral outcomes are the result of different mechanisms at any level of analysis. Two types of homoplasy are relevant: parallel and convergent evolution (West-Eberhard, 2003). *Parallel evolution* is suggested by similar learning phenomena occurring in species that share the same cell-molecular mechanisms but use different mechanisms at higher levels (e.g., different neurotransmitters or neural circuits). *Convergent evolution* is consistent with species that exhibit different mechanisms at all levels underlying the same learning phenomenon. The view that evolution has led to vast genetic changes that preclude extensive homologies (e.g., Mayr, 1963; Simpson, 1964) is contradicted by contemporary genetics. Genetics has revealed a considerable amount of homology in protein structure and gene sequences across animal phyla that were already evolving independently during the Cambrian, more than 540 Ma (see Chapter 1). Phenotypic change is often achieved by the recruitment of old genes in the organization of new structures and functions. What are the implications of these discoveries for comparative learning and cognition?

Notice that mechanistic levels are hierarchically nested (see Figure 3.1). For example, the same associative structure (S→S learning) or second-messenger system (cAMP) could be involved in different learning phenomena. This modular arrangement is suggested by the fact that brain processes are generally conserved, which implies a potential for parallel evolution of learning and cognitive mechanisms. An example from the visual system illustrates this point. Although the eyes of vertebrates, insects, and cephalopods are functionally equivalent, their morphology and development suggest parallel evolution. However, they share the homologous gene *Pax6* involved in the regulation of the light-sensitive pigment rhodopsin (Fernald, 2004). *Pax6* is involved in light detection even in animals that lack eyes (jellyfish) and in algae that exhibit phototaxis. Conservation of *Pax6* across kingdoms reflects constraints on the number of molecules sensitive to light. Likewise, similar learning phenomena in different species (or in the same species but across different domains: foraging, reproduction, defensive, etc.) can be based on different neurotransmitter systems and yet share the same cell-molecular processes for synaptic plasticity.

3.1.4 Species differences in learning phenomena

When different learning phenomena are found in different species, the key questions are (1) Have the underlying mechanisms diverged? (2) Are behavioral differences caused by the divergence of *contextual factors*, that is, sensory-perceptual, motivational-emotional, and motor mechanisms (Bitterman, 1975)? Differences in the functional relationship between changes in the environmental conditions and changes in behavior can be the result of different learning mechanisms, but many factors influence behavior (Figure 3.2). An animal may, for example, stop eating a particular type of food because of an inability to detect it, an acquired aversion, satiation, or a motor deficit that prevents food procurement. The effects of these *contextual factors* highlight the fact that learning, cognition, and behavior are not strictly equivalent. This reflects a *learning–performance dichotomy*.

Contextual factors cannot be eliminated or even equated across species, so comparative research generally focuses on varying factors known to affect learning and cognition while

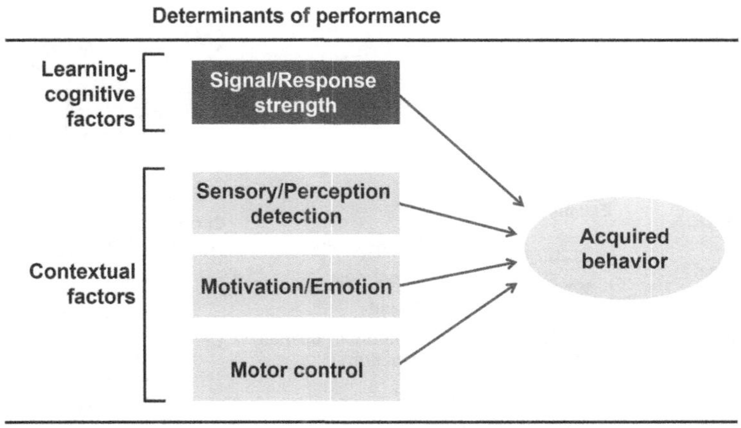

Figure 3.2 **Factors affecting acquired behavior.** Factors that affect acquired behavior can be divided into two broad categories: learning-cognitive and contextual (sensory detection, perception, motivation, motor control). (Modified from Papini, 2021; reproduced with permission from Taylor & Francis.)

asking whether different species respond to such factors with similar behavioral adjustments. This is called ***control by systematic variation*** (Bitterman, 1975) and indicates an emphasis on the search for functional relationships (Wright, 2013). Instead of asking, for example, whether rats learn the runway task faster than turtles, researchers ask whether runway learning depends on the same variables in rats and turtles.

3.2 Invertebrate learning

We start by describing learning and cognition in invertebrates. In terms of their neural organization, some invertebrates exhibit few neurons, which results in less connectivity (e.g., neural circuits), offering a starting point for a comparative analysis of learning and cognition.

3.2.1 Cnidarian neurons

Cnidarians (jellyfish, coral, sea anemones) are radially symmetrical animals with sensory neurons, motor neurons, and interneurons organized in a ***diffuse nervous system*** (Figure 3.3-A). A bicycle wheel is an example of radial symmetry: no left or right side. Fossils similar to living cnidarians have been found in rocks dated to 544 to 650 Ma. The neurobiological properties of cnidarian neurons can provide clues about the evolutionary origin of simple neural circuits.

Intracellular recordings from neurons of the jellyfish *Cyanea capillata* illustrate basic physiological properties of neurons common to all animals (Anderson & Schwab, 1984). The ***resting potential*** of a neuron is slightly negative (inside negatively charged). ***Depolarization*** occurs when a stimulus applied to the cell makes the interior of the neuron electrically less negative or even positive relative to the extracellular space.

Figures 3.3-B and C show that electrical stimulation of various intensities can produce both action potentials and graded potentials (Anderson, 1985). ***Graded potentials*** are local depolarizations proportional to the intensity of the stimulus. When the size of the graded potential reaches a threshold, an ***action potential*** (***AP***) is generated presynaptically. APs are

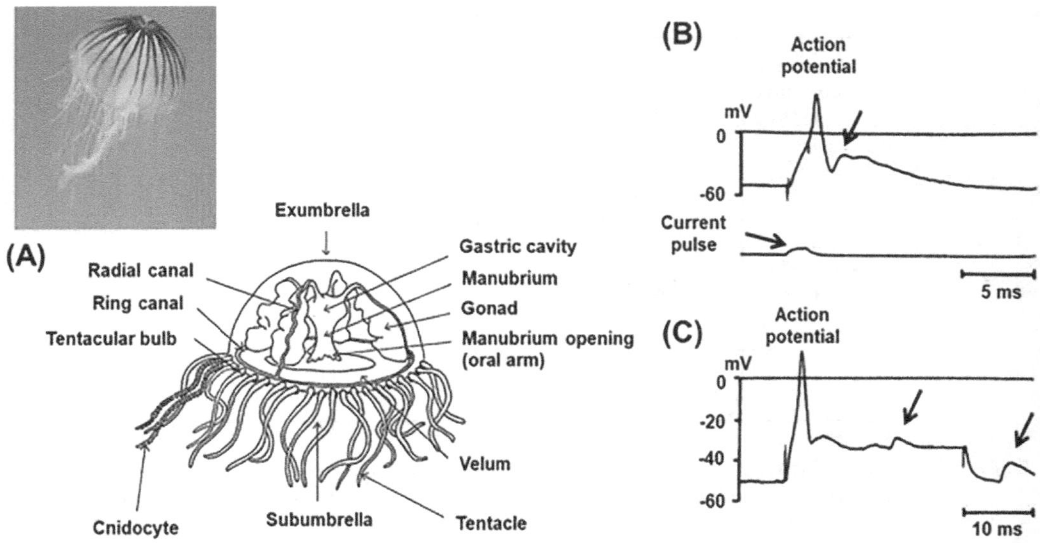

Figure 3.3 **Properties of cnidarian neurons.** **(A)** The jellyfish *Crapedacusta sowerbyi* (from Hroudova et al., 2012; with permission from *PLoS One*). **(B)** Intracellular recording from neurons of the jellyfish *Cyanea capillata*. A short pulse (2 ms) evokes a single action potential followed by graded depolarizations (arrow). **(C)** A longer current pulse also evokes an action potential followed by graded depolarizations (arrows). (**B** and **C** from: Anderson & Schwab, 1984; with permission from the University of Chicago Press.) (Photo from Creative Commons https://search.creativecommons.org, by Fool4myCanon, license CC BY 2.0.)

all-or-none depolarizations of the neuron that travel through the neuron's axon at constant speed and amplitude.

In a *chemical synapse*, the arrival of an AP at the axon terminal causes the release of *neurotransmitter* molecules stored in vesicles. Neurotransmitters diffuse into the synaptic cleft, some attaching to a receptor protein in the postsynaptic membrane. This opens channels permeable to specific *ions*, like sodium (Na^+) and calcium (Ca^{2+}), thus allowing these ions to flow through the membrane. Cell membranes are semipermeable, that is, they keep ions at different concentrations inside relative to outside of the cell. As a result, when an ion channel opens, ions tend to rush toward the side where they are less concentrated. The inflow of positively charged ions generates a graded excitatory potential in the postsynaptic cell (called an *excitatory postsynaptic potential, EPSP*). If sufficiently intense to reach a threshold, this depolarization will cause the neuron to fire an AP.

Chemical transmission can be bidirectional in cnidarians. Cell recordings show that when an AP is generated in the postsynaptic neuron, small depolarizations can occur about 1 ms later in the presynaptic neuron. Such an "echo" does not occur if the postsynaptic neuron exhibits only an EPSP (Anderson, 1985).

Cnidarian neurons also exhibit inhibitory synapses, that is, transmission that results in an *inhibitory postsynaptic potential* (*IPSP*). The inflow of negatively charged ions like chloride (Cl^-) causes *hyperpolarization*—the inside of the postsynaptic neuron becomes even more negatively charged. This makes it more difficult for the postsynaptic neuron to generate an AP. Whether a synapse is excitatory or inhibitory depends on the postsynaptic receptor. Receptors that allow Na^+ to enter the postsynaptic neuron are excitatory (e.g., acetylcholine), whereas receptors that facilitate the influx of Cl^- are inhibitory (e.g., GABA). These are all familiar properties of neurons from similar studies in other species.

Cnidarian neurons share several additional properties with the neurons of other animals (Bosch et al., 2017; Spencer, 1989), including:

- The synaptic cleft in chemical synapses is about 12 to 20 nm.
- The time it takes for the neurotransmitter to travel through the synaptic cleft and stimulate the postsynaptic neuron is within the range observed in other species.
- Cnidarians also exhibit *electrical synapses* in which APs travel with almost no delay between adjacent neurons, as in the swimming motor network of the jellyfish *Polyorchis penicillatus*.
- Like in most invertebrates, axons are not *myelinated*, and thus the speed of conduction depends on the thickness of the axon. Cnidarian nervous systems feature giant fibers in a circuit that controls swimming movements.
- Neurotransmitter vesicles are variable in shape.
- Synaptic transmission includes acetylcholine, glutamate, GABA, glycine, and serotonin.
- Neurotransmitter release depends on calcium influx into the axon terminal.
- The same synaptic receptors studied in other animals have also been identified.
- Neurogenesis.

Cnidarians do not exhibit the distinction between central and peripheral nervous systems typical of bilateral animals. Rather, neurons are distributed in diffuse nets. Figure 3.4

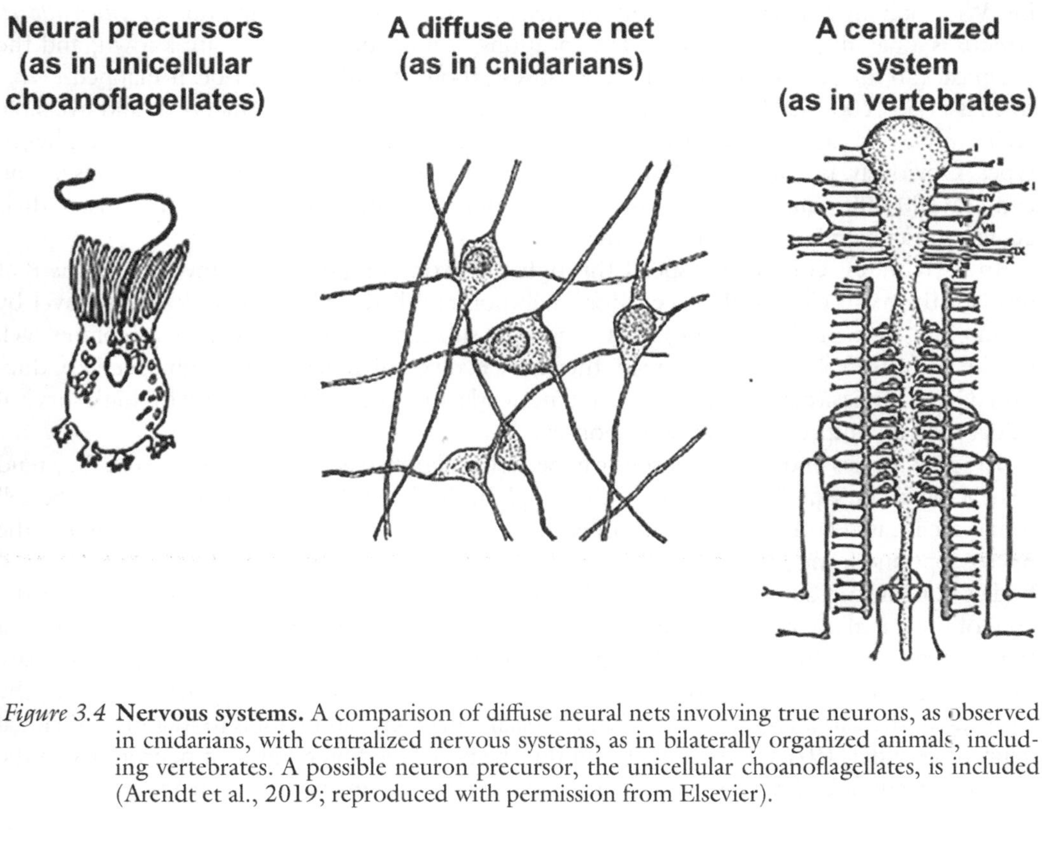

Figure 3.4 **Nervous systems.** A comparison of diffuse neural nets involving true neurons, as observed in cnidarians, with centralized nervous systems, as in bilaterally organized animals, including vertebrates. A possible neuron precursor, the unicellular choanoflagellates, is included (Arendt et al., 2019; reproduced with permission from Elsevier).

illustrates these systems and implies an evolutionary sequence starting from unicellular choanoflagellates (protists), which could be precursors of true neurons, just as diffuse systems could be precursors of centralized systems (Arendt et al., 2019).

3.2.2 The nervous systems of bilateral animals

In bilaterally symmetrical species (all phyla except for comb jellies, sponges, placozoans, and cnidarians), neurons are organized into nervous systems that exhibit some general features. For example, they extend in an anterior–posterior axis and usually present an anterior enlargement (called *brain* in vertebrates). Because bilateral animals generally move forward, the head first encounters new stimuli, and therefore, it usually contains sensory receptors for vision, taste, olfaction, etc., and nearby neurons to process sensory information. In some groups, segmentation of the body is paralleled by a similar segmentation of the nervous system in cell clusters called *ganglia* that contain circuits controlling movement in specific body segments. In other groups, bilateral symmetry is typical of the larval stage, but adults exhibit a different type of symmetry, such as in echinoderms (sea urchins, starfish). They are still considered to be bilateral animals because of their early development.

Bilateral animals have distinct *central* and *peripheral nervous systems* (*CNS, PNS*). The CNS includes ganglia and the tracts that interconnect them, usually located ventrally with respect to the digestive system, except in chordates, in which the CNS is dorsal. The nerves, sensory receptors, and motor endings connected to muscles and internal organs form the PNS.

Some neural features have played a key role in research on learning. Nervous systems with few neurons facilitate the identification of correlates between single cell activity and behavior. With only 302 neurons, the CNS of the adult hermaphrodite nematode *Caenorhabditis elegans* is a paradigm of simplicity. The locations of individual neurons are known, and the chemical (about 5,000) and electrical synapses (about 2,000) have all been mapped (WormAtlas et al., 2002–2018). The genome of *C. elegans* has also been mapped, and available techniques, such as fluorescent imaging, permit *in vivo* genetic analysis of learning phenotypes. Obviously, not all invertebrates are this simple. A ganglion in the CNS of an insect can contain 100,000 neurons packed in a cubic millimeter, making it difficult to register their activity concurrently with their behavior.

In vertebrates, conduction speed through the axon is regulated by myelin sheaths that insulate the axon electrically except for small points called *nodes of Ranvier*. APs travel by "jumping" from node to node, thus achieving substantial speed. Most invertebrates lack myelin sheaths in their CNSs; instead, they have evolved giant axons for high-speed conduction. Giant axons are usually part of neural networks that control behaviors with high survival value, such as antipredator escape responses.

In some species, individual neurons can be easily identified across animals because they tend to develop in the same location within the ganglion. In the mollusk *Aplysia californica*, the cell somas are located around the outside of each ganglion, facilitating their observation under the microscope and intracellular recordings during a behavioral experiment. This outer layer of cell bodies contains no axons or dendrites. Monopolar neurons project a single axon toward the core of the ganglion, called the neuropil, and the dendritic branches emanate from the part of the axon closest to the cell soma. In bipolar neurons, typical of vertebrates, dendrites emanate from the soma. The position of a neuron in the ganglion, its spontaneous firing pattern, the pathway of the axon, and its connection to specific neurons can be used to identify individual neurons (Kandel, 1976). Experiments can thus be performed on equivalent neurons (with the same connections and neurochemical properties) in every animal of the same species.

3.2.3 *Properties of habituation*

Learning phenomena exhibited by a wide range of animal species are usually classified as associative (classical and operant conditioning) and nonassociative (habituation, dishabituation, pseudoconditioning, and sensitization). Habituation is the simplest and most general form of behavioral plasticity (Harris, 1943). As discussed in Chapter 2, all animals exhibit reflexive behavior (e.g., orienting toward the source of stimulation or showing some protective response). Reflexes are responses tuned to provide a fitness advantage in the presence of a particular stimulus that has been encountered over many generations. Variation in the threshold for a stimulus to elicit a response allows the organism to adjust to the current environment. The threshold is affected by the animal's current motivational state, state of attention, and history (Staddon, 2016). Ongoing feeding, courting, and other activities could be disrupted as the animal switches to a risk-assessment mode. ***Habituation*** reduces the orienting or protective response to a particular event when that event is mild and repetitive, therefore minimizing the disruption of other activities. Habituation can be thought of as increasing the threshold to respond to a stimulus as a result of previous exposure.

Ten properties characterize habituation, nine of them represented in Figure 3.5 (Rankin et al., 2009). These properties provide criteria for classifying an instance of behavioral change as habituation. Any response that fulfills these criteria depends on synaptic transmission in the CNS.

1. Exponential reduction of behavior. Response decrement during repeated stimulation is usually a negative exponential function of the number of stimulus presentations.
2. Spontaneous recovery. A period of rest without stimulation can restore the strength of a habituated response the next time the habituation stimulus is presented.
3. Habituation of recovery. Successive episodes of spontaneous recovery result in progressively less recovery of the habituated response, suggesting retention across the resting period.
4. Interstimulus interval effect. The shorter this interval, the faster and deeper the habituation.
5. Stimulus intensity effect. The weaker the stimulus, the faster the habituation.
6. Below-zero habituation. Once habituation has occurred, extra stimulus presentations reduce the subsequent recovery of the response as if habituation would have continued in the absence of a response to a stimulus—hence the qualifier "below-zero."
7. Generalization of habituation. After habituation, testing with stimuli different from the original reduces response suppression. Habituation is stimulus specific.
8. Dishabituation. The presentation of a novel, intense stimulus intermixed with the presentation of the habituation stimulus can lead to substantial recovery of a habituated response to the original stimulus. Dishabituation distinguishes between central and peripheral causes of response decrement. Only behavioral decrements caused by neural interactions (i.e., central) are considered examples of habituation. Peripheral mechanisms of response decrement include ***sensory adaptation*** (less activation of sensory receptors after repeated stimulation) and ***muscular fatigue*** (reduction in muscle contractions after repeated activation).
9. Habituation of dishabituation. The ability of a dishabituation stimulus to restore the response diminishes after repeated presentations.
10. Long-term habituation. In some training protocols, response decrement can last days and even weeks.

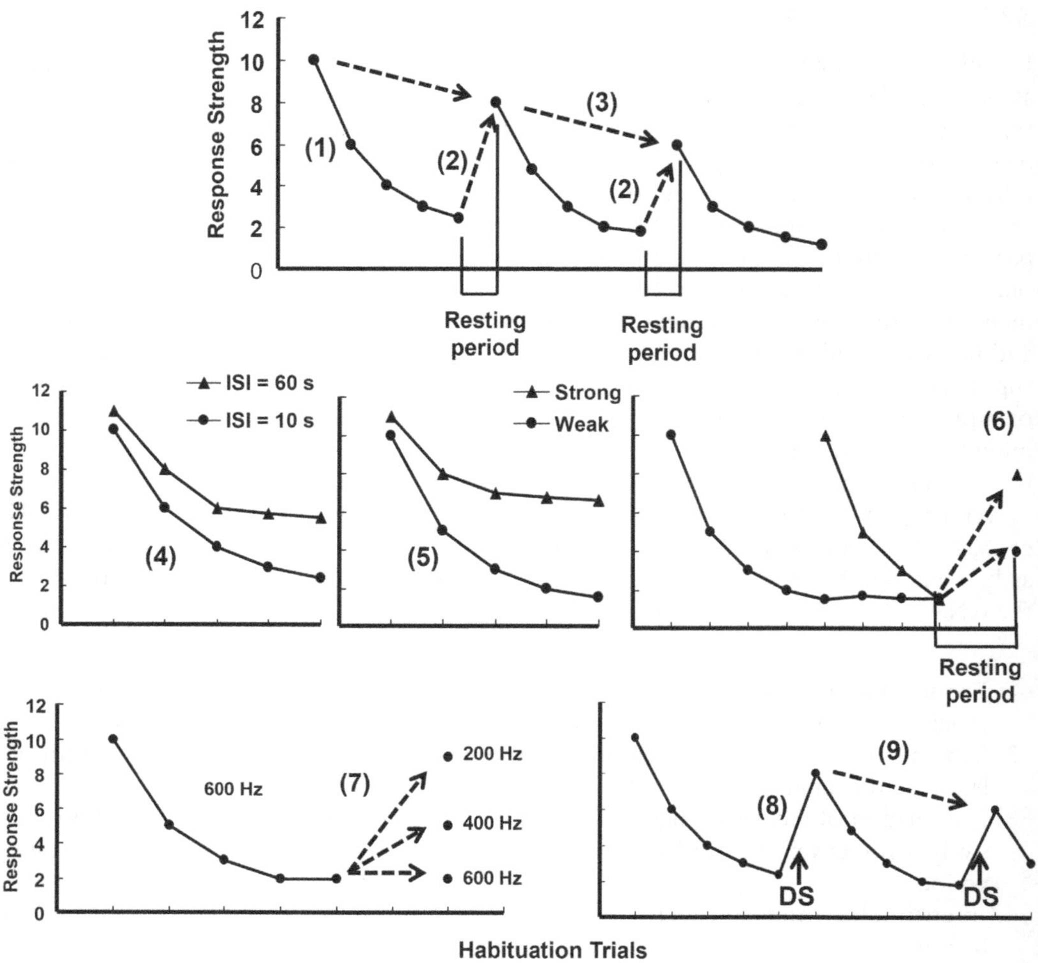

Figure 3.5 **Properties of habituation.** The numbers in parentheses correspond to each of these properties, as described in the text. DS, dishabituation stimulus. (From Papini, 2021; reproduced with permission from Taylor & Francis.)

These properties describe changes in behavior during the presentation of the habituation stimulus. When conditions between groups are different (e.g., different interstimulus intervals, different stimulus intensities), then training and testing conditions are confounded. One way to clarify this would be to test the two groups under the same conditions. Rats exposed to a noise every 2 s show greater response decrement than when exposed every 16 s (property #4, Figure 3.5). However, when the total number of noise presentations is held constant, then tests under a variety of intervals common to groups previously trained with different interstimulus intervals revealed that responding was more suppressed after training with 16 s rather than 2 s intervals (Davis, 1970).

So these training and testing conditions lead to opposite effects on behavior. It is plausible that long interstimulus intervals promote context-stimulus associations that reduce responding because exposure to the context makes the presentation of the habituation stimulus less surprising. In turn, context–stimulus associations would imply that long-term habituation can be treated as an associative phenomenon (Wagner, 1979). As shown in what follows, short- and long-term habituation are based on different cell-molecular mechanisms, a fact consistent with the view that long-term effects are based on associative learning.

3.2.4 *Habituation in cnidarians*

The diffuse nervous systems of cnidarians can acquire, store, and retrieve information gained from experience, as illustrated by the habituation of protective responses (Haralson & Haralson, 1988; Johnson & Wuensch, 1994; Logan, 1975; Rushforth et al., 1963). For example, bodily contractions induced by mechanical stimuli decrease gradually with repeated stimulation in hydras (*Hydra pirardi*), jellyfish (*Aurelia aurita*), and sea anemones (*Anthopleura elegantissima*). After sea anemones have been habituated to the repeated stimulation of a specific body location, responding increases as the test location is farther removed from the training location—a generalization gradient. Moreover, if the animal remains undisturbed for an hour, reintroducing the habituation stimulus leads to the spontaneous recovery of the response, but the habituation that follows can be faster than the original habituation. Long-term habituation over several days was reported in sea anemones. When jellyfish habituated to a tactile stimulus were shaken for 2 s (their home tank was gently moved in a circular fashion), reexposure to the tactile stimulus caused the dishabituation of the defensive response, suggesting that habituation was caused by changes in synaptic transmission.

3.3 Behavioral and neural plasticity in nonassociative learning

3.3.1 *Habituation and dishabituation*

Animals with the simplest nervous systems display some degree of behavioral plasticity, suggesting that the modifiability of nerve connections is a basal property of nerve tissue. *Synaptic plasticity* refers to the ability of synaptic transmission to adjust because of the use and disuse of neural connections. This is the basis of learning by individual experience, as was discovered through the study of nonassociative learning in simple systems.

Some defensive responses of mollusks, such as the gill-withdrawal reflex (GWR) of *Aplysia californica*, exhibit habituation and dishabituation (Cohen et al., 1997). *A. californica* is a marine slug that breathes by circulating water through its gill. Tactile stimuli (e.g., a water jet) applied to several structures induce gill retraction, a reflex that protects a vulnerable and vital organ (Figure 3.6). The dishabituation experiment requires consideration of temporal parameters. Ideally, performance in the trial immediately following the presentation of the dishabituation stimulus should be compared to the performance of a control group that did not receive the dishabituation stimulus but was exposed to the same sequence with the habituation stimulus. This distinguishes dishabituation from spontaneous recovery (see Figure 3.5) and eliminates peripheral factors (e.g., sensory adaptation, muscular fatigue) as sources of the response decrement observed during habituation.

3.3.2 *Short-term and long-term habituation*

Habituation can help us understand one of the most intriguing aspects of neural function: How is information acquired and stored in the CNS? The following sections capitalize on

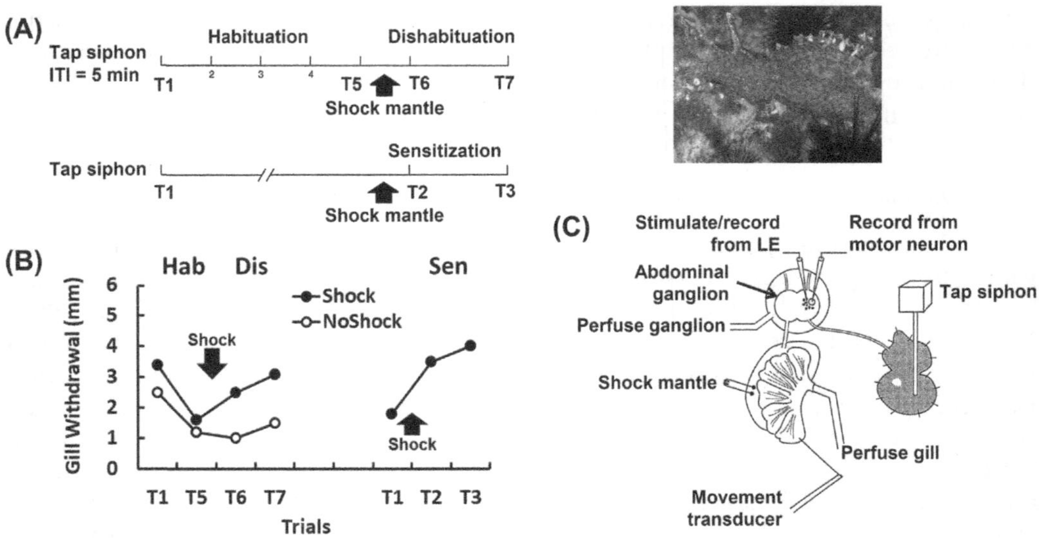

Figure 3.6 **Nonassociative learning.** Procedure to study habituation (Hab), dishabituation (Dis), and sensitization (Sen) of the GWR in *A. californica* (Cohen et al., 1997; reproduced with permission from the *Journal of Neuroscience*). **(A)** A tapping stimulus is used to induce the GWR; a shock applied to the mantle is used to induce dishabituation. ITI: intertrial interval. **(B)** Once habituated, a single shock applied to the mantle resulted in the recovery of the GWR—dishabituation. A nonhabituated GWR to tapping is enhanced by the single administration of a shock—sensitization. (Sensitization is described later in this chapter.) **(C)** These phenomena can be produced even when the relevant neural circuit is maintained outside the animal. The siphon is isolated from the rest of the body except for the siphon nerve, which carries sensory information into the abdominal ganglion. Such neural activity can be recorded with microelectrodes. The abdominal ganglion is also isolated from the body except for its connections to the gill via several nerves. Motoneurons stimulate the gill muscle and produce its contraction. LE: a specific neuron in the abdominal ganglion. (Photo from Creative Commons https://search.creativecommons.org, by kstolzenbach, license CC0 1.0.)

the extensive analyses of habituation in two model systems: the nematode *C. elegans* and the mollusk *A. californica*.

Two habituation phenomena are distinguished by the speed of recovery of the habituated response after training. In *short-term habituation*, the response recovers almost completely within hours. In *long-term habituation*, the response can remain suppressed for days after training. Different mechanisms are engaged depending on the number and temporal distribution of trials. In *A. californica*, 40 trials administered in a single session led to complete recovery a day after training (short-term habituation), but the response remained habituated for a week after 40 trials distributed over four daily sessions of 10 trials (long-term habituation) (Carew et al., 1972).

3.3.3 Neural basis of short-term habituation: C. elegans

The *tap-withdrawal response* (*TWR*) has been used to study habituation in *C. elegans*. Tapping the plate where the animal is placed produces a vibration of the substrate that induces reverse swimming. Reverse swimming also occurs spontaneously and can be induced by thermal stimuli (a heated plate placed close to the nematode but without touching the animal or the medium through which the animal is moving).

Short-term habituation of the TWR shows many properties of habituation, including dishabituation (Rankin et al., 1990). Dishabituation is observed when the habituated TWR recovers after a mild shock to the head of the animal, suggesting that the mechanisms of habituation involve synaptic changes. Although reverse swimming responses elicited by tapping are mediated by the same locomotor circuit underlying spontaneous reverse swimming, when the TWR is habituated, the number and frequency of spontaneous reverse swimming responses is not affected (McEwan & Rankin, 2013). Similarly, reverse swimming elicited by a thermal stimulus is not affected by prior habituation of that response by tapping. This suggests that habituation of the TWR occurs within the pathway involving mechanoreceptors rather than in the circuit controlling swimming. If the latter were true, habituation of the TWR should have affected both spontaneous reverse swimming and the response elicited by stimuli other than tapping.

3.3.4 Neural basis of short-term habituation: A. californica

The GWR of *A. californica* has a monosynaptic pathway connecting sensory neurons (SNs) carrying information from the siphon and motoneurons innervating the gill muscles (Figure 3.7). The critical synapse is located in the abdominal ganglion. This ganglion can be isolated and maintained in a seawater solution long enough to perform habituation experiments (Castellucci & Kandel, 1974). The nerve carrying sensory information from the siphon can be electrically stimulated (habituation stimulus), and activity of one of the critical

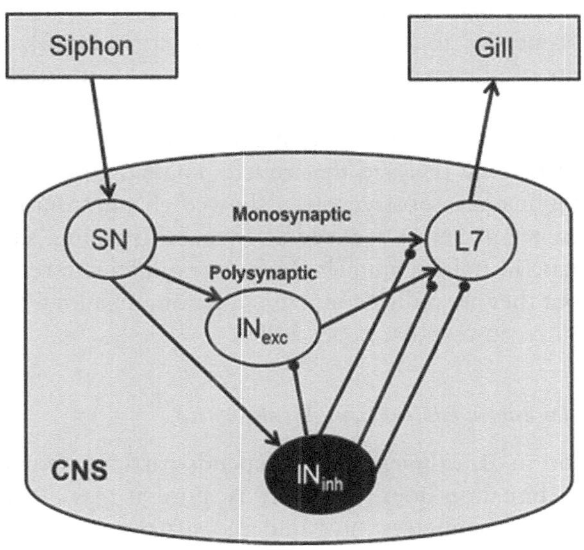

Figure 3.7 **Circuit of the gill-withdrawal reflex of *A. californica*.** The monosynaptic circuit involves direct synaptic connections between the mechanosensory neurons of the siphon (SN) and the motoneurons located in the abdominal ganglion (L7). SNs also connect with excitatory and inhibitory interneurons (IN_{exc}, IN_{inh}) in a polysynaptic circuit. The motoneurons have been individually identified. Habituation of the gill-withdrawal reflex (GWR) occurs in these sensory-motor synapses. (From Papini, 2021; reproduced with permission from Taylor & Francis.)

motoneurons, L7, can be monitored as an output (response). Repeated activation of the SN does not affect its own ability to generate an AP, but the EPSP elicited on L7 decreases in magnitude. Unlike mammals, this EPSP change is not caused by interneurons but by the repeated activation of the sensory-motor synapse. Interestingly, if L7 is repeatedly stimulated, its ability to produce an AP is not diminished, suggesting that the source of synaptic plasticity is in the presynaptic SN or in the sensory-motor synapse.

Because short-term habituation of the GWR is mediated by a single synapse that undergoes a decrease in its elicited amplitude, the phenomenon is known as ***homosynaptic depression***. Homosynaptic depression is caused by a decrease in the amount of glutamate neurotransmitter released by the SN as a result of repeated APs. This repeated activation reduces the influx of Ca^{2+} into the axon terminals of SNs, thus decreasing the amount of glutamate released into the synapse. Therefore, short-term habituation of the GWR in *A. californica* is mainly a presynaptic phenomenon.

3.3.5 Neural basis of long-term habituation: C. elegans

Despite its extreme simplicity, the nematode *C. elegans* can form a long-term memory of habituation lasting at least 24 h. Short-term habituation training involving 80 tapping stimuli delivered every 60 s (massed training) can be compared with long-term habituation involving the same number of stimuli but distributed in 4 blocks of 20 stimuli each, separated by a 1-h resting interval (spaced training). When tested a day later, massed training yielded no evidence of retention of habituation, whereas spaced training let to retention of habituation of the TWR.

Long-term habituation was impaired by disruption of protein synthesis with a heat shock (immersing nematodes in a bath at 32°C for 40 min) and also in mutants lacking a glutamate transporter in the SNs needed to detect tapping (Rose et al., 2002). In such mutants, SNs have reduced amounts of glutamate at the axon terminals. Consistent with these findings, a mutant lacking a subunit of the glutamate receptor present in interneurons of the TWR circuit showed normal short-term habituation but no evidence of long-term habituation. Moreover, fluorescent tagging revealed that vesicles containing glutamate (presynaptic), as well as receptors for glutamate (postsynaptic), showed changes during habituation. Glutamate transporter presence in SNs is reduced after spaced training, suggesting that there is less release of glutamate in trained animals. Moreover, glutamate receptor subunits do not change in numbers, but they are reduced in size, suggesting that long-term habituation training reduces the size of synapses (Rose et al., 2003).

3.3.6 Neural basis of long-term habituation: A. californica

Long-term habituation in *A. californica* also depends partly on homosynaptic depression, just like short-term habituation does, but there is more at play. To establish a long-term memory, the sensory cells themselves must undergo structural changes. Homosynaptic depression was observed after spaced training involving five daily sessions, each with 10 stimulations of the siphon (Castellucci et al., 1978). EPSPs obtained from L7 after 1, 7, or 21 days of habituation training were significantly depressed relative to those of control animals not exposed to spaced training. These L7 EPSPs were obtained after a single AP in the SN. How could such functional changes be sustained over a retention interval of several days?

Long-term habituation is achieved in part by the functional deactivation of sensory-motor synapses. Only about 30% of the synaptic connections of SNs with L7 are active in a habituated response, whereas about 90% of such connections are active in controls. Although the actual connections remain in place, long-term habituation training reduces the number of active sensory-motor synapses. Interestingly, this ***functional disconnection*** is rapidly reversed by a dishabituation stimulus (Carew et al., 1979). An electric shock to the head 2 h after habituation training reinstates the GWR when animals are reexposed to the habituation stimulus 2 h later to about 70% of the original strength. The response level of habituated animals not exposed to the head shock is about 10% of the original strength.

3.4 Cellular bases of sensitization

3.4.1 *Short-term sensitization*

There are three consequences to the presentation of an intense stimulus. First, the more intense the stimulus, the lesser the habituation (Figure 3.5, property #5). Second, if the response has habituated, then the presentation of an intense stimulus restores response strength (Figure 3.5, property #8). Third, nonhabituated responses elicited by repeated presentations of an intense stimulus can increase in strength—this is called ***sensitization*** (Figure 3.6-B). Whereas habituation is stimulus specific, sensitization is characterized by increased responsivity to stimuli in general.

Short-term sensitization involves an increase in response strength that dissipates within a few hours after training. Short-term sensitization in *C. elegans* can be induced by exposing nematodes to two taps separated by 2 min (baseline), followed by a train of taps for 600 ms (training), and finally, after 2 min, two new taps separated by 2 min (test). Control animals received five taps separated by 2-min intervals. Whereas the control group exhibited no change in the TWR, the sensitization group showed a significant increase in the TWR from baseline to testing (Rankin et al., 1990).

3.4.2 *Dishabituation and short-term sensitization in A. californica*

Research with *A. californica* shows the generalized effects of exposure to intense stimuli. Initial trials habituated the GWR in different animals either by stimulating the siphon or by stimulating the purple gland with a water jet (the purple gland ejects a dark secretion, called inking behavior, that can camouflage the animal from a predator; Carew et al., 1971). Then, all animals received a single, strong shock administered to the head. Subsequent trials with the siphon-habituated animals revealed dishabituation of the GWR when stimulated with the water jet at the siphon and increased responding of the gill when stimulated at the purple gland. On the other hand, purple gland–habituated animals exhibited dishabituation of the GWR when stimulated in the purple gland and a facilitation of the gill response when stimulated in the siphon. So a shock to the head generally facilitated both habituated and nonhabituated reflexes, indicating its influences on several reflexive pathways (Figure 3.6-B).

The training protocol involved in dishabituation experiments includes two sensory inputs: habituation stimulus (e.g., siphon tactile stimulation) and dishabituation stimulus (e.g., head shock). Thus, the circuit underlying dishabituation is more complex than that of habituation (Figure 3.8). Several electrophysiological findings point to the localization of dishabituation in this circuit (axo-axonic synapses enclosed in dotted lines in the figure). For example, if a microelectrode is used to stimulate L7 repeatedly, the subsequent elicitation of the GWR is ***not*** facilitated; since dishabituation involves increased activation of L7, this finding suggests that the site of plasticity is presynaptic (Carew et al., 1971).

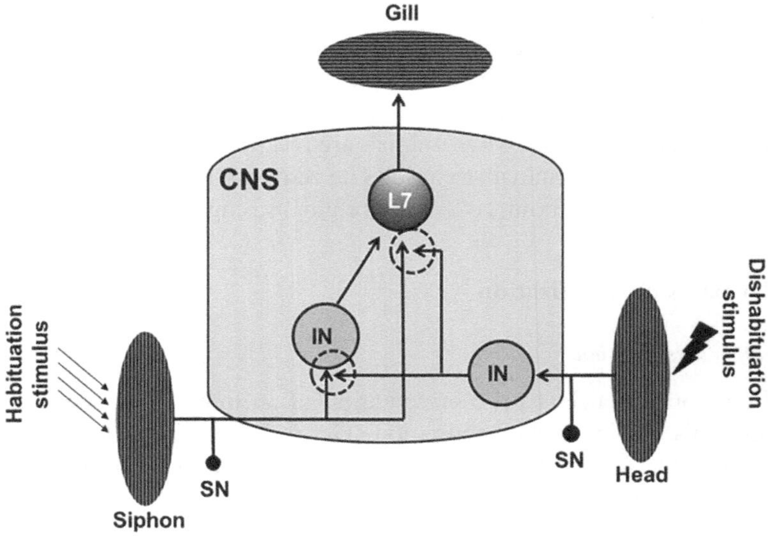

Figure 3.8 **The circuit for dishabituation of the GWR in *A. californica*.** Arrows represent excitatory synapses. Sensory neurons (SN) from the siphon (habituation stimulus) and from the head (dishabituation stimulus) connect to interneurons (IN) that make synaptic contact with the motoneuron L7, which contracts the gill. The SN from the siphon also makes direct connection with L7 (monosynaptic pathway, Figure 3.7). Modifiable axo-axonic synapses are marked with a dotted outline. (From Papini, 2021; reproduced with permission from Taylor & Francis.)

Short-term habituation is based on homosynaptic depression, but stimulation of SNs in the head facilitates conduction through the synapse depressed by habituation training (Castellucci & Kandel, 1976). The dishabituation input restores the amplitude of the EPSPs recorded in L7. These SNs establish axo-axonic synapses with the SNs innervating the siphon, and these connections cause the siphon-L7 synapse to be dishabituated. This is called *heterosynaptic facilitation* because the facilitation of the siphon-L7 synapse is achieved by a second synapse, itself not changed during training. Just as habituation and dishabituation involved opposite changes in EPSPs at the L7 neuron, they also appear to involve, respectively, decreases and increases in the amount of glutamate neurotransmitter released at the sensory-motor synapse.

Facilitatory interneurons activated during dishabituation training release serotonin as their neurotransmitter (Brunelli et al., 1976; Glanzman et al., 1989). If the isolated abdominal ganglion is bathed in a serotonin-rich solution after habituation training, EPSP amplitude in L7 is restored, much as done by dishabituation stimuli. Synaptic facilitation is prevented by the application of the serotonin antagonist cinanserin. Moreover, depletion of serotonin by the administration of a serotonin neurotoxin reduces dishabituation. The serotonin bath also facilitates nondepressed synapses, a fact interpreted as short-term sensitization. Serotonin is responsible for initiating a cascade of effects in siphon SNs that leads to increased synaptic efficacy (Braha et al., 1990; Figure 3.9). Serotonin binds to at least two types of receptors in these synapses, each increasing cytoplasmatic levels of two proteins acting as second messengers: cyclic adenosine monophosphate (cAMP) and diacylglycerol (DAG). In turn, these activate their own protein kinase, PKA and PKC, respectively.

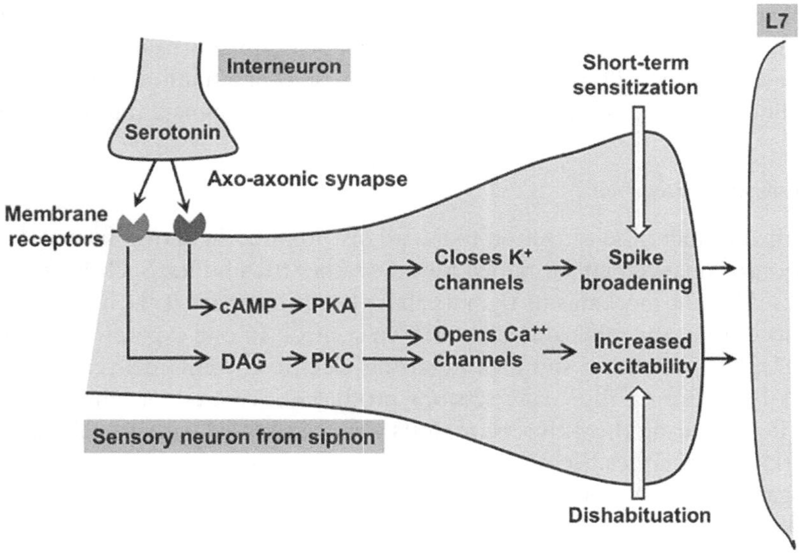

Figure 3.9 **Mechanisms of nonassociative learning.** Molecular processes underlying dishabituation and short-term sensitization of the GWR in *A. californica*. Neural plasticity occurs in the sensory neuron as a result of activation by excitatory interneurons making axo-axonic contact. The release of serotonin activates second messenger proteins (cAMP, DAG), which, in turn, activate their own protein kinases (PKA, PKC). Habituated synapses can be dishabituated by increased excitability, a mechanism that results in the opening of calcium (Ca^{2+}) channels, the mobilization of vesicles, and the release of large quantities of neurotransmitter into the synapse. Nondepressed synapses can be activated by spike broadening, a mechanism depending on the closing of potassium (K^+) channels that keeps the depolarization caused by an AP acting on the axon's terminal for a longer-than-normal period. cAMP: cyclic adenosine monophosphate. DAG: diacylglycerol. PKA: protein kinase A. PKC: protein kinase C. (From Papini, 2021; reproduced with permission from Taylor & Francis.)

If the abdominal ganglion is exposed to a cAMP analog, the siphon-L7 synapse is facilitated, but other synapses involving nonsensory cells are not facilitated (Brunelli et al., 1976). Increased cAMP levels at the axon terminals have two effects on the permeability of ion channels located in the cell membrane. First, through its action on cytoplasmatic enzymes, cAMP closes some potassium (K^+) channels in the cell membrane, thus reducing K^+ outflux to the outside of the SN. Normally, an AP depolarizes the cell by allowing massive influx of positively charged sodium ions (Na^+) into the cell; this induces an outflux of positively charged K^+ that repolarizes the cell. APs last longer than usual because this K^+ outflux is reduced in stimulated SNs. This is called *spike broadening*. This influence of cAMP is mediated by PKA, a cytoplasmatic enzyme that can modify ion channels.

Increased levels of DAG activate PKC, which lengthens the time during which Ca^{2+} channels remain open, thus increasing Ca^{2+} influx into the SN. Ca^{2+} facilitates the release of neurotransmitter into the synapse by mobilizing vesicles toward the cell membrane. This effect, also mediated in part by PKA in a synergistic fashion, results in the *increased excitability* of SNs.

Spike broadening and increased excitability are independent from each other and work best under different synaptic conditions (Byrne & Hawkins, 2015). If the synapse has been depressed by habituation training, then increased influx of Ca^{2+} and the mobilization of vesicles (increased excitability) can dishabituate the synapse. However, nondepressed synapses are predominantly facilitated by the closing of K^+ channels (spike broadening). Thus, although behaviorally similar, the cell-molecular mechanisms of dishabituation and short-term sensitization are different, although both increase the release of glutamate into the synapse.

3.4.3 Long-term sensitization

Increasing the number of sensitization trials and distributing them over several days leads to a type of response enhancement sustained for days rather than hours. Such *long-term sensitization* involves different mechanisms than its short-term counterpart. Long-term sensitization can be induced using the same animal as its own control. In one experiment (Antzoulatos & Byrne, 2007), a sensitization stimulus (a strong electric current) delivered on one side of the animal's body during four daily sessions produced increased withdrawal of the siphon (Figure 3.10-A). During the fifth session, tests were conducted with a weak electric stimulus applied to the tail in either the same (ipsilateral) or opposite (contralateral) side relative to the training area. Sensitization occurred only when the test stimulus was administered on the ipsilateral side; a test stimulus applied to the contralateral side produced similar responses and EPSPs to that of a nontrained control (Figure 3.10-B).

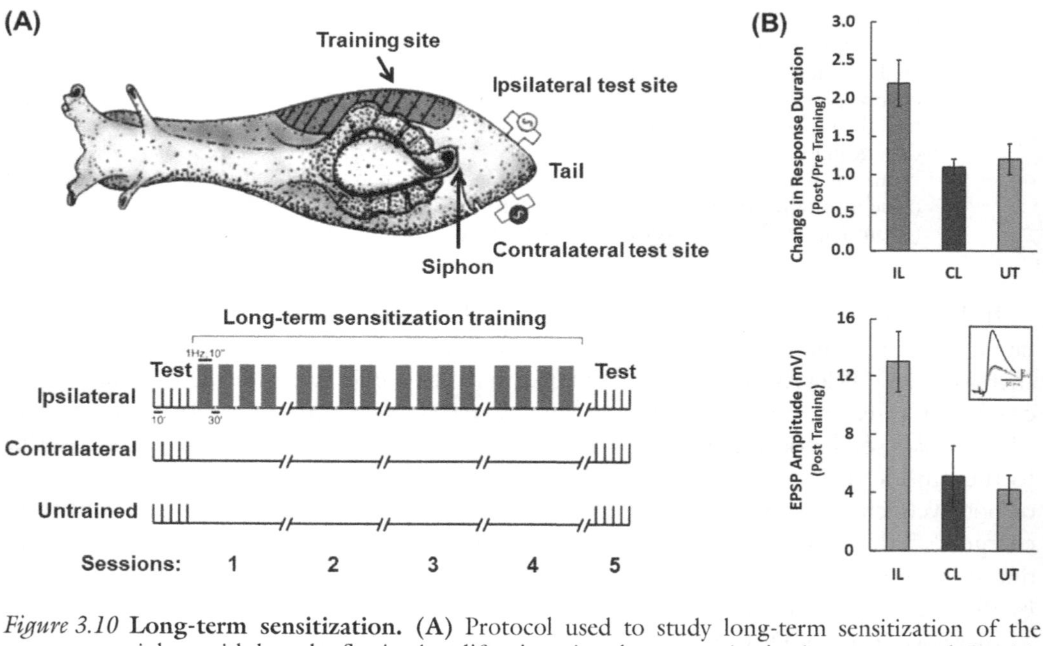

Figure 3.10 **Long-term sensitization. (A)** Protocol used to study long-term sensitization of the siphon-withdrawal reflex in *A. californica* using the same animal as its own control. Sensitization training involved stimulating one side of the animal with a strong electric discharge. Four sessions were administered. Test stimuli were applied on the tail either ipsilaterally or contralaterally to the training side, before and after training. Test stimuli were weaker and shorter electric discharges. **(B)** Ipsilateral (IL) testing led to increased siphon withdrawal compared to either contralateral (CL) testing in the same animal or testing in an untrained (UT) control. Similar results were observed in terms of the peak EPSPs recorded in motor neurons controlling the siphon-withdrawal reflex. (From Antzoulatos & Byrne, 2007; reproduced with permission from the *Journal of Neuroscience*.)

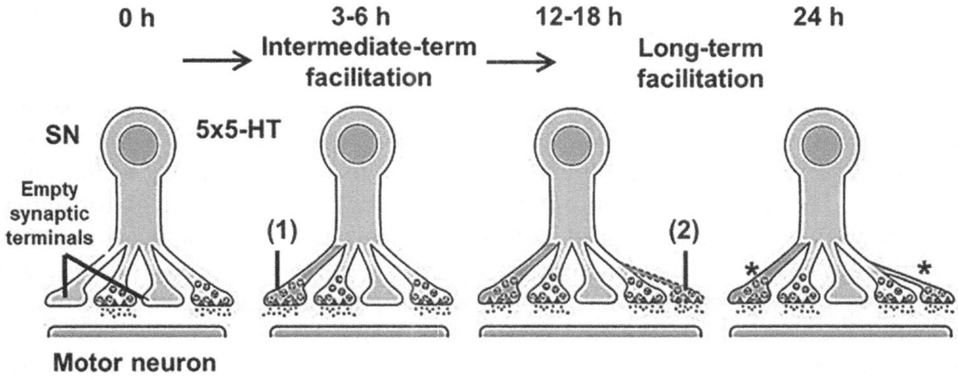

Figure 3.11 **Structural changes in long-term sensitization.** These changes in *A. californica* are induced by repeated baths in serotonin (5 × 5-HT) in the sensory-motor synapse. Initially (1), there is a rapid clustering of synaptic vesicles in preexisting, but silent varicosities. Later (2), new synaptic varicosities develop in the sensory neuron (SN). These new varicosities are functionally active (asterisks) and maintain response facilitation in long-term sensitization. (From Bailey & Kandel, 2008; reproduced with permission from Elsevier.)

During long-term sensitization training, the increased release of glutamate from the SN causes the clustering of AMPA glutamate receptors in the postsynaptic (L7) membrane, which facilitates synaptic transmission, thus increasing L7 activity. This clustering of AMPA receptors induced by sensitization training depends on proteins that are also active during synaptic formation in early development (Glanzman, 2006; Li et al., 2009).

In addition, long-term sensitization involves an increase in the number of axon terminals in SNs that synapse with L7 (Figure 3.11; Bailey & Kandel, 2008). These new connection sites, called ***varicosities***, are functional. Repeated serotonin baths and cAMP injections, both known to induce heterosynaptic facilitation, also increase varicosities. Gene expression is mediated by CREB (cAMP response element-binding protein), a protein that controls the transcription of specific genes, many of which help build new synapses (Martin et al., 1997). Treating SNs with protein-synthesis inhibitors eliminates long-term sensitization induced by serotonin without affecting short-term sensitization (Montarolo et al., 1986).

Experiments with cultured cells make it possible to identify the cell components needed for the development of varicosities. Surprisingly, varicosities develop only in cultures with intact motoneurons (Glanzman et al., 1990). Thus, although sensitization is mainly a presynaptic phenomenon, the induction of varicosities in the SN requires the presence of the motoneuron, suggesting the action of retrograde signals from L7 to the SN (Glanzman, 2013).

In conclusion, although short-term learning effects in *A. californica* involve functional adjustments in synaptic transmission, long-term habituation and sensitization require structural changes in sensory and motor neurons that preserve the information for longer periods.

3.4.4 Evolution of sensitization in mollusks

The ability to identify neurons individually can be used to understand the evolutionary history of nonassociative learning phenomena. Suppose that "increased excitability" and "spike broadening," two mechanisms of response facilitation described previously, are considered neuromodulatory phenotypes of *Aplysia*'s mechanosensory neurons. Could homologous neurons be tested for these phenotypes in a group of mollusks with known phylogenetic relationships?

Wright et al. (1996) followed a four-step approach to answer this question. First, six species of mollusks were selected for analysis (Genera: *Bulla*, *Akera*, *Aplysia*, *Dolabella*, *Bursatella*, and *Dolabrifera*). Second, their phylogenetic relationships were determined by morphological characters. Third, SNs homologous to those in *Aplysia*'s tail (stimulated in dishabituation and sensitization experiments) were identified in each species in terms of their location, size, and resting physiology. Finally, the presence or absence of the two serotonin-induced neuromodulatory phenotypes, increased excitability and spike broadening, was determined for each species and mapped into the phylogenetic tree.

This phylogenetic analysis shows that increased excitability evolved before spike broadening in these SNs since increased excitability but not spike broadening was found in two basal groups: *Akera* and *Bulla*. Moreover, increased excitability and spike broadening have apparently been lost in the tail SNs of *Dolabrifera*'s recent ancestors, since both traits were found in *Aplysia*, *Dolabella*, and *Bursatella*. Consistent with these results, *Dolabrifera* produced no evidence for short-term or long-term sensitization (Wright, 1998). Interestingly, *Aplysia* and *Dolabrifera* exhibit comparable levels of habituation of the mantle-withdrawal response, showing that *Dolabrifera* is capable of some forms of learning. Moreover, the increased excitability but not spike broadening in *Bulla* is a basal condition, whereas the absence of spike broadening in *Dolabrifera* is due to evolutionary reversal.

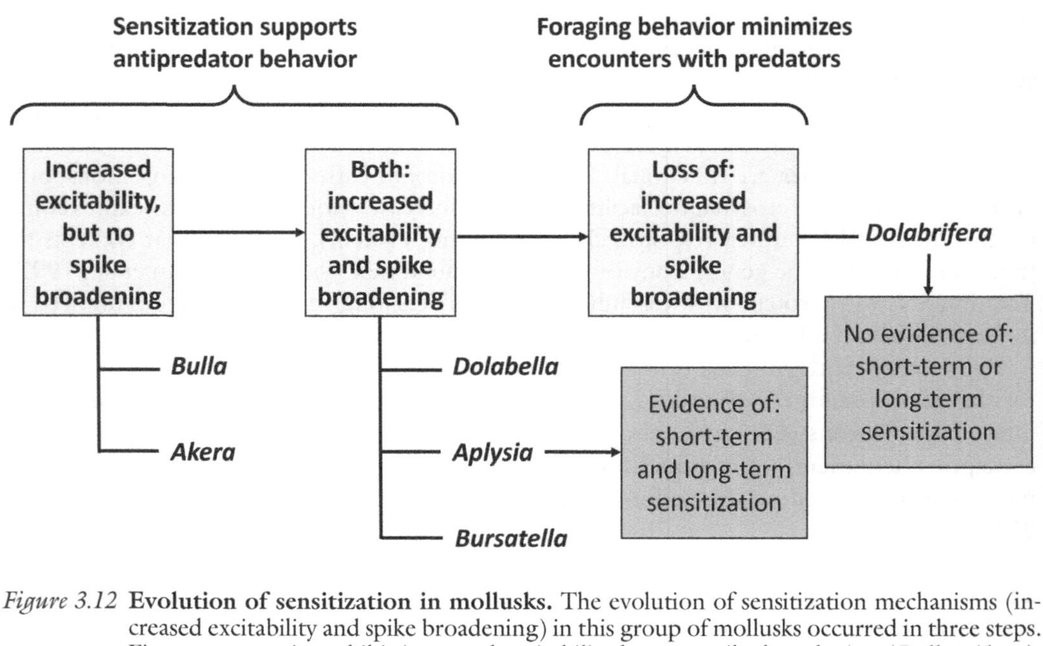

Figure 3.12 **Evolution of sensitization in mollusks.** The evolution of sensitization mechanisms (increased excitability and spike broadening) in this group of mollusks occurred in three steps. First, some species exhibit increased excitability but not spike broadening (*Bulla*, *Akera*). Second, some species exhibit both mechanisms (*Dolabella*, *Aplysia*, *Bursatella*). But, third, one species (*Dolabrifera*) has apparently lost both mechanisms and exhibits no evidence of either short-term or long-term sensitization. This evolutionary reversal may be related to the peculiar predator-avoidance strategy of these mollusks. (The information in this figure combines findings reported by Wright (1998), Wright et al. (1996), and Himstead and Wright (2018).

Sensitization likely evolved as an antipredator mechanism. Individual *Aplysia* that survived a lobster attack exhibit sustained sensitization relative to undisturbed animals, including increased excitability of SNs (Mason et al., 2014). In the absence of sensitization, how does *Dolabrifera* deal with predators? *Dolabrifera* evolved a specific pattern of daily activity that tends to avoid predatory encounters (Himstead & Wright, 2018). Most of the day, these tropical mollusks remain inactive under boulders in a tidal pool. When the tide falls below the water level of their pool during the middle of the day, they emerge to forage for food for about 1 to 3 h and then return to their hiding places. It is possible that *Dolabrifera* lost the neural mechanisms for sensitization because of its efficient avoidance of predators. These findings are summarized in Figure 3.12.

There is a connection between aversive learning (as in these examples of sensitization) and predatory encounters that may cause tissue damage. Most experiments with *A. californica* are based on aversive stimuli that activate SNs in the skin (Walters, 1991). These cells are in a prime location to detect life-threatening injury. Skin damage generates sustained discharges from both damaged and surviving SNs during a few seconds following tissue injury. The CNS receives high-frequency discharges much like those during sensitization training. This is followed by synaptic facilitation and cellular repair processes that likely involve the growth of axon terminals. Such synaptic facilitation can last for weeks and sensitize reflexes initiated by contact near the injured area. This suggests an evolutionary connection between cellular changes following injury and sensitization. Learning mechanisms based on nociceptive signals may have evolved early in response to the emergence of predator–prey interactions and thus are common to many species (Walters, 2018).

3.4.5 *Generality of the neural mechanisms of nonassociative learning*

Do the mechanisms of habituation, dishabituation, and sensitization described previously for nematodes and mollusks apply to vertebrates? These nonassociative learning phenomena have been documented in many species (Harris, 1943), but similarity in learning phenomena does not imply homology of mechanisms (see Figure 3.1). For example, although dishabituation and sensitization in *A. californica* involve an increase in behavior based on a similar cellular circuit (Figure 3.8), they depend on different cell-molecular mechanisms: increased excitability vs. spike broadening, respectively (Figure 3.9). These differences are consistent with differences in the type and timing of stimuli used to observe the phenomena as well as different developmental timetables for their emergence (Marcus et al., 1988). Dishabituation can be observed early in development, whereas sensitization emerges about 50 days later. It has been difficult to characterize vertebrate nonassociative learning at the cellular level, as done with nematodes and mollusks, because of the relative complexity of the vertebrate CNS. Let us consider the mechanisms of synaptic plasticity implicated in habituation, the simplest learning phenomenon.

In *A. californica* (mollusk), short-term habituation of the GWR seems to depend on presynaptic changes, namely, a reduction in the release of glutamate in the SN (or interneuron) making synaptic contact with the motoneuron—homosynaptic depression. In *C. elegans* (nematode), short-term habituation of the TWR also seems to depend on presynaptic changes affecting the release of glutamate in mechanoreceptors sending sensory signals to motoneurons. In these species, long-term habituation is regulated by protein synthesis affecting the expression of glutamate receptors in SNs (Yu & Rankin, 2022). What about habituation in vertebrates?

A potentially useful neurobiological technique to study habituation in vertebrates, given their enormous neural complexity, involves imaging the movement of Ca^{2+} ions through cell membranes in specific brain locations. Recall that Ca^{2+} ions facilitate the fusion of neurotransmitter vesicles to the axon membrane, resulting in the release of neurotransmitter. Ca^{2+} imaging has been applied to the study of habituation in larvae of the zebrafish (*Danio rerio*), a vertebrate (Marquez-Legorreta et al., 2022).

The behavioral procedure involves placing individual larvae in a dish and projecting a black spot from underneath the dish. The animal then escapes the stimulus by emitting a C-start response (the initiation of which resembles a "C") triggered by a pair of brainstem giant neurons, called Mauthner cells. The C-start response decreases in frequency as the stimulus is projected repeatedly. The rate of habituation depends on the interstimulus interval, and an intense light dishabituates the response (Figure 3.5, properties #4 and #8). Similar results were observed using an auditory stimulus to elicit the C-start response (Figure 3.13).

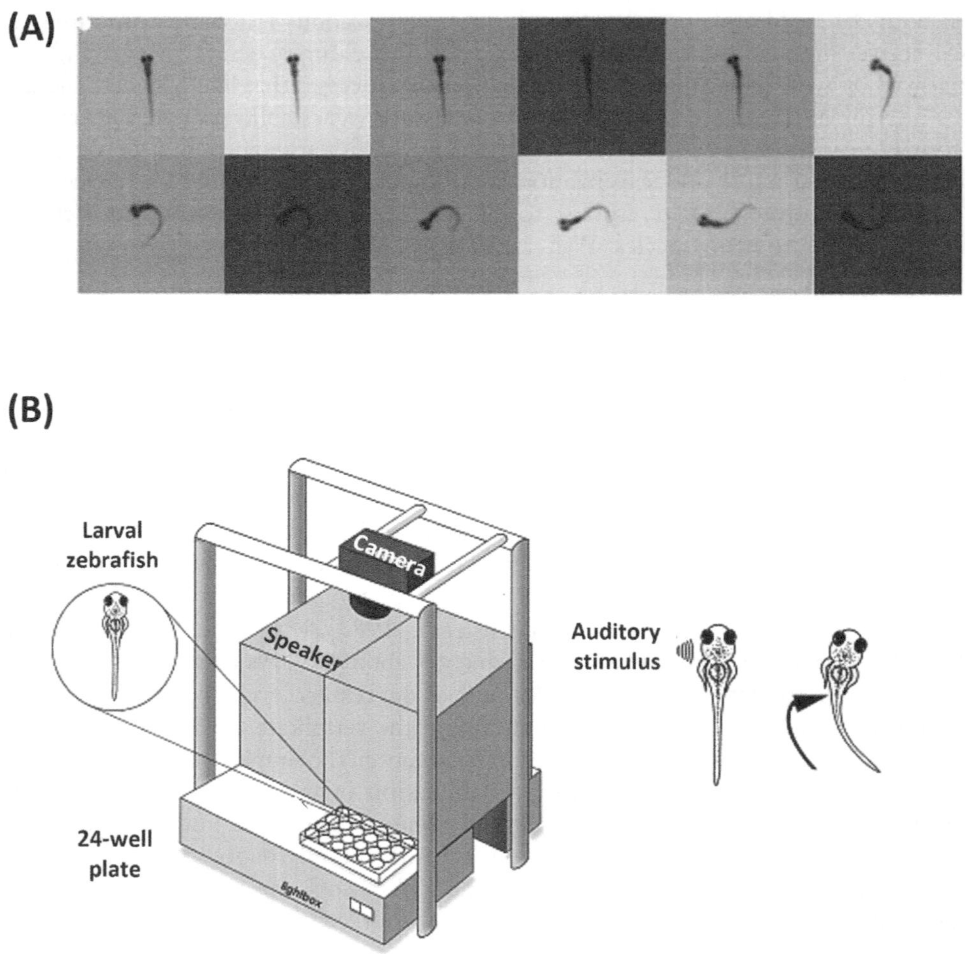

Figure 3.13 **Habituation in zebrafish. (A)** The elicitation of the C-start response by an auditory stimulus in a larval zebrafish. **(B)** The instrument used to habituate the C-start response to an auditory stimulus in zebrafish. (From Roberts et al., 2011; reproduced with permission from PLoS One.)

Ca^{2+} imaging during habituation provides a visual display of neurons distributed in the entire brain that are decreasing their level of activation across trials. Neurons that show strong and moderate levels of habituation were located mainly in the tectum, a region involved in vision, and their activity was correlated with behavior. Additional research showed that glutamate receptors are implicated in short- and long-term habituation of the C-start response, and the long-term effect also requires gene expression and protein synthesis, in striking similarity with long-term habituation in mollusks and nematodes (Roberts et al., 2013).

3.5 Associative learning and cognition in invertebrates

3.5.1 Associative learning in basal invertebrates

Two forms of associative learning are relevant in this and the following sections: ***Pavlovian*** and ***operant conditioning*** (for procedures and terminology, see Chapter 2). Despite their diffuse neural net (see Figure 3.4), cnidarians do exhibit associative learning. Pavlovian conditioning was reported in the sea anemone *Cribrina xanthogrammica* (Haralson et al., 1975). Animals were first habituated to Light, then exposed to Light→Shock pairings, and finally to Light-only extinction trials. Light was the ***conditioned stimulus*** (CS) and Shock was the ***unconditioned stimulus*** (US). Control groups were given training with either Light-only, Shock-only, or random Light/Shock presentations. Electrodes located at the sides of the anemone column recorded body and tentacle contractions during the signal (CRs, ***conditioned responses***). Experimental subjects exhibited habituation during the initial Light-only trials, followed by a gradual increase in the amplitude of the CR during Light→Shock pairings and by a reduction of the CR during extinction trials. CS→US pairings led to higher CRs than in any of the controls, which ruled out an explanation of the increased CR via nonassociative effects, such as sensitization and pseudoconditioning.

Most animal phyla are bilaterally symmetrical and exhibit central and peripheral nervous systems (see Figure 1.14). The simplest bilaterally symmetrical animals are the flatworms (Phylum Platyhelminthes; e.g., planaria). Two species of flatworms, *Dugesia dorotocephala*

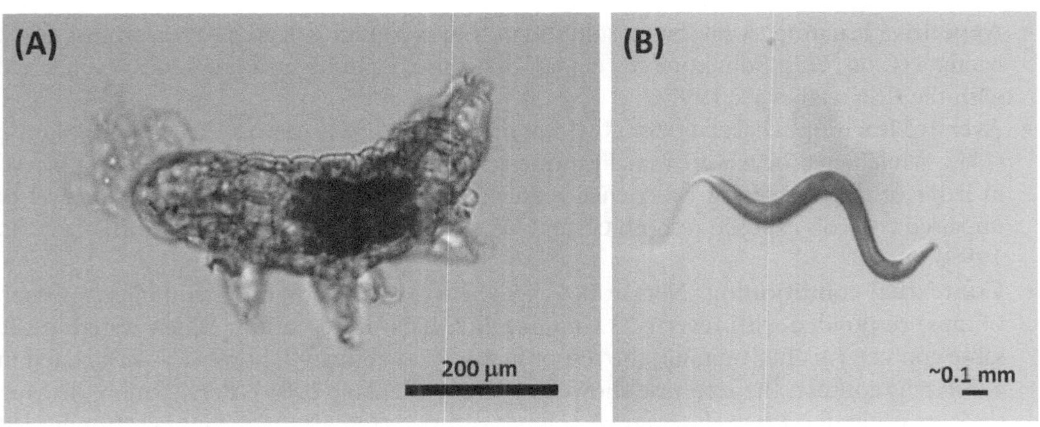

Figure 3.14 **Simple animals. (A)** The tardigrade *Dactylobiotus dispar*. (Photo by S. Pack, S. Blinova, and R. Ali, courtesy of Theodore Dumas.) **(B)** The nematode *Caenorhabditis elegans*. (Photo courtesy of Mark McCormick.)

and *D. tigrine*, exhibit Pavlovian conditioning (Baxter & Kimmel, 1963; Jacobson et al., 1967). Animals exposed to Light→Shock pairings showed higher CR levels than animals exposed to unpaired Light and Shock presentations, to backward Shock→Light pairings, and to simultaneous LightShock pairings. Thus, nonassociative effects were insufficient to explain these behavioral changes. There is conflicting evidence concerning the ability of planaria to form long-term memories; positive results were reported for memory of familiar places (Shomrat & Levin, 2013), but no evidence of retention for directional preferences modified by exposure to electric shock was also reported (Abbott & Wong, 2008).

Tardigrades, commonly called "water bears" (Phylum Tardigrada), are among the smallest bilaterally organized animals (less than 1 mm long; Figure 3.14-A). They display a remarkable capacity to enter a state of suspended animation called "tun" for months when exposed to environmental conditions that would threaten survival for most animals (e.g., unusually low temperatures, extreme desiccation, or a vacuum). When normal environmental conditions return, tardigrades "revive" and exhibit typical behavior.

The mechanisms leading to the tun state offer a unique opportunity to study metabolic aspects of learning. In one study (Zhou et al., 2019), tardigrades (*Dactylobiotus dispar*) maintained in water and fed with algae were isolated to determine responses to various stimuli (e.g., lights, electrical discharges). In one condition, a Blue light (CS) was presented for 20 s and followed by a 400-μA Shock lasting 2.5 s (US). The unconditioned response (UR) to the Shock was a shortening of the body. One hour after a single Blue→Shock pairing, animals exhibited a shortening of the body (CR) when exposed to the Blue light. Controls exposed only to the Shock (US only), to a White light (novel stimulus), to the Blue light without the Shock (CS only), to a backward Shock→Blue light pairing, or to random presentations of the Blue light and Shock displayed no changes in body length. Animals given conditioning trials with other wavelengths of Light preceding Shock failed to exhibit a CR when tested with the Blue light. This indicates that the change in behavior was CS specific. Retention was detected when animals were tested one hour after training but not after 4 hours.

The nematode *C. elegans* (Phylum Nematoda) exhibits both nonassociative learning (as described previously in this chapter) and associative learning (Figure 3.14-B). Experiments provided evidence of the following conditioning effects in *C. elegans*, all with appropriate nonassociative controls (Yu & Rankin, 2022):

- **Appetitive learning.** A salt-based solution (CS) was paired with access to a layer of *E. coli* bacteria (food, US). Subsequently, nematodes showed a preference for a location marked with the CS (Wen et al., 1997).
- **Aversive learning.** Diacetyl odor (CS) was paired with exposure to an acetic acid solution (US). While nematodes were initially attracted to the diacetyl odor (tracking a spot placed in front of them), pairing experience reduced this tracking response below the level of unpaired controls exposed to both CS and US separated by 30-s intervals (Morrison et al., 1999).
- **Contextual conditioning.** Nematodes exposed to a mechanosensory stimulus (a stream of taps) responded with reversed swimming that habituated rapidly. When tested in the same context 1 h after training, the response was still habituated; however, when tested in a different context, the response showed recovery (Rankin, 2000). Furthermore, leaving the nematodes for 1 h in the training context without presenting the tapping stimulus led to a loss of habituation (contextual extinction), whereas leaving the nematodes for 1 h in the training context before habituation training retarded subsequent habituation (contextual latent inhibition; Figure 3.15).

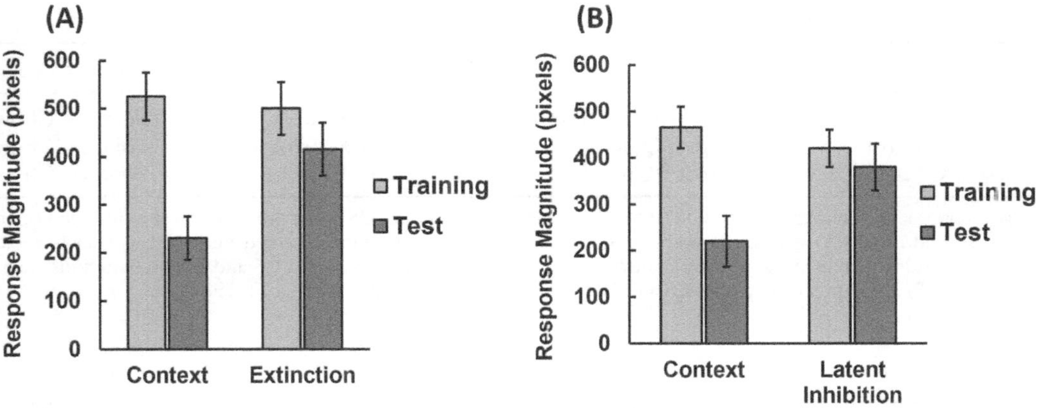

Figure 3.15 **Habituation in a nematode.** Effects of two different manipulations of the context on the retention of a habituated response in the nematode *C. elegans* (Rankin, 2000; reproduced with permission from the American Psychological Association). **(A)** Extensive exposure to the training context after training (extinction) leads to a loss of habituation. **(B)** Extensive preexposure to the training context before training (latent inhibition) leads to a failure of the context to control habituation.

Experiments with earthworms (*Lumbricus terrestris*; Phylum Annelida) show that pseudoconditioning plays a considerable role in aversive situations (Abramson & Buckbee, 1995), reaffirming the need for appropriate control conditions. Worms respond to a neutral stimulus after US-only training, thus giving the impression of conditioning. Another species of segmented worm, the leech (*Hirudo medicinalis*), shows evidence of Pavlovian conditioning. When tactile stimulation (CS) was paired with electric shock (US) applied to the posterior end of the animal, the CS potentiated the *shortening reflex*, a defensive CR that can be objectively measured (Sahley & Ready, 1988).

3.5.2 Associative learning in mollusks

Conditioning has been studied in some detail in two groups of mollusks (Phylum Mollusca): cephalopods (octopuses, cuttlefish) and gastropods (snails). Cephalopods have traditionally been considered behaviorally and neurologically complex invertebrates (Shigeno et al., 2018). Classical conditioning of sign tracking to a flashing light (CS) signaling food (US), but not to unpaired presentations, was described in cuttlefish (*Sepia officinalis*; Purdy et al., 1999). Similarly, octopuses (*Octopus cyanea*) learned to attack a computer-generated moving stimulus (CS) paired with food (US) and to approach the goal box of a runway to collect food (Papini & Bitterman, 1991). Octopuses (*O. bimaculoides*) learned to locate one of six escape routes (with the other five blocked) when the water level in the tank was lowered to simulate low-tide conditions (Boal et al., 2000). A subsequent test demonstrated significant retention of the escape behavior after a week.

Aversive classical conditioning has been demonstrated in several species of mollusks. *A. californica* exhibits the gill withdrawal to a tactile stimulus (CS+) paired with shock (US) but not to another tactile stimulus presented alone (CS-; Carew et al., 1983). *Hermissenda crassicornis* demonstrates Pavlovian conditioning with high-speed rotation as the US. Rotation stimulates the statocysts, the animal's vestibular organ, inhibiting locomotion and inducing

Table 3.1 Second-order conditioning in the snail *Limax maximum*

Group	*Phase 1*	*Phase 2*	*Preference test*
Experimental	Carrot→Quinidine	Potato→Carrot	Potato < Chow
Phase 1 Control	Carrot/Quinidine	Potato→Carrot	Potato ~ Chow
Phase 2 Control	Carrot→Quinidine	Potato/Carrot	Potato ~ Chow

Note. Carrot and Potato are odors (CSs). Quinidine is an aversive odor (US). The preference test pitted the Potato odor (second-order CS) against a novel odor (rat Chow). Experimental animals showed a greater tendency to avoid the Potato odor than animals in either control group. Controls received unpaired CS and US presentations (indicated by "/") in Phase 1 or unpaired CS and CS presentations in Phase 2 (Sahley et al., 1981).

a shortening of the foot. Light→Rotation pairings reduced the normal positive phototactic response, whereas Food→Rotation pairings inhibited feeding reflexes (Farley et al., 1997).

Limax maximum provided evidence of second-order conditioning, blocking, and the US-preexposure effect (Sahley et al., 1981), all well-known from experiments with vertebrates (see Chapter 4). The second-order conditioning demonstration is described in Table 3.1. First-order conditioning involved pairings between the odor of Carrot and Quinidine sulfate (CS1→US), a bitter substance with aversive properties. During second-order conditioning training, Potato odor was paired with the Carrot odor (i.e., CS2→CS1). Finally, animals were given a preference test between the Potato odor and rat Chow, a novel odor. Controls received unpaired training during either the first-order or second-order phase. Only experimental animals exhibited an aversion to the second-order signal (CS2, Potato odor) during the preference test, spending less time in that side of the apparatus.

Are these examples of Pavlovian or of operant conditioning? A hint that some feeding responses are Pavlovian is provided by an experiment with the snail *Helix aspersa*. Odor→Food pairings induced a conditioned response consisting of lowering the posterior tentacles toward the food source. This response, which occurred at a lower frequency in unpaired controls, was not affected by omission training (Ungless, 1998). In *omission training*, the occurrence of a response cancels the delivery of an appetitive reinforcer. If the response is operant and thus controlled by its history of consequences, it should decrease in strength, but Pavlovian responses are elicited by antecedent stimuli (CS) and are less sensitive to their consequences. The fact that snails continued to lower their tentacles even though this response caused food omission suggests that the behavior is Pavlovian in nature.

3.5.3 Associative learning in arthropods

The green crab *Carcinus maenas* shows both Pavlovian and operant conditioning. Pairings of a mild tactile stimulus applied to the carapace (CS) with an air puff to the eye (US) resulted in anticipatory eye-withdrawal responses compared to unpaired, backward, US-only, and CS-only controls (Abramson & Feinman, 1988). Crabs can also learn to press a lever for food reinforcement. Master–yoked comparisons demonstrate that response–reinforcer pairings are critical for maintaining lever pressing (Abramson & Feinman, 1990). In a *master–yoked design*, training involves pairs of animals labeled "master" and "yoked." In this experiment with green crabs, the master animal was subjected to omission training such that a response caused the reinforcer to be omitted in its environment. However, the master's response also omitted the food for the yoked animal, whether or not the yoked animal responded. If this is an operant response (controlled by its food outcome), then master animals should respond at a higher level than yokes, as was the case for crabs. However, if the response depends on antecedent stimuli (a Pavlovian response), then master and yoked should respond at about the same level. The master–yoked design equates all the stimuli in the environments of masters and yokes, but the response-reinforcer contingency operates consistently only for master animals.

Insects are the most frequently used invertebrates in learning research because their complex sensory systems and refined behaviors support demonstrations of learning and cognition rivaling those involving vertebrates. Free-flying honeybees (***Apis mellifera***) can be trained to drink sucrose from a cup and then fly back to the hive. They digest a small part of this solution, regurgitate the rest in the colony, and return to the cup's location after a few minutes. One or more trials can be administered in each of these visits, and the bee can fly many times between the lab and the hive in a single day. Visual, olfactory, and magnetic stimuli have been successfully used in a wide variety of compound conditioning experiments (***compound stimuli*** have two or more elements, e.g., color-odor). With honeybees, research with invertebrates moved beyond simple demonstrations of conditioning to tackle more complex questions (Bitterman, 1988, 1996; Chittka, 2017).

Table 3.2 A demonstration of within-compound associations in honeybees

Phase 1 *Compound conditioning*	*Phase 2* *Differential conditioning*	*Choice test* *Preference*
OrangeJazmin→Sucrose YellowLemon→Sucrose	Jazmin→Sucrose Lemon-only	Orange > Yellow

Note. A single group of honeybees received these training trials. For some honeybees, Phase 2 involved Lemon→Sucrose and Jazmin-only (stimulus ***counterbalance***), and these animals preferred Yellow > Orange. For simplicity, subgroups established for counterbalancing purposes are not included in this table.

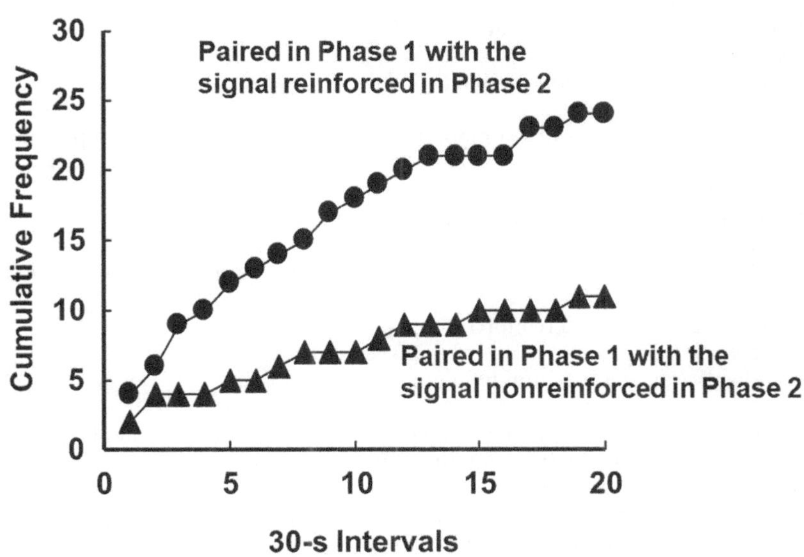

Figure 3.16 **Within-compound associations in honeybees.** The cumulative frequency of responding during the test (see Table 3.2). (From Couvillon & Bitterman, 1982; reproduced with permission from the American Psychological Association.)

Consider the following demonstration of within-compound associations (Couvillon & Bitterman, 1982). *Within-compound associations* refer to relationships among the elements of a compound stimulus, such as one involving both colors and odors presented adjacent to a drop of sucrose (Table 3.2). Bees received training with OrangeJazmin→Sucrose and YellowLemon→Sucrose; then, Jazmin→Sucrose (reinforced) and Lemon-only (nonreinforced) trials. In a final test, bees preferred Orange to Yellow (Figure 3.16). Preference for Orange indicates that Lemon-only trials in Phase 2 reduced the value of Yellow by virtue of the Lemon→Yellow within-compound association established in Phase 1.

Table 3.3 provides a partial list of learning phenomena reported in honeybees using a variety of techniques, types of stimuli, and behavioral measures. These learning phenomena were originally described in experiments with rats and pigeons. The fact that honeybees also exhibit them is a remarkable example of the stability of learning phenomena across species.

Table 3.3 Partial list of learning phenomena reported for honeybees and vertebrates

Phenomenon and brief characterization
Backward blocking
Impaired response to an element of a compound trained with a second element reinforced in a subsequent phase.
Compound–component discrimination
Discriminating between a compound and its elements reinforced separately.
Concurrent blocking
Impaired response to an element of a compound trained with a second element reinforced in separate trials within the same session.
Conditional discrimination
One of two alternatives is correct in the presence of one conditional stimulus, but the second alternative is correct in the presence of another conditional stimulus.
Context conditioning
Discriminating between two contexts, one paired with reinforcement and the other with nonreinforcement.
Discrete-trial avoidance learning
Respond in the presence of a signal to avoid shock.
Escape learning
Respond in the presence of shock to terminate it.
Forward blocking
Impaired response to an element of a compound trained with a second element previously reinforced.
Free-operant avoidance learning
Respond with a minimum interresponse time to postpone shock.
Latent inhibition
Nonreinforced preexposure to the signal retards subsequent acquisition during CS→US training.
Omission training
Withhold responding to receive a reinforcer.
Overlearning extinction effect
Faster extinction after extra acquisition training.
Overshadowing
Decreased responding to a CS, A, after reinforced presentations with a second CS, AB+, compared to reinforced trials by itself, A+ (the opposite of potentiation).
Partial delay of reinforcement extinction effect
Slower extinction after training with a random mixture of immediate and delayed reinforcement compared with consistent immediate reinforcement.
Partial reinforcement extinction effect
Slower extinction after training with partial reinforcement rather than with continuous reinforcement.

(*Continued*)

Table 3.3 (Continued)

Phenomenon and brief characterization
Potentiation
Increased responding to a CS, A, after reinforced presentations with a second CS, AB+, compared to reinforced trials by itself, A+ (the opposite of overshadowing).
Probability matching
Choice of an alternative matches the probability of reinforcement for that alternative.
Progressive improvement in spatial reversals
Faster discrimination learning after repeated reversals of cue validity.
Second-order conditioning
Responding to a signal paired with another signal originally paired with the reinforcer.
Spontaneous recovery in extinction
Recovery of an extinguished response after a period of rest.
Successive negative contrast
Less responding for a small reward after training with a large reward compared to a small-reward control.
Summation of excitation
Greater response to a compound signal after individual reinforcement of its elements.
Transfer along a continuum
Acquisition of an easy discrimination with stimuli from a given sensory modality facilitates the subsequent acquisition of a difficult discrimination with stimuli from the same modality.
US-preexposure effect
Preexposure to unsignaled USs retards subsequent acquisition during CS→US training.
Within-compound associations
Responding to an element of a compound is affected by subsequent modification of another element of the compound.

Note. The control groups were omitted for brevity.

3.5.4 Learning mutants in fruit flies

Mutations can be induced by applying chemicals, X-rays, or other mutagens on germ cells. This has been done extensively in *Drosophila* fruit flies. Behavioral screening identifies abnormalities that can be attributed to mutations. Then these animals are bred to obtain many homozygous mutants that can be studied. Such screening has uncovered *learning mutants* that exhibit abnormalities in acquisition, storage, retrieval, and/or behavioral expression of acquired information. Ideally, a learning mutation that affects acquisition would disrupt acquisition in all learning tasks, but such a result is not commonly observed. Moreover, behavior in a learning task can be affected by contextual factors, such as sensory or motor mechanisms, an issue that can be resolved by including appropriate controls (see Figure 3.2).

Research with *Drosophila* fruit flies has identified several genes involved in learning (Hoy, 2013; McGuire et al., 2005). These mutations affect cellular and synaptic processes involved in learning, development, and fertility. Behavioral analyses have uncovered several gene functions (Table 3.4). A mutation known as *dunce* leads to normal appetitive and aversive conditioning, but forgetting is faster than normal, leading to deficits in short- and long-term memory in operant visual learning (Gong et al., 1998) and to acquisition deficits in olfactory conditioning (Tully & Quinn, 1985). However, *dunce* mutants exhibit a normal forgetting curve in a heat-avoidance task (Mariath, 1985). Thus, gene function must be qualified by the learning task in which such a function is assessed.

An interesting picture is emerging of the genetics of olfactory conditioning in *Drosophila*. In olfactory conditioning, fruit flies are exposed in groups to A→Shock and B-only trials (with A and B representing two odor signals, usually counterbalanced). Tests involve a choice between the two odors in the absence of shocks. The training–test interval can be

Table 3.4 Some genes affecting olfactory conditioning in fruit flies

Gene	*Learning effect*	*Action*
dunce	Defective STM	Affects the cAMP pathway (cAMP phosphodiesterase)
rutabaga	Defective STM	Affects the cAMP pathway (type I adenylyl cyclase)
NF1	Defective STM	Affects the cAMP pathway (neurofibromatosis 1)
volado	Defective STM	Cell-adhesion protein affects presynaptic plasticity
fasciclin II	Defective STM	Cell-adhesion protein affects prynaptic plasticity
leonardo	Defective STM	Affects synaptic transmission
synapsins	Defective STM	Affects neurotransmitter release
amnesiac	Defective MTM	Stimulates cAMP synthesis
radish	Defective ARM	Selective effects on ARM
notch	Defective LTM	Affects presynaptic plasticity
staufen	Defective LTM	Affects synaptic plasticity
crammer	Defective LTM	Affects cysteine protease
cabbage	Defective STM-LTM	?
turnip	Defective STM-LTM	Affects the protein kinase C pathway
latheo	Defective acquisition	Affects synaptic plasticity?
linotte	Retarded acquisition	Structural brain defects

Note: STM: short-term memory. MTM: middle-term memory. ARM: anesthesia-resistant memory. LTM: long-term memory. Most of these genes exert their effects in neurons of the mushroom bodies—the anterior ganglia in the insect CNS. The main exceptions are *amnesiac*, expressed in dorsal paired medial neurons, and *crammer*, expressed in glial cells.

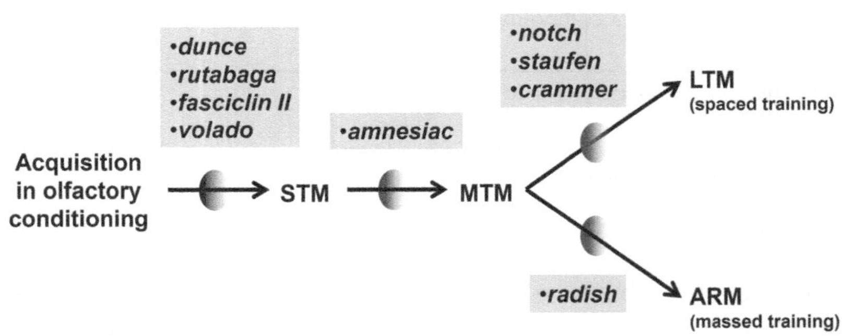

Figure 3.17 **Learning mutants in *Drosophila*.** These mutants exhibit specific dysfunction in some stage of the learning process. ARM: anesthesia-resistant memory. LTM: long-term memory. MTM: middle-term memory. STM: short-term memory.

in the order of minutes (short-term memory), hours (middle-term memory), or more than a day (long-term memory). In some groups, the standard test procedure is administered after the flies receive a cold shock, which involves placing the flies for 2 min in glass vials prechilled on ice. Memory retention after cold shock is referred to as ***anesthesia-resistant memory***. Administering a single training trial or several trials on a massed schedule leads to short-term, middle-term, and anesthesia-resistant retention of conditioning, whereas spaced training results in long-term retention and is disrupted by cold shock (i.e., it involves protein synthesis). The distinction among types of memory is supported by the selective effects of various mutations on olfactory conditioning (Figure 3.17).

The pathway from genes to behavior is mediated by neural circuitry. Several techniques have been used to map the neural circuit underlying olfactory conditioning in *Drosophila* (Fiala & Riemensperger, 2017). The resulting picture (Figure 3.18) shares a fundamental

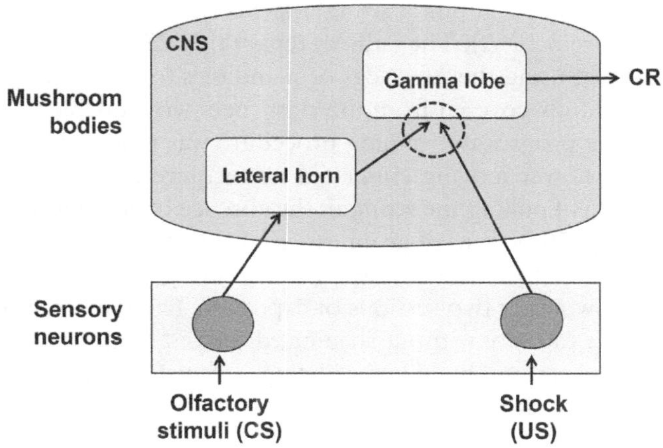

Figure 3.18 **Neural circuit of conditioning in *Drosophila*.** Convergence of CS and US inputs in the gamma lobe of the mushroom bodies in fruit flies during olfactory conditioning. CNS: central nervous system. CR: conditioned response. (From Papini, 2021; reproduced with permission from Taylor & Francis.)

property with similar circuits underlying other forms of associative learning, such as nictitating membrane conditioning in rabbits and fear conditioning in rats (see Chapter 4): the convergence of CS and US inputs into specific neural regions induces synaptic plasticity in response to their temporal contiguity.

3.5.5 *Invertebrate cognition*

Animal cognition is fully characterized in Chapters 8 through 11, but for the purpose of this section, *cognition* is identified with the stages of information processing (encoding, storage, and retrieval) involved in problem solving (although its meaning will be further extended in section 3.6 on behavioral plasticity in aneural organisms). The bodies, nervous systems, behavioral repertoires, ecology, social organization, and evolution of invertebrates are so different from those of vertebrates in general, and of mammals and birds in particular, that the question of "cognition in invertebrates" may sound farfetched. But despite these differences, invertebrates and vertebrates must cope with similar problems, including procuring food, attracting mates, and finding safe locations. Although their nervous systems are organized in unique ways, their neurons have familiar properties, and their environments include time and space, two physical dimensions underlying the evolution of learning and cognition.

As with nonassociative and associative learning, a meaningful start is to ask what types of behavioral phenomena described in any invertebrate species could qualify as cognitive. The question of mechanism will arise once dependable behavioral data on invertebrate cognition are presented. Examples of cognition in invertebrates can be found in research with insects and cephalopods, including species in both groups that exhibit complex nervous systems and behavior.

Consider the following problem posed to bumblebees (*Bombus terrestris*) foraging for sucrose (Alem et al., 2016). If a drop of sucrose is placed on top of a blue artificial flower, the bee will drink the sucrose immediately. After this training, if the sucrose is covered partially, but the bee has access to it, then it will still drink it. Now, the flower is moved progressively under the cover, but the bee can pull a string attached to the flower to bring it closer and access the reward (Figure 3.19-A). The authors report that 23 of 40 bees trained in this task learned to pull the string using their forelegs or mandibles to move the flower closer. When tested with the sucrose fully covered from the start, bees were unable to solve this problem in their first trial, so the progressive training procedure was required. Moreover, naïve bees that could not see the flower moving closer did not acquire the behavior, whereas trained individuals were capable of pulling the string in the absence of visual feedback from the moving flower. Interestingly, 50 bees were given experience with the sucrose on the blue flower and then were shown the fully covered target with the string; two individuals actually solved the problem on their own after two sessions of exposure. These innovators, individuals that exhibit problem-solving capacity without shaping, displayed an unusual amount of exploratory behavior, trying several methods before being successful. The behavior of innovators provides an example of cognition.

Bumblebees are highly social and visually oriented. Naïve individuals that observe trained demonstrators pull the string to obtain sucrose may imitate them. After pretraining to obtain sucrose from the blue flower, observers were allowed to see a trained bee pull the string and drink the sucrose 10 times, although no direct interaction was allowed. When placed in the problem situation, 15 of 25 observers successfully pulled the string on the first trial. Another group of observers that did not see a trained bee pull from the flower (instead pulled by the experimenter using nylon thread), but saw a bee drinking the sucrose once the flower was in place, did not learn the string-pulling task. This control rules out an alternative in terms of stimulus enhancement, such that drinking from the flower simply enhanced the likelihood that bees would interact with objects near the flower.

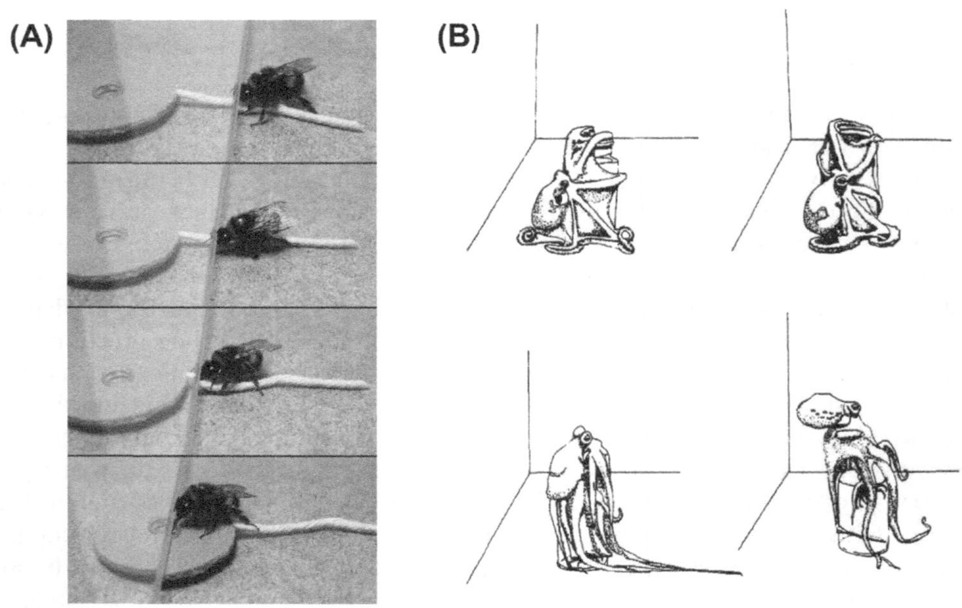

Figure 3.19 **Problem-solving behavior. (A)** A bumblebee (*Bombus terrestris*) has learned to pull from a string to move an artificial flower with a drop of sucrose on the center (round disc) that was made inaccessible by a translucent cover (photo by Sylvain Alem, courtesy of Lars Chittka). **(B)** An octopus (*Octopus vulgaris*) explores a glass jar, opens the lid, inserts an arm, and seizes the crab (reproduced with permission from Elsevier). See text for references.

Cephalopods (octopuses, cuttlefish) also show problem-solving capacity associated with sustained exploratory behavior (Mather & Dickel, 2017). In one experiment with octopuses (*Octopus vulgaris*) housed in individual tanks (Fiorito et al., 1990), a glass jar with a lid containing a crab (a typical prey) was placed in the center of the tank and left there for 5 min. It took individual octopuses about five trials to approach, open the jar, and seize the crab. Repeating this procedure across days resulted in the development of a more efficient predatory sequence, which can be attributed to operant conditioning (Figure 3.19-B). Unscrewing the lid for the first time is a candidate for a cognitive phenomenon, although the fact that these animals displayed a persistent exploratory behavior, even after solving this problem many times, suggests the possibility that the solution was a byproduct of tactual exploration of the jar and lid.

Field observations provide intriguing evidence of possible tool use in the octopus *Amphioctopus marginatus* (Finn et al., 2009). Individuals have been observed to carry discarded coconut shells for some distance under their body to later use them as shelters. One individual was observed to arrange the halves to create a housing device.

These possible cognitive abilities of insects and cephalopods may be dismissed as instances of associative learning. On the one hand, doing so expands the breadth of capabilities consistent with associative learning. On the other hand, complex problem-solving abilities often derive from a combination of behavioral flexibility and conditioning to develop into capacities used for solving new problems. A classic example is provided by the learning set phenomenon (see Chapter 1, ***Brain size and intelligence***). After solving many discriminations between two stimuli, animals may need fewer trials to solve new discriminations, as if they learned to learn. The main conclusion of this research on learning and cognition in invertebrates is that some of the effects are strikingly like those observed in mammals (see Chapters 4–6) despite the remoteness of their common ancestor. But are the underlying mechanisms homologous or homoplastic?

3.5.6 Parallel evolution from common cell-molecular mechanisms

From a comparative perspective, the remarkable generality of conditioning phenomena across species can be understood in reference to one of three evolutionary concepts: deep homology, massive convergence, or parallel evolution of learning mechanisms (see Chapter 1). The framework developed in Figure 3.1 provides the criteria for organizing the evidence.

Homology requires similarity due to inheritance from a common ancestor. If homologous learning mechanisms imply similarity at all four levels of analysis, then deep homology can be safely dismissed since the nervous systems of animal phyla have evolved largely independently from each other. Thus, there is no area in the CNS of *Aplysia* or *Drosophila* that would be homologous with the vertebrate amygdala, a brain area important for associative learning (see Chapter 4). Whereas all neurons have the same properties (see Figure 3.3), the systems, qua systems, have evolved independently, suggesting that similarities in learning mechanisms among animals from diverse phyla must be homoplastic.

Homoplasy, similar mechanisms evolved independently, is suggested by the potential function of associative learning mechanisms. Similarities in learning phenomena probably arose from the evolution of brain circuits sensitive to a key aspect of associative learning: ***contiguity***. Circuits sensitive to the temporal or spatial contiguity among events can be based on different architectures yet satisfy similar ecological functions. The acquisition of information about cause–effect and part–whole relationships is common to most, if not all, ecological conditions (Dickinson, 1980). That is, effects never happen without a cause, and causes precede effects;

part–whole relationships refer to assumptions that wholes are made of parts that can be separated without altering the identity of the whole.

Homoplasy is still vague because it could entail massive ***convergence***, supported by different underlying mechanisms for behavior at all levels, or ***parallel evolution***, consistent with shared cell-molecular mechanisms but dissimilar mechanisms at higher levels. Available evidence points to parallel evolution based on homologous cell-molecular processes. Given the strong functional correspondence between the neurons of cnidarians (the simplest animals with neurons) and those of other animals, it may be argued that some fundamental properties of the cellular machinery of neurons were established early in animal phylogeny and are thus homologous across species.

One such candidate involves second-messenger systems. The neurotransmitter in chemical synapses is the first messenger inducing electrochemical potentials in the postsynaptic cell. Repeated synaptic activation can engage ***second messengers***, such as the cascade involving cyclic adenosine-monophosphate (cAMP) and the cAMP-response element binding protein (CREB), which, in turn, can induce changes in synaptic function leading to short- and long-term memory formation. Conditioning is based on long-term memory, and it involves cellular changes mediated by gene transcription, such as the upregulation or downregulation of synaptic receptors (Kandel, 2012).

The role of the cAMP-CREB cascade in long-term memory tasks has been described in divergent phyla including the nematode *C. elegans*, the mollusk *A. californica*, the arthropod *D. melanogaster*, and rodents (Figure 3.20). Feeding starved *C. elegans* several times

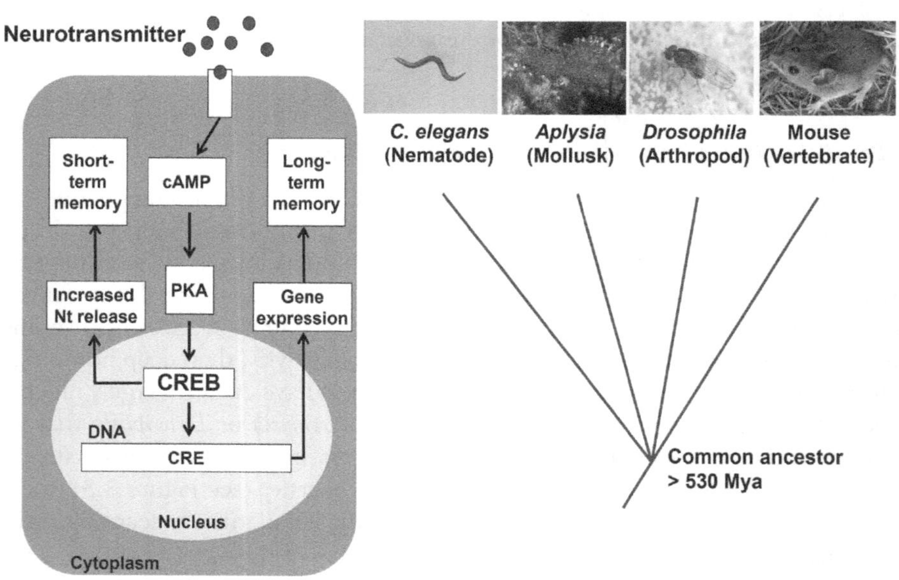

Figure 3.20 **Cellular mechanisms of learning.** Similarity in the role of cyclic adenosine monophosphate (cAMP) in short- and long-term memory among distantly related phyla suggests parallel evolution based on homologous cell-molecular mechanisms. CREB: cAMP response element-binding protein. DNA: deoxyribonucleic acid. PKA: protein kinase A. (Photo of *C. elegans* courtesy of Mark McCormick; other photos from Creative Commons https://search.creativecommons.org; *Aplysia* by kstolzenbach, license CC0 1.0; *Drosophila* by treegrow, license CC BY 2.0; mouse by grongar, license CC BY 2.0.)

in the presence of the chemical butanone induces an attraction to this substance that can be detected more than a day afterward. This long-term memory is dependent upon the cAMP-CREB cascade, as suggested by learning mutants (Kauffman et al., 2010).

In *Aplysia*, long-term sensitization (a phenomenon with a cellular basis similar to that of conditioning) is triggered by interneurons releasing the neurotransmitter serotonin to affect SNs carrying information from the sensitizing stimulus (analogous to the reinforcer; see Figure 3.9). SNs respond by increasing the production of cAMP, which, in turn, activates protein kinase A (PKA), a cAMP-dependent protein. PKA enters the cell nucleus where it activates CREB. CREBs are transcriptional factors that induce gene expression—necessary to alter synaptic transmission—thus providing the basis for long-term changes in synaptic plasticity (Alberini et al., 1994).

In *Drosophila* fruit flies, mutations that affect various aspects of long-term memory compromise the cAMP-CREB cascade leading to gene expression (McGuire et al., 2005). In mice (*Mus musculus*), deletion of the CREB gene leads to impairments in tasks involving long-term memory, such as contextual fear conditioning and spatial learning (Kaplan & Abel, 2003). Therefore, learning in species with divergent nervous systems can still be based on homologous cell-molecular mechanisms, much like the evolution of different types of eyes is based on similar light-sensitive molecules, as mentioned previously.

3.6 Behavioral plasticity in aneural organisms

3.6.1 Some conceptual issues

Did learning abilities evolve before the emergence of nervous systems? A key question is whether single-cell organisms (e.g., bacteria, protists) and multicellular organisms lacking nervous tissue (e.g., plants, fungi) are capable of *conditioned responses*. Such ability would suggest the possibility of a memory of the goal object or event. Most comparative psychologists approach a question such as this through the eyes of Morgan's (1894) canon of parsimony. Morgan's canon demands evidence based on sound methodology before complex psychological capacities are granted to any organism. Intelligent "behavior" can be ascribed to any living organism, biological process, and even objects, but are such attributions warranted?

As reviewed in this chapter, memory formation rests on the notion of *synaptic plasticity* (e.g., Kandel, 2001; Takeuchi et al., 2014). What we are calling memory are the changes in synaptic transmission that occur after experience with specific stimulus conditions by either the use of circulating neurotransmitter receptors (short-term) or by the synthesis of such receptors via gene expression (long-term). This view cannot be extrapolated directly to *aneural organisms*—organisms lacking neurons. However, direct experience with specific stimulus conditions could be encoded by cells, independently or in addition to whatever information may also be encoded in neural circuits via synaptic plasticity. This notion follows from *epigenetics*, that is, the mechanisms of gene expression (Abraham et al., 2019; Bédécarrats et al., 2018). This cellular view of memory seems in principle applicable to at least some aneural organisms, especially single-cell bacteria and protists.

Homology in learning mechanisms among neural and aneural organisms could, in principle, be found only at the cell-molecular level (see Figure 3.1). Homology at any of the other levels is precluded by the absence of neural circuitry. The study of behavioral plasticity in aneural organisms can provide clues about the adaptive advantage introduced by the evolution of neural circuits. The first task is to catalog the learning phenomena that have been demonstrated in aneural organisms in situations analogous to those used with animals, particularly in terms of control conditions and with attention devoted to evidence of anticipatory responses (Papini, 2025).

In the corrected edition of their influential *Principles of Animal Psychology*, Maier and Schneirla (1935, p. 9) dedicated the first chapter to "fundamental characteristics of behavior: plants and protista." (Chapter 1 provides a view of the taxonomy of living organisms.) They pointed out that some properties of behavior present in multicellular animals are observed in organisms without nervous systems, such as bacteria and protists, including the ability to recognize optimal conditions promoting life. The bacterium *Spirillum*, for example, congregates in areas rich in oxygen, which they first reach by swimming randomly. Once an oxygen gradient is detected, individuals tend to reverse their movement when transitioning from a rich- to a poor-oxygen medium, which results in their congregation. Detecting gradients in the environment is a basic capacity important to sustain life (e.g., chemical gradients) and promote growth (e.g., light gradients, especially obvious in plants). Detecting gradients can be accomplished via simultaneous or successive sampling of the environment; the latter requires some kind of memory in order to detect whether you are moving up or down the gradient.

The capacity of protists to modify their behavior based on individual experience was also known to these early comparative psychologists. For example, experiments with *Paramecium* drawn into a capillary too thin for them to easily swing around induced substantial attempts at backing until, eventually, they were able to turn around and exit the capillary. Repeating the situation several times resulted in them reversing their movement as soon as placed inside the capillary. Maier and Schneirla (1935, p. 34) concluded that these and similar examples were reminiscent of "learning in higher animals in that they are attributable to the individual's own experience [. . .] However, the behavior changes they permit are very temporary in nature, and the organism reverts each time to its original condition with no trace of the experience being evidenced in its subsequent activities." These results provide additional confirmation of the value of protein synthesis in synaptic transmission in neural organisms.

3.6.2 Learning in aneural organisms

3.6.2.1 Bacteria and archaea

Chapter 1 provides a brief characterization of bacteria and archaea, their similarities as prokaryotes, and their differences. There is limited information on the behavior of archaea, a prerequisite for studies of behavioral plasticity, but interest is increasing given the genome mapping of several species. For example, the swimming behavior of *Methanocaldococcus villosus* suggests that these microorganisms swim either in a straight line or in a zigzag pattern described as "relocate-and-seek" behavior (Herzog & Wirth, 2012). These types of study may provide the basis for exploring the ability to adjust swimming as a function of individual experience in archaea.

Flagellate bacteria, like *E. coli*, also swim by changing from moving in a straight line (called "runs"), when the flagellum rotates either clockwise or counterclockwise, to abrupt changes in direction caused by a reversal of the rotating movement (called "twiddles" or "tumbles;" Koshland, 1980). Such changes allow *E. coli* to detect and track increasing concentrations of nutrients, a behavior called *chemotaxis*. Similar changes in the direction of movement caused by archaella rotation (functionally equivalent to the flagella of bacteria) were observed in the archaeon *Halobacterium salinarium* induced by blue light, which acts as a repellent stimulus (Grishanin et al., 1996).

Chemotaxis in *E. coli* has sensory and motor components, and it involves the ability to compare successive samples of concentrations at different times or locations. When *E. coli* is in a nutrient-poor environment or exposed to repellents, they tumble and redirect their movement. However, when exposed to a nutrient-rich environment, the frequency of tumbling is reduced, at least temporarily. Such reduction in tumbling is related to the level of occupancy of the chemical receptor located in the anterior end of the bacterium (Berg & Tedesco, 1975). Although this phenomenon may resemble habituation as described in animals, it is perhaps more appropriately described as sensory adaptation (Parkinson & Revello, 1978). Archaea and bacteria evolved different structures for motility (the archaellae and flagella already mentioned), but the cellular machinery in terms of chemoreceptor arrays is apparently shared (Briegel et al., 2015). The signaling pathways implicated in sensory adaptation and the proteins controlling flagellar movement have been identified (Porter et al., 2011). Given these homologies, it would not be surprising to find evidence of behavioral plasticity in archaea, like there is for bacteria.

Some of the cellular components present in bacteria are familiar to those studying animal learning at the cellular level. Bacteria that form biofilms (bacteria clusters attached to a surface) display a form of cellular communication based on ion channels much as done by neurons in animals. cAMP, a key cellular component of long-term memory (see Figure 3.20), is an attractant used by bacteria to aggregate in large numbers (Lyon et al., 2021). This suggests that some components of the cellular machinery available in prokaryotes might have been coopted to play a role in plasticity with the evolution of neurons.

3.6.2.2 *Protists*

Compared to prokaryotes, single-cell eukaryotes are larger in size, have their DNA segregated inside the cell's nucleus, and have more genes and proteins that regulate cellular processes. Their membranes are also more flexible than those of prokaryotes, allowing for new forms of feeding behavior, such as engulfing prey in *Amoeba*.

Protists also display ion-channel-dependent electrochemical potentials akin to the neuron's all-or-none APs and graded potentials already described. APs in these protists are accompanied by the opening of Ca^{2+} channels and followed by the opening of K^+ channels that restore the cell's resting potential (Wan & Jékely, 2021). Such APs are involved in a variety of movements. Importantly, repetitive cycles of excitation can lead to a reduction in movement similar to sensory adaptation at the level of the receptor.

In the protist *Stentor*, some stimuli that initially produce a contraction lose their effectiveness after repeated presentations (Rajan et al., 2023; Wood, 1988a; Figure 3.21-A). Mechanical stimulation has little or no effect, but contractions are potentiated by a combination of mechanical and electrical stimulation. A 15-min resting period restored the original level of body contraction, a phenomenon reminiscent of the spontaneous recovery of a habituated response in animals. However, further experiments revealed sensory adaptation, which depended on a reduction in receptor potential induced by mechanical stimulation, while APs, when they occurred, were undiminished across stimulus presentations (Figure 3.21-B; Wood, 1988b).

The slime mold *Physarum polycephalum* is a large, visible to the naked eye, single-cell, amoeboid protist containing numerous nuclei, and can grow pseudopodia in any direction.

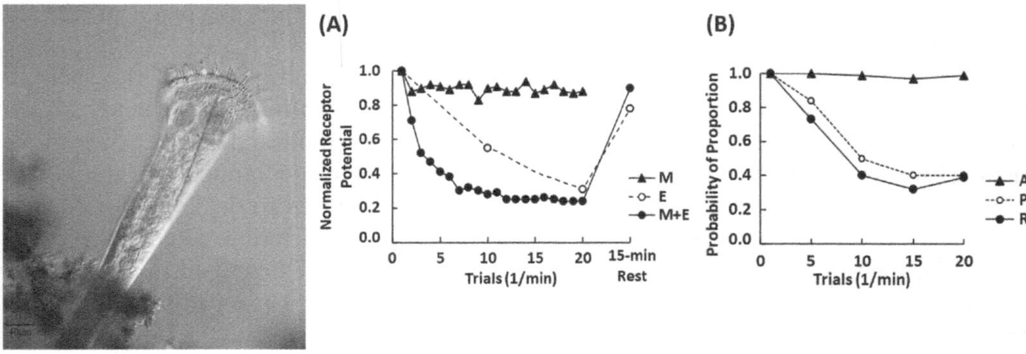

Figure 3.21 **Behavioral plasticity in *Stentor*. (A)** Sensory adaptation of body contractions in *Stentor* measured in terms of the electrochemical potential in the receptor. M: mechanical. E: electrical. M+E: mechanical plus electrical. (From Wood, 1988a; reproduced with permission from the Society for Neuroscience.) **(B)** Sensory adaptation in *Stentor* depends on reduction in receptor potentials but not in action potentials. AP: action potential. Pr: probability. RP: receptor potential. (From Wood, 1988b; reproduced with permission from the Society for Neuroscience.) Photo "Un Stentor con vestido" by Proyecto Agua/Water Project, licensed under CC BY-NC-SA 2.0, from Creative Commons, https://wordpress.org/openverse/?referrer=creativecommons.org.

Experiments with *Physarum* involving multiple trials show evidence of a response (i.e., growth) decrement bearing some properties of habituation.

In one experiment (Boisseau et al., 2016), *Physarum* organisms were placed in a Petri dish connected with a second dish containing food through a bridge of agar gel. For one group, the bridge contained a mild quinine solution (Q); for a second group, the bridge contained caffeine (CAF); and for a third group (C), the bridge was clean. Whereas the agar gel is neutral, both quinine and caffeine are repellents; in their presence, *Physarum* arrests growth and only progress if concentrations are mild. The dependent variable was the time it took for each individual *Physarum* to cross the bridge and enter the baited dish.

During trials 1 through 5, the time to cross the bridge was reduced exponentially, a typical outcome of habituation experiments with animals. On trial 6 (discrimination test), each group was divided into two subgroups, one exposed to the habituation stimulus (e.g., Q→Q) and the other to the novel stimulus (e.g., Q→CAF). Crossing time remained low for the habituation stimulus but increased significantly for the novel stimulus. Thus, *Physarum* discriminated these stimuli, something also typical of habituation in animals.

On trials 7–8 (resting period), all individuals were exposed to the agar gel bridge and crossed it with short latencies.

Finally, on trial 9 (discrimination test), the same test conducted on trial 6 was repeated. Interestingly, individual *Physarum* showed partial recovery of the latency to the habituation stimulus after a 2-day resting period, reminiscent of spontaneous recovery but strong recovery of long latencies to the nonhabituation stimulus.

With respect to associative learning, experiments with three species of amoebae show evidence of Pavlovian conditioning (Carrasco-Pujante et al., 2021). In the absence of either the CS or US, individual amoebae in a Petri dish move in all directions from the location where they are placed. If a weak electric field is applied, then they overwhelmingly move toward the cathode side of the Petri dish (the negative pole); if in the presence of the electric field, now functioning as a potential CS, a peptide (US) secreted by the amoeba's prey is placed in the anode side (the positive pole), then most individual amoebae move toward the US (anode) side and against their tendency to approach the CS (cathode) side.

The key test is to place trained amoebae back in the situation in the presence of the CS but in the absence of the US. In the posttraining CS-only test, more than 70% of trained individual amoebae of all three species moved in the direction associated with the US (anode) during training. If the CS and US were presented simultaneously during training, then about half the amoebae move in the direction of the CS and the rest in the direction of the US. However, during the CS-only test, more than 75% of amoebae that had previously moved in the direction of the US (anode) repeated the same movement.

Additional controls provide the following evidence. If both CS and US were placed in the cathode side, 98% of amoebae move in the US (cathode) direction in a subsequent CS-only test, suggesting that exposure to both CS and US did not cause them to move toward the anode as it was observed after training. Amoebae first exposed to the US (anode) later showed normal movement toward the CS (cathode) when tested in the absence of the US, suggesting that simple exposure to the US did not generate movement toward the anode.

After training with the simultaneous CS-US procedure, amoebae were also exposed to the CS-only for 30 min three times, each session separated by a 5-min interval in a neutral medium. Although the authors described this in terms of forgetting, "extinction" may be a more appropriate term if the CS-only condition resulted in biochemical changes in the amoebae that eliminated responding. Individual amoebae of all three species reversed their movement after 20 to 50 min of exposure to just the CS. If this is an example of forgetting, then this result agrees with Maier and Schneirla's (1935) conclusion mentioned previously about the short-term nature of behavioral changes in protists.

Early experiments suggested that *Paramecium* could be trained to cling to the side of a clean wire previously paired with bacteria (food) and even showed retention of that response 3 h after training, compared to untrained controls (Gelber, 1958). Subsequent research with *Paramecium caudatum*, a ciliate protist that proliferates in freshwater and marine environments, provided evidence of several conditioning phenomena (Hennessey et al., 1979). The designs and results of these experiments are summarized in Table 3.5. Individual paramecia normally swam in a sinusoidal trajectory that was observed using time-lapse photography. Swimming was interrupted by the presentation of a brief shock (US), which induced a backward jerk produced by reversed cilia rotation. The presentation of a vibratory CS (a shaking of the substrate produced by a tone) did not initially disrupt swimming, but after several CS→US pairings, swimming was disrupted by CS presentations. These experiments provided robust evidence of conditioning in individual paramecia, including appropriate controls for *pseudoconditioning* and *sensitization*. Interestingly, there was evidence of 24-h retention, suggesting that training resulted in the development of a long-term memory.

As mentioned previously, epigenetic mechanisms offer one potential explanation of behavioral plasticity in single-celled organisms (Ginsburg & Jablonka, 2009). For example, in the case of habituation in the slime mold described previously, repetitive stimulation of the membrane receptor for quinine might lead to epigenetic inhibition in the expression of the gene coding for such receptor. With fewer membrane receptors, growth over an area containing a diluted solution of quinine might continue to occur, but at a slower rate, thus allowing the protist to reach the food. Some of these processes involving gene expression are mediated by cAMP and protein kinases (Schaap, 2021), familiar cell-molecular cascades mediating learning in animals.

Table 3.5 Classical conditioning experiments in *Paramecium caudatum*

Experiment	*Groups*	*Purpose*	*Terminal performance*
1	300 Hz CS 400 Hz CS 500 Hz CS	Vary CS	All groups displayed acquisition, but the 400–500 Hz CS showed the fastest acquisition
2	Paired CS→US Unpaired CS, US	Controls for pseudoconditioning and sensitization	Higher response level in paired than in unpaired subjects
3	Paired CS→US Random CS, US	Truly random control	Higher response level in paired than in random subjects
4	CS→US, CS-only, CS→US	Acquisition, extinction, reacquisition	Response increased in acquisition, decreased in extinction, and increased again in reacquisition
5	RI = 24 h, retrained Original training Unpaired training	Long-term memory	Higher initial response level for retrained subjects than for originally trained or unpaired subjects
6	300 Hz→US 500 Hz-only	Differential conditioning with counterbalanced CSs	Higher response to the positive CS than to the negative CS

Note: For paired subjects, the CS and US overlapped during the last 2 s of the 4-s CS, and responses were measured during the initial 2 s of the CS. For unpaired subjects, the US was presented 7 s after CS offset. To assess pseudoconditioning, responses in the unpaired condition were measured during the initial 2 s of CS presentation. To assess sensitization, responses were measured during the 2 s immediately preceding the presentation of the US. The CS was a 4-s vibration stimulus. The US was a 2-s shock. The dependent variable was calculated by dividing the total number of responses by the number of subjects in each group. The response was an interruption of swimming behavior during the presentation of the CS or before US presentation depending on the training condition. The intertrial interval varied between 10 s and 20 s depending on the experiment. (From Hennessey et al., 1979.)

3.6.2.3 Plants

Plants lack neurons but have a variety of differentiated cell types and respond to stimuli including light, gravity, touch, stimuli originating from other plants, insufficient water, and excessive salt. Movement is typically not appreciable for an observer unless via time-lapse photography. In some unusual cases, plant movement can be observed in real time. ***Mimosa pudica***, for example, folds its leaves immediately upon a touch stimulus, and the Venus flytrap ***Dionaea muscipula***, a carnivorous plant, closes two modified leaves that trap an insect walking on the internal side. These observable movements suggest a system capable of reacting in a reflex-like manner.

Mimosa's leaf-folding response, called a seismonastic response, can be elicited by mechanical and electrical stimuli. Once folded, it takes about 15 min for the leaves to return to their original position. Such extended recovery time poses some practical limitations to reproduce learning phenomena with temporal parameters like those used with animals. Still, repeated stimulation of ***Mimosa*** leaves results in a reduction of the seismonastic response that shows some of the properties of habituation (Applewhite, 1972). For example, a habituated response spontaneously recovers its strength after a long resting period and habituates more slowly with longer interstimulus intervals (Figure 3.22), as in habituation in animals. An electrical discharge after habituation elicited the seismonastic response, thus making it impossible to observe dishabituation but showing a capacity for stimulus selectivity.

Mechanical stimulation of ***Mimosa*** leaves generates an electrochemical signal that travels through the central stem of the leaf (called rachilla) and stimulates a motor organ located

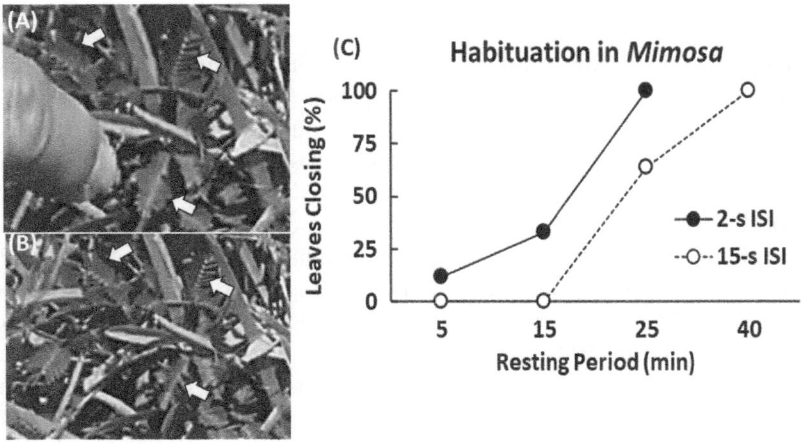

Figure 3.22 **Behavioral plasticity in *Mimosa*. (A)** *Mimosa* leaves stimulated by touch (mechanical stimulus). **(B)** Stimulated leaves fold rapidly (seismonastic response), but nonstimulated leaves from the same plant remain extended. **(C)** *Mimosa* leaves from 14 different plants were floated in water in a dish that could be raised and suddenly dropped from a 0.4 cm height to trigger the seismonastic response. One tip of a closed leaf would not be in contact with water. This was applied at ISIs (interstimulus intervals) of 2 or 15 s until the leaves were again in contact with the water. The figure shows the responses to two additional stimuli administered at the end of the resting period. (From Applewhite, 1972, Table 1. Photos by M. R. Papini from a personal video.)

at the base of the rachilla (called pulvinus), where it triggers a rapid change in ion channels that results in the outflow of water from the leaf. It is this "hydraulic" change that causes the leaves to fold (Hagihara & Toyota, 2020). Ion channels for chloride, potassium, and calcium are involved in this process, all familiar components of electrochemical potentials in neurons. However, it is not yet known whether habituation of the seismonastic response is caused by changes in one or more of these ion channels.

3.6.2.4 *Fungi*

Most species of fungi are multicellular, but some are unicellular, like yeast. Fungi respond to a variety of stimuli, display patterns of growth akin to foraging behavior, and emit chemical signals that influence other organisms whether in mutualistic or parasitic fashion (Aleklett & Boddy, 2021). But do they display behavioral plasticity?

In one experiment (Fukasawa et al., 2020), fungi of the species *Phanerochaete velutina* were placed on a piece of wood in the middle of a platform. The body of the fungus, the mycelium, grew in all directions. Subsequently, a sterilized piece of wood providing nutrients for the fungus was placed on one side of the platform. The mycelium grew to cover this wood. After 48 days, the fungus was placed on a new platform without nutrients, and its growth was monitored for 8 days. Measurements of the mycelium showed a significant bias to grow toward the side where the nutrients used to be rather than to the opposite side of the platform. These results suggested a kind of memory of the location of the nutrients. However, as the authors pointed out, additional controls are needed (e.g., growth direction in mycelia treated in the same manner but in the absence of nutrients).

3.6.2.5 *Basal animal phyla*

Three animal phyla are usually classified at the base of the animal evolutionary tree: sponges (Porifera), placozoans (Placozoa), and comb jellies (Ctenophora) (Dunn et al., 2015). Sponges and placozoans exhibit cell differentiation, but there is no evidence of neurons or muscles or that their ancestors had neurons that were lost in the subsequent evolution of these lineages (Musser et al., 2021). In sponges, tactile stimuli applied to epithelial cells can induce the closure of the pores, but such irritability is due to individual cells acting in isolation. Some cells show conduction of electrochemical potentials that depend on Ca^{2+} and K^{+} ions, as in neurons (Leys, 2015). Nitric oxide, a gaseous signaling molecule present in all animals, including sponges, could be the precursor of the neuropeptide and neurotransmitter signaling systems of neurons (Jékely, 2021). However, no ***neuropeptides***—short chains of amino acids that play a role in communication between neurons—have been described in sponges.

Placozoans are small, flat, ciliated, free-swimming animals living in marine environments (Schierwater & Eitel, 2015). Their six differentiated cell types produce a variety of neuropeptide-receptor systems used in cell signaling. Exposing *Trichoplax adhaerens* to various neuropeptides revealed specific responses, including crinkling (reduction in size lasting several minutes), turning (rotation around a fixed axis), and flattening and churning (increasing body size; stretching, contracting, and rotating movements) (Varoqueaux et al., 2018). These behaviors seem to be components of feeding. Feeding is characterized by directed movement (chemotaxis) toward the food source, usually algae, based on the collective activity of ventral ciliated cells acting in isolation from each other and from the attractant. Their response likely depends on sensory receptors located in the cilia (Senatore et al., 2017).

Comb jellies are small predatory animals that feed on plankton, live in marine environments, exhibit bioluminescence (i.e., they emit light) and iridescence (i.e., they change color depending on the angle of illumination), and are hermaphroditic. Comb jellies have evolved a neuromuscular system that controls predatory behavior and appears to be based on different mechanisms from those observed in other animals (Norekian & Moroz, 2020; Tamm, 2014). Neurotransmitters present in all other animals are either absent (e.g., serotonin, dopamine, noradrenaline, adrenaline, acetylcholine, etc.) or expressed in nonneural cells (e.g., gamma-amino butyric acid, GABA, has been found in their muscle cells but not in neurons). Neural transmission in comb jellies could be based on glutamate. Recent phylogenetic analyses based on the properties of voltage-gated calcium channels (Senatore et al., 2016) and on gene linkages at the chromosome level (Schultz et al., 2023) suggest that comb jellies represent a sister group to all other phyla, including the sponges.

Virtually nothing is known about learning and neural plasticity in sponges, placozoans, or comb jellies (Moroz, 2015). An analysis of learning in ctenophores would be especially interesting given that their nervous system evolved independently from that of cnidarians and bilaterians. Cnidarians (e.g., jelly fish, coral, sea anemones) have neurons with very similar properties to those of bilaterians but organized in a diffuse neural net, much as do ctenophores. Evidence of both associative and nonassociative learning in cnidarians described previously in this chapter suggests that learning experiments with ctenophores might produce similar results.

3.6.3 *What are nervous systems good for?*

The research reviewed in the previous section raises some interesting questions.

First, *is there compelling evidence of learning in aneural organisms?* As already mentioned, progress in comparative psychology is guided by Morgan's (1894) canon, according to which a higher psychological capacity should not be postulated when a lower capacity can explain the available facts. On this basis, the evidence of learning in aneural organisms appears suggestive in some cases and robust in others. When the evidence is inconclusive, it may be that modeling experiments after analogous studies of learning in animals may be inappropriate. Perhaps the definitions of some key phenomena need to be tailored to aneural organisms.

Take habituation as a case in point. Habituation is typically distinguished from sensory adaptation (changes of sensory receptors) and muscular fatigue (changes of muscles involved in behavior) as a phenomenon occurring in the CNS. Obviously, this definition would not work for unicellular organisms since the distinction between central and peripheral does not apply. But bacteria and protists express receptor proteins that respond to various stimuli and have motor components (e.g., cilia) that might become less active as a function of repeated stimulation. So although the central-vs.-peripheral logic cannot be applied in terms of cells, an analogous view applied to single-celled organisms might help us understand response decrement in habituation-like situations. A lesson from studies with aneural organisms is that the building blocks of learning, including sensing stimuli, adjusting movement based on experience, and making decisions about resources important to sustain life, likely evolved before nervous systems.

Second, ***where the evidence for learning seems compelling, is it consistent with homology, convergence, or parallel evolution relative to animal learning?*** Learning between aneural and neural organisms either represents independently evolved, convergent forms of plasticity—in which case there should be no correspondence at any level—or represents parallel evolution based on homologous cell-molecular mechanisms providing the basis for independently evolved mechanisms at higher levels. Consider *Mimosa*'s response to mechanical stimulation again. At the circuit level (equivalent to the neurobiological level in animals) (Figure 3.1), the vascular system of this plant and the nervous system of animals have evolved independently and function via different processes. Yet at the molecular level, potassium, chloride, and calcium ion channels are important for cell signaling in both groups of organisms. Indeed, ion channels important for synaptic transmission predate the evolution of animals (Moran et al., 2015).

Third, if many of the components and capacities for learning predate the evolution of nervous systems, and if relevant epigenetic mechanisms may have been available to at least some aneural organisms, ***what capacities did the evolution of neurons allow that were not possible before?*** A central property of neurons is their ability to receive signals, generate electrochemical signals, and transmit to other neurons via chemical and electrical synapses. Such cell-to-cell communication, called ***synaptic transmission***, requires close contact between neurons (less than 20 nm).

Alternatively, cells can communicate by ***volume transmission***, that is, by releasing various types of proteins, including steroid hormones, peptides, and other signaling molecules. Volume transmission does not require proximity between cells and works well in animals because of the evolution of a circulatory system that provides mobility to such molecules over relatively long distances. In single-celled organisms that form colonies, the absence of a circulatory system and their small body size set the efficiency of volume transmission to the diffusion rates of the molecules involved. These limitations suggest that one advantage of synaptic transmission is that it allowed for the evolution of relatively large body plans and active behavior as different parts could be coordinated by fast neural signaling between cells located in remote bodily structures (Schmidt-Rhaesa et al., 2015).

Even the limited nervous system of *C. elegans*, with its 302 neurons, opens up this animal's *umwelt* to new resources and threats that need to be detected and evaluated before actions are selected—approach, withdrawal, or avoidance. The longer life span of a simple animal like

C. elegans, compared to that of a single-cell organism, enhances the evolutionary benefits of behavioral plasticity, conferring an advantage for investing in long-term memory circuits that store previous experience that can be used to enhance individual fitness. Synaptic plasticity of the kind involved in learning also allows for specificity, that is, for the mapping of specific events into a restricted set of connections, leaving other connections to represent different events (Kandel et al., 2021).

Synaptic transmission was probably already present in pre-Cambrian animals and then rapidly evolved during the Cambrian, when there is fossil evidence for the emergence of predatory behavior (Monk & Paulin, 2014). Cambrian animals show an adaptive radiation of body plans. Before the Cambrian, the Ediacaran fauna includes mainly animals that either filtered food particles or grazed on bacterial mats (see Chapter 1). Cambrian innovations include hard exoskeleton, eyes, and complex foraging patterns preserved as traces in the ocean floor (Briggs et al., 1994; Crimes, 1992). Selective pressures may have favored the evolution of neurons capable of generating APs that propagate at fast speeds based on the coordinated activity of various ion channels.

Glossary

Action potential (AP) An all-or-none electrochemical potential transmitted through the neuron's axon at constant speed and amplitude.

Aneural organism Organisms lacking neurons, including bacteria, archaea, protists, plants, fungi, sponges, and placozoans.

Anticipatory responses Responses occurring before a specific outcome.

Brain An anterior enlargement of the vertebrate CNS.

Central and peripheral nervous system (CNS, PNS) The CNS includes the neural tissue located in the ganglia (invertebrates) or in the brain and spinal cord (vertebrates). The PNS includes nerves connecting the CNS with receptors, organs, and glands.

Chemical synapse The arrival of an action potential at the axon terminal causes the release of a neurotransmitter into a synapse.

Chemotaxis A tendency to move toward (positive) or away (negative) from a chemical source.

Cognition Psychological processes involving perception, learning, memory, decision-making, action selection, thinking, and (in humans) language.

Compound stimulus A stimulus that includes two or more elements.

Conditioned response (CR)/Unconditioned response (UR) In Pavlovian conditioning, the CR is acquired through pairings between a CS and US, whereas the UR is elicited by the US with little or no training.

Conditioned stimulus (CS)/Unconditioned stimulus (US) In Pavlovian conditioning, the CS is an initially "neutral" stimulus that acquires signaling value by virtue of being paired with a US. The US is capable of eliciting URs after little or no training.

Contextual factors In comparative learning, factors other than learning that can influence behavior (e.g., motivation, perception, motor).

Contiguity In associative learning, the temporal or spatial proximity between stimuli or between stimuli and responses.

Control by systematic variation Manipulating a variable in a given task to determine if behavior changes in similar ways in two or more species.

Convergent evolution Similar learning phenomena based on different mechanisms at all levels.

Counterbalance Assignment of animals to different combinations or sequences of stimuli while keeping constant the relationships between stimuli.

Depolarization A change in the neuron's resting potential that makes the interior of the cell electrically less negative or positive relative to the extracellular space.

Diffuse nervous system The nervous system of cnidarians and ctenophores is dispersed in the body without a clear differentiation between central and peripheral systems.

Dishabituation The presentation of an intense stimulus can reactivate an otherwise habituated response to a second stimulus.

Electrical synapse A synapse in which the electrochemical potential crosses directly from the presynaptic to the postsynaptic neuron without neurotransmitter release.
Epigenetics Cell-molecular processes that regulate gene expression.
Excitatory and inhibitory postsynaptic potentials (EPSP, IPSP) A depolarizing (EPSP) or hyperpolarizing (IPSP) gradual potential induced in the postsynaptic neuron by the release of neurotransmitter by the presynaptic neuron.
Functional disconnection A reduction in the efficacy of a synapse because of habituation.
Ganglion (plural: Ganglia) A cluster of neurons in the CNS of invertebrates.
Graded potentials A change in a neuron's electrochemical potential proportional to the stimulus that provoked it.
Habituation A decrease in the response to a stimulus that results from its repetitive presentation. Short-term habituation is an example of nonassociative learning. Long-term habituation may involve associative learning between the habituation stimulus and context present during training.
Heterosynaptic facilitation The facilitation of transmission through a synapse because of a third neuron modifying the excitability of the presynaptic neuron via an axo-axonic synapse.
Homology Similarity in characters across species due to inheritance from a common ancestor.
Homoplasy Similarity in characters across species that evolved independently due to common ecological pressures. Homoplasy includes convergence, parallel evolution, and evolutionary reversal.
Homosynaptic depression A decrease in the excitability of a synapse.
Hyperpolarization Action potentials that cause the interior of the postsynaptic neuron to become more negative than during a resting potential.
Increased excitability An increase in the amount of neurotransmitter release by lengthening the time during which calcium channels remain open.
Ion An electrically charged atom or molecule. Sodium (Na^+) and chloride (Cl^-) are two ions important for electrochemical transmission in neurons.
Learning (associative, nonassociative) Acquiring, storing, and retrieving information that results from experience. Associative learning results from a single occurrence or from repeated experience with two or more events that occur in temporal or spatial contiguity. Nonassociative learning occurs when organisms modify their response to a single event after repeated presentations.
Learning mutants In *Drosophila* fruit flies, these are mutations affecting one or more learning processes.
Learning–performance dichotomy A distinction between the acquisition of information and changes in behavior. The absence of behavioral change does not necessarily imply the lack of acquisition.
Master–yoked design Equating the learning environment of two animals by allowing one of them (master) to control events in its own environment and also in the other animal's environment (yoked). Used to disentangle the contribution of Pavlovian and operant contingencies to the occurrence of a particular behavior in a learning task.
Muscular fatigue Exhaustion of the muscles (after repeated stimulation) resulting in the inability to perform a response.
Neurotransmitter A chemical released at the axon's terminals by an incoming action potential. Neurotransmitters diffuse in synapses and reach the postsynaptic membrane, where they activate specific receptors, inducing graded potentials.
Nodes of Ranvier Sections without myelin in an axon that allow ion channels to be activated by action potentials.
Omission training In the presence of a stimulus, a response causes the withdrawal of an appetitive reinforcer that would otherwise occur.
Operant or instrumental conditioning Situations in which outcomes depend on the occurrence of a response.
Parallel evolution Independent evolution of similar learning phenomena based on homologous cell-molecular mechanisms.
Pavlovian or classical conditioning Situations in which stimuli occur in close temporal or spatial contiguity, such that one becomes a signal for the other.
Pseudoconditioning In Pavlovian conditioning, exposure to the US can lead to a novel stimulus, eliciting the UR even in the absence of specific training.
Resting potential The electrochemical potential of a nonstimulated neuron.
Second messenger Component of an intracellular cascade triggered by synaptic transmission and playing a role in gene expression.

Sensitization An increase in the strength of a response because of the repeated presentation of a relatively intense stimulus. Short- and long-term sensitization depend on the duration of the behavioral change.
Sensory adaptation A reduction in the response of a sensory receptor to a stimulus because of repeated stimulation.
Spike broadening A reduction of potassium outflow that extends the time during which a neurotransmitter is released after an action potential.
Synaptic plasticity The capacity of some synapses to modify their function as a result of use and disuse.
Synaptic transmission Passage of information between neurons via the release of neurotransmitter in chemical synapses.
Varicosities Sites where neurons establish synaptic connections.
Volume transmission Communication between cells based on the release of molecules, such as peptides.
Within-compound associations Links between the elements of a compound stimulus arising from their simultaneous presentation.

References

Abbott, S. M., & Wong, G. K. (2008). The conditioning and memory retention of planaria (Dugesia tigrina) for directional preferences. *Bios*, *79*, 160–170. https://doi.org/10.1893/0005-3155-79.4.160
Abraham, W. C., Jones, O. D., & Glanzman, D. L. (2019). Is plasticity of synapses the mechanism of long-term memory storage? *npj Science of Learning*, *4*, 9. https://doi.org/10.1038/s41539-019-0048-y
Abramson, C. I., & Buckbee, D. A. (1995). Pseudoconditioning in earthworms (*Lumbricus terrestris*): Support for nonassociative explanations of classical conditioning phenomena through an olfactory paradigm. *Journal of Comparative Psychology*, *109*, 390–397. https://doi.org/10.1037/0735-7036.109.4.390
Abramson, C. I., & Feinman, R. D. (1988). Classical conditioning of the eye withdrawal reflex in the green crab. *Journal of Neuroscience*, *8*, 2907–2912. https://doi.org/10.1523/JNEUROSCI.08-08-02907.1988
Abramson, C. I., & Feinman, R. D. (1990). Lever-press conditioning in the crab. *Physiology and Behavior*, *48*, 267–272. https://doi.org/10.1016/0031-9384(90)90311-q
Alberini, C. M., Ghirardi, M., Metz, R., & Kandel, E. R. (1994). C/EBP is an immediate-early gene required for the consolidation of long-term facilitation in Aplysia. *Cell*, *76*, 1099–1114. https://doi.org/10.1016/0092-8674(94)90386-7
Aleklett, K., & Boddy, L. (2021). Fungal behaviour: A new frontier in behavioural ecology. *Trends in Ecology & Evolution*, *36*, 9. https://doi.org/10.1016/j.tree.2021.05.006
Alem, S., Perry, C. J., Zhu, X., Loukola, O. J., Ingraham, T., Søvik, E., & Chittka, L. (2016). Associative mechanisms allow for social learning and cultural transmission of string pulling in an insect. *PLoS Biology*, *14*. https://doi.org/10.1371/journal.pbio.1002564
Anderson, P. A. V. (1985). Physiology of a bidirectional, excitatory chemical synapse. *Journal of Neurophysiology*, *53*, 821–835. https://doi.org/10.1152/jn.1985.53.3.821
Anderson, P. A. V., & Schwab, W. E. (1984). An epithelial cell-free preparation of the motor nerve net of *Cyanea*. *Biological Bulletin*, *166*, 396–408.
Antzoulatos, E. G., & Byrne, J. H. (2007). Long-term sensitization training produces spike narrowing in *Aplysia* sensory neurons. *Journal of Neuroscience*, *27*, 676–683. https://doi.org/10.1523/JNEUROSCI.4025-06.2007
Applewhite, P. B. (1972). Behavioral plasticity in the sensitive plant. *Mimosa*. *Behavioral Biology*, *7*, 47–53. https://doi.org/10.1016/S0091-6773(72)80187-1
Arendt, D., Bertucci, P. Y., Achim, K., & Musser, J. M. (2019). Evolution of neuronal types and families. *Current Opinion in Neurobiology*, *56*, 144–152. https://doi.org/10.1016/j.conb.2019.01.022
Bailey, C. H., & Kandel, E. R. (2008). Synaptic remodeling, synaptic growth and the storage of long-term memory in *Aplysia*. In W. S. Sossin, J. C. Lacaille, V. F. Castellucci, & S. Belleville (Eds.), *Progress in brain research* (Vol. 169, pp. 179–198). Elsevier.
Baxter, R., & Kimmel, H. D. (1963). Conditioning and extinction in the planarian. *American Journal of Psychology*, *76*, 665–669. https://doi.org/10.2307/1419718

Bédécarrats, A., Chen, S., Pearce, K., Cai, D., & Glanzman, D. L. (2018). RNA from trained *Aplysia* can induce an epigenetic engram for long-term sensitization in untrained *Aplysia*. *eNeuro*, *5*. https://doi.org/ENEURO.0038-18.2018

Berg, H. C., & Tedesco, P. M. (1975). Transient response to chemotactic stimuli in *Escherichia coli*. *Proceedings of the National Academy of Sciences*, *72*, 3235–3239. https://doi.org/10.1073/pnas.72.8.3235

Bitterman, M. E. (1975). The comparative analysis of learning. *Science*, *188*, 699–709. https://doi.org/10.1126/science.188.4189.699

Bitterman, M. E. (1988). Vertebrate-invertebrate comparisons. In H. J. Jerison & I. Jerison (Eds.), *Intelligence and evolutionary biology* (pp. 251–275). Springer-Verlag.

Bitterman, M. E. (1996). Comparative analysis of learning in honeybees. *Animal Learning and Behavior*, *24*, 123–141. https://doi.org/10.3758/BF03198961

Bitterman, M. E., & Woodard, W. T. (1976). Vertebrate learning: Common processes. In R. B. Masterton, C. B. G. Campbell, M. E. Bitterman, & N. Hotton (Eds.), *Evolution of brain and behavior in vertebrates* (pp. 169–189). Erlbaum.

Boal, J. G., Dunham, A. W., & Williams, K. T. (2000). Experimental evidence for spatial learning in octopuses (*Octopus bimaculoides*). *Journal of Comparative Psychology*, *114*, 246–252. https://doi.org/10.1037/0735-7036.114.3.246

Boisseau, R. P., Vogel, D., & Dussutour, A. (2016). Habituation in non-neural organisms: Evidence from slime moulds. *Proceedings of the Royal Society, B*, *283*. http://doi.org/10.1098/rspb.2016.0446

Bosch, T. C. G., Klimovich, A., Domazet-Lošo, T., Gründer, S., Holstein, T. W., Jékely, G., Miller, D. J., Murillo-Rincon, A. P., Rentzsch, F., Richards, G. S., Schröder, K., Technau, U., & Tuste, R. (2017). Back to the basics: Cnidarians start to fire. *Trends in Neuroscience*, *40*, 92–105. https://doi.org/10.1016/j.tins.2016.11.005

Braha, O., Dale, N., Hochner, B., Klein, M., Abrams, T. W., & Kandel, E. R. (1990). Second messengers involved in the two processes of presynaptic facilitation that contribute to sensitization and dishabituation in *Aplysia* sensory neurons. *Proceedings of the National Academy of Sciences USA*, *87*, 2040–2044. https://doi.org/10.1073/pnas.87.5.2040

Briegel, A., Ortega, D. R., Huang, A. N., Oikonomou, C. M., Gunsalus, R. P., & Jensen, G. J. (2015). Structural conservation of chemotaxis machinery across Archaea and Bacteria. *Environmental Microbiology Reports*, *7*, 414–419. https://doi.org/10.1111/1758-2229.12265

Briggs, D. E. G., Erwin, D. H., & Collier, F. J. (1994). *The fossils of the Burgess Shale*. Smithsonian Institution Press.

Brunelli, M., Castellucci, V. F., & Kandel, E. R. (1976). Synaptic facilitation and behavioral sensitization in *Aplysia*: Possible role of serotonin and cyclic AMP. *Science*, *194*, 1178–1181. https://doi.org/10.1126/science.186870

Byrne, J. H., & Hawkins, R. D. (2015). Nonassociative learning in invertebrates. *Cold Spring Harbor Perspectives in Biology*, *7*. https://doi.org/10.1101/cshperspect.a021675

Carew, T. J., Castellucci, V. F., & Kandel, E. R. (1971). An analysis of dishabituation and sensitization of the gill-withdrawal reflex in *Aplysia*. *International Journal of Neuroscience*, *2*, 79–98. https://doi.org/10.3109/00207457109146995

Carew, T. J., Castellucci, V. F., & Kandel, E. R. (1979). Sensitization in Aplysia: Restoration of transmission in synapses inactivated by long-term habituation. *Science*, *205*, 417–419. https://doi.org/10.1126/science.451611

Carew, T. J., Hawkins, R. D., & Kandel, E. R. (1983). Differential classical conditioning of a defensive withdrawal reflex in *Aplysia californica*. *Science*, *219*, 397–400. https://doi.org/10.1126/science.6681571

Carew, T. J., Pinsker, H. M., & Kandel, E. R. (1972). Long-term habituation of a defensive withdrawal response reflex in *Aplysia*. *Science*, *175*, 451–454. https://doi.org/10.1126/science.175.4020.451

Carrasco-Pujante, J., Bringas, C., Malaina, I., Fedetz, M., Martínez, L., Pérez-Yarza, G., Dolores Boyano, M., Berdieva, M., Goodkov, A., López, J. I., Knafo, S., & De la Fuente, I. M. (2021). Associative conditioning is a robust systemic behavior in unicellular organisms: An interspecies comparison. *Frontiers in Microbiology*, *12*, 707086. https://doi.org/10.3389/fmicb.2021.707086

Castellucci, V. F., Carew, T. J., & Kandel, E. R. (1978). Cellular analysis of long-term habituation of the gill-withdrawal reflex of *Aplysia californica*. *Science*, *202*, 1306–1308. https://doi.org/10.1126/science.214854

Castellucci, V. F., & Kandel, E. R. (1974). A quantal analysis of the synaptic depression underlying habituation of the gill-withdrawal reflex in *Aplysia*. *Proceedings of the National Academy of Sciences USA*, *71*, 5004–5008. https://doi.org/10.1073/pnas.71.12.5004

Castellucci, V. F., & Kandel, E. R. (1976). Presynaptic facilitation as a mechanism for behavioral sensitization in *Aplysia*. *Science*, *194*, 1176–1178. https://doi.org/10.1126/science.11560
Chittka, L. (2017). Bee cognition. *Current Biology*, *27*, R103–7R1059. https://doi.org/10.1016/j.cub.2017.08.008
Cohen, T. E., Kaplan, S. W., Kandel, E. R., & Hawkins, R. D. (1997). A simplified preparation for relating cellular events to behavior: Mechanisms contributing to habituation, dishabituation, and sensitization of the *Aplysia* gill-withdrawal reflex. *Journal of Neuroscience*, *15*, 2886–2899. https://doi.org/10.1523/JNEUROSCI.17-08-02886.1997
Couvillon, P. A., & Bitterman, M. E. (1982). Compound conditioning in honeybees. *Journal of Comparative and Physiological Psychology*, *96*, 192–199. https://doi.org/10.1037/h0077869
Crimes, T. P. (1992). The record of trace fossils across the Proterozoic-Cambrian boundary. In J. H. Lipps & P. W. Signor (Eds.), *Origin and early evolution of the Metazoa* (pp. 177–202). Plenum.
Davis, M. (1970). Effects of interstimulus interval length and variability on startle-response habituation in the rat. *Journal of Comparative and Physiological Psychology*, *72*, 177–192. https://doi.org/10.1037/h0029472
Dickinson, A. (1980). *Contemporary animal learning theory*. Cambridge University Press.
Dunn, C. W., Leys, S. P., & Haddock, S. H. D. (2015). The hidden biology of sponges and ctenophores. *Trends in Ecology & Evolution*, *30*, 282–291. https://doi.org/10.1016/j.tree.2015.03.003
Eddy, T. J., Gallup, G. G. Jr., & Povinelli, D. J. (1993). Attribution of cognitive states to animals: Anthropomorphism in comparative perspective. *Journal of Social Issues*, *49*, 87–101. https://doi.org/10.1111/j.1540-4560.1993.tb00910.x
Farley, J., Reasoner, H., & Janssen, M. (1997). Potentiation of phototactic suppression in *Hermissenda* by a chemosensory stimulus during compound conditioning. *Behavioral Neuroscience*, *111*, 320–341. https://doi.org/10.1037/0735-7044.111.2.320
Fernald, R. D. (2004). Evolving eyes. *International Journal of Developmental Biology*, *48*, 701–705. https://doi.org/10.1387/ijdb.041888rf
Fiala, A., & Riemensperger, T. (2017). Localization of a memory trace: Aversive associative olfactory learning and short-term memory in Drosophila. In J. H. Byrne (Ed.), *Learning and memory: A comprehensive reference* (2nd ed., Vol. 1, pp. 475–482). Elsevier.
Finn, J. K., Tregenza, T., & Tregenza, N. (2009). Defensive tool use in a coconut-carrying octopus. *Current Biology*, *19*, R1069–R1070. https://doi.org/10.1016/j.cub.2009.10.052
Fiorito, G., von Planta, C., & Scotto, P. (1990). Problem-solving ability of *Octopus vulgaris* Lamarck (Mollusca, Cephalopoda). *Behavioral and Neural Biology*, *53*, 217–230. https://doi.org/10.1016/0163-1047(90)90441-8
Fukasawa, Y., Savoury, M., & Boddy, L. (2020). Ecological memory and relocation decisions in fungal mycelial networks: Responses to quantity and location of new resources. *ISME Journal*, *14*, 380–388. https://doi.org/10.1038/s41396-019-0536-3
Gelber, B. (1958). Retention in *Paramecium aurelia*. *Journal of Comparative and Physiological Psychology*, *51*, 110–115. https://doi.org/10.1037/h0049093
Ginsburg, S., & Jablonka, E. (2009). Epigenetic learning in non-neural organisms. *Journal of Bioscience*, *34*, 633–346. https://doi.org/10.1007/s12038-009-0081-8
Glanzman, D. L. (2006). The cellular mechanisms of learning in *Aplysia*: Of blind men and elephants. *Biological Bulletin*, *210*, 271–279. https://doi.org/10.2307/4134563
Glanzman, D. L. (2013). Synaptic mechanisms of induction and maintenance of long-term sensitization memory in *Aplysia*. In R. Menzel & P. R. Benjamin (Eds.), *Handbook of behavioral neuroscience, Vol. 22. Invertebrate learning and memory* (pp. 206–220). Elsevier.
Glanzman, D. L., Kandel, E. R., & Schacher, S. (1990). Target-dependent structural changes accompanying long-term synaptic facilitation in *Aplysia* neurons. *Science*, *249*, 799–802. https://doi.org/10.1126/science.2389145
Glanzman, D. L., Mackey, S. L., Hawkins, R. D., Dyke, A. M., Lloyd, P. E., & Kandel, E. R. (1989). Depletion of serotonin in the nervous system of Aplysia reduces the behavioral enhancement of gill withdrawal as well as the heterosynaptic facilitation produced by tail shock. *Journal of Neuroscience*, *9*, 4200–4213. https://doi.org/10.1523/JNEUROSCI.09-12-04200.1989
Gong, Z., Xia, S., Liu, L., Feng, C., & Guo, A. (1998). Operant visual learning and memory in *Drosophila* mutants *dunce*, *amnesiac*, and *radish*. *Journal of Insect Physiology*, *44*, 1149–1158. https://doi.org/10.1016/s0022-1910(98)00076-6
Grishanin, R. N., Bibikov, S. I., Altschuler, I. M., Kaulen, A. D., Kazimirchuk, S. B., Armitage, J. P., & Skulachev, V. P. (1996). delta psi-mediated signalling in the bacteriorhodopsin-dependent photoresponse. *Journal of Bacteriology*, *178*, 3008–3014. https://doi.org/10.1128/JB.178.11.3008-3014.1996

Hagihara, T., & Toyota, M. (2020). Mechanical signaling in the sensitive plant *Mimosa pudica* L. *Plants*, *9*, 587. https://doi.org/10.3390/plants9050587
Haralson, J. V., Groff, C. I., & Haralson, S. J. (1975). Classical conditioning in the sea anemone, *Cribrina xanthogrammica*. *Physiology and Behavior*, *15*, 455–460. https://doi.org/10.1016/0031-9384(75)90259-0
Haralson, S. J., & Haralson, J. V. (1988). Habituation in the sea anemone, *Anthopleura elegantissima*: Spatial discrimination. *International Journal of Comparative Psychology*, *1*, 245–253.
Harris, J. D. (1943). Habituatory response decrement in the intact organism. *Psychological Bulletin*, *40*, 385–422. https://doi.org/10.1037/h0053918
Hennessey, T. M., Rucker, W. B., & McDiarmid, C. G. (1979). Classical conditioning in paramecia. *Animal Learning & Behavior*, *7*, 417–423. https://doi.org/10.3758/BF03209695
Herzog, B., & Wirth, R. (2012). Swimming behavior of selected species of Archaea. *Applied and Environmental Microbiology*, *78*, 1670–1674. https://doi.org/10.1128/AEM.06723-11
Himstead, A., & Wright, W. G. (2018). Precise foraging schedule in an intertidal euopisthobranch mollusk. Marine & Freshwater *Behaviour and Physiology*, *51*, 131–141. https://doi.org/10.1080/10236244.2018.1505430
Hoy, M. A. (2013). *Insect molecular genetics*. Elsevier.
Hroudova, M., Vojta, P., Strnad, H., Krejcik, Z., Ridl, J., Paces, J., Vicek, C., & Paces, V. (2012). Diversity, phylogeny, and expression patterns of Pou and six homeodomain transcription factors in hydrozoan jellyfish *Craspedacusta sowerbyi*. *PLoS One*, *7*, e36420. https://doi.org/10.1371/journal.pone.0036420
Jacobson, A. L., Horowitz, S. D., & Fried, C. (1967). Classical conditioning, pseudoconditioning, or sensitization in the planarian. *Journal of Comparative and Physiological Psychology*, *64*, 73–79. https://doi.org/10.1037/h0024808
Jékely, G. (2021). The chemical brain hypothesis for the origin of nervous systems. *Philosophical Transactions of the Royal Society London, B376*, 20190761. https://doi.org/10.1098/rstb.2019.0761
Johnson, M. C., & Wuensch, K. L. (1994). An investigation of habituation in the jellyfish *Aurelia aurita*. *Behavioral & Neural Biology*, *61*, 54–59. https://doi.org/10.1016/S0163-1047(05)80044-5
Kandel, E. R. (1976). *Cellular basis of behavior*. Freeman.
Kandel, E. R. (2001). The molecular biology of memory storage: A dialogue between genes and synapses. *Science*, *294*, 1030–1038. https://doi.org/10.1126/science.1067020
Kandel, E. R. (2012). The molecular biology of memory: cAMP, PKA, CRE, CREB-1, CREB-2, and CPEB. *Molecular Brain*, *5*, 14. https://doi.org/10.1186/1756-6606-5-14
Kandel, E. R., Koester, J. D., Mack, S. H., & Siegelbaum, S. A. (2021). *Principles of neural science*. McGraw Hill. http://web.stanford.edu/~shenoy/GroupPublications/PNS-6thEdition-SectionV-Motor-Chapter39-BMIs.pdf
Kaplan, M. P., & Abel, T. (2003). Genetic approaches to the study of synaptic plasticity and memory storage. *CNS Spectrums*, *8*(8), 597–610. https://doi.org/10.1017/s1092852900018873
Kauffman, A. L., Ashraf, J. M., Corces-Zimmerman, M. R., Landis, J. N., & Murphy, C. T. (2010). Insulin signaling and dietary restriction differentially influence the decline of learning and memory with age. *PLoS ONE*, *8*, 5 https://doi.org/10.1371/journal.pbio.1000372
Koshland, D. E. Jr. (1980). Bacterial chemotaxis in relation to neurobiology. *Annual Review of Neuroscience*, *3*, 43–75. https://doi.org/10.1146/annurev.ne.03.030180.000355
Leys, S. P. (2015). Elements of a "nervous system" in sponges. *Journal of Experimental Biology*, *218*, 581–591. https://doi.org/10.1242/jeb.110817
Li, H. L., Huang, B. S., Vishwasrao, H., Sutedja, N., Chen, W., Jin, I., Hawkins, R. D., Bailey, C. H., & Kandel, E. R. (2009). Dscam mediates trans-synaptic interactions for remodeling of glutamate receptors in *Aplysia* during de novo and learning-related synapse formation. *Neuron*, *26*, 527–540. https://doi.org/10.1016/j.neuron.2009.01.010
Logan, C. (1975). Topographic changes in responding during habituation to waterstream stimulation in sea anemones (*Anthopleura elegantissima*). *Journal of Comparative and Physiological Psychology*, *89*, 105–117. https://doi.org/10.1037/h0076660
Lyon, P., Keijzer, F., Arendt, D., & Levin, M. (2021). Reframing cognition: Getting down to biological basics. *Philosophical Transactions of the Royal Society, B376*, 20190750. https://doi.org/10.1098/rstb.2019.0750
Maier, N. R. F., & Schneirla, T. C. (1935). *Principles of animal psychology*. McGraw-Hill.
Marcus, E. A., Nolen, T. G., Rankin, C. H., & Carew, T. J. (1988). Behavioral dissociation of dishabituation, sensitization, and inhibition in *Aplysia*. *Science*, *241*(4862), 210–213. https://doi.org/10.1126/science.3388032

Mariath, H. A. (1985). Operant conditioning in *Drosophila melanogaster* wild-type and learning mutants with defects in the cyclic AMP metabolism. *Journal of Insect Physiology*, *31*, 779–787. https://doi.org/10.1016/0022-1910(85)90071-X
Marquez-Legorreta, E., Constantin, L., Piber, M., Favre-Bulle, I. A., Taylor, M. A., Blevins, A. S., Giacomotto, J., Bassett, D. S., Vanwalleghem, G. C., & Scott, E. K. (2022). Brain-wide visual habituation networks in wild type and *fmr1* zebrafish. *Nature Communications*, *13*, 895. https://doi.org/10.1038/s41467-022-28299-4
Martin, K. C., Casadio, A., Zhu, H., Yaping, E., Rose, J. C., Chen, M., Bailey, C. H., & Kandel, E. R. (1997). Synapse-specific, long-term facilitation of Aplysia sensory to motor synapses: A function for local protein synthesis in memory storage. *Cell*, *26*, 927–938. https://doi.org/10.1016/s0092-8674(00)80484-5
Mason, M. J., Watkins, A. J., Wakabayashi, J., Buechler, J., Pepino, C., Brown, M., & Wright, W. G. (2014). Connecting model species to nature: Predator-induced long-term sensitization in Aplysia californica. *Learning and Memory*, *21*, 363–367. https://doi.org/10.1101/lm.034330.114
Mather, J. A., & Dickel, L. (2017). Cephalopod complex cognition. *Current Opinion in Behavioral Sciences*, *16*, 131–137. https://doi.org/10.1016/j.cobeha.2017.06.008
Mayr, E. (1963). *Animal species and evolution*. Harvard University Press.
McEwan, A. H., & Rankin, C. H. (2013). Mechanosensory learning and memory in *Caenorhabditis elegans*. In R. Menzel & P. R. Benjamin (Eds.), *Invertebrate learning and memory* (pp. 91–111). Elsevier.
McGuire, S. E., Deshazer, M., & Davis, R. L. (2005). Thirty years of olfactory learning and memory research in *Drosophila melanogaster*. *Progress in Neurobiology*, *76*, 328–347. https://doi.org/10.1016/j.pneurobio.2005.09.003
Monk, T., & Paulin, M. G. (2014). Predation and the origin of neurons. *Brain, Behavior and Evolution*, *84*, 246–261. https://doi.org/https://doi.org/10.1159/000368177
Montarolo, P. G., Goelet, P., Castellucci, V. F., Morgan, J., Kandel, E. R., & Schacher, S. (1986). A critical period for macromolecular synthesis in long-term heterosynaptic facilitation in *Aplysia*. *Science*, *234*, 1249–1254. https://doi.org/10.1126/science.3775383
Moran, Y., Barzilai, M. G., Liebeskind, B. J., & Zakon, H. H. (2015). Evolution of voltage-gated ion channels at the emergence of Metazoa. *Journal of Experimental Biology*, *218*, 515–525. https://doi.org/10.1242/jeb.110270
Morgan, C. L. (1894). *An introduction to comparative psychology*. Scott.
Moroz, L. L. (2015). Convergent evolution of neural systems in ctenophores. *Journal of Experimental Biology*, *218*, 598–611. https://doi.org/10.1242/jeb.110692
Morrison, G. E., Wen, J. Y. M., Runciman, S., & van der Kooy, D. (1999). Olfactory associative learning in Caenorhabditis elegans is impaired in lrn-1 and lrn-2 mutants. *Behavioral Neuroscience*, *113*(2), 358–367. https://doi.org/10.1037/0735-7044.113.2.358
Musser, J. M., Schippers, K. J., Nickel, M., Mizzon, G., Kohn, A. B., Pape, C., Ronchi, P., Papadopoulos, N., Tarashansky, A. J., Hammel, J. U., Wolf, F., Liang, C., Hernández-Plaza, A., Cantalapiedra, C. P., Achim, K., Schieber, N. L., Pan, L., Ruperti, F., Francis, W. R., . . . Arendt, D. (2021). Profiling cellular diversity in sponges informs animal cell type and nervous system evolution. *Science*, *374*, 717–723. https://doi.org/10.1126/science.abj2949
Norekian, T. P., & Moroz, L. L. (2020). Comparative neuroanatomy of ctenophores: Neural and muscular systems in *Euplokamis dunlapae* and related species. *Journal of Comparative Neurology*, *528*(3), 481–501. https://doi.org/10.1002/cne.24770
Papini, M. R. (2002). Pattern and process in the evolution of learning mechanisms. *Psychological Review*, *109*, 186–201. https://doi.org/10.1037/0033-295X.109.1.186
Papini, M. R. (2021). *Comparative psychology. Evolution and development of brain and behavior*. Taylor & Francis.
Papini, M. R. (2025). Behavioral plasticity in aneural organisms. *Psychological Review, 132*(5), 1074–1089. https://doi.org/10.1037/rev0000483
Papini, M. R., & Bitterman, M. E. (1991). Appetitive conditioning in *Octopus cyanea*. *Journal of Comparative Psychology*, *105*, 107–114. https://doi.org/10.1037/0735-7036.105.2.107
Parkinson, J. S., & Revello, P. T. (1978). Sensory adaptation mutants of *E. coli*. *Cell*, *15*, 1221–1230. https://doi.org/10.1016/0092-8674(78)90048-x
Porter, S., Wadhams, G., & Armitage, J. (2011). Signal processing in complex chemotaxis pathways. *Nature Reviews Microbiology*, *9*, 153–165. https://doi.org/10.1038/nrmicro2505

Purdy, J. E., Roberts, A. C., & Garcia, C. A. (1999). Sign tracking in cuttlefish (*Sepia officinalis*). *Journal of Comparative Psychology*, *113*, 443–449. https://doi.org/10.1037/0735-7036.113.4.443

Rajan, D., Makushok, T., Kalish, A., Acuna, L., Bonville, A., Correa Almanza, K., Garibay, B., Tang, E., Voss, M., Lin, A., Barlow, K., Harrigan, P., Slabodnick, M. M., & Marshall, W. F. (2023). Single-cell analysis of habituation in Stentor coeruleus. *Current Biology*, *33*, 241–251. https://doi.org/10.1016/j.cub.2022.11.010

Rankin, C. (2000). Context conditioning in habituation in the nematode *C. elegans*. *Behavioral Neuroscience*, *114*, 496–505. https://doi.org/10.1037/0735-7044.114.3.496

Rankin, C. H., Abrams, T., Barry, R. J., Bhatnagar, S., Clayton, D. F., Colombo, J., Coppola, G., Geyer, M. A., Glanzman, D. L., Marsland, S., McSweeney, F. K., Wilson, D. A., Wu, C. F., & Thompson, R. F. (2009). Habituation revisited: An updated and revised description of the behavioral characteristics of habituation. *Neurobiology of Learning and Memory*, *92*, 135–138. https://doi.org/10.1016/j.nlm.2008.09.012

Rankin, C. H., Beck, C. D. O., & Chiba, C. M. (1990). *Caenorhabditis elegans*: A new model system for the study of learning and memory. *Behavioural Brain Research*, *37*, 89–92. https://doi.org/10.1016/0166-4328(90)90074-o

Roberts, A. C., Bill, B. R., & Glanzman, D. L. (2013). Learning and memory in zebrafish larvae. *Frontiers in Neural Circuits*, *7*. https://doi.org/10.3389/fncir.2013.00126

Roberts, A. C., Reichl, J., Song, M. Y., Dearinger, A. D., Moridzadeh, N., Lu, E. D., Pearce, K., Esdin, J., & Glanzman, D. L. (2011). Habituation of the C-start response in larval zebrafish exhibits several distinct phases and sensitivity to NMDA receptor blockade. *PLoS One*, *6*, e29132. https://doi.org/10.1371/journal.pone.0029132

Rose, J. K., Kaun, K. R., Chen, S. H., & Rankin, C. H. (2003). GLR-1, a non-NMDA glutamate receptor homolog, is critical for long-term memory in Caenorhabditis elegans. *Journal of Neuroscience*, *23*, 9595–9599. https://doi.org/10.1523/JNEUROSCI.23-29-09595.2003

Rose, J. K., Kaun, K. R., & Rankin, C. H. (2002). A new group-training procedure for habituation demonstrates that presynaptic glutamate release contributes to long-term memory in *Caenorhabditis elegans*. *Learning and Memory*, *9*, 130–137. https://doi.org/10.1101/lm.46802

Rushforth, N., Burnett, A., & Maynard, R. (1963). Behavior in *Hydra*. Contraction responses of *Hydra pirardi* to mechanical and light stimuli. *Science*, *139*, 760–761. https://doi.org/10.1126/science.139.3556.760

Sahley, C. L., & Ready, D. F. (1988). Associative learning modifies two behaviors in the leech, *Hirudo medicinalis*. *Journal of Neuroscience*, *8*, 4612–4620. https://doi.org/10.1523/JNEUROSCI.08-12-04612.1988

Sahley, C. L., Rudy, J. W., & Gelperin, A. (1981). An analysis of associative learning in a terrestrial mollusk. I. Higher-order conditioning, blocking, and a transient US pre-exposure effect. *Journal of Comparative Physiology-A*, *144*, 1–8. https://doi.org/10.1007/BF00612791

Schaap, P. (2021). From environmental sensing to developmental control: Cognitive evolution in dictyostelid social amoebas. *Philosophical Transactions of the Royal Society*, *B376*. https://doi.org/10.1098/rstb.2019.0756

Schierwater, B., & Eitel, M. (2015). Placozoa. In *Evolutionary developmental biology of invertebrates 1: Introduction, Non-Bilateria, Acoelomorpha, Xenoturbellida, Chaetognatha* (pp. 107–114). Springer.

Schmidt-Rhaesa, A., Harzsch, S., & Purschke, G. (2015). *Structure and evolution of invertebrate nervous systems*. Oxford University Press.

Schultz, D. T., Haddock, S. H. D., Bredeson, J. V., Green, R. E., Simakov, O., & Rokhsar, D. S. (2023). Ancient gene linkages support ctenophores as sister to other animals. *Nature*. https://doi.org/10.1038/s41586-023-05936-6

Senatore, A., Hamad, R., & Phuong, L. (2016). Physiology and evolution of voltage-gated calcium channels in early diverging animal phyla: Cnidaria, Placozoa, Porifera and Ctenophora. *Frontiers in Physiology*, *7*. https://doi.org/10.3389/fphys.2016.00481

Senatore, A., Reese, T. S., & Smith, C. L. (2017). Neuropeptidergic integration of behavior in *Trichoplax adhaerens*, an animal without synapses. *Journal of Experimental Biology*, *220*, 3381–3390. https://doi.org/10.1242/jeb.162396

Shigeno, S., Andrews, P. L. R., Ponte, G., & Fiorito, G. (2018). Cephalopod brains: An overview of current knowledge to facilitate comparison with vertebrates. *Frontiers in Physiology*, *9*. https://doi.org/10.3389/fphys.2018.00952

Shomrat, T., & Levin, M. (2013). An automated training paradigm reveals long-term memory in planarians and its persistence through head regeneration. *Journal of Experimental Biology, 216*, 3799–3810. https://doi.org/10.1242/jeb.087809
Simpson, G. G. (1964). Organisms and molecules in evolution. *Science, 146*, 1535–1538. https://doi.org/10.1126/science.146.3651.1535
Spencer, A. N. (1989). Chemical and electrical synaptic transmission in the Cnidaria. In P. A. V. Anderson (Ed.), *Evolution of the first nervous systems* (pp. 33–53). Plenum.
Staddon, J. E. R. (2016). *Adaptive behavior and learning*. Cambridge University Press.
Takeuchi, T., Duszkiewicz, A. J., & Morris, R. G. M. (2014). The synaptic plasticity and memory hypothesis: Encoding, storage and persistence. *Philosophical Transactions of the Royal Society, B369*. http://dx.doi.org/10.1098/rstb.2013.0288
Tamm, S. L. (2014). Cilia and the life of ctenophores. *Invertebrate Biology, 133*, 1–46. https://doi.org/10.1111/ivb.12042
Tully, T., & Quinn, W. G. (1985). Classical conditioning and retention in normal and mutant *Drosophila melanogaster. Journal of Comparative Physiology, 157*, 263–277. https://doi.org/10.1007/BF01350033
Ungless, M. A. (1998). A Pavlovian analysis of food-attraction conditioning in the snail *Helix aspersa. Animal Learning and Behavior, 26*, 15–19. https://doi.org/10.3758/BF03199158
Varoqueaux, F., Williams, E. A., Grandemange, S., Truscello, L., Kamm, K., Schierwater, B., Jékely, G., & Fasshauer, D. (2018). High cell diversity and complex peptidergic signaling underlie placozoan behavior. *Current Biology, 28*, 3495–3501. https://doi.org/10.1016/j.cub.2018.08.067
Wagner, A. R. (1979). Habituation and memory. In A. Dickinson & R. A. Boakes (Eds.), *Mechanisms of learning and motivation* (pp. 53–82). Erlbaum.
Walters, E. T. (1991). A functional, cellular, and evolutionary model of nociceptive plasticity in *Aplysia. Biological Bulletin, 180*, 241–251. https://doi.org/10.2307/1542394
Walters, E. T. (2018). Nociceptive biology of molluscs and arthropods: Evolutionary clues about functions and mechanisms potentially related to pain. *Frontiers in Physiology, 9*. https://doi.org/10.3389/fphys.2018.01049
Wan, K. Y., & Jékely, G. (2021). Origins of eukaryotic excitability. *Philosophical Transactions of the Royal Society, B376*. https://doi.org/10.1098/rstb.2019.0758
Wen, J. Y. M., Kumar, N., Morrison, G., Rambaldini, G., Runciman, S., Rousseau, J., & van der Kooy, D. (1997). Mutations that prevent learning in *C. elegans. Behavioral Neuroscience, 111*, 354–368. https://doi.org/10.1037//0735-7044.111.2.354
West-Eberhard, E. J. (2003). *Developmental plasticity and evolution*. Oxford University Press.
Wood, D. C. (1988a). Habituation in *Stentor*: Produced by mechanoreceptor channel modification. *Journal of Neuroscience, 8*, 2254–2258. https://doi.org/10.1523/JNEUROSCI.08-07-02254.1988
Wood, D. C. (1988b). Habituation in *Stentor*: A response-dependent process. *Journal of Neuroscience, 8*, 2248–2253. https://doi.org/10.1523/JNEUROSCI.08-07-02248.1988
WormAtlas, Altun, Z. F., Herndon, L. A., Wolkow, C. A., Crocker, C., Lints, R., & Hall, D. H. (Eds.). (2002–2018). http://www.wormatlas.org
Wright, A. A. (2013). Functional relationships for investigating cognitive processes. *Behavioural Processes, 93*, 4–24. https://doi.org/10.1016/j.beproc.2012.11.003
Wright, W. G. (1998). Evolution of nonassociative learning: Behavior analysis of a phylogenetic lesion. *Neurobiology of Learning and Memory, 69*, 326–337. https://doi.org/10.1006/nlme.1998.3829
Wright, W. G., Kirschman, D., Rozen, D., & Maynard, D. (1996). Phylogenetic analysis of learning-related neuromodulation in molluscan mechanosensory neurons. *Evolution, 50*, 2248–2263. https://doi.org/10.1111/j.1558-5646.1996.tb03614.x
Yu, A. J., & Rankin, C. H. (2022). Learning and memory in the nematode Chaenorhabditis elegans. In M. Krause, K. L. Hollis, & M. R. Papini (Eds.), *Evolution of learning and memory mechanisms* (pp. 15–32). Cambridge University Press.
Zhou, S., DeFranco, J. P., Blaha, N. T., Dwivedy, P., Culver, A., Nallamala, H., Chelluri, S., & Dumas, T. C. (2019). Aversive conditioning in the tardigrade, *Dactylobiotus dispar. Journal of Experimental Psychology: Animal Learning and Cognition, 45*, 405–412. https://doi.org/10.1037/xan0000218

4 Associative learning: Acquisition

4.1 Introduction

Interactions between the organism and the environment may leave a neural record of the experienced events. Gaining information about such interactions is the domain of *associative learning*—the processes that can produce behavior appropriate to the relationships between stimuli and between stimuli and responses. *Acquisition* refers to the processes that store that information, whereas *conditioning* refers to the procedures used to study associative learning. Associative learning has the potential to affect behavior, but such behavioral plasticity depends on several additional factors, including genetic predispositions, maturation, perception, motor skills, motivation, etc.

This chapter centers on the behavioral and brain mechanisms underlying acquisition. This knowledge is important in its own right but also because these are the building blocks of other functions, including rule learning and social learning. Associative learning also informs our understanding of behavioral disorders. Psychologists studying conditioning concentrate mainly on the procedures of Pavlovian or classical conditioning and operant or instrumental conditioning (see Chapter 2 for conditioning terminology).

4.2 Associative processes

4.2.1 Contiguity

4.2.1.1 Contiguity in Pavlovian conditioning

When one stimulus is presented shortly before another stimulus (a paradigm called *delay* or *forward conditioning*), the first stimulus becomes a signal for the impending presentation of the second stimulus. This is referred to as *excitatory conditioning* to differentiate it from *inhibitory conditioning*, in which the first stimulus becomes a signal for the absence of the second stimulus (see Section 4.4).

The fact that most studies of associative learning utilize delay conditioning highlights the importance of temporal and spatial *contiguity*. However, excitatory conditioning can occur even when the signal does not bear a forward relation with the reinforcer and even when they are not strictly contiguous in time. In *trace conditioning*, there is a temporal gap between the offset of the conditioned stimulus (CS) and the onset of the unconditioned stimulus (US; also called *outcome*, O). Excitatory conditioning is said to occur to the sensory trace left by the signal after its presentation (Pavlov, 1927). In *simultaneous conditioning*, the onset and offset of both CS and US coincide in time, whereas in *backward conditioning*, the US occurs

DOI: 10.4324/9781003401957-6

before the CS. The most common control group against which to compare responding in these conditioning procedures is an ***explicitly unpaired group***, in which the CS and US are presented in the same session but separated by an interval of time sufficient to minimize acquisition by the CS.

Although trace, simultaneous, and backward conditioning are generally less effective than delay conditioning, they have all produced evidence of excitatory conditioning. Their apparent weakness results from performance deficits rather than learning deficits. That is, the absence of behavior does not necessarily imply a failure of learning (see Section 4.2.3). In these paradigms, acquisition, usually measured in terms of responses evoked by the signal, can be assessed in terms of the reinforcing properties of signals, as suggested by an experiment based on ***sensory preconditioning*** (Matzel et al., 1988). In Phase 1 of their experiment (Table 4.1), three groups received forward (F) sensory preconditioning training in which the target signal, Click, was paired with another signal, Tone (Click→Tone). At this point, these signals have no reinforcement history. In Phase 2, the Tone is paired with Shock in a forward (F), simultaneous (S), or backward (B) arrangement. The effects of these training regimes were assessed in tests in which the Click, originally paired with the Tone, was presented alone (no Tones or Shocks during these tests). If rats learned the Click→Tone association in Phase 1, then hearing the Click should activate the ***representation*** of the Tone (i.e., a neural record that corresponds to the perception of the Tone). Critically, if excitatory associations between the Tone and Shock were established in Phase 2 in the forward, simultaneous, and backward paradigms, then the Click should induce fear responses in all these conditions. By virtue of forward conditioning in Phase 1, the Click could do what the Tone could not do in the simultaneous and backward situations: elicit a response. The necessity of the Click→Tone pairings in Phase 1 is confirmed by a group that received the two stimuli explicitly unpaired but then received the Tone→Shock pairings in Phase 2 (Group U-F).

Figure 4.1 shows the results in terms of a latency to complete 5 s of licking at the tube delivering water during Test 1 and Test 2; the longer the latency, the greater the fear because fear tends to suppress appetitive behavior. Rats exhibited a strong fear response during trials with the Click (Test 1), whether fear conditioning involved forward (F-F), simultaneous (F-S), or backward (F-B) pairings between the Tone and the Shock in Phase 2. Groups U-U and U-F suggest that nonassociative factors, such as sensitization and pseudoconditioning, were not sufficient to elicit responding to the Click. Furthermore, responding to the Tone (Test 2) was robust in Group F-F but not in Groups F-S and F-B. Therefore, a CS eliciting weak responding due to simultaneous or backward pairing with the US in Phase 2 was nonetheless capable of supporting levels of sensory preconditioning like those of a forward CS. These results suggest that temporal contiguity between signal and reinforcer is a fundamental component

Table 4.1 Classical conditioning and temporal contiguity

Group	*Phase 1 (SPC)*	*Phase 2 (Conditioning)*	*Test 1*	*Results*	*Test 2*	*Results*
F-F	Click→Tone	Tone→Shock	Click?	Robust	Tone?	Robust
F-S	Click→Tone	Tone→Shock	Click?	Robust	Tone?	Weak
F-B	Click→Tone	Shock→Tone	Click?	Robust	Tone?	Weak
U-F	Click, Tone	Tone→Shock	Click?	Weak	Tone?	Robust
U-U	Click, Tone	Tone, Shock	Click?	Weak	Tone?	Weak

Note. B: backward pairings. F: forward pairings. S: simultaneous pairings. U: unpaired stimuli. Robust: a strong response to the stimulus. Weak: the stimulus did not evoke much responding.

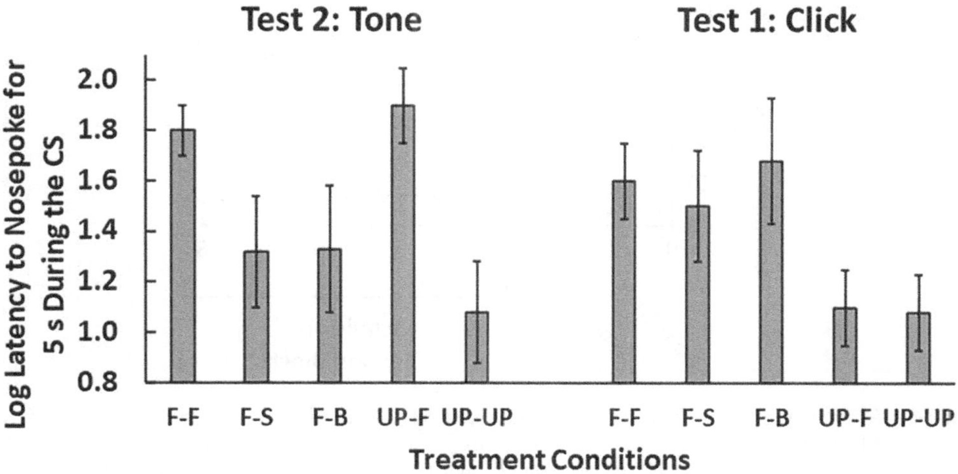

Figure 4.1 **Role of contiguity in conditioning.** Rats received training as described in Table 4.1. Test 1 with the Click CS shows similar levels of sensory preconditioning after forward (F), simultaneous (S), or backward (B) pairings between Tone and Shock, but low responding when Tone and Shock were unpaired. Test 2 with the Tone shows that only forward (F) Tone-Shock pairings supported responding to the Tone. A forward relationship is necessary for a CS to elicit conditioned responses but temporal contiguity, whether in F, S, or B paradigm, is sufficient for acquisition. (From Matzel et al., 1988; reproduced with permission from Elsevier.)

of classical conditioning, independent of the temporal order between stimuli. Forward (or delay) conditioning, however, does endow the CS with a strong response-eliciting power.

4.2.1.2 Contiguity in operant conditioning

To determine whether the contiguity between response and outcome influences operant conditioning, researchers have used a variety of designs. Every operant contingency contains a Pavlovian contingency embedded in it. As shown in Figure 2.7 (Chapter 2), every time an operant response (R) occurs, there is a pairing between the signal (S^D) and the outcome (O), one that is functionally analogous to a Pavlovian stimulus–outcome pairing, S→O. Thus, one strategy has been to compare the behavior of animals trained in an operant procedure against the behavior of animals trained according to a Pavlovian procedure. For example, if the operant condition delivers food (or avoids shock) every time there is a response in the presence of an antecedent stimulus, then the Pavlovian equivalent delivers food (or avoids shock) only when the antecedent stimulus is presented. Under these conditions, when the operant and Pavlovian contingencies lead to similar behavioral changes, then the Pavlovian S→O contingencies are sufficient to explain the effects. If, however, operant contingencies lead to greater behavioral change than Pavlovian contingencies, then the R→O contingency makes a significant contribution to behavioral change (Sheffield, 1965).

An important difference is that the O occurs only when there is a response in the operant procedure but occurs in all trials in the Pavlovian procedure. An ingenious technique, known as ***master–yoked design***, was introduced to equate two groups in terms of the number and temporal distribution of outcomes during a conditioning session. In this procedure, pairs of animals are randomly assigned to either the master or the yoked condition. Master

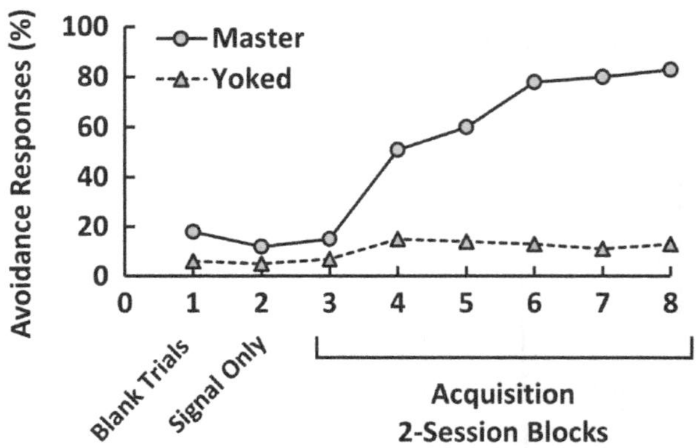

Figure 4.2 **Master–yoked design.** In a master–yoked design, goldfish (*Carassius auratus*) trained as Masters acquired avoidance behavior faster and to a higher level than Yoked controls. (From Overmier & Papini, 1986; reproduced with permission from the American Psychological Association.)

animals control their own outcomes, but they also control the outcomes delivered to the yoked animals. Thus, in the food case, if the master makes a response and obtains food, the yoked also obtains food irrespective of its behavior. The same occurs with shock avoidance: Master and yoked animals get the same number and distribution of shocks as a function of the master's behavior. Under these conditions, if a response is an operant, it should increase in frequency depending on the outcome with which it was paired. Therefore, master animals should respond more than yoked animals. Figure 4.2 shows that master goldfish acquired a swimming response to avoid shock faster than yoked animals (Overmier & Papini, 1986), a result suggesting that the R→O contingency contributes to acquisition beyond the contribution of the Pavlovian S→O contingency. In the absence of a difference in behavior in master and yoked animals, the behavioral change could be entirely accounted for in terms of the Pavlovian S→O contingency.

In other cases, master and yoked groups produce similar acquisition performance, suggesting that Pavlovian contingencies could be sufficient to generate the appearance of operant behavior. For example, approach to an appetitive CS has been shown to be mostly dependent upon Pavlovian contingencies using the master–yoked design in a variety of situations, including sexual reinforcement with quail (Crawford & Domjan, 1993) and food reinforcement with rats (Harris et al., 2013). Thus, apparent purposefulness in behavior does not necessarily imply that the behavior is a function of its consequences. This issue is discussed in what follows with the introduction of the distinction between actions and habits.

4.2.2 Comparative and developmental generality of contiguity

The importance of contiguity in associative learning can be assessed by determining its generality across species (comparative) and across the lifespan of individual organisms (developmental). Comparative aspects were covered in Chapter 3 with examples of associative learning in animals with diffuse nervous systems, like cnidarians (sea anemones, jellyfish), and in animals with central nervous systems, such as the nematode *Caenorhabditis elegans.* Consider the experiment described in Table 4.2 (Nishijima & Maruyama, 2017). Nematodes display an unconditioned rejection of the chemical 1-nonanol, whereas they are attracted

Table 4.2 Pavlovian conditioning in *C. elegans*

Group	*Training*	*Test*	*Results*
Paired	1-Nonanol→KCl	1-Nonanol	Preference for 1-nonanol
Vehicle	Ethanol→KCl	1-Nonanol	Avoidance of 1-nonanol
Unpaired	1-Nonanol, KCl	1-Nonanol	
Signal only	1-Nonanol	1-Nonanol	
Reinforcer only	KCl	1-Nonanol	
Naïve	No training	1-Nonanol	

Note. CS: 1-nonanol, an odor that induces avoidance response. US: KCl, potassium chloride, a taste that triggers approach. Nematodes were released in a plate that was marked with the CS and/or US for a number of trials separated by either a short or a long interval. All animals were tested on the plate that only had the CS odor.

to the taste of potassium chloride (KCl). Pairing 1-nonanol with KCl, a CS→US pairing, reversed the avoidance of 1-nonanol in a subsequent CS-only test. By contrast, all the control groups, including an unpaired group, displayed avoidance of 1-nonanol. Therefore, CS→US contiguity was critical to establishing this behavioral change.

The relevance of contiguity is also highlighted by developmental research in rat fetuses. A mammalian fetus is immersed in amniotic fluid rich in chemical substances derived from the mother's diet. It is possible to present stimuli and record responses in the developing fetus. The importance of contiguity has been assessed in experiments pairing gustatory and olfactory stimuli in gestation day 20 (typically, a day before birth). Lemon solutions are irritants and induce activity and wiping responses. In one experiment (Smotherman & Robinson, 1991), rat fetuses were exposed to a 10-μL oral infusion of sucrose (CS) followed seconds later by lemon (US). After three such pairings, the activity level in the presence of the signal was measured and compared to that of control animals exposed to Lemon→Sucrose backward pairings (US→CS), to Sucrose→Saline pairings, to Sucrose-only trials (CS-only control), and to Lemon-only trials (US-only controls). In a final test, animals trained with CS→US pairings responded significantly more to Sucrose than any of the controls. These findings highlight the importance of temporal contiguity for associative learning in developing mammals.

4.2.3 Learning/performance dichotomy

Because instrumental learning involves the reinforcement of a specific response, it is tempting to identify learning with performance, but this would not be valid. Associative learning is not the same as behavioral change but more like neural change that may manifest in behavior. In *latent learning* (Tolman & Honzik, 1930), rats explored a complex maze without receiving food reinforcement. When food was introduced in the maze's goal box, these animals showed faster acquisition of the direct route to the goal than animals that encountered food from the first trial. The implication is that rats were learning about the maze while engaged in exploratory behavior. The neural record of exploration altered behavior when food became available. The learning–performance dichotomy cautions that apparent failures of acquisition may represent failures of performance. How much of our prior experience remains latent until the right conditions are present for that learning to influence behavior?

In some cases, acquisition can be virtually identical in groups treated differentially, but groups could diverge when conditions change. For example, groups trained with large and small rewards often produce similar asymptotic performance, but a transition to extinction reveals differences. Figure 4.3-A shows that lever pressing reinforced with 1 or 12 food pellets per trial was similar at the end of acquisition and yet extinction was faster in animals that received the larger reward (Papini et al., 2001). Perhaps the behavioral measure (responses per minute) suffered from a ceiling effect and no longer discriminated these conditions by the end of acquisition. *Ceiling effects* (and *floor effects*, when the behavioral change is decremental) reflect a lack of sensitivity of the response measure or the presence of a biological limit for a particular response—the frequency of lever pressing can increase up to a maximum.

The acquisition of new information can influence behavior only when the strength of a signal surpasses a *response threshold*. Consider a visual discrimination problem in a T-maze where a rat receives food for approaching a lighted arm but no food for approaching a dark arm (L+/D-). In such experiments, the position of L and D arms varies over trials to minimize reliance upon spatial cues (left arm, right arm). Under these conditions, rats usually display *position habits* (consistent choice of one arm), which yields food in 50% of the trials because each arm is L+ in half the trials. To test whether the rat was learning anything about the L+/D- discrimination while exhibiting a position habit, Spence (1945) implemented a reversal of cue validity (L-/D+). This reversal retarded acquisition of the visual discrimination (Figure 4.3-B). Thus, the animal was indeed learning about the discrimination, albeit not enough to break the position habit—hence the notion that such learning was below a response threshold.

Performance failure can reflect acquisition failure or *retrieval failure*. If behavior during learning reflects both acquisition and retrieval, then manipulations that facilitate retrieval should enhance behavior, even if no additional training for acquisition is provided. In a series of experiments with rats (Miller, 1982), behavior was facilitated by exposure to some aspect of the training context (e.g., the start box of the maze). These *reminder treatments* facilitated

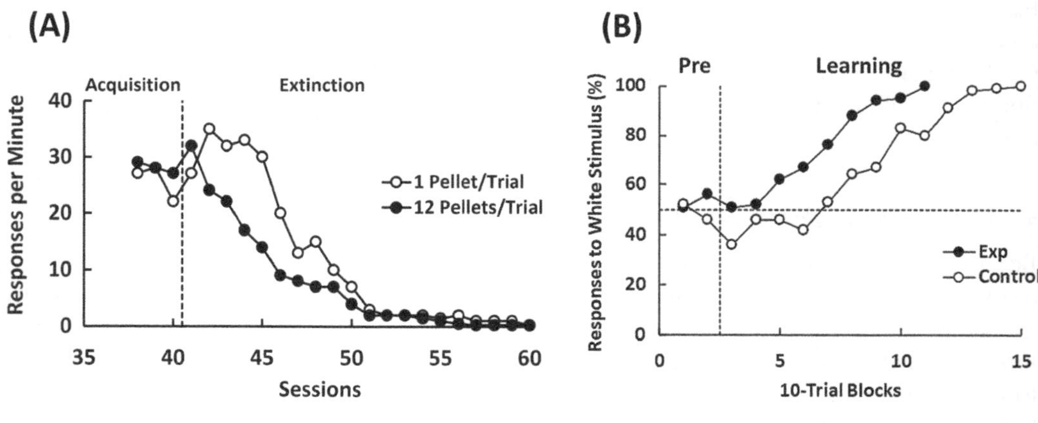

Figure 4.3 **Learning and performance. (A)** Nondifferential asymptotic performance in acquisition obscured the influence of reward magnitude on performance (1 vs. 12 pellets) due to a ceiling effect on the dependent variable. (From Papini et al., 2001; reproduce with permission from Elsevier.) **(B)** Rats solving a visual discrimination in which stimuli change positions across trials often fall into rigid position habits, choosing one side for many trials. In this experiment, the validity of the stimuli was reversed when rats were in a position habit, and the reversal retarded the solution of the problem. This showed that rats were actually learning about the stimulus-outcome relationship, but such learning was not affecting performance as they were engaged in a position habit. (From Spence, 1945; reproduced with permission from the American Psychological Association.)

the retrieval of critical information. Consistent with this assumption, reminder treatments had no effect when administered early in training while the animal was still acquiring information but facilitated acquisition when administered during intermediate or later training sessions. These results suggest that learning curves reflect both acquisition and retrieval.

4.2.4 *What is learned in Pavlovian conditioning?*

The presentation of a CS closely followed by a US endows the signal with the ability to elicit a CR. Two explanations for this have been proposed based on the idea that each event causes a unique pattern of neural activity—the representations of the stimulus events.

In one view, the acquired response emerges because the presentation of the CS activates a representation of the US—an *S→S association*. In this case, the CS has acquired ***informational value***, that is, the CS leads to behavior indicative of the US's modality, intensity, and hedonic value as well as its spatial and temporal location. In another view, the acquired response may emerge because the presentation of the CS activates a representation of the CR—an *S→R association*. In this case, the CR is elicited without mediation by the US representation.

Both explanations are plausible because the CS occurs in close temporal contiguity to both the US and the CR. The ***outcome-devaluation technique*** is used to distinguish between the S→R and S→S accounts of Pavlovian conditioning. Devaluing the US after acquisition should affect behavior if the US representation is activated (S→S learning) but not if the US representation is bypassed (S→R learning).

Table 4.3 describes the design of an outcome-devaluation experiment (Holland & Rescorla, 1975 US). Consider the two groups labeled "FOC" (first-order conditioning). In Phase 2, food-restricted rats received pairings of a Tone (CS) and Food (appetitive US). As a result, the Tone elicited an increase in Activity, an appetitive response anticipating food. In the Devaluation phase, rats in the experimental group received access to Food and immediately after eating were placed in a high-speed Rotation apparatus (aversive US; Rotation causes nausea and leads to food rejection). Control rats were exposed to Rotation.

In a final test, experimental animals exposed to the Tone in the absence of Food or Rotation responded significantly less than controls. This result suggests that, in Devaluation, the Tone activated a representation of Food because of Tone→Food pairings in Phase 2, but the Food had become aversive after Food→Rotation pairings. Thus, the Tone signaled an aversive reinforcer and therefore reduced activity. Because Rotation was not paired with Food during Phase 2, control animals showed no comparable reduction in activity.

Table 4.3 Design of an outcome-devaluation experiment

Group	*Phase 1*	*Phase 2*	*Devaluation*	*Test*	*Results*
FOC-E	L→Food	T→Food	Food→Rotation	T?	Exp < Con
FOC-C	L→Food	T→Food	Rotation	T?	
SOC-E	L→Food	T→L	Food→Rotation	T?	Exp = Con
SOC-C	L→Food	T→L	Rotation	T?	

Note. Design used by Holland and Rescorla (1975) to demonstrate the outcome-devaluation effect in first-order conditioning (FOC) and second-order conditioning (SOC). L: Light CS, T: Tone CS. Rotation: High-speed rotation was used to generate a sickness-like state aimed at devaluing the reinforcer. Rats in Group FOC-E (experimental) responded less during the final Test than rats in Group FOC-C (control), suggesting that the first-order CS reactivated a representation of the (now devalued) Food. By contrast, the second-order CS was not affected by Food devaluation as Group SOC-E responded at about the same rate as Group SOC-C.

It is also possible to devalue a reinforcer by motivational means, for example, by giving rats free food after acquisition but before testing. Satiated animals responded less to the Tone than food-restricted animals. All together, these results suggest that the Tone evoked a CR via activation of the Food representation—an S→S association. When food was devalued by either sickness or satiation, then responding to the CS was reduced.

Researchers noticed that rats exposed to food devaluation continued to respond during the Tone, although sated animals responded less than controls. Subsequent experiments have tried various methods to establish complete rejection of the food and thus the complete absence of behavior, and yet some amount of responding is almost always observed. It is unclear whether this residual responding reflects incomplete learning of the aversion, incomplete expression of aversive learning during testing, or S→R learning (Holland, 2008). This could be important for some clinical treatments aiming at changing reinforcer value by pairing it with either appetitive (anxiety paired with calm words of affirmation) or aversive stimuli (cigarette smoking paired with pictures of black lungs). S→R learning may hinder the efficacy of these treatments.

One approach to testing S→R associations is to assume that if the evidence fails to support S→S associations, then learning must be of the S→R type. Researchers have invoked S→R associations when behavior is unaffected by reinforcer devaluation. For example, the same devaluation technique that influenced responding in first-order classical conditioning did not work on second-order conditioning (Holland & Rescorla, 1975). As also shown in Table 4.3, after Light→Food pairings in Phase 1 (first-order conditioning), rats received Tone→Light pairings in Phase 2 (second-order conditioning) until they responded to the Tone. Subsequent devaluation of Food did not affect responding to the Tone, the second-order signal, suggesting that second-order conditioning is based on S→R associations, that is, a type of learning not mediated by an active US representation.

In addition to informational value, Pavlovian conditioning also endows the signal with motivational and emotional properties: *reinforcement value*. A signal for food can acquire appetitive value like that of food itself. In this case, the signal is said to function as a *secondary* or *conditioned reinforcer* (*primary reinforcer* is the unconditioned property of food to increase the probability of a behavior with which it is paired). The reinforcement value of signals can be used to detect conditioning when signals lack the ability to elicit a response. We have seen that USs and reinforcers can both elicit responses and reinforce associations. We have also described the ability of CSs and S^Ds to promote behavior, and in what follows, we will learn that, by virtue of their learning history, signals can also reinforce associations. A below-threshold CS may fail to elicit a consistent response, but it may still act as a conditioned reinforcer (Rescorla, 1980). The informational and reinforcement values of a signal are independent from each other, but both depend on conditioning (see **4.3.4 Conditioned reinforcement**).

4.2.5 *What is learned in operant conditioning?*

Thorndike (1911) suggested that new behaviors are acquired gradually through a process involving the gradual strengthening of successful responses and the weakening of unsuccessful ones. "Success" was defined as achieving the goal object (e.g., food, water). This *law of effect* states that operant learning depends on the outcomes (consequences or effects) of actions. Such outcomes were suggested to strengthen an association between the stimuli perceived at the time the successful response was emitted and the response that led to the outcome. This became known as the *S→R theory of operant conditioning*, which you will note is like the S→R account of Pavlovian conditioning mentioned previously. The parsimony of a unified account of both kinds of conditioning led to much empirical testing.

S→R associations are difficult to demonstrate empirically, although they make good neural sense. Synaptic plasticity in connections involving sensory and motor neurons is common in neural circuitry underling learning, as described for simple systems in Chapter 3. In operant conditioning, S→R associations are understood as ***habits*** that are automatically elicited by stimuli without a clear expectation of their consequences, as the automatic performance of complex actions by an experienced person (e.g., driving by taxi drivers).

Habits are distinguished from ***actions***, responses guided by outcome expectancies (e.g., learning to drive a car). Actions require S→S associations in which the second "S" refers to an expectation of the reinforcer activated by the preceding stimulus. Extended operant training can render an action (sensitive to reinforcer devaluation) into a habit (insensitive to reinforcer devaluation; Adams & Dickinson, 1981). The effect of extended training fits the notion that expectancy-guided actions become automatic habits with extensive practice. These results suggest Thorndike's law of effect was partially correct but was incomplete. S→R associations are gradually learned and contribute to the acquisition of new behaviors.

The outcome-devaluation technique, discussed with respect to Pavlovian conditioning, can also be useful in operant conditioning. This might imply that S-S associations modulate operant behavior. In one experiment (Colwill & Rescorla, 1985), two responses (Lever Pressing, Chain Pulling) were paired with different reinforcers (Food Pellets, Sucrose Solution). Rats rapidly learn to obtain rewards by pressing a lever with a forepaw and pulling a chain hanging from the ceiling of the conditioning box.

Subsequently, one reinforcer, say Pellets, was devalued by pairing it with a toxin (lithium chloride, LiCl) that induces gastrointestinal Sickness. In a final test, the two responses were available (Table 4.4). Rats responded less to the Lever, previously paired with the devalued reinforcer (Pellets), than to the Chain, paired with the nondevalued reinforcer (Sucrose). The Lever (S) evoked a representation of Pellets (S), which had been devalued by being paired with Sickness, thus reducing responding to the lever. However, as in previous demonstrations of devaluation, rats continued to press the lever at a low rate, potentially reflecting a weak S-R association.

Classical and operant conditioning involve both S→S and S→R associations depending on the situation, either separate or integrated as an S→R→O chain. Some have proposed that other associations may be learned about during operant conditioning (de Wit & Dickinson, 2009), such as the relationship between representations of the Response and Outcome (R→O), Outcome and Response (O→R), and a hierarchical relationship in which the

Table 4.4 Reinforcer devaluation in operant conditioning

Phase 1 (Acquisition)	*Phase 2 (Devaluation)*	*Test responding*
Lever→Pellets Chain→Sucrose	Pellets→LiCl (Sickness) Sucrose-only	Lever < Chain

Note. In Phase 1, the same animal was exposed to the two responses (Lever Pressing, Chain Pulling) paired with different reinforcers (Food Pellets, Sucrose Solution). In Phase 2, Pellets were paired with lithium chloride (LiCl), a toxin that leads to gastrointestinal Sickness, whereas Sucrose was presented on its own. Finally, given a choice, rats preferred the response whose reinforcer had not been paired with LiCl. Different animals received all possible combinations of responses and reinforcers (see ***counterbalance***, Chapter 2), but they were not included in this table for simplicity. Thus, for other animals, Sucrose was paired with LiCl and Pellets were presented on their own, and so on.

stimulus activates a representation containing both the response and outcome: S→[R→O]. Each of these has received some degree of support, suggesting that operant conditioning entails learning about a complex, dynamic interaction of stimuli, responses, and outcomes. The evidence for these additional associative links is discussed in Chapter 6.

4.2.6 Hierarchical associations: occasion setting

Serial compounds (e.g., Tone→Click→Food) can lead to a type of learning that seems to have unique properties. When a short Click stimulus is followed by Food if preceded by a long, diffuse Tone, but not if presented by itself (Click-only), the Tone facilitates responding to the Click. In this case, the Tone is called an *occasion setter* because it sets the occasion for responding to the Click (Fraser & Holland, 2019; Leising et al., 2025). Three properties of such response facilitation are highlighted here: (1) The occasion setter fails to control behavior on its own; (2) occasion setters continue to facilitate responding to another CS even after extensive nonreinforced presentations—they are insensitive to extinction treatments; and (3) response facilitation transfers to other CSs trained with other occasion setters. Let us consider these properties.

Pigeons do not show specific behavioral changes to diffuse stimuli, but diffuse stimuli can become occasion setters. In one experiment (Rescorla, 1985), pigeons pecked at a localized Light that signaled Food when preceded by a diffuse Tone (T→L→F) but did not respond on Light-only or Tone-only trials. This illustrates the first property listed previously, that is, occasion setters fail to control behavior on their own. Moreover, the occasion-setting ability of the Tone was not disrupted whether the Tone was previously paired with Food or with the absence of Food. In fact, previous Tone→Food pairings did not transform the Tone more easily into an occasion setter. These results suggest that Pavlovian conditioning and occasion setting result in dissociable stimulus properties.

The second property was also tested on pigeons. After the training described earlier, the Tone was repeatedly presented alone (an extinction procedure). In a subsequent test, the Tone retained its ability to facilitate responding to the Light (Rescorla, 1985). The occasion-setting function appears to be intact after various conditioning treatments of the diffuse stimulus.

The third property, transfer, was examined in an experiment in which rats received concurrent training with the following trials (Holland, 1995). One serial compound involved the presentation of a Clicker followed by a Door Light terminating with Food delivery (C→DL→F), whereas a second serial compound involved a Panel Light followed by a Tone terminating with Food delivery (PL→T→F). There were also DL-only and T-only trials designed to establish C and PL as occasion setters. The two lights (DL, PL) were lights placed in different locations. The first stimulus in the serial compound was the occasion setter (C, PL), whereas the second stimulus was the discriminative stimulus (DL, T). Animals also received trials with Noise followed by Food in half of the trials (N→F) and by itself in the other half (N-only); this discriminative stimulus was not preceded by any specific stimulus, but it was reinforced just as frequently as the other discriminative stimuli (DL and T). The occasion setters facilitated responding to their respective discriminative stimulus (C→DL, PL→T) and to the discriminative stimulus trained in the other serial compound (C→T, PL→DL). However, the occasion setters failed to facilitate responding to the Noise, which had not been trained as part of a serial compound. Thus, occasion setters can facilitate responding to other CSs provided they have also been trained as part of a serial compound. This illustrates the third property of occasion setters, namely, transfer.

These properties of occasion setting attracted attention because they seem to contrast with those of typical CSs. Rather than eliciting or provoking responses directly, as done by typical signals, occasion setters modulate responding to other stimuli. Modulation implies that the occasion setter controls the validity of the CS→US association in a hierarchical manner rather than exerting control over one element of the association, either the CS or US.

Animals are exposed to ambiguous situations in nature. For example, stimuli predictive of food may be approached when conditions are safe but not when there are signs the reward may be absent or that predators may be nearby. Contextual or discrete cues acting as occasion setters may disambiguate these two situations, producing signal approach in one case but signal avoidance in the other. Moreover, "context" may refer to external stimuli characterizing a particular location or can also encompass internal states arising from motivational, emotional, or circadian changes.

One example of an internal context is provided by the aftereffects of drugs (Palmatier & Bevins, 2008). For example, rats treated with Nicotine received training in which a Noise was paired with Sucrose (Nic→N→S), whereas the same rats treated with CDP (chlordiazepoxide, an anxiolytic drug) were exposed to pairings between a Light and Sucrose (CDP→L→S). On separate trials in which a placebo was administered instead of the drug, the rats received the CS but not the sucrose. The internal states induced by Nicotine and CDP facilitated responding to the Noise and Light CSs, but their facilitatory effect transferred across discriminations (e.g., Nic→L, CDP→N). Importantly, neither the Noise nor the Light controlled behavior when presented alone. It makes intuitive sense that occasion setters facilitate responding for various signals of the same reward.

4.2.7 Neurobiology of stimulus contiguity in mammals

4.2.7.1 Long-term potentiation and depression

Close contiguity in time or space between stimuli, responses, and outcomes is an important factor in conditioning. To be sure, contiguity is not the only factor influencing conditioning. Evidence shows that behavior can exhibit change even when minutes elapse between the signal and the reinforcer, and that behavior can fail to change even under contiguous S→S training. Still, under most conditions, contiguity is a significant factor in conditioning, a fact that also makes sense from a neurobiological perspective. Individual neurons often receive inputs from a variety of sources, and their coincidence in time can induce synaptic changes that increase the likelihood of activity in the postsynaptic neuron when the inputs coincide again.

The idea that stimuli, responses, and outcomes can be encoded by changes in synaptic connections caused by their concurrent activation, referred to as ***activity-dependent synaptic plasticity***, was first suggested by Ramón y Cajal (1911), who speculated that the repeated use of preexisting connections between neurons could lead to structural changes in dendrites and axons that would enhance their connectivity. In the same vein, Hebb (1949) suggested that the activation of two neurons sharing a synapse could increase the efficiency of that synapse, especially if the action potential of the presynaptic neuron reaches the postsynaptic neuron before the latter is activated by other presynaptic neurons. This became known as a ***Hebbian synapse***. This position is now summarized by the famous colloquialism, "Cells that fire together wire together."

Evidence consistent with the concept of Hebbian synapse was provided decades later by experiments stimulating a circuit in the hippocampus. Using rabbits, Bliss and Lømo (1973) reported that repeated, strong stimulation of axons in the perforant path that provides input into the hippocampus from the entorhinal cortex increased the subsequent response of neurons in the dentate gyrus of the hippocampus that receive the incoming action potentials (Figure 4.4). This hippocampal circuit was intensely studied in a slice of brain tissue kept alive for several hours in a special bath. Such a *brain slice* technique allows for more precise stimulation and recording of neural activity than would be the case with the entire animal.

A demonstration of this phenomenon, called *long-term potentiation* (*LTP*), involved three steps: weak stimuli to the performant path elicited a weak response in the dentate gyrus; then, perforant-path axons were stimulated with a burst of strong stimuli; finally, tests with the weak stimulus produced an enhanced response relative to the response elicited before activation with the strong stimuli (Figure 4.5). LTP displays three properties relevant for an understanding of learning. First, *persistence*: The elevated responsiveness of the postsynaptic neuron remains stable from hours to weeks, making it a suitable substrate for long-term memory. Second, *specificity*: Strong stimulation of one pathway activates that pathway but not a pathway that converges on the same neurons of the dentate gyrus that was not subjected to a burst of strong stimuli. Third, *associativity*: Strong stimulation of one pathway will increase the ability of a second pathway stimulated with a weak stimulus provided the two are activated simultaneously.

Subsequent experiments also showed that synaptic transmission can be reduced by a type of activity-dependent synaptic plasticity that could help explain response inhibition. This phenomenon, called *long-term depression* (*LTD*), can be induced in the hippocampus by the administration of a low-frequency burst of stimuli (Figure 4.5). Dudek and Bear (1992) administered 900 pulses at a rate of one to three pulses per second to Shaffer collateral axons originating in the CA3 region and making synaptic connection with pyramidal neurons of the CA1 region. Subsequent recording of activity in the dendrites of the pyramidal neurons in CA1 demonstrated reduced excitability after the administration of test pulses. LTP and LTD have been found in a variety of brain areas and species; Figure 4.5 shows examples from the optic tectum of the frog *Xenopus*. These results also show that both LTP and LTD are

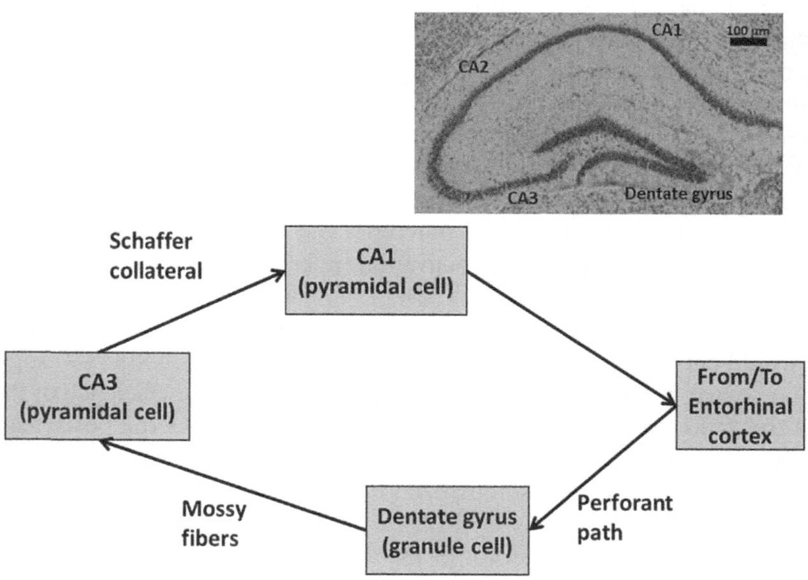

Figure 4.4 **Hippocampal circuit used in LTP and LTD experiments.** This circuit is repeated serially in adjacent slices of hippocampal tissue. (Hippocampal photo by M. R. Papini.)

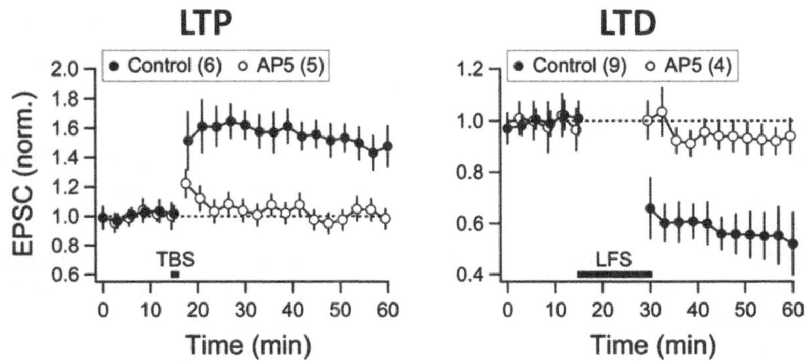

Figure 4.5 **Long-term potentiation (LTP) and long-term depression (LTD) in the amphibian optic tectum.** AP5: an antagonist of the N-methyl-D aspartate (NMDA) glutamate receptor. LFS: low-frequency stimulation. TBS: theta burst stimulation. (From Du et al., 2009; with permission from the Proceedings of the National Academy of Sciences USA.)

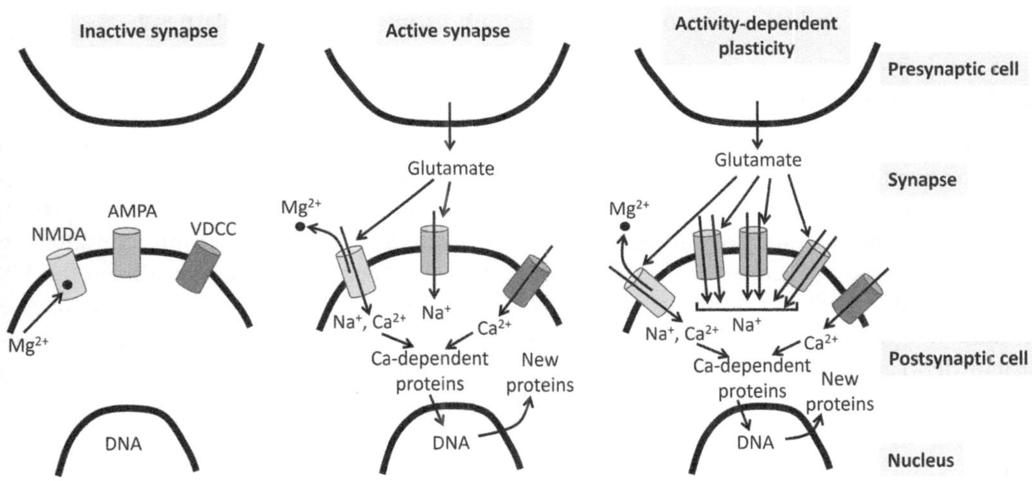

Figure 4.6 **AMPA-NMDA receptors.** The neurotransmitter glutamate can activate two types of receptors that are jointly expressed in some synapses: the AMPA and NMDA receptors. In the inactive synapse (left), NMDA receptors are blocked by magnesium (Mg^{2+}) ions. In active synapses (middle), when AMPA receptors are active, the magnesium block is released and an influx of sodium (Na^{+}) and calcium (Ca^{2+}) ions enter the postsynaptic cell. Voltage-dependent calcium channels (VDCC) also open, thus increasing calcium influx. Calcium triggers an intracellular molecular cascade that can stimulate gene transcription in the neuron's nucleus (DNA), leading to the synthesis of new AMPA receptors. This is the basis for activity-dependent synaptic plasticity (right), critical for the formation of long-term memories.

blocked by AP5, an antagonist of the neurotransmitter glutamate. Thus, understanding the connection between LTP/LTD and learning requires an understanding of glutamate receptors (e.g., AMPA and NMDA receptors).

Activity-dependent synaptic plasticity in glutamate receptors is represented in Figure 4.6 and briefly described in the next paragraphs, while the following section connects these cellular processes with behavior.

Excitatory synaptic activity is regulated by various neurotransmitters, including glutamate. Glutamate binds with two types of receptors important for conditioning: *AMPA receptors* (alpha-amino-3-hydroxy-5-methyl-4-isoxazolepropionate acid) and *NMDA receptors* (N-methyl-D-aspartate). This action of glutamate is achieved by opening the receptor to the influx of sodium (Na^+) inside the postsynaptic neuron. Na^+ is a positively charged ion that makes the inside of the neuron more positive, increasing the likelihood that the neuron will generate action potentials.

When the presynaptic neuron (e.g., the Schaffer collateral in the hippocampus) releases glutamate in its axon terminals, stimulation of AMPA receptors in the pyramidal cells of CA1 generates excitatory postsynaptic potentials that bring the pyramidal neuron close to firing action potentials. If this pyramidal cell is activated by the AMPA receptors, then NMDA receptors also present in the postsynaptic membrane can become active. Whereas AMPA receptors are activated by glutamate, NMDA receptors require both glutamate binding and a depolarized pyramidal cell before they can be activated. These two factors open the NMDA receptor by removing a magnesium (Mg^{2+}) block, thus allowing for the influx of two positively charged ions: Na^+ and Ca^{2+} (calcium). It is the influx of Ca^{2+} into the postsynaptic cell that is critical for LTP and LTD. AP5 blocks the NMDA receptor thus preventing the release of Mg^{2+} and the influx of Ca^{2+}, therefore disrupting synaptic plasticity.

4.2.7.2 From brain slice to behavior

Although this influence of AMPA receptors on NMDA receptors was described in relation to the hippocampal circuit, similar arrangements are present in other brain regions. This mechanism is therefore thought to apply to a variety of conditioning phenomena (Nicoll, 2017). To visualize the relevance of this AMPA-NMDA mechanism for conditioning, consider the circuit illustrated in Figure 4.7. In this circuit, a neuron receives a strong input from the US pathway and an initially weak input from the CS pathway. The weak input would release glutamate binding to both AMPA and NMDA receptors, but this is unlikely to generate sufficient depolarization to produce a strong signal. However, if this weak input is contiguous

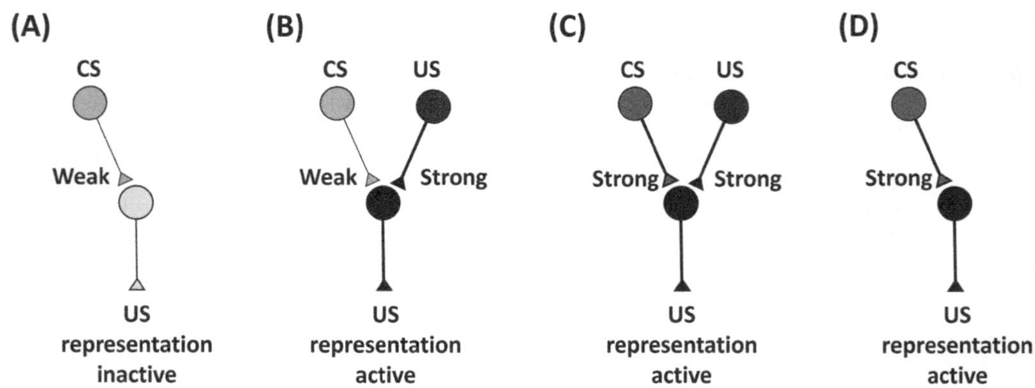

Figure 4.7 **Synaptic plasticity.** An application of activity-dependent synaptic plasticity to Pavlovian conditioning. **(A)** Initially, the CS input cannot activate the US representation. **(B)** The coincidence of a weak signal input with a strong reinforcer input that activates the US representation strengthens the CS input **(C)**. **(D)** Finally, the CS has acquired the ability to activate the US representation by itself.

in time to a strong input from the US pathway, then AMPA receptors will depolarize the postsynaptic neuron, and because glutamate is binding to the NMDA receptor, this receptor will open and Ca^{2+} will flow into the postsynaptic cell. The coincidence of the two inputs in time would then increase the strength of the connection between CS and US pathways. Eventually, just the activation of the CS input should be enough to depolarize the postsynaptic neuron.

The associative property of LTP suggests that the overlap in time of inputs bringing information from the CS and US might be necessary for contiguity to be detected at the neural level. Neurons that receive such convergence of inputs are referred to as *coincidence detectors*. Knowledge derived from the brain slice technique is applicable to the behavior of the entire animal, since factors that modulate LTP in the brain slice also affect behavior in learning tasks.

In fear conditioning, for example, neural inputs originating from a Tone paired with Shock converge in the lateral amygdala (LA). Coincidence detectors in the LA are pyramidal cells receiving auditory information from the thalamus and cortex (weak synapses) and pain signals from spinal cord neurons receiving nociceptive information (strong synapses). If these inputs arrive at similar times, then Hebbian synaptic plasticity would strengthen the weak inputs so that they alone can depolarize the pyramidal neuron in the LA and eventually lead to behavioral, physiological, and autonomic responses associated with fear conditioning (Figure 4.8).

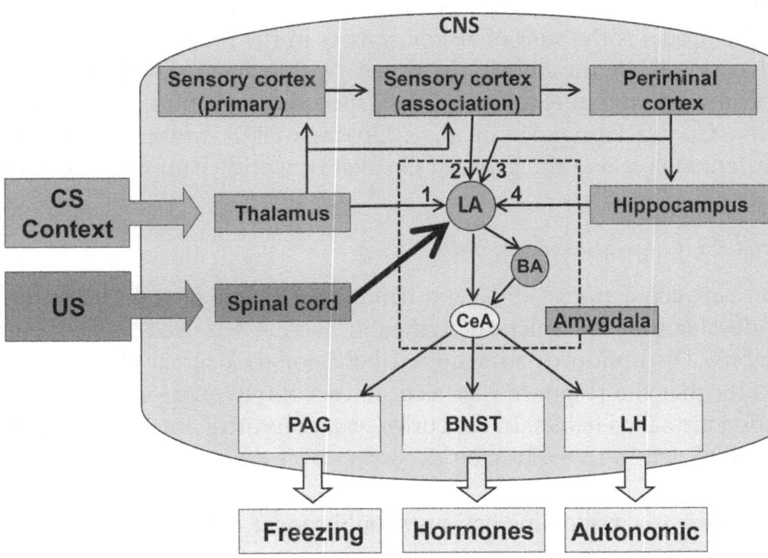

Figure 4.8 **Brain circuit of fear conditioning.** Inputs from the CS, context, and US converge in the lateral amygdala (LA). CS and context processing converge in the amygdala via the thalamus (#1) or after cortical and hippocampal processing (#2–4). From the LA, information moves into the basal amygdala (BA) or directly into the central amygdala (CeA), which distributes impulses to areas that control various responses, including the periaqueductal gray (PAG) responsible for freezing, the bed nucleus of the stria terminalis (BNST) controlling the release of stress hormones, and the lateral hypothalamus (LH) triggering autonomic responses, such as changes in heart rate. (Modified from Papini, 2021; reproduced with permission from Taylor & Francis.)

A key demonstration of the connection between LTP at the cellular level and conditioning at a behavioral level would require that both phenomena are mediated by Ca^{2+} influx into postsynaptic pyramidal cells in the LA related to NMDA receptor activity. LTP in brain slices of LA tissue is linked to a type of NMDA receptor containing a subunit known as NR2B (NMDA receptors vary in the type of subunits they express). Experiments with ifenprodil, a drug that selectively blocks NMDA receptors with an NR2B subunit, prevented both LTP in LA slices (Müller et al., 2009) and fear acquisition in the entire animal (Rodrigues et al., 2001). These findings imply that an LTP-like process in the LA is triggered during fear conditioning.

It is important to note that the use of a single line denoting a pathway directly from one CS node to one US node is an oversimplification utilized to make the connections easier to identify and to elucidate interactions between different areas. As discussed in Chapter 2, each CS and US is represented by a distinct population of neurons and pattern of neuronal activity.

Additionally, most contemporary models of learning and cognition consist of multilayer neural networks that include an input layer, one or more hidden unit layers, and an output layer. These types of models are referred to as neurally plausible, which means that the properties of the model are consistent with what we know to be the properties of neuronal activity. The input, hidden, and output layers correspond to the sensory, association, and motor cortices in the brain.

Association cortex does not directly receive sensory input, nor does it directly control motor activity, which is similar to the hidden unit layer. In most multilayer neural networks, there is no exact correspondence between the pattern of activity in the hidden unit layer and the sensory world the model is experiencing. The connections between the sensory, hidden, and motor layers are formed through experience and processes akin to LTP and LTD, and the output of the model is the sum of all the activity in the hidden unit layer, much like an organism's behavior may be the sum of the activity within and across brain networks. These models have been successful in text recognition, speech recognition, surgical assistance, and self-driving cars (Gomez-Fernandez et al., 2020) as well as winning at *Jeopardy!* against champion Ken Jennings and at the game of Go against world champion Lee Sedol.

4.2.7.3 S→S and S→R associations in the brain

The distinction between actions (S→S) and habits (S→R) was introduced in Section 4.2.4. The outcome-devaluation experiment described in Table 4.4 is used to distinguish between actions and habits. Disruption of an acquired behavior to a signal after its reinforcer was devalued indicates that the response is an action; by contrast, responses insensitive to reinforcer devaluation are called habits. In appetitive situations involving food reinforcement, the transition from S→S action to S→R habit occurring over extensive training is mediated by a shift in the relevant brain circuit.

A lesion in a brain area regulating actions should render the operant response insensitive to reinforcer devaluation even after minimal training, whereas a lesion in an area controlling habits should leave the operant behavior sensitive to reinforcer devaluation even after extended training. Two areas of the rat's dorsal striatum fit these functions. Early in training, the ***dorsomedial striatum*** controls the formation of lever-pressing actions, such that a lesion in this area converts the action into a habit resistant to reinforcer devaluation (Yin et al., 2005). Conversely, lesions of the ***dorsolateral striatum*** disrupt the conversion of an action into a habit, rendering the response vulnerable to reinforcer devaluation even after extensive training (Yin et al., 2004).

The transition from action to habit also occurs during spatial learning. Consider a rat in a T-maze receiving a reward for turning right (Figure 4.9). This problem can be solved either by learning to approach a location or stimulus based on S→S associations (action) or by performing a particular response based on S→R associations (habit).

In one experiment (Packard & McGaugh, 1996), rats were trained in a T-maze with constant start and goal boxes and tested after either 8 or 16 training sessions by releasing them from a new location. After 8 training sessions, rats tended to show place learning, thus approaching the location where they were reinforced before—an action. However, after 16 sessions, rats tended to make a left turn, the same response they were trained to perform, ending in the wrong arm of the maze—a habit.

During such tests, either the hippocampus or the caudate nucleus (dorsal striatum) was inactivated with lidocaine (a local anesthetic that disables neurons for a short time without damaging them). Hippocampal inactivation impaired test performance after 8 sessions but not after 16 sessions of training; inactivation of the caudate nucleus impaired performance after 16 sessions but not after 8 sessions. Thus, the transition from expectancy-guided actions to habits involves a shift in brain control from limbic (hippocampus) to dorsal striatum (caudate) areas. Interestingly, the transition from action to habit is accelerated by negative emotions, including sources of emotional stress and physical pain (Gasbarri et al., 2014). Aversive conditions tend to promote an automatic, habitual mode of responding.

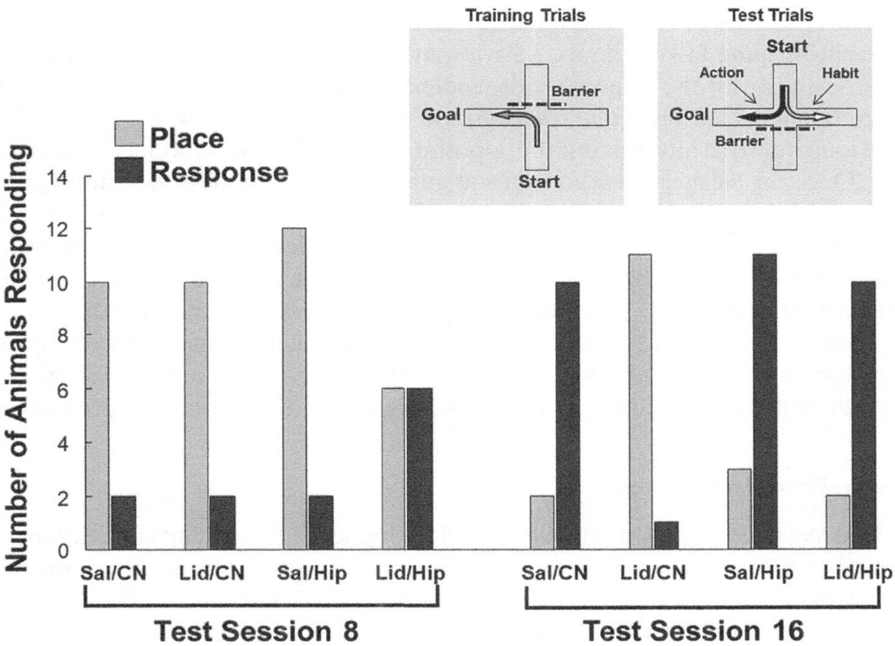

Figure 4.9 **Neural control of place and response learning.** Rats were trained to run from the start to the goal in a plus maze. During two key tests after either 8 or 16 training sessions, rats were released from the test position. After 8 training sessions, rats approached the goal, thus making the opposite response turn relative to training (action learning). However, after 16 trials, they turned left, thus ending in the incorrect arm (habit learning). Reversible inactivation of the hippocampus (Hip) with lidocaine infusions (Lid) disrupted action learning relative to saline infusions (Sal), whereas inactivation of the caudate nucleus (CN) disrupted habit learning. (From Packard & McGaugh, 1996; reproduced with permission from Elsevier. Maze drawings from Papini, 2021; reproduced with permission from Taylor & Francis.)

4.3 Acquisition factors

4.3.1 Beyond contiguity: salience, magnitude, and temporal factors

Many factors affect the rate of conditioning. Whether in Pavlovian or operant situations, the *salience* of stimuli and the *magnitude* or value of the reinforcers are directly related to the speed of acquisition and may affect the asymptotic or terminal level of the acquired response. According to some learning theories (e.g., Rescorla & Wagner, 1972), stimulus salience affects the rate of conditioning, whereas reinforcer magnitude affects the asymptotic level. Additionally, temporal factors affecting acquisition include the distribution of trials in time, the duration of the signals, and the interval between signals and reinforcers. These effects are illustrated by the results of experiments in which a factor is systemically varied during acquisition. For example, in the conditioned suppression task, in which animals lever pressing for food are exposed to Pavlovian Tone→Shock pairings, as the intensity of the Tone increases, the suppression of lever pressing increases (Kamin, 1965). One way to understand salience and magnitude effects is in terms of the degree to which the stimuli are discriminated from the ever-present context—a figure–background problem.

Temporal factors affecting acquisition include the distribution of trials in time, the duration of the signals, and the interval between signals and reinforcers. In a variety of situations, when trials are separated by a long interval, acquisition tends to be faster than training with short intervals—the *trial-spacing effect.* But experiments involving gradual changes from long to short intervals or vice versa indicate that the change in behavior can be asymmetrical.

In the autoshaping task with rats, a Pavlovian procedure in which a brief presentation of a lever (CS) ends with the response-independent delivery of food pellets (US), rats exhibit higher levels of lever pressing (*sign tracking*) and lower levels of magazine entries (*goal tracking*) with long intertrial intervals but the opposite behavioral organization with short intertrial intervals. Once the balance between sign and goal tracking is established, gradual transitions in the intertrial interval tend to preserve the original distribution of these responses. Thus, a short-to-long interval transition tends to produce lower levels of sign tracking at intertrial intervals that would normally produce high levels of lever pressing, because goal tracking continues to be prominent. Vice versa, a long-to-short interval transition promotes sign tracking even under intervals that would usually suppress such behavior, because goal tracking continues to be low (Thomas & Papini, 2020). Thus, whereas a particular factor might have a predictable effect, such effects need to be evaluated in the context of prior experience.

4.3.2 Signal→outcome relevance

Signal→outcome relevance (also known as "belongingness," "constraints on learning," "preparedness," and "associative selectivity") refers to the proposal that some combinations of signals, responses, and outcomes are more easily associated than others. These terms reflect a departure from a principle of *equipotentiality*, according to which the same mechanisms apply to learning involving any combination of stimuli or responses (Domjan, 1997). Several findings suggest that learning mechanisms are adaptively specialized for the resolution of species-typical ecological problems. The main alternative to signal–outcome relevance is that these findings are explained in terms of *contextual variables*—sensory-perceptual, motivational-emotional, or motor factors.

Consider an example (Garcia & Koelling, 1966). When rats were exposed to pairings between a taste or an audiovisual signal with either X-ray irradiation (which induces nausea) or electric shock (which causes peripheral pain), they seemed to learn the Taste→Nausea and Audiovisual→Pain associations better than the Taste→Pain and Audiovisual→Nausea associations.

In one experiment with controls for nonassociative effects (Miller & Domjan, 1981), rats were trained with one of two signals paired with one reinforcer, while the other reinforcer was presented by itself the following day (Table 4.5). This training procedure ensured that each rat was exposed to both reinforcers, only one of which was paired with the target signal. Rats were initially trained to lick water from tubes inserted on the left and right of a panel. During conditioning, licking water from one of the tubes produced a flashing light (a visual CS) or saccharin (a taste CS). The USs (Shock or LiCl) were delivered 60 s after the first lick that produced the signal (Light or Sac). Additional controls received either Light or Sac paired with a harmless injection of isotonic saline. To control for reinforcer exposure, rats trained with Shock were exposed to LiCl the following day, whereas rats trained with LiCl were exposed to Shock the following day. In a final preference test, rats trained with the Shock rejected the drinking tube that produced the Light more than the tube that yielded Sac, but rats trained with LiCl rejected the drinking tube that yielded Sac more than the tube that produced the Light. Thus, Light→Shock worked better than Light→LiCl, whereas Sac→LiCl worked better than Sac→Shock (Figure 4.10). Because both CSs and both USs

Table 4.5 A demonstration of signal-outcome relevance in Pavlovian conditioning

Group	*Days 1–3* *Habituation*	*Day 4* *Paired reinforcer*	*Day 5* *Unpaired reinforcer*	*Day 7* *Test*
Light-LiCl	Water	Light→LiCl	Shock	Water vs. Light
Sac-LiCl	Water	Sac→LiCl	Shock	Water vs. Sac
Light-Shock	Water	Light→Shock	LiCl	Water vs. Light
Sac-Shock	Water	Sac→Shock	LiCl	Water vs. Sac
Light-Saline	Water	Light→Saline	Saline	Water vs. Light
Sac-Saline	Water	Sac→Saline	Saline	Water vs. Sac

Note. Day 6 was a resting day. Light: drinking water from a spout activated a flashing light. Saccharin (Sac): drinking from a spout that yielded a 0.15% saccharin solution. LiCl: an intraperitoneal injection of lithium chloride that produces gastrointestinal sickness and nausea. Saline: an intraperitoneal injection of isotonic saline solution used as a control for the injection procedure. Notice that there was a single signal→outcome pairing and that all the rats were exposed to both reinforcers (LiCl and Shock).

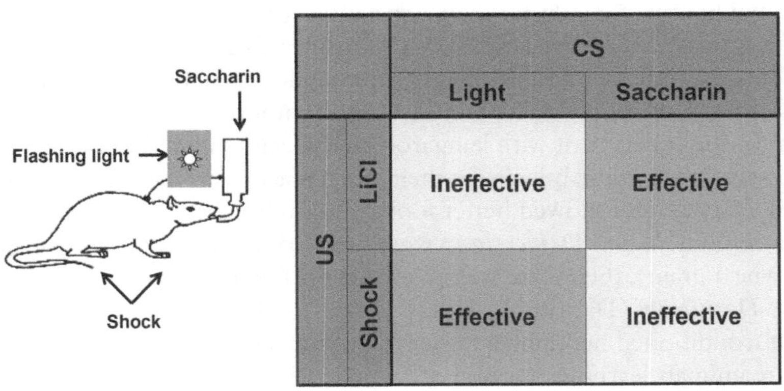

Figure 4.10 **Design and results of experiments showing signal–outcome relevance.** Two signals are combined with two reinforcers. One combination of each type leads to strong acquisition, whereas the other is less effective.

were effective in one combination, failure of the other combination to yield evidence of conditioning cannot be attributed to the use of inadequate stimuli. These results are consistent with signal→outcome relevance.

The ideal approach to determine that ecological pressures lead to evolutionary divergence in learning mechanisms is to compare closely related species adapted to different environments (Domjan & Galef, 1983). Signal→outcome relevance could reflect the operation of an adaptive learning mechanism for animals with a generalized diet that are often sampling novel foods, including poisonous foods. This selective pressure could favor the evolution of mechanisms for the rapid acquisition of food aversions that would minimize the intake of poison. This hypothesis was tested using feeding-specialist vs. feeding-generalist species of kangaroo rats. Generalist species (*Dipodomys merriami*) consume grains, seeds, and plant materials, whereas specialists (*D. microps*) are almost exclusively restricted to the leaves of chenopod plants, like shadscale. These two species differ in diet but belong to the same genus, live in the Owens Valley of California, have similar body size and shape, and can be maintained in the laboratory under similar conditions. Consistent with the hypothesis of adaptive specializations, the generalist *D. merriami* acquired taste aversion faster than the specialist *D. microps* (Daly et al., 1982).

Additional evidence consistent with signal→outcome relevance comes from an artificial selection study with fruit flies (Dunlap & Stephen, 2014). Four populations of flies were exposed to training protocols that predicted different degrees of reproductive success combining colors and odors (CSs) with quinine (an aversive US). For one group, Odor was a reliable predictor of Quinine, but Color was not; a second group had Color reliably predicting Quinine, whereas Odor was unreliable. Finally, for two control groups, Color and Odor were either both highly reliable or both unreliable.

After training, flies were given a choice to lay eggs in a context marked with the Color or Odor experienced during training. The experimenter determined the probability that the eggs would be allowed to hatch in each condition, thus introducing differential reproductive success paired with the choice of context, which, in turn, depended on previous training. After 40 generations of selective breeding, fruit flies demonstrated faster learning with Odor after Odor→Quinine selection but faster learning with Color after Color→Quinine selection when these signals had been reliable predictors of reproductive success. Learning about Color or Odor when signals have been unreliably paired with reproductive success in previous generations was not differential.

These results suggest the possibility that some associations carry such an adaptive weight that animals would learn them faster than associations that have not influenced reproductive success in the animal's ancestors (Dunlap & Dexheimer, 2022; Stahlman & Leising, 2024).

Some problems of interpretation highlight the complexity of these phenomena. First, could contextual factors (sensory-perceptual, motivational-emotional, and motor) explain some of these effects? In the experiment with kangaroo rats, species differed not only in the strength of their food aversion learning but also in their initial reaction to the sunflower seeds. Perhaps the generalist *D. merriami* showed better food aversion because of ***neophobia***—reluctance to consume novel foods. When *D. merriami* were exposed to a novel food for which it was less neophobic (wheat grain), then there was no evidence of food aversion and no difference with the specialist *D. microps* (Daly et al., 1982). Rapid food aversion conditioning could thus result from unconditioned neophobia rather than from signal→outcome relevance.

Second, are animals learning but not performing? For example, Sac→Shock pairings led to better conditioning when a temporal delay was interpolated between the signal and the US (Krane & Wagner, 1975). While no aversion was detected with a 5-s delay, a substantial aversion to Sac developed with delays of 30 and 210 s. Flavored solutions thus require a considerable signal–outcome interval to be associated with either gastrointestinal poisoning or peripheral pain. Similarly, although the initial results suggested that audiovisual stimuli failed to become associated with nausea, subsequent studies reported positive results. In one experiment (Batson & Best, 1979), pairings of a novel context with LiCl blocked subsequent acquisition of a Sac→LiCl association in the same context. Such blocking suggests that the context had been associated with the nausea induced by LiCl.

Third, what is the appropriate procedure for demonstrating signal→outcome relevance? For example, in the fruit fly study, two conditioned stimuli were paired with a single outcome. In the original demonstrations, however, two stimuli and two outcomes were used, and relevance was suggested by the interaction between these conditions (Figure 4.10). This design shows that both signals and both outcomes are viable but only when presented in a specific arrangement. Thus, the fruit fly experiment would require the addition of a second outcome to fully demonstrate signal→outcome relevance (Dwyer, 2015).

An implication of the research on food aversions is that natural selection can achieve the fine-tuning of a particular behavioral process by adjusting contextual factors (e.g., neophobia, stimulus trace dynamics) without necessarily modifying associative mechanisms.

4.3.3 Signal–context interactions

Events always occur in a context, and therefore, contextual cues can acquire signal value just as do temporally discrete signals. *Contextual conditioning* is especially strong when no discrete stimulus signals an outcome—e.g., so-called unsignaled US presentations. Unlike signals, contextual cues are present over longer periods and include external stimuli (visual, auditory, tactile) as well as internal states (drug-induced states, emotions, motivations).

Context manipulations can affect learning about the signal. Consider the two examples described in Table 4.6. First, *latent inhibition*, a retardation of acquisition to a CS that was preexposed by itself before conditioning (more on latent inhibition in Chapter 5). A change in context between CS preexposure and CS→US conditioning eliminates the latent inhibition effect: acquisition is similar (not retarded) to that of a group not given signal preexposure (Westbrook et al., 2000). Second, the presentation of unsignaled USs inflates the value of the context, which, in turn, leads to retardation of acquisition during subsequent CS→US training. This phenomenon, called the *US-preexposure effect*, is also disrupted by a change in context between reinforcer preexposure and conditioning (Tomie, 1976).

Table 4.6 Two examples of contextual modulation in classical conditioning

Disruption of latent inhibition by a context shift			
	Phase 1	*Phase 2*	
Group	*Preexposure*	*Conditioning*	*Result in Phase 2*
1	X: Tone-only	X: Tone→Shock	Acquisition: 1 < 2
2	Y: Tone-only	X: Tone→Shock	
Disruption of the US-preexposure effect by a context shift			
	Phase 1	*Phase 2*	
Group	*Preexposure*	*Conditioning*	*Result in Phase 2*
1	X: Food	X: Light→Food	Acquisition: 1 < 2
2	Y: Food	X: Light→Food	

Note. X and Y represent two contexts with different visual, auditory, olfactory, tactile, and other sensory properties. Notice that in both examples, Group 2 receives training in different contexts across Phases 1 and 2. 1 < 2: slower acquisition in Group 1 than Group 2.

4.3.4 Conditioned reinforcement

A US evokes an UR due to an evolutionary history in which similar US→UR events enhanced the reproductive success of the organism's ancestors. In Pavlovian conditioning, a CS comes to elicit a CR due to CS→US pairings. The CS has effects like those of the US. Against the backdrop of many environmental stimuli, the CS indicates when a CR may have adaptive value. In operant conditioning, the probability of behavior increases or decreases if passed responses were followed by reinforcement or nonreinforcement, respectively. An outcome (US) used to establish a new operant behavior is referred to as a *primary reinforcer*. Alternatively, if a signal (CS) becomes a substitute for the outcome (US) during conditioning, then that signal could be used as a *conditioned* or *secondary reinforcer* to increase the probability of an operant response.

Note the similarity in the use of the term "conditioned" for Pavlovian and operant procedures; an operant outcome (US) requires no training to elicit a response (UR) and act as a primary reinforcer for operant behavior, whereas a Pavlovian signal requires training to elicit a response and act as a conditioned reinforcer for operant behavior. A signal that activates a state similar to that activated by an outcome will have acquired biological relevance and could be a substitute for the outcome. If the outcome is food, then a signal paired with food elicits a similar pattern of neural activity to that of food. If the outcome is attention and affection (a hug), then signals ("good job") paired with hugs can result in a similar pattern of neural activity as a hug. After sufficient conditioning, it is as if you were receiving a hug when hearing "good job." Support for this interpretation comes from the finding that rats respond to a CS with the CR appropriate to the US with which that CS was paired. In a test during which rats were drinking plain water, the CS paired with sucrose elicited sucrose-related responses, but the CS paired with quinine elicited bitter-related responses (Delamater et al., 1986). It was as if the water tasted sweet during one CS and bitter during the other.

The establishment of a conditioned reinforcer has profound implications. Many stimuli (e.g., songs, people, smells) around you were at one time likely paired with a US (e.g., a delicious dish at a restaurant, a satisfying gulp of water, a pleasurable exchange with a partner, a painful experience with a hot plate) and may now have the ability to reinforce or punish your behavior despite their seemingly neutral status. Money has no particular phylogenetic value but it is an excellent reinforcer for many people because of its positive relationship to primary reinforcers. Most human operant learning probably involves some form of conditioned reinforcement (Hull, 1951), including those considered problematic. The subtle way conditioned reinforcers are established suggests their involvement in the maintenance of many problematic human behaviors, such as addiction (Keller & Schoenfeld, 1950).

Training a conditioned reinforcer consists of two phases. In Phase 1, a stimulus is repeatedly paired with a primary reinforcer. In Phase 2, the conditioned reinforcement value of the stimulus is measured by delivering it after a new response. There are, however, several alternative ways in which the neutral stimulus is presented in Phase 1 (Table 4.7). In Group 1, a neutral stimulus may be presented in a purely Pavlovian procedure. Alternatively, as in Group 2, Phase 1 may involve training an operant response followed by a stimulus and a primary reinforcer. Lastly, in Group 3, Phase 1 involves an operant discrimination, such that a target operant response is reinforced in the presence of a stimulus (S^1) but not in its absence. The stimulus may be discrete (Light, Tone) or it could be the sensory feedback associated with making a response. Groups 1 and 2 include nonreinforced presentations of the conditioned reinforcer (i.e., extinction) in Phase 2 to assess its strength. Consequently, while the conditioned reinforcer is being assessed, its strength is weakened, and new extinction learning is

Table 4.7 Alternative designs for establishing a conditioned reinforcer

Alternatives	*Phase 1*	*Phase 2*
1	$S^1 \rightarrow O/S^2$	$R \rightarrow S^1$ vs. $R \rightarrow S^2$
2	$R^1 \rightarrow S^1 \rightarrow O/R^1 \rightarrow S^2$	$R^1 \rightarrow S^1$ or $R^2 \rightarrow S^1$ vs. $R^1 \rightarrow S^2$ or $R^2 \rightarrow S^2$
3	$S^1 \rightarrow R \rightarrow O/S^2 \rightarrow R$	$S^2 \rightarrow R \rightarrow S^1 \rightarrow R \rightarrow O$

Note. Alternative procedures are presented in the first column. S^1: initially neutral stimuli. O: outcomes or primary reinforcers. S^2: a within-subject control stimulus not paired with O is included in each procedure. In Group 3, S^2 serves as its own control cue, which is expected to maintain responding in Phase 2 but not in Phase 1. R^1, R^2: two operant responses.

occurring. Group 3 solves this problem by establishing a conditioned reinforcer (S^1) in Phase 1, which is then maintained in Phase 2 while S^1 serves as a conditioned reinforcer for S^2.

If not accounted for, conditioned reinforcement can pose problems when assessing learning and behavior change. For example, investigators wanted to measure how well rats learn a spatial discrimination when a delay was inserted in between the correct spatial response and food delivery. In a T-maze, a rat traverses the straight alley of a T-maze, which dead-ends at a left and right arm. In some mazes, each arm has distinct features (visual pattern and texture) that extend into a goal box at the end of each arm. If the rat arrives at the correct arm, then after some delay (e.g., 60 s), food is delivered at the end of the arm. As discussed previously (see **4.2.1 Contiguity**), learning is negatively impacted by poor contiguity and, thus, any delay between making a response (e.g., making a left or right turn in the T-maze) and receiving the reinforcer should disrupt acquisition.

In mazes like this, delays do disrupt learning, but rats are able to learn the correct response with as much as a 10-min delay (Wolfe, 1934), even though the acquisition of another response, lever pressing, is eliminated by as little as a 1-min delay between the lever press and reinforcer (Dickinson et al., 1992). Conditioned reinforcement may play a role in circumventing the effects of a delay in the T-maze (Hull, 1943).

Take a moment to try and spot the conditioned reinforcer in this example and identify the procedure from those in Table 4.7 that would establish it. The conditioned reinforcer would be the distinct features of the arm associated with the correct response, and it most closely resembles Group 2 from the table. A correct response followed by a conditioned reinforcer (e.g., a particular arm color) mimics the effects of a primary reinforcer delivered immediately after the correct response. It is "as if" the rat received food after making the correct response simply by encountering the unique features of the arm (the conditioned reinforcer) paired with food.

To reduce the influence of conditioned reinforcement, the features that make the goal arm distinct from the incorrect arm could be eliminated. However, two cues remain, spatial and kinesthetic. The correct arm occupies a distinct location in space, and the kinesthetic feedback from making a turn in one direction is distinct from that of making a turn in the other direction.

A variation of a T-maze that eliminates the association between the direction of an arm choice and whether the arm was correct has been used to evaluate the role of conditioned reinforcement in maze performance (Figure 4.11-A; Grice, 1948). After traversing the start alley, the rats could enter a left or right arm, each with distinct brightness, either black or white. The brightness of the box indicated the correct arm, making this a visual, not spatial, discrimination. The choice arms led into a separate delay section of each arm where the rats

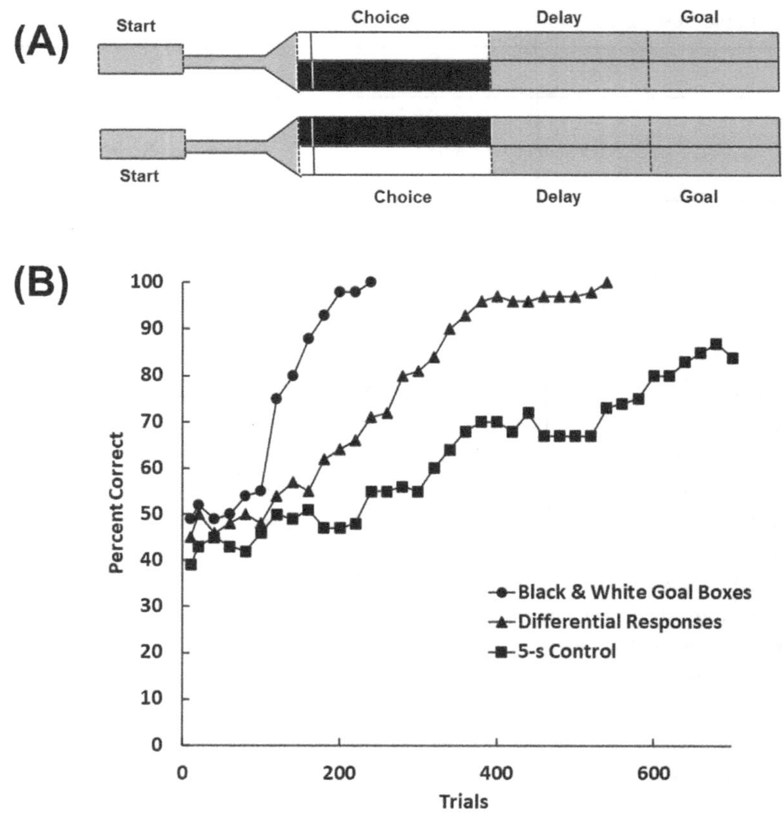

Figure 4.11 **Conditioned reinforcement. (A)** Maze used to train a visual discrimination. The start box was painted gray. The choice boxes were either white or black. In some trials, the black compartment required a right turn and in other trials a left turn. The delay and goal boxes were painted gray. Reinforcement for a correct response was delivered in the goal box. **(B)** The maze shown above was modified in a second experiment (see text). Correct responses were lowest in the 5-s delay control, greater when the response acquired secondary reinforcer value, and greatest when the brightness of the delay boxes matched those in the goal boxes so they acquired conditioned reinforcement value. (From Grice, 1948; reproduced with permission from the American Psychological Association.)

were contained for some delay before a door opened to the goal box. The delay sections of the correct and incorrect arms were gray, thus reducing or even eliminating secondary reinforcement due to distinct cues in the arms preceding reinforcement. Furthermore, kinesthetic conditioned reinforcers were eliminated by moving the position of the choice arms across trials, such that the correct arm was located to the left on some trials and to the right on others.

Using this procedure, rats were found to learn the discrimination with delays of 5 s or less, which are much shorter delays than the 10-min delay reported previously (Wolfe, 1934). A second experiment used a 5-s delay for all rats and manipulated the type of conditioned reinforcer present using a modified version of the maze shown in Figure 4.11-A (Grice, 1948).

In a control group, the conditions were the same as previously described. In a different group, the choice boxes and the goal boxes were painted white or black. The delay boxes for both responses were gray. Thus, the correct stimulus in the choice box, black, was the same as in the correct goal box, also black, which thus could acquire conditioned reinforcing value.

In yet another group, one of the choice arms required the rats to traverse a 15-degree incline, whereas the other arm included two blocks positioned in the choice box in a way that required the rat to go around them. The incline and the blocks were encountered equally often in the black and white arms, but only one of the distinct responses was the correct response.

The results of this second experiment indicated that the control group acquired the discrimination in a median of 580 trials, whereas the group exposed to different responses (incline vs. blocks) required 295 trials, and the group exposed to the black and white stimuli also in the goal box required 155 trials (Figure 4.11-B). Thus, pairings the black and white stimuli with the appropriate outcome in the goal box resulted in the stimuli being effective conditioned reinforcers. Similarly, a unique response paired with food acted as an effective conditioned reinforcer, thus facilitating acquisition. This result suggests that the sensory feedback from making a response can act as an effective conditioned reinforcer.

Thus, conditioned reinforcers can facilitate acquisition by bridging the temporal delay between a response and delivery of a primary reinforcer. Clicker training is used to train animals for various purposes, including as service dogs and to receive needed medicine or vaccinations without tranquilizers in animals kept in captivity at zoos and rescue centers (Pryor, 2002). Clicker training proceeds as in Group 2, Table 4.7. The animal performs a target behavior, a single click is produced by a handheld device, and a treat is delivered as soon as possible. Clicker training raises another important issue. Competing behaviors will be reinforced by occurring in proximity to the primary reinforcer. Delivering the clicker immediately after the target behavior reduces the likelihood that competing, nontarget behaviors would be reinforced.

There is general agreement about a few properties of conditioned reinforcement (Kelleher & Gollub, 1962). First, the effectiveness of a conditioned reinforcer is determined by the intensity of the primary reinforcer, the frequency of pairings with the primary reinforcer, and the interval between the conditioned reinforcer and primary reinforcer. As in Group 3, Table 4.7, extended chains can be established by pairing a neutral stimulus with a conditioned reinforcer. Second, conditioned reinforcers require continued pairings with a primary reinforcer to maintain their value. Third, conditioned reinforcers can be established by pairing with the delivery of an appetitive stimulus or the removal of an aversive stimulus. Finally, conditioned reinforcers are subject to generalization. Stimuli resembling the conditioned reinforcer will have behavioral effects proportional to their similarity (e.g., "good job" and "great work").

These properties highlight the distinction between a conditioned reinforcer and a marking stimulus. A ***marking stimulus*** is presented immediately after the correct and incorrect responses and then again immediately before reinforcement and nonreinforcement. In a spatial or visual discrimination, a marking stimulus facilitates acquisition when there is a temporal delay between the target response and the outcome, just as in conditioned reinforcement.

Lieberman et al. (1979) trained rats on a visual discrimination in an alley maze with a 1-min delay between the correct response and reinforcement. In the marking group, the rats were picked up and moved to the delay box after correct and incorrect responses and then again picked up and moved from the delay to the goal box. In the control group, rats ran unaided into the delay and start box. Rats in the marking group learned the task with the 1-min delay, but rats in the control group never performed above chance.

Visual and auditory stimuli also serve as marking stimuli. Marking stimuli are effective because they increase the salience of a response. When parents overreact to a toddler saying a curse word ("What did he say?!"), they may not reinforce or punish but inadvertently mark the verbal behavior such that it becomes more salient to the toddler. Whereas marking stimuli act on the salience of an action, conditioned reinforcers seem to promote S→R learning as the effectiveness of a conditioned reinforcer is unimpaired by devaluation of the outcome with which it was paired (Parkinson et al., 2005).

4.3.5 Operant contingencies

Most previous descriptions of operant conditioning have emphasized the case in which a response such as lever pressing or running leads to an outcome such as food. Under many conditions, R→O pairings lead to an increase in the amplitude, frequency, or probability of the response. But this represents only one of several possible arrangements, all having some influence on behavior.

A more complete view of operant procedures distinguishes between appetitive and aversive outcomes and between the presentation and the removal of the outcome contingent on the occurrence of a response (Table 4.8). *Appetitive reinforcers* support instrumental behavior when their presentation is contingent on the occurrence of a response (R→O). By contrast, *aversive reinforcers* support instrumental behavior when their removal is contingent on the occurrence of the response (R→noO).

Food, water, and electric shocks are easily classified as appetitive or aversive, but other outcomes cannot be easily assigned to one of these categories a priori. For example, rats acquired a lever-pressing response reinforced by the delivery of a weak electric current to a deep brain location (Olds & Milner, 1954). Moreover, some responses that prevented stimulation of other brain areas also increased in frequency. Thus, brain stimulation can produce either appetitive or aversive reinforcement effects. The attribution of hedonic properties to brain structures was possible because of the effects of response-contingent intracranial stimulation.

4.3.5.1 Positive reinforcement

In *positive reinforcement* (Table 4.8), the occurrence of a response is paired with the occurrence of the outcome (R→O) and the absence of the response is paired with the absence of the outcome (noR→noO). In the runway procedure, animals learn to move from a start

Table 4.8 Operant contingencies

Name	*Outcome*	*Contingencies*	*Response change*
Positive reinforcement	Appetitive	R→O | noR→noO	Increase
Punishment	Aversive	R→O | noR→noO	Decrease
Omission training	Appetitive	R→noO | noR→O	Decrease
Escape conditioning	Aversive, appetitive	R→Ooff | noR→O	Increase
Avoidance conditioning	Aversive, appetitive	R→noO | noR→O	Increase

Note. Reinforcers or outcomes (O) are characterized in terms of external events such as food (appetitive) and shock (aversive). In each case, the arrangement involves one outcome when the response (R) occurs and another when it fails to occur (noR). In escape, "Ooff" implies that the reinforcer is terminated. In avoidance, "noO" implies that the aversive reinforcer is averted.

to a goal box to obtain food or water. In a Skinner box, animals press a lever that results in the delivery of an outcome. Positive reinforcement usually increases response frequency or strength.

Early in training, positive reinforcement increases the probability of several responses, including the target response. As training continues, response variability is reduced, only to reemerge when reinforcement conditions change (Antonitis, 1951). This effect of operant reinforcement on response variability permits the development of new skills from behavioral precursors, a process called *shaping*. In shaping a target response (e.g., teaching a rat to run in circles), the experimenter starts by defining a remote precursor (e.g., turn the head to a side) and reinforce it consistently until the response increases in frequency. Then, the experimenter may require an additional response before a reinforcer is again delivered (e.g., a head turn plus forward locomotion). The target behavior emerges gradually as a function of such differential reinforcement.

Positive reinforcement can also generate response variability. Pryor et al. (1969) used positive reinforcement to generate novel jumping behaviors in a porpoise (*Steno bredanensis*). Pigeons trained to peck eight times across two keys, in any sequence, learned to emit novel sequences, different from the previous 50 sequences! Yoked controls receiving the same reward frequency but independently of sequence novelty exhibited lower response variability (Page & Neuringer, 1985).

4.3.5.2 Punishment

In ***punishment*** (Table 4.8), an instrumental response is followed by an aversive outcome. Whereas electrical discharges can be seen as artificial stimuli, the pain they induce is the efficient cause of this aversive reinforcer. Likely counterparts of laboratory experiments on punishment using electric shocks are predator–prey encounters and territorial aggression among conspecifics (Stamps, 1998). Punishment can suppress behavior, but its effectiveness depends upon special conditions.

Experiments with pigeons (Azrin & Holz, 1966) and rats (Church, 1969) have identified some factors that facilitate the effects of punishment on behavior. In a typical experiment, a response is first shaped and maintained with positive reinforcement (e.g., Lever Pressing→Food) and subsequently exposed to punishment (e.g., Lever Pressing→Shock). The degree of response suppression depends on the following factors:

- Intense and long shocks introduced with their maximum intensity from the outset of punishment are more effective than a gradual increase in shock intensity.
- Even short temporal delays between the response and the punishing stimulus make punishment less effective.
- Partial punishment is less effective than continuous punishment.

4.3.5.3 Omission

Omission (Table 4.8) prevents or postpones the occurrence of a reward. In a runway procedure, approaching the goal is rewarded only if the animal takes longer than some minimum amount of time (Logan, 1960). Operant responses decrease in frequency when omission contingencies are implemented, but whether a response will be sensitive to omission is difficult to anticipate *a priori*. Pavlovian responses—characterized by control by stimulus–stimulus relations, rather than any relation between behavior and its consequences—are resistant to omission training.

4.3.5.4 *Escape*

In *escape conditioning* (Table 4.8) the response removes an aversive stimulus (e.g., shock, water immersion, lighted surface). In the water maze, the animal is conditioned to escape from immersion in water by climbing on a platform (Morris, 1984). There are two sources of reinforcement in escape procedures: the termination of the aversive reinforcer (*negative reinforcement*) and a safety period that follows the response (*positive reinforcement*). Just as food is rewarding when hungry, safety is rewarding in the presence of threat or pain. Consistent with an appetitive interpretation, escape conditioning is affected by anticipatory factors. Animals learn to escape faster when the transition in shock intensity (Campbell & Kraeling, 1953) or water temperature (Woods et al., 1964) is Large→Small than when it is Large→Intermediate. Thus, anticipating a larger aversive reduction increases the rewarding effect of escaping into relative safety.

4.3.5.5 *Avoidance*

In *avoidance conditioning*, the response prevents an aversive event that would otherwise occur (Table 4.8). The aversive event must be signaled by a discriminative stimulus, S^D, whether an external stimulus or the trace of a previous event. As in escape conditioning, sources of reinforcement include the termination of the S^D (negative reinforcement) and the presence of safety signals provided by the response itself (positive reinforcement). Several procedures are used to study avoidance conditioning:

- In one-way active avoidance, an S^D in one compartment signals that crossing to an adjacent compartment will prevent the shock. One compartment is paired with shock delivery and the other with safety. One-way avoidance is facilitated by intense shocks and long safety periods.
- In two-way active avoidance, an S^D signals the impending presentation of shock unless the animal moves to another compartment. Both compartments are paired with shock and safety in different trials. This procedure can induce conflict because the animal must approach a compartment previously paired with shock or leave a compartment that was once safe.
- In discriminative avoidance, the animal chooses between a safe option (e.g., right arm of a T-maze) and one paired with shock (e.g., the left arm).
- In Sidman avoidance, shocks are delivered at a constant rate (e.g., every 15 s), but a response postpones the following upcoming shock (e.g., by 45 s). Traces of previous responses and shocks provide information about the forthcoming shocks. Sidman avoidance usually generates steady response rates.
- In passive (or inhibitory) avoidance, a response (e.g., entering a dark compartment, stepping off a platform) is punished by shock in training and the latency to emit that response in the absence of shock increases when tested usually at least one day after training.

As in escape conditioning, anticipatory processes also play a role in avoidance conditioning. In a one-way avoidance task, rats were trained to move to a safe compartment in the presence of an S^D to avoid shock. One group was maintained in safety for 30 s, whereas a control group was kept in safety for only 1 s. After avoidance acquisition, the safety period was unexpectedly reduced from 30 s to 1 s, whereas safety was maintained at 1 s in the control group. Downshifted animals exhibited a deterioration of avoidance behavior (Cándido et al., 1992). This effect is analogous to a deterioration of behavior that occurs after a downshift in food magnitude or quality (Flaherty, 1996). Safety and food downshifts also seem to depend on the same neurochemical mechanisms, as they are both attenuated by the administration of anxiolytics (Torres et al., 1994). The violation of an expectation (of longer safety or larger food reward) shows that behavior is regulated by anticipatory processes.

4.4 Inhibitory conditioning

4.4.1 Summation and retardation tests

Some Pavlovian training procedures lead to a stable form of response inhibition. In ***inhibitory conditioning*** procedures, the outcome occurs in the absence of the signal. Predictors for the explicit absence of food can redirect foraging behavior or engage other behaviors. Several procedures have been devised to capture this basic form of learning (Table 4.9). In ***conditioned inhibition training***, a stimulus is paired with the outcome except when it is accompanied by a second stimulus, which thus becomes a signal for outcome omission (i.e., A+/AB-). In ***differential conditioning***, one stimulus is paired with the outcome whereas another is presented alone (i.e., A+/B-). In ***backward conditioning***, the outcome precedes the stimulus, which therefore signals an outcome-free period (i.e., +→B-). In the ***explicitly unpaired procedure***, unsignaled reinforcers occur in a particular context except when a signal is presented (i.e., +, B-); thus, this signal predicts outcome omission.

Excitatory conditioning and inhibitory conditioning are in opposition. A CS signaling the presentation of a US usually elicits a response. A CS signaling US omission may elicit a specific response, such as withdrawal from the location where food would otherwise be delivered, but often, the recorded response does not change during the presentation of the inhibitor. This creates two problems for any demonstration of inhibitory conditioning: detection (how can it be revealed?) and validation (is it inhibitory conditioning or something else?).

4.4.1.1 Detection

In some cases, a stimulus signaling outcome omission induces a response opposite to that induced by a stimulus signaling outcome presentation. If a signal for food elicits goal tracking, then one for food omission would tend to elicit goal withdrawal (Papini & White, 1994).

Table 4.9 Examples of procedures involving reinforcer omission

Procedure	*Training*	*Test*
Conditioned inhibition training	Tone→Food, ToneLight-only	Light?
Differential conditioning	Tone→Food, Light-only	Light?
Backward conditioning	Food→Light	Light?
Explicitly unpaired procedure	Context→Food, ContextLight-only	Light?

Note. In these procedures, the Light can acquire inhibitory strength because it informs that Food will not be available for some time. Conditioned inhibition, backward conditioning, and the explicitly unpaired procedure can lead to the Light acquiring inhibitory strength, whereas differential conditioning results in the light acquiring little-to-no inhibitory strength.

However, an inhibitory signal may induce no obvious change in behavior. In these cases, two indirect tests based on the opposition between excitatory and inhibitory conditioning have been proposed to reveal inhibitory conditioning (Rescorla, 1969):

In the *summation test*, the presumed inhibitor is compounded with a known exciter. Since excitation and inhibition are opposites, the compound should elicit less response than the exciter alone. A common inhibitor is the symbol of a circle with a diagonal line through it; such a sign that includes a sketch of a mobile phone is expected to inhibit phone use (phone use would be permitted in the absence of the diagonal line).

In the *retardation test*, pairing of the presumed inhibitor with an outcome should retard the acquisition of excitatory conditioning relative to a control stimulus. A driver used to stop at a red light may require extensive training to learn to instead drive forward through a red light.

Consider the appetitive experiment with rats described in Table 4.10 (Pearce & Kaye, 1985). In the experimental group, a Tone was followed by Click and Food (Tone→Click→Food),

Table 4.10 A demonstration of inhibitory conditioning

Group	*Training*	*Test*
Summation:		
Exp	Tone→Click→Food, ToneLight-only	Click vs. ClickLight
Con	Tone-only, Click→Food, ToneLight-only	Click vs. ClickLight
Retardation:		
Exp	Tone→Click→Food, ToneLight-only	Light→Food
Con	Tone-only, Click→Food, ToneLight-only	Light→Food

Note. This design involves a variation of conditioned inhibition training. The exciter is the Tone and the inhibitor is the Light. In the experimental group (Exp), the Light presented together with the Tone (which predicts Food) is not reinforced. Therefore, the Light informs that the expected Food will not occur (the food is expected because of the Tone). In the control group (Con) the Tone is presented by itself, and thus, it does not predict Food. Notice that both groups receive the same number of presentations of each stimulus (Tone, Click, Light, and Food) but differ in the relationship between the Tone and Food.

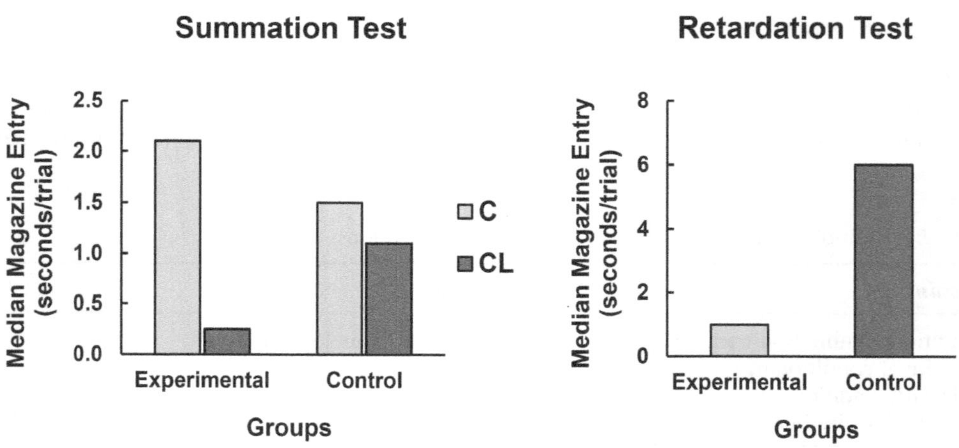

Figure 4.12 **A demonstration of inhibitory conditioning.** Results of the experiment described in Table 4.10 demonstrating inhibitory conditioning using summation and retardation tests. (From Pearce & Kaye, 1985; reproduced with permission from the American Psychological Association.)

and thus the Tone and Click became signals for Food. In other trials, a ToneLight simultaneous compound was never followed by Food. Did the Light become an inhibitory signal of Food omission? The control group received the same stimuli, except that the Tone was unpaired with respect to the Click→Food pairing. Notice that both groups received equal exposure to all the stimuli but differed in the relationship between the Tone and Click→Food: either serial or unpaired. After training, half the animals were exposed to a summation test and half to a retardation test (Figure 4.12).

The summation test showed greater disruption of goal tracking on ClickLight trials than on Click trials in the experimental group than in the control group. The presumed inhibitor (Light) reduced responding to a known exciter (Click). The retardation test indicated a lower level of goal tracking to the Light in the experimental than in the control group (acquisition to the Light was retarded). Thus, the treatment administered to the Light in the experimental group (but not in the control group) led to inhibitory conditioning.

4.4.1.2 Validation

To determine that a signal that seems to suppress behavior has developed inhibitory conditioning requires control conditions that discard any other mechanism that could lead to response suppression in the absence of inhibitory conditioning (Papini & Bitterman, 1993). The following are some of these alternative mechanisms:

- *Reduced generalized excitation.* Excitation generalizing from the exciter to the inhibitor will tend to be reduced in the experimental condition by nonreinforced presentations of the inhibitor. This is especially problematic if the control signal is a novel stimulus at the time of testing. Key question: Does the experimental group show more inhibition than the control group or less excitation? Solution: Use a control stimulus with a similar nonreinforcement history as that of the presumed inhibitor.
- *Differential generalization of excitation.* What matters is not the identity of the stimuli (Light, Click) but their relationship to the outcome. Key question: Would the results provide evidence for inhibitory conditioning if the Click rather than the Light had been used as the inhibitor? Solution: Counterbalance the stimuli across subjects, such that Click may be the exciter and Light the inhibitor for some animals and vice versa for others.
- *Attentional enhancement.* Suppose animals are given conditioned inhibition training involving Light→Food and LightTone-only trials. If animals respond more to the Light alone than to the LightTone compound, then they are attending to the Tone because the discrimination is unsolvable if the Tone is ignored. Key question: Is responding to the exciter in the summation test reduced by inhibitory conditioning or by increased attention to the inhibitor? Solution: Evidence of retardation of acquisition after the same acquisition training would suggest that training produced inhibitory conditioning; enhanced attention cannot lead to both summation and retardation.
- *Attentional decrement.* Nonreinforced presentations of a signal may reduce attention—latent inhibition. Key question: Is excitatory acquisition by the inhibitor retarded by its inhibitory strength or by reduced attention? Solution: Provide evidence of both summation and retardation after the same acquisition training; attentional decrement cannot account for both effects.
- *Contextual blocking.* Unsignaled reinforcers can condition the context and thus retard acquisition to the signal. Key question: Is retardation produced by the inhibitory strength of the signal or by contextual blocking? Solution: Run the retardation test in a different context; inhibitory conditioning to a CS should transfer across contexts.

- *Stimulus generalization decrement.* In a summation test, responding to the exciter plus the inhibitor may be suppressed not because of inhibition but because the exciter is perceived as different from the stimulus experienced in acquisition when it was presented alone. Key question: Is the exciter modulated by the inhibitor or just perceived as a different stimulus? Solution: Arrange a summation test in which the exciter for both experimental (with the presumed inhibitor) and control conditions are tested in compound with a second stimulus to equate perceptual similarity.

These alternatives challenge demonstrations of inhibitory conditioning because these processes (e.g., generalization, contextual blocking, etc.) have been independently corroborated. These problems illustrate the complexity of demonstrating cause-and-effect relationships in experimental psychology. There are important implications for failures of control. Imagine developing a therapy for a disorder without understanding the mechanism by which the therapy works.

A therapeutic technique for posttraumatic stress known as eye movement desensitization and reprocessing (EMDR) requires participants to synchronize their eye movements while retelling a traumatic event, a training that may inhibit traumatic memories. There are several possible mechanisms for patient improvement: the synchronization of eye movements and retelling of the traumatic event, just the retelling of the event, the placebo effect, and some interaction of these factors. The use of proper controls can help identify whether EMDR provides an advantage greater than any other alternative. Thus, proper demonstrations of inhibitory conditioning, as well as therapeutic techniques, require appropriate controls and convergent evidence from two or more tests.

4.4.2 Neurobiology of inhibitory conditioning

The inhibition of fear is important in its own right and also because of implications for emotional disorders in humans, such as phobia and posttraumatic stress disorder. Signals for shock omission, as in the explicitly unpaired procedure (see Table 4.9), have traditionally been thought of as *safety signals.* Given what is known about the neurobiology of fear conditioning (see Figure 4.8), one would expect that a signal for fear inhibition would reduce activity in the amygdala. An experiment with mice (*Mus musculus*) trained in the explicitly unpaired procedure showed that neural activity in the lateral amygdala (LA) is inhibited by the presentation of a Tone acting as a safety signal (Rogan et al., 2005). Such inhibition coincides with the arrival of information from the auditory thalamus. Simultaneously, the safety signal increased neural activity in the caudate-putamen area (dorsal striatum). This area is not essential for fear conditioning but is important for approach responses. Interestingly, behavioral experiments demonstrated that a signal for shock omission can also induce approach responses (Leclerc & Reberg, 1980). Thus, a safety signal that inhibits fear-related responses, such as freezing, can also induce appetitive responses by reducing neural activity in the amygdala while increasing it in the striatum.

The reduction in amygdala activity during the presentation of a safety signal appears to be under cortical control. The integrity of the insular cortex is crucial for fear inhibition. Temporary and reversible inactivation of the insular cortex eliminated the effects of a safety signal on social freezing in animals previously exposed to inescapable shocks (Christianson et al., 2011). Interestingly, the insular cortex is compromised in individuals suffering from posttraumatic stress disorder (Hughes & Shin, 2011), suggesting that a homologous circuit underlies fear inhibition in mammals.

4.5 Schedules of reinforcement

The R→O contingency is rarely perfect in the real world. This is described by *schedules of reinforcement* (Ferster & Skinner, 1957; Skinner, 1938). In the Skinner box situation, an animal (typically a rat or pigeon) receives access to a manipulandum (a lever or a localized light) that, if operated behaviorally (lever pressing or key pecking), leads to the delivery of an outcome (pellets or grain). In *free-operant training*, the animal can emit the operant response at any moment during the session. In *discrete-trial training*, response contingencies are separated by intertrial intervals and are typically characterized by the presentation of S^Ds. Many of the experiments reviewed previously involved discrete-trial procedures.

The simplest schedules are *continuous reinforcement* (every response is reinforced) and *extinction* (every response is nonreinforced). Between these two extremes lie a variety of schedules in which not every response has the same outcome—*partial reinforcement*. Two basic ways to schedule partial reinforcement are as a function of responses emitted and as a function of time. Moreover, simple schedules can be combined to yield complex schedules of reinforcement. Table 4.11 describes common schedules and their asymptotic behavioral effects, and Figure 4.13 presents an idealized version of asymptotic behavior in some basic schedules.

Table 4.11 Some examples of schedules of reinforcement

Schedule (acronym)	*Definition and main behavioral effects*
Fixed Ratio (FR)	Reinforcers for "x" responses, with "x" having always the same value. Well-established behavior involves a postreinforcement pause, followed by a high response rate. Example: In FR 10, every 10th response is reinforced.
Variable Ratio (VR)	Reinforcers for "x" responses, with "x" varying from cycle to cycle. VR schedules lead to steady, high response rates. Example: In VR 10, on average, the 10th response is reinforced.
Differential Reinforcement of High Rates (DRH)	Reinforcers for a response provided it occurs within a certain time since the previous response. This leads to high response rates. Example: "x" number of responses must occur within "y" seconds to obtain a reinforcer.
Differential Reinforcement of Low Rates (DRL)	Reinforcers for a response provided it occurs after a minimum time since the previous response. DRL schedules lead to low response rates. Example: In DRL 10 s, a reinforcer is delivered only if no responses have occurred during the last 10 s.
Progressive Ratio (PR)	Reinforcers for "x" responses, with "x" increasing according to some defined value. PR schedules are used to study reinforcer value. Example: In PR with step = 5, reinforcers are delivered after 1, 6, 11, 16, 21 . . . responses.
Fixed Interval (FI)	Reinforcers for the first response occurring after a fixed time ends. Each interval starts from the delivery of a reinforcer. Postreinforcement pause, followed by gradual increase in response rate (called the *FI scallop*). Example: In FI 10 s, the first response emitted after 10 s is reinforced.
Variable Interval (VI)	Reinforcers for a response occurring after a variable time ends. VI schedules lead to steady, intermediate response rates. Example: In VI 10 s, the first response after an interval averaging 10 s is reinforced.
Fixed Time (FT) and Variable Time (VT)	Analogous to FI and VI, except there is no response requirement (i.e., Pavlovian). Time schedules are used to control the effects of reinforcer distribution on behavior. Example: FT 60 s delivers a reinforcer every 60 s.

(*Continued*)

Table 4.11 (Continued)

Schedule (acronym)	*Definition and main behavioral effects*
Progressive Interval (PI)	Analogous to PR, except based on an increasing time interval. PI schedules simulate time-based food depletion. Example: In PR with step = 10 s, reinforcers are delivered to the first response registered after 1 s, 11 s, 21 s . . . etc.
Multiple (MULT)	At least two simple schedules, presented in succession, each with a correlated stimulus and each ending in reinforcement. MULT schedules are used to study behavioral contrast between different reinforcement conditions. Example: A MULT FI 10 s FR 10 delivers a reinforcer according to each simple schedule.
Mixed (MIX)	The same as MULT schedules except for the lack of correlated stimuli for each simple schedule (i.e., the same discriminative stimulus for all components).
Chain (CHAIN)	Responding on a simple schedule under a correlated stimulus is reinforced by a transition to a second schedule with a different correlated stimulus. The last schedule reinforces a response.
Tandem (TAND)	The same as a CHAIN schedule, except the same stimulus is presented in all the components. Comparing performance in CHAIN and TAND schedules has been used to study conditioned reinforcement since the stimulus transition in CHAIN schedules is missing in TAND schedules, but the schedules are otherwise identical. Example: In a TAND FI 10 s FR 10, the 10th response after 10 s have elapsed is reinforced.
Concurrent (CONC)	Two responses are available simultaneously, each with its own schedule and each providing reinforcement. Different locations provide contrasting stimuli. Used to study the relationship between responses and reinforcers, as in matching experiments.

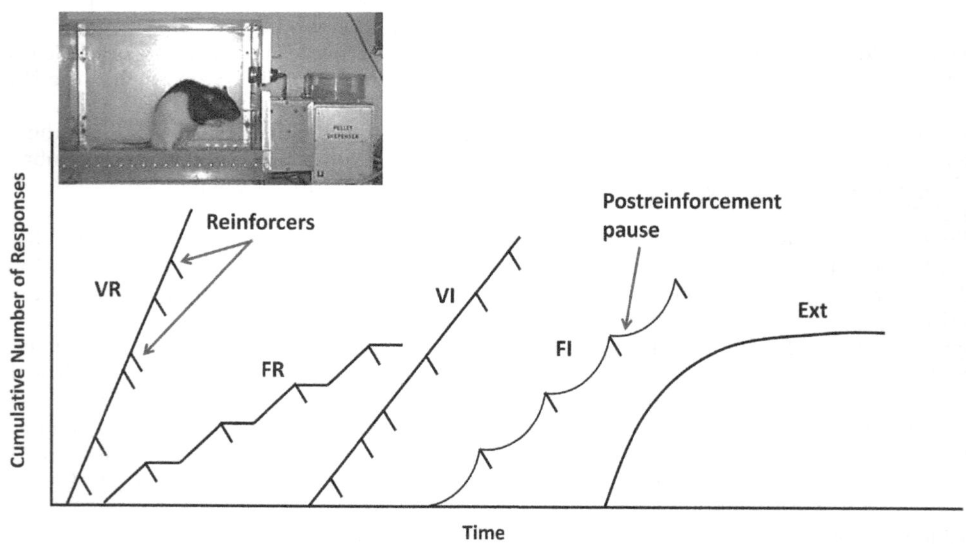

Figure 4.13 **Idealized representation of asymptotic operant behavior maintained by basic schedules of reinforcement.** Variable schedules maintain a constant response rate (VR: variable ratio; VI: variable interval). Fixed schedules (FR: fixed ratio; FI: fixed interval) yield a postreinforcement pause. In extinction (Ext), nonreinforcement leads to gradual response reduction (although the function presented here is an idealized version). (Photograph by M. R. Papini.)

Schedules can be arranged to mimic natural situations. Time-based schedules are analogous to food resources that either take time to replenish after consumption (a flower's nectar) or appear according to a certain cycle (prey active at night). Response-based schedules resemble a foraging situation in which an animal is collecting food in a patch. The higher the rate of responding (searching in a patch), the higher the rate of reinforcement; but, of course, the rate of reinforcement also determines the rate of responding. The causal relationship between responses and reinforcers is reciprocal. Not surprisingly, the allocation of responses and the obtained reinforcements often match, so it is deviations from such matching that are interesting (Poling et al., 2011).

Discrete-trial procedures break down the reciprocal causality between responding and reinforcement, making it possible to manipulate probability of reinforcement as an independent variable. In one experiment (Wilson et al., 1964), rhesus monkeys (*Macaca mulatta*) were trained in a Red/Blue discrimination in which one alternative yielded food on 70% of the trials and the other on the remaining 30% (70:30 problem). Both types of trials were intermixed randomly, and errors led to a correction procedure that kept the probability of reinforcement for each alternative as scheduled. Under such conditions, animals exhibited ***maximization***, that is, they chose the alternative paired with the largest reinforcement probability in most of the trials. Monkeys did show a tendency toward ***matching*** on 50:50 problems, when the alternatives were equally reinforced. Interestingly, this matching originated from a tendency to avoid on one trial the side rewarded on the preceding trial. Sequential effects suggest that matching can be a byproduct of local processes operating across trials (Shimp, 1982).

Some schedules of reinforcement have specific properties. For example, the ***fixed-interval scallop*** involves a patterned distribution of responses that occurs after extensive training on FI schedules. Animals typically show response suppression immediately after reinforcement—postreinforcement pause—followed by a transition to a higher response rate. The length of the postreinforcement pause tends to be directly proportional to the size of the temporal interval. ***Interval timing***, the ability to estimate temporal intervals in the order of seconds to hours, plays an important role in the development of the FI scallop. In a FI schedule, the highest degree of temporal control is represented by responding immediately upon the termination of the interval, whereas the poorest is represented by responding at a constant rate. Comparative research shows a higher degree of temporal control in rats, woodmice, cats, and monkeys (mammals) than in pigeons, doves, turtles, and tilapia fish (Lejeune & Wearden, 1991). The evolutionary significance of these species differences remains elusive. Chapter 8 reviews interval timing in detail.

4.6 What is a reinforcer?

Reinforcers are generally conceptualized as stimuli with biological relevance to an organism. In Pavlovian conditioning, a reinforcer (called a US) can be said to strengthen the value of a CS with which it is paired. But USs also usually have an observable behavioral consequence: the UR. For example, food elicits not only approach, but once inside the oral cavity, food elicits salivation, chewing, swallowing, and similar consummatory behaviors. Would food have reinforcing value if these behaviors were prevented? An experiment with pigeons looked at this problem.

Pigeons were first pretrained to consume grain from a lighted hopper. Once pecking at grain was established, pigeons were exposed to a key light paired with the activation of the hopper. However, although pigeons were allowed to see the food as during pretraining, a translucent piece of plastic prevented them from consuming the food. They still developed conditioned key pecking to the key light, much as they did when food was fully accessible (Zentall & Hogan, 1975). Thus, having learned the conditions that facilitated access to grain during pretraining, just observation of the grain was sufficient to shape a new response—pecking at the key light. Of course, this could just be an example of second-order conditioning or secondary reinforcement discussed previously in this chapter. In either case, a reinforcer seemed to have been a stimulus in this case, whether because it was directly accessible or because key pecking was paired with the hopper light as a conditioned reinforcer.

There is a view of a reinforcer that looks at it not as a stimulus but as a highly likely response. According to this idea, pecking at food has a higher probability of occurrence if access to food was restricted for the pigeon than pecking at a key light. Thus, a response that has a lower probability of occurrence, L, can be reinforced (i.e., increase in strength) if it is followed by a response that has a higher probability of occurrence, H, provided that L is closely followed by H in time. This is called *Premack's principle* (Premack, 1959).

To derive this idea, the independent rates of responses were first determined. Cebus monkeys, which have a tendency to handle and operate different types of objects, were exposed to an apparatus that had different objects that could be manipulated (Premack, 1959). The responses were (1) pressing a lever, (2) operating a hinged door, and (3) pushing back a door. These responses were freely available to the monkeys during several sessions to determine the independent rate of occurrence. Under these conditions, the mean rates of responses for these three actions were 50, 20, and 100 responses, respectively.

When two of these responses were available simultaneously, but without an explicit operant contingency, their frequencies did not change much from what was observed when only one response was available at a time. When lever pressing was closely followed by door pushing, then the frequency of lever pressing went from 50 responses to 120 responses. When door pushing was no longer contingent on pressing the lever (i.e., extinction of lever pressing), lever pressing decreased in frequency until reaching a rate lower than that recorded during independent testing in a few sessions.

A second experiment used first-grade children to test this notion of reinforcement (Premack, 1959). Children had access to a pinball machine and chocolate candies. When there was no contingency between these responses, some children preferred the pinball machine while others preferred the candy (62% to 39%, respectively, called "manipulators" and "eaters"). When manipulators had access to candy followed by access to the pinball machine, eating candy increased in every child. However, the reversed contingency (pinball to candy) had little or no effect on eating candy. Similar results, although less dramatic, were observed for eaters.

As can be suspected, Premack's principle has been extensively used in applied settings. In clinical settings with children, one advantage of this procedure is that it uses actions that are already present in the behavioral repertoire. These activities can also be used to encourage active engagement with a number of behaviors. However, many studies failed to provide data on the independent frequency of the behaviors used, and in other cases, the conclusions were qualitative rather than quantitative (Herrod et al., 2022). Still, Premack's principle remains a more active area of enquiry in applied settings than in basic research.

4.7 Situational generality of associative learning

This chapter emphasized the acquisition process as studied mostly in rodents and birds, but conditioning phenomena are also general across training situations. Classifying a phenomenon as an instance of conditioning implies that most, if not all, of the properties of

Table 4.12 Common conditioning tasks

Pavlovian conditioning				
Preparation	*CS*	*US*	*Measured CR*	*Species*
Salivary conditioning	Visual, auditory	Food	Drops of saliva	Dogs
Autoshaping	Visual	Food	Key pecking	Pigeons
Autoshaping	Lever presentation	Food	Lever pressing	Rats
Appetitive training	Visual, auditory	Food	Magazine entry	Rats
Eyelid conditioning	Visual, auditory	Air puff	Eyelid closure	Rabbits
Conditioned suppression	Visual, auditory	Shock	Suppression ratio	Rats
Fear conditioning	Tone, context	Shock	Freezing	Rats
Conditioned taste aversion	Flavor	Toxin	Consumption	Rats
Operant conditioning				
Preparation	*S^D*	*O*	*R*	*Species*
Runway	Spatial cues	Food	Latency	Rats
T-maze	Spatial, visual	Food	Percent correct	Rats
Skinner box	Visual, auditory	Food	Key pecking	Pigeons
Skinner box	Visual, auditory	Food	Lever pressing	Rats
Active avoidance	Visual, auditory	Shock	Latency	Rats

conditioning apply to that phenomenon, thus leading to new discoveries, theoretical integration, and applied interventions. The paradigms included in Table 4.12 vary in their components, but they exhibit the same acquisition phenomena. What about other stimuli, outcomes, and responses?

4.7.1 *Interoceptive signals*

Visual and auditory stimuli can be easily manipulated and precisely defined, but conditioning is supported by more unusual stimuli. Rats can be trained to use cues arising from different levels of food restriction as Pavlovian signals for shock. Thus, rats shocked after 0 h of food restriction but not after 24 h showed more freezing when tested after 0 h than after 24 h of food restriction; the opposite was the case when shocked after 24 h but not after 0 h of food restriction (Davidson et al., 1992).

Drug discrimination studies illustrate the ability of animals to discriminate between the internal cues induced by different drugs (Mombelli, 2022). Morphine-trained rats may respond to other opioids but not to nonopioid compounds. Studies involving internal states as S^Ds need to eliminate the potential role of cues that originate in distinct responses induced by the drugs or other procedures. A pigeon may behave differently when injected with cocaine versus pentobarbital, so that the sensory feedback generated by these distinct movements, rather than the internal states, may be discriminative stimuli for responding.

4.7.2 *Sexual reinforcement*

Pavlovian conditioning based on *sexual reinforcement* in both male and female quail (*Coturnix japonica*) has been extensively documented (Domjan & Gutiérrez, 2019). Quail are polygynous birds that exhibit a high frequency of mating behavior. Males exposed to a visual

Figure 4.14 **Sexual reinforcement.** Male Japanese quail (*Coturnix japonica*) develop sexual behavior by simple exposure to a model. Effective models include the taxidermically prepared head and neck section. These models act also as effective signals. (Photograph courtesy of Michael Domjan.)

stimulus (CS) paired with copulation with a receptive female (US) exhibit more goal tracking (approach to the area where the female is released) than controls receiving unpaired CS and US presentations. Sexual conditioning displays many properties of conventional preparations, including a CS→US interval gradient and second-order conditioning. For example, the goal-tracking response reaches its maximum strength with CS→US intervals of 30 s and becomes progressively weaker with intervals of up to 1,200 s (Akins et al., 1994). However, longer CS→US intervals support a more general search response. As in other cases, the absence of behavioral change does not imply the absence of conditioning.

Males develop copulatory behavior with exposure to a taxidermic model. Such predisposition indicates that processes other than classical conditioning contribute to the organization of sexual behavior in quail. Especially effective are models that include the head, neck, and body shape of a female (Figure 4.14). If such a model is used as a CS for a live female, copulatory responses increase even further. Sexual reinforcement in rats yields similar effects to those observed in other situations. In one experiment, male rats were preexposed to an Almond-scented pad (CS) and later given exposure to an Almond-scented female followed by Ejaculation (US). After five trials of preexposure to the CS, these males exhibited less preference for an Almond-scented female than controls that had received only one preexposure to the Almond odor (Quintana et al., 2018), an effect reminiscent of latent inhibition.

4.7.3 Conditioned immunomodulation

Classical conditioning also affects neural-immune interactions. The immune system includes a set of organs and functions that provide protection against pathogens. In one experiment, mice were administered conditioned taste aversion training in which access to Saccharin (CS) was followed by an injection of the drug cyclophosphamide (US)—a drug that induces sickness and leads to conditioned taste aversion. However, mice exposed to several CS→US pairings died at an unexpectedly high rate. Further research showed that cyclophosphamide also suppresses immune function. Thus, the signal had inadvertently acquired the ability to cause immunosuppression (Ader & Cohen, 1982).

Pavlovian conditioning can also enhance immune function. For example, mice administered cyclophosphamide in the presence of visual and auditory cues and later challenged with sheep red blood cells exhibited enhanced antibody production in the presence of the CS compared to controls (Krank & MacQueen, 1988). Cyclophosphamide initially suppresses immune function, but that suppression would eventually give way to an immune boost as the immune system recovers. With extensive training, the compensatory immune boost becomes conditioned to the audiovisual stimulus and results in a stronger antibody response than in controls after exposure to a novel immune threat. Since Pavlovian signals can suppress or enhance immune function, this phenomenon is known as conditioned immunomodulation.

4.7.4 Conditioning of allergies

Pavlovian conditioning also affects the development of allergies. This was suggested by a case study of a patient who was allergic to roses and exhibited symptoms even when exposed to an artificial rose. Experiments with rats (MacQueen et al., 1989) and humans (Gauci et al., 1994) suggest that signals of allergens that induce the release of enzymes from mast cells can, after some pairings, induce the release of the same enzymes.

4.7.5 Drug tolerance

The repeated administration of some drugs of abuse (e.g., heroin, cocaine, alcohol) results in the development of withdrawal symptoms after a period of abstinence. Withdrawal symptoms involve aversive feelings that promote relapse. Additionally, periodic drug administration results in the development of *drug tolerance*—requiring increasing doses to obtain the same result initially produced by a small dose. Stimuli present before and during drug administration can acquire control over these responses, causing withdrawal symptoms, cravings leading to relapse, and tolerance. Morphine tolerance has been explained in terms of Pavlovian conditioning (Siegel, 1999). The UR to morphine is hypoalgesia, which gives way to hyperalgesia as the drug is metabolized. The context signals the hypoalgesic effects of morphine (US) as well as the hyperalgesia that cancels it out. Tolerance is based on the development of a conditioned *compensatory response*. This compensatory response is both the UR induced by hypoalgesia and the compensatory CR induced by stimuli associated with the drug.

Pain sensitivity can be measured by placing a rat on a heated plate and recording the latency to lick a paw. Shorter latencies suggest more rapid pain perception. This hot-plate procedure helped demonstrate that morphine tolerance occurs because of conditioned hyperalgesia (Siegel et al., 1978). Rats experiencing the effects of morphine in a particular context exhibited shorter paw-lick latencies (and hence greater hyperalgesia) when subsequently exposed to the context alone compared to rats receiving unpaired exposure to context and morphine. Furthermore, rats made tolerant to large doses of heroin by pairing this drug with a context during many trials and later given the terminal dose (to which they had become tolerant) in a novel context were more likely to die than rats tested in the familiar environment (Siegel et al., 1982). Rats tested in the novel context were susceptible to the lethal effects of heroin because the novelty of the context prevented the activation of compensatory conditioned responses that would have reduced the effects of the drug (Siegel, 2016).

The examples reviewed in this section demonstrate the generality of Pavlovian conditioning across a spectrum of stimulus conditions, reinforcers, and response systems. Similar generality has been found in studies of instrumental conditioning. Conditioning mechanisms are so ubiquitous that their relevance to behavior, cognition, and physiology in a wide range of situations can hardly be overestimated.

Glossary

Acquisition Processes leading to the development of some neural record of experienced events that can potentially affect behavior.

Actions Outcome-dependent behaviors, sensitive to the outcome-devaluation test.

Activity-dependent synaptic plasticity Changes in the connection between two neurons resulting from their concurrent activation.

Alpha responses A response based on the same motor system as the conditioned response but occurring in the absence of pairings between the conditioned and unconditioned stimuli.

AMPA receptors A type of excitatory glutamate receptor. When associated with NMDA receptors in the same synapses, repeated stimulation of the synapse can lead to the synthesis of new AMPA receptors. This process is involved in some instances of synaptic plasticity underlying learning.

Appetitive reinforcers Reinforcers an organism is willing to invest time and effort to obtain.

Associative learning Establishing links between stimuli, reinforcers, and/or outcomes by experience.

Attentional decrement Acquired reduction in the processing of a stimulus. In latent inhibition, attentional decrement may originate in extensive nonreinforced presentations of a stimulus.

Attentional enhancement Acquired enhancement in the processing of a stimulus. In conditioned inhibition training (A+/AB-), discriminative behavior (more responding in A trials than in AB trials) can only be achieved if the presence of B is detected. This might increase attention to this stimulus.

Aversive reinforcers Reinforcers an organism is willing to invest time and effort to eliminate.

Avoidance conditioning Responses that postpone or prevent an aversive reinforcer. The aversive reinforcer occurs in the absence of a response.

Backward conditioning In Pavlovian conditioning, a procedure in which the unconditioned stimulus precedes in time the presentation of the conditioned stimulus.

Brain slice A technique involving a section of neural tissue maintained in a cell culture used to stimulate and record neural activity. This technique is used in demonstrations of long-term potentiation and depression.

Ceiling and floor effects Limits of behavior or of the dependent measure that do not allow for further changes in behavior to be recorded, either toward the top of the scale (ceiling) or the bottom of the scale (floor).

Coincidence detectors Neurons that respond to the contiguity between inputs arriving from different afferent pathways by increasing the strength of synaptic transmission.

Compensatory response Some Pavlovian conditioning procedures lead to a conditioned response that is opposite to the unconditioned response.

Conditioned or Secondary reinforcer A reinforcer whose value comes from conditioning experience, that is, a conditioned stimulus previously paired with an unconditioned stimulus.

Conditioned response (CR) In a Pavlovian conditioning procedure, the response to the conditioned stimulus that develops (i.e., it is absent in early trials) as a result of experiencing pairings between the conditioned and unconditioned stimuli.

Conditioned stimulus (CS) In a Pavlovian conditioning procedure, a signal for the occurrence or omission of another stimulus (a conditioned or unconditioned stimulus).

Conditioned immunomodulation Ability of signals for drugs that affect immune system activity to produce anticipatory immune responses. Such signals can enhance or suppress immune activity depending on the effects of the drug used in the experiment.

Conditioned inhibition training A Pavlovian conditioning procedure in which a stimulus is reinforced by itself (A→US) but not when presented with a second stimulus (AB-only). The goal is to demonstrate that the added stimulus (B) evokes inhibitory conditioning.

Conditioning Procedures used to study associative learning.

Contextual conditioning Conditioning to the static features of the environment in which training takes place.

Contextual variables Factors affecting behavior in learning experiments, including sensory-perceptual, motor, and motivational factors, that are not related to learning.

Contiguity When two or more stimuli are adjacent in time or space, they are said to be contiguous. Contiguity is a key factor in associative learning.

Continuous reinforcement Every conditioned stimulus (Pavlovian) or every response (operant) is paired with an outcome.

Delay or forward conditioning A Pavlovian conditioning procedure involving the presentation of a conditioned stimulus followed by (and often overlapping with) an unconditioned stimulus.

Differential conditioning In Pavlovian conditioning, a procedure in which one stimulus is paired with the unconditioned stimulus (A+) while another is presented by itself (B-).

Discrete-trial training A training procedure in which the opportunity to respond is marked by a conditioned stimulus (Pavlovian) or an unconditioned stimulus (operant). Signals are present only during specific periods.

Discriminative stimulus (S^D) In an operant conditioning procedure, a signal in the presence of which a response will produce some outcome.

Divergence Evolution of a difference in a particular phenotype in different lineages in the descendants of ancestors that originally expressed the same phenotype. Divergence is responsible for the evolution of new species.

Drug tolerance Stimuli paired with some drugs supporting addictive behavior trigger a compensatory response that tends to cancel out the positive effect of the drug. As a result, after repeated administrations of the drug, increasing doses are required to obtain the same effect.

Equipotentiality A principle loosely based on Pavlov's (1927) notion that any stimulus can become a conditioned stimulus. Equipotentiality was challenged by a variety of findings suggesting that some combinations of stimuli, responses, and outcomes lead to faster acquisition.

Escape conditioning Acquisition of a response that removes an aversive reinforcer.

Excitatory conditioning In Pavlovian conditioning, any procedure in which the conditioned stimulus signals the presentation or occurrence of the unconditioned stimulus.

Explicitly unpaired procedure In Pavlovian conditioning, a procedure in which the conditioned and unconditioned stimuli are never presented in close contiguity.

Extinction After conditioning training, a series of trials in which every conditioned stimulus (Pavlovian) or response (operant) is presented by itself, in the absence of the outcome.

Fixed-interval scallop A pattern of operant responding in fixed-interval schedules in which a reinforcer is followed by a pause in responding, in turn followed by the gradual increase in response rate until the next reinforcer is delivered.

Free-operant training A training procedure in which the operant response is continuously available.

Goal tracking During Pavlovian conditioning, the tendency to approach the site where the unconditioned stimulus will be delivered during the presentation of the conditioned stimulus.

Habits Responses to a stimulus that are at least partially independent of the current value of their associated outcome. Habitual behavior is said to be outcome independent and less sensitive to the outcome-devaluation technique.

Hebbian synapse Hebb (1949) suggested that the activation of a presynaptic neuron reaching a postsynaptic neuron just before the latter is activated increases the ability of the presynaptic neuron to influence the postsynaptic neuron in the future. Hebbian synapses exhibit experience-dependent plasticity.

Homology Phenotypic similarity among individuals of different species resulting from inheritance from a common ancestor.

Homoplasy Phenotypic similarity among individuals of different species that evolved independently and are the result of common ecological pressures. Three types of homoplasy are usually distinguished: convergence (similarities among distantly related species), parallel evolution (similarities among closely related species), and evolutionary reversal (similarities between descendants and remote ancestors).

Informational value, reinforcement value Signals for outcomes are said to indicate when or where the reinforcer will occur (informational value) but also acquire the ability to strengthen responses that are followed by their presentation or omission (reinforcement value).

Inhibitory conditioning In Pavlovian conditioning, any procedure in which the conditioned stimulus signals the omission of the unconditioned stimulus.

Interoceptive signals Stimuli originating in the internal state of the animals can control behavior as typical conditioned or discriminative stimuli.

Interval timing Estimating the duration of intervals in the seconds-to-hours range.

Latent inhibition A learning phenomenon involving retardation of acquisition following nonreinforced presentation of the signal, whether a conditioned stimulus (Pavlovian) or a discriminative stimulus (operant).

Latent learning A learning phenomenon in which exposure to some stimuli produce little or no evidence of behavioral change until an outcome is introduced in the situation. The introduction of a reinforcer shows that the organism was actually learning something about the situation although little or no behavioral change had been observed.

Law of effect Thorndike's (1911) proposal that a response is strengthened by positive consequences and weakened by negative consequences.

Learning mechanisms Processes postulated to explain learning phenomena. At least four mechanistic levels are recognized: psychological, neurobiological, neurochemical, and cell-molecular (see **Chapter 3**, Figure 3.1).

Learning phenomenon Behavioral differences between at least two training conditions generated under controlled conditions.

Long-term potentiation (LTP) and depression (LTD) A neural phenomenon involving the strengthening or weakening of specific synapses resulting from high- or low-frequency stimulation.

Magnitude Size of a reinforcer.

Master–yoked design Pairs of animals are randomly assigned to either the master or the yoked condition. During training, the behavior of the master animal determines the occurrence of events in its own environment and also in the environment of the yoked animal. The behavior of yoked animals is irrelevant as far as the events in their own environment. This design equates environmental conditions across master and yoked animals, but only master animals have operant control over events. Yoked animals are exposed to a Pavlovian procedure.

Matching The choice of an option is about as frequent as the frequency with which that option is reinforced.

Maximization Exclusive or near-exclusive choice of the option paired with an outcome in the majority of the trials.

Negative reinforcement An operant contingency in which a response removes or prevents an aversive reinforcer. The aversive reinforcer occurs in the absence of a response.

Neophobia Tendency to reject novel stimuli.

NMDA receptors A type of excitatory glutamate receptor. When associated with AMPA receptors in the same synapses, NMDA receptors respond to glutamate only when the neuron is also activated. The activation of NMDA receptors initiates a cellular cascade that can lead to the synthesis of new AMPA receptors, thus facilitating synaptic transmission. This process is involved in conditioning.

Nonassociative learning Evidence of behavioral change due to experience but in the absence of pairings between conditioned and unconditioned stimuli.

Nucleus accumbens A striatal nucleus implicated in reward.

Omission An operant contingency in which a response is paired with the withdrawal of an appetitive reinforcer, which is presented in the absence of the response.

Operant or instrumental conditioning A response-dependent procedure in which the occurrence of a response in a given situation or stimulus leads to an outcome, such as the presentation or omission of a reinforcer.

Outcome Used in reference to the US (Pavlovian conditioning) or the reinforcer (operant conditioning). Outcomes are typically biologically significant stimuli, such as food, water, and pain.

Outcome-devaluation technique A procedure in which the unconditioned stimulus (Pavlovian) or the reinforcer (operant) after acquisition training is subjected to a change that reduces its ability to support behavior (e.g., by pairing an appetitive stimulus such as food with an aversive consequence such as intoxication with lithium chloride). A technique used to distinguish between actions and habits.

Partial reinforcement Only a fraction of all conditioned stimuli (Pavlovian) or responses (operant) are paired with an outcome, while the rest are presented in the absence of the outcome.

Pavlovian or classical conditioning A response-independent procedure involving the pairing in time or space of at least two stimuli, such that one signals the occurrence or omission of the other.

Periaqueductal gray A nucleus surrounding the cerebral aqueduct in the mammalian rhombencephalon implicated in the organization of defensive behaviors, including freezing in fear conditioning and the processing of nociceptive signals (pain).

Position habit In a discrimination with a discriminative stimulus (visual, auditory, olfactory, etc.), the position of this stimulus is shifted across trials to minimize reliance on spatial cues (right vs. left). Typically, before the development of discriminative behavior, animals tend to consistently choose one of the two options (right or left) for a number of trials. As a result of such position habits, the response would be reinforced in about 50% of the trials.

Positive reinforcement An operant contingency in which a response leads to the presentation of an appetitive reinforcer and the absence of the response is paired with the absence of the reinforcer.

Premack's principle A response with a higher probability of occurrence, H, will reinforce (i.e., strengthen) one with a lower probability of occurrence, L, if the two are contingent: L→H.

Primary reinforcer A biologically significant stimulus whose response-evoking power requires little or no experience.

Pseudoconditioning The development of a response to a stimulus similar to the conditioned response that occurs after pairings between conditioned and unconditioned stimuli, but in the absence of such pairings.

Punishment An operant contingency in which a response is paired with the occurrence of an aversive reinforcer.

Reinforcement The organism's reception of a reinforcer.

Reinforcer In either Pavlovian or operant conditioning procedures, the biologically significant event that supports associative learning. Typical reinforcers include food, water, sex, pain, water immersion, loud noises, and similar events.

Reminder treatment After some amount of training has been administered, presenting only a fraction of the training situation can improve performance if this is done occasionally and in the absence of reinforcement. Theoretically, these treatments are thought to involve the reactivation of memory related to the training task.

Representation A neural record equivalent to an external event (stimulus) or a response performed by the organism.

Response threshold A theoretical level of response strength below which behavioral changes are not observed despite the occurrence of acquisition.

Retardation test A test used to demonstrate inhibitory conditioning. After training, the presumed inhibitor is reinforced. If acquisition of excitation is retarded relative to an appropriate control, then one interpretation is that retardation is caused by inhibitory conditioning.

S→R association Theoretically, the acquisition of a link between the internal representations of the stimulus (S) and the response (R). S→R associations are the basis of habits and are said to be independent of the current value of the outcome that led to their development.

S→S association Theoretically, the acquisition of a link between the internal representations of two stimuli (S). S→S associations are the basis for the acquisition of actions, that is, behaviors guided by an active representation of their outcome.

Safety signals Stimuli paired with the absence of an aversive reinforcer, which is otherwise present.

Salience Intensity of a stimulus.

Schedules of reinforcement Arrangements describing contingencies between responses and outcomes in operant conditioning.

Second-order conditioning A Pavlovian conditioning phenomenon involving two phases of training. In Phase 1, a conditioned stimulus is paired with an unconditioned stimulus (A→US). In Phase 2, a second conditioned stimulus is paired with the first conditioned stimulus (B→A). Responding to the second conditioned stimulus (B) provides evidence that the first conditioned stimulus (A) had acquired reinforcing value. Control involved unpaired presentations of the stimuli in Phase 1 (A, US) but not in Phase 2 (B→A) and paired presentation in Phase 1 (A→US) but unpaired presentations in Phase 2 (B, A). Second-order conditioning depends on paired experience in both phases.

Sensitization An increase in the strength of the response to a neutral stimulus as a result of exposure to an unconditioned stimulus.

Sensory preconditioning A Pavlovian conditioning phenomenon involving two training phases. In Phase 1, two neutral stimuli are paired in close contiguity (A→B). In Phase 2, the second stimulus from Phase 1 is now paired with an unconditioned stimulus (B→US). In a final test, the first stimulus from Phase 1 is presented. The phenomenon involves the occurrence of a conditioned response to the first stimulus from Phase 1 (A), although it was never directly paired with the unconditioned stimulus. A demonstration of this phenomenon requires at least two control conditions, one in which Phase 1 events are unpaired (A, B) but Phase 2 events are paired (B→US) and another one in which Phase 1 events are paired (A→B) but Phase 2 events are unpaired (B, US). Sensory preconditioning required paired experience in both phases of training.

Sexual reinforcement Response outcomes involving copulation, whether in males or females.

Shaping Differential reinforcement of responses progressively closer in form to a terminal response.

Sign tracking During Pavlovian conditioning, the tendency to approach the conditioned stimulus.

Signal–outcome relevance Also known as constraints on learning, preparedness, and associative selectivity; the notion that some arrangements between signals, responses, and outcomes lead to faster acquisition in either Pavlovian or operant situations.

Simultaneous conditioning In Pavlovian conditioning, the complete overlap in time of the conditioned and unconditioned stimuli.

Summation test A test used in demonstrations of inhibitory conditioning. In this test, the presumed inhibitor is compounded with a separately trained exciter. The goal is to determine whether the animal responds less to this compound than to the exciter alone. One possible interpretation is that inhibition reduced excitation elicited by the exciter.

Trace conditioning In Pavlovian conditioning, a procedure in which there is a temporal gap between the offset of the conditioned stimulus and the onset of the unconditioned stimulus.

Trial-spacing effect A learning phenomenon in which acquisition is faster the longer the intertrial interval in both Pavlovian and instrumental situations.

Truly random control A Pavlovian procedure in which the conditioned and unconditioned stimuli are programed to occur randomly. This procedure may include some occasional pairings.

Unconditioned stimulus (US) In a Pavlovian conditioning procedure, a biologically significant event with sufficient salience or magnitude to elicit an unconditioned response (e.g., food, water, pain).

US-preexposure effect A learning phenomenon in which unsignaled presentations of the unconditioned stimulus (US) retard subsequent conditioning when that unconditioned stimulus is signaled by a conditioned stimulus.

References

Adams, C., & Dickinson, A. (1981). Actions and habits: Variations in associative representations during instrumental learning. In N. E. Spear & R. R. Miller (Eds.), *Information processing in animals: Memory mechanisms* (pp. 143–165). Erlbaum.

Ader, R., & Cohen, N. (1982). Behaviorally conditioned immunosuppression and murine systemic lupus erythematosus. *Science*, *215*, 1534–1536. https://doi.org/10.1126/science.7063864

Akins, C. K., Domjan, M., & Gutiérrez, G. (1994). Topography of sexually conditioned behavior in male Japanese quail (*Coturnix japonica*) depends on the CS-US interval. *Journal of Experimental Psychology: Animal Behavior Processes*, *20*, 199–209. https://doi.org/10.1037/0097-7403.20.2.199

Antonitis, J. J. (1951). Response variability in the white rat during conditioning, extinction, and reconditioning. *Journal of Experimental Psychology*, *42*, 273–281. https://doi.org/10.1037/h0060407

Azrin, N. H., & Holz, W. C. (1966). Punishment. In W. K. Honig (Ed.), *Operant behavior: Areas of research and application* (pp. 380–447). Appleton-Century-Crofts.

Batson, J. D., & Best, P. J. (1979). Drug-preexposure effects in flavor-aversion learning: Associative interference by conditioned environmental stimuli. *Journal of Experimental Psychology: Animal Behavior Processes*, *5*, 273–283. https://doi.org/10.1037/0097-7403.5.3.273

Bliss, T. V. P., & Lømo, T. (1973). Long-lasting potentiation of synaptic transmission in the dentate area of the anaesthetized rabbit following stimulation of the performant path. *Journal of Physiology (London)*, *232*, 331–356. https://doi.org/10.1113/jphysiol.1973.sp010273

Campbell, B. A., & Kraeling, D. (1953). Response strength as a function of drive level and amount of drive reduction. *Journal of Experimental Psychology*, *45*, 97–101. https://doi.org/10.1037/h0060223

Cándido, A., Maldonado, A., Megías, J. L., & Catena, A. (1992). Successive negative contrast in one-way avoidance learning in rats. *Quarterly Journal of Experimental Psychology*, *45B*, 15–32.

Christianson, J. P., Jennings, J. H., Ragole, T., Flyer, J., Benison, A. M., Barth, D., Watkins, L. R., & Maier, S. F. (2011). Safety signals mitigate the consequences of uncontrollable stress via a circuit involving the sensory insular cortex and bed nucleus of the stria terminalis. *Biological Psychiatry, 70*, 458–464. https://doi.org/10.1016/j.biopsych.2011.04.004

Church, R. M. (1969). Response suppression. In B. A. Campbell & R. M. Church (Eds.), *Punishment and aversive behavior* (pp. 111–156). Appleton-Century-Crofts.

Colwill, R. M., & Rescorla, R. A. (1985). Postconditioning devaluation of a reinforcer affects instrumental responding. *Journal of Experimental Psychology: Animal Behavior Processes, 11*, 120–132. https://doi.org/10.1037/0097-7403.11.1.120

Crawford, L. L., & Domjan, M. (1993). Sexual approach conditioning: Omission contingency tests. *Animal Learning & Behavior, 21*, 42–50. https://doi.org/10.3758/BF03197975

Daly, M., Rauschenberger, J., & Behrends, P. (1982). Food aversion learning in kangaroo rats: A specialist-generalist comparison. *Animal Learning and Behavior, 10*, 314–320. https://doi.org/10.3758/BF03213716

Davidson, T. L., Flynn, F. W., & Jarrard, L. E. (1992). Potency of food deprivation intensity cues as discriminative stimuli. *Journal of Experimental Psychology: Animal Behavior Processes, 18*, 174–181. https://doi.org/10.1037/0097-7403.18.2.174

de Wit, S., & Dickinson, A. (2009). Associative theories of goal-directed behaviour: A case for animal–human translational models. *Psychological Research, 73*, 463–476. https://doi.org/10.1007/s00426-009-0230-6

Delamater, A. R., LoLordo, V. M., & Berridge, K. C. (1986). Control of fluid palatability by exteroceptive Pavlovian signals. *Journal of Experimental Psychology: Animal Behavior Processes, 12*, 143–152. https://doi.org/10.1037/0097-7403.12.2.143

Dickinson, A., Watt, A., & Griffiths, W. J. (1992). Free-operant acquisition with delayed reinforcement. *Quarterly Journal of Experimental Psychology B: Comparative and Physiological Psychology, 45B*, 241–258.

Domjan, M. (1997). Behavior systems and the demise of equipotentiality: Historical antecedents and evidence from sexual conditioning. In M. E. Bouton & M. S. Fanselow (Eds.), *Learning, motivation, and cognition* (pp. 31–51). American Psychological Association.

Domjan, M., & Galef, B. G. Jr. (1983). Biological constraints on instrumental and classical conditioning: Retrospect and prospect. *Animal Learning and Behavior, 11*, 151–161. https://doi.org/10.3758/BF03199643

Domjan, M., & Gutiérrez, G. (2019). The behavior system for sexual learning. *Behavioural Processes, 162*, 184–196. https://doi.org/10.1016/j.beproc.2019.01.013

Du, J., Wei, H., Wang, Z., Wong, S. T., & Poo, M. (2009). Long-range retrograde spread of LTP and LTD from optic tectum to retina. *Proceedings of the National Academy of Sciences USA, 106*, 18890–18896. www.pnas.org/doi/pdf/10.1073pnas.0910659106

Dudek, S. M., & Bear, M. F. (1992). Homosynaptic long-term depression in area CA1 of the hippocampus and the effects of NMDA receptor blockade. *Proceedings of the National Academy of Sciences, USA, 89*, 4363–4367. https://doi.org/10.1073/pnas.89.10.4363

Dunlap, A. S., & Dexheimer, A. F. (2022). Experimental evolution and mechanisms for prepared learning. In M. Krause, K. L. Hollis, & M. R. Papini (Eds.), *Evolution of learning and memory mechanisms* (pp. 71–88). Cambridge University Press.

Dunlap, A. S., & Stephens, D. W. (2014). Experimental evolution of prepared learning. *Proceedings of the National Academy of Sciences USA, 111*, 11750–11755. https://doi.org/10.1073/pnas.1404176111

Dwyer, D. M. (2015). Experimental evolution of sensitivity to a stimulus domain alone is not an example of prepared learning. *Proceedings of the National Academy of Sciences USA, 112*, E385. https://doi.org/10.1073/pnas.1420871112

Ferster, C. B., & Skinner, B. F. (1957). *Schedules of reinforcement*. Appleton-Century-Crofts.

Flaherty, C. F. (1996). *Incentive relativity*. Cambridge University Press.

Fraser, K. M., & Holland, P. C. (2019). Occasion setting. *Behavioral Neuroscience, 133*(2), 145–175. https://doi.org/10.1037/bne0000306

Garcia, J., & Koelling, R. A. (1966). Relation of cue to consequence in avoidance learning. *Psychonomic Science, 4*, 123–124. https://doi.org/10.3758/BF03342209

Gasbarri, A., Pompili, A., Packard, M. G., & Tomaz, C. (2014). Habit learning and memory in mammals: Behavioral and neural characteristics. *Neurobiology of Learning and Memory, 114*, 198–208. https://doi.org/10.1016/j.nlm.2014.06.010

Gauci, M., Husband, A. J., Saxarra, H., & King, M. G. (1994). Pavlovian conditioning of nasal tryptase release in human subjects with allergic rhinitis. *Physiology and Behavior*, *55*, 823–825. https://doi.org/10.1016/0031-9384(94)90066-3

Gomez-Fernandez, M., Higley, K., Tokuhiro, A., Welter, K., Wong, W. K., & Yang, H. (2020). Status of research and development of learning-based approaches in nuclear science and engineering: A review. *Nuclear Engineering and Design*, *359*, 110479. https://doi.org/10.1016/j.nucengdes.2019.110479

Grice, G. R. (1948). The relation of secondary reinforcement to delayed reward in visual discrimination learning. *Journal of Experimental Psychology*, *38*, 1–16. https://doi.org/10.1037/h0061016

Harris, J. A., Andrew, B. J., & Kwok, D. W. (2013). Magazine approach during a signal for food depends on Pavlovian, not instrumental, conditioning. *Journal of Experimental Psychology: Animal Behavior Processes*, *39*, 107–116. https://doi.org/10.1037/a0031315

Hebb, D. O. (1949). *The organization of behavior: A neuropsychological theory*. Wiley.

Herrod, J. L., Snyder, S. K., Hart, J. B., Frantz, S. J., & Ayres, K. M. (2022). Applications of the Premack principle: A review of the literature. *Behavior Modification*, *47*(1), 219–246. https://doi.org/10.1177/01454455221085249

Holland, P. C. (1995). Transfer of occasion setting across stimulus and response in operant feature positive discriminations. *Learning and Motivation*, *26*(3), 239–263. https://doi.org/10.1016/0023-9690(95)90014-4

Holland, P. C. (2008). Cognitive versus stimulus-response theories of learning. *Learning & Behavior*, *36*, 227–241. https://doi.org/10.3758/lb.36.3.227

Holland, P. C., & Rescorla, R. A. (1975). The effect of two ways of devaluing the unconditioned stimulus after first- and second-order appetitive conditioning. *Journal of Experimental Psychology: Animal Behavior Processes*, *1*, 355–363. https://doi.org/10.1037/0097-7403.1.4.355

Hughes, K. C., & Shin, L. M. (2011). Functional neuroimaging studies of post-traumatic stress disorder. *Expert Reviews in Neurotherapeutics*, *11*, 275–285. https://doi.org/10.1586/ern.10.198

Hull, C. L. (1943). *Principles of behavior: An introduction to behavior theory*. Appleton-Century-Crofts.

Hull, C. L. (1951). *Essentials of behavior*. Yale University Press.

Kamin, L. J. (1965). Temporal and intensity characteristics of the conditioned stimulus. In W. F. Prokasy (Ed.), *Classical conditioning: A symposium* (pp. 118–147). Appleton-Century-Crofts.

Kelleher, R. T., & Gollub, L. R. (1962). A review of positive conditioned reinforcement. *Journal of the Experimental Analysis of Behavior*, *5*(4 Suppl.), 543–597. https://doi.org/10.1901/jeab.1962.5-s543

Keller, F. S., & Schoenfeld, W. N. (1950). *Principles of psychology: A systematic text in the science of behavior*. Appleton-Century-Crofts.

Krane, R. V., & Wagner, A. R. (1975). Taste aversion learning with delayed shock US: Implications for the "generality of the laws of learning". *Journal of Comparative and Physiological Psychology*, *88*, 882–889. https://doi.org/10.1037/h0076417

Krank, M. D., & MacQueen, G. M. (1988). Conditioned compensatory responses elicited by environmental signals for cyclophosphamide-induced suppression of antibody production in mice. *Psychobiology*, *16*, 229–235.

Leclerc, R., & Reberg, D. (1980). Sign-tracking in aversive conditioning. *Learning and Motivation*, *11*, 302–317. https://doi.org/10.1016/0023-9690(80)90003-X

Leising, K. J., Nerz, J., Solorzano-Restrepo, J., & Bond, S. R. (2025). Are you studying occasion setting? A review for inquiring minds. *Comparative Cognition and Behavior Reviews*, *20*, 1–40. https://doi.org/10.3819/CCBR.2025.200002

Lejeune, H., & Wearden, J. H. (1991). The comparative psychology of fixed-interval responding: Some quantitative analyses. *Learning and Motivation*, *22*, 84–111. https://doi.org/10.1016/0023-9690(91)90018-4

Lieberman, D. A., McIntosh, D. C., & Thomas, G. V. (1979). Learning when reward is delayed: A marking hypothesis. *Journal of Experimental Psychology: Animal Behavior Processes*, *5*, 224–242. https://doi.org/10.1037/0097-7403.5.3.224

Logan, F. A. (1960). *Incentive*. Yale University Press.

MacQueen, G., Marshall, J., Perdue, M., Siegel, S., & Bienenstock, J. (1989). Pavlovian conditioning of rat mucosal mast cells to secrete rat mast cell protease II. *Science*, *243*, 83–85. https://doi.org/10.1126/science.2911721

Matzel, L. D., Held, F. P., & Miller, R. R. (1988). Information and expression of simultaneous and backward associations: Implications for contiguity theory. *Learning and Motivation*, *19*, 317–344. https://doi.org/10.1016/0023-9690(88)90044-6

Miller, R. R. (1982). Effects of intertrial reinstatement of training stimuli on complex maze learning in rats: Evidence that "acquisition" curves reflect more than acquisition. *Journal of Experimental Psychology: Animal Behavior Processes*, *8*, 86–109. https://doi.org/10.1037/0097-7403.8.1.86

Miller, V., & Domjan, M. (1981). Specificity of cue to consequence in aversion learning in the rat: Control for US-induced differential orientations. *Animal Learning and Behavior*, *9*, 339–345. https://doi.org/10.3758/BF03197841

Mombelli, E. (2022). Animal models of drug addiction. In S. Della Sala (Ed.), *Encyclopedia of behavioral neuroscience* (2nd ed., Vol. 1, pp. 674–681). Elsevier. https://doi.org/10.1016/B978-0-12-819641-0.00118-3

Morris, R. (1984). Developments of a water-maze procedure for studying spatial learning in the rat. *Journal of Neuroscience Methods*, *11*, 47–60. https://doi.org/10.1016/0165-0270(84)90007-4

Müller, T., Albrecht, D., & Gebhardt, C. (2009). Both NR2A and NR2B subunits of the NMDA receptor are critical for long-term potentiation and long-term depression in the lateral amygdala of horizontal slices of adult mice. *Learning & Memory*, *16*, 395–405. https://doi.org/10.1101/lm.1398709

Nicoll, R. A. (2017). A brief history of long-term potentiation. *Neuron*, *93*, 281–290. https://doi.org/10.1016/j.neuron.2016.12.015

Nishijima, S., & Maruyama, I. N. (2017). Appetitive olfactory learning and long-term associative memory in *Caenorhabditis elegans*. *Frontiers in Behavioral Neuroscience*, *11*, 80. https://doi.org/10.3389/fnbeh.2017.00080

Olds, J., & Milner, P. (1954). Positive reinforcement produced by electrical stimulation of septal area and other regions of the rat brain. *Journal of Comparative and Physiological Psychology*, *47*, 419–427. https://doi.org/10.1037/h0058775

Overmier, J. B., & Papini, M. R. (1986). Factors modulating the effects of teleost telencephalon ablation on retention, relearning, and extinction of instrumental avoidance behavior. *Behavioral Neuroscience*, *100*, 190–199. https://doi.org/10.1037//0735-7044.100.2.190

Packard, M. G., & McGaugh, J. L. (1996). Inactivation of hippocampus or caudate nucleus with lidocaine differentially affects expression of place and response learning. *Neurobiology of Learning and Memory*, *65*, 65–72. https://doi.org/10.1006/nlme.1996.0007

Page, S., & Neuringer, A. (1985). Variability is an operant. *Journal of Experimental Psychology: Animal Behavior Processes*, *11*, 429–452. https://doi.org/10.1037/0097-7403.11.3.429

Papini, M. R. (2021). *Comparative psychology. Evolution and development of brain and behavior*. Taylor & Francis.

Papini, M. R., & Bitterman, M. E. (1993). The two-test strategy in the study of inhibitory conditioning. *Journal of Experimental Psychology: Animal Behavior Processes*, *19*, 342–352. https://doi.org/10.1037/0097-7403.19.4.342

Papini, M. R., Ludvigson, H. W., Huneycutt, D., & Boughner, R. L. (2001). Apparent incentive contrast effects in autoshaping with rats. *Learning and Motivation*, *32*, 434–456. https://doi.org/10.1006/lmot.2001.1088

Papini, M. R., & White, N. (1994). Performance during signals for reward omission. *Learning and Motivation*, *25*, 45–64. https://doi.org/10.1006/lmot.1994.1003

Parkinson, J. A., Roberts, A. C., Everitt, B. J., & Di Ciano, P. (2005). Acquisition of instrumental conditioned reinforcement is resistant to the devaluation of the unconditioned stimulus. *Quarterly Journal of Experimental Psychology Section B*, *58*, 19–30. https://doi.org/10.1080/02724990444000023

Palmatier, M. I., & Bevins, R. A. (2008). Occasion setting by drug states: Functional equivalence following similar training history. *Behavioural Brain Research*, *195*(2), 260–270. https://doi.org/10.1016/j.bbr.2008.09.009

Pavlov, I. P. (1927). *Conditioned reflexes*. Oxford University Press.

Pearce, J. M., & Kaye, H. (1985). Strength of the orienting response during inhibitory conditioning. *Journal of Experimental Psychology: Animal Behavior Processes*, *11*, 405–420. https://doi.org/10.1037/0097-7403.11.3.405

Poling, A., Edwards, T. L., Weeden, M., & Foster, T. M. (2011). The matching law. *Psychological Record*, *61*, 313–322. https://doi.org/10.1007/BF03395762

Premack, D. (1959). Toward empirical behavior laws: I. Positive reinforcement. *Psychological Review*, *66*(4), 219–233. https://doi.org/10.1037/h0040891
Pryor, K. (2002). *Don't shoot the dog!* (3rd ed.). Ringpress Books.
Pryor, K. W., Haag, R., & O'Reilly, J. (1969). The creative porpoise: Training for novel behavior. *Journal of the Experimental Analysis of Behavior*, *12*, 653–661. https://doi.org/10.1901/jeab.1969.12-653
Quintana, G. R., Jackson, M., Nasr, M., & Pfaus, J. G. (2018). Effect of CS preexposure on the conditioned ejaculatory preference of the male rat: Behavioral analyses and neural correlates. *Learning and Memory*, *25*, 513–521. https://doi.org/10.1101/lm.048108.118
Ramón y Cajal, S. (1911). *Histologie du système nerveux de l'homme et des vertébrès* (Vol. II). Maluine.
Rescorla, R. A. (1969). Pavlovian conditioned inhibition. *Psychological Bulletin*, *72*, 77–94. https://doi.org/10.1037/h0027760
Rescorla, R. A. (1980). *Pavlovian second-order conditioning: Studies in associative learning*. Erlbaum.
Rescorla, R. A. (1985). Conditioned inhibition and facilitation. In R. R. Miller & N. S. Spear (Eds.), *Information processing in animals: Conditioned inhibition* (pp. 299–326). Erlbaum.
Rescorla, R. A., & Wagner, A. R. (1972). A theory of Pavlovian conditioning: Variations in the effectiveness of reinforcement and nonreinforcement. In A. H. Black & W. F. Prokasy (Eds.), *Classical conditioning II: Current research and theory* (pp. 64–99). Appleton Century Crofts.
Rodrigues, S. M., Schafe, G. E., & LeDoux, J. E. (2001). Intra-amygdala blockade of the NR2B subunit of the NMDA receptor disrupts the acquisition but not the expression of fear conditioning. *Journal of Neuroscience*, *21*, 6889–6896. https://doi.org/10.1523/JNEUROSCI.21-17-06889.2001
Rogan, M. T., Leon, K. S., Perez, D. L., & Kandel, E. R. (2005). Distinct neural signatures for safety and danger in the amygdala and striatum of the mouse. *Neuron*, *46*, 309–320. https://doi.org/10.1016/j.neuron.2005.02.017
Sheffield, F. D. (1965). Relation between classical conditioning and instrumental learning. In W. F. Prokasy (Ed.), *Classical conditioning* (pp. 302–322). Appleton-Century-Crofts.
Shimp, C. P. (1982). Reinforcement and the local organization of behavior. In M. L. Commons, R. J. Herrnstein, & H. Rachlin (Eds.), *Quantitative analyses of behavior. Vol. 2. Matching and maximizing accounts* (pp. 111–130). Ballinger.
Siegel, S. (1999). Drug anticipation and drug addiction. *Addiction*, *94*, 1113–1124. https://doi.org/10.1046/j.1360-0443.1999.94811132.x
Siegel, S. (2016). The heroin overdose mystery. *Current Directions in Psychological Science*, *25*, 375–379. https://doi.org/10.1177/0963721416664404
Siegel, S., Hinson, R. E., & Krank, M. D. (1978). The role of predrug signals in morphine analgesic tolerance: Support for a Pavlovian conditioning model of tolerance. *Journal of Experimental Psychology: Animal Behavior Processes*, *4*, 188–196. https://doi.org/10.1037/0097-7403.4.2.188
Siegel, S., Hinson, R. E., Krank, M. D., & McCully, J. (1982). Heroin "overdose" death: The contribution of drug-associated environmental cues. *Science*, *216*, 436–437. https://doi.org/10.1126/science.7200260
Skinner, B. F. (1938). *The behavior of organisms*. Appleton-Century-Crofts.
Smotherman, W. P., & Robinson, S. R. (1991). Conditioned activation of fetal behavior. *Physiology and Behavior*, *50*, 73–77. https://doi.org/10.1016/0031-9384(91)90500-N
Spence, K. W. (1945). An experimental test of continuity and non-continuity theories of discrimination learning. *Journal of Experimental Psychology*, *35*, 253–266. https://doi.org/10.1037/h0060794
Stahlman, W. D., & Leising, K. J. (2024). The behavioral origins of phylogenic responses and ontogenic habits. *Journal of the Experimental Analysis of Behavior*, *121*(1), 27–37. https://doi.org/10.1002/jeab.892
Stamps, J. (1998). Territoriality. In G. Greenberg & M. Haraway (Eds.), *Comparative psychology: A handbook* (pp. 761–770). Garland.
Thomas, B. L., & Papini, M. R. (2020). Shifts in intertrial interval duration in autoshaping with rats: Implications for path dependence. *Learning & Motivation*, *72*, 101687 https://doi.org/10.1016/j.lmot.2020.101687
Thorndike, E. L. (1911). *Animal intelligence*. Macmillan.
Tolman, E. C., & Honzik, C. H. (1930). Introduction and removal of reward and maze performance in rats. *University of California Publications in Psychology*, *4*, 257–275.
Tomie, A. (1976). Retardation of autoshaping: Control by contextual stimuli. *Science*, *192*, 1244–1246. https://doi.org/10.1126/science.192.4245.1244

Torres, C., Morales, A., Megías, j. L., Cándido, A., & Maldonado, A. (1994). Flumazenil antagonizes the effect of diazepam on negative contrast in one-way avoidance learning. *Behavioral Pharmacology*, *5*, 637–641. https://doi.org/10.1097/00008877-199410000-00010

Westbrook, R. F., Jones, M. L., Bailey, G. K., & Harris, J. A. (2000). Contextual control over conditioned responding in a latent inhibition paradigm. *Journal of Experimental Psychology: Animal Learning and Cognition*, *26*, 157–173. https://doi.org/10.1037/0097-7403.26.2.157

Wilson, W. A., Oscar, M., & Bitterman, M. E. (1964). Visual probability learning in the monkey. *Psychonomic Science*, *1*, 71–72. https://doi.org/10.3758/BF03342795

Wolfe, J. B. (1934). The effect of delayed reward upon learning in the white rat. *Journal of Comparative Psychology*, *17*, 1–21. https://doi.org/10.1037/h0070755

Woods, P. J., Davidson, E. H., & Peters, R. J. Jr. (1964). Instrumental escape conditioning in a water tank: Effects of variations in drive stimulus intensity and reinforcement magnitude. *Journal of Comparative and Physiological Psychology*, *57*, 466–470. https://doi.org/10.1037/h0046640

Yin, H. H., Knowlton, B. J., & Balleine, B. W. (2004). Lesions of dorsolateral striatum preserve outcome expectancy but disrupt habit formation in instrumental learning. *European Journal of Neuroscience*, *19*, 181–189. https://doi.org/10.1111/j.1460-9568.2004.03095.x

Yin, H. H., Ostlund, S. B., Knowlton, B. J., & Balleine, B. W. (2005). The role of the dorsomedial striatum in instrumental conditioning. *European Journal of Neuroscience*, *22*, 513–523. https://doi.org/10.1111/j.1460-9568.2005.04218.x

Zentall, T. R., & Hogan, D. E. (1975). Key pecking in pigeons produced by pairing keylight with inaccessible grain. *Journal of the Experimental Analysis of Behavior*, *23*(2), 199–206. https://doi.org/10.1901/jeab.1975.23-199

5 Associative learning: Integration

5.1 Introduction

This chapter integrates basic notions of learning with other psychological processes that also affect behavior, like attention, motivation, and emotion. In addition, the acquisition processes covered in Chapter 4 will be viewed in the light of more complex situations, including postacquisition phenomena and effects related to the processing of compound stimuli. We start by looking at extinction, a fundamental postacquisition process that poses some challenges to our understanding of learning.

5.2 Extinction and learning

5.2.1 Procedure, phenomenon, mechanism

Like many other concepts in the field of learning, *extinction* has at least three meanings. As a *procedure*, it refers to the presentation of the CS alone, after CS→US pairings (Pavlovian) or the omission of the reinforcer for a previously reinforced response (operant). In both cases, the omission of the reinforcer in a situation in which either a reinforced CS or response has led to an increase in behavior now leads to an opposite change in behavior, that is, a decrease. This change in behavior is the *phenomenon* of extinction. Extinction also invokes a set of constructs that have been introduced as *mechanisms* to explain the phenomenon, such as the weakening of an association. The same distinction between procedure, phenomenon, and mechanism applies to acquisition, habituation, avoidance, and similar concepts.

Why has a response decreased in frequency? Because the reinforcer has been omitted (procedure), because the omission of the reinforcer led to the extinction of the response (phenomenon), or because omitting the reinforcer weakened an association established during acquisition (mechanism).

5.2.2 Unlearning vs. parallel associations

Consider extinction in a Pavlovian procedure. In acquisition, CS→US pairings increase the occurrence of some behavior. In extinction, CS-only presentations reduce the response previously acquired. Does extinction eliminate the CS→US association, or does it lead to a different type of learning?

Pavlov (1927) noticed that the salivary response could be recovered by a variety of postextinction treatments (Figure 5.1). First, a resting period without CS presentations caused an extinguished response to recover when the CS was presented again—*spontaneous recovery*. Second, response recovery also occurred after stimulation with a novel stimulus—*disinhibition*.

DOI: 10.4324/9781003401957-7

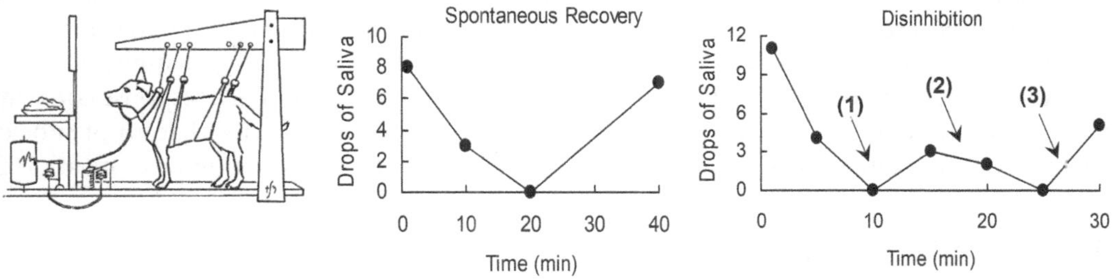

Figure 5.1 **Pavlov's salivary conditioning procedure with dogs.** These behavioral graphs come from quantitative data presented by Pavlov (1927). The middle panel illustrates extinction and spontaneous recovery. The salivary response decreases across three trials separated by 10-min intervals, but introducing a resting period of 20 min causes the relapse of the response. The right panel shows that a novel stimulus presented three times often causes a relapse of the response in a subsequent trial, a phenomenon Pavlov named disinhibition. Notice that the relapse of the response is lower than the response level during the first extinction trial. Incomplete relapse suggests that some unlearning might have taken place, whereas behavior relapse suggests that unlearning was incomplete.

In one experiment with dogs, Pavlov himself entered the training room and talked to the animal for about 2 minutes. A subsequent CS presentation revealed a substantial disinhibition of the salivary response. Third, an extinguished response also recovered its strength after unsignaled US presentations—*reinstatement.* Rats receiving acquisition training with a CS in one context (A) and extinction in another context (B) exhibit response recovery when the signal is presented either in the original acquisition context (A) or in a third, new context (C)—*renewal* (Bouton & Bolles, 1979). ABA and ABC renewal suggests that extinction performance is context specific. Similar effects have also been described using operant procedures (also notice some parallels with habituation phenomena; see Figure 3.5). The relapse of behavior illustrated by these four phenomena implies that extinction does not lead to the complete unlearning of the CS→US association, but, if not unlearning, what causes the response to decrease during extinction?

Pavlov (1927) suggested that extinction after excitatory conditioning leads to the development of an inhibitory association that temporarily blocks the response without eliminating the excitatory CS→US association. By assuming that the inhibitory link was easier to disrupt than the excitatory link, Pavlov's hypothesis accounted for spontaneous recovery, disinhibition, and reinstatement. In these cases, the inhibitory link was disrupted by introducing ambiguity via a resting period or a novel stimulus, or by disambiguating the value of the extinguished stimulus via an unsignaled reinforcer presentation. More recent data suggest it may not be the inhibitory link that is easier to disrupt but rather whatever learning comes second. Rats trained with a stimulus as a conditioned inhibitor in Phase 1 (A+, AB-) followed by training as an excitor in Phase 2 (B+) demonstrated renewal and spontaneous recovery of inhibition (Fiori et al., 1994; Sissons & Miller, 2009). Second-learned associations are easier to disrupt than first-learned associations.

Conversely, one may ask whether there are procedures that strengthen the extinction memory such that they reduce or even eliminate these postextinction effects. This has been studied in detail for the renewal effect. Renewal is reduced by extensive extinction training (Denniston, Chang et al., 2003), by extinction in three different contexts before testing in yet another context (Chelonis et al., 1999), and by conditioned inhibition training after extinction and before testing (Rauhut et al., 2001). These results and the fact that the relapse of behavior is often incomplete (as shown in Figure 5.1) suggest that extinction may also result in some amount of unlearning of the associations established during acquisition.

Extinction is a fundamental aspect of learning. In fact, the extinction of a response confirms that the response was acquired through experience. A change in behavior that is not subject to extinction is likely to be the result of other processes, such as maturation or motivation.

5.3 Perception and learning

The detection of events within external and internal environments is the initial step in the process of learning (see Chapter 2). Although organisms are confronted with a multiplicity of stimuli across several sensory modalities, usually, only some of them acquire control over behavior. How does such selective control develop?

5.3.1 Compound conditioning

Most natural stimuli involve multisensory stimulation. For example, ducklings imprinted to their mother may initially respond to the movement of a large object (the mother) but eventually learn to respond to a set of stimuli that include auditory, visual, and thermal elements (see Chapter 7). The study of ***compound conditioning***, that is, learning about the elements of a complex stimulus, suggests that the conditioning of an element can be affected by the strength of the accompanying elements. Four examples are presented in Table 5.1

Table 5.1 Examples of compound conditioning

(1) Overshadowing				
Group	*Training*		*Tests*	*CR to Tone in Test*
Exp	ToneLight→Shock		Tone?	Less in Exp than Con
Con	Tone→Shock		Tone?	
(2) Forward Blocking				
Group	*Phase 1*	*Phase 2*	*Test*	*CR to Tone in Test*
Exp	Light→Shock	ToneLight→Shock	Tone?	Less in Exp than Con
Con	Click→Shock	ToneLight→Shock	Tone?	
(3) Concurrent Blocking				
Group	*Training*		*Test*	*CR to Tone in Test*
Exp	LightTone→Shock, Light→Shock		Tone?	Lowest in Exp than Controls
Con-1	LightTone→Shock, Shock		Tone?	
Con-2	LightTone→Shock		Tone?	
Con-3	LightTone→Shock, Light-only		Tone?	
(4) Backward Blocking				
Group	*Phase 1*	*Phase 2*	*Test*	*CR to Tone in Test*
Exp	ToneLight→Shock	Light→Shock	Tone?	Less in Exp than Con
Con	ToneLight→Shock	Click→Shock	Tone?	
(5) Feature-positive discriminations				
Group	*Training*		*Result*	
Exp	ToneLight→Shock, Tone-only		More CR to compound than to Tone	

(*Continued*)

Table 5.1 (Continued)

(6) Positive patterning		
Group	*Training*	*Result*
Exp	ToneLight→Shock, Tone-only, Light-only	More CR to compound than elements

Note. "Tone," "Light," and "Shock" are used to illustrate these effects. In actual experiments, the CSs and USs used may be different. In each case, several control conditions have been reported in the literature. The "ToneLight" phrase indicates the simultaneous presentation of the Tone and the Light (compound). The question mark indicates a nonreinforced test of the stimulus. A comma separates different trials after some intertrial interval. There is also a "feature-negative discrimination" with the Tone reinforced only when not accompanied by the feature: ToneLight-only, Tone→Shock (Light is the feature). There is also a "negative patterning" with the compound nonreinforced but the elements reinforced: ToneLight-only, Tone→Shock, Light→Shock.

Suppose a compound signal with two elements is reinforced in a delay paradigm until the animal responds consistently (ToneLight→Food). In *overshadowing* (Pavlov, 1927), each element of the compound (say Tone) presented in isolation elicits less responding than it would if that element had been reinforced by itself (Tone→Food). Overshadowing also questions the sufficiency of temporal contiguity for acquisition because the Tone was equally contiguous to food whether it was presented by itself or as part of a ToneLight compound. This effect is especially strong when the overshadowing stimulus (Light) is more intense than the overshadowed stimulus (Tone).

A similar deficit occurs when one of the elements in a compound stimulus is reinforced individually, either before (forward), during (concurrent), or after (backward) compound conditioning. Suppose that animals receive Light→Shock pairings in Phase 1, followed by ToneLight→Shock pairings in Phase 2, and ending with a Tone-only test. Responding to the Tone (added in Phase 2) is usually lower than in a condition in which the light was not conditioned in Phase 1. Prior conditioning of one element interferes with subsequent conditioning of any element added to the original, an effect called *forward blocking* (Kamin, 1969). Similarly, mixing the two trials randomly within a session (Light→Food and ToneLight→Food) also leads to a deficit in responding to the Tone. This is called *concurrent blocking* (or cue-validity effect; Wagner, 1969). Forward blocking and concurrent blocking suggest that responding to the redundant element of a compound is severely restricted. There is also a *backward blocking* effect induced by a sequence of phases opposite to that of forward blocking (Blaser et al., 2004). Backward blocking suggests a retrospective reevaluation process whereby the experience in Phase 2 changes a memory acquired during Phase 1.

5.3.2 Overshadowing and blocking effects

Forward blocking fostered a relativistic view of learning that counters a classic assumption according to which the elements of a compound gain and lose strength independently—the *independence rule* (Couvillon & Bitterman, 1991). Studies of blocking have stimulated the development of two classes of relativistic theories since the 1970s. First, a class of models posits that the elements of a compound stimulus compete for a limited amount of associability, stimulus value, or attention. These models view forward blocking as arising from a deficit of storage. For example, the model proposed by Rescorla and Wagner (1972) is based on the premise that the reinforcer supports a maximum amount of conditioning, such that acquisition by one element of the compound reduces the strength available for other elements—*shared associative strength*. Thus, preconditioning of an element captures most of the available strength, thus preventing the added element from gaining further strength despite a seemingly effective degree of temporal contiguity with the reinforcer.

A second class of models assumes that contiguity is sufficient for conditioning but not for performance. The comparator hypothesis (Stout & Miller, 2007) suggests that the blocking stimulus (called "comparator") activates a representation of the reinforcer with similar strength as the activation induced by the blocked stimulus. When the strengths of the reinforcer representations activated by the blocked and blocking stimuli are similar, the conditioned response to the signal is attenuated, thus leading to forward blocking.

Both classes of relativistic theories have led to counterintuitive predictions. For example, competition models correctly predict that changes in reinforcer magnitude between Phases 1 and 2 attenuate forward blocking (Pearce & Hall, 1980). Similarly, the comparator hypothesis rightly predicts that extinction of the comparator stimulus after Phase 2 attenuates blocking (Denniston, Savastano et al., 2003). It is unclear whether a single theoretical principle will be able to account for these effects or whether different mechanisms are engaged under different conditions.

5.3.3 *Signal–context interactions*

As discussed in Chapter 4, reinforcer presentations always occur in a context, and therefore, contextual cues can acquire signal value, just as temporally discrete conditioned stimuli. "Signal value" refers to the ability of a stimulus (whether a CS or context) to predict the occurrence of some event, such as the US. Unlike signals, contextual cues are present over longer periods and include external stimuli (visual, auditory, tactile) as well as internal states (conditions induced by drugs, emotions, motivations).

The emergence of the conditioned response is determined by the signal value of the CS relative to the context (Gibbon & Balsam, 1981). All other things being equal, if a US is delivered at the end of a CS, then the shorter the CS (trial duration: T), the stronger the response to the CS; the shorter the interval between successive reinforcers (cycle: C), the

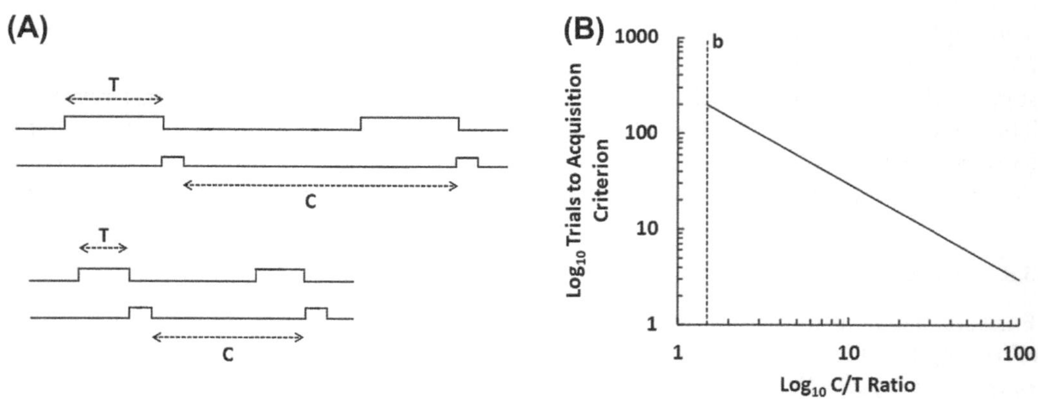

Figure 5.2 **The C/T ratio. (A)** Two training procedures that have the same C/T ratio but different absolute values for T and C (C and T are twice the length in the top compared to the bottom graph). **(B)** The figure represents the relationship between a measure of acquisition speed (trials to criterion) and the C/T ratio. The function tends to be linear on double logarithmic scales. "b" is a threshold (C/T = 1.5) below which there is no evidence of acquisition.

stronger the response to the context. Thus, responding to the CS emerges faster with a short T, but responding to the context emerges faster with a short C. Under many conditions, responding to the CS and to the context compete for expression, so that the CR should be directly related to T but inversely related to C. The weaker the context, the more likely the animal will respond to the CS. The results of a wide range of classical conditioning experiments demonstrate that the emergence of the CR to the CS is a negative function of the C/T ratio—called the *expectancy ratio*. As the C/T ratio increases, and independently of the absolute values of C and T, the CR tends to emerge after a smaller number of CS→US pairings. Two training conditions with different C and T values would lead to similar acquisition rates if the C/T ratios are the same. Thus, as an example, autoshaping training with a 5-s CS (T) and a 60-s intertrial interval (C) should produce similar acquisition rates to autoshaping training with a 15-s CS and a 180-s intertrial interval because 60/5 = 180/15.

5.4 Attention and learning

When we are in a stadium watching a soccer game, our senses are exposed to many stimuli. A friend sitting by our side might notice a change in our behavior and could wonder what caused it. Although we are sensing multiple stimuli, our behavior may be influenced by only one or a few of them. This stimulus selectivity could have resulted in a response to brilliant dribbling in the field or to the sight and smell of a nearby burger. Stimulus selectivity is one way to represent the intervening variable of *attention*, which can enhance or disrupt conditioning to a stimulus.

5.4.1 Latent inhibition

Attentional decrement due to repetitive exposure to a stimulus may cause *latent inhibition*, defined as a retardation of acquisition during CS→US pairings (Phase 2) after repeated CS-only presentations (Phase 1). Notice that the procedure to induce latent inhibition, CS-only presentations in Phase 1, is the same as that used in extinction, except that the CS is presented before conditioning, not after conditioning as in extinction. Additionally, we have already discussed in Chapters 2 and 3 how repeated presentation of a stimulus results in habituation of the behavior initially elicited by the stimulus. A noise or light will elicit an orienting response initially, but this will decrease with repeated presentations. In this case, conditioning, rather than simple exposure to the stimulus, is used to detect latent inhibition in Phase 2 as a retardation in the acquisition of the response relative to a control not exposed to CS-only presentations.

Latent inhibition was found in a variety of training conditions with mammals. Extensive Tone-only presentations retarded subsequent acquisition of a nictitating membrane CR in rabbits (Solomon et al., 1974). The nictitating membrane is a second eyelid that rabbits (and other species) have that closes when the eye is stimulated; it is a protective response. Is latent inhibition another procedure for conditioning an inhibitor, as the name would suggest? One of the two most common methods for testing an inhibitor is a summation test. An inhibitor is paired with a conditioned excitor trained separately, and excitatory responding to the excitor is compare to other groups in which the excitor is paired with a neutral stimulus (i.e., not excitatory or inhibitory). When a summation test of a Tone CS was presented in compound with a transfer excitor (a Light previously paired with Shock), the Tone with extensive preexposure disrupted responding to the Light, but it did so to the same extent as the Tone in a group without preexposure. Thus, the ToneLight compound was equally novel in both groups, as the Light had always been presented by itself. This result suggested that latent inhibition was the result of reduced attention to the Tone rather than the development of inhibitory conditioning to the Tone (i.e., converting the Tone into a signal for the absence of shock). In this case, the Tone should have suppressed responding to the Light only after extensive preexposure but not when the Tone had not been preexposed. Therefore, the word "inhibition" in latent inhibition should not be interpreted as suggesting that nonreinforced exposure to a novel stimulus leads to inhibitory conditioning (Rescorla, 1971).

Latent inhibition has also been described extensively in fear conditioning experiments with mice, in conditioned taste aversion with rats, and in a variety of tasks with human participants. As you might suspect, the strength of latent inhibition (i.e., the extent of the retardation of acquisition) increases with the number of CS preexposures, is reduced by a change in the stimulus from preexposure to conditioning (i.e., stimulus generalization decrement), is reduced with changes in the context from preexposure to conditioning, and is also reduced by changes in the motivational state from preexposure to conditioning. Many of these findings must be qualified, as numerous exceptions and opposite effects have been reported. Consider the issue of the contextual control of latent inhibition as an example. In conditioned taste aversion, preexposure to the CS (Saline solution) followed by pairings of the CS with sickness induced by lithium chloride (LiCl, a toxin inducing gastrointestinal sickness) as the US in the same context may (Morón et al., 2002) or not (Manrique et al., 2004) affect the size of latent inhibition depending on seemingly trivial changes in procedure, such as the number of trials of preexposure to the context before CS preexposure sessions start.

Whereas attentional decrement may account for a variety of latent inhibition effects, there are other factors at play. In one case (Ishii et al., 1999), the target stimulus was preexposed either by itself or in compound with a second stimulus (Table 5.2). Then, animals were conditioned either with the same or the alternate preexposure stimulus (e.g., preexposed to A and conditioned with A vs. AB). Any of the two changes from preexposure to conditioning reduced the size of latent inhibition, suggesting that the CS (whether A or AB) suffered from stimulus generalization decrement.

There are also hidden sources of information during CS preexposure that might affect the strength of latent inhibition, such as the motivational state of the animal. In one experiment (Killcross & Balleine, 1996), rats were preexposed to two stimuli, one while they were hungry and the other while they were thirsty (Hungry: A, Thirsty: B). Then, half the rats were trained with three stimuli (A, B, C), each paired with pellets (solid, more related to hunger), while the other half received training with the same three stimuli but paired with saline solution (liquid, more relevant to thirst). Training involved pairing each CS with the

Table 5.2 Latent inhibition after stimulus changes from preexposure to conditioning

Preexposure	*Conditioning*	*Results*
Water	A→US	
A	A→US	Strong latent inhibition
AB	A→US	Attenuated latent inhibition
Water	AB→US	
A	AB→US	Attenuated latent inhibition
AB	AB→US	Strong latent inhibition

Note. A and B were Vinegar and Sucrose flavors, counterbalanced across experiments. The US was LiCl. Animals preexposed to Water provided a nonpreexposure control condition. Only a subset of the testing conditions included in the study is presented here (from Ishii et al., 1999).

Table 5.3 Role of motivation on latent inhibition

Group	*Preexposure*	*Conditioning*	*Results*
Hunger	Hungry: A Thirsty: B	Hungry & Thirsty: A→Pellet Hungry & Thirsty: B→Pellet Hungry & Thirsty: C→Pellet	Acquisition to A retarded
Thirst	Hungry: A Thirsty: B	Hungry & Thirsty: A→Saline Hungry & Thirsty: B→Saline Hungry & Thirsty: C→Saline	Acquisition to B retarded

Note. A, B, and C were auditory stimuli (Tone, Clicker, white Noise). The USs were Pellets or Saline solution. The dependent variable was the number of magazine entries in the cup where the USs were delivered, but during the CS (i.e., before US delivery). C was a nonpreexposed, control stimulus (from Killcross & Balleine, 1996).

appropriate US (e.g., A→Pellet, B→Pellet, C→Pellet) while recording head entries in the magazine where either the pellets or saline were delivered during the presentation of each CS. During training, all animals were both hungry and thirsty (Table 5.3). In the Pellet condition, rats showed retardation of acquisition to A, the stimulus preexposed while the animal was hungry (relative to B, preexposed while thirsty, and C, not preexposed), whereas in the Saline condition, retardation was observed to B, the stimulus preexposed while the animal was thirsty (relative to A, preexposed while hungry, and C, not preexposed). These results suggest that during CS preexposure, animals learned that the CS was unrelated to their current motivational state, whether hungry or thirsty. As a result, acquisition to a CS paired with a US relevant to their motivational state during preexposure was retarded.

It is tantalizing to imagine the implications of such a result. For example, two people attend a party after a week of relative social isolation preparing for an exam (Person A) or after a week of fasting for religious reasons (Person B). The stimuli each person is exposed to at the party (people, places, music, etc.) will condition at different rates (when paired with food and pleasure) during the party depending on their motivational state (social or food deprivation) when preexposed during the previous week. Person A listened to a new song that was released at the start of the week of relative social isolation, equivalent to preexposure that the song is irrelevant for social bonding, and now, the song plays while Person A is engaged in a warm embrace (US) with a friend at the party. That song will acquire less associative strength, which translates into the strength of the CR, than a different song that was not preexposed or the same song preexposed for Person B during a week in which they were hungry.

Several factors contribute to latent inhibition, including attentional processes. For example, hunger may have increased attention to food-related events, and when food failed to occur during preexposure, the heightened attentional state may have enhanced learning that the CS was unrelated to hunger, thus retarding acquisition to the CS when it was paired with a hunger-relevant US. Consistent with this view, food or water restriction during CS preexposure enhanced attention to the CS so that subsequent fear conditioning (i.e., a different motivational situation) reduced latent inhibition (i.e., more CR strength) relative to a group of animals that were not deprived of food or water (De La Casa, 2013). Similarly, CS preexposure in animals that had just been subjected to a reward downshift event hypothesized to increase attention also exhibited reduced latent inhibition since attention during CS preexposure was preserved (De La Casa et al., 2018).

Attentional processes also seem to be involved in latent inhibition with human participants, a fact that has been used as a biomarker for the early detection of schizophrenia. It has been hypothesized that participants high in schizotypy have trouble ignoring irrelevant (i.e., preexposed) stimuli, which leads to a reduced latent-inhibition effect. One task implemented with patients who scored high in schizotypy compared to low-schizotypy controls involved exposure to a target letter (S) together with four nontarget letters (D, M, T, V) during preexposure. The test stage involves presenting the target letter always followed by X (S→X), a control letter always followed by X (H→X), and the other letters followed by X on some trials but not on other trials. Participants are asked to press a key when they predicted that X would be presented. Healthy volunteers exhibited slower reaction times to X when it followed the preexposed stimulus than the control stimulus, a latent inhibition effect that developed rapidly during testing, whereas participants high in schizotypy showed a latent inhibition effect that developed much later in testing (Granger et al., 2020). Latent inhibition may be sensitive to the neurochemical basis of schizophrenia symptoms. Patients with psychotic symptoms that improve with dopamine blockers may not show latent inhibition before treatment but may exhibit the effect after treatment. In mice, the repeated presentation of a stimulus is accompanied by a reduction in dopamine release in the striatum that predicts the subsequent development of a latent inhibition effect (Kutlu et al., 2022). However, patients with schizophrenia symptoms that show a latent inhibition effect may exhibit normal dopamine levels in the striatum but high glutamate levels in the anterior cingulate cortex (Demjaha et al., 2014). Thus, latent inhibition may be a tool to detect the neurochemical basis of schizophrenia symptoms, whether based on dopamine or glutamate deficiency, and thus predict which psychopharmacological treatment has a greater chance of success in specific patients.

Repeated presentations of the CS by itself are procedurally similar to habituation (see Chapter 3). Boughner and Papini (2006) compared the degree of habituation during the CS preexposure phase of latent inhibition in rats trained in an autoshaping paradigm and found that the strength of habituation did not predict the strength of latent inhibition. These results suggest that latent inhibition cannot be reduced to only long-term habituation. Nonetheless, if latent inhibition and long-term habituation are somehow related, then latent inhibition should be a widespread learning phenomenon across species.

5.4.2 *Comparative studies of latent inhibition*

Demonstrations of latent inhibition in vertebrates other than mammals are rare. In some cases, preexposure to the CS is preceded by training the animal to receive the reward, which has the potential to induce contextual conditioning. In these cases, not reinforcing the CS in an excitatory context may convert it into an inhibitor (see inhibitory conditioning, Chapter 4). Having learned that the CS predicts the absence of the US may subsequently retard acquisition during CS→US training, which may look like latent inhibition. When this potential confound is not present, then the results of comparative latent inhibition studies are less consistent. Here are some examples.

Wynne and Delius (1995) reported that pigeons failed to show latent inhibition after preexposure to a context in which they were later conditioned to peck by apomorphine administration. Apomorphine induces pecking in pigeons, a behavior that can be conditioned to the context. In a series of experiments with goldfish (*Carassius auratus*), Shishimi (1985) reported no evidence of latent inhibition after systematic variations in the type of signal (visual, auditory), reinforcer (electric shock, food), number of preexposure trials (0–160 trials), and training procedure (classical and operant conditioning).

In mammals, preexposure to a CS also retards conditioning when the CS is used as the inhibitor in a conditioned inhibition paradigm (i.e., A+, AB-, with "B" being the preexposed stimulus). This also suggests that latent inhibition does not involve inhibitory conditioning, as mentioned previously, but rather an attentional deficit affecting signal processing independently of its role in a conditioning situation (Rescorla, 1971). In goldfish, however, CS preexposure does not affect the course of conditioned inhibition training (Shishimi, 1985). Goldfish acquired a White→Shock, WhiteRed-only (W+, WR-) discrimination equally well whether Red (the flickering red light acting as the negative stimulus) was preexposed or not. In this experiment, training involved classical conditioning of which visual stimuli (White and Red lights) were used as signals and swimming over a barrier as the response. Notice that discriminating between W and WR is not possible without attending to R or to the WR configuration. As shown in Figure 5.3, the mean level of performance of preexposed goldfish was lower than that of nonpreexposed goldfish, but the discrimination was learned equally well. The mean performance group difference suggests that the effect of preexposure was to reduce responsiveness to stimuli rather than modify attention to a specific stimulus.

In some cases, nonreinforced CS preexposure can enhance subsequent CS→US conditioning—a reversed latent inhibition effect. In one experiment (Morin et al., 1990), Atlantic salmon (*Salmo salar*) preexposed to an olfactory stimulus (L-cysteine diluted in water) during 20 trials, followed the next day by 20 Odor→Shock pairings, showed enhanced CS→US acquisition as measured in terms of heart rate relative to a nonpreexposed control. A similar reversed latent inhibition effect was reported in preweanling 10-day-old rats after

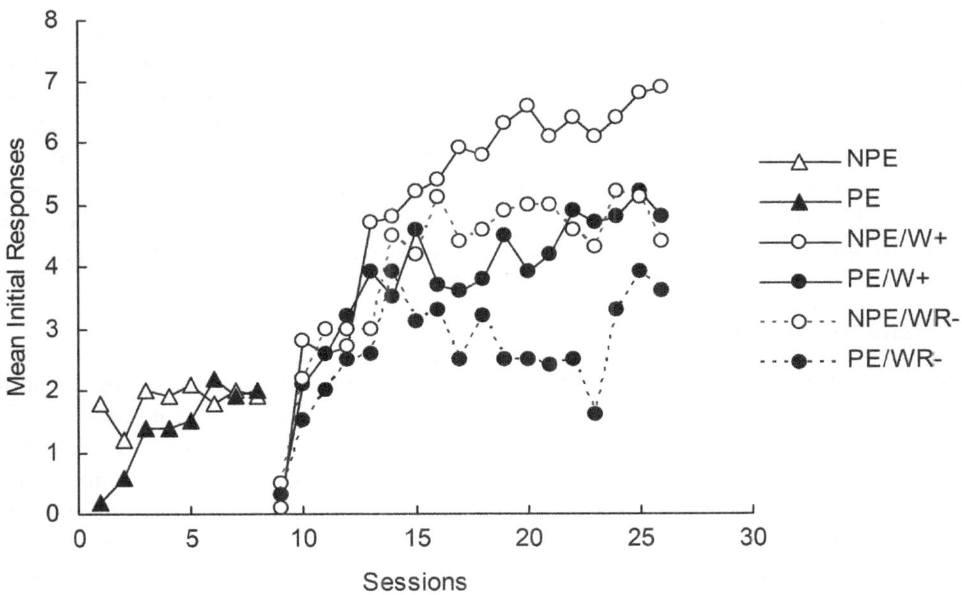

Figure 5.3 **Latent inhibition studies in goldfish.** Groups of goldfish were either preexposed (PE) or nonpreexposed (NPE) to a flickering red light (R) and then trained to discriminate a white stimulus (W+) from a compound of the white stimulus and red light (WR-). The discrimination was solved by PE (continuous lines) and NPE groups (dashed lines), showing no evidence that PE modified attention to R. (From Shishimi, 1985; reproduced with permission from the American Psychological Association.)

relatively few preexposure trials (Hoffman & Spear, 1989), thus suggesting interesting parallels between comparative and developmental data that have not been explored in detail.

There are also some demonstrations of latent inhibition in nonmammalian vertebrates in aversive conditioning situations. Fish respond to odors diffusing from damage skin from conspecifics, a natural consequence of predation. In lemon damselfish (*Pomacentrus moluccensis*), preexposure to an Odor subsequently retards conditioning during an Odor→Alarm episode, relative to preexposure to Saline water (Mitchell et al., 2011). Conditioning was measured in terms of suppression of foraging behavior. Similar latent inhibition of predator odors was reported in frog tadpoles (*Pelophylax perezi*; Gonzalo et al., 2013).

Latent inhibition has also been reported in invertebrates. In honeybees, stimulus preexposure later retarded acquisition in an aversive situation (Abramson & Bitterman, 1986). Interestingly, unlike in rats (Rescorla, 1971, mentioned previously), stimulus preexposure suppressed responding to a known excitor during a summation test. Chandra et al. (2010) reported increased retardation of acquisition as a function of variations in the number of preexposure trials from zero (control) up to 50 nonreinforced presentations of the CS. Honeybees were conditioned by pairings of an Odor (CS) and Sucrose (US), and the proboscis extension was the CR. However, these animals had pretraining conditioning with sucrose, which could have influenced the effect. In two species of crayfish (*Orconectes virilis* and *O. rusticus*), preexposure to goldfish odor later retarded acquisition of defensive behavior when the odor was paired with an alarm substance (Acquistapace et al., 2003).

The common procedures implemented in habituation (see Chapter 3) and latent inhibition experiments merit further consideration. Attentional decrement was invoked in both effects, and yet there are well-documented failures of latent inhibition, whereas habituation has been reported in a wide range of species. An important difference between these two effects lies in the testing procedures. While habituation is usually assessed at the time the stimulus is being presented, latent inhibition is assessed in a subsequent acquisition phase of CS→US pairings. Latent inhibition seems to assess the degree to which the CS preexposure experience transfers to conditioning with the same CS. To have a better understanding of failures to observe latent inhibition, it is useful to look at related tasks also thought to depend on attentional decrement and determine whether there is covariation of experimental outcomes. We turn to one such task in this coming section, also involving transfer of training.

5.4.3 ***Intra- vs. extradimensional transfer***

Suppose that a group of animals is trained in a visual discrimination involving compound stimuli with Colors (Red, Yellow) and Lines (Horizontal, Vertical). "Color" and "Line" are visual dimensions. Training is arranged so that Color is relevant but Line is irrelevant, as described in Table 5.4. The correct strategy is to respond to Red, not to respond to Yellow, and to ignore Horizontal and Vertical. In other words, attend to the Color dimension but ignore the Line dimension. The crucial test is to determine the relative difficulty of learning a subsequent discrimination in which the previously relevant dimension continues to be relevant (***intradimensional transfer***) or one in which the previously irrelevant dimension becomes relevant (***extradimensional transfer***).

After training, animals received transfer discrimination training involving new Colors (Green, Blue) and new Lines (Slash: /; Backslash: \). For the intradimensional condition, Color continues to be relevant: Respond to Green but not to Blue and ignore the Lines. However, for the extradimensional condition, Line orientation has now become relevant: Respond to Slash but not to Backslash and ignore Colors. In monkeys and rats, intradimensional transfer

Table 5.4 An example of an intradimensional vs. extradimensional transfer design

Group	*Training*	*Transfer*
Intradimensional (Color-Color transfer)	**Red**Horizontal→Food **Red**Vertical→Food **Yellow**Horizontal→Nothing **Yellow**Vertical→Nothing	**Green**Slash→Food **Green**Backslash→Food **Blue**Slash→Nothing **Blue**Backslash→Nothing
Extradimensional (Color-Line transfer)	**Red**Horizontal→Food **Red**Vertical→Food **Yellow**Horizontal→Nothing **Yellow**Vertical→Nothing	Green**Slash**→Food Green**Backslash**→Nothing Blue**Slash**→Food Blue**Backslash**→Nothing

Note. The elements of the compound in the relevant dimension are in **bold**. The task was instrumental, but the response requirement has been ignored in Table 5.4 for simplicity. Color and Lines were counterbalanced, but, again, this feature was ignored in the table for simplicity.

facilitates learning relative to extradimensional transfer. The initial training reduces attention to the irrelevant dimension of the visual compound, thus interfering with the acquisition of a task that requires focusing attention on that dimension (Sutherland & Mackintosh, 1971). In the example, a reduction of attention to Line orientation during training causes a retardation of acquisition when Line orientation becomes relevant in transfer.

Because goldfish showed reversed latent inhibition effects, one can ask whether they exhibit other effects that also depend on attention. Dimensional transfer effects were studied using a complex design with goldfish as subjects (Table 5.4). Goldfish have well-developed vision, and thus, it is possible to present the type of complex stimuli required for a demonstration of dimensional transfer effects. In these experiments, stimuli were presented in a circular target in which a black Line was superimposed on a Color background. Thus, "RedHorizontal" was a red target with a black horizontal line.

Interestingly, goldfish learned these complex transfer problems, but their performance was equally effective whether the transfer was intra- or extradimensional (Couvillon et al., 1976). These results suggest the possibility that the mechanisms responsible for attentional modulation of associative learning are weak or absent in nonmammalian vertebrates. The alternative hypothesis suggests that these behavioral effects reflect species differences in contextual factors, such as inappropriate conditions of preexposure training, rather than a divergence in learning mechanisms. Detailed behavioral and neurobiological analyses in a comparative framework are required to arrive at stronger conclusions.

5.4.4 *Perceptual learning*

Latent inhibition involves a decrement in learning about a stimulus after preexposure. However, repeated exposure to stimuli can enhance learning by increasing attention to the perceptual differences between stimuli (more on this in Chapter 10). Such *perceptual learning* involves experience, and it leads to a stable change in perception (Mitchell & Hall, 2014). For example, a trained geologist or a wine enthusiast will distinguish far more differences among rocks or wines than persons with limited experience. Such perceptual skills are best acquired after extensive opportunity to compare variations of the target stimulus. In one experiment (Gibson & Walk, 1956), rats that had been extensively exposed to triangles and circles on the walls of their cages subsequently learned to discriminate these stimuli faster than controls not exposed to these visual stimuli. Preexposure did not involve any specific training, whereas the discrimination was acquired when the choice of one stimulus was reinforced with food, but the choice of the other was not. Similar results have been reported with other sensory systems (e.g., flavors, tactile stimuli) and with other species (e.g., chickens, humans), suggesting perceptual learning is a general phenomenon.

Experiments show that perceptual learning is facilitated by extensive opportunity to compare the stimuli subsequently involved in discrimination training. For example (Symonds & Hall, 1995), preexposure to two flavors in an interleaving fashion across trials (A-B-A-B-. . .) facilitated their discrimination (A+, B-) more than preexposure to these flavors in blocks of trials (A-A-A-. . . B-B-B-. . .). Interleaving exposure seems to promote attention to the elements that differentiate the two stimuli involved in the comparison. Such attention may be also enhanced by the introduction of a common element. Thus, if preexposure involves AX and BX, with "X" being a common element, subsequent discrimination between A and B is enhanced relative to groups lacking such common element. Table 5.5 shows the design of a flavor aversion experiment involving a common element (Lemon or Quinine) presented during preexposure to the flavors. The discrimination between the two compounds, one paired with the toxin LiCl and the other presented by itself, developed faster for the group preexposed to the compounds with a common element than for the group that had no such common element (Mackintosh et al., 1991).

Two theoretical possibilities were suggested to account for results such as these (McLaren et al., 1989). One possibility is that extensive preexposure to the common element after AX-, BX- training caused attention to X to be reduced more than to either of the two unique elements (i.e., more latent inhibition to X than to either A or B). Such an extensive reduction in attention to X could have facilitated the discrimination between A and B. A second possibility is that the common element encourages the development of inhibitory associations between the elements that are unique to each stimulus. This would work in the following manner.

AX training involves the acquisition of excitatory associations between A and X, such that subsequent exposure to X evokes a representation of A and vice versa. The same would be true for X and B during BX trials. Consequently, a representation of B will be evoked by X during AX trials. Over trials, the direct experience of B on BX trials will come to be discriminated from the representation of B elicited on AX trials, a process facilitated by the conversion of A into a signal for the absence of B (i.e., an inhibitor of B). The same would

Table 5.5 Design of a perceptual learning experiment with a common element

Group	*Preexposure*	*Discrimination*	*Results*
LSal-LSuc	Lemon-Saline Lemon-Sucrose	Lemon-Saline→LiCl Lemon-Sucrose→Nothing	Faster discrimination
QSal-QSuc	Quinine-Saline Quinine-Sucrose	Lemon-Saline→LiCl Lemon-Sucrose→Nothing	Faster discrimination
LSal-QSuc	Lemon-Saline Quinine-Sucrose	Lemon-Saline→LiCl Lemon-Sucrose→Nothing	Slower discrimination
QSal-LSuc	Quinine-Saline Lemon-Sucrose	Lemon-Saline→LiCl Lemon-Sucrose→Nothing	Slower discrimination

Note. Additional groups are omitted for simplicity. Notice that the top two groups were preexposed to two compounds with a common element (either Lemon or Quinine), whereas the lower two groups were preexposed to compounds without a common element. During discrimination training, all the groups were trained to differentiate one compound paired with LiCl from a different compound presented by itself (Nothing). Preexposure with a common element facilitated the discrimination between Saline and Sucrose, whether the common element was present during discrimination training (first group) or the common element was a different flavor (second group).

also occur during BX trials, with B inhibiting a representation of A. This mechanism would further differentiate A and B in terms of their perception, thus facilitating their discrimination (Figure 5.4). The same process is occurring as you are learning to discriminate the concepts of "latent inhibition" from "perceptual learning," which share many common elements. Ideally, when asked to discriminate latent inhibition from perceptual learning on an exam or in a conversation, inhibitory connections will prevent you from thinking about the unique properties of perceptual learning. This illustrates the tension between discrimination and generalization.

Evidence consistent with inhibitory associations was obtained in the experiment described in Table 5.5. Discrimination between A and B was facilitated whether the common element during preexposure was also present during discrimination (Lemon) or the common element during preexposure (Quinine) and discrimination training (Lemon) were different. The key factor was that the presence of a common element during preexposure generated inhibitory associations between the unique elements of each compound. For the geologist and wine enthusiast mentioned previously, a rock and a sip of wine would also be informing them about related rock and wine stimuli that are absent in that perceptual experience.

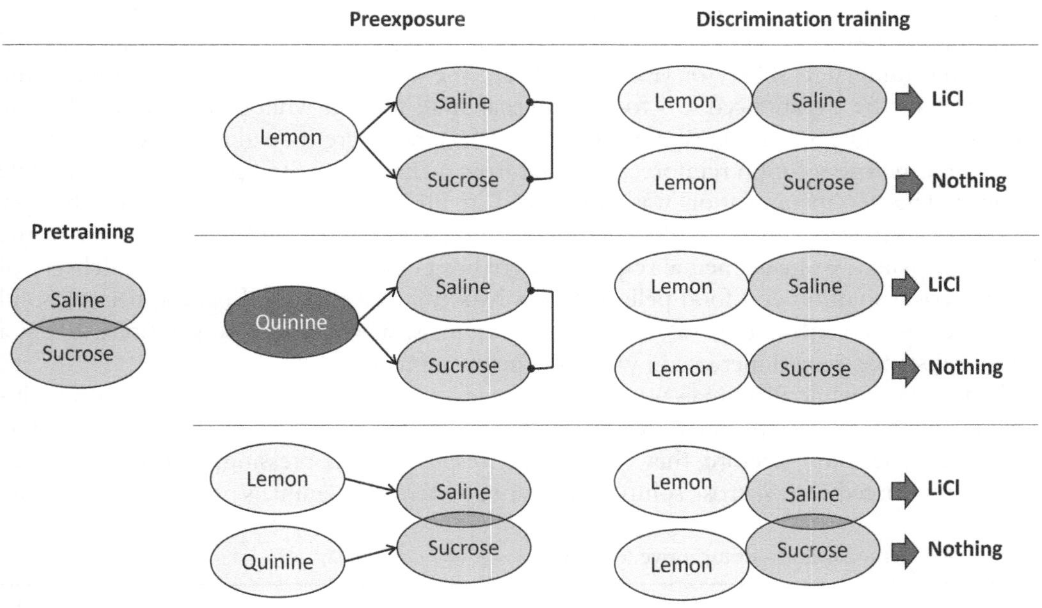

Figure 5.4 **Hypothetical explanation of perceptual learning.** Before training (Pretraining), Saline and Sucrose stimuli have some unique and some common elements. During Preexposure, inhibitory associations develop between the unique elements of Saline and Sucrose stimuli promoted by the presence of a common stimulus (either Lemon or Quinine). In the absence of a common element (bottom condition), Saline and Sucrose continue to share some proportion of elements (an additional control present in Table 5.5 is omitted from this figure for clarity). The Discrimination develops faster in the top two conditions because Saline and Sucrose are more distinct stimuli than in the bottom condition. Notice that Saline and Sucrose become more distinct because of the presence of a common stimulus during Preexposure, whether that stimulus is present (top condition, Lemon) or absent (middle condition, Quinine) during Discrimination.

5.5 Motivation and learning

It is noon, and Nancy is crossing the street, walking fast toward that burger place at the corner. What factors determine Nancy's behavior? She has probably had a cheeseburger for lunch before in this restaurant. Experience provides the knowledge needed to direct behavior toward a specific goal. But why is Nancy doing this right now? She had the same knowledge about burgers at 10 a.m., but then, she was busy sorting some documents in her office. Well, it is lunchtime, and Nancy is hungry. Whereas learning gives directionality to behavior, ***motivation*** is an internal state that changes the value of biological and conditioned stimuli to provide the impetus to initiate a behavior. As with attention, motivation is also influenced by learning, and the integration of these determines behavior. After all, Nancy is having her lunch at noon, an acquired social convention.

5.5.1 Incentive value

How do objects acquire incentive value? Why is a cheeseburger appealing to some but not to others? We learned previously that the internal state, whether food deprived or water deprived during preexposure to a stimulus, plays a role in learning that the preexposed stimulus does not change motivation (e.g., a reduction in hunger). By the same rule, the internal state present when a US is consumed can enhance its incentive value as a reinforcer.

To demonstrate this type of ***incentive learning***, animals must be shifted in their internal state from hungry to thirsty or vice versa. Then, the key factor in incentive learning is the relevance of the experienced US to the internal state present while it is received. In one experiment (Table 5.6; Dickinson & Dawson, 1989), rats were trained in Phase 1 to press a lever for a sucrose solution reinforcer and pull from a chain for a food pellet reinforcer while hungry. The key manipulation was introduced in Phase 2, when some rats were hungry whereas others were thirsty. Under these motivational conditions and in the absence of the lever and chain (i.e., instrumental responses were not possible), they received free delivery of both sucrose solution and food pellets. It was hypothesized that food pellets, being a solid substance, would increase in value for hungry animals, whereas sucrose solutions, being a liquid substance, would increase in value for thirsty animals.

In a final test while all animals were thirsty, the lever was available in the absence of all reinforcers. For rats in Group Thirst, experiencing the sucrose solution while thirsty increased its incentive value, and therefore, they engaged the response, lever pressing, that had been previously reinforced with sucrose solution to a larger extent than animals previously reinforced

Table 5.6 A demonstration of incentive learning

Group	*Phase 1*	*Phase 2*	*Test*	*Results*
Thirst	Hungry: Lever→Sucrose Hungry: Pull→Pellet	Thirsty: Sucrose Thirsty: Pellet	Thirsty: Lever?	5.9(*)
	Hungry: Lever→Pellet Hungry: Pull→Sucrose	Thirsty: Sucrose Thirsty: Pellet	Thirsty: Lever?	3.1
Hunger	Hungry: Lever→Sucrose Hungry: Pull→Pellet	Hungry: Sucrose Hungry: Pellet	Thirsty: Lever?	3.1(ns)
	Hungry: Lever→Pellet Hungry: Pull→Sucrose	Hungry: Sucrose Hungry: Pellet	Thirsty: Lever?	3.6

Note. The results are expressed in terms of responses per minute. The difference in behavior was significant for Group Thirst (*) but nonsignificant for Group Hunger (ns). (From Dickinson & Dawson, 1989)

with pellets for pressing the lever. Group Hunger shows that this effect is not just a matter of experiencing these rewards and these internal states but a function of the appropriate connection between them. Thus, for animals in Group Hunger, a test under thirst made no difference because they had experienced the sucrose solution in Phase 2 under hungry conditions.

A change in internal state can invigorate a response that was associated in the past with a reward that reduced that internal state, even if that response was acquired under a different internal state. Thus, animals that learned to lever press for sucrose solution while hungry would press the lever more if they also experienced sucrose solutions while thirsty. The relevance of a liquid solution to the internal state of thirst increased the value of that reward.

5.5.2 Wanting and liking

If I say that I would like to have some pizza, somebody listening to me will conclude that I must like pizza. Our intuitions tell us that wanting and liking a reward are interchangeable. Moreover, we have known for some time that there is a brain reward system connecting areas in the mesencephalon (e.g., ventral tegmental area, VTA) with striatal (e.g., nucleus accumbens, NAc) and cortical regions (e.g., prefrontal cortex, PFC) whose activity relates to the incentive value of a reward. These connections are based on neurons that release dopamine as their neurotransmitter. Early research with rats subjected to dopamine depletion in the brain showed that while they would not consume food, they reacted with signs of pleasure (or aversion) when the reward was placed in their mouths (Berridge et al., 1989).

Such signs were observed in the so-called taste reactivity test, in which the facial expressions of rats tasting various solutions is videotaped with a camera placed underneath the animal's head (Grill & Norgren, 1978). Figure 5.5 shows four expressions, one of which is exhibited in response to sucrose (rhythmic tongue movements, B), which stimulates taste receptors for sweet solutions and is highly palatable for rats, and the other in response to quinine (gapes, D), which stimulates receptors for bitter solutions that rats actively reject. Animals that were subjected to a treatment that depletes dopamine and induces a reluctance to eat still showed normal facial expressions to various substances, including sucrose and quinine. Conversely, electrical stimulation of the lateral hypothalamus, which raises dopamine levels and induces food consumption, failed to enhance liking facial expressions. These findings reveal a distinction between "liking," as indicated by facial expressions, and "wanting," as indicated by consumption. Similar facial expressions have been observed in response to the same taste solutions in humans and other primates, providing information about the generality of liking of various solutions.

These findings also led to a more general distinction between "wanting" a reward and "liking" a reward. *Wanting* relates to the salience of reward signals and to activity in the dopaminergic reward system. Wanting is responsible for cravings induced by exposure to stimuli associated with US delivery or reinforcer consumption, which acquire incentive salience. Wanting therefore plays a major role in our interaction with incentives that increase dopamine release, including food, having relevance to our understanding of disorders like obesity and addiction (Morales & Berridge, 2020). However, *liking* appears to be under the control of a set of regions of the nucleus accumbens, the ventral pallidum, and the parabrachial nucleus in the brainstem. Microinfusions of opioids in the anterior regions of these areas (so-called hot spots) increase positive facial expressions, whereas the same microinfusions in the posterior region of these areas (so-called cold spots) reduces positive facial expressions (Berridge & Kringelbach, 2015).

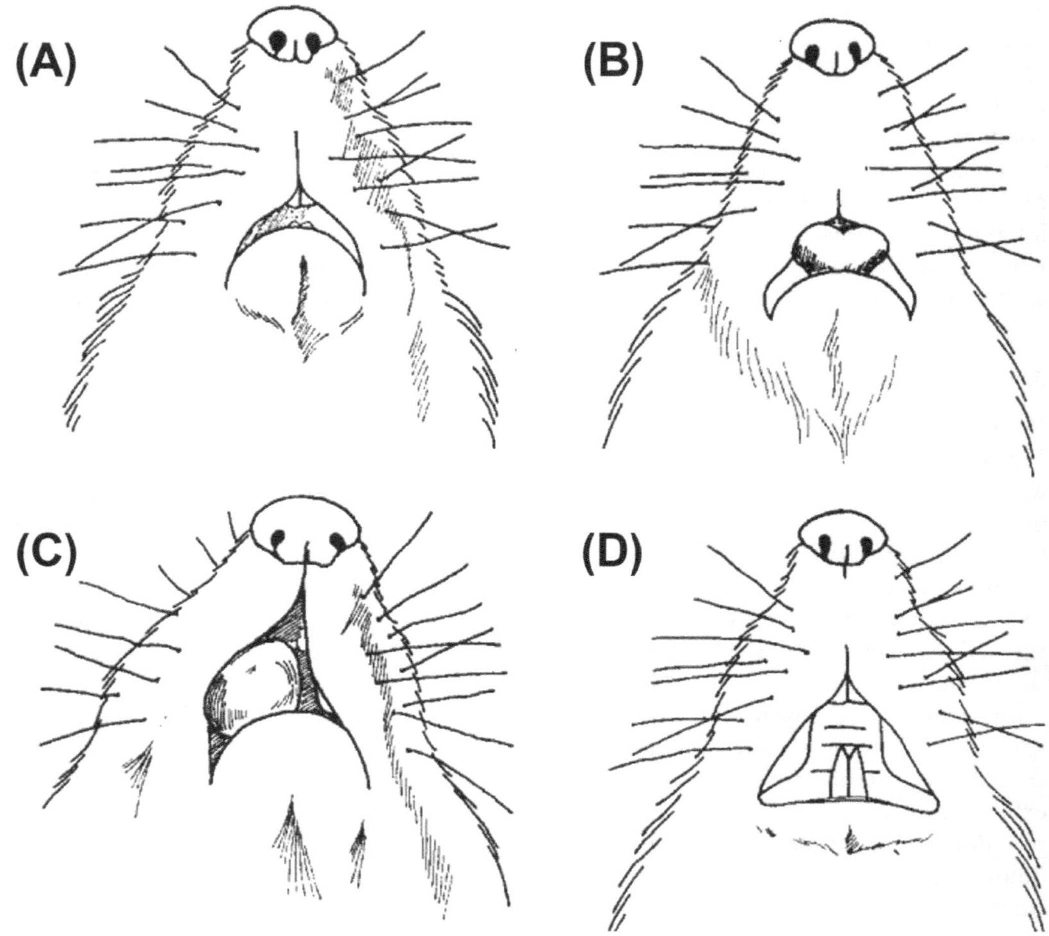

Figure 5.5 **Facial expressions of rats in response to taste solutions. (A):** rhythmic mouth movements (symmetric movement of the lower jaw). **(B):** rhythmic tongue protrusions (tongue emerges on the midline covering the upper incisors). **(C):** lateral tongue movements (tongue emerges on the side of the mouth). **(D):** gapes (lower jaw lowers and the corners of the mouth retract, forming a triangular opening). Mouth movements and tongue protrusions **(A–C)** are typical responses to sucrose (a sweet taste), whereas gapes **(D)** occur in response to quinine (a bitter taste). (From Grill & Norgren, 1978; reproduced with permission from *Brain Research*.)

5.6 Emotion and learning

The distinction between "motivation" and "emotion" is not so clear-cut as one might think, especially because of the inconsistency with which these concepts are defined. Both concepts refer to internal states, both can promote behavior, and both usually refer to external events. Hunger, as an example of a motivational state, may induce food searching behavior that is all about reestablishing a nutritional or energetic equilibrium. Fear, as an example of an emotional state, may induce protective responses, such as freezing or escape, aimed at surviving a threat. Thus, distinguishing between motivation and emotion is somewhat arbitrary, perhaps based more on traditional treatments of these concepts in psychology than about objective differences (Berridge, 2018).

5.6.1 Fear/threat

Organisms are surrounded by threatening situations, and to the extent that they survive the threat, it is obviously adaptive to learn about these situations as fast as possible. *Fear* learning plays a defensive function allowing organisms to cope with predators, aggressive conspecifics, and some natural phenomena as sources of threat. The study of mammalian fear conditioning is arguably the area that has made most progress toward an understanding of this form of learning at lower levels of analysis (see Figure 3.1). From an evolutionary perspective, the neural mechanisms supporting the protective emotion of fear likely evolved as part of an antipredator suite of characters. The origin of fear mechanisms in mammals may be connected to the active lifestyle of early chordates. The tail and lateral muscles of Cambrian chordates, such as *Pikaia*, suggest these animals had an active lifestyle that may have included a repertoire of evasive and escape behaviors when threatened by predators. Characters with clear defensive function, such as the armors of agnathan and placoderm fish, evolved rapidly during the Cambrian, more than 500 Ma, but were absent in fossil specimens from pre-Cambrian rocks (Randle & Sansom, 2019).

Consistent with this view, the behavior and brain mechanisms engaged in threatening situations exhibit evolutionary conservation. For example, goldfish (*Carassius auratus*) and zebrafish (*Danio rerio*), whose common ancestor with mammals may have lived about 400 Ma (see Figure 1.13, Chapter 1), rapidly acquire avoidance behavior and contextual fear conditioning, exhibit extinction when shocks are discontinued, and show modulation by factors that also influence mammalian learning under similar conditions, such as shock intensity and blockage of NMDA receptors (Kenney et al., 2017; Lal et al., 2018; Overmier & Papini, 1986). Furthermore, fear learning in bony fish depends on the dorsomedial telencephalon (Portavella et al., 2004; see also Chapter 1), a region homologous to the mammalian amygdala, known to play a central role in fear and avoidance conditioning in mammals.

There are multiple sources of evidence supporting the notion that fear conditioning is accompanied by an unconditioned negative emotional response that can be conditioned to a CS in rodents. For example, rats that experienced Light→Shock pairings that induced peripheral pain subsequently acquired a new response to escape from the Light, even in the absence of subsequent shocks (McAllister et al., 1974). Conditioned fear has sufficient emotional intensity to support the development of a new response by itself.

Rodents tend to remain motionless in anticipation of physical pain, such as when placed in a situation previously associated with shock-induced pain. This *freezing* response (a behavioral index of fear) is also observed when rats and mice are exposed to the odor of a predator (Ferrero et al., 2011). Fear conditioning is also accompanied by the release of stress hormones, such as glucocorticoids (Cordero et al., 1998), and by the activation of endogenous opioids in the brain that reduce sensations of pain (hypoalgesia; McNally, 2009). For example, prior exposure to shock lengthens the duration a rat will wait before flicking its tail away from a potentially dangerous heat source (Chance et al., 1977). Thus, whereas it is not possible to directly observe the emotion of fear (or any emotion, for that matter), evidence such as that described here provides a strong indication that anticipating peripheral pain is accompanied in rodents by a negative emotional response.

5.6.2 Neurobiology of fear

As happens often in this book, topics developed in each chapter are interconnected with those covered in other chapter. Chapters 4 and 5 outlined some of the basic circuitry underlying fear conditioning (see Figure 4.8) and avoidance conditioning (see Figure 6.5). This section illustrates the application of neurobiological knowledge to understand some of the topics covered herein but in the realm of fear conditioning. These include CS and contextual conditioned fear, fear extinction, and the consolidation and reconsolidation of fear memories.

5.6.2.1 Discrete and contextual conditioned fear

Consider again the circuit presented in Figure 4.8. Stimulus inputs to this network include discrete CSs, such as tones or odors, and contextual stimuli, such as the chamber in which the experience takes place. These inputs (discrete and context) converge with the US input (usually a shock) in the lateral amygdala (LA). Stimuli activate peripheral receptors that send axons to a subcortical thalamic nucleus, the medial geniculate nucleus (MGN) in the case of a Tone CS, from which it is distributed to LA and then to the basal amygdala (BA)—labeled (1) in the figure, and also to the cortex. The connection from MGN to LA is a so-called quick-and-dirty pathway because it delivers CS information about an impending threat, but it does not provide perceptual detail. For example, Tone→Shock pairings lead to normal fear conditioning, whether in terms of freezing or heart rate responses (an autonomic index of fear), in rats with damage to auditory processing areas of cortex. But lesions of the MGN disrupt fear conditioning of both freezing and heart rate responses based on a Tone CS (LeDoux et al., 1984).

As shown in Figure 5.6, however, if the auditory cortex is intact, then Tone→Shock pairings induce plasticity in that area. Signal information travels from the thalamus to various cortical areas, some of which provide more detailed information about the CS to the amygdala. Thus, for responding to a threatening shadow, the quick-and-dirty pathway may be enough, but identifying the signal as a particular pattern of auditory stimulation (e.g., a

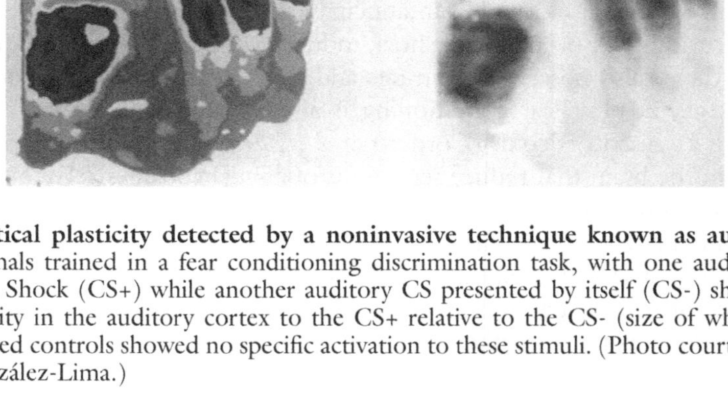

Figure 5.6 **Cortical plasticity detected by a noninvasive technique known as autoradiography.** Animals trained in a fear conditioning discrimination task, with one auditory CS paired with Shock (CS+) while another auditory CS presented by itself (CS-) showed enhanced activity in the auditory cortex to the CS+ relative to the CS- (size of white spot). Nontrained controls showed no specific activation to these stimuli. (Photo courtesy of Francisco González-Lima.)

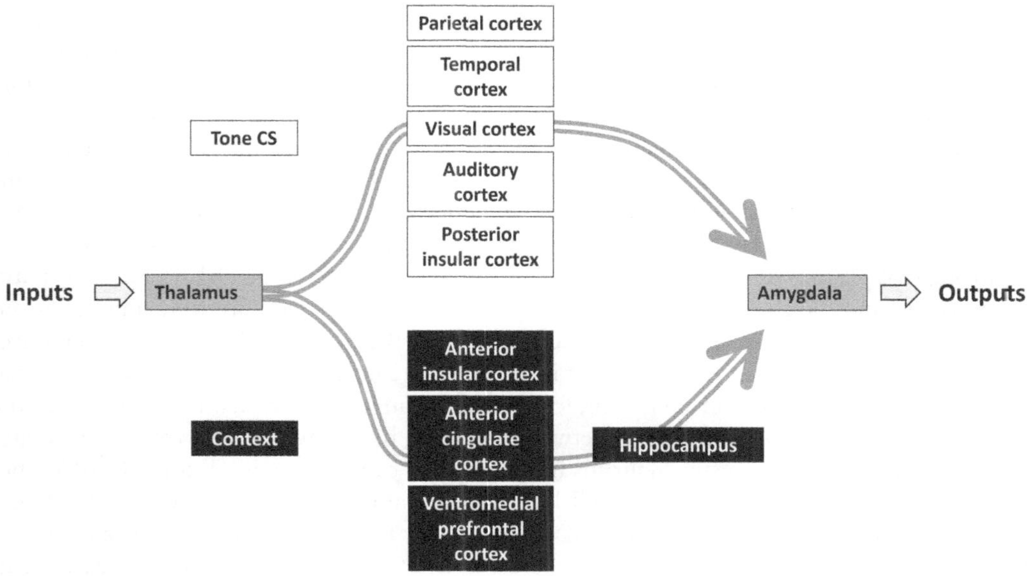

Figure 5.7 **Neurobiology of fear conditioning.** A summary of brain areas involved in fear conditioning to a Tone CS (white boxes) and to the context (black boxes).

hawk call) requires cortical input. However, auditory CSs and multimodality (e.g., olfactory and visual) contextual stimuli are likely to rely on different sensory processing pathways. Not surprisingly, then, lesions of an area of cortex more tightly linked to auditory processing, the posterior insular cortex, disrupted the freezing response to a Tone previously paired with Shock but not fear conditioning to the context (Brunzell & Kim, 2001; Figure 5.7).

Of course, encounters with signals for pain or threats also occur in a context, but in this case, fear conditioning is mediated by different structures. Unsignaled shocks administered in the presence of a distinct set of static cues (auditory, visual, or tactile features) would induce freezing responses during subsequent encounters with only the static cues. Functional magnetic resonance imaging (fMRI) studies with humans have identified the ventral hippocampus, the anterior insular cortex, and some areas in the prefrontal cortex as being critical for contextual fear conditioning (Lang et al., 2009). A summary of these findings is presented in Figure 5.7.

In fear, as in other domains, the ability to behave according to context allows for impressive behavioral plasticity (Maren et al., 2016). The same behaviors can be adaptive in one context and maladaptive in another. Displaying fear to a snake when encountering it in its natural environment is a protective emotion, yet the same paralyzing and arousing fear would be misplaced when observing a snake in a zoo setting.

5.6.2.2 *Fear extinction*

Neurobiological studies on fear extinction shed light on whether extinction involves new learning opposing the original acquisition (an inhibitory association) or the unlearning of the previously acquired CS→US association. As is often the case, both hypotheses appear to be correct. To illustrate this point, it is necessary to introduce a developmental dimension.

Preweanling infant rats (about 17 days of age; weaning usually occurs at 21 days of age in rats) exhibit no evidence of spontaneous recovery, reinstatement, or renewal effects after extinction of fear conditioning, which suggest that extinction erased the CS→US association. By contrast, postweanling rats (about 24 days of age) exhibit all these effects, suggesting that extinction in these animals was incomplete and behavior was being suppressed by new learning of an inhibitory association (Kim & Richardson, 2010). A key developmental outcome in rats is that the hippocampus becomes fully functional during this developmental period.

In preweanling, 17-day-old rats, fear extinction is driven mainly by a pathway from the ventromedial prefrontal cortex (vmPFC) to the basolateral amygdala (BLA), whereas pathways connecting the BLA with the hippocampus and the vmPFC are not fully functional yet. The vmPFC decreases the firing rate of neurons in the BLA during CS extinction (Herry et al., 2008), suggesting that the vmPFC is involved in the unlearning of the CS→US association, the preeminent mechanism during fear extinction in immature rats. In adults, when the brain is fully mature, communication between the BLA, hippocampus, and vmPFC facilitates memory formation. As a result, neurons in the vmPFC can activate inhibitory (GABAergic) neurons located in the intercalated cell layers of the amygdala, which then inhibit freezing responses during CS presentation in extinction—a new CS→NoUS inhibitory association (Ganella et al., 2018). Therefore, whereas extinction may promote the unlearning of CS→US fear associations in infants (and perhaps, to a lesser extent, in adults), the same procedure may result in the learning of a new inhibitory CS→NoUS fear association during fear extinction in adult animals.

5.6.2.3 Consolidation and reconsolidation of fear memories

At the cell-molecular level, the consolidation of newly acquired fear conditioning requires the synthesis of new proteins through the activation of cellular processes that modify synaptic transmission (see Figure 3.20). Perhaps more interesting, though, is that the presentation of the CS or context opens a window for synaptic plasticity of the original fear memories after acquisition has taken place. During this window, reactivated memories of acquisition are accompanied by another episode of protein synthesis and thus become modifiable again, either to be strengthened or weakened. Presenting the CS or context after acquisition in the absence of the US can lead either to extinction or to a procedure known as ***reconsolidation***.

These two procedures differ in the extent to which the CS is presented. Extensive presentations lead to extinction, but a brief CS presentation is used in studies of reconsolidation. As a procedure, reconsolidation is similar to the reminder treatments described in Chapter 4 to explore the issue of retrieval failure. Reminder treatments illustrated how a short exposure to a component of the training situation could strengthen the memory of the task, an effect that was interpreted as the result of extra retrieval practice. Reconsolidation studies focus on the cell-molecular consequences of such reminder treatments.

Consider contextual fear as an example. On day 1, there is a single acquisition session with one shock delivered midway into a 3-min session. On day 2, animals exposed to fear extinction are placed in the same context for 30 min, whereas animals exposed to reconsolidation are exposed to the context for only 3 min. As shown in the previous section, fear extinction leads to both the weakening of the original association and the development of a new inhibitory association. This new learning would require protein synthesis. However, if even a short exposure to the context also opens a window of synaptic plasticity, then protein synthesis would also be implicated. Inhibition of protein synthesis should, therefore, increase freezing after extinction, as it would interfere with extinction learning, but it should decrease freezing after the reconsolidation procedure, because reconsolidation tends to strengthen the original

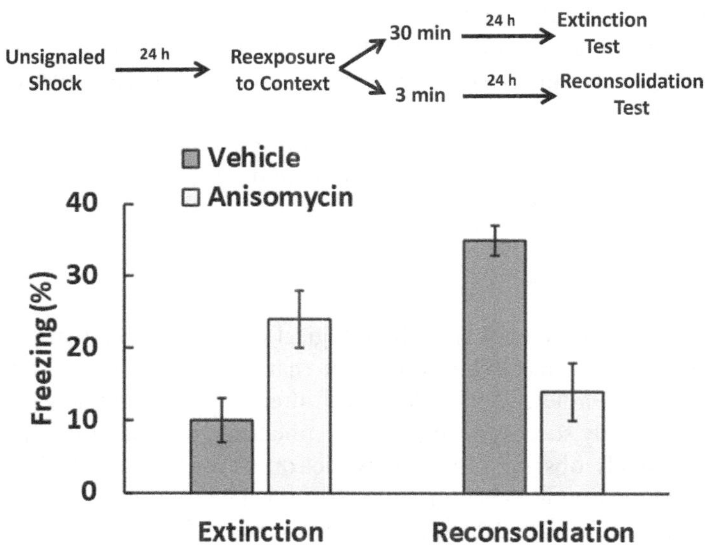

Figure 5.8 **Extinction vs. reconsolidation of fear.** Effects of inhibition of protein synthesis by infusions of anisomycin in the locus coeruleus on extinction and reconsolidation of contextual fear. (From Arihara et al., 2023; reproduced with permission from the *Journal of Neuroscience*.)

memory. Several brain regions are involved in these processes, one of them being the locus coeruleus (LC), a nucleus in the brainstem whose noradrenergic neurons project to a variety of regions involved in fear conditioning, including the amygdala, hippocampus, and medial prefrontal cortex. Protein synthesis can be inhibited by the administration of the antibiotic anisomycin directly into the LC immediately after the appropriate experience.

Figure 5.8 shows the results of such an experiment with mice (Arihara et al., 2023). Anisomycin infused immediately after extinction training led to an increase in freezing when animals were tested a day after. This result is consistent with the hypothesis that noradrenergic output from the LC is important to consolidate extinction memories. By contrast, anisomycin infusion into the LC immediately after reconsolidation treatment led to a reduction of freezing 24 h after. This suggests that brief exposure to the context would preserve or even strengthen the original fear memory provided protein synthesis is not inhibited. In addition, neuronal activation was assessed in terms of the number of neurons that expressed the protein c-Fos, a marker of neuronal depolarization. According to this measure, contextual fear conditioning in mice resulted in higher levels of neural activation not only in the LC but also in the lateral amygdala (LA) and central amygdala (CeA) after both extinction and reconsolidation treatments. Amygdala activation is consistent with a wealth of research showing the participation of these nuclei in fear conditioning (e.g., see Figure 4.8).

5.6.3 Frustration

In an operant conditioning situation, mammals exposed to signals for rewards like food and water learn to expect them. In this context, a reward *expectation* refers to a pattern of neural activity consistent with that elicited by the reward itself. In other words, when the signal is presented, it is as if the animal is experiencing a form of the reward. Consequently, when the signals are present but the rewards fail to occur (i.e., extinction) or are devalued in quality or quantity, the animal is experiencing an unexpected reward downshift, that is, the current reward has lower value than the expected reward. This disparity leads to an aversive emotional response in mammals. Such reward downshifts, referred to as ***surprising nonreward*** (Papini, 2003); surprising because signals were previously paired with a better reward and nonreward because the reward is either completely or partially omitted. Surprising nonreward has two properties. First, surprising nonreward elicits a state of ***primary*** (or ***unconditioned***) ***frustration*** that can induce immediate aftereffects and, second, support the acquisition of ***secondary*** (or ***conditioned***) ***frustration*** (Amsel, 1992).

5.6.3.1 Aftereffects

Aftereffects refer to the behavioral and physiological consequences of surprising nonreward in the seconds to minutes that follow the event that reflect the aversive nature of primary frustration (Papini & Dudley, 1997). A typical aftereffect of surprising nonreward is the invigoration of previously successful responses, a phenomenon called the ***extinction burst*** or ***frustration effect***, usually observed in early extinction trials (Skinner, 1938) or immediately after unexpected reward omissions (Amsel & Roussel, 1952). If given the option, rats learn to escape from a place associated to surprising nonreward. Rats trained to approach a goal box where they received food pellets subsequently learned to jump to another compartment when the food was either omitted or reduced in amount (Daly, 1974). This learning phenomenon, called ***escape from frustration***, is consistent with an aversive emotional state. Pigs (*Sus scrofa*) trained to press a panel with their snout to receive food and then shifted to extinction exhibited increased plasma levels of glucocorticoid hormones (markers of emotional stress) and displayed increased aggressive behavior (pushing, biting, and fighting; Dantzer et al., 1980). ***Extinction-induced aggression*** and increased levels of stress hormones after surprising nonreward have been observed in other species. You may have observed this at a fast-food restaurant or grocery store if a child is disappointed when a parent rejects a demand.

5.6.3.2 Anticipatory effects

Exposure to surprising nonreward can induce the formation of a long-term memory that, when reactivated, can influence behavior. Unlike aftereffects, anticipatory effects are less restricted in time. ***Successive negative contrast*** (SNC) is an example of an anticipatory effect. Rats and other mammals exposed to a surprising downshift in reward magnitude (Large→Small) reject the downshifted reward more than control animals only exposed to the Small reward. SNC was reported in human babies, monkeys, rats, mice, dogs, and opossums trained in situations involving operant responses such as running or lever pressing and consummatory responses such as fluid consumption (Papini, 2014). Figure 5.9 shows an example of consummatory SNC in the white-eared opossum (*Didelphis albiventris*) exposed to successive downshifts from 32% to 4% sucrose versus unshifted controls always exposed to 4% sucrose (Papini et al., 1988). Further experiments with rodents demonstrate that SNC is correlated with high plasma levels of glucocorticoid hormones, is increased by corticosterone treatment, and is reduced by treatment with anxiolytic drugs and opioid agonists (Papini et al., 2015). SNC reflects the suppressive effects of secondary frustration on behavior directed at a previously rewarding source (i.e., anticipating a frustrative outcome).

5.6.3.3 Comparative and developmental studies

SNC has failed to appear in experiments with a variety of nonmammalian vertebrates. Figure 5.10 maps the distribution of SNC on a tree depicting the phylogenetic relationship

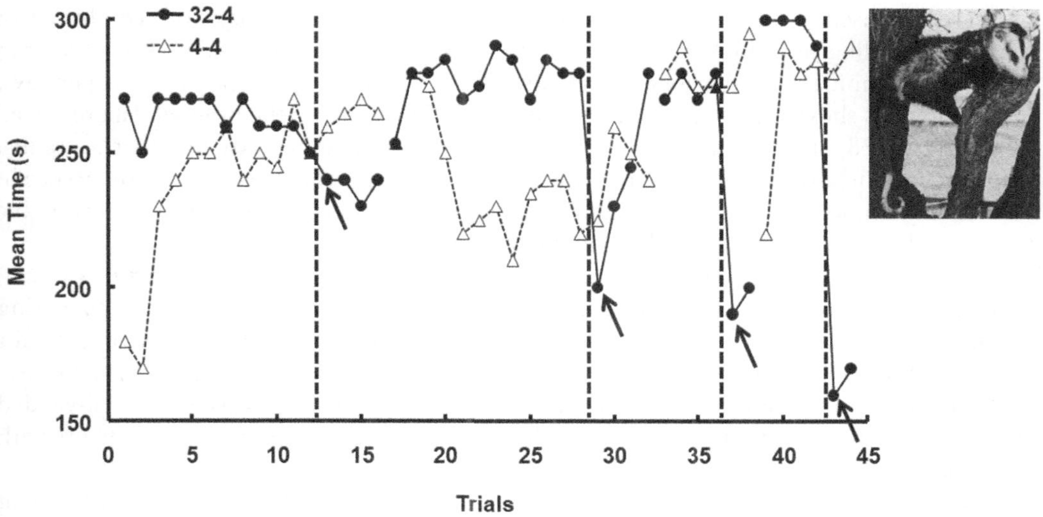

Figure 5.9 **cSNC in the opossum.** Time licking for either 32% or 4% sucrose. The dashed line marks the downshift to 4% sucrose (32–4) sucrose. Four downshifts were administered. The arrows mark a reduction in sucrose intake in downshifted opossums (32–4) relative to unshifted controls (4–4). (From Papini et al., 1988; reproduced with permission from the Psychonomic Society.)

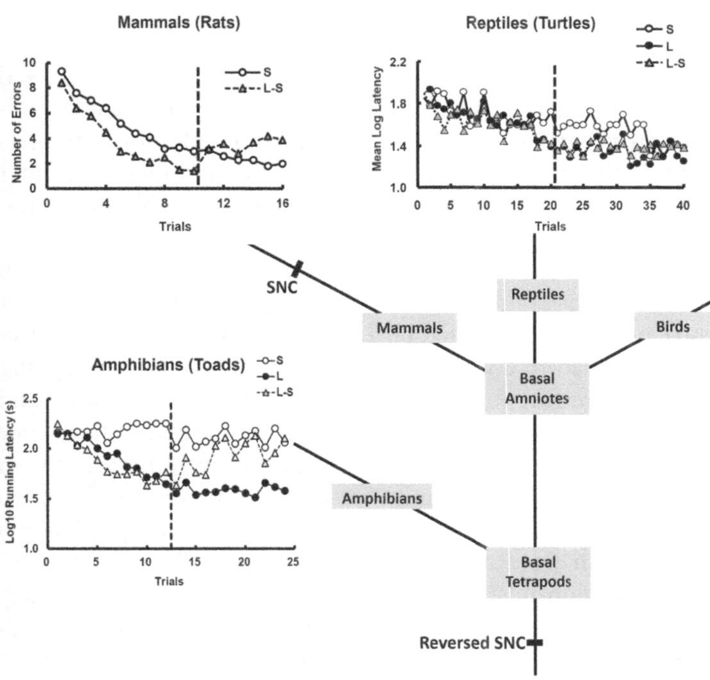

Figure 5.10 **Results from reward downshift experiments with four species of tetrapods.** The dashed lines mark the downshift from a large to a small reward (L-S). One or two unshifted controls were included in these experiments (L-L, S-S). These experiments involved instrumental behaviors. Toad figure from Muzio et al., 2011 (reproduced with permission from PLoS One). Pigeon figure from Papini, 1997 (reproduced with permission from the American Psychological Association). Turtle figure from Papini & Ishida, 1994 (reproduced with permission from Taylor & Francis). Rat figure from Elliott, 1928 (public domain).

of the species used in these experiments. These experiments involve analogous conditions of training, including the reinforcer (food or water), responses (runway running, key pecking in pigeons, consummatory behavior), and the use of spaced training conditions (1 trial per day). Only mammals show the SNC effect, represented in this figure by the original data reported by Elliott (1928) in rats. In other vertebrates, reward downshift leads to either a gradual adjustment or no change in behavior. However, the sensitivity of behavior to the difference in reward magnitude before the downshift indicates that the absence of SNC is not attributable to an inability of reward magnitude to influence behavior.

As a further example, consider an experiment involving goldfish (*Carassius auratus*) trained to swim from a start-box to a goal-box of a straight alley for a food reward consisting of either 4 or 40 worms (Lowes & Bitterman, 1967). Response latencies decreased faster for the group receiving the large reward, suggesting that the magnitude difference had a differential impact on behavior. Subsequently, a downshift from 40 to 4 worms per trial yielded virtually no change in behavior. These results with goldfish are typical of experiments with pigeons, turtles, and toads.

The distribution of SNC across vertebrates is not an isolated event. Two other learning phenomena also involving surprising nonreward also fail to appear in spaced-trial experiments with turtles, toads, and goldfish (Papini, 2014):

- *Partial reinforcement extinction effect* (*PREE*): Greater persistence in extinction after training with partial rather than continuous reinforcement.
- *Magnitude of reinforcement extinction effect* (*MREE*): Greater persistence in extinction after training with small rather than large rewards.

The SNC, PREE, and MREE also fail to appear in preweanling rats, 11 to 21 days old (Amsel, 1992), again demonstrating a parallel between comparative and developmental studies of learning (see **5.4.2 Comparative studies of latent inhibition**). In addition, adult rats exhibit a performance analogous to that of nonmammalian vertebrates and infant rats after treatment with benzodiazepine anxiolytics, opioid agonists, and lesions of limbic structures, such as the amygdala (Ortega et al., 2017).

As with attention, conflicting evidence on the effects of surprising nonreward has been reported, especially with birds. For example, pigeons and chickens exposed to extinction after reward training display aggressive behavior to a stuffed bird, a live pigeon, or a mirror reflection (Papini et al., 2019). Pigeons trained in a visual discrimination directed wing-flapping responses to the negative signal. Interestingly, as discriminative behavior developed and thus nonreward became less surprising, these aggressive responses diminished in frequency (Terrace, 1972). As mentioned previously, similar aggressive responses were reported with mammals (rats, pigs, monkeys) exposed to reward omissions directed at conspecifics or to inanimate objects present in the situation (see section on **Aftereffects**). Starlings (*Sturnus vulgaris*) exposed to a reward downshift from mealworms to turkey crumbs reduced consummatory behavior below the level of an unshifted group always exposed only to turkey crumbs—a consummatory SNC effect (Freidin et al., 2009). Spaced-trial experiments with pigeons demonstrate reversed SNC and MREE (Papini, 1997) but clear PREEs (Papini et al., 2002).

One approach to resolving these discrepancies is to compare the effects of factors that tap on lower mechanistic levels (see Figure 3.1). In one experiment (Thomas & Papini, 2003), pigeons trained under partial or continuous reinforcement in a runway received treatment with drugs known to attenuate (chlordiazepoxide), enhance (nicotine), or have no effect

Table 5.7 Neurochemical analysis of the PREE in rats and pigeons

Drug	*System*	*Effect in Rats*	*Effect in Pigeons*
Chlordiazepoxide	GABA	Reduce PREE	No effect
Nicotine	Acetylcholine	Enhance PREE	Reduce PREE
Haloperidol	Dopamine	No effect	Reduce PREE

Note. Chlordiazepoxide is used to reduce anxiety in psychiatric patients and acts on the benzodiazepine site of the $GABA_A$ (gamma-amino-butytic acid) receptor, where it increases the receptor's affinity for GABA. Nicotine is a stimulant drug that binds to a subclass of cholinergic receptors known as nicotinic. Haloperidol, a dopamine receptor antagonist, is used to reduce hallucinations and delusions in schizophrenic patients.

(haloperidol) on the PREE in rats. In pigeons, however, the effects were different (Table 5.7). This result suggests that although behaviorally similar across rats and pigeons, the neurochemical mechanisms underlying the PREE have evolved independently (i.e., homoplasy rather than homology; see Chapter 1).

5.6.4 *Frustration, memory update, and emotional activation*

Effects involving surprising nonreward suggest a distinction between (1) *memory update*, adjusting reward value as conditions change in the environment and (2) *emotional activation*, tagging such changes in reward as emotionally significant (Papini, 2003). In the PREE, a transition from reward to nonreward across two successive trials tends to be followed by a decrement in behavior in the subsequent trial, reflecting memory update. Acquiring information of such changes is one of the main functions of conditioning mechanisms common to all vertebrates. Memory update can be characterized either in terms of the strengthening and weakening of the signal value of a stimulus paired with rewards of different magnitude or quality, including nonreward, or as the acquisition of opposite types of information that compete for expression, such as excitatory and inhibitory associations between signal and reinforcer. These are cognitive processes that encode knowledge about changes in environmental events.

In the PREE, there is also a difference in the rate of change across trials. When shifted to extinction, behavior changes slowly after acquisition with partial reinforcement but rapidly after acquisition with continuous reinforcement, a difference related to emotional activation. Emotion is recruited when reward changes are significant, that is, when the degree of disparity between the obtained and expected rewards surpasses a threshold.

This has been studied in the consummatory SNC task in which sucrose concentrations can be varied with precision. Three groups of rats receiving access to either 32%, 24%, or 16% sucrose during preshift sessions (training concentrations) were downshifted to a lower concentration (test concentrations) so as to generate test/training ratios ranging between 0.06 and 1. The amount of time licking the solution (called goal-tracking time) was recorded during these downshift sessions, and the results were analyzed in terms of the absolute value of the preshift and postshift concentration, the difference between them, and their ratio. The results showed that when the test/training ratios were used to represent the results, the function of these three groups overlapped extensively (Figure 5.11). The implication is that, at least within a range of sucrose concentrations, equal test/training ratios produce similar levels of behavioral suppression after a reward downshift, independently of their absolute sucrose concentrations involved (Papini & Pellegrini, 2006). Similar dependence of behavior on the test/training ratios of rewards were described in other situations. Moreover, it is likely

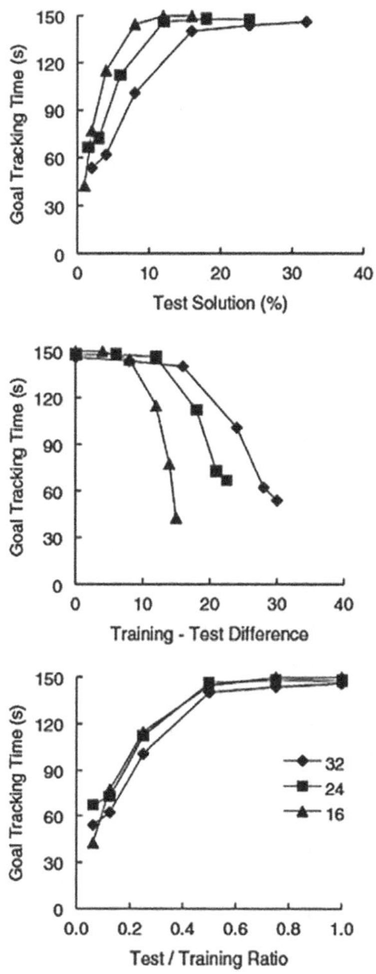

Figure 5.11 **Test/Training reward ratios in the cSNC task.** Three groups of rats receiving access to 32%, 24%, or 16% sucrose were downshifted to several sucrose concentrations chosen to generate specific test/training ratios. The results indicate that behavior of these animals diverged when the results were represented in terms of the absolute sucrose concentrations (top) or the training–test difference (middle). However, the functions overlapped extensively when the results were represented in terms of the test/training ratios. (From Papini & Pellegrini, 2006; reproduced with permission from Elsevier.)

that similar ratio invariance may be found in rats exposed to aversive situations involving escape from shock (Nation et al., 1974), escape from low temperatures (Woods et al., 1964), and one-way avoidance with different periods of safety (Cándido et al., 1992).

5.6.5 *Neurobiology of fear and frustration in vertebrates*

Goldfish trained under spaced-trial conditions exhibit avoidance learning (Portavella et al., 2003). Moreover, avoidance learning depends on the medial pallium, an area of the fish telencephalon homologous to the mammalian amygdala (Portavella et al., 2004).

Toads learn to anticipate (exhibiting increased heart rate) and actively avoid sites associated with hypertonic solutions that dehydrate them—a life-threatening situation for amphibians (Daneri et al., 2007). Such avoidance behavior is accompanied by neural activation in the medial pallium, an area of the amphibian telencephalon homologous to the mammalian amygdala (Puddington et al., 2016). Likewise, pigeons trained to peck at a key for food show suppression of key-pecking performance when it is punished with electric shock (Azrin, 1959), and such suppression is alleviated by treatment with benzodiazepine anxiolytics that enhance GABAergic transmission (Mansbach et al., 1988).

Thus, goldfish, toads, and pigeons, neither one exhibiting SNC after reward downshift, share with mammals some of the components of the brain circuit (amygdala) and psychopharmacology (GABAergic transmission) of avoidance learning and conflict (Korn et al., 2017). These results suggest deep homologies in the brain circuit underlying fear and avoidance conditioning among vertebrates, with the amygdala being a central component of that circuit.

The amygdala is also a component of the circuit activated by reward downshifts. In the instrumental SNC task, lesions restricted to the BLA reduced the response to a reward downshift in a runway situation (Salinas et al., 1996). Similar lesions in the BLA also eliminate the consummatory SNC effect relative to sham controls (Kawasaki et al., 2017). Chemogenetic inactivation of the CeA disrupts consummatory SNC (Guarino et al., 2020). Lesions of the hippocampus and anterior cingulate cortex, which impair contextual fear conditioning, also affect instrumental (Franchina & Brown, 1971) and consummatory (Ortega et al., 2011) SNC effects. These neurobiological effects add to the behavioral and psychopharmacological results pointing to similar mechanisms underlying fear and frustration (Gray & McNaughton, 2000).

These results suggest evolutionary relationships between fear conditioning and secondary frustration. An intriguing possibility is that the anticipatory emotional activation responsible for effects such as SNC is based on brain mechanisms that evolved in early mammals from the circuit responsible for fear conditioning (Papini, 2003). This evolutionary hypothesis predicts substantial overlap in the genes expressed during fear and frustration events, especially in the amygdala (Sabariego et al., 2013).

5.7 Choice and learning

Most of the learning situations described in this and the preceding chapters focused on tasks in which a single option is available for responding. The present chapter has integrated learning with a variety of other processes to highlight the widespread role of learning to understand behavior. This section asks how learning contributes to choosing among response options. Can the principles that apply to the acquisition of a response be useful to understand choice? As we will see, some new concepts are needed to understand choice behavior.

Prior experience plays a key role when we are making decisions, whether in terms of short-term consequences or in terms of more remote consequences. The simplest choice is between responding or not responding—this is called *forced choice*. Not responding usually means doing something else that is incompatible with responding. In a simple conditioning situation, a rat facing a lever or a pigeon in front of a lighted response key may respond or do something else. Forced choices highlight the idea that choice is actually present in all situations; it is a more general concept in its application than one might anticipate.

But that "something else" can be made explicit. For example, a rat may have two levers, or a pigeon may face two response keys. This is usually referred to as a *free choice*. Some choices allow for immediate correction, whereas in other cases, corrections are not possible without having to start the process again. If I try on a jacket at the store and if feels uncomfortable, I can try another one; but if I am at the movie theater and do not like the movie I am watching, I would have to go back to the start and buy a ticket to watch a different movie (or just leave the movie theater). As usual, let us first consider a simple choice situation: How would an animal that has two options paired with the same outcome distribute its choices?

5.7.1 *Matching*

A pigeon has learned to respond by pecking at one of two keys to obtain access to grain in a free-operant situation in which both responses are continuously available. The distribution of choices tends to match the distribution of reinforcers if the reinforcers are available based on time. For example, pecking at one key is reinforced on a variable-interval 60 s (VI 60 s) schedule, but pecking at the other is also rewarded on a VI 60 s schedule. These schedules are typically run continuously, which means that as the pigeon is responding to the right key, the time in the VI schedule on the left key is also running. In this environment, a pigeon would collect the largest amount of food by pecking at one key for some time, but occasionally switching to the other key, staying there if it has received food, but then again occasionally checking the other key.

It soon became obvious that pigeons would keep switching from one response key to the other, so a brief delay was introduced, called a change-over delay, so that reward would be delivered only 1.5 s after a switch was detected. This reduced the frequency of switching. Using this procedure and varying the VI schedules across a range of intervals, the pigeon's distribution of response choices tended to match the distribution of rewards (Figure 5.12-A). This regularity became known as the *matching law* (Herrnstein, 1961). In relative terms, the matching law can be represented as:

$$R_1 / (R_1 + R_2) = r_1 / (r_1 + r_2),$$

where R_1 and R_2 are two responses (pecking at the right or left key) and r_1 and r_2 are the reward schedules associated with each response. Such matching is unsurprising because in an instrumental situation, behavior and reinforcements are causing each other: behavior produces rewards, but rewards control behavior.

The application of the matching law to single schedules of reinforcement, where animals face a forced choice, helps highlight a major point. In a forced-choice situation, there is a target response (e.g., key pecking, R_t), and there are other responses (R_o) that the animal can engage in, such as walking around, cleaning its feathers, flapping a wing, etc. This can be represented as:

$$R_t / (R_t + R_o) = r_t / (r_t + r_o), \text{ or } R_t / R_o = r_t / r_o$$

Thus, the rate of responding to an available option is a function not only of the outcomes delivered by that response but of rewards available for other responses in that situation. This notion has been applied successfully to a variety of situations beyond pigeons pecking at response keys.

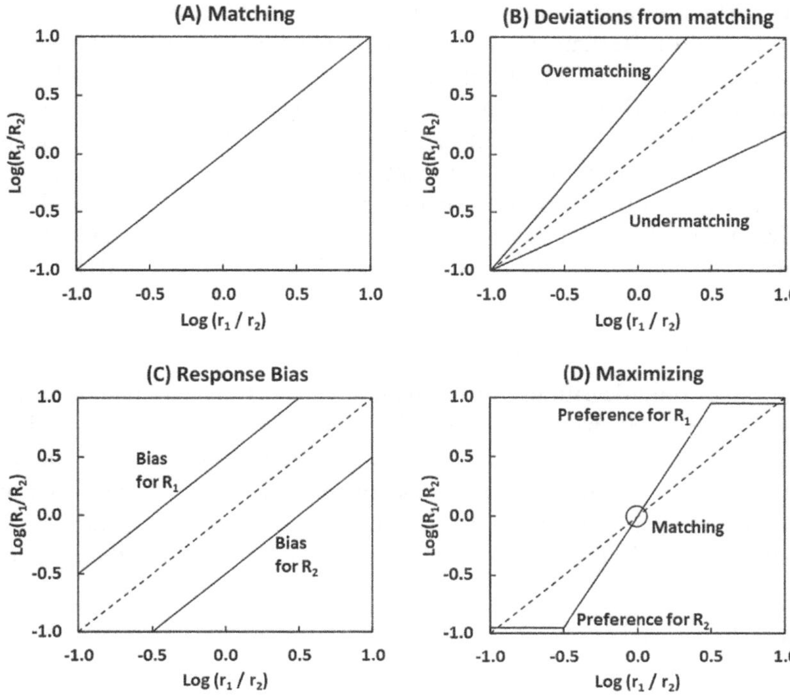

Figure 5.12 **Choice and reinforcement.** Four outcomes in choice experiments with two alternatives associated with two schedules of reinforcement. **(A)** Strict matching: Relative allocation of responses is equal to the relative rates of reinforcement. **(B)** Deviations from matching: overmatching and undermatching. These can be accommodated by adding free parameters to the matching equation (see text). **(C)** Response biases move the relationship in one or the other direction depending on which response is preferred. **(D)** Maximizing: the almost exclusive choice of one response.

5.7.2 *Matching and drug dependence*

Consider the case of drug dependence. Humans seem to be especially prone to consume a variety of substances. A substance use disorder (SUD) is defined as the persistent use of a drug even when that behavior is associated to significant negative outcomes that seem to exceed the drug's positive effects. Individuals with a SUD may lose friendships and sources of income and may see their physical health deteriorate and yet persist in their drug use. However, after having used a drug persistently, a person may enter a period of instability in their drug use, quitting and relapsing several times until, in many cases, consumption is reduced or even eliminated. Such remissions can occur because of treatment or even spontaneously. One study with Vietnam veterans who regularly used opioids while in the war found that 88% of them remitted when they returned to the US (Robins, 1993). Some used opioids occasionally, but their social environment was cited by many as a deterrent for opioid use. What factors caused these changes in drug use?

The matching law suggests that the availability of reinforcing activities other than drug taking is one such factor. In terms of the equation shown previously, R_o and its corresponding rewards limit the allocation of effort and time to the target response. For example, rats reduce self-administration of methamphetamine if they have concurrent access to wheel running

(Miller et al., 2012). Similar results were reported in experiments with human participants based on the notion of alternative sources of reinforcement suggested by the matching law (Acuff et al., 2023). Basically, when immediate alternative rewards are available, drug consumption decreases, whether it is alcohol, cocaine, cannabis, or heroin. But, vice versa, when the reward value of a drug is higher than the reward value of alternative sources, the choice of drug consumption increases over that of the alternatives. To be sure, substance use behavior depends on many factors that make it a complex phenomenon in terms of both behavior and neurobiology. Drugs cause extensive changes in the brain reward system that account for the difficulties of sustained remission in some cases (Koob & Volkow, 2016; see Chapter 6).

5.7.3 *Undermatching, overmatching, and maximizing*

There are some important deviations from matching. Factors that determine some of these deviations include low sensitivity to relative rates of reinforcement, cost of switching between alternatives, amount of experience with the choice procedure, and a bias to select one response over the alternative. Since the matching law has a descriptive function, these deviations can be accommodated by adding free parameters to the matching equation. A free parameter is a number obtained from the actual data that one is modeling (Baum, 1974). Thus, the equation becomes:

$$R_t / R_o = b(r_t / r_o)^s$$

where *b* represents response bias and *s* reflects the sensitivity to the relative rate of reinforcement. When both responses are similar (e.g., pressing the right vs. left lever), the animal will tend to be equally biased and $b = 1$. A stronger preference for one response over the other can be modeled by adopting a value of $b > 1$. Response bias is influenced by the effort to perform the response, the values of the rewards associated with the responses, or unconditioned tendencies to prefer one response over the other (e.g., some rats exhibit spatial preferences). Similarly, matching is represented by $s = 1$, but with reduced sensitivity to reward rates, $s < 1$. The values adopted for these free parameters to fit behavioral data depend on whether the data reflect ***undermatching*** or ***overmatching*** (Figure 5.12-B, C).

The original experiments on matching involved concurrent VI-VI schedules in which reinforcer probability in each alternative varies independently of the animal's behavior. What do animals do if they are responding on a concurrent VR-VR schedule? A variable-ratio schedule (VR) is one in which rewards depend on a variable number of responses within a given average. For example, a VR 10 schedule will deliver food every 10 responses on average. Notice, however, that the faster the animal responds, the sooner it will be rewarded. Thus, it is not surprising that when exposed to a concurrent VR-VR schedule, animals tend to respond almost exclusively to the VR with the lowest ratio value (Herrnstein & Loveland, 1975). This is called ***maximizing*** (Figure 5.12-D).

In the case of a concurrent VR-VI schedule, reinforcement depends on behavior in the VR option, but it also depends on time in the VI component. Thus, animals should prefer the VR option most of the time, but they should also occasionally switch to the VI option (DeCarlo, 1985).

5.7.4 *Delay discounting*

An otherwise valuable reward can lose value if delivered after a relatively long temporal delay. This effect, called *delay discounting*, leads to some interesting choice phenomena. In one

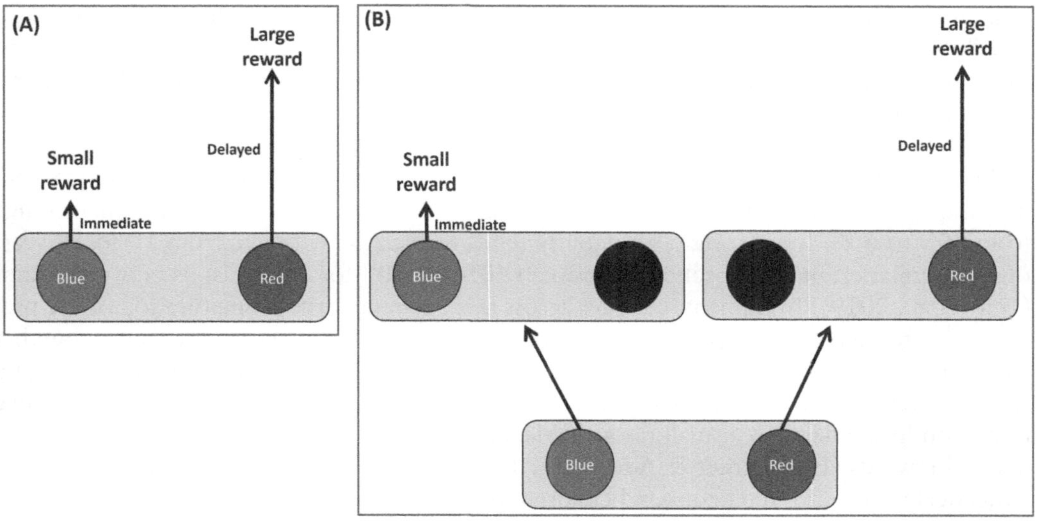

Figure 5.13 **Delay discounting design. (A)** When given a choice between an immediate, small reward and a delayed, large reward, animals tend to be impulsive and select the immediate reward (Blue). **(B)** However, if a choice discrimination is interpolated before the final response, then animals tend to exert self-control and select the large, delayed reward (Red).

experiment (Rachlin & Green, 1972), pigeons obtained a small, immediate reward by pecking at one key but a large, delayed reward (delayed by 4 s) by pecking at a different key. These keys were presented simultaneously. Under these conditions, pigeons showed a bias to choose the small, immediate reward over the large, delayed reward, thus exhibiting choice *impulsivity*. However, when an initial choice between the two rewards (i.e., a precommitment) was interpolated before the pigeon could opt for the keys leading to these rewards, rats and pigeons showed *self-control*, that is, they tended to choose the alternative leading to a large, delayed reward (Figure 5.13).

These results suggest that the value of a reward is diminished when there is a waiting time, but the structure of the situation may determine the direction of the choice. For example, you would probably prefer $100 today to $500 ten days from now (impulsivity), but you would reverse your preference (self-control) if the choice was to receive $100 in 30 days vs. $500 in 40 days, even though the large reward is delayed by 10 days in both cases. One solution to this problem is to assume that the functions discounting the values of these rewards cross over at some point in time. Thus, when rewards are delivered closer in time to the choice response, the small reward is valued more than the large reward, but when rewards are delivered after a longer delay, the values reverse. These so-called *hyperbolic delay functions* can be described by a simple equation:

$$V = M \,/\, 1 + kD$$

where the subjective value of the reward (V) is directly related to its magnitude (M) but inversely related to its delay (D). In this equation, k is a constant that determines the rate of decay of reward value and can vary across individuals (Odum, 2011). Impulsive choice is connected to substance use disorders, excessive eating, poor self-care, and gambling. Longitudinal studies that use delay discounting questionnaires show that k predicts the likelihood that an individual will develop specific behavioral disorders. For example, cigarette smokers usually show steep hyperbolic delay functions in these tests (i.e., large *k* values), and this measure predicts their drug use, financial well-being, physical fitness, eating habits, health, and household savings (Snider et al., 2019).

Like most learning phenomena, delay discounting seems to have a genetic component, but it is also open to malleability through experience. Estimates of heritability in humans range from 30% to 60%. Interestingly, heritability tends to increase with age from 12 to 18 years of age. Similar estimates for rats vary between 40% and 50% for comparisons between strains (Gray et al., 2019). In humans, changes across this age range parallel maturation of the prefrontal cortex, a prime component of the brain circuit involved in delay discounting together with the striatum, insular cortex, and anterior cingulate cortex, as shown by brain imaging studies (Wesley & Bickel, 2014). Self-control can also be trained. Exposure to a gradual reduction in the delay to a small reward (Mazur & Logue, 1978) or extensive training with delayed rewards (Eisenberger & Adornetto, 1986) increases the frequency of choosing the large, delayed reward in pigeons and children, respectively.

Glossary

Attention Stimulus selectivity. Attention implies responding to only some of the stimuli present in a situation.

Backward blocking Training first with a compound CS (AB+) followed by training with one of the elements (A+), and ending with a test of the other CS (B?). In the test, B is responded less than a control stimulus not subjected to the A+ training. Backward blocking suggests retrospective reevaluation of A.

Compound conditioning Conditioning with a CS made with two or more elements, such as tone and light (represented, for example, as AB+).

Concurrent blocking Training with a compound CS (AB+) and one of the elements (A+) in trials distributed within the same session (also called cue–validity effect).

Contextual conditioning Presenting unsignaled USs in a given situation.

Delay discounting A conditioning paradigm in which the onset of the CS precedes, usually for a few seconds, and either ends or overlaps with the onset of the US.

Disinhibition Presenting a novel stimulus usually results in a relapse of the extinguished response.

Escape from frustration Emitting a novel response, usually involving some effort, to exit a context in which the animal has just experience a reward omission or reduction.

Expectancy ratio A ratio between the interreinforcement interval (C) and the duration of the CS (T), represented as the C/T ratio. Equal C/T ratios result in similar acquisition rates, independently of the absolute values of C and T.

Expectation A pattern of brain activity similar to that induced by an actual object. For example, an expectation of pizza involves brain activity similar to that occurring when seeing or tasting pizza.

Extinction As a procedure, presenting the CS after CS-US pairings or emitting the operant response after instrumental reinforcement of that response. As a phenomenon, the reduction in an acquired response after the US or reinforcer is withheld. As a mechanism, the development of an inhibitory association or the weakening of the association established during acquisition.

Extinction burst A transient increase in the rate of an operant response, usually during the early trials of appetitive extinction, when the reward fails to occur.

Extinction-induced aggression Withholding a reward can induce aggressive behavior, especially if another animal is present in the situation.

Fear An emotional response induced by signals of threat or danger that promotes behaviors such as freezing, escape, and avoidance.

Forced choice A situation in which the choice is to respond or not to respond.

Forward blocking Training first with a CS (A+) followed by training with a compound stimulus (AB+) and ending with a test of the other CS (B?). In the test, B is responded less than a control stimulus not subjected to the A+ training.

Free choice Having more than one option to respond, say A and B. The animal can respond to A, to B, not respond to any of the options, or respond to both options.
Freezing Absence of movement, except for breathing, typically observed in the presence of a signal for pain in a fear conditioning situation.
Frustration An emotional response induced by the unexpected omission, reduction, or delay in the occurrence of an appetitive reinforcer. Frustration may promote a variety of responses, from suppression to invigoration, escape, and avoidance.
Frustration effect The invigoration of a response immediately after an unexpected reward omission.
Hyperbolic delay functions A mathematical function describing the reduction in value of a reinforcer as a function of the delay to its presentation or availability.
Impulsivity Tendency to select the option that yields the least delay to reinforcement, even if better, more delayed reinforcers are available.
Incentive learning Assigning value to a stimulus as a function of the internal motivational state or the animal.
Independence rule In compound conditioning, when learning about each of the elements of a compound proceeds separately from the other elements.
Latent inhibition Presentations of a CS by itself (A-) later retards acquisition when that CS is paired with a US (A+).
Liking A motivational process related to facial expressions induced by tasting substances such as sucrose and quinine. Liking depends on the activity of opioidergic neurons located in restricted regions, including the nucleus accumbens and ventral pallidum.
Magnitude of reinforcement extinction effect (MREE) Greater persistence of behavior in extinction after training with a small reward than after training with a large reward.
Matching law The relative rate of responding is similar to the relative rate of reinforcement for that response.
Maximizing Responding exclusively or almost exclusively to one of the available options.
Motivation The internal state providing impulse for behavior but not direction.
Overmatching A distribution of responses in a choice situation in which one option controls a greater relative proportion of the responses than the other options.
Overshadowing In compound conditioning, reinforcing a compound (AB+) usually leaves one of the elements less capable of inducing responding in a test (B?) compared to a situation in which that element was trained by itself (B+).
Partial reinforcement extinction effect (PREE) Greater persistence of behavior in extinction after training with partial reinforcement than after training with continuous reinforcement.
Perceptual learning Exposure to two or more stimuli later facilitates their discrimination when one is paired to reinforcement.
Primary frustration An aversive emotional state induced by the unexpected omission or reduction of a reward.
Reconsolidation After acquisition, brief or limited presentations of the signal can enhance or reduce subsequent responding to that signal. As in original consolidation, reconsolidation opens up a window for protein synthesis that can alter the original memory.
Reinstatement The presentation of an unsignaled US often results in a relapse of an extinguished response the next time the CS is presented.
Renewal Extinguishing a response in a context different from that of the original acquisition shows a relapse of that extinguished response if tested in the original acquisition context or in a new context.
Secondary (or conditioned) frustration Anticipating the possibility of being frustrated if approaching a stimulus or situation previously associated with the unexpected omission or reduction of a reward.
Self-control Choosing an option that will produce a more delayed, usually larger reward over an option that will produce a more immediate, usually smaller reward.
Shared associative strength In compound conditioning, learning about one element depends on how much learning has occurred about the other elements present in a trial. The fundamental principle behind the Rescorla-Wagner model of conditioning.
Spontaneous recovery Interpolating a resting period with no CSs or USs usually leads to the relapse of a conditioned response when the CS is presented again.
Successive negative contrast The unexpected downshift from a large to a small reward, whether in quality or quantity, leads to a transient deterioration of the response compared to the response of a control condition in which animals experienced only the small reward.

Surprising nonreward The unexpected omission or reduction of reward value.
Taste reactivity test Detecting changes in facial expression triggered by taste stimuli.
Undermatching A distribution of responses in a choice situation in which one option controls a smaller relative proportion of the responses than the other options.
US-preexposure effect A retardation of acquisition during CS-US training after previous unsignaled presentations of the US in the same context.
Wanting A motivational process related to the salience of stimuli predicting reward and responsible for cravings. Wanting depends on activity in the dopaminergic reward system of the brain.

References

Abramson, C. I., & Bitterman, M. E. (1986). Latent inhibition in honeybees. *Animal Learning & Behavior*, *14*, 184–189. https://doi.org/10.3758/BF03200054

Acquistapace, P., Hazlett, B. A., & Gherardi, F. (2003). Unsuccessful predation and learning of predator cues by crayfish. *Journal of Crustacean Biology*, *23*(2), 364–370. https://doi.org/10.1163/20021975-99990346

Acuff, S. F., MacKillop, J., & Murphy, J. G. (2023). A contextualized reinforcer pathology approach to addiction. *Nature Reviews in Psychology*, *2*, 309–323. https://doi.org/10.1038/s44159-023-00167-y

Amsel, A. (1992). *Frustration theory*. Cambridge University Press.

Amsel, A., & Roussel, J. (1952). Motivational properties of frustration: I. Effect on a running response of the addition of frustration to the motivational complex. *Journal of Experimental Psychology*, *43*, 363–368. https://doi.org/10.1037/h0059393

Arihara, Y., Fukuyama, Y., & Kida, S. (2023). Consolidation, reconsolidation, and extinction of contextual fear memory depend on de novo protein synthesis in the locus coeruleus. *Brain Research Bulletin*, *202*, 110746. https://doi.org/10.1016/j.brainresbull.2023.110746

Azrin, N. H. (1959). A technique for delivering shock to pigeons. *Journal of the Experimental Analysis of Behavior*, *2*, 162–163. https://doi.org/10.1901/jeab.1959.2-161

Baum, W. M. (1974). On two types of deviation from the matching law: Bias and undermatching. *Journal of the Experimental Analysis of Behavior*, *22*, 231–242. https://doi.org/10.1901/jeab.1974.22-231

Berridge, K. C. (2018). Evolving concepts of emotion and motivation. *Frontiers in Psychology*, *9*. https://doi.org/10.3389/fpsyg.2018.01647

Berridge, K. C., & Kringelbach, M. L. (2015). Pleasure systems in the brain. *Neuron*, *86*, 646–664. https://doi.org/10.1016/j.neuron.2015.02.018

Berridge, K. C., Venier, I. L., & Robinson, T. E. (1989). Taste reactivity analysis of 6-hydroxydopamine-induced aphagia: Implications for arousal and anhedonia hypotheses of dopamine function. *Behavioral Neuroscience*, *103*, 36–45. https://doi.org/10.1037//0735-7044

Blaser, R. E., Couvillon, P. A., & Bitterman, M. E. (2004). Backward blocking in honeybees. *Quarterly Journal of Experimental Psychology*, *57B*, 349–360. https://doi.org/10.1080/02724990344000187

Boughner, R. L., & Papini, M. R. (2006). Appetitive latent inhibition in rats: Preexposure performance does not predict conditioned performance. *Behavioural Processes*, *72*, 42–51. https://doi.org/10.1016/j.beproc.2005.11.015

Bouton, M. E., & Bolles, R. C. (1979). Role of conditioned contextual stimuli in reinstatement of extinguished fear. *Journal of Experimental Psychology: Animal Behavior Processes*, *5*(4), 368–378. https://doi.org/10.1037/0097-7403.5.4.368

Brunzell, D. H., & Kim, J. J. (2001). Fear conditioning to tone, but not to context, is attenuated by lesions of the insular cortex and posterior extension of the intralaminar complex in rats. *Behavioral Neuroscience*, *115*, 365–375. https://doi.org/10.1037//0735-7044.115.2.365

Cándido, A., Maldonado, A., Megías, J. L., & Catena, A. (1992). Successive negative contrast in one-way avoidance learning in rats. *Quarterly Journal of Experimental Psychology*, *45B*, 15–32.

Chance, W. T., White, A. C., Krynock, G. M., & Rosecrans, J. A. (1977). Autoanalgesia: Behaviorally activated antinociception. *European Journal of Pharmacology*, *44*(3), 283–284. https://doi.org/10.1016/0014-2999(77)90076-0

Chandra, S. B. C., Wright, G. A., & Smith, B. H. (2010). Latent inhibition in the honey bee, *Apis mellifera*: Is it a unitary phenomenon? *Animal Cognition*, *13*, 805–815. https://doi.org/10.1007/s10071-010-0329-6

Chelonis, J. J., Calton, J. L., Hart, J. A., & Schachtman, T. R. (1999). Attenuation of the renewal effect by extinction in multiple contexts. *Learning and Motivation*, *30*, 1–14. https://doi.org/10.1006/lmot.1998.1022

Cordero, M. I., Merino, J. J., & Sandi, C. (1998). Correlational relationship between shock intensity and corticosterone secretion on the establishment and subsequent expression of contextual fear conditioning. *Behavioral Neuroscience*, *112*, 885–891. https://doi.org/10.1037//0735-7044.112.4.885

Couvillon, P. A., & Bitterman, M. E. (1991). How honeybees make choices. In L. Goodman & R. C. Fischer (Eds.), *The behaviour and physiology of bees* (pp. 116–130). CAB International.

Couvillon, P. A., Tennant, W. A., & Bitterman, M. E. (1976). Intradimensional vs. extradimensional transfer in the discriminative learning of goldfish and pigeons. *Animal Learning and Behavior*, *4*, 197–203. https://doi.org/10.3758/BF03214035

Daly, H. B. (1974). Reinforcing properties of escape from frustration aroused in various learning situations. *Psychology of Learning and Motivation*, *8*, 187–231. https://doi.org/10.1016/S0079-7421(08)60455-7

Daneri, M. F., Papini, M. R., & Muzio, R. N. (2007). Common toads (*Bufo arenarum*) learn to anticipate and avoid hypertonic saline solutions. *Journal of Comparative Psychology*, *121*, 419–427. https://doi.org/10.1037/0735-7036.121.4.419

Dantzer, R., Arnone, M., & Mormade, P. (1980). Effects of frustration on behaviour and plasma corticosteroid levels in pigs. *Physiology and Behavior*, *24*, 1–4. https://doi.org/10.1016/0031-9384(80)90005-0

DeCarlo, L. T. (1985). Matching and maximizing with variable-time schedules. *Journal of the Experimental Analysis of Behavior*, *43*, 75–81. https://doi.org/10.1901/jeab.1985.43-75

De La Casa, L. G. (2013). Food and water deprivation disrupts latent inhibition with an auditory fear conditioning procedure. *Behavioural Processes*, *100*, 54–57. https://doi.org/10.1016/j.beproc.2013.07.022

De La Casa, L. G., Mena, A., Ruiz-Salas, J. C., Quintero, E., & Papini, M. R. (2018). Reward devaluation disrupts latent inhibition in fear conditioning. *Learning & Behavior*, *46*, 49–59. https://doi.org/10.3758/s13420-017-0282-1

Demjaha, A., Egerton, A., Murray, R. M., Kapur, S., Howes, O. D., Stone, J. M., & McGuire, P. K. (2014). Antipsychotic treatment resistance in schizophrenia associated with elevated glutamate levels but normal dopamine function. *Biological Psychiatry*, *75*, e11–e13. https://doi.org/10.1016/j.biopsych.2013.06.011

Denniston, J. C., Chang, R. C., & Miller, R. R. (2003). Massive extinction treatment attenuates the renewal effect. *Learning and Motivation*, *34*, 68–86. https://doi.org/10.1016/S0023-9690(02)00508-8

Denniston, J. C., Savastano, H. I., Blaisdell, A. P., & Miller, R. R. (2003). Cue competition as a retrieval deficit. *Learning and Motivation*, *34*, 1–31. https://doi.org/10.1016/S0023-9690(02)00505-2

Dickinson, A., & Dawson, G. R. (1989). Incentive learning and the motivational control of instrumental performance. *Quarterly Journal of Experimental Psychology*, *41B*, 99–112. https://doi.org/10.1080/14640748908401185

Eisenberger, R., & Adornetto, M. (1986). Generalized self-control of delay and effort. *Journal of Personality and Social Psychology*, *51*, 1020–1031. https://doi.org/10.1037/0022-3514.51.5.1020

Elliott, M. H. (1928). The effect of change of reward on the maze performance of rats. *University of California Publications in Psychology*, *4*, 19–30.

Ferrero, D. M., Lemon, J. K., Fluegge, D., Pashkovski, S. L., Korzan, W. J., Datta, S. R., Spehr, M., Fendt, M., & Liberles, S. D. (2011). Detection and avoidance of a carnivore odor by prey. *Proceedings of the National Academy of Science USA*, *108*, 11235–11240. https://doi.org/10.1073/pnas.1103317108

Fiori, L. M., Barnet, R. C., & Miller, R. R. (1994). Renewal of Pavlovian conditioned inhibition. *Animal Learning & Behavior*, *22*, 47–52. https://doi.org/10.3758/BF03199955

Franchina, J. J., & Brown, T. S. (1971). Reward magnitude shift effects in rats with hippocampal lesions. *Journal of Comparative and Physiological Psychology*, *76*, 365–370. https://doi.org/10.1037/h0031375

Freidin, E., Cuello, M. I., & Kacelnik, A. (2009). Successive negative contrast in a bird: Starlings' behavior after unpredictable negative changes in food quality. *Animal Behaviour*, *77*, 857–865. https://doi.org/10.1016/j.anbehav.2008.12.010

Ganella, D. E., Nguyen, L. D., Lee-Kardashyan, L., Kim, L. E., Paolini, A. G., & Kim, J. H. (2018). Neurocircuitry of fear extinction in adult and juvenile rats. *Behavioural Brain Research, 351*, 161–167. https://doi.org/10.1016/j.bbr.2018.06.001

Gibbon, J., & Balsam, P. D. (1981). Spreading association in time. In C. M. Locurto, H. S. Terrace, & J. Gibbon (Eds.), *Autoshaping and conditioning theory* (pp. 219–253). Academic Press.

Gibson, E. J., & Walk, R. D. (1956). The effect of prolonged exposure to visually presented patterns on learning to discriminate them. *Journal of Comparative and Physiological Psychology, 49*, 239–242. https://doi.org/10.1037/h0048274

Gonzalo, A., López, P., & Martín, J. (2013). Adaptive forgetting in Iberian green frog tadpoles (*Pelophylax perezi*): Learned irrelevance and latent inhibition may avoid predator misidentification. *Journal of Comparative Psychology, 127*(1), 39. https://doi.org/10.1037/a0032043

Granger, K. T., Talwar, A., & Barnett, J. H. (2020). Latent inhibition and its potential as a biomarker for schizophrenia. *Biomarkers in Neuropsychiatry, 3*, 100025. https://doi.org/10.1016/j.bionps.2020.100025

Gray, J. A., & McNaughton, N. (2000). *The neuropsychology of anxiety: An enquiry into the functions of the septo-hippocampal system*. Oxford University Press.

Gray, J. C., Sanchez-Roige, S., de Wit, H., MacKillop, J., & Palmer, A. A. (2019). Genomic basis of delayed reward discounting. *Behavioural Processes, 162*, 157–161. https://doi.org/10.1016/j.beproc.2019.03.006

Grill, H. J., & Norgren, R. (1978). The taste reactivity test. I. Mimetic responses to gustatory stimuli in neurologically normal rats. *Brain Research, 143*, 263–279. https://doi.org/10.1016/0006-8993(78)90568-1

Guarino, S., Conrad, S. E., & Papini, M. R. (2020). Frustrative nonreward: Chemogenetic inactivation of the central amygdala abolishes the effect of reward downshift without affecting alcohol intake. *Neurobiology of Learning and Memory, 169*, 1–7. https://doi.org/10.1016/j.nlm.2020.107173

Herrnstein, R. J. (1961). Relative and absolute strength of response as a function of frequency of reinforcement. *Journal of the Experimental Analysis of Behavior, 4*, 267–272. https://doi.org/10.1901/jeab.1961.4-267

Herrnstein, R. J., & Loveland, D. H. (1975). Maximizing and matching on concurrent ratio schedules. *Journal of the Experimental Analysis of Behavior, 24*, 107–116. https://doi.org/10.1901/jeab.1975.24-107

Herry, C., Ciocchi, S., Senn, V., Demmou, L., Müller, C., & Lüthi, A. (2008). Switching on and off fear by distinct neuronal circuits. *Nature, 454*, 600–606. https://doi.org/10.1038/nature07166

Hoffman, H., & Spear, N. E. (1989). Facilitation and impairment of conditioning in the preweanling rat after prior exposure to the conditioned stimulus. *Animal Learning and Behavior, 17*, 63–69. https://doi.org/10.3758/BF03205213

Ishii, K., Haga, Y., & Hishimura, Y. (1999). Distractor effect on the latent inhibition of conditioned flavor aversion in rats. *Japanese Psychological Research, 41*, 229–238. https://doi.org/10.1111/1468-5884.00123

Kamin, L. J. (1969). Predictability, surprise, attention, and conditioning. In B. A. Campbell & R. M. Church (Eds.), *Punishment and aversive behavior* (pp. 279–296). Appleton-Century-Crofts.

Kawasaki, K., Annicchiarico, I., Glueck, A. C., Morón, I., & Papini, M. R. (2017). Reward loss and the basolateral amygdala: A function in reward comparisons. *Behavioural Brain Research, 331*, 205–213. https://doi.org/10.1016/j.bbr.2017.05.036

Kenney, J. W., Scott, I. C., Josselyn, S. A., & Frankland, P. W. (2017). Contextual fear conditioning in zebrafish. *Learning & Memory, 24*, 516–523. https://doi.org/10.1101/lm.045690.117

Killcross, S., & Balleine, B. (1996). Role of primary motivation in stimulus preexposure effects. *Journal of Experimental Psychology: Animal Behavior Processes, 22*, 32–42. https://doi.org/10.1037//0097-7403.22.1.32

Kim, J. H., & Richardson, R. (2010). New findings on extinction of conditioned fear early in development: Theoretical and clinical implications. *Biological Psychiatry, 67*, 297–303. https://doi.org/10.1016/j.biopsych.2009.09.003

Koob, G. F., & Volkow, N. D. (2016). Neurobiology of addiction: A neurocircuitry analysis. *Lancet Psychiatry, 3*, 760–773. https://doi.org/10.1016/S2215-0366(16)00104-8

Korn, C. W., Vunder, J., Miró, J., Fuentemilla, L., Hurlemann, R., & Bach, D. R. (2017). Amygdala lesions reduce anxiety-like behavior in a human benzodiazepine-sensitive approach-avoidance conflict test. *Biological Psychiatry, 82*, 522–531. https://doi.org/10.1016/j.biopsych.2017.01.018

Kutlu, M. G., Zachry, J. E., Melugin, P. R., Tat, J., Cajigas, S., Isiktas, A. U., Patel, D. D., Siciliano, C. A., Schoenbaum, G., Sharpe, M. J., & Calipari, E. S. (2022). Dopamine signaling in the nucleus accumbens core mediates latent inhibition. *Nature Neuroscience*, *25*, 1071–1081. https://doi.org/10.1038/s41593-022-01126-1

Lal, P., Tanabe, H., Suster, M. L., Ailani, D., Kotani, Y., Muto, A., Itoh, M., Iwasaki, M., Wada, H., Yaksi, E., & Kawakam, K. (2018). Identification of a neuronal population in the telencephalon essential for fear conditioning in zebrafish. *BMC Biology*, *16*, 45. https://doi.org/10.1186/s12915-018-0502-y

Lang, S., Kroll, A., Lipinski, S. J., Ridder, S., Christmann, C., Schad, L. R., & Flor, H. (2009). Context conditioning and extinction in humans: Differential contribution of the hippocampus, amygdala, and prefrontal cortex. *European Journal of Neuroscience*, *29*, 823–832. https://doi.org/10.1111/j.1460-9568.2009.06624.x

LeDoux, J. E., Sakaguchi, A., & Reis, D. J. (1984). Subcortical efferent projections of the medial geniculate nucleus mediate emotional responses conditioned to acoustic stimuli. *Journal of Neuroscience*, *4*, 683–698. https://doi.org/10.1523/JNEUROSCI.04-03-00683.1984

Lowes, G., & Bitterman, M. E. (1967). Reward and learning in the goldfish. *Science*, *157*, 455–457. https://doi.org/10.1126/science.157.3787.455

Mackintosh, N. J., Kaye, H., & Bennett, C. H. (1991). Perceptual learning in flavour aversion conditioning. *Quarterly Journal of Experimental Psychology*, *43B*, 297–322.

Manrique, T., Molero, A., Ballesteros, M. A., Morón, I., Gallo, M., & Fenton, A. A. (2004). Time of day-dependent latent inhibition of conditioned taste aversions in rats. *Neurobiology of Learning and Memory*, *82*, 77–80. https://doi.org/10.1016/j.nlm.2004.04.003

Mansbach, R. S., Harrod, C., Hoffman, S. M., Nader, M. A., Lei, Z., Witkin, J. M., & Barrett, J. E. (1988). Behavioral studies with anxiolytic drugs: V. Behavioral and in vivo neurochemical analyses in pigeons of drugs that increase punished responding. *Journal of Pharmacology and Experimental Therapeutics*, *246*, 114–120.

Maren, S., Phan, K. L., & Liberzon, I. (2016). The contextual brain: Implications for fear conditioning, extinction and psychopathology. *Nature Reviews Neuroscience*, *14*, 417–428. https://doi.org/10.1038/nrn3492

Mazur, J. E., & Logue, A. W. (1978). Choice in a "self-control" paradigm: Effects of a fading procedure. *Journal of the Experimental Analysis of Behavior*, *30*, 11–17. https://doi.org/10.1901/jeab.1978.30-11

McAllister, W. R., McAllister, D. E., Weldin, G. H., & Cohen, J. M. (1974). Intertrial interval effects in classically conditioned fear to a discrete conditioned stimulus and to situational cues. *Journal of Comparative and Physiological Psychology*, *87*, 582–590. https://doi.org/10.1037/h0036993

McLaren, I. P. L., Kaye, H., & Mackintosh, N. J. (1989). An associative theory of the representation of stimuli: Applications to perceptual learning and latent inhibition. In R. G. M. Morris (Ed.), *Parallel distributed processing: Implications for psychology and neurobiology* (pp. 102–130). Clarendon Press, Oxford University Press.

McNally, G. P. (2009). The roles of endogenous opioids in fear learning. *International Journal of Comparative Psychology*, *22*, 153–169. https://doi.org/10.46867/ijcp.2009.22.03.02

Miller, M. L., Vaillancourt, B. D., Wright, M. J., Jr., Aarde, S. M., Vandewater, S. A., Creehan, K. M., & Taffe, M. A. (2012). Reciprocal inhibitory effects of intravenous d-methamphetamine self-administration and wheel activity in rats. *Drug and Alcohol Dependance*, *121*, 90–96. https://doi.org/10.1016/j.drugalcdep.2011.08.013

Mitchell, C., & Hall, G. (2014). Can theories of animal discrimination explain perceptual learning in humans? *Psychological Bulletin*, *140*, 283–307. https://doi.org/10.1037/a0032765

Mitchell, M. D., McCormick, M. I., Ferrari, M. C. O., & Chivers, D. P. (2011). Friend or foe? The role of latent inhibition in predator and non-predator labelling by coral reef fishes. *Animal Cognition*, *14*, 707. https://doi.org/10.1007/s10071-011-0405-6

Morales, I., & Berridge, K. C. (2020). "Liking" and "wanting" in eating and food reward: Brain mechanisms and clinical implications. *Physiology & Behavior*, *227*, 13152. https://doi.org/10.1016/j.physbeh.2020.113152

Morin, P.-P., Dodson, J. J., & Doré, F. Y. (1990). Facilitative effect of preexposure on hear-rate conditioning to an olfactory cue in Atlantic salmon (*Salmo salar*). *Journal of Comparative Psychology*, *104*, 340–344. https://doi.org/10.1037/0735-7036.104.4.340

Morón, I., Manrique, T., Molero, A., Ballesteros, M. A., Gallo, M., & Fenton, A. (2002). The contextual modulation of conditioned taste aversions by the physical environment and time of day is similar. *Learning & Memory*, *9*, 218–223. https://doi.org/10.1101/lm.52202

Muzio, R. N., Pistone Creydt, V., Iurman, M., Rinaldi, M. A., Sirani, B., & Papini, M. R. (2011). Incentive or habit learning in amphibians? *PLoS One*, *6*, e25798. https://doi.org/10.1371/journal.pone.0025798

Nation, J. R., Wrather, D. M., & Mellgren, R. L. (1974). Contrast effects in escape conditioning of rats. *Journal of Comparative and Physiological Psychology*, *86*, 69–73. https://doi.org/10.1037/h0035962

Odum, A. L. (2011). Delay discounting: I'm a k, you're a k. *Journal of the Experimental Analysis of Behavior*, *96*, 427–439. https://doi.org/10.1901/jeab.2011.96-423

Ortega, L. A., Solano, J. L., Torres, C., & Papini, M. R. (2017). Reward loss and addiction: Opportunities for cross-pollination. *Pharmacology, Biochemistry, and Behavior*, *154*, 39–52. https://doi.org/10.1016/j.pbb.2017.02.001

Ortega, L. A., Uhelski, M., Fuchs, P. N., & Papini, M. R. (2011). Impairment of recovery from incentive downshift after lesions of the anterior cingulate cortex: Emotional or cognitive deficits? *Behavioral Neuroscience*, *125*, 988–995. https://doi.org/10.1037/a0025769

Overmier, J. B., & Papini, M. R. (1986). Factors modulating the effects of teleost telencephalon ablation on retention, relearning, and extinction of instrumental avoidance behavior. *Behavioral Neuroscience*, *100*, 190–199. https://doi.org/10.1037/0735-7044.100.2.190

Papini, M. R. (1997). Role of reinforcement in spaced-trial operant learning in pigeons (*Columba livia*). *Journal of Comparative Psychology*, *111*, 275–285. https://doi.org/10.1037/0735-7036.111.3.275

Papini, M. R. (2003). Comparative psychology of surprising nonreward. *Brain, Behavior and Evolution*, *62*, 83–95. https://doi.org/10.1159/000072439

Papini, M. R. (2014). Diversity of adjustments to reward downshift in vertebrates. *International Journal of Comparative Psychology*, *27*, 420–445.

Papini, M. R., & Dudley, R. T. (1997). Consequences of surprising reward omissions. *Review of General Psychology*, *1*, 175–197. https://doi.org/10.1037/1089-2680.1.2.175

Papini, M. R., Fuchs, P. N., & Torres, C. (2015). Behavioral neuroscience of psychological pain. *Neuroscience and Biobehavioral Reviews*, *48*, 53–69. https://doi.org/10.1016/j.neubiorev.2014.11.012

Papini, M. R., & Ishida, M. (1994). Role of magnitude of reinforcement in spaced-trial instrumental learning in turtles (*Geoclemys reevesii*). *Quarterly Journal of Experimental Psychology*, *47B*, 1–13. https://doi.org/10.1080/14640749408401344

Papini, M. R., Mustaca, A. E., & Bitterman, M. E. (1988). Successive negative contrast in the consummatory responding of didelphid marsupials. *Animal Learning and Behavior*, *16*, 53–57. https://doi.org/10.3758/BF03209043

Papini, M. R., & Pellegrini, S. (2006). Scaling relative incentive value in consummatory behavior. *Learning and Motivation*, *37*, 357–378. https://doi.org/10.1016/j.lmot.2006.01.001

Papini, M. R., Penagos-Corzo, J. C., & Pérez-Acosta, A. M. (2019). Avian emotions: Comparative perspectives on fear and frustration. *Frontiers in Psychology*, *9*, 2707. https://doi.org/10.3389/fpsyg.2018.02707

Papini, M. R., Thomas, B. L., & McVicar, D. G. (2002). Between-subject PREE within-subject reversed PREE in spaced-trial extinction with pigeons. *Learning and Motivation*, *33*, 485–509. https://doi.org/10.1016/S0023-9690(02)00006-1

Pavlov, I. P. (1927). *Conditioned reflexes: An investigation of the physiological activity of the cerebral cortex*. Oxford University Press.

Pearce, J. M., & Hall, G. (1980). A model for Pavlovian learning: Variations in the effectiveness of conditioned but not of unconditioned stimuli. *Psychological Review*, *87*, 532–552. https://doi.org/10.1037/0033-295X.87.6.532

Portavella, M., Salas, C., Vargas, J. P., & Papini, M. R. (2003). Involvement of the telencephalon in spaced-trial avoidance learning in the goldfish (Carassius auratus). *Physiology and Behavior*, *80*(1), 49–56. https://doi.org/10.1016/s0031-9384(03)00208-7

Portavella, M., Torres, B., Salas, C., & Papini, M. R. (2004). Avoidance response in goldfish: Emotional and temporal involvement of medial and lateral telencephalic pallium. *Neuroscience Letters*, *24*, 2335–2342. https://doi.org/10.1523/JNEUROSCI.4930-03.2004

Puddington, M. M., Daneri, M. F., Papini, M. R., & Muzio, R. N. (2016). Telencephalic neural activation following passive avoidance learning in a terrestrial toad. *Behavioural Brain Research*, *315*, 75–82. https://doi.org/10.1016/j.bbr.2016.08.003

Rachlin, H., & Green, L. (1972). Commitment, choice and self-control. *Journal of the Experimental Analysis of Behavior*, *17*, 15–22. https://doi.org/10.1901/jeab.1972.17-15
Randle, E., & Sansom, R. S. (2019). Bite marks and predation of fossil jawless fish during the rise of jawed vertebrates. *Proceedings of the Royal Society, B*, *286*, 20191596. https://doi.org/10.1098/rspb.2019.1596
Rauhut, A. S., Thomas, B. L., & Ayres, J. J. B. (2001). Treatments that weaken Pavlovian conditioned fear and thwart its renewal in rats: Implications for treating human phobias. *Journal of Experimental Psychology: Animal Behavior Processes*, *27*, 99–114. https://doi.org/10.1037/0097-7403.27.2.99
Rescorla, R. A. (1971). Summation and retardation tests of latent inhibition. *Journal of Comparative and Physiological Psychology*, *75*, 77–81. https://doi.org/10.1037/h0030694
Rescorla, R. A., & Wagner, A. R. (1972). A theory of Pavlovian conditioning: Variations in the effectiveness of reinforcement and nonreinforcement. In A. H. Black & W. F. Prokasy (Eds.), *Classical conditioning II* (pp. 64–99). Appleton-Century-Crofts.
Robins, L. N. (1993). Vietnam veterans' rapid recovery from heroin addiction: A fluke or normal expectation? *Addiction*, *88*, 1041–1054. https://doi.org/10.1111/j.1360-0443.1993.tb02123.x
Sabariego, M., Morón, I., Gómez, M. J., Donaire, R., Tobeña, A., Fernández-Teruel, A., Martínez-Conejero, J. A., Esteban, F. J., & Torres, C. (2013). Incentive loss and hippocampal gene expression in inbred Roman high-(RHA-I) and Roman low-(RLA-I) avoidance rats. *Behavioural Brain Research*, *257*, 62–70. https://doi.org/10.1016/j.bbr.2013.09.025
Salinas, J. A., Parent, M. B., & McGaugh, J. L. (1996). Ibotenic acid lesions of the amygdala basolateral complex or central nucleus differentially effect the response to reductions in reward. *Brain Research*, *742*, 283–293. https://doi.org/10.1016/S0006-8993(96)01030-X
Shishimi, A. (1985). Latent inhibition experiments with goldfish (*Carassius auratus*). *Journal of Comparative Psychology*, *99*, 316–327. https://doi.org/10.1037/0735-7036.99.3.316
Sissons, H. T., & Miller, R. R. (2009). Spontaneous recovery of excitation and inhibition. *Journal of Experimental Psychology: Animal Behavior Processes*, *35*(3), 419–426. https://doi.org/10.1037/a0014815
Skinner, B. F. (1938). *The behavior of organisms*. Appleton-Century.
Snider, S. E., DeHart, W. B., Epstein, L. H., & Bickel, W. K. (2019). Does delay discounting predict maladaptive health and financial behaviors in smokers? *Health Psychology*, *38*, 21–28. https://doi.org/10.1037/hea0000695
Solomon, P. R., Brennan, G., & Moore, J. W. (1974). Latent inhibition of the rabbit's nictitating membrane response as a function of CS intensity. *Bulletin of the Psychonomic Society*, *4*(5-A), 445–448. https://doi.org/10.3758/BF03334250
Stout, S. C., & Miller, R. R. (2007). Sometimes-competing retrieval (SOCR): A formalization of the comparator hypothesis. *Psychological Review*, *114*, 759–783. https://doi.org/10.1037/0033-295X.114.3.759
Sutherland, N. S., & Mackintosh, N. J. (1971). *Mechanisms of animal discrimination learning*. Academic Press.
Symonds, M., & Hall, G. (1995). Perceptual learning in flavor aversion conditioning: Roles of stimulus comparison and latent inhibition of common stimulus elements. *Learning and Motivation*, *26*, 203–219. https://doi.org/10.1016/0023-9690(95)90005-5
Terrace, H. S. (1972). By-products of discrimination learning. *Psychology of Learning and Motivation*, *5*, 195–265. https://doi.org/10.1016/S0079-7421(08)60442-9
Thomas, B. L., & Papini, M. R. (2003). Mechanisms of spaced-trial runway extinction in pigeons. *Learning and Motivation*, *34*, 104–126. https://doi.org/10.1016/S0023-9690(02)00506-4
Wagner, A. R. (1969). Frustrative nonreward: A variety of punishment. In B. A. Campbell & R. M. Church (Eds.), *Punishment and aversive behavior* (pp. 157–181). Appleton-Century-Crofts.
Wesley, M. J., & Bickel, W. K. (2014). Remember the future II: Meta-analyses and functional overlap of working memory and delay discounting. *Biological Psychiatry*, *75*, 435–448. https://doi.org/10.1016/j.biopsych.2013.08.008
Woods, P. J., Davidson, E. H., & Peters, R. J., Jr. (1964). Instrumental escape conditioning in a water tank: Effects of variations in drive stimulus intensity and reinforcement magnitude. *Journal of Comparative and Physiological Psychology*, *57*, 466–470. https://doi.org/10.1037/h0046640
Wynne, B., & Delius, J. D. (1995). Sensitization to apomorphine in pigeons: Unaffected by latent inhibition but still due to classical conditioning. *Psychopharmacology*, *119*, 414–420. https://doi.org/10.1007/BF02245857

6 Associative learning: Interactions

6.1 Introduction

Thus far, the emphasis has been on analyzing separately the contribution of Pavlovian and operant conditioning to behavior, their common and unique procedural features, and their basic mechanisms. We have shown that the underlying processes are distinct using the *omission* experiment to illustrate this point (see Chapter 4, Table 4.8). But in real life, whether in a natural setting or in the lab, behavior is the result of both conditioning processes and other contributing factors, including perception, attention, motivation, emotion, and many others. Chapter 6 focuses on areas in which these two conditioning processes interact in the production of behavior.

To view what we mean by "interaction" more clearly, consider a simple situation: a rat trained in a runway to pick up food in the goal box. This animal is hungry, so the behavior is motivated by food, but the rat must learn to move from the start to the goal box of the runway to find the food. In this sense, this rat is in an operant situation because obtaining the reward is contingent upon the animal's behavior of approaching the goal box. This is a *positive reinforcement* contingency.

But notice that once it receives the food, this event occurs in the context of goal-box stimuli and, in a real sense, the animal experiences a Pavlovian pairing between these stimuli and food. The implication is that every encounter with food, shock, or even a "trivial" encounter with a light or a tone occurs in the presence of other stimuli. The animal's brain will encode these coincidences automatically. Thus, although approaching the goal in a runway is an operant behavior, such behavior can be influenced by Pavlovian learning that connects the stimuli in the runway to the delivery of a reward in the goal box. In this example, both operant and Pavlovian processes propel the rat to move toward the goal box.

As we will see, in other situations, the two processes compete for the control of behavior producing all sorts of interactions. As an example, suppose the same rat that receives food in the goal box of the runway also receives a foot shock in the goal box on a random 50% of the trials (i.e., partial punishment). The approach behavior is likely to be interfered by avoidance responses as the rat is exposed to this mixture of outcomes, food and shock. The approach response is now partially punished by the shock and the stimuli in the runway (especially in the goal box) are now paired with both food and shock in a Pavlovian manner. Such a complex situation may generate an approach–avoidance conflict resulting in behavioral hesitation as goal-box stimuli are becoming ambivalent in terms of their hedonic value. Analogous real-life situations are relatively common. For example, animals may forage in areas where food and predators have been frequently detected, and employees may need to approach a manager that has been both supportive and strict in the past. That foraging area and manager have become ambivalent and may generate a similar type of approach–avoidance hesitation.

DOI: 10.4324/9781003401957-8

6.2 Interactions between elicited and reinforced behaviors

6.2.1 Equipotentiality

Learning theory has been influenced by a principle of ***equipotentiality***, according to which any stimulus can become a signal for any reinforcer and any response can be influenced by its consequences. Equipotentiality probably originated in Pavlov's (1927) experiments showing that almost any type of stimulus could be used as a CS for food. However, there is abundant evidence showing many exceptions to this principle, suggesting that perhaps the idea should be abandoned. An example shows that this is not as simple a problem as it may appear. Responses such as lever pressing, which many thought to be arbitrary and artificial (i.e., there are no levers in nature for animals to press) can be easily established using either ***shaping by successive approximations*** (a purely operant procedure) or an ***autoshaping*** procedure in which the presentation of a retractable lever functions as a CS for food (a response-independent, Pavlovian procedure). Both procedures easily lead to rats pressing levers, as has been done in thousands of experiments. Such results conform to Thorndike's (1911) law of effect, according to which an appetitive outcome contingent on a response increases the future probability of occurrence of the response—an equipotentiality scenario.

When similar procedures were applied to a variety of responses (e.g., sniffing, digging, or rearing), evidence showed that the probability of some responses were increased by response-contingent reinforcement, but others exhibited no detectable changes. In one experiment (Shettleworth, 1975), hamsters were reinforced with food for engaging in a variety of responses shown in Figure 6.1. The time spent scrabbling, digging, and rearing increased in frequency almost immediately after food was presented contingent with these

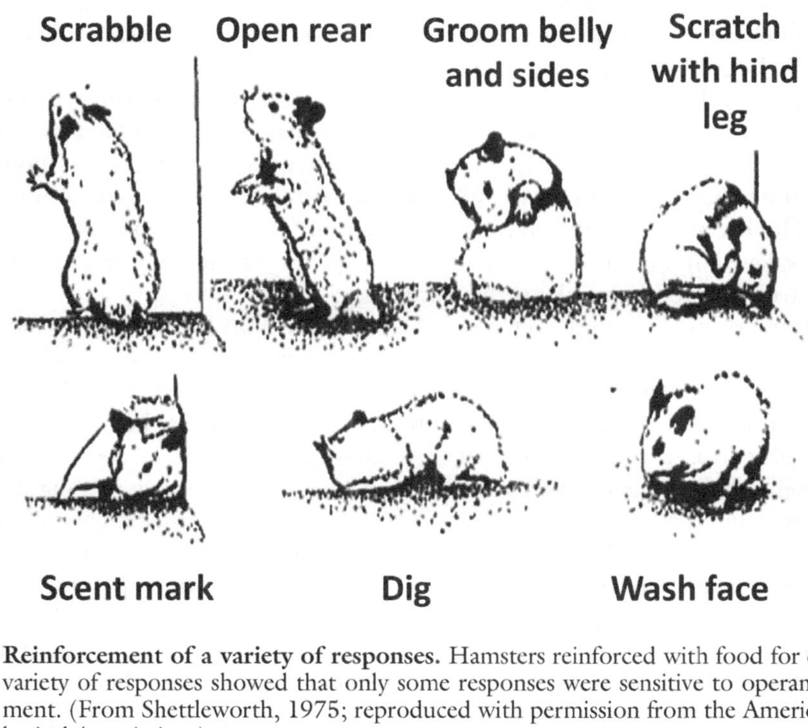

Figure 6.1 **Reinforcement of a variety of responses.** Hamsters reinforced with food for exhibiting a variety of responses showed that only some responses were sensitive to operant reinforcement. (From Shettleworth, 1975; reproduced with permission from the American Psychological Association.)

responses. However, scratching, scent marking, and face washing were barely influenced by the response-contingent reinforcer, and only after a considerable number of reinforcements. Behaviors that increased after food reinforcement were also behaviors that were observed to increase in a separate group of hungry animals subjected to food restriction relative to free-fed animals. By contrast, behaviors that exhibited little or no increase with the delivery of food reinforcement were reduced in a separate group of hungry animals. These results suggested that operant reinforcement with food was effective with behaviors that were part of the natural behavioral repertoire of hamsters when foraging.

Additional research suggested that the insensitivity of some of these responses to operant reinforcement was related to the degree to which there was a stimulus that supported the elicitation of the response. In a series of experiments with rats, Pearce et al. (1978) showed that the frequency of scratching behavior increased following the introduction of response-contingent food provided that the rat wore a collar around its neck. The collar could be assumed to produce itching stimulation that elicited scratching, thus increasing the normal frequency of occurrence of the response, which could then be further enhanced by operant reinforcement. Even yawning, which was found in dogs to show little increase to response-contingency food delivery, increases in frequency under some reinforcer contingencies in humans and monkeys (Baenninger, 1997). Thus, several factors contribute to the shaping of a response by operant reinforcement. These include its connection to the natural repertoire associated with the reinforcer used in training, and whether a stimulus is present that supports a baseline level of a behavior that is sufficient for the behavior to come under the control of its consequences.

6.2.2 Misbehavior

Skinner (1938) presented extensive evidence on the power of reinforcement to shape and control the behavior of rats in his book *The Behavior of Organisms.* Years later, Breland and Breland (1961) published a series of results that revealed the limits of reinforcement in a paper entitled *The Misbehavior of Organisms*, in obvious reference to Skinner's book. In their article, the Brelands detailed cases in which conventional operant training of their subjects failed either because the behavior never changed its frequency or because although initially successful, the behavior eventually ceased to be supported by reinforcement in the expected direction. The Brelands had created a company to train animals to exhibit a variety of behavior to be displayed in museums, zoos, and even in TV shows and commercials. One example will suffice to illustrate the problems they faced.

The training routine involved a raccoon as a bandit, with its natural black band of fur covering its eyes like a bandanna, performing a bank robbery. The raccoon was trained to pick up multiple coins and drop them into a small metallic box. The raccoon was initially reinforced with food for picking up one coin, and this shaping process had the intended result as the animal increased the frequency of this behavior. Then, the raccoon was required to drop the coin into the metallic box as if the animal was saving money in a piggy bank. This behavior was reinforced with food, which the raccoon would immediately pick up and eat. After some initial success, the problem started when the raccoon would readily pick up the coin but would spend a lot of time manipulating it rather than dropping it into the box. This behavior consistently delayed the delivery of the contingent food. Eventually, the raccoon was required to pick up two coins and drop them into the metallic box, but then the raccoon refused to release the coins and spent full minutes rubbing them together "in a most miserly fashion" (Breland & Breland, 1961, p. 682). Coins were dipped in the box but not dropped.

This resulted in a failure to receive food, but the refusal to drop the coins nonetheless persisted until the project was abandoned.

One interpretation of this phenomenon is that the operant contingencies involving food were at conflict with the species-typical, food-handling behavior of the raccoon. Initially, the coin was established as a Pavlovian conditioned stimulus (CS) for food (the unconditioned stimulus, US) as its manipulation was paired with food delivery intended to reinforced the response. However, the presence of food elicited several food-related behaviors that were incompatible with the target response of dropping the coin in the metallic box. One is reminded of the autoshaping phenomenon in rats mentioned previously. In this Pavlovian procedure (Atnip, 1977), the presentation of a retractable lever for a few seconds (the CS) is paired with the delivery of food (the US). The rat does not need to respond to the lever in this Pavlovian, response-independent procedure, but rats would typically approach and direct a number of responses to the lever, including biting, manipulating, and pushing it, all of which can be detected automatically. The type of responses observed in autoshaping are also the result of an interaction between the type of CS and the type of US used in training. As mentioned in Chapter 2, rats can be autoshaped in a cold environment if the lever predicts the turning on of a heat lamp for a few seconds (the US) provided the lever (the CS) is covered by acrylic fur, but not if it is a regular, aluminum lever. Conversely, the fur lever does not promote much lever pressing if it is paired with food, but the aluminum lever promotes autoshaping (Davey et al., 1989). Thus, the raccoon's refusal to drop the coin appears to have been the result of Pavlovian responses related to the manipulable nature of the coin (raccoons are nocturnal and usually hold food objects with their hands to identify and assess them) and the use of food as a US. Raccoons are not born with a tendency to display these behaviors toward coins but only exhibited them when coins became signals for food during their training. These responses interfered with the intended operant behavior of dropping the coin in the metallic box, thus leading to the failure of the project.

6.2.3 *Adjunctive behavior*

In typical learning experiments, there are moments during the training session when reinforcers are delivered, but there are also moments in which nothing important (to the animal) is actually happening. If the animal is not responding for the reinforcer, what is the animal doing during these periods? A study with pigeons was designed to track behavioral changes on a continuous basis during a session (Staddon & Simmelhag, 1971). Pigeons were exposed to response-independent food deliveries at regular intervals of 30 s while observers scored the occurrence of several behaviors. Surprisingly, two distinct sets of responses increased in frequency at different moments during the interreinforcement interval that were labeled terminal and adjunctive behaviors. ***Terminal responses*** peaked at the end of the interval, before food delivery, and involved such activities as goal tracking and pecking at the food cup. These behaviors are consistent with the impending availability of food, that is, approaching the location where food will be delivered and pecking just like they would do when food (grain) becomes available. This was not surprising, as you previously learned in Chapter 2 about these as consummatory behaviors elicited by the sensory properties of a US.

Other preparatory behaviors are associated with the affective properties of a US. Staddon and Simmelhag (1971) referred to a second set of preparatory responses, called ***adjunctive behaviors***, that occur early in the interreinforcement interval, starting to increase in frequency immediately after food delivery. During these periods, pigeons turned away from the proximity of the food cup and started to peck at the floor. Since these behaviors were observed after extensive exposure to the periodic schedule of food delivery, these animals had learned when the food would become available, called ***temporal conditioning*** (Pavlov, 1927). Temporal conditioning explained the occurrence of terminal responses on trials when food was not delivered, which provides a hint as to the function of adjunctive behaviors as coping or replacement behaviors that occur when food is not likely to appear (Staddon, 1977). A variety of adjunctive behaviors, such as drinking water or running in a wheel, are induced during a timed period of food absence (Figure 6.2). This finding relates to similar evidence from other situations showing that animals respond to CSs conveying information about the absence of reward by engaging in other behaviors (e.g., withdrawal from signals of food omission or the postreinforcement pause in fixed-interval schedules, as described in Chapter 4).

These behaviors were characterized as "adjunctive" because they seem attached to operant (or terminal) responses. One adjunctive behavior that has been studied extensively is known as ***schedule-induced polydipsia*** (*SIP*). A rat pressing a lever for food delivered every 60 s on average, but also having continuous access to water in the conditioning box, will consume about half its body weight in water during the time between reinforcer availability throughout a 3-h session (Falk, 1961). Excessive drinking under similar conditions of intermittent reinforcement extends to other solutions, including alcohol (Moreno & Flores, 2012). Other behaviors also occur in excess during a period of low reinforcement probability, including, for example, aggressive behavior directed at another animal (Campagnoni et al., 1986) or excessive activity in a running wheel (Staddon & Ayres, 1975). In fact, the type of adjunctive behavior is determined by whatever is present in the situation.

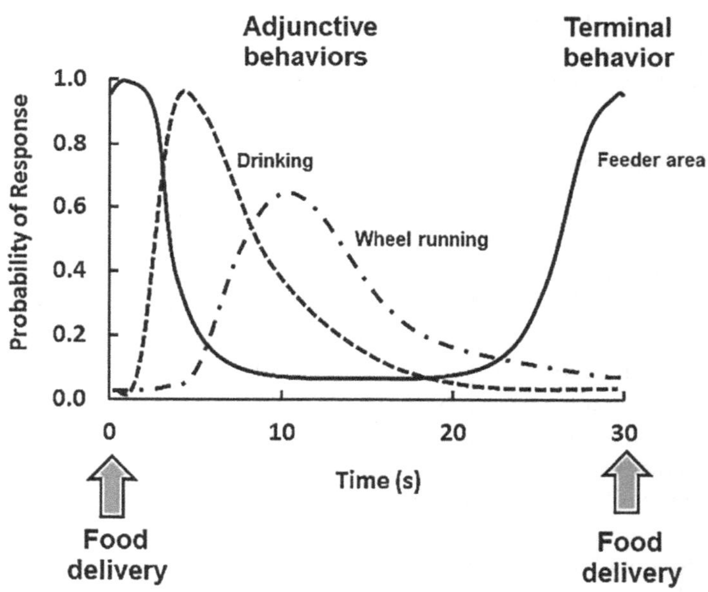

Figure 6.2 **Terminal and adjunctive behaviors.** Dynamic changes of terminal and adjunctive behaviors during the interval between successive food deliveries. When food is delivered at regular intervals, the animal tends to approach the location where food will be delivered as the interval is near its end (terminal behavior). Early in the interval, the animal engages in alternative behaviors (adjunctive behaviors). Drinking and wheel running are used in this figure, but the type of behavior depends on the available options in the situation. (Modified from Papini, 2021; reproduced with permission from Taylor & Francis.)

The high intensity of adjunctive behaviors may reflect the elicitation of emotional behavior (e.g., frustration), which is induced by periods of low reward probability (Papini & Dudley, 1997). Reward omissions also invigorate dominant responses. Rats given two successive opportunities to press a lever for food exhibited an increase in lever pressing in the second component when food was unexpectedly omitted in the first component (Stout et al., 2003). In a natural foraging situation, increased emotional arousal may function to move the animal away from a depleted source of food and promote exploratory foraging (Papini, 2003; Papini et al., 2022). However, in a confined environment (as in lab procedures), emotional activation may invigorate responses that are supported by the situation, such as drinking if water is available.

Although adjunctive behaviors tend to occur during periods of low reinforcement rates, the rewards that do occur in the situation could influence their development. The delivery of a piece of food increases the probability of behaviors that immediately precede it, but food delivery can also increase the probability of more distal responses, even if this effect is smaller. Thus, food could reinforce adjunctive behavior even in the presence of a temporal gap.

One way to test this notion is to impose a delay between the last occurrence of licking for water and food delivery. If licking is an adjunctive behavior, this should not affect its occurrence; by contrast, if licking is actually an operant response, a delay should affect its occurrence. SIP is reduced more by a 30-s delay than by a 15-s delay between the last lick for water and food delivery (López-Crespo et al., 2004). Moreover, using a ***master–yoked design*** (see Chapter 4 for more information of the master–yoked design), according to which master animals were reinforced with food 30 s after the first 20 licks on a water tube, led to more licking than did yoking the same reward rate independently of the 20-lick requirement (Killeen & Pellón, 2013). Therefore, in addition to its other potential functions, in some instances there is an operant component in adjunctive behavior since it is influenced by reinforcement in a manner consistent with operant conditioning.

6.2.3.1 Brain mechanisms of schedule-induced polydipsia

In SIP, rats that could be lever pressing for food or engaging in other food-related behavior are instead consuming water. As mentioned, this is an interaction between the operant contingency and the natural behaviors (URs) elicited by intermittent food delivery. As in many other behavioral phenomena, there are measurable individual differences in SIP. Some rats develop polydipsia rapidly and to a high level of drinking (HD rats), whereas others exhibit low drinking under the same conditions (LD rats). These differences provide a basis for exploring neural phenotypes.

One study evaluated the distribution of ***dopamine receptors*** (known as D1 and D2) and the expression levels of c-Fos, a protein that indexes neuronal activity, in HD and LD rats in the SIP task (Pellón et al., 2011). After substantial training, HD and LD rats were consuming about 16 and 6 ml of water during the session, respectively. HD rats exhibited higher concentrations of D2 receptors, whereas LD rats showed higher concentration of D1 receptors. These differences were observed in several areas related to the reward system of the brain, including the ventral tegmental area, nucleus accumbens, amygdala, and medial prefrontal cortex.

Interestingly, when licks are analyzed as a function of volume of fluid intake (licks/mL), then LD rats took 39 licks to drink a milliliter of water, whereas HD rats needed 88 licks to consume the same amount. Thus, LDs were more efficient than HDs, suggesting that the excess licking in HD rats may reflect stereotypical motor responses under the control of dopamine D2 receptors. Although licking seems to be the same across animals, the underlying mechanisms vary in relation to the role of these dopamine receptors in different animals. LD rats seem to behave in a manner consistent with operant conditioning, maximizing water intake with each lick, whereas the behavior of HD rats seems more related to automatic Pavlovian responses.

6.2.4 A defensive response system

Rats quickly learn to run (e.g., in a wheel or through an alley) if doing so terminates a threat (e.g., Bolles et al., 1966). When placed in a box in which they have been shocked, they quickly learn to jump to the safety of a platform (Maatsch, 1959). These forms of avoidance learning are rapidly acquired and are robust, and it takes massive numbers of extinction trials without shock administration for the behavior to reduce its strength. Even then, a single shock quickly reinstates the avoidance behavior at full strength.

We previously showed that some behaviors are less sensitive to positive reinforcement than others, and the same can be said of behaviors exposed to negative reinforcement. While running and jumping are easily acquired to avoid aversive stimuli involving pain, other behaviors are acquired with greater difficulty due to an interaction of the Pavlovian and instrumental contingencies. If a naïve rat is placed in a conditioning box equipped with a single lever that can be pressed to avoid a shock, then this rat will have difficulty acquiring the lever-pressing response.

Consider the following procedure. A Tone is presented for up to 10 s, and its termination coincides with shock delivery unless the rat pressed the lever during the 10-s Tone, in which case no shock is delivered. This procedure is similar to classical fear conditioning, and in fact, to the extent the animal fails to press the lever, that is exactly what it experiences: Tone→Shock pairings. However, unlike in a standard Pavlovian procedure, there is an operant component since the behavior has the reliable consequence of preventing the shock. Rats readily acquire lever-pressing behavior when it is followed by food, and rats can readily acquire avoidance behavior, so why is this procedure so problematic for rats (D'Amato & Schiff, 1964)?

Under these conditions, it can take hundreds of trials for rats to acquire the lever-pressing response to avoid shocks, which implies the animal is receiving many shocks that are potentially avoidable. When the avoidance response involves jumping over a hurdle or running, avoidance is typically acquired with very little training. Bolles (1970) suggested that animals under threat will readily learn an avoidance response if the response is part of a preorganized response system that has a defensive function. These responses were called *species-specific defense reactions*, a behavior that was assumed to have an adaptive evolutionary history. Shock delivery is analogous to an encounter with a predator or an aggressive conspecific, and in such a situation, animals must learn all there is to learn very fast, with the least number of trials, to survive.

So natural selection has favored the evolution of a preorganized repertoire of behaviors with an antipredator function that can be summarized as *freeze, flight, or fight*. Freezing involves a total absence of movement, a common conditioned response in Pavlovian fear conditioning with rodents, which is adaptive because predators (e.g., snakes, birds of prey) tend to locate their prey mainly on the basis of movement. Thus, freezing minimizes detection. Fleeing involves escaping the threat and seeking a safer place if one is available and it has obvious survival value. Freezing will be dominant if the animal has learned that there are no safe locations in the environment in which it encounters a threat, such as the small conditioning box typically used in fear conditioning experiments. However, rats will actively flee if they have learned that there are safer locations that can be reached.

Fight involves a so-called defensive attack. When the distance between the predator and prey is minimal, the prey may actually attack the predator aggressively as a last resort.

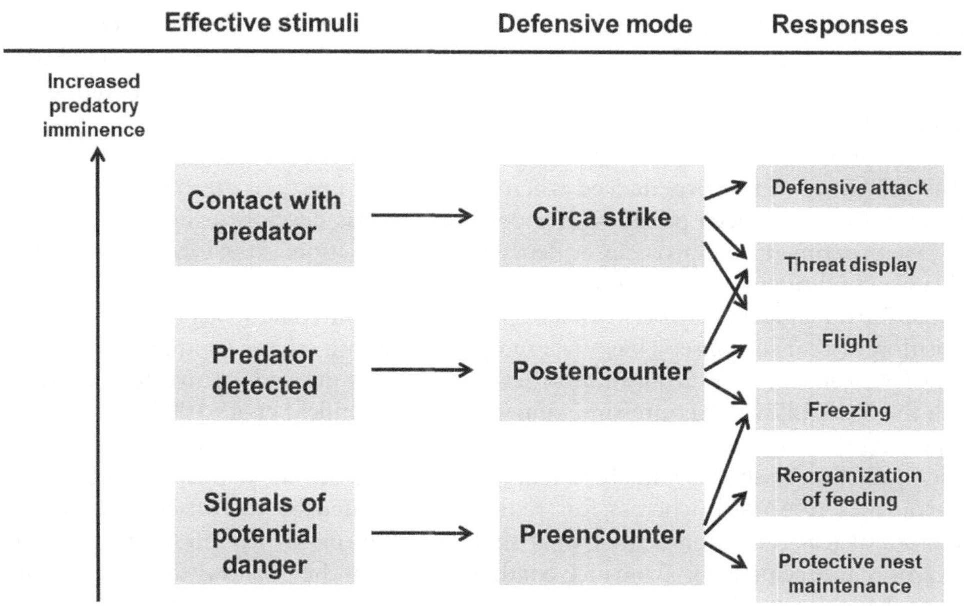

Figure 6.3 **The rat's defensive behavior system.** Three levels are represented in this figure: effective stimuli, defensive modes, and specific responses. This model is based on Fanselow (1994). (From Papini, 2021, reproduced with permission from Taylor & Francis.)

The rat's defensive *behavior system* is presented in Figure 6.3. Notice the freeze, flee, and fight components, but there is nothing there suggesting that manipulating an object will allow the rat to avoid a predator or an aggressive conspecific. The training situation outlined previously for a rat will elicit these defensive behaviors as soon as the animal experiences a shock. If the experiment is done in a typical conditioning box, the Tone paired with Shock will rapidly elicit freezing responses, a response that would compete for expression with lever pressing. A rat that is freezing cannot press a lever. This situation illustrates once again the conflict between Pavlovian and operant behaviors, with a CS eliciting a response that is incompatible with the emission of the operant behavior that would prevent or eliminate the shock. Interestingly, if rats are trained to freeze to avoid a Shock, then this avoidance response is rapidly acquired (Bolles & Riley, 1973).

Notice the correspondence between the notions of species-specific defense responses and misbehaviors described previously. They correspond to situations involving aversive and appetitive reinforcers, respectively, but in both cases, there is a conflict between the elicited Pavlovian response and the reinforced operant response that leads to behavioral interference. Such interactions reflect the contributions of natural selection to the shaping of behavioral skills and the importance of individual learning experience in the development of behavior.

6.3 Escape and avoidance learning

6.3.1 Avoidance conditioning

Part of the driving force behind escape and avoidance learning is provided by the reinforcing power of eliminating a source of aversiveness. A traditional issue in the field of learning has been to point out that successful avoidance carries the seed of its own extinction, provided that the avoidance response is actually and purely shaped by avoiding the aversive outcome. The puzzle has been this: How can a behavior motivated by shock be maintained when its occurrence eliminates the shock? The paradox is that successful avoidance should lead to its own extinction.

One response to this paradox has been to point out that avoidance is in part maintained by the reduction of fear experienced when the avoidance response terminates the stimulus that has occasionally been paired with shock and that has developed the ability to induced fear. One experiment that provides evidence for fear reduction as the mechanism underlying avoidance conditioning was reported by Kamin (1957). This experiment was based on the fact that introducing a delay between a response and its outcome tends to interfere with the acquisition of that response. Thus, for example, if pressing a lever produces food, but only after a few seconds, then acquisition of lever pressing is delayed relative to a condition in which the food follows lever pressing immediately (Wilkenfield et al., 1992).

Applying that logic to the case of avoidance, fear in such a situation is elicited by the onset of the signal for the shock (initially functioning as a CS since the animal has not yet learned the avoidance response), whereas fear reduction is elicited by the offset of such a signal. Therefore, if fear reduction (rather than shock prevention) is hypothesized to be a major source of reinforcement for avoidance conditioning, then the goal was to delay the offset of the signal for shock relative to the avoidance response but at the same time keeping shock avoidance constant. Thus, an avoidance response canceled shock delivery in all conditions but led to the offset of the signal for shock with increasing delays.

As shown in Figure 6.4, delays of 0 (no delay), 2.5, 5, and 10 s were implemented in different groups. The evidence showed that the increase in the delay led to progressively greater

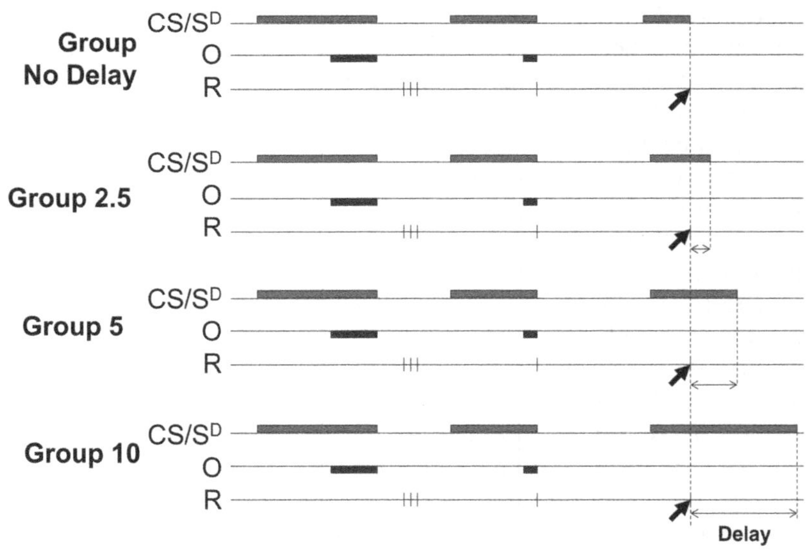

Figure 6.4 **Role of fear reduction in avoidance conditioning.** Schematic representation of the design used by Kamin (1957) to determine whether avoidance learning was dependent upon shock prevention or fear reduction. The signal (CS/S^D) acquired the ability to induce fear because of early pairings with the shock (O, the outcome) before the animal acquired the avoidance response. The response (R) prevents the Shock in all groups, but the response ends the CS/S^D with increasing delays. The longer this delay, the greater the disruption of avoidance learning.

disruption in avoidance conditioning, even though in all cases, the responses avoided the shock. Thus, delaying the relationship between the occurrence of the avoidance response and the reinforcing event of fear reduction disrupted avoidance conditioning, even if the shock was actually avoided (Kamin, 1957).

6.3.2 *Escape conditioning*

In a typical avoidance conditioning experiment, the same response that leads to avoiding the shock before it is presented also leads to escaping the Shock once it has started. Thus, the escape response must occur in the presence of pain induced by the Shock, so it is likely that fear reduction plays less of an important role in escape conditioning compared to pain reduction.

In one experiment (Ehrman & Overmier, 1976), two groups of dogs received training in comparable situations during Phase 1, except that one group was able to escape and avoid shock, whereas the other was only able to escape (Table 6.1). The required response (R) was to jump over a barrier in a two-compartment shuttle box. Importantly, each trial was initiated in both groups by the onset of a visual signal (V). In Phase 2, both groups were confined to one of the compartments (jumping was not possible), and they received differential Pavlovian conditioning with two auditory CSs, one paired with Shock and the other presented alone. This training aimed at conditioning the auditory CS predicting Shock with the ability to evoke fear.

Having acquired the jumping response to deal with Shock, either avoid or escape, the question of interest was whether animals exposed to the Pavlovian CS for Shock, T, in the two-compartment situation would jump over the barrier. Notice that T should elicit fear, but it was not trained in relation to the jumping response, R. Thus, T induces fear, and if the animal has learned that it can jump to avoid shock (in Group Avoidance), then T is expected to increase the jumping response just as much as V. However, if the animal has just learned to escape from the shock (in Group Escape), then T's induction of fear should not affect the jumping response, just as V should not.

The results were the following. First, groups did not respond when C was presented during the test; C was a control stimulus never paired with shock, so a lack of responding was consistent with this training. Second, animals in Group Avoidance increased their shuttling over the barrier in the Test when either V or T were presented. For these animals, fear motivated their avoidance behavior. Third, animals in Group Escape failed to show an increase in

Table 6.1 Design of an experiment on the role of fear in escape conditioning

Group	*Instrumental baseline*	*Pavlovian phase*	*Test*
Avoidance	V→R→noSh	T→Sh, C→noSh	V→R? T→R? C→R? V→noR→Sh
Escape	VSh→R→endSh	T→Sh, C→noSh	V→R? T→R? C→R? VSh→noR→Sh

Note. V was a visual signal. T and C were auditory signals (such as Tone and Click sound). R was the shuttling response over a barrier. Sh was the shock. During the instrumental baseline, animals in Group Avoidance could avoid the shock by shuttling over the barrier during the visual stimulus (V). However, animals in Group Escape could not avoid, but they could escape the shock by jumping over the barrier once the shock started. To equate groups, the visual stimulus (V) was presented to all the animals. In the Test, each signal (V, T, C) was presented while the animal could shuttle over the barrier.

the jumping response in the presence of either V or T. For these animals, fear did not motivate the avoidance response. These results are consistent with the view that conditioned fear plays a more prominent role in avoidance than in escape conditioning.

6.3.3 Neurobiology of avoidance learning

Avoidance learning is connected to fear conditioning. The initial presentation of a signal for shock followed by shock prior to the development of an avoidance response is functionally similar to a CS→US Pavlovian pairing in the same manner as implemented in the fear conditioning paradigm (see Chapter 4). Such pairing would result in a freezing CR.

However, avoidance learning goes beyond Pavlovian fear conditioning to include negative reinforcement. On occasion, there is evidence of interference between the two types of learning. If a CR such as freezing is elicited by the CS but the required avoidance response involves locomotion, then these responses compete for expression, and avoidance learning can be significantly impaired, as described previously in this chapter (see the concept of species-specific defense response). Such impairment suggests that the Pavlovian process develops before the avoidance response emerges. As mentioned previously, when the required avoidance response and the Pavlovian response match, then the acquisition of avoidance is facilitated. In situations in which the two responses compete for expression, the development of the avoidance response requires the inhibition of incompatible responses.

The brain circuit underlying fear conditioning has a key component: the amygdala (see Figure 4.8). Inputs from the CS and US pathways converge in the ***basolateral amygdala*** (BLA), and they are transferred to the ***central amygdala*** (CeA), from which they are distributed to several nuclei controlling various outputs. The output connecting the CeA to the ***periaqueductal gray*** (PAG) is responsible for freezing.

In one example of avoidance discussed previously, requiring the animal to jump over a barrier to avoid a shock, such active avoidance learning requires a disruption of the CeA→PAG pathway to minimize response incompatibility between freezing elicited by the signal and the active avoidance response supported by its consequences (i.e., termination and then avoidance of shock). As expected, lesions of the CeA, which impair fear conditioning, actually facilitate active avoidance learning and even promote such learning in animals that are prone to excessive freezing to the signal (Choi et al., 2010). Avoidance learning was also linked to the period of safety following the response as a source of positive reinforcement (see Table 4.8, Chapter 4). Consistent with this, interfering with the pathway connecting the BLA to a major component of the reward system, the ***nucleus accumbens*** (NAc), also disrupts active avoidance learning (Ramirez et al., 2015). Different outputs from the BLA are controlling both Pavlovian fear conditioning leading to freezing and instrumental avoidance conditioning promoting active behavior (Figure 6.5).

A seemingly puzzling aspect of avoidance learning is that after extensive training, avoidance can continue despite evidence of reduced fear to the signal (Mineka, 1979). For example, stress hormones are elevated early in avoidance training but return to basal levels after extensive training, even though the avoidance response continues to occur. Thus, avoidance is subject to a similar transition from action to habit that applies to appetitive behaviors (see Chapter 4), a transition also reflected in terms of brain mechanisms. For example, extensively trained avoidance responses are no longer vulnerable to amygdala lesions (Poremba & Gabriel, 1999), suggesting that responding to the signal eventually becomes independent of fear reduction—the outcome of the response (i.e., S→R habit).

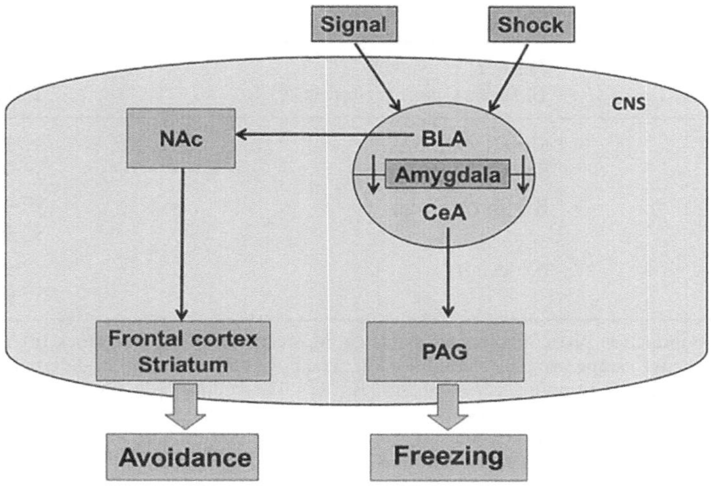

Figure 6.5 **Proposed brain circuit for avoidance conditioning.** Initially, in training, pairing of a signal with shock causes fear conditioning leading to freezing. This is mediated by the basolateral (BLA) and central amygdala (CeA) through connections with the periaqueductal gray (PGA). Figure 4.8 provides a detailed description of the neurobiology of fear conditioning. The development of avoidance requires the inhibition of freezing and the activation of the active avoidance response. This is mediated by the nucleus accumbens (NAc) through its connections with the prefrontal cortex and dorsal striatum. (Modified from Papini, 2021; reproduced with permission from Taylor & Francis.)

6.3.4 Learned helplessness

Avoidance learning is hampered by prior exposure to *inescapable shocks*, a phenomenon called *learned helplessness* (Overmier & Seligman, 1967; Seligman & Maier, 1967). A demonstration of learned helplessness includes three groups trained over two phases, administered in different contexts and requiring different responses (Table 6.2). In Phase 1, two groups involve a master–yoked comparison, and therefore, they are matched in the number and distribution of shocks but differ in terms of Response→noShock pairings. Master animals are usually trained in escape conditioning, whereas training is purely Pavlovian for Yoked animals since Shock presentations and omissions depend on the performance of master animals. The third group is exposed to the same situation and treated in the same way as the Master and Yoked groups, except that no shocks are ever administered to these animals. This NoShock control indicates whether the conditions of Phase 2 support avoidance learning in untreated animals and the extent of the deficit, if any, afforded by escape training in Master animals during Phase 1. In Phase 2, all animals receive active escape/avoidance training.

The typical outcome in Phase 2 is that the Master and NoShock groups show similar avoidance acquisition, and both acquire faster than Yoked animals. Learned helplessness is not produced by exposure to painful stimuli, because the Yoked and Master groups differ in Phase 2 despite being exposed to the same amount of shock in Phase 1. Moreover, Master and NoShock animals usually acquire avoidance behavior at about the same rate, also showing that learned helplessness is not the result of exposure to painful stimuli. Rather, learned helplessness results from exposure to inescapable painful stimuli.

Table 6.2 Design of learned helplessness experiments

Group	*Phase 1* *Induction phase (context X)*	*Phase 2* *Test phase (context Y)*
Master	Sh→R_1→noSh Sh→noR_1→Sh	S^D→R_2→noSh S^D→noR_2→Sh
Yoked	R_1, Sh or no Sh	S^D→R_2→noSh S^D→noR_2→Sh
NoShock	No events	S^D→R_2→no Sh S^D→noR_2→Sh

Note. Typically, the induction phase involves escapable (in Masters) vs. inescapable shock (in Yoked), whereas the test phase involves active escape-avoidance conditioning. Training is administered in different contexts (X and Y) and usually requires different responses across phases (R_1, R_2). The key group is the Yoked. Learned helplessness occurs when conditioning in Phase 2 proceeds more slowly in Group Yoked than in the other two groups. Notice that the master–yoked design guarantees equal amount and distribution of shocks for Masters and Yokes during the induction phase. Sh: shock. S^D: discriminative stimulus.

One key factor is *controllability*—the contingency between the animal's behavior and the shocks. Also interesting is that the animals in the NoShock condition must already have learned that their behaviors have effects on their environment. This is not surprising, given that their bedding moves when they step on it, water flows from their drinking tubes when licked, and their cage mate moves when prodded. Skinner (1953) suggested that animals can learn about the general value of behaving because of the sensory effects of doing so (e.g., a baby shaking a rattle or an artist receiving visual feedback in the form of color on a canvas). Sensory effects also consistently precede biological reinforcers (e.g., a cup moves before you drink from it).

The effects of exposure to inescapable shocks, which contradict the animal's prior experience with its environment, are widespread. Learned helplessness involves several cognitive and behavioral changes (Overmier & Murison, 2005). For example, animals may learn that there is no contingency between their own behavior and aversive stimulation during exposure to inescapable shocks. Such learning could subsequently discourage active coping in situations involving aversive stimuli—hence the label "helplessness." Consistent with this hypothesis, previous exposure to escape conditioning attenuates learned helplessness.

The induction phase also seems to lead to attentional deficits that reduce the salience of the animal's own behavior. Increasing response salience by marking the behavior with an exteroceptive stimulus (e.g., a noise when the animal makes a particular movement) attenuates learned helplessness. The escape response also serves as a signal of the end of the aversive event and the beginning of a period of safety.

Experiments have shown that an audiovisual stimulus presented at the time of the termination of the aversive event or the start of the safety period reduced learned helplessness. Inescapable shocks may also reduce activity levels, making it difficult to cope with novel situations. Although a reduction in activity can affect behavior in some situations, learned helplessness also affects response inhibition, interfering with the acquisition of passive avoidance (withholding a response to avoid shock) and choice, interfering with the acquisition of a discrimination between two options (choosing between a left vs. right response with equal motor demands).

Inescapable shocks can also reinforce postural adjustments that reduce pain. Thus, learned helplessness can arise because a response that reduces pain, acquired in Phase 1, is incompatible with the response required during Phase 2. Rats explicitly trained in Phase 1 to escape from shock by remaining inactive were more impaired than yoked controls in Phase 2—a reversed learned helplessness effect (Balleine & Job, 1991). Although the controllability hypothesis has received the bulk of attention, controllability of aversive events is only one of several contributing factors!

Inescapable shock can also affect social behavior. Yoked rats given training with inescapable shocks and later placed as intruders into an established colony were defeated more frequently by resident males and received a greater number of bites in aggressive encounters than either master animals that had experienced escapable shocks or controls not exposed to shocks (Williams & Lierle, 1986). By contrast, learning to escape shocks before exposure to inescapable shocks reduced the frequency of defeat. This treatment is called ***immunization*** because it renders inescapable shocks less effective in generating learned helplessness. Just as inescapable shocks lead to deficits in social interactions, repeated defeat by aggressive resident males leads to deficits in escape conditioning (Williams & Lierle, 1988).

Let us apply what we have learned to a real-life scenario. Some situations are not physically harmful but may be stressful and inescapable (e.g., taking a particular college course). Alana has joined a gymnastics team, but she feels the practices are unbearable. She is exhibiting symptoms of emotional stress. Her parents agreed to let her leave the gym at the end of the season but are requiring her to keep her current commitment to the team because she is not in any danger. She feels as though she is in an inescapable situation.

As her parents or teammates, what could you do to reduce her stress level and prevent learned helplessness? Using the techniques reviewed above, you could start to mark instances in which she exhibits control over her environment by verbally praising her ("great job going inside to get an umbrella"). You could add a salient signal that you present near the end of every practice (e.g., a sign that says "5 min left") or add a stimulus immediately after practice that signals a period of safety (e.g., ice cream). Without any intervention, just as the rats did in Williams and Lierle (1986), the inescapable situation may have resulted in Alana being less likely to act to remove herself from a future danger (e.g., domestic abuse). However, the manipulations suggested here would reduce the effects of the inescapable situation and increase the probability she acts to escape from a future danger.

6.4 Impulsivity and self-control

6.4.1 The marshmallow test

The ***marshmallow test*** is commonly used in studying ***impulsivity*** and delay of gratification in young children (Mischel et al., 1989). In this task, a researcher places a single marshmallow in front of a child and indicates that it may be eaten at any time with one important proviso: The researcher is going to briefly leave the room, and if the child waits to eat until the researcher returns, a second marshmallow will be added to the bounty. If the child eats the marshmallow before the researcher returns, then the child receives no additional marshmallow. Young children that can resist temptation have been shown to have better educational and life outcomes, even many years after the test occurred (e.g., Michaelson & Munakata, 2020).

The marshmallow test allows for many procedural variations. For example, delays may be lengthened, instructions may be changed, the nature of the treat and the context itself may be manipulated, etc. The key aspect of this test is to pit short-term and long-term consequences of the child's behavior against one another. The opportunity to immediately consume the marshmallow and eschew the candy that would have been delivered later is tough for many children to pass up. Even those that manage to wait appear to express conflict behavior.

Consider the Pavlovian–operant interaction embedded in the marshmallow test. A Pavlovian relationship exists between the appearance of the marshmallow (the CS) and its pleasing taste (the US) because of prior experience of the child with candy. Pavlovian salivation (i.e., the CR) could be observed in the presence of the marshmallow. Furthermore, the presentation of a desirable food could elicit food-handling behavior, such as reaching for the candy and placing it in the mouth.

This Pavlovian contingency is contrasted against the operant contingency in the following way: An additional marshmallow will be available if the child can avoid eating the one that is within reach at this time. This situation is reminiscent of the raccoon dealing with the problem of releasing a coin that had become a signal for food (see section on misbehavior). Hence, the usual behaviors produced by the presentation of candy are in mutual conflict with the behavior that would produce a greater reinforcer.

When immediate outcomes control behavior at the expense of opportunities for better but more delayed reinforcers, we might call the behavior ***impulsive***. Conversely, when immediate reinforcers are avoided in favor of better but more delayed reinforcers, the behavior may be characterized as *self-control* (Beran & Parrish, 2022). All such cases are representative of circumstances in which the animal is simultaneously inclined to behave in two mutually incompatible ways by virtue of multiple sets of controlling contingencies (see section on behavioral specializations and the brain in Chapter 1 and on delay discounting in Chapter 5).

6.4.2 Self-control in other animals

Comparative psychologists have adapted elements of the marshmallow test to investigate impulsivity and self-control in nonhuman animals, finding some remarkable similarities to human behavior. An African grey parrot named Griffin was presented with the opportunity to consume a less-preferred food item sooner or to wait up to 15 min to eat a more-preferred treat (Koepke et al., 2015). Griffin almost always waited to consume the more-desirable food, but while he waited, he engaged in behaviors that resembled those of children who were successful on the marshmallow task, including preening, sleeping, vocalizing, and manipulating the available reward.

A comparative study (Brucks et al., 2022) including several species of parrots found that these behaviors are common in effective waiting. Great green macaws, blue-throated macaws, and blue-headed macaws had comparable success in waiting for a better food item, though they were more impulsive than African grey parrots. These ancillary behaviors during the waiting period were observed in all species, although they differed in their tolerance of relatively long waiting periods. For example, Griffin frequently succeeded even with a 15-min delay, but none of these other parrots waited for longer than 1 minute.

There are significant differences in task demands, reinforcer quality, behavioral histories, and laboratory practices between the two studies just cited. Griffin, for example, had had training in responding to a verbal command, "wait," from his caretakers that might have provided a cognitive skill needed to delay gratification, that is, to have a more effective control of the Pavlovian component of this task. Other African grey parrots that had no such training could only wait for seconds before consuming the food item available, demonstrating that the Pavlovian component of the task overcame the operant contingency (Vick et al., 2010).

One variation of the task highlights the need to test self-control within an ecologically valid problem for the animal. Thinking back to the comic from Chapter 1 (Figure 1.1), should all animals receive the same test for self-control? The cleaner wrasse fish (*Labroides dimidiatus*), a species that lives in the Great Barrier Reef, removes parasites and other material from the bodies of their clients. This is mutually beneficial for the cleaner wrasse and the clients. Some clients, however, will leave the area if they are not tended to first, whereas others stay in the area and can be serviced with less urgency. To maximize their intake, the cleaner wrasse services the touchy clients first and then tends to the regulars.

Bshary and Grutter (2002) tested this behavior in a laboratory procedure in which the fish were first given simultaneous access to two stimuli (A and B). Choosing stimulus A gave fish access to a reinforcer, and the trial ended. However, choosing stimulus B gave fish access to the same reinforcer, but after consumption, stimulus A and its reinforcer were also made available. The cleaner wrasse successfully learned to select stimulus B. Under the same conditions, other animals have not fared so well on this ephemeral reinforcer task (Zentall, 2020).

Other variations of the marshmallow and ephemeral reinforcer task in rats and pigeons provided evidence that self-control is frequently predicted by and may be wholly reduced to ***delay discounting***. Recall from Chapters 2 and 5, that in delay discounting the value of a reinforcer is reduced (or discounted) by the delay to access it. An easy approximation to get the future value of a reinforcer is to simply divide its absolute value by the delay to access it (e.g., 4 s of food access divided by 4 s of delay). However, multiplying the delay by the slope of a hyperbolic ***discounting function*** is a better approximation. How does this work in the marshmallow task?

If a delay were added before access to the sooner, smaller reinforcer and participants were required to commit to the sooner, smaller or later, larger reinforcer, then at the time of the response the value of both reinforcers would be reduced, however, because of the lower starting value of the smaller reinforcer and the discounting function, the lower reward, A, would be reduced to a greater extent (Figure 6.6). This is akin to asking an addict to commit to abstinence well before they might encounter a choice between drinking now (sooner, smaller reinforcer) and quality family time later (later, larger reward) – more on this below. This same finding with different delay values was replicated with pigeon pecking keys and rats pressing different levers in the ephemeral reinforcer task (Zentall et al., 2017).

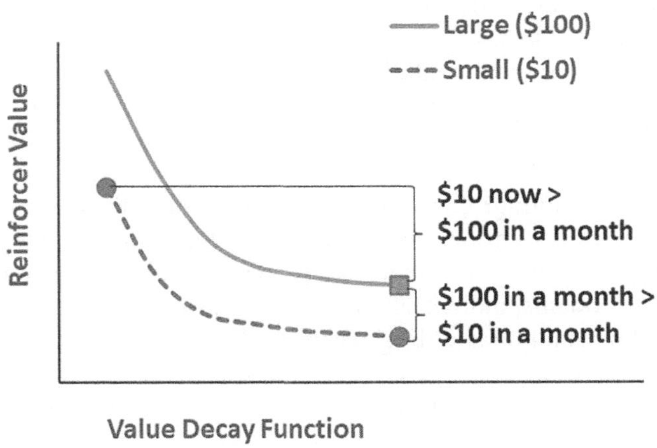

Figure 6.6 **The discounting function.** These theoretical functions correspond to the discount experienced by a Small vs. a Large reinforcer (e.g., money) as a function of the length of the time delay from the choice to the reception of the reinforcer. When the choice is close in time to reinforcement, then Small is preferred to Large. However, when the choice is removed in time, then Large is preferred to Small.

The implications of the value of discounting functions in predicting self-control have been largely overlooked because self-control, in an evolutionary context, has little value. In natural situations, the promise of access to a large, delayed reinforcer is rarely made, and it would not justify passing over an immediate reinforcer, even if relatively small (Zentall, 2020). Indeed, impulsivity, the opposite to self-control, is more likely to be selected.

6.4.3 Substance-use disorders and impulsivity

The behavioral characteristics of *substance-use disorders* (*SUDs*) are tied to the language of impulsivity. SUDs involve risky and impulsive drug-seeking and drug-taking behaviors that can harm a person's personal and professional relationships and that are directed at a psychoactive drug. Notice the analogy to the impulsive behavior of children. In the marshmallow test, a child may struggle to ignore a piece of candy for the requisite amount of time and thus fail to earn a second piece. Similarly, a person suffering from an SUD may struggle to withhold drug-seeking and consumption and thus suffer numerous aversive consequences. In both cases, the situation can be viewed as a problem of the allocation of behavior across time and space. Much of the behavior of a person with an SUD may come to revolve around a substance that has a powerful rewarding effect, exacting a cost on behavior that would otherwise be supported by other reinforcers.

A drug can be defined by its effect on behavior. Like any reinforcer, drugs vary in their ability to influence behavior. Some drugs generate dependence but largely spare an individual's behavioral repertoire, such as caffeine. Psychoactive drugs like methamphetamine and heroin are such powerful reinforcers that they can lead to abuse and even criminal behavior to acquire and consume them. SUDs are characterized by a failure of self-control skills that would otherwise suppress or inhibit such behavior (Jentsch & Pennington, 2013; Jentsch et al., 2014). Without such inhibition, Pavlovian processes controlling cravings and operant processes leading to drug-seeking behavior and compulsive drug-taking behavior proceed unimpeded.

People suffering from an SUD show a greater degree of delay discounting of other rewards (Bickel et al., 2015; Kollins, 2003; see delay discounting in Chapter 5). Delay discounting in this context implies that delaying the delivery of other reinforcers renders them less effective at controlling behavior than would be the case for a person without an SUD. This may manifest as greater sensitivity for immediate reinforcers at the expense of more significant reinforcers available on a more delayed fashion (Stahlman & Catania, 2022).

But what is the cause and what is the effect? Does the development of an SUD lead to an increase in in delay discounting? Consistent with this possibility, exposing rats to stimulants produces steeper delay-discounting effects (Gipson & Bardo, 2009; Mendez et al., 2010). Are individuals who already have a tendency to discount delayed rewards more likely to develop an SUD? In rodents, individual differences in delay discounting predict a tendency toward drug self-administration and drug-seeking behavior (Anker et al., 2009; Marusich & Bardo, 2009; Perry et al., 2005). Therefore, research with animal models suggests that it is a mixture of both, which implies a positive feedback loop that can lead a person to a serious SUD.

Recall that adding a previous commitment enhanced self-control in pigeons (Rachlin & Green, 1972). A prior commitment may work not by "enhancing self-control" per se but by altering the delay discounting functions so that behavior more closely conformed to the notion of self-control. This same logic has been applied to substance use: cigarette smoking. Recall from Chapter 2 that tobacco products are the cause of 90% of lung cancer cases, the leading cause of death among cancers. Part of the difficulty of quitting is due to the immediate effects of nicotine compared to the delayed effects of cancer (~20-year delay). Azrin and Powell (1968) invented a case for cigarettes that, once closed, remains closed for 2 h. After removing a cigarette from the case, the user now has the option of keeping the case open to have access to another cigarette after completing the first one or choosing the delayed health benefits of not smoking another cigarette immediately after the first by closing the case. In most cases, this prior commitment strategy is effective, and the individuals closed the case. This device reduced smoking by taking advantage of the delay-discounting function!

6.4.4 *Neurobiology of substance use disorders*

The development of an SUD is often stereotyped and predictable. A person's initial use of a substance with abuse potential may be powerfully and positively reinforcing. Once the drug-taking behavior has been established, a new motivational system seems to develop that requires continuous drug use. Such drug use generates a motivational system that becomes activated by the absence of the drug and that triggers an aversive internal state referred to as ***drug withdrawal.*** A state of drug withdrawal elicits drug-seeking behaviors that are reinforced by the reduction in the internal aversive state. At this point, drug use may simply aim at reducing the aversive state of withdrawal, with drug taking leading to little or no positive effects characteristic of the initial experience with the drug. Withdrawal symptoms vary widely across different drugs. Caffeine withdrawal may lead to headaches, lethargy, difficulty in thinking, and irritability, whereas heroin withdrawal may lead to serious and painful consequences. There is substantial overlap in the neural systems underlying SUDs.

6.4.4.1 *Reward circuitry*

Early neuroscience research led to the discovery of a ***brain reward system*** (Figure 6.7). The neural regions implicated in reward are distributed, but the following are key components of this system. The ***ventral tegmental area*** (*VTA*) sends dopaminergic projections to the basal telencephalon, particularly the ***nucleus accumbens*** (*NAc*), and to the ***prefrontal cortex*** (*PFC*). The VTA has been implicated in establishing the incentive value of rewards. Indeed, stimulation of VTA neurons has been demonstrated to reinforce behavior (e.g., Fields et al., 2007; Olds & Milner, 1954; Phillips et al., 1989), producing patterns of responding comparable to those of traditional reinforcers, such as food and sucrose. Intracranial administration of drugs of abuse, such as opioids, into the VTA similarly reinforces behavior. The dopaminergic axons leaving the VTA in their way to the NAc are activated with the acute delivery of various drugs of abuse, including alcohol, nicotine, cannabis, and opioids (Di Chiara & Imperato, 1988), as well as natural rewards. This suggests a central role for these dopaminergic pathways in reward processes.

The NAc receives projections from VTA (as well as extensive projections from other limbic areas), and its neural activity is critical in the reinforcing effects of drugs and natural rewards. For example, animals will self-administer both stimulants, like cocaine (Rodd-Henricks et al., 2002) and opioids (Goeders et al., 1984) into the NAc. The ***ventral pallidum*** receives inputs from NAc, and direct manipulations of this pathway produce concomitant effects. For example, administration of receptor antagonists in the ventral pallidum eliminates the reinforcing properties of ethanol (June et al., 2003), and lesions of the ventral pallidum eliminate the reinforcing effects of cocaine and heroin (Hubner & Koob, 1990).

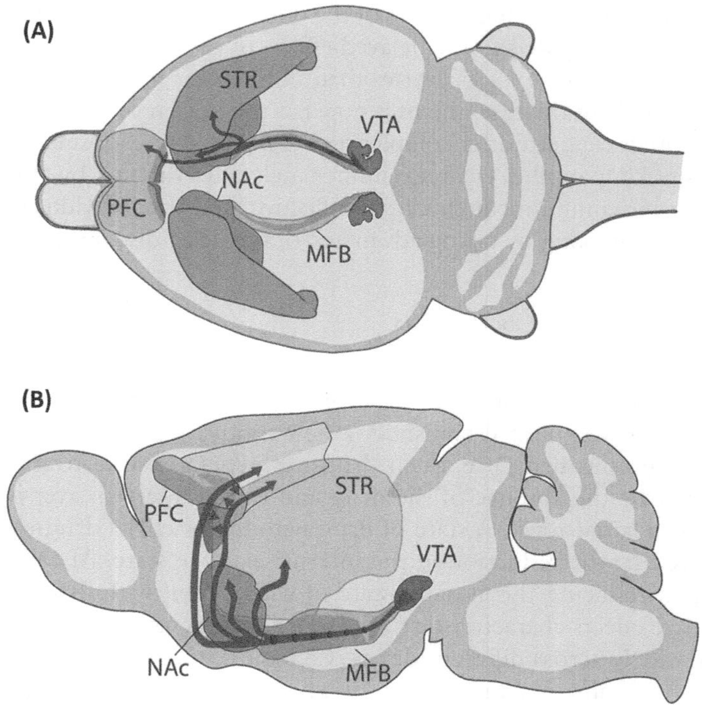

Figure 6.7 **The brain reward system. (A)** A dorsal view of the main pathway, the medial forebrain bundle (MFB) originating in the ventral tegmental area (VTA) and projecting dopaminergic neurons to two main regions, the nucleus accumbens (NAc) and the prefrontal cortex (PFC). There are also projections to the dorsal striatum (STR) as well as to other areas not included in this illustration. **(B)** A lateral view of the reward system with the same components as above. (From Reynolds & Flores, 2021; reproduced with permission from Frontiers in Neural Circuits.)

6.4.4.2 *Withdrawal symptoms and circuitry*

After drug use has become chronic, there is a shift in the motivational components of drug-taking behavior. A drug now produces less of a positive effect, but abstaining from drug use results in a host of negative effects characteristic of withdrawal. This has led to the widespread notion that whereas the initial development of drug dependence can be described in terms of positive reinforcement, drug-seeking behavior after chronic use could be described in terms of negative reinforcement as the drug reduces the negative state created by drug withdrawal. This requires a clarification on terminology.

Traditionally, operant contingencies have been defined in terms of the occurrence or omission of external events that can affect the subsequent probability of emitting the target response. The *APA Dictionary of Psychology* defines reinforcer as "a stimulus or circumstance that produces reinforcement when it occurs in a dependent relationship, or contingency, with a response. Also called reinforcing stimulus" (https://dictionary.apa.org/reinforcer). For example, ***positive reinforcement*** involves the occurrence of a reinforcing outcome contingent on a response (R→O), whereas ***negative reinforcement***, as in ***avoidance*** and ***escape*** conditioning, involves the omission or termination of a reinforcing outcome contingent on a response (R→noO). Both will result in an increase in the probability of an operant response.

There are correlated internal states that are also varying. For example, food reduces an aversive state of hunger, and pain interferes with an appetitive state of comfort. However, it is the external events that define these contingencies, not their correlated internal states. Drug procurement can then be instrumentally reinforced because the drug eliminates an aversive internal state of withdrawal. Is this a case of positive reinforcement or escape conditioning? According to the present criterion, drug-procurement behavior while under the influence of withdrawal symptoms illustrates positive reinforcement: The reinforcer is the drug (external event), not the removal of withdrawal symptoms (internal state), and the result is an increase in drug procurement.

There is variability across drugs and individuals in these withdrawal symptoms, but they often include anxiety, stress, irritability, malaise, and a reduced interest in natural rewards. Drug use at this stage serves largely the function of alleviating the aversive symptoms of withdrawal. At this point, an SUD is characterized by neurobiological changes distinct from those in initial drug use. Although dopaminergic transmission in the brain reward system originating in the VTA is heightened for a new user, a fact that corresponds with the initial positive reinforcing effect of the drug, this positive effect is substantially reduced during drug withdrawal in both rodents and humans (Martinez et al., 2007; Volkow et al., 1997, 2007; Weiss et al., 1992). A person with an SUD typically lacks interest in other rewards, a symptom related to these changes in the brain reward circuit (e.g., Barr & Phillips, 1999; Grieder et al., 2014).

Other neural systems change in response to an increased *tolerance* of the drug. With opioids, for example, the expectation of drug effects triggers a compensatory response that attenuates the effects of the drug, such that increasing doses are needed to achieve the same high as earlier in the process. Opioid tolerance is dependent on Pavlovian conditioning that renders the drug less effective. Rats chronically exposed to heroin in the same context (where the context acts as a signal for the posteffects of the drug) develop tolerance. However, research shows that a dose that is physiologically manageable in the usual context can cause death when the animal receives the same dose in a novel context (Siegel et al., 1982). The novelty of the context did not trigger the compensatory responses, so a tolerable dose in a familiar context can become lethal in a new context (see section on drug tolerance, Chapter 4).

Receptors for stress hormones (e.g., corticotropin releasing factor, CRF; norepinephrine) in the *amygdala* are upregulated during drug withdrawal (i.e., expressed in larger numbers), contributing to irritability, sensitivity to external stimulation, and other behavior characteristic of stress. Elevated stress hormones (e.g., CRF, corticosterone) are also found during withdrawal along the *hypothalamic-pituitary-adrenal axis*, a circuit involved in the regulation of stress hormones.

Activity in the dopaminergic reward system is inhibited, especially by an input from the *lateral habenula* (LHb) into the VTA (Clerke et al., 2021). The LHb plays an important role in several mental disorders, including SUD and depression. During drug withdrawal, activity in LHb neurons projecting to the *rostromedial tegmental nucleus* (*RMTg*) increases significantly. Such activity activates GABAergic neurons in the RMTg which then inhibit dopaminergic neurons in the VTA, thus reducing activity in the brain reward system. This LHb influence on the VTA may be responsible for such symptoms of SUDs as *anhedonia*, the inability to feel pleasure and to exhibit interest for natural rewards. This has led to therapeutic interventions targeting LHb neurons to alleviate the effects of drug withdrawal, including a tendency toward impulsivity.

6.5 Pavlovian control of operant behavior

6.5.1 Conditioned suppression

In the preceding sections, we described the results of experimental circumstances in terms of the interactions between Pavlovian and operant responses. Often, that interaction led to competition for expression, as in the case of misbehavior, but in some cases, the interaction facilitated learning, as when rats were trained to freeze as an avoidance response for shock. In these cases, the experimenters were not interested in investigating explicitly the interactions between Pavlovian and operant contingencies, but this is precisely the goal of the experiments reviewed in this section.

We briefly mentioned in Chapter 4 a fear conditioning paradigm known as conditioned suppression (also known as conditioned emotional response). *Conditioned suppression* combines two aspects of behavior common to many situations: searching for food and avoiding predators. When an animal is searching for food, it also needs to be alert about potential predators. I may be snacking while driving, but if I hear somebody honking behind me, I would likely stop eating the snack to pay attention to the traffic. The Honk acts as a CS for potential danger, and its occurrence while I am eating peanuts from a bag will likely suppress my interest in food, at least momentarily.

This situation was modeled in the lab using a design involving two phases of training and a test. What is important and interesting about this design is that two pieces of knowledge that are acquired separately can be combined during the test to reveal their interaction. The conditioned suppression design is presented in Table 6.3.

There are many variations of this paradigm. In the example presented here, a rat is first trained to press a Lever to obtain a Food pellet (Phase 1). When Lever pressing is established as an operant response, the Lever is removed from the conditioning box, and the animal receives a series of Tone-Shock pairings (Phase 2). Within a few pairings, the animal starts freezing in response to the presentation of the Tone. Finally, the rat has access again to the Lever, and now the Tone is presented occasionally (Test). Thus, the two types of training administered separately are juxtaposed to determine whether the Pavlovian CS can exert any control over the operant response despite the fact these two components were never trained together (i.e., the rat has never before encountered the Lever and Tone in the same session).

In these tests, the Food and Shock are usually not presented so as to assess the effect of the Pavlovian CS on the operant response in the absence of reinforcers. The control group goes through the same process, except that in Phase 2, the Tone and Shock are presented in

Table 6.3 Conditioned suppression paradigm to study fear conditioning

Group	*Phase 1: Operant*	*Phase 2: Pavlovian*	*Test*
Experimental	LeverPressing→Food	Tone→Shock	LeverPressing+Tone
Control	LeverPressing→Food	Tone, Shock	LeverPressing+Tone

Note. Groups differ only in Phase 2: Pavlovian. The experimental condition involves CS→US pairings (Tone→Shock), whereas the control condition involves unpaired presentations of the CS and US (Tone, Shock). Food and Shock are usually not presented during the Test.

an unpaired fashion. Thus, the Tone will become a good signal for Shock in the Experimental condition but not in the Control condition.

The typical outcome of a conditioned suppression experiment shows that in the absence of the Tone, there is a relatively high rate of Lever pressing, but as the Tone is presented, the animal enters into a freezing mode, and the operant response is strongly suppressed. During freezing, all behavior ceases, and only breathing movements are observed. Lever pressing is restored after the Tone is turned off. The degree of suppression of the operant response is typically calculated with a *suppression ratio*:

$$\textbf{Suppression ratio} = \frac{\textbf{Responses during the CS}}{\textbf{Responses during the CS} + \textbf{Responses before the CS}}$$

In the example we are following, and assuming the duration of the CS is 30 s, then the suppression ratio is equal to lever presses during the 30 s of CS presentation, divided by the sum of responses during the CS plus responses during an equal 30-s period right before the CS is presented. Thus, a suppression ratio of 0.5 implies that the animal responded just as much during the CS as it was responding before the CS. In other words, the CS did not affect operant responding. The control condition in Table 6.3 would tend to exhibit a suppression ratio close to 0.5 because the unpaired CS and US presentation did not convert the CS in a reliable signal for the US. However, if the animal was responding at a high rate before the CS and the presentation of the CS disrupted its behavior, then the ratio would tend to approach

(A)

Group	Phase 1	Phase 2	Test
Blocking	N→Sh	LN→Sh	L?
Control 1	----	LN→Sh	L?
Control 2	----	N→Sh	L?

(B)

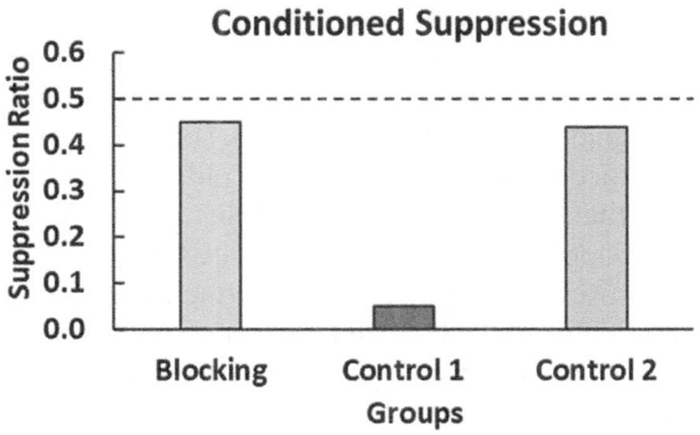

Figure 6.8 **A demonstration of blocking using conditioned suppression. (A)** This table describes the design. **(B)** The bar graph plots the results reported numerically in Kamin (1969, p. 282). Suppression ratios close to zero indicate strong fear conditioning (i.e., almost complete suppression of operant responses), whereas ratios close to 0.5 provide no evidence that the presentation of the CS affected behavior relative to the behavior of the animal immediately prior to CS presentation.

zero. In conditioned suppression, therefore, a suppression ratio close to zero implies strong fear conditioning (i.e., significant suppression of the operant response by the CS for shock that would induce freezing behavior). Behavioral observations show that, indeed, the reason for a suppression ratio close to zero is the elicitation of a strong freezing response by a CS previously paired with shock (Bouton & Bolles, 1980).

The use of the conditioned suppression paradigm is illustrated with data reported by Kamin (1969) in his original research on blocking. You may recall blocking from our treatment of this phenomenon in Chapters 4 and 5. In *blocking*, animals fail to respond to a CS paired with the US if that CS is accompanied by another signal previously paired with the same US. Kamin used a White Noise (N) and a Light (L) as the CSs and Shock as the US. In the Blocking condition, animals received N→Shock pairings in Phase 1, followed by LN→Shock pairings in Phase 2. Control conditions received no treatment in Phase 1 but LN→Shock pairings (Control 1) or just N→Shock pairings (Control 2) during Phase 2. All animals were tested with L, the added CS in the Blocking condition (Figure 6.8-A). Pretraining of N impaired responding to L, even though L was perfectly capable of suppressing operant behavior in the test, as shown by Control 1.

Notice the suppression ratios for these three conditions (Figure 6.8-B). For the Blocking and Control 2 conditions, the ratios were close to 0.5, that is, no evidence of fear conditioning. Notice, however, that suppression to L in Control 1 was almost complete, showing that the L acquired control over the operant response even though it was presented together with N in an LN compound. The difference was that L was redundant in the Blocking condition as the US was signaled by N but not in the Control 1 condition in which both L and N were good signals for the shock.

6.5.2 *Pavlovian–instrumental transfer*

The basic structure of the conditioned suppression paradigm can be extended to understand how a Pavlovian CSs can facilitate or interfere with operant behavior, depending on the conditions. This is the realm of *Pavlovian–instrumental transfer* (*PIT*) designs in which two kinds of learning trained separately are combined during a final test (recall that operant = instrumental; see Chapter 2). One comes from a Pavlovian conditioning phase and the other from an operant conditioning phase, although the order of these phases is irrelevant.

Consider the experiment described in Figure 6.9-A (Overmier & Bull, 1969). In the Operant Phase, a single group of animals received avoidance training in which the performance of a response during a signal, A, avoided a foot Shock (of course, the Shock was delivered in the absence of the avoidance response). Before the avoidance response was established, there were A→Shock pairings that endowed A with the ability to elicit fear. In the Pavlovian Phase and in the absence of an opportunity to respond, three CSs were presented. The previously trained CS, A, was now presented by itself in an extinction procedure; two new CSs were given differential fear conditioning, B paired with Shock whereas C was presented alone. Finally, a Test was administered in which each of the three CSs from the Pavlovian Phase were presented while the animal had the ability to perform the avoidance response shaped in the Operant Phase. As usual, this test was administered in the absence of Shocks.

The results are presented in terms of response latency—the time it took the animals to respond in the presence of a signal (Figure 6.8-B). During the Operant Phase, response latency was very short, indicating that the animals responded as soon as the signal, A, was presented. That is, the animals had learned to avoid the shock effectively. In the Test, however, previous extinction of A eliminated its ability to induce an avoidance response, as revealed

(A)

Operant Phase	Pavlovian Phase	Test
A→R→noShock	A→noShock	A→R?
A→noR→Shock	B→Shock	B→R?
	C→noShock	C→R?

(B)

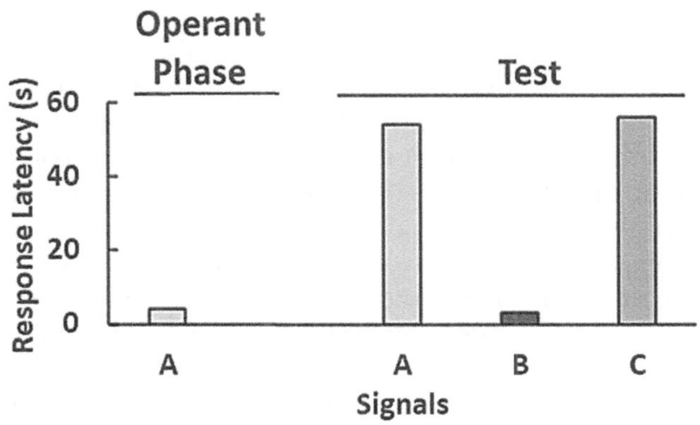

Figure 6.9 **Pavlovian–instrumental transfer. (A)** A look at the design of this experiment involving an Operant Phase, a Pavlovian Phase, and a Test. **(B)** The results expressed in terms of response latency. (From Overmier & Bull, 1969; reproduced with permission from the American Psychological Association.)

by a long latency to respond. Control CSs showed that a fear-inducing CS, B, had acquired the ability to trigger the avoidance response even though B had never been trained in avoidance conditioning. Finally, C, having been presented by itself, lacked the ability to trigger the avoidance response.

One explanation of these results suggests that a mediational state of fear is the common element across the Operant and Pavlovian Phases supporting this case of transfer. The animals had learned what to do in the presence of a signal for fear during operant training (perform the avoidance response), and whether that fear was triggered by a new signal did not matter much.

6.5.2.1 *General and specific PIT*

The example just described highlights the fact that the influence of a Pavlovian signal on operant behavior depends on a common element provided by a mediational state of fear. Similar results would be obtained in the common element across Pavlovian and operant phases were an appetitive state induce by a reward, such as food or sucrose. For example, a Pavlovian signal for food pellets would bias choice for an operant response previously associated with food pellets and away from a response previously paired with sucrose, but a Pavlovian signal for sucrose would bias choice in the opposite direction (Kruse et al., 1983). In cases like this, the common element is a shared expectancy specific to the outcome common between the Pavlovian CS and the operant response.

The original explanation for cases involving interactions between Pavlovian signals and operant behavior centered on the notion of general affective states (Rescorla & Solomon, 1967). The suggestion was that a Pavlovian CS induced an emotional state that heightened performance of an operant behavior whose consequence involved the same emotional state but interfered with operant responses mediated by the opposite affective state. This provided a simple explanation for the effectiveness of the conditioned suppression paradigm. In this case, the Pavlovian CS induced an aversive affective state that interfered with the appetitive state modulating lever pressing for food. Consequently, strong activity in the aversive state inhibited appetitive motivation, thus resulting in the suppression of appetitive behavior.

This account fails to predict the quite specific transfer illustrated by Kruse et al.'s (1983) experiment just described. In this case, both food pellets and sucrose solutions are appetitive, which makes it difficult to assume that different types of appetitive affective states would interfere with each other. More likely, it is the sensory components of these two rewards that makes them different and allows for an outcome-specific type of transfer.

There are, in fact, two forms of PIT, as illustrated in Figure 6.10. The example given in the preceding paragraph is called *specific transfer* because the Pavlovian CS enhances a response associated with the same outcome as the Pavlovian signal. The common elements between the two components are the sensory properties of the outcomes. Thus, the operant response paired with the same outcome as that signaled by the Pavlovian CS is enhanced over the level of the response paired with a different outcome and over the baseline level of responding in the absence of any signal.

A second form of transfer involves comparisons between a Pavlovian signal and a single operant response; in this case, the comparison is how the Pavlovian signal affects the operant response relative to a baseline condition (e.g., responding in the absence of the Pavlovian

Pavlovian-to-instrumental transfer (PIT)

	(A) Specific transfer	(B) General transfer
Pavlovian training	Tone→Pellet Light→Sucrose	Tone→Pellet Light→Nothing
Operant training	Right Lever→Pellet Left Lever→Sucrose	Lever→Pellet
PIT test	CS: Same > Different Tone: Right Lever > Left Lever Light: Right Lever < Left Lever	Tone: Lever>Baseline Light: Lever=Baseline

Results

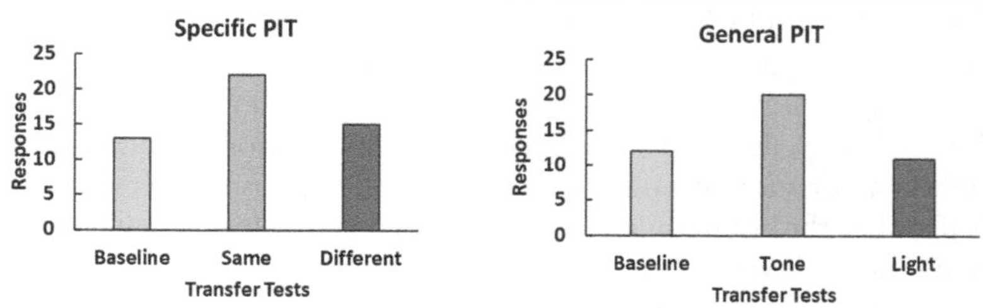

Figure 6.10 **Specific and general Pavlovian–instrumental transfer. (A)** A typical design and results of a specific PIT experiment. **(B)** A typical design and results of a general PIT experiment.

signal). This is called *general transfer*, and a typical result is that the response is enhanced during the presentation of the Pavlovian signal paired with the same outcome, relative to the level exhibited by the operant response during the presentation of the control CS or during baseline, in the absence of any CS. The implication of general transfer is that the CS enhances a general motivational state that increases performance for a response reinforced with a motivationally equivalent reward.

Specific and general transfer designs can be combined in a single experiment to determine whether these two effects are dissociable, that is, whether a single manipulation would affect one but not the other. Table 6.4 shows an example of such a combined design (Corbit et al., 2007). In Phase 1 (Pavlovian), an animal receives three distinct types of Pavlovian trials involving three CSs (A, B, C) and three USs (X, Y, Z). These trials can be described as A→X, B→Y, and C→Z. In Phase 2 (operant), two responses are reinforced with different outcomes: R1→X and R2→Y. Presenting A in the transfer Test would bias the choice toward R1 rather than R2 (same rewards), whereas presenting B could bias the choice toward R2, rather than R1 (also same rewards). These results represent specific transfer. In the same experiment, presentations of C may boost performance of both R1 and R2 relative to baseline responding. This occurs despite the fact that R1 and R2 had a history of producing X and Y as their outcomes rather than Z, the outcome associated with the Pavlovian signal C. This illustrates general transfer.

To show that these effects are dissociable within the same experiment, a subgroup of animals trained as described above is kept hungry, whereas a second subgroup is given access to food until they are no longer hungry. This manipulation changes the motivational state of the animals, devaluing the rewards via satiation.

The results showed that under hunger motivation, both effects were present. Specific transfer was observed in that CSs A and B increased the response paired with the same US. That is, when Pavlovian signal A was presented, animals responded more to the lever previously paired with the same outcome than to the lever paired with the alternative outcome, and the same was true when Pavlovian signal B was presented. Similarly, general transfer under hunger motivation was observed in that animals responded more to both levers (R1 + R2) when Pavlovian signal C was presented than during the baseline, when no signal was presented.

By contrast, when the animals were satiated, responding went down for all CSs. However, the differences in responding to R1 vs. R2 in the presence of A and B were preserved, suggesting that specific transfer is not outcome dependent, whereas the difference between general responding (R1 + R2) vs. baseline responding was eliminated, suggesting that general

Table 6.4 Combined design for specific and general PIT

Pavlovian	*Instrumental*	*Tests*	
		PIT, hungry	*PIT, sated (devalued)*
A→X	R1→X	A: R1 > R2	A: R1 > R2
B→Y	R2→Y	B: R1 < R2	B: R1 < R2
C→Z		C: (R1 + R2) > BL	C: (R1 + R2) = BL

Note. A, B, C: Pavlovian CSs. R1, R2: operant responses. X, Y, Z: outcomes (rewards). BL: baseline (responding in the absence of any CS). For the Tests, half the animals are tested under the same motivational condition prevailing in previous phases (hungry), and the rest are tested after having free access to food (sated). Satiation was implemented as a procedure that devalued the USs motivationally.

transfer was outcome dependent. That is, outcome devaluation did not affect specific transfer, but it eliminated general transfer. The differential response of specific and general transfer to outcome devaluation within the same experimental conditions suggests that these effects are based on different mechanisms.

6.5.2.2 Neurobiology of PIT

A neuroscience approach is helpful to further differentiate specific and general transfer effects in their underlying mechanisms. Brain regions implicated in transfer effects include the NAc and the amygdala, but additional regions differ as a function of transfer type. Corbit and Balleine (2005) reported that specific transfer can be selectively attenuated by lesions of the basolateral amygdala, which do not affect general transfer, but that general transfer is eliminated by lesions of the central nucleus of the amygdala, which do not affect specific transfer—a double dissociation effect. In a follow-up study (Corbit & Balleine, 2011), these researchers found that different regions of the NAc contributed to transfer effects. Figure 6.11 shows the location of these lesions and the results. Lesions to the NAc shell eliminated specific transfer, whereas lesions of the NAc core spared specific transfer. The opposite result was observed relative to general transfer, where lesions of the NAc core eliminated the effect, whereas lesions of the NAc shell had no observable consequence on this effect.

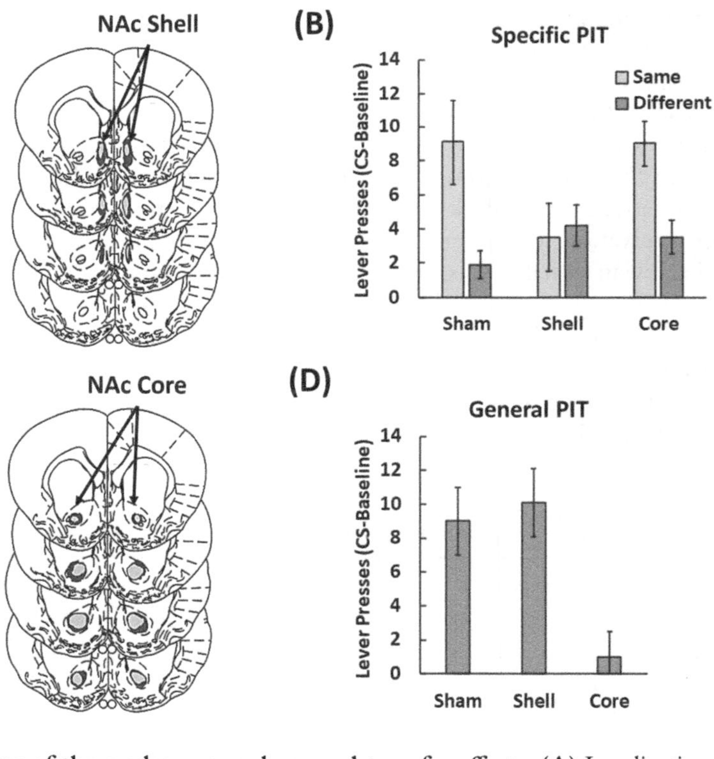

Figure 6.11 **Lesions of the nucleus accumbens and transfer effects. (A)** Localization of the experimental lesions in the nucleus accumbens shell (NAc Shell). **(B)** Lesions of the NAc shell (but not of the core) eliminated specific transfer. **(C)** Localization of lesions of the nucleus accumbens core (NAc Core). **(D)** Lesions of the NAc core (but not of the NAc shell) disrupted general PIT. PIT: Pavlovian–instrumental transfer. (From Corbit & Balleine, 2005; reproduced with permission from the *Journal of Neuroscience*.)

6.5.2.3 Relevance of PIT

Pavlovian and operant conditioning processes can be isolated in the lab and studied to determine their properties and the way they influence behavioral, physiological, and neurobiological processes. But in real life and in natural situations, organisms encounter situations where these processes combine in complex ways, as shown by the PIT effects. For this reason, PIT is usually brought into the context of understanding phenomena of applied relevance, such as mental disorders (Garbusow et al., 2022). The main lesson to learn from PIT effects is that Pavlovian signals can acquire control over operant behavior even in the absence of explicit training. So the key is to consider situations that induce people to behave in ways that lead to maladaptive behavior.

Consider a person who has undergone treatment for an alcohol substance disorder and has remained sober for a number of weeks. What are risky situations for this person? Alcohol drinks are usually served in glasses that have specific shapes and sizes depending on the type of drink. For example, whisky, beer, and wine are typically consumed in very specific types of glasses. If our imaginary person used to be particularly prone to drink whisky, a whisky glass has probably become a Pavlovian signal capable of influencing behavior. So an invitation by friends to meet in a pub where our person can be exposed to whisky glasses might induce the urge to drink whisky and affect the person's choice at a critical time. In the context of an SUD, this urge is called craving. *Cravings* can be viewed as conditioned responses elicited by Pavlovian cues associated with drug consumption. This episode could induce the *relapse* of a habit that the person is trying to eliminate with therapy. Research shows that cravings are connected to episodes of relapse of drug intake (Vafaie & Kober, 2022).

Similar applications of the PIT conceptual framework are viable for situations in which Pavlovian signals develop a powerful grip on behavior. Two additional examples come to mind: social media and obesity. The prevalence of social media has resulted in a "new" type of fear, the *fear of missing out* (Dogan, 2019). This is such an important motivational source that it drives some individuals to be dependent on feedback from social media platforms and to experience a kind of withdrawal when access is prevented, which has led to treating this behavior in a similar way to an SUD.

A cross-cultural meta-analysis of data suggests, not surprisingly, that social media dependence is more prevalent in collectivist societies than in individualist societies (31% vs. 14%; Cheng et al., 2021). Clearly, notifications of incoming messages previously paired to the informational value of the message can act as powerful Pavlovian signals that modulate choice in operant behavior. Thus, a professional in a business meeting in which important data are being presented may decide to divert attention to the phone to check on an incoming text, potentially causing serious problems. In this context, the fear of missing out has consequences that remind us of the inhibition of appetitive behavior during the presentation of a Pavlovian CS for shock in the conditioned suppression paradigm discussed previously.

Similarly, a person suffering from obesity responds predominantly to visual cues of food rather than to the homeostatic need for feeding. Individuals with obesity have a blunted neural response to lipids relative to nonobese controls in dopaminergic areas within the brain reward system, such as the nucleus accumbens. Such reduced response to lipids was observed even after substantial weight loss maintained for up to 3 months, which could explain the high rate of relapse into obesity after a successful diet (van Galen et al., 2023). It is likely that Pavlovian signals for highly palatable food items continue to exert their effects long after the person has lost weight, an effect that reminds us of the insensitivity of specific transfer to reward devaluation. The power of such Pavlovian signals, probably visual or olfactory, over operant behavior related to eating may explain the high rate of weigh regain in persons with obesity (Stopyra et al., 2021).

Glossary

Adjunctive behavior Behavior induced by intermittent reinforcement during periods when food delivery is unlikely. Compare to *terminal response.*

Amygdala A series of regions in the ventral portion of the telencephalon that participates in a variety of behavioral functions, including aversive emotions.

Anhedonia Reduced or absent feelings of pleasure (e.g., lack of motivation for palatable foods).

Autoshaping A Pavlovian response-independent procedure in which a localized stimulus (CS) is used as a signal for a reward (US). In pigeons, a localized Light is a signal for Grain. In rats, the presentation of a retractable Lever is a signal for food Pellets. Autoshaping generates signal-centered behavior (e.g., key pecking, lever pressing).

Avoidance Behavior that prevents the prevention of an aversive stimulus. See negative reinforcement.

Basolateral amygdala (BLA) Region of amygdala that receives converging sensory inputs, as in signals and reinforcers. The BLA projects to several regions, including the central amygdala and the nucleus accumbens.

Behavior system A hierarchical organization of behaviors primarily concerned with a specific function, such as defensive or feeding behavior. Behavior systems were inferred from studies showing the responses that are activated by specific outcomes of biological importance, such as food or pain.

Blocking Reduced responding to a CS trained in compound with a second CS previously paired to the same US. The previously trained CS is said to block the added CS, reducing its ability to elicit responses despite being paired to the US.

Brain reward system A projection of dopaminergic neurons originating in the ventral tegmental area (VTA) sending axons to several brain regions, including the nucleus accumbens (NAc) and the prefrontal cortex (PFC).

Central amygdala (CeA) A region of the amygdala important for regulation of emotion, stress, and threat-related behavior. The CeA receives inputs from the basolateral amygdala and projects to various regions, including the periaqueductal gray (PAG).

Conditioned suppression Reduction of appetitive operant behavior during the presentation of a Pavlovian signal for an aversive stimulus.

Controllability The ability of an animal to control biologically relevant events in its environment.

Craving Urge to procure a specific outcome, such as a type of food or a drug.

Delay discounting The reduced value of a delayed reinforcer relative to rewards that are presented more immediately in time.

Dopamine A neurotransmitter (and neurotransmitter receptor) playing a major function in the brain reward system originating in the ventral tegmental area (VTA) and projecting to striatal and prefrontal regions. These dopaminergic connections play an important role in establishing a stimulus as a reward.

Equipotentiality The suggestion that associations can be established between any stimulus, reinforcer, and behavior, whether with Pavlovian or operant conditioning procedures.

Escape Behavior that results in the termination of ongoing aversive stimulation. See negative reinforcement.

Fear of missing out In the context of social media, the aversive feeling of being left outside by a social group.

Freeze, flight, or fight When confronted with a threat, some animals (e.g., rats) cease all movement if no escape is available (freezing), escape from the situation if a route is available (flight), or attack the source of aversiveness if there is no other alternative (fight).

General transfer The facilitation or interference of operant performance by Pavlovian signals by virtue of their shared affective characteristics, usually assessed relative to the operant response in the absence of the Pavlovian signal. Compare with specific transfer.

Hypothalamic-pituitary-adrenal axis (HPA axis) A circuit involving neural and hormonal signals activated by aversive situations.

Immunization Learning to escape from an aversive event prevents or reduces the impairment of avoidance behavior when aversive events are escapable. Immunization treatments are related to learned helplessness.

Impulsivity Tendency to prefer a small immediate reward to a large but delayed reward. See marshmallow test, self-control.

Inescapable shock Aversive stimulus that cannot be terminated by any response.

Lateral habenula (LHb) A diencephalic nucleus exerting an inhibitory influence over the brain reward system, either directly or via the rostromedial tegmental nucleus.

Learned helplessness Impairment of avoidance learning resulting from prior exposure to inescapable aversive stimulation.

Marshmallow test An experimental paradigm developed to investigate self-control in children.

Master–yoked design A design in which an experimental group controls outcomes for both itself (master) and a paired animal (yoke). The master–yoke design equates pairs of animals in terms of the frequency and distribution in time of reinforcers while allowing master animals to control the reinforcer (operant) while yoked animals experience outcomes independently of their behavior (Pavlovian).

Negative reinforcement Process by which behavior is made more probable in the future by virtue of contingent termination or prevention of aversive stimulation. See avoidance and escape.

Nucleus accumbens (NAc) Portion of ventral striatum implicated in the brain reward system. It is subdivided into core and shell, the former implicated in general transfer and the latter in specific transfer.

Omission An operant contingency in which a reward is presented, unless a response occurs, in which case the reward is withheld.

Pavlovian–instrumental transfer (PIT) Separately trained Pavlovian signals can exert control over operant responses when they are first combined. Pavlovian CSs can either facilitate or interfere ongoing operant behavior.

Periacqueductal grey (PAG) Brain region involved in producing the conditioned freezing response characteristic of fear. The PAG receives inputs from the central nucleus of the amygdala.

Positive reinforcement Process that increases the future probability of a behavior closely paired in time with the delivery of an appetitive reinforcer.

Prefrontal cortex (PFC) The most anterior portion of the frontal cortex. This is a highly differentiated region both anatomically and functionally. Different regions of the PFC are concerned with reward processes, delayed responses, and emotional reactions.

Relapse In the context of an SUD, the reinstatement of drug-seeking behavior after a period without access to the drug. Relapse may be related to exposure to Pavlovian signals of the drug that preserved control over operant behavior.

Rostromedial tegmental nucleus (RMTg) A brainstem nucleus that receives projections from the lateral habenula and sends inhibitory GABAergic fibers to the ventral tegmental nucleus. RMTg activation is related to the inhibition of the brain reward system.

Schedule-induced polydipsia Excessive drinking produced by intermittent food reinforcement. See adjunctive behavior.

Self-control The ability to postpone gratification when a larger reward is available more remotely in time.

Shaping by successive approximations The gradual development of a target response by the reinforcement of progressively closer versions of that response.

Species-specific defense reaction (SSDR) A set of preorganized defensive responses activated by threatening stimuli.

Specific transfer The facilitation of operant performance by Pavlovian signals because of shared sensory features of the outcomes paired with the response and the signal. Compared with general transfer.

Substance use disorders (SUDs) A disorder characterized by the compulsive use of chemical substances. Engaging in behaviors characterized by chronic drug-seeking and drug-taking behavior even to the exclusion of other reinforcers and despite aversive consequences.

Temporal conditioning Presenting USs in the absence of CSs but at regular time intervals.

Terminal response Behavior characterized by temporal approach to food under various reinforcement schedules. Compare with ***adjunctive behavior***.

Tolerance Condition in which chronic drug use results in a diminution of the positively reinforcing qualities of the drug. See also withdrawal.

Ventral pallidum A region of the basal ganglia that receives inputs from the nucleus accumbens and sends projections to other regions of the basal ganglia and to the lateral habenula. The ventral pallidum is implicated in the reinforcing effects of stimuli (e.g., drugs).

Ventral tegmental area (VTA) A brainstem nucleus (tegmentum) that plays a key function in the dopaminergic brain reward system by projecting to the nucleus accumbens and prefrontal cortex, among other regions.

Withdrawal In the context of a SUD, the aversive feelings triggered by drug deprivation. Withdrawal states play a major role in the relapse of drug-seeking behavior.

References

Anker, J. J., Zlebnik, N. E., Gliddon, L. A., & Carroll, M. E. (2009). *Behavioural Pharmacology, 20*(5–6), 406–414. https://doi.org/10.1097/FBP.0b013e3283305ea2

Atnip, G. W. (1977). Stimulus- and response-reinforcer contingencies in autoshaping, operant, classical, and omission training procedures in rats. *Journal of the Experimental Analysis of Behavior, 28*(1), 59–69. https://doi.org/10.1901/jeab.1977.28-59

Azrin, N. H., & Powell, J. (1968). Behavioral engineering: The reduction of smoking behavior by a conditioning apparatus and procedure. *Journal of Applied Behavior Analysis, 1*(3), 193–200. https://doi.org/10.1901/jaba.1968.1-193

Baenninger, R. (1997). On yawning and its functions. *Psychonomic Bulletin & Review, 4*(2), 198–207. https://doi.org/10.3758/BF03209394

Balleine, B., & Job, R. S. (1991). Reconsideration of the role of competing responses in demonstrations of the interference effect (learned helplessness). *Journal of Experimental Psychology: Animal Behavior Processes, 17*(3), 270–280. https://doi.org/10.1037/0097-7403.17.3.270

Barr, A. M., & Phillips, A. G. (1999). Withdrawal following repeated exposure to d-amphetamine decreases responding for a sucrose solution as measured by a progressive ratio schedule of reinforcement. *Psychopharmacology, 141*, 99–106. https://doi.org/10.1007/s002130050812

Beran, M. J., & Parrish, A. E. (2022). Distinguishing mechanisms of behavioral inhibition and self-control. In M. Krause, K. L. Hollis, & M. R. Papini (Eds.), *Evolution of learning and memory mechanisms* (pp. 375–391). Cambridge University Press.

Bickel, W. K., MacKillop, J., Madden, G. J., Odum, A. L., & Yi, R. (2015). Experimental manipulations of delay discounting and related processes: An introduction to the special issue. *Journal of the Experimental Analysis of Behavior, 103*(1), 1–9. https://doi.org/10.1002/jeab.133

Bolles, R. C. (1970). Species-specific defense reactions and avoidance learning. *Psychological Review, 77*(1), 32–48. https://doi.org/10.1037/h0028589

Bolles, R. C., & Riley, A. L. (1973). Freezing as an avoidance response: Another look at the operant-respondent distinction. *Learning and Motivation, 4*, 268–275. https://doi.org/10.1016/0023-9690(73)90016-7

Bolles, R. C., Stokes, L. W., & Younger, M. S. (1966). Does CS termination reinforce avoidance behavior? *Journal of Comparative and Physiological Psychology, 62*(2), 201–207. https://doi.org/10.1037/h0023678

Bouton, M. E., & Bolles, R. C. (1980). Conditioned fear assessed by freezing and by the suppression of three different baselines. *Animal Learning and Behavior, 8*, 429–434. https://doi.org/10.3758/bf03199629

Breland, K., & Breland, M. (1961). The misbehavior of organisms. *American Psychologist, 16*(11), 681–684. https://doi.org/10.1037/h0040090

Brucks, D., Petelle, M., Baldoni, C., Krasheninnikova, A., Rovegno, E., & von Bayern, A. M. P. (2022). Intra- and interspecific variation in self-control capacities of parrots in a delay of gratification task. *Animal Cognition, 25*, 473–491. https://doi.org/10.1007/s10071-021-01565-6

Bshary, R., & Grutter, A. S. (2002). Experimental evidence that partner choice is a driving force in the payoff distribution among cooperators or mutualists: The cleaner fish case. *Ecology Letters, 5*(1), 130–136. https://doi.org/10.1046/j.1461-0248.2002.00295.x

Campagnoni, F. R., Lawler, C. P., & Cohen, P. S. (1986). Temporal patterns of reinforcer-induced general activity and attack in pigeons. *Physiology and Behavior, 37*(4), 577–582. https://doi.org/10.1016/0031-9384(86)90289-1

Cheng, C., Lau, Y. C., Chan, L., & Luk, J. W. (2021). Prevalence of social media addiction across 32 nations: Meta-analysis with subgroup analysis of classification schemes and cultural values. *Addictive Behaviors, 117*. https://doi.org/10.1016/j.addbeh.2021.106845

Choi, J. S., Cain, C. K., & LeDoux, J. E. (2010). The role of amygdala nuclei in the expression of auditory signaled two-way active avoidance in rats. *Learning and Memory, 17*, 139–147. https://doi.org/10.1101/lm.1676610

Clerke, J. A., Congiu, M., & Mameli, M. (2021). Neuronal adaptations in the lateral habenula during drug withdrawal: Preclinical evidence for addiction therapy. *Neuropharmacology, 192*, 108617. https://doi.org/10.1016/j.neuropharm.2021.108617

Corbit, L. H., & Balleine, B. W. (2005). Double dissociation of basolateral and central amygdala lesions on the general and outcome-specific forms of Pavlovian-instrumental transfer. *Journal of Neuroscience, 25*(4), 962–970. https://doi.org/10.1523/JNEUROSCI.4507-04.2005

Corbit, L. H., & Balleine, B. W. (2011). The general and outcome-specific forms of Pavlovian-instrumental transfer are differentially mediated by the nucleus accumbens core and shell. *Journal of Neuroscience*, *31*(33), 11786–11794. https://doi.org/10.1523/JNEUROSCI.2711-11.2011

Corbit, L. H., Janak, P. H., & Balleine, B. W. (2007). General and outcome-specific forms of Pavlovian-instrumental transfer: The effect of shifts in motivational state and inactivation of the ventral tegmental area. *European Journal of Neuroscience*, *26*(11), 3141–3149. https://doi.org/10.1111/j.1460-9568.2007.05934.x

D'Amato, M. R., & Schiff, D. (1964). Long-term discriminated avoidance performance in the rat. *Journal of Comparative and Physiological Psychology*, *57*(1), 123–126. https://doi.org/10.1037/h0046678

Davey, G. C. L., Phillips, J. H., & Witty, S. (1989). Signal-directed behavior in the rat: Interactions between the nature of the CS and the nature of the UCS. *Animal Learning & Behavior*, *17*, 447–456. https://doi.org/10.3758/BF03205225

Di Chiara, G., & Imperato, A. (1988). Drugs abused by humans preferentially increase synaptic dopamine concentrations in the mesolimbic system of freely moving rats. *Proceedings of the National Academy of Sciences USA*, *85*(14), 5274–5278. https://doi.org/10.1073/pnas.85.14.5274

Dogan, V. (2019). Why do people experience the fear of missing out (FoMO)? Exposing the link between the self and the FoMO through self-construal. *Journal of Cross-Cultural Psychology*, *50*(4), 524–538. https://doi.org/10.1177/0022022119839145

Ehrman, R. N., & Overmier, J. B. (1976). Dissimilarity of mechanisms for evocation of escape and avoidance responding in dogs. *Animal Learning and Behavior*, *4*(3), 347–351. https://doi.org/10.3758/BF03214063

Falk, J. L. (1961). Septal stimulation as a reinforcer of and an alternative to consummatory behavior. *Journal of the Experimental Analysis of Behavior*, *4*(3), 213–217. https://doi.org/10.1901/jeab.1961.4-213

Fanselow, M. S. (1994). Neural organization of the defensive behavior system responsible for fear. *Psychonomic Bulletin and Review*, *1*(4), 429–438. https://doi.org/10.3758/BF03210947

Fields, H. L., Hjelmstad, G. O., Margolis, E. B., & Nicola, S. M. (2007). Ventral tegmental area neurons in learned appetitive behavior and positive reinforcement. *Annual Reviews in Neuroscience*, *30*, 289–316. https://doi.org/10.1146/annurev.neuro.30.051606.094341

Garbusow, M., Ebrahimi, C., Riemerschmid, C., Daldrup, L., Rothkirch, M., Chen, K., Chen, H., Belanger, M. J., Hentschel, A., Smolka, M. N., Heinz, A., Pilhatsch, M., & Rapp, M. A. (2022). Pavlovian-to-instrumental transfer across mental disorders: A review. *Neuropsychobiology*, *81*(5), 418–437. https://doi.org/10.1159/000525579

Gipson, C. D., & Bardo, M. T. (2009). Extended access to amphetamine self-administration increases impulsive choice in a delay discounting task in rats. *Psychopharmacology*, *207*, 391–400. https://doi.org/10.1007/s00213-009-1667-4

Goeders, N. E., Lane, J. D., & Smith, J. E. (1984). Self-administration of methionine enkephalin into the nucleus accumbens. *Pharmacology, Biochemistry, and Behavior*, *20*(3), 451–455. https://doi.org/10.1016/0091-3057(84)90284-3

Grieder, T. E., Herman, M. A., Contet, C., Tan, L. A., Vargas-Perez, H., Cohen, A., Chwalek, M., Maal-Bared, G., Freiling, J., Schlosburg, J. E., Clarke, L., Crawford, E., Koebel, P., Repunte-Canonigo, V., Sanna, P. P., Tapper, A. R., Roberto, M., Kieffer, B. L., Sawchenko, P. E., Koob, G. F., van der Kooy, D., & George, O. (2014). VTA CRF neurons mediate the aversive effects of nicotine withdrawal and promote intake escalation. *Nature Neuroscience*, *17*(12), 1751–1758. https://doi.org/10.1038/nn.3872

Hubner, C. B., & Koob, G. F. (1990). The ventral pallidum plays a role in mediating cocaine and heroin self-administration in the rat. *Brain Research*, *508*(1), 20–29. https://doi.org/10.1016/0006-8993(90)91112-T

Jentsch, J. D., Ashenhurst, J. R., Cervantes, M. C., Groman, S. M., James, A. S., & Pennington, Z. T. (2014). Dissecting impulsivity and its relationships to drug addictions. *Annals of the New York Academy of Sciences*, *1327*(1), 1–26. https://doi.org/10.1111/nyas.12388

Jentsch, J. D., & Pennington, Z. T. (2013). Reward, interrupted: Inhibitory control and its relevance to addictions. *Neuropharmacology*, *76*(B), 479–486. https://doi.org/10.1016/j.neuropharm.2013.05.022

June, H., Foster, K., McKay, P., Seyoum, R., Woods, J. E. II, Harvey, S. C., Eiler, W. J. A. II, Grey, C., Carroll, M. R., McCane, S., Jones, C. M., Yin, W., Mason, D., Cummings, R., Garcia, M., Ma,

C., Sarma, P. V. V. S., Cook, J. M., & Skolnick, P. (2003). The reinforcing properties of alcohol are mediated by GABAA1 receptors in the ventral pallidum. *Neuropsychopharmacology*, *28*, 2124–2137. https://doi.org/10.1038/sj.npp.1300239

Kamin, L. J. (1957). The retention of an incompletely learned avoidance response. *Journal of Comparative and Physiological Psychology*, *50*(5), 457. https://doi.org/10.1037/h0044226

Kamin, L. J. (1969). Predictability, surprise, attention, and conditioning. In B. A. Campbell & R. M. Church (Eds.), *Punishment aversive behavior* (pp. 279–296). Appleton-Century-Crofts.

Killeen, P. R., & Pellón, R. (2013). Adjunctive behaviors are operants. *Learning & Behavior*, *41*(1), 1–24. https://doi.org/10.3758/s13420-012-0095-1

Koepke, A. E., Gray, S. L., & Pepperberg, I. M. (2015). Delayed gratification: A grey parrot (*Psittacus erithacus*) will wait for a better reward. *Journal of Comparative Psychology*, *129*(4), 339–346. https://doi.org/10.1037/a0039553

Kollins, S. H. (2003). Delay discounting is associated with substance use in college students. *Addictive Behaviors*, *28*(6), 1167–1173. https://doi.org.10.1016/S0306-4603(02)00220-4

Kruse, J. M., Overmier, J. B., Konz, W. A., & Rokke, E. (1983). Pavlovian conditioned stimulus effects upon instrumental choice behavior are reinforcer specific. *Learning and Motivation*, *14*(2), 165–181. https://doi.org/10.1016/0023-9690(83)90004-8

López-Crespo, G., Rodríguez, M., Pellón, R., & Flores, P. (2004). Acquisition of schedule-induced polydipsia by rats in proximity to upcoming food delivery. *Animal Learning & Behavior*, *32*(4), 491–499. https://doi.org/10.3758/BF03196044

Maatsch, J. L. (1959). Learning and fixation after a single shock trial. *Journal of Comparative and Physiological Psychology*, *52*(4), 408–410. https://psycnet.apa.org/doi/10.1037/h0048310

Martinez, D., Narendran, R., Foltin, R. W., Slifstein, M., Hwang, D. R., Broft, A., Huang, Y., Cooper, T. B., Fischman, M. W., Kleber, H. D., & Laruelle, M. (2007). Amphetamine-induced dopamine release: Markedly blunted in cocaine dependence and predictive of the choice to self-administer cocaine. *American Journal of Psychiatry*, *164*(4), 622–629. https://doi.org/10.1176/ajp.2007.164.4.622

Marusich, J. A., & Bardo, M. T. (2009). Differences in impulsivity on a delay discounting task predict self-administration of a low unit dose of methylphenidate in rats. *Behavioural Pharmacology*, *20*(5–6), 447–454. https://doi.org/10.1097/FBP.0b013e328330ad6d

Mendez, I. A., Simon, N. W., Hart, N., Mitchell, M. R., Nation, J. R., Wellman, P. J., & Setlow, B. (2010). Self-administered cocaine causes long-lasting increases in impulsive choice in a delay discounting task. *Behavioral Neuroscience*, *124*(4), 470–477. https://doi.org/10.1037/a0020458

Michaelson, L. E., & Munakata, Y. (2020). Same data set, different conclusions: Preschool delay of gratification predicts later behavioral outcomes in a preregistered study. *Psychological Science*, *31*(2), 193–201. https://doi.org/10.1177/0956797619896270

Mineka, S. (1979). The role of fear in theories of avoidance learning, flooding, and extinction. *Psychological Bulletin*, *86*(5), 985. https://doi.org/10.1037/0033-2909.86.5.985

Mischel, W., Shoda, Y., & Rodriguez, M. L. (1989). Delay of gratification in children. *Science*, *244*(4907), 933–938. https://doi.org/10.1126/science.2658056

Moreno, M., & Flores, P. (2012). Schedule-induced polydipsia as a model of compulsive behavior: Neuropharmacological and neuroendocrine bases. *Psychopharmacology*, *219*(2), 647–659. https://doi.org/10.1007/s00213-011-2570-3

Olds, J., & Milner, P. (1954). Positive reinforcement produced by electrical stimulation of septal area and other regions of rat brain. *Journal of Comparative and Physiological Psychology*, *47*(6), 419–427. https://doi.org/10.1037/h0058775

Overmier, J. B., & Bull, J. A. (1969). On the independence of stimulus control of avoidance. *Journal of Experimental Psychology*, *79*(3, Pt.1), 464–467. https://doi.org/10.1037/h0026985

Overmier, J. B., & Murison, R. (2005). Trauma and resulting sensitization effects are modulated by psychological factors. *Psychoneuroendocrinology*, *30*(10), 965–973. https://doi.org/10.1016/j.psyneuen.2005.04.012

Overmier, J. B., & Seligman, M. E. (1967). Effects of inescapable shock upon subsequent escape and avoidance responding. *Journal of Comparative and Physiological Psychology*, *63*(1), 28. https://doi.org/10.1037/h0024166

Papini, M. R. (2003). Comparative psychology of surprising nonreward. *Brain, Behavior and Evolution*, *62*(2), 83–95. https://doi.org/10.1159/000072439

Papini, M. R. (2021). *Comparative psychology: Evolution and development of brain and behavior* (3rd ed.). Taylor & Francis.

Papini, M. R., & Dudley, R. T. (1997). Consequences of surprising reward omissions. *Review of General Psychology*, *1*(2), 175–197. https://doi.org/10.1037/1089-2680.1.2.175

Papini, M. R., Guarino, S., Hagen, C., & Torres, C. (2022). Incentive disengagement and the adaptive significance of frustrative nonreward. *Learning and Behavior*, *50*, 372–388. https://doi.org/10.3758/s13420-022-00519-3

Pavlov, I. P. (1927). *Conditioned reflexes: An investigation of the physiological activity of the cerebral cortex*. Oxford University Press.

Pearce, J. M., Colwill, R. M., & Hall, G. (1978). Instrumental conditioning of scratching in the laboratory rat. *Learning and Motivation*, *9*(3), 255–271. https://doi.org/10.1016/0023-9690(78)90009-7

Pellón, R., Ruíz, A., Moreno, M., Claro, F., Ambrosio, E., & Flores, P. (2011). Individual differences in schedule-induced polydipsia: Neuroanatomical dopamine divergences. *Behavioural Brain Research*, *217*(1), 195–201. https://doi.org/10.1016/j.bbr.2010.10.010

Perry, J. L., Larson, E. B., German, J. P., Madden, G. J., & Carroll, M. E. (2005). Impulsivity (delay discounting) as a predictor of acquisition of IV cocaine self-administration in female rats. *Psychopharmacology*, *178*, 193–201. https://doi.org/10.1007/s00213-004-1994-4

Phillips, A. G., Blaha, C. D., & Fibiger, H. C. (1989). Neurochemical correlates of brain-stimulation reward measured by ex vivo and in vivo analyses. *Neuroscience & Biobehavioral Reviews*, *13*(2–3), 99–104. https://doi.org/10.1016/S0149-7634(89)80017-X

Poremba, A., & Gabriel, M. (1999). Amygdala neurons mediate acquisition but not maintenance of instrumental avoidance behavior in rabbits. *Journal of Neuroscience*, *19*(21), 9635–9641. https://doi.org/10.1523/JNEUROSCI.19-21-09635.1999

Rachlin, H., & Green, L. (1972). Commitment, choice, and self-control. *Journal of the Experimental Analysis of Behavior*, *17*(1), 15–22. https://doi.org/10.1901/jeab.1972.17-15

Ramirez, F., Moscarello, J. M., LeDoux, J. E., & Sears, R. M. (2015). Active avoidance requires a serial basal amygdala to nucleus accumbens shell circuit. *Journal of Neuroscience*, *35*(8), 3470–3477. https://doi.org/10.1523/JNEUROSCI.1331-14.2015

Rescorla, R. A., & Solomon, R. L. (1967). Two-process learning theory: Relationships between Pavlovian conditioning and instrumental learning. *Psychological Review*, *74*(3), 151. https://doi.org/10.1037/h0024475

Reynolds, L. M., & Flores, C. (2021). Mesocorticolimbic dopamine pathways across adolescence: Diversity in development. *Frontiers in Neural Circuits*, *8*(15), 735625. https://doi.org/10.3389/fncir.2021.735625

Rodd-Henricks, Z. A., McKinzie, D. L., Li, T. K., Murphy, J. M., & McBride, W. J. (2002). Cocaine is self-administered into the shell but not the core of the nucleus accumbens of Wistar rats. *Journal of Pharmacology and Experimental Therapeutics*, *303*(3), 1216–1226. https://doi.org/10.1124/jpet.102.038950

Seligman, M. E., & Maier, S. F. (1967). Failure to escape traumatic shock. *Journal of Experimental Psychology*, *74*(1), 1–9. https://doi.org/10.1037/h0024514

Shettleworth, S. J. (1975). Reinforcement and the organization of behavior in golden hamsters: Hunger, environment, and food reinforcement. *Journal of Experimental Psychology: Animal Behavior Processes*, *1*(1), 56–87. https://doi.org/10.1037/0097-7403.1.1.56

Siegel, S., Hinson, R. E., Krank, M. D., & McCully, J. (1982). Heroin "overdose" death: The contribution of drug-associated environmental cues. *Science*, *216*, 436–437. https://doi.org/10.1126/science.7200260

Skinner, B. F. (1938). *The behavior of organisms: An experimental analysis*. Appleton-Century-Crofts.

Skinner, B. F. (1953). *Science and human behavior*. Macmillan.

Staddon, J. E. R. (1977). On Herrnstein's equation and related forms. *Journal of the Experimental Analysis of Behavior*, *28*(2), 163–170. https://doi.org/10.1901/jeab.1977.28-163

Staddon, J. E. R., & Ayres, S. L. (1975). Sequential and temporal properties of behavior induced by a schedule of periodic food delivery. *Behaviour*, *54*(1–2), 26–49. https://doi.org/10.1163/156853975X00317

Staddon, J. E. R., & Simmelhag, V. L. (1971). The "superstition" experiment: A reexamination of its implications for the principles of adaptive behavior. *Psychological Review*, *78*(1), 3–43. https://doi.org/10.1037/h0030305

Stahlman, W. D., & Catania, A. C. (2022). Faustian bargains: Short-term and long-term contingencies in phylogeny, ontogeny, and sociogeny. *Journal of the Experimental Analysis of Behavior*, *119*(1), 192–202. https://doi.org/10.1002/jeab.812

Stopyra, M. A., Friederich, H. C., Lavandier, N., Monning, E., Bendszus, M., Herzog, W., & Simon, J. J. (2021). Homeostasis and food craving in obesity: A functional MRI study. *International Journal of Obesity*, *45*, 2464–2470. https://doi.org/10.1038/s41366-021-00920-4

Stout, S. C., Boughner, R. L., & Papini, M. R. (2003). Reexamining the frustration effect in rats: Aftereffects of surprising reinforcement and nonreinforcement. *Learning and Motivation*, *34*(4), 437–456. https://doi.org/10.1016/S0023-9690(03)00038-9

Thorndike, E. L. (1911). *Animal intelligence: Experimental studies.* Macmillan Press. https://doi.org/10.5962/bhl.title.55072

Vafaie, N., & Kober, H. (2022). Association of drug cues and craving with drug use and relapse: A systematic review and meta-analysis. *JAMA Psychiatry*, *79*(7), 641–650. https://doi.org/10.1001/jamapsychiatry.2022.1240

van Galen, K. A., Schrantee, A., ter Horst, K. W., la Fleur, S. E., Booij, J., Constable, R. T., Schwartz, G. J., DiLeone, R. J., & Serlie, M. J. (2023). Brain responses to nutrients are severely impaired and not reversed by weight loss in humans with obesity: A randomized crossover study. *Nature Metabolism*, *5*, 1059–1072. https://doi.org/10.1038/s42255-023-00816-9

Vick, S. J., Bovet, D., & Anderson, J. R. (2010). How do African grey parrots (*Psittacus erithacus*) perform on a delay of gratification task? *Animal Cognition*, *13*, 351–358. https://doi.org/10.1007/s10071-009-0284-2

Volkow, N. D., Wang, G. J., Fischman, M. W., Foltin, R. W., Fowler, J. S., Abumrad, N. N., Vitkun, S., Logan, J., Gatley, S. J., Pappas, N., Hitzemann, R., & Shea, C. E. (1997). Relationship between subjective effects of cocaine and dopamine transporter occupancy. *Nature*, *386*(6627), 827–830. https://doi.org/10.1038/386827a0

Volkow, N. D., Wang, G. J., Telang, F., Fowler, J. S., Logan, J., Jayne, M., Ma, Y., Pradhan, K., & Wong, C. (2007). Profound decreases in dopamine release in striatum in detoxified alcoholics: Possible orbitofrontal involvement. *Journal of Neuroscience*, *27*(46), 12700–12706. https://doi.org/10.1523/JNEUROSCI.3371-07.2007

Weiss, F., Markou, A., Lorang, M. T., & Koob, G. F. (1992). Basal extracellular dopamine levels in the nucleus accumbens are decreased during cocaine withdrawal after unlimited-access self-administration. *Brain Research*, *593*(2), 314–318. https://doi.org/10.1016/0006-8993(92)91327-B

Wilkenfield, J., Nickel, M., Blakely, E., & Poling, A. (1992). Acquisition of lever-press responding in rats with delayed reinforcement: A comparison of three procedures. *Journal of the Experimental Analysis of Behavior*, *58*(3), 431–443. https://doi.org/10.1901/jeab.1992.58-431

Williams, J. L., & Lierle, D. M. (1986). Effects of stress controllability, immunization, and therapy on the subsequent defeat of colony intruders. *Animal Learning & Behavior*, *14*(3), 305–314. https://doi.org/10.3758/BF03200072

Williams, J. L., & Lierle, D. M. (1988). Effects of repeated defeat by a dominant conspecific on subsequent pain sensitivity, open-field activity, and escape learning. *Animal Learning & Behavior*, *16*(4), 477–485. https://doi.org/10.3758/BF03209389

Zentall, T. R. (2020). Enhancing "self-control": The paradoxical effect of delay of reinforcement. *Learning & Behavior*, *48*(1), 165–172. https://doi.org/10.3758/s13420-019-00407-3

Zentall, T. R., Case, J. P., & Berry, J. R. (2017). Rats' acquisition of the ephemeral reward task. *Animal Cognition*, *20*(3), 419–425. https://doi.org/10.1007/s10071-016-1065-3

7 Social learning

7.1 Introduction

This chapter focuses on the role of early learning in the development of social behavior mainly in birds and mammals. The evolutionary origin of social behaviors is connected to sexual reproduction. Finding sexually receptive conspecifics involves a spectrum of social interactions, including competition, territoriality, courtship, copulation, and parental care, among others. In addition to learning, social behavior is based on attention, emotion, cognition, and other processes. Individual behaviors (e.g., reflexes, conditioning, etc.) are the backbone of social learning.

The study of social learning is complicated by the fact that the experimenter often has little control over social interactions. For example, the behavior of a singing male sparrow can induce a female to approach the male's territory, which, in turn, influences the male to respond, and so on (see Chapter 11). Moreover, the actual behaviors can vary from pair to pair and across situations. In some lines of research, naturalistic observations have given way to experimental research in which a key aspect of the social situation is defined objectively. For example, play-back vocalizations and substitute mothers are used in place of the original stimuli for greater control. These settings are more similar to typical studies of learning in individuals. However, they also simplify the social situation, such that key aspects of the natural phenomenon could be lost in the laboratory setting. The complexity of social phenomena is considerable, and their development is often intricate, involving interactions between genetic, physiological, and experiential factors.

7.2 From individual to social learning

7.2.1 Individual recognition

Individual recognition is a prerequisite for social bonding among specific individuals, as in monogamous species. Individual recognition can only be achieved through learning in a social context since the individual to be recognized is not predetermined. In this sense, it is a problem analogous to filial imprinting in that it involves extensive exposure to a particular individual. In Australian budgerigars (*Melopsittacus undulatus*), small parrots that nest in colonies, monogamous pairs are established for life. Budgerigars recognize individuals by the colors and patterns of feather markings of the head and by the size and color of the eye's iris (Brown & Dooling, 1992, 1993). Experiments with real and computer-generated images of conspecifics show that markings that provide information about the individual's sex, age, and group are perceptually salient. Budgerigars discriminate face color more easily than body

DOI: 10.4324/9781003401957-9

color, which may be how they recognize members of their breeding colony. During courtship, males rapidly contract the pupil in the presence of potential mates, and female budgerigars, but not males, easily discriminate faces with different iris size. The size and color of the iris may provide information about the male's age.

Individual recognition is also required in structured groups in which access to resources depends on the individual's position in the social hierarchy. In primates that live in groups characterized by a leadership structure, displaying inappropriate behavior toward a dominant member can result in injury. Chimpanzees (*Pan troglodytes*) shown pictures of individuals from their group with whom they have had aggressive interactions exhibit an increase in heart rate, whereas heart rate decreased when watching pictures of strangers. By contrast, their heart rate did not change when exposed to pictures of companions (Boysen & Berntson, 1989). Experiments with chimpanzees and rhesus monkeys suggest that the eyes are preferentially used in individual recognition tasks (Parr et al., 2000).

Individual recognition must then be based on either the outcomes derived from interactions with specific group members or an observed interaction among group members (e.g., the winner of a contest for a mate). Such interactions may be related to sexual and reproductive behaviors, as with the budgerigars, or to aggressive encounters, as with the chimpanzees. The studies described detect individual recognition once the learning process has been completed, and thus, we have limited information as to what type of experience leads to the development of individual recognition.

7.2.2 Kin recognition

Animals follow simple rules of thumb to distinguish kin from others. Perhaps the simplest proxy for *kin recognition* is to discriminate familiar from unfamiliar individuals. If two animals have grown up in close proximity, there is a good chance that they are genetically related; strangers, however, are likely to come from outside the circle of relatives. With respect to the parents, "familiarity" and "relatedness" can be easily dissociated in cross-fostering experiments in which some pups are moved to be reared in a different litter by an unrelated mother, whereas others stay in their original litter. Cross-fostering designs help distinguish the contribution of maternal behavior from biological factors, including inheritance, to the development of a particular behavior, such as kin recognition. In cases in which it is the maternal behavior that contributes to the behavior, then there is a clear role of learning in the development of the behavior. In some cases, kin recognition depends on maternal interactions, whereas in other cases, kin recognition appears to involve something other than simple familiarity.

In the Galapagos mockingbird (*Nesomimus parvulus*), kin recognition appears to be based on operant learning. Adult birds are more likely to help a breeding pair when they were fed by both adults in the nest than when they were fed by only one or by none of them (Curry & Grant, 1990). Nestlings are usually fed by their parents, and so this associative rule of thumb would normally lead to the allocation of helping behavior by the helper to its kin, the breeding pair.

By contrast, female ground squirrels (*Spermophilus beldingi*) discriminate relatives even when they have been reared apart by different mothers (Mateo, 2017). In the laboratory, newborns were cross-fostered among different mothers to create various combinations. As adults, females reared apart engaged in less aggressive behavior when they were siblings than when they were unrelated. Therefore, kin recognition appears to be based on both familiarity and relatedness. An intriguing possibility is that the information essential for kin recognition in ground squirrels is acquired during intrauterine development (Robinson & Smotherman, 1991). Rat fetuses are capable of responding to a variety of sensory stimuli and of acquiring preferences that affect their postnatal behavior through associative learning, so a similar mechanism may account for kin recognition in ground squirrels.

7.2.3 Feeding and social learning

Social interactions can have a long-lasting effect on behavior through ***social learning***. Interactions between a naive rat (called the observer) and a rat that has eaten distinctively flavored food (the demonstrator) lead to the development of a preference for that flavor in the observer (Figure 7.1). Analyses of this type of interaction have revealed the information and context in which such information is used. For example, the preference does not develop simply because of exposure to the flavor. Moreover, observer rats exposed to demonstrators that have eaten a cinnamon-flavored food do not prefer to build a nest using shredded paper scented with cinnamon (Galef et al., 1994). This suggests that the flavor preference is specific for feeding. Reliance on social information is heightened when rats live in uncertain or unfavorable environments (Galef et al., 2008).

Social interactions can change an animal's own experience with food. For example, female spotted hyenas (*Crocuta crocuta*) given meat poisoned with lithium chloride (LiCl) and tested individually rejected that type of meat, even days after the conditioning episode. (LiCl is a toxin that induces gastrointestinal sickness.) However, the same female hyena would readily consume the meat in a social group; group feeding reversed the aversion (Yoerg, 1991). Social learning is actively promoted when the individuals involved in the interaction are close kin. In primates, the mother–infant bond provides information about food safety for the infant. Infant Japanese macaques (*Macaca fuscata*) can reverse a food aversion (produced by Food→LiCl pairings) if their mother consumes the food in their presence (Hikami et al., 1990).

These socially mediated reversals of conditioned food aversions can be understood as examples of ***counterconditioning***. In the original demonstration of counterconditioning (Pavlov, 1927), pain induced by electric shock (CS) was used as a signal for food (US). Although

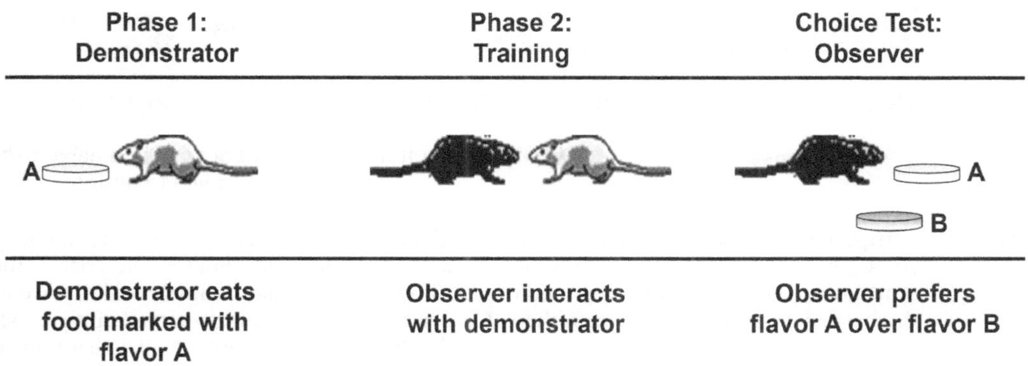

Figure 7.1 **Social transmission of food preferences.** Phase 1: the demonstrator rat is exposed to the target flavor. Phase 2: the demonstrator and observer rats interact socially. Choice test: the observer can choose between the flavor previously given to the demonstrator and a novel flavor. Social learning is manifested by the observer's preference for the flavor given originally to the demonstrator. (Based on Galef et al., 1994; from Papini, 2021; reproduced with permission from Taylor & Francis.)

the shock applied to a dog's leg initially elicited leg flexion, after several pairings with food, the shock started to elicit salivation. Pairings with food had shifted the hedonic value of the shock from aversive to appetitive. Similarly, as shown previously, food previously paired with intoxication shifts its aversive valence when paired with appetitive social interactions, especially involving the mother.

7.2.4 Predator recognition

Predatory pressures have contributed significantly to the evolution of social behavior, from large aggregates of fish swimming coordinately, called fish schools, to herds of herbivore mammals in the African plains. Grouping can be advantageous to individuals if it facilitates antipredator defense (Griffin, 2004). Fish schools can also foster learning of ***predator recognition***, even in the absence of direct contact with the predator. Zebra fish, *Brachydanio rerio*, form schools even in aquarium tanks. If damaged skin fluids (US) obtained from a fish with skin damage are pumped into the tank, the school shows an ***alarm reaction*** (UR) consisting of swimming and staying at the bottom of the tank for several minutes (Suboski et al., 1990). The damaged skin contains an alarm substance released when a predator has caught a zebra fish. Thus, the defensive reaction of the surviving members of the school would confer them protection against a nearby predator.

An extension of this effect suggests how predator recognition is learned and transmitted socially (Figure 7.2). Pairing a neutral odor such as morpholine (CS) with the alarm

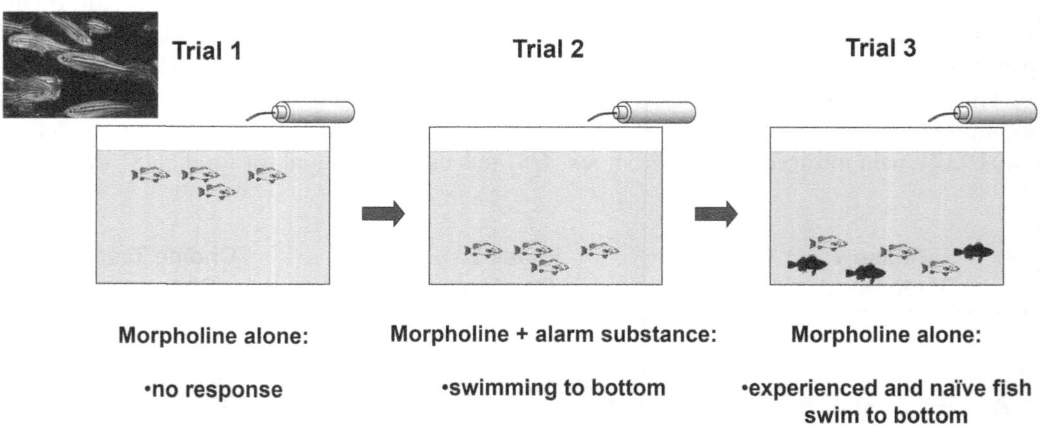

Figure 7.2 **Antipredator social learning in zebra danio fish,** *Brachydanio rerio.* On Trial 1, an undisturbed group shows no specific response to a neutral odor, morpholine. On Trial 2, the same group is exposed to a compound of morpholine and the alarm substance. Fish dive to the bottom of the tank and remain there. On Trial 3, the same animals trained in the previous trial and a few naïve fish (dark) are exposed only to the morpholine. Notice that trained fish respond to the morpholine by diving to the bottom, unlike on Trial 1. Moreover, naïve animals never exposed to the alarm substance or to morpholine acquire recognition of the morpholine as an alarm substance by social learning. (Based on Suboski et al., 1990; from Papini, 2021; reproduced with permission from Taylor & Francis; photo from Creative Commons https://search.creativecommons.org, by Oregon State University, license CC BY-SA 2.0.)

substance (US) results in the odor acquiring warning properties similar to those of the alarm substance—a case of Pavlovian conditioning. The CS increases the probability that the fish would evade (CR) an approaching predator. Surprisingly, zebra fish that never encountered the alarm substance but were exposed to the CS together with the CR of experienced fish also acquired the antipredator behavior (CR) to the CS. Such learning is based on observing the alarm reaction of other fish in the group, suggesting that what we called here a CR (the alarm reaction to the CS) also acts, at least in part, as a US.

A similar example of learning to recognize a predator has been described in blackbirds (*Turdus merula*). A blackbird displaying active defense in the presence of a predator (e.g., an owl) can attract other blackbirds and induce *mobbing*—harassment of a predator by a group of potential prey. Experiments show that a naïve blackbird learns to mob a model if it observes this model together with another blackbird displaying defensive behaviors. In one experiment, mobbing was induced in one blackbird (the demonstrator) by exposing it to an owl, while a second blackbird (the observer) could not see the owl, but it could see the demonstrator and a plastic bottle. In subsequent tests, the observer blackbird displayed mobbing behavior toward the bottle (Curio et al., 1978). Conditioning can thus lead to the social transmission of predator recognition in some species.

7.2.5 Social reinforcement

The behavior of a social animal is affected by social reinforcement just as food reinforcement shapes the behavior of a hungry animal. *Social reinforcement* refers to a change in behavior that triggers responses in recipient group members, such as physical contact for humans (e.g., a hug) or protection of an offspring in distress by a mammalian mother. Two examples illustrate social reinforcement.

Female marmoset monkeys (*Callithrix jacchus*) regularly give birth to twins. The mother provides care and nurture for the infants, but other members of the family and even unrelated adults also contribute to caring for the twins. The demands of caring for twins are likely related to the fact that the maternal behavior of female marmosets depends on infant care experience, which requires motivation to learn about infant care. The reinforcing effect of responding to an infant in distress was shown in an experiment with female marmosets. These females learned to press a lever while listening to an infant's distress call for an opportunity to stop the distress call and turned on the lights of an adjacent compartment, where they could see a replica of an infant (Pryce et al., 1993). Control conditions showed that lever pressing was maintained at higher levels only when the response stopped the distress call. It is surprising that such a reinforcer was effective at all because no direct contact with an infant was involved.

Mice can be trained to press a lever to have an opportunity to interact with another mouse. This social interaction test permits various neural manipulations while the animal is learning a response via social reinforcement (Solié et al., 2022). These experiments showed that the dopaminergic reward system originating in the *ventral tegmental area* (*VTA*) and projecting to the nucleus accumbens and prefrontal cortex is critical for the effectiveness of social reinforcement. These VTA neurons are maximally active when the mouse is interacting with an unfamiliar conspecific, but their activity is reduced after repeated interactions with the same conspecific, thus reflecting the development of an expectancy of interacting with a specific individual. Thus, social reinforcement seems to engage the same reward system in the brain activated by other rewards, such as food and water.

7.2.6 From social reinforcement to reproductive success

A functional advantage of predicting biologically important events lies in the organism's ability to prepare for their imminent arrival (Hollis, 1982). One possibility is that territorial males would be more effective at defending their territory or copulating with a receptive female if these events were signaled. In turn, this would suggest that conditioning mechanisms providing information about impending events have adaptive significance.

Experiments with blue gourami fish (*Trichogaster trichopterus*) and Japanese quail (*Coturnix japonica*) show that males gain a reproductive advantage when the arrival of males and females is signaled. In both species, males defend small territories against intruders, and females rarely mate with males lacking a territory. A territorial male faces the problem of discriminating between an intruder male and a receptive female. Failure to discriminate leads to maladaptive behavior, such as courting a male intruder or attacking a female.

In one experiment (Hollis et al., 1995), a group of blue gourami males received Pavlovian conditioning training in which a Light (CS) was paired with the presentation of another Male (US), whereas another group received exposure to the Light and the intruder Male in an explicitly unpaired control procedure. In a subsequent test, 10/11 males exposed to Pavlovian pairings won the encounter, whereas only 1/11 males exposed to explicitly unpaired events chased away the intruder. Winning also had long-lasting effects. When, 2 days later, these males were confronted with new intruders without the benefit of a CS, 6/11 experimental

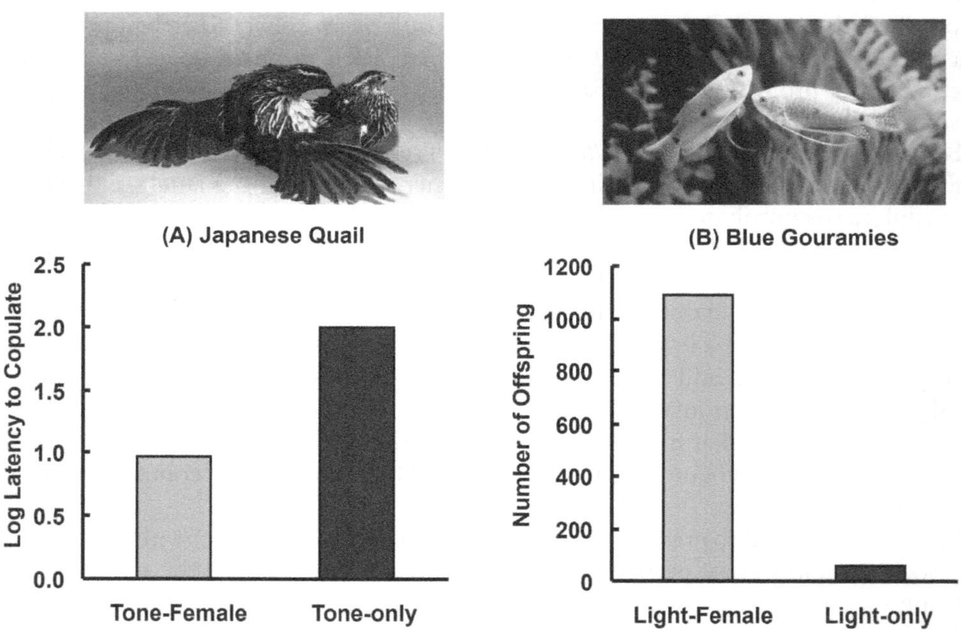

Figure 7.3 **Social reinforcement and reproductive success. (A)** Japanese quail (*Coturnix japonica*) males copulated faster (i.e., shorter latencies) when the female was signaled by a Tone than when the Tone was not paired with a female (Gutiérrez & Domjan, 1996; reproduced with permission from the American Psychological Association). **(B)** Blue gourami (*Trichogaster trichopterus*) males sired more offspring when the female was signaled by a Light than when the Light had not been paired with females (Hollis et al., 1997; reproduced with permission from the American Psychological Association). (Quail photo courtesy of B. Cusato and M. Burns-Cusato; blue gourami photo courtesy of K. Hollis.)

males won their second contest, whereas none of the 11 explicitly unpaired males won theirs. Once a male wins a contest, its chances of staying a winner improve, whereas the chances of winning for losers worsen. Notice that winning a contest does not depend on the male's phenotype but on the presence vs. absence of a signal. Conditioning mechanisms are available to all the males, but those in the experimental group had the opportunity to utilize them.

In another experiment (Gutiérrez & Domjan, 1996), male quail received discrimination training in which Tone-1 signaled the Female (CS+), whereas Tone-2 signaled her absence (CS-). In a subsequent test, pairs of males were placed in the same arena and given exposure to a tone. Individuals were chosen so that the same tone had been the CS+ for one male (Tone-1) but the CS- for the other (Tone-2). CS+ males copulated faster with the female than CS- males (Figure 7.3-A). When the CS+ was presented, males rapidly approached the area where the female usually appeared in the arena. By contrast, the CS- induced little or no behavioral change in the male. This anticipatory approach elicited by the CS+ conferred a copulatory advantage. In fact, male quail exposed to a CS+ for a receptive female released more sperm cells than CS- males (Domjan et al., 1998).

Experiments with blue gourami males show that paired training can have reproductive benefits (Hollis et al., 1997). In this case, it was possible to compare the number of offspring produced by males exposed to Light→Female pairings versus those produced by males given unpaired presentations of Light and Female. Paired males produced a larger number of offspring than unpaired males (Figure 7.3-B). The reason for this difference was related to the discrimination problem mentioned previously. Unpaired males were more likely to be aggressive toward the female, whereas Pavlovian males readily courted the incoming female.

7.2.7 Imitation

Consider the following problem posed to bumblebees (*Bombus terrestris*) foraging for sucrose (Alem et al., 2016). If placed on top of a blue artificial flower with a drop of sucrose in the center, the bee drinks the sucrose immediately. Next, the flower is moved progressively under a cover, but if the bee pull a string attached to the flower, then it can bring the flower closer and access the reward (see Figure 3.19-A and section **3.5.5 Invertebrate cognition**). The authors reported that 23 of 40 bees (58%) exposed to this task actually learned to pull from the string using their forelegs or mandibles. In a final test, naïve individuals observed trained demonstrators pulling the string to obtain sucrose. When the naïve observers were placed in the problem situation, 15 of 25 observers (60%) successfully pulled from the string on the first trial. A control group of observers did not see a trained bee pull the string to access the flower (which was pulled by the experimenter using a thin nylon thread) but saw a bee drinking the sucrose once the flower was in place. None of the bees in this control group learned the string-pulling task.

What makes this example especially striking is that this apparent imitation is relatively rare in nature. *Imitation* involves an observer's copying an action performed by a model more or less precisely. But several possibilities need to be discarded before an example like that of the bumblebee is taken as evidence of imitation. It is possible that the mere presence of another bumblebee attracted the observer to the location—called *social facilitation*. Perhaps observing the platform moving led the observer to pay special attention to the setting or manipulandum—called *local enhancement*. These alternatives, combined with trial-and-error learning, may help the animal develop a response that looks like imitation. One way to control for these alternatives is to use a *two-action method*, that is, a procedure in which observers perform one specific action exhibited by the model to obtain a reward.

Using this method, observer pigeons watched demonstrators press a lever to obtain food either by pecking at it or by stepping on it (Zentall et al., 1996). Both responses led to reward, so they had the same consequence. When observers were tested in the presence of the lever, they tended to perform the same response they had observed from the demonstrator, either pecking or stepping on the lever. Interestingly, if observers were trained to perform both responses for food and later observed a demonstrator perform only one of the responses, they tended to imitate the demonstrator in a subsequent test (McGregor et al., 2006). Pigeons displayed similar levels of imitation whether the demonstrators were rewarded for every response, were only occasionally rewarded, or were in extinction. These results suggests that imitation was largely determined by the Response→Outcome contingency applied to the demonstrator's behavior. This is called *blind imitation*.

Imitation is also distinguished from *emulation*, in which the demonstrator's and the observer's response leads to an outcome, but the two responses may not match precisely. This suggests the observer is focused on the functional consequence of the response modeled by the demonstrator rather than on the response's precise topography. Chimpanzees observing a demonstrator use a rake to procure food later used the rake in different ways to obtain food. So although the form of the response was different, the outcome of the behavior was the same (Tomasello et al., 1987). These observations on emulation fit the notion of *vicarious reinforcement*, according to which "the behavior of an observer is modified on account of the reinforcement administered to a model" (Bandura & Walters, 1963, p. 4).

The pressures that result in selection of mechanisms that promote kin recognition are easy to identify and understand. Although more obscure, selection for imitation, emulation, and local enhancement is equally relevant. The Pavlovian or operant contingency in effect for one animal in an environment is likely to be true for others. If you approach a vending machine and use an app to retrieve food, then that same contingency will likely (though, frustratingly, not always) be in effect for me. Thus, selection has likely occurred for organisms that increase the probability of the same behavior (imitation), similar behaviors (emulation), and behaviors that increase contact (local enhancement) when the observed behavior results in appetitive outcomes or avoidance of aversive outcomes (Skinner, 1986). Of course, an organism's umwelt limits the kinds of stimuli that can be learned about. Solitary species with few predators are much less likely to learn about social cues than species in which individuals frequently interact with each other or with predators. A great example is gaze following. Attending to the gaze of a conspecific is likely to increase detection of potential mates, nutrient sources, and predators. However, it will only gain control of behavior if the observer attends to the head of the demonstrator.

7.3 Imprinting in precocial birds

7.3.1 Properties

The ability of young precocial birds, such as ducklings or hatchlings, to learn to recognize their mother is referred to as *filial imprinting*. As a result of such recognition learning, the young bird follows its mother and exhibits distress if the mother is not present in its surrounding. As experience with the situation develops, the recognition process expands to other features of the "mother configuration" and even to siblings. The imprinting process can be induced in the laboratory due to a striking property: Young precocial birds can develop attachments to arbitrary objects. Ducklings easily become attached to humans, following them around and responding to their presence and absence in much the same way as they would respond to their biological mother.

Arbitrary objects and their stimulus features are not equally effective in controlling the *following response*—a behavior that reduces the distance between the chick and its mother. Objects that include movement are particularly effective (Rosa-Salva et al., 2018). A stuffed duck pushed around in a circular motion by a motor, a block of rubber moved back and forth on rails by an electric train motor, and a geometric pattern on a rotating cylinder have been noted as effective stimuli. For example (Eiserer & Swope, 1980), animals from several precocial species exposed to either a stationary light or to the same light with a rotating lens—the type used in emergency vehicles—developed strong approach to the rotating light, demonstrating that movement makes an imprinting stimulus especially effective. Static stimuli can be effective if they are very salient (Eiserer, 1980a). Ducklings were just as imprinted to a set of three stationary light bulbs of different colors as to the same lights when they moved continuously. However, 100-W bulbs were more effective than 7.5-W bulbs. Therefore, it is not movement per se that facilitates imprinting but rather the conspicuousness of the stimulus, as a large, moving hen would be in the natural situation.

One advantage of arbitrary stimuli is that their elements can be manipulated (e.g., intensity, color, shape, speed of movement) to identify the features that control behavior. For example, a stuffed model can be scrambled to produce a variety of patterns (Figure 7.4). Dark-reared chicks (*Gallus gallus*) generally prefer the natural model to the scrambled models

Figure 7.4 **Stimulus control of imprinting.** Manipulation of a naturalistic stimulus (the stuffed model shown at the top) to determine which element of the configuration controls preference for the imprinting stimulus (Johnson & Horn, 1988; reproduced with permission from Elsevier). Scrambled configurations including the head and neck regions, such as the one on the bottom right, are as effective as the naturalistic model.

but are indifferent when the choice is between the natural model and any scrambled model that includes the head and neck regions (Johnson & Horn, 1988). Thus, preference for the natural model is mostly based on the head-neck region. Interestingly, they are also indifferent between the natural model and stuffed models displaying prominent head-neck regions, such as that of a bird from a different species or of a polecat, a small carnivorous mammal.

Imprinting learning occurs only within a *sensitive* (or *critical*) *period*. Thus, young precocial birds have a limited time window to become imprinted to an object, and if they failed to do so, their ability to develop an attachment is restricted. The limits of this sensitive period are not rigid and are modulated by several factors (Michel & Tyler, 2005), suggesting that imprinting is not a purely maturational process that unfolds independently of environmental influences. There are also species differences in the degree of malleability of sensitive periods. Five-month-old ducks (*Anas platyrhynchos*), but not 5-month-old chickens (*Gallus gallus*), reared in visual isolation developed strong approach tendencies to the set of red-green-blue lights moving horizontally (Eiserer, 1980b). The sensitive period can also be extended by pharmacological treatments. Domestic chickens (*Gallus domesticus*) exhibit no evidence of imprinting when exposed to a model after the second posthatching day, but the same model induces chicks to follow the imprinting model up to 8 days after hatching when treated with ketamine (a noncompetitive N-methyl-D-aspartate receptor, NMDA, antagonist; Parsons & Rogers, 1997).

Attachments derived from imprinting are not completely irreversible. In one experiment (Salzen & Meyer, 1968), domestic chicks were exposed to one of two artificial stimuli (green ball for half of the animals, yellow sponge for the rest) hanging from the cage's ceiling during 3 days. During a subsequent test session, simultaneous access to both stimuli indicated that chicks strongly preferred the one to which they had been exposed. Next, each chick was exposed for 3 days to the other object (e.g., the sponge for those previously exposed to the ball and vice versa) and tested again with both objects. Now, chicks exhibited preference for the more recently exposed stimulus, thus reversing their original attachment. This new preference was still present after 3 more days during which the chicks were not exposed to either stimulus. A second attachment to another stimulus, called *secondary imprinting*, is less stable than primary imprinting and can be disrupted by a variety of procedures, including preexposing chicks (*Gallus gallus*) to a live hen (Boakes & Panter, 1985).

7.3.2 Motivational factors

Imprinting can be treated as an example of *perceptual learning* because it involves the development of object recognition by mere exposure. However, recognition works hand-in-hand with motivation to approach and remain in close proximity to the object. The response of following the imprinting object is not itself the imprinting phenomenon, but it shows that imprinting is both a matter of learning and motivation. The young precocial bird is compelled to perform any response that minimizes the distance to the imprinting stimulus.

In an early demonstration, 1- to 2-day old ducklings (*Anas rubripes tristis* and *A. platythynchos*) were placed in a box with two compartments separated by a translucent wall. The chick was in one of these compartments and a moving yellow cylinder (the imprinting stimulus) was in the other. Furthermore, a peck on a small key placed in one of the walls of the chick's compartment illuminated the stimulus compartment and set the imprinting stimulus in motion for 40 s. Chicks rapidly learned to respond to the key (acquisition) and stopped pecking at the key when this behavior no longer activated the imprinting stimulus (extinction). While these are properties of responses acquired through instrumental conditioning with conventional reinforcers such as food or water, this pecking response persisted even after hundreds of presentations of the imprinting stimulus, giving no evidence of "satiety," as would be the case with responses reinforced by food or water (Peterson, 1960). Furthermore, reinforcing this response on a fixed-interval schedule produced the typical scallop pattern (see Figure 4.15) when ducklings received water as the reinforcer, but no such pattern was observed when the response activated the imprinting stimulus (DePaulo & Hoffman, 1981).

An interesting demonstration of the dissociation between recognition learning and the following response of imprinted ducklings was provided by an experiment based on *omission training* (see Table 4.8). Ducklings were first imprinted to a moving bottle and, once the following response was strong, they received omission training. During omission training, the imprinting stimulus was constantly moving unless the animal approached the section of the box that was closest to the stimulus, in which case the stimulus was turned off for 8 s. Ducklings rapidly adjusted to this situation by withdrawing from the closest area and sitting on a remote part of the apparatus. This allowed for the activation of the imprinting stimulus, which the ducklings followed from the distance. Eventually, the ducklings would again approach the object and restart the cycle (Hoffman et al., 1969a).

The motivational properties of imprinting are evident in other behaviors. Young precocial birds imprinted on a stimulus exhibit *distress vocalizations* when the stimulus is removed. These vocalizations are brief "peeps" of 3 to 4 kHz that also occur in aversive situations (when experiencing food deprivation or low body temperature). Interestingly, distress calls can also be influenced by instrumental conditioning, much like the following response. Using a *master–yoked design* (see Chapter 4), master animals could activate the imprinting stimulus by emitting distress calls. Such calls also activated the imprinting stimulus for yoked animals but independently of their behavior. Master animals emitted more distress calls than yoked controls (Hoffman et al., 1966). In the natural environment, distress calls communicate that something potentially dangerous is occurring, eliciting corrective actions from the mother.

When the imprinting stimulus is presented independently of the chick's behavior and relatively frequently, few distress calls are recorded. Furthermore, eating and drinking tend to occur when the imprinting stimulus is activated (Hoffman et al., 1969b). This pattern of responding is clear when the imprinting stimulus is presented frequently, but it breaks down when presentations are spaced apart by 2 min. The presentation of the imprinting stimulus switches the young bird into an appetitive mode, facilitating eating and drinking. However, these behaviors tend to be suppressed when the imprinting stimulus is off and the animal is in an aversive mode, as suggested by distress calls. Moreover, the administration of electric shocks when the imprinting stimulus is off, making these periods more aversive, leads to a stronger following response (Ratner, 1976), whereas injections of morphine (an opioid receptor agonist that reduces aversiveness) diminish the frequency of distress calls elicited by removal of the imprinting stimulus (Panksepp et al., 1978).

7.3.3 Learning factors

A few days after hatching, Peking ducklings (*Anas platyrhynchos*) respond to various attributes of their mother hen, including her call (auditory) and presence (visual). Experiments also show that they prefer the species-typical call to that of another species, even when this call is accompanied by a stuffed model of an animal of their own species. How do these auditory and visual stimuli become effective?

Duckling embryos incubated in social isolation, which deprives them from hearing the calls of their mother and siblings, and devocalized, which deprives them from hearing their own calls, do not exhibit preference for the Peking call over the call of a chicken (Gottlieb, 1978). By contrast, socially reared ducklings show strong preference for the species-typical call over a chicken call. The source of *embryonic experience* lies in vocalizations emitted by the mother, by siblings in other eggs within the nest, and even by the embryo's own vocalizations.

These results suggest that the duckling initially responds strongly to some aspect of the imprinting stimulus, but after a few days of interaction with the object, previously ineffective elements of the imprinting configuration develop control over the following response. Ducklings exposed to an object in motion eventually develop a strong approach response even when the object is stationary. By contrast, birds exposed only to the stationary object develop a weak following response (Hoffman et al., 1972). A similar preference develops for a visual stimulus accompanied by the species-typical maternal call. In one experiment (Bolhuis & Honey, 1994), a group of ducklings was exposed to a compound stimulus that included a shape projected on a screen (visual feature) accompanied by the maternal call (auditory feature), while a second group received unpaired exposure to the same features, each presented in different sessions. When given a choice between the familiar shape and a novel shape in the absence of the auditory feature, ducklings in the group trained with the audio-visual compound exhibited stronger preference for the visual feature than ducklings exposed to the same stimuli in an unpaired fashion.

To explain results like these, Hoffman and Ratner (1973) suggested that some feature of the compound imprinting stimulus has a greater initial strength to elicit the following response and to reduce separation fear. The feature with high initial strength (e.g., movement, plumage color, social interaction with siblings, maternal call) could vary across species depending on ecological factors. For example, auditory features would be more important for sympatric species sharing the same habitat and similar plumage, whereas visual features could be more important for species that have evolved a unique plumage pattern. Strong features act as USs, endowing accompanying stimuli with strength (CSs) by virtue of temporal and spatial contiguity (Figure 7.5-A). Thus, static stimuli could be thought of as initially neutral CSs that acquire the capacity to induce the following response because of their simultaneous pairing with salient US features. This is known as the *classical conditioning theory of imprinting*.

The configural nature of the imprinting stimulus is an aspect that differs from more typical studies of classical conditioning in which the CS and US are separate events that occur at different times and locations. In imprinting, CS and US are features of the same compound stimulus, a characteristic that makes it more difficult to manipulate these features to generate conditioning phenomena. In turn, the configural nature of the imprinting stimulus invites a view in terms of *within-compound associations*—links between the elements of a compound stimulus established by virtue of their joined occurrence (see Chapter 3). As mentioned previously, visual stimuli are more preferred when they were paired with the maternal call than when the visual and auditory features were unpaired. Further experiments show that separate presentations of the auditory feature (the maternal call) reduced the duckling's preference for the visual feature (geometric shapes) whether they occurred before or after exposure to the audiovisual compound (Table 7.1). Presenting the auditory feature without the visual feature reduced the strength of the within-compound association between these features, thus decreasing the ability of the visual stimulus to elicit a preference (Bolhuis & Honey, 1994).

The imprinting stimulus also introduces a motivational factor (see previous section). For instance, if the stimulus is presented in alternating minutes (e.g., present, absent, present,

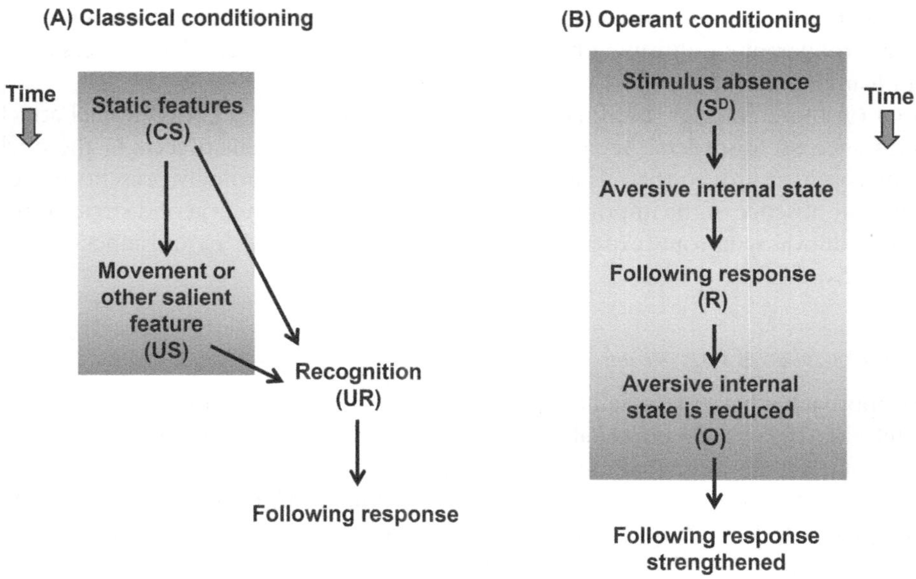

Figure 7.5 **Role of associative learning in the development of filial imprinting in precocial birds.** **(A)** Classical conditioning allows initially ineffective features of the imprinting stimulus (e.g., static features; conditioned stimulus, CS) to become part of the configuration the animal recognizes and follows by virtue of pairing with salient stimuli (e.g., movement; unconditioned stimulus, US). **(B)** Operant conditioning contributes to the strengthening of the following response (operant response, R) by reducing an aversive internal state induced by the withdrawal of the imprinting stimulus (outcome, O). The triggering factor is the absence of the salient stimulus (discriminative stimulus, S^D).

Table 7.1 Within-compound associations in imprinting

Group	*Phase 1*	*Phase 2*	*Preference test results*
Compound-Element	CallTriangle	Call	Triangle ~ Circle
Compound first	CallTriangle	Nothing	Triangle > Circle
Element-Compound	Call	CallTriangle	Triangle ~ Circle
Compound second	Nothing	CallTriangle	Triangle > Circle

Note. Call: the maternal call (auditory). Triangle: the image of a triangle projected on a screen (visual). Circle: the image of a circle projected on a screen (visual). In the preference test, orientation toward the triangle and circle were about the same for chicks exposed to isolated calls, whether before or after compound exposure. Design used by Bolhuis and Honey (1994).

and so forth), ducklings would eventually emit most of their distress calls during the periods in which the stimulus is absent, suggesting that the imprinting stimulus acquires the ability to reduce fear. Interestingly, chicks left in an empty environment do not emit distress calls initially but only after being exposed to the imprinting stimulus. Thus, the imprinting stimulus induces the need for its presentation and, consequently, the distress that accompanies its absence. This is consistent with the finding that morphine injections reduce distress calls and naloxone injections increase them (Panksepp et al., 1978). Morphine is an opioid agonist that reduces pain, fear, and frustration, whereas naloxone is an opioid antagonist that prevents endogenous opioids from activating their receptors. The following response is subjected to operant conditioning because it is paired with an object that reduces an aversive state of fear (Figure 7.5-B).

Based on these findings, Hoffman (1987) suggested a parallel between filial attachment and substance-use disorders. According to this hypothesis, salient objects in the duckling's early environment induce the release of endogenous opioids naturally present in the brain, such that the absence of the imprinting stimulus leads to the induction of distress comparable to the withdrawal symptoms experienced by a person afflicted with a substance-use disorder who is deprived of the drug.

7.3.4 Neurobiology of imprinting

Several approaches have identified the processes underlying the development of filial imprinting (McCabe, 2019; Nakamori et al., 2013). Animals exposed to an imprinting stimulus, but not control animals reared in darkness or exposed to constant light, exhibit activation in an area known as the ***intermediate and medial mesopallium*** (*IMM*). Such activity could reflect the storage of the imprinting memory, the processing of visual or auditory stimuli, or motor coordination. However, IMM neurons were active in experiments involving visual or auditory imprinting, suggesting that it is not exclusively linked to one sensory system. The IMM is also active during the acquisition of passive avoidance, when chicks learn to suppress a previously punished response, thus suggesting that its activity does not reflect motor activation.

In a series of experiments (McCabe et al., 1981, 1982), lesions of the IMM area before the development of imprinting led to a permanent acquisition deficit. Animals showed a deficient following response and were indifferent when given a choice between the familiar stimulus and a novel one. Lesions of the IMM after the development of imprinting also reduced preference for the imprinting stimulus. Comparing IMM lesions with sham lesions (the same surgical treatment, except that the brain tissue is not affected) and to lesions of similar size located in other areas showed that the effects of IMM lesions are not caused by the size of the lesion but by its location. Additional observations show that IMM lesions do not impair feeding behavior or the accuracy of pecking at a moving target. Thus, these lesions do not impair imprinting because they cause deficits in vision, motivation, or motor coordination. The implication is that information critical to filial imprinting is encoded by IMM neurons.

Imaging techniques show that brain activation changes after exposure to the imprinting object in brain areas that send their outputs to the IMM. Two such areas are the hyperpallium apicale (IHA) and the hyperpallium densocellulare (HDR). In one experiment (Nakamori et al., 2013), chicks placed in an activity wheel watched a moving dot in a screen. When training involved a red circle, presentation of a blue square induced escape responses, but the opposite was the case when training involved the blue square. Brain images of behaving chicks showed that the activity patterns corresponding to the red and blue stimuli were similar in animals that had not received training. By contrast, chicks trained with a blue square exhibited differential activation depending on the stimulus. Tests with the blue square produced strong responses in the IHA and in the HDR, both visual areas sending projections to the IMM. However, in these chicks, responses to the red square were restricted to the IHA (Table 7.2).

An analysis of several neuroanatomical features of IMM neurons in chicks exposed to imprinting training for either 20 min (underexposed) or 140 min (overexposed) provides information for the type of change underlying imprinting (Horn et al., 1985). Animals overexposed to the imprinting stimulus exhibit larger synapses between the axons of incoming neurons and the dendrites of IMM neurons. The enlarged synaptic region corresponds to the

Table 7.2 Neural plasticity induced by imprinting to a visual image

Training	*Test*	*IHA*	*Intermediate area*	*HDR*
Blue square	Blue square	High	Low	High
	Red circle	High	No activity	No activity
No training	Blue square	High	High	High
	Red circle	High	High	High

Note. Images of neural activity obtained when chicks are watching the imprinting stimulus, a blue square. Activity in the IHA (hyperpallium apicale) and HDR (hyperpallium densocellulare) is strong, with low activity in the intermediate area for chicks trained with the blue square. By contrast, untrained chicks showed no boundaries in activity in these two areas when exposed to the blue square. The red circle is a control stimulus. Based on Nakamori et al., 2013.

postsynaptic membrane where neurotransmitter receptors are located. This suggests that one effect of imprinting training is to induce the production of additional neurotransmitter receptors that facilitate synaptic transmission, such as *NMDA receptors* (see Chapter 4). Substances that bind selectively to NMDA receptors indicate a proliferation of such receptors after training (McCabe & Horn, 1988), and NMDA antagonists (substances that prevent receptors from being activated) infused into the IMM area decrease the strength of imprinting (Brock et al., 1996). MNDA receptors contain subunits known as NR1 and NR2, each with several alternative variations. Two variations identified as NR2A and NR2B change during the initial days after hatching. During the sensitive period, the proportion of NR2B subunits in cells located in the hyperpallium dorsale (HD) increases immediately after imprinting but remains low in chicks that are not imprinted to a stimulus. By contrast, the concentration of NR2A subunits remains unchanged during this period. Inhibition of NR2B subunits in the HD interferes with activity in the IMM needed to establish imprinting (Nakamori et al., 2010). It is possible, therefore, that the length of the sensitive period requires the proliferation of NR2B subunits in NMDA receptors located in the HD. This induces plasticity in IMM neurons that encode the imprinting memory. The sensitive period ends when the expression of these NR2B subunits is reduced.

The reduction in preference for the imprinting stimulus after IMM lesions is more drastic when the stimulus is arbitrary (a rotating box) than when it is natural (a rotating stuffed model). Preference for the natural stimulus is reduced by the lesion, but it is still above chance. Further experiments indicate that the preference for the naturalistic stuffed model is present 24 h after hatching but absent 2 h after hatching, and it requires walking experience to emerge. These observations suggest that filial imprinting actually involves two independent processes (Horn, 1991). One is the emergence of a predisposition to recognize naturalistic objects (perhaps a head-neck configuration), and another is the acquisition of a detailed representation of the imprinting stimulus. This second learning process depends on IMM neurons.

Whereas the predisposition could be a unique attribute of filial imprinting, the learning mechanism need not be unique. For example, the development of a detailed representation of the hen could involve classical conditioning (e.g., within-compound associations) and perceptual learning (e.g., mere-exposure learning), both processes known to occur in other species and situations. In the natural environment, predispositions and learning processes act together and reinforce each other. An emerging predisposition can direct attention selectively to a specific set of cues (e.g., head-neck region), whereas the learning process builds a more comprehensive representation adding stimulus features that accompany the head-neck configuration. Learning is what permits a precocial chick to eventually recognize a collection of attributes as parts of the same "mother" configuration.

7.3.5 Sexual imprinting

Filial imprinting during early development affects the social behavior of adult precocial birds, a phenomenon called ***sexual imprinting***. This is a case of ***latent learning*** in which a long interval interpolates between the acquisition of information and its behavioral expression (see Chapter 4). Ducklings imprinted to humans tend to direct their adult courtship behavior to humans rather than ducks. This concept is no doubt familiar to you from popular cultural references insinuating that a person has chosen to marry someone just like their parent. In the popular TV show *How I Met Your Mother*, all of the main characters question their mate selections after a friend mentions this observation. In an experimental setting, a young precocial bird would seem to learn both to recognize a particular object (filial imprinting) and to develop a sexual preference for objects similar to the original one (sexual imprinting). Consistent with this hypothesis, chicks receiving IMM lesions soon after hatching show deficits in filial imprinting (as discussed earlier) and display no clear sexual preference as adults (Bolhuis et al., 1989). Moreover, studies in which filial and sexual imprinting are induced and tested with arbitrary stimuli show a correlation between filial and sexual preferences (Vidal, 1980).

The nature of the stimulus presented in a test of sexual preference, as well as the social experience of the juvenile bird, can also affect adult sexual preferences. Chicks imprinted to an arbitrary stimulus and subsequently exposed to conspecifics exhibit a sexual preference for a stuffed natural model later in life rather than for the artificial imprinting model to which they were attached (Vidal, 1980). Therefore, the establishment of a filial attachment does not rigidly determine adult sexual preferences.

There is diversity in the extent to which social interactions determine adult sexual preferences in birds. In zebra finches (*Taeniopygia guttata*), adult males direct their courtship singing to conspecific females or to female Bengalese finches (*Lonchura striata*), depending on whether they were reared by zebra or Bengalese finches, respectively. Zebra finch males exposed during development first to conspecifics and later to Bengalese finches exhibit ***dithering behavior***: They direct courtship singing and other social behaviors to females of both species. The sexual preference of ditherer males is stable over time and restricted—they do not court females from other finch species. These males exhibit ***double sexual imprinting*** (ten Cate, 1986). Interestingly, if male zebra finches are raised with conspecifics and Bengalese finches simultaneously, they prefer females of their own species (Immelmann, 1972). This preeminence of conspecifics arises from early social interactions between the developing zebra finch and its parents. Zebra parents tend to direct both feeding and aggressive responses to the young zebra finches rather than to young Bengalese finches.

In zebra finches, the sensitive period for sexual imprinting can be extended by social experience. Socially isolated animals show some degree of plasticity up to about 100 days of age; at about 150 days of age, sexual preferences are no longer malleable. Behavioral plasticity in isolated birds is correlated with the proliferation of dendritic spines in telencephalic areas known to be important for sexual imprinting, the nidopallium and mesopallium (Bischof et al., 2002). In these two areas, the density of dendritic spines increases in isolation and is drastically reduced when the animal is exposed to a live model within the first 100 days of life. A similar reduction in dendritic spines can be induced by chemical stimulation in brain slices from these areas. Stimulation with TEA (tetraethilamonia) causes a pattern of neural activation that enhances conductivity at some synaptic sites. This phenomenon, known as

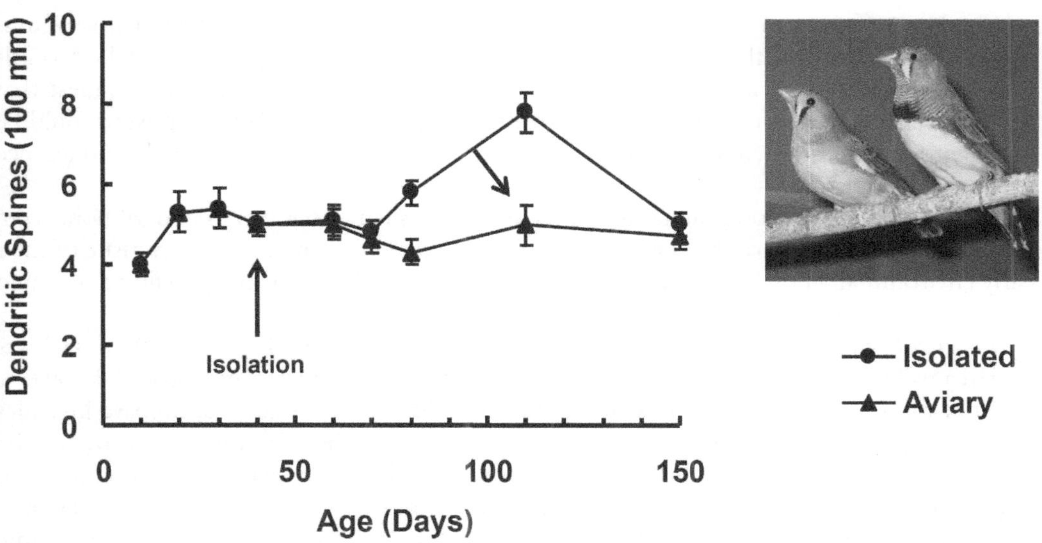

Figure 7.6 **Neural basis of sexual imprinting.** Density of dendritic spines in the medial nido-mesopalllium of zebra finches in birds reared either in isolation since postnatal day 40 or in an aviary. The arrow shows the reduction in spine density that occurs in isolated birds exposed to a social environment from 100 to 107 days of age. (From Bischof et al., 2002; reproduced with permission from Elsevier; photo courtesy of Brent Cooper.)

long-term potentiation (see Chapter 4), also causes a reduction in dendritic spines. Moreover, dendritic spines are kept at low levels if animals are raised in social contact with other birds. Thus, the availability of a model triggers a learning process that seems to exhaust available plasticity in the telencephalon. Interestingly, dendritic spines decrease even in the absence of social or chemical stimulation to reach basal levels by the time the animals are about 150 days old (Figure 7.6). It is unclear what causes a decrease in spine density in isolated animals, but one possibility is that the animal develops a preference to nonsocial (biologically inappropriate) stimuli available in the environment of the isolated bird.

7.3.6 Imprinting-like phenomena in other species

The two most important criteria used to identify potential cases of imprinting are learning by simple exposure and during a sensitive period. There are no clear examples of filial imprinting in other species, but there some examples of early learning in other species that exhibit these two features.

In altricial chicks, recognition can be assessed in terms of the begging response. Upon arrival of a parent to the nest, nestlings open their mouths vigorously, a response that induces the parent to deliver food. Experiments with blackbird chicks (*Turdus merula*) removed from the nest a few days after hatching and reared in darkness suggest that the development of parent recognition involves exposure learning. Nestlings were exposed to a stuffed model during feeding sessions and later given a preference test between the familiar model and a novel model at ages 10 to 23 days after hatching. Preference for the familiar model was strongest in 11-day-old chicks, suggesting the presence of a sensitive period (Junco, 1988). Obviously, these nestlings are exposed to operant conditioning training since begging (response) is paired with food (reinforcer) in the presence of a parent in the nest (discriminative stimulus). Thus, it is possible that conditioning rather than exposure is responsible for the acquisition of a preference for a familiar visual object. However, further experiments suggest that the preference develops even in the absence of food reinforcement. Thus, exposure could be sufficient for acquisition, although food reinforcement would strengthen the filial preference (Junco, 1993).

Species that exhibit long-range migratory behavior, such as sea turtles and salmon, seem to learn through exposure the chemical stimuli and magnetic signature characteristic of their early environment (Lohmann et al., 2008). The adult animal uses memory to find a hatching site during breeding.

Chemical imprinting directs the migratory behavior of salmon. Salmon hatch in freshwater streams in the northern continents and then undergo a developmental process known as smoltification—morphological, physiological, and behavioral changes that prepare juveniles as they migrate from fresh water to marine environments. While fish then swim toward the sea, they are exposed to the chemicals in the streams where they hatched—the imprinting migration. Salmon eventually swim upstream of rivers to engage in reproductive behavior—the homing migration. Adults usually die after breeding. Salmon tend to return to the same rivers where they hatched, a behavior suspected to be based on chemical imprinting. Salmon exposed to a water current containing the amino acid L-cysteine during one entire day at various stages during the smoltification phase and exposed to L-cysteine after smoltification was over showed a decrease in heart rate typically observed when exposed to familiar stimuli. Such changes peaked for fish exposed to the chemical stimulus between day 21 and 28 of the smoltification phase but not earlier or later, suggesting a sensitive period (Morin et al., 1989).

The brain mechanisms for the imprinting and homing migrations have been described in Pacific salmon (Ueda, 2016). Early exposure to the hatching environment during the imprinting migration triggers the release of hormones from the brain-pituitary-thyroid axis that stimulate the expression of a gene coding for a key component of the NMDA receptor in the basal telencephalon: the NR1 subunit. Expression of the gene coding for the NR1 subunit peaks and then decreases after day 7 of exposure to the hatching environment. This mechanism is thought to trigger the formation of a chemical imprinting memory that will later guide the adult toward the breeding site. Gonadal hormones are involved in the homing migration of the adult salmon into fresh water. Concentrations of the gonadotropin-releasing hormone in the olfactory bulbs peak when salmon are exposed to stimuli from the hatching streams. This is accompanied by enhanced expression of the gene coding for the NR1 subunit of the NMDA receptor in the olfactory bulb, a process thought to be responsible for the retrieval of the imprinting memory established during the imprinting migration.

Imprinting-like phenomena have also been described in mammals. In goats (*Capra hircus*), a precocial mammal, the mother rather than the offspring rapidly forms a bond with the newborn if exposed shortly after giving birth—implying a sensitive period (Gubernick et al., 1979). A mother given access to a newborn for 5 min after birth would several hours later accept this animal (and all its siblings), allowing them to nurse. Infants that spent 8 or more hours with their own mother were vigorously rejected. This ability to form new attachments hours after giving birth suggests that the sensitive period for *maternal imprinting* is not precisely timed. Chemical stimuli in the mother's saliva and milk probably allow the mother to recognize her own infants and reject alien ones (Gubernick, 1980).

Rats also show an imprinting-like effect during the first 10 postnatal days—a sensitive period. During this period, pairing an odor (CS) with electric current (US) leads to the development of a preference for the odor. Paradoxically, pain acts as an appetitive reinforcer for newborn rats. Similar experience with pain after 11 days of age supports aversion to the odor, as it happens in adults. Pain thresholds are about the same as in older rats, so these preferences are not due to insensitivity to pain in infants. Acquired odor preferences rather than aversions prevent newborns from developing a rejection to olfactory cues associated with the mother (Moriceau & Sullivan, 2005). During the sensitive period, pups are restricted to the nest, where the mother engages in rough handling that induces distress vocalizations in the pups. If the sensitive period is disrupted by infusions of the stress hormone corticosterone in the amygdala, then infants exhibit odor aversion rather than preference (Figure 7.7-A). Alternatively, if the sensitive period is extended by infusing a corticosterone antagonist into the amygdala, then infants exhibit odor preferences rather than aversion (Figure 7.7-B; Moriceau et al., 2006).

7.4 Early social learning

7.4.1 Attachment

A rat mother and her pups interact in a complex manner during nursing and maternal care. Does this mean that the mother and pup have established an attachment? ***Attachment*** refers to the bond that develops between the mother and her infants, and it is usually defined by three properties (Ainsworth, 1972):

- The attachment object is recognized and discriminated from other objects.
- The attachment object is preferred over other objects.
- Removal of the attachment object induces aversive responses.

Filial imprinting in precocial birds fits these criteria and is thus an example of attachment. What about the mother–infant bond in mammals? In the case of rats, neither the mother nor the pups seem to exhibit ***individual recognition***. In rats, maternal behavior can be prolonged

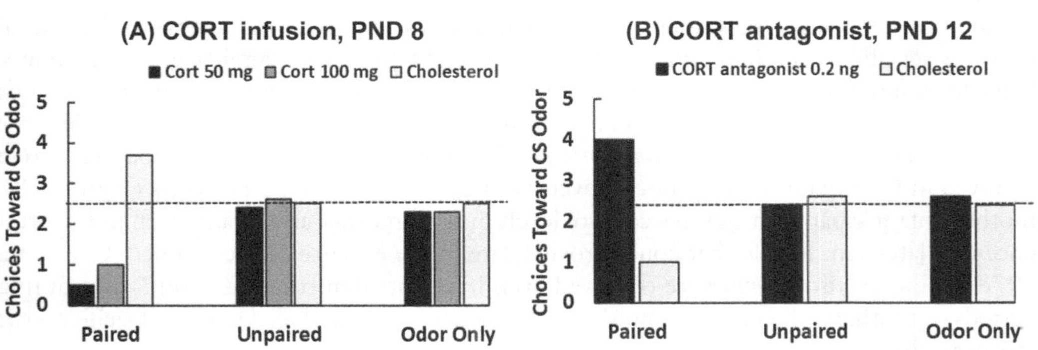

Figure 7.7 **Odor→Shock conditioning in infant rats.** Choices of the odor in paired (CS→US), unpaired (CS, US), or presented by itself (odor-only) procedures. Shock was the unconditioned stimulus (US). **(A)** Animals received infusions of two doses of the stress hormone corticosterone (or a control infusion of cholesterol) in the amygdala during postnatal day (PND) 8 (sensitive period). **(B)** Animals received an infusion of the corticosterone antagonist mifepristone in the amygdala (or a control infusion of cholesterol) in PND 12 (after the sensitive period). (From Moriceau et al., 2006; reproduced with permission from the *Journal of Neuroscience*.)

almost indefinitely by replacing older pups with younger ones. A mother would also nurse alien pups so long as they acquired the odors of her litter (Leon, 1975). Thus, the mother appears to respond to the pup's odor in a generic sense rather than on an individual basis. Pups, in turn, do not discriminate between their own mother and alien mothers, so long as they are lactating females and their diets are the same. Pups respond to chemical cues in the milk that can be affected by the female's diet.

Both mothers and pups also respond to separation by exhibiting aversive reactions, but these reactions do not demonstrate individual recognition. For example, plasma levels of the stress hormone corticosterone are raised when mothers are deprived of their litter, but controls show that these changes are due to handling during the experimental procedure rather than to the absence of the pups (Smotherman et al., 1977). Pups separated from their mother emit distress vocalizations, but these calls are reduced if the pups are placed in a warm environment (Blumberg et al., 1992). Distress calls can be induced by a variety of aversive treatments, including novelty, handling, and administering electric currents. In turn, mothers reunited with pups exposed to these treatments show high levels of plasma corticosterone (Smotherman et al., 1977). Thus, rat mothers and pups respond adequately to different levels of distress in the absence of individual recognition. Rats and other species of mammals with similar mother–infant bonds do not meet the criteria for attachment.

In other mammals, there is evidence that at least the mother recognizes her offspring individually. For example, sheep can discriminate the odor of their own lamb from that of others (Kendrick et al., 1992), and northern elephant seals (*Mirounga angustirostris*) recognize their infants on the basis of the infant's vocalizations (Petrinovich, 1974).

7.4.2 Attachment in primates

The most extensive evidence of attachment comes from the study of the mother–infant bond in primates. For example, squirrel monkey mothers (*Saimiri sciureus*) recognize their own offspring and prefer them to other infants, including familiar alien infants (Rosenblum, 1968), and infants also recognize their mother and discriminate her from other females (Kaplan & Russell, 1974).

Additional studies suggest that the aversive response of mothers and infants to short separation is specific to the pair and is not spared by the presence of familiar group members. Separation-induced stress can be measured in terms of plasma concentrations of ***corticosteroid hormones*** (e.g., corticosterone in rodents, cortisol in primates). These hormones reflect the degree of activation of the ***hypothalamic-pituitary-adrenal axis***, a neuroendocrine system involved in the organism's response to aversive situations. In squirrel monkeys (Figure 7.8), mother–infant separation elevates cortisol levels in both mother and infant, even in the presence of a late-term female that could provide care in the absence of the mother (Coe et al., 1978). High cortisol levels were observed even in infants that received "aunt" care during periods of mother–infant separation, showing that separation-induced stress is specific to the mother's absence.

Separation stress has a significant impact on the organism's general health. In rhesus monkeys (*Macaca mulatta*), maternal separation increases cortisol levels and decreases bacteria normally found in the intestinal flora, such as *Lactobacillus*, that buffer the organism against the proliferation of pathogens like *Salmonella* (Bailey & Coe, 1999). A decrease of the intestinal flora following maternal separation makes the infant rhesus monkey prone to infections by pathogens usually kept at subclinical levels. Social isolation in cebus monkeys (*Cebus apella*) also impairs the immune system, increasing vulnerability to disease (Kling

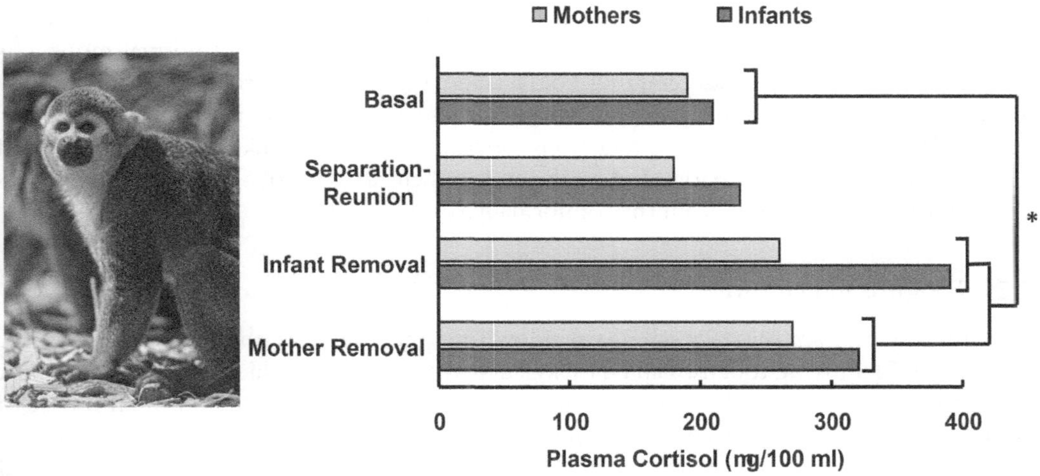

Figure 7.8 **Mother–infant separation in monkeys.** Plasma cortisol levels in infant and mother squirrel monkeys exposed to separation and reunion. The asterisk marks the significant comparisons in plasma cortisol levels. (Coe et al., 1978; reprinted with permission from Elsevier; photo from Creative Commons https://search.creativecommons.org, by Tambako the Jaguar, license CC BY-ND 2.0.)

et al., 1992). Thus, infant primates are under selective pressure to develop and maintain an attachment to their mother.

7.4.3 *Early social restriction*

Rhesus monkeys can also learn an attachment to an artificial object with certain qualities. Infants separated from their mother 6 to 12 h after birth and housed individually exhibited a strong attachment to a blanket used to cover the wire floor of the cage, reacting violently when the blanket was removed from the cage (Harlow, 1971). In monkeys, attachment is acquired to an object that provides a certain quality of tactile stimulation. Such *contact comfort* has primary reinforcing value for the infant and also for their mothers (Livingstone, 2022). Attachment is not derived through conditioning by association with the nourishment provided by the mother but through contact comfort with the mother. Thus, infants that could choose between surrogate mothers built with either wire or cloth preferred to be close to the cloth surrogate mother even when the wire mother provided milk. These infants spent enough time with the wire mothers to obtain nourishment and then shifted to the cloth mother for the remaining time (Harlow & Zimmerman, 1959). Moreover, in a fear-inducing situation (the release of a mechanical toy or exposure to a novel place), infants sought contact with the cloth mother. Unlike infants reared with cloth mothers, those raised with wire mothers showed low levels of play and exploratory behavior in such situations.

However, early rearing with the cloth mother affected adult social behavior, so various "therapies" were tried with these infants. Adding rocking movement to the surrogate mother or rearing with a dog led only to a modest improvement in social skills, although dog-reared monkeys were more likely to initiate social interactions, and their social interactions were more complex (Capitanio, 1985). The most successful treatment of socially restricted infant rhesus monkeys was provided by normally reared monkeys called "therapists" (Harlow &

Suomi, 1971). In one study, 6-month-old socially isolated monkeys were permitted to join 3-month-old normally reared monkeys for 2 h per day. A 3-month-old normal monkey is sufficiently mature to provide clinging contact and yet too young to behave aggressively toward socially isolated monkeys. In a few weeks, these monkeys were clinging to each other and displaying vigorous, playful interactions. Socially-restricted monkeys gradually stopped displaying maladaptive behaviors, and by the end of their first year of age, their behavior was essentially indistinguishable from that of normally reared monkeys.

7.5 Tool use and culture

The study of ***tool-use behavior*** offers a window into the cognitive abilities of animals (see Chapter 8). Identifying tool use can be tricky, such as a situation in which a horse rubs against a tree to scratch an itch. However, genuine tool use requires manipulation of an object to achieve a specific end (e.g., to procure otherwise inaccessible food). The horse is not manipulating the tree, so this would not qualify as tool use. A chimpanzee picking up a stick and inserting it into a hole to retrieve termites would qualify. The components of this behavior are constrained by their common goal.

Among apes, chimpanzees (*Pan troglodytes*) are known for their use of tools to procure resources. As mentioned, adults feed on termites collected with twigs they insert into the termite nest, they select stronger sticks to extract the marrow from the bones of dead animals, and they use leaves as sponges to drink water. In some cases, male chimpanzees tear up leaves to attract females as part of a courtship display. Some of these behaviors are typical of specific populations of chimpanzees rather than of the species, a fact suggesting local culture.

A ***culture*** can be defined as a set of standardized practices acquired or developed by one or a few innovators that spread to other group members and are passed across generations via social learning. This definition of culture, not universally accepted, is applicable to nonhuman animals because it makes no reference to language. The feeding behavior of chimpanzees provides an indication of their potential to develop culture (Whiten et al., 2005). In fact, when two high-ranking adult female chimpanzees were taught one of two methods for retrieving food using a stick and returned to their separate groups, 81% of the observer chimpanzees adopted the method taught to the demonstrator. Two months later, 84% of chimpanzees were still using the same method despite the presence of the other method used by a minority of chimpanzees in the population. In the wild, 10 different chimpanzee communities can be distinguished based on the unique method by which they fish for termites (Boesch et al., 2020).

Consider the range of possible relationships between chimpanzees and oil palm nuts (McGrew, 1992). Chimpanzees live in several groups located in the rainforests of central and western Africa (Figure 7.9). In some populations of Senegal (West Africa), chimpanzees live in habitats where there are no oil palm nuts available, suggesting that these are not indispensable for their survival. In Kasoje, Tanzania (Central Africa), there are oil palm nuts, and they are readily consumed by monkeys and pigs, but chimpanzees ignore them. At Gombe, also in Tanzania, chimpanzees eat just the outer pulp of the nut, discarding the kernel. But at Bossou, Guinea (West Africa), chimpanzees access the kernel by cracking the nut with a pair of stones—a hammer and an anvil. Although other species have been observed to use stones as either hammers (Egyptian vultures crack ostrich eggs by throwing a stone) or anvils (California sea otters smash mollusk shells against a rock held in their belly while floating on the water), only primates have been observed to use both hammer and anvil in conjunction. The use of stone tools to open oil palm nuts at Bossou sets that population apart from others and raises the question of the ontogenetic origin of such practices.

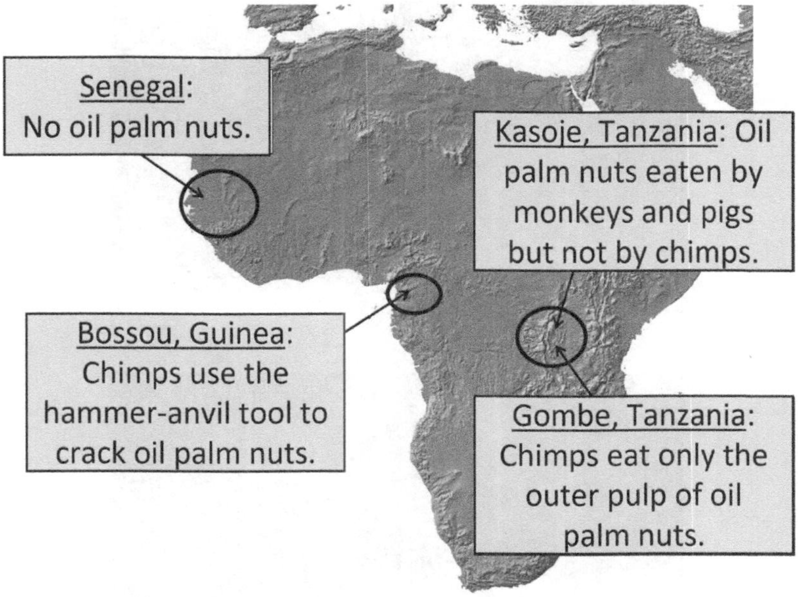

Figure 7.9 **Differences in tool use among populations of chimpanzees.** Different populations of chimpanzees are currently geographically isolated. As far as the hammer–anvil tool, there are important differences across populations that have been attributed to cultural factors—practices passed across generations by social learning. (Map from Creative Commons, www.creativecommons.com, by Newport Geographic, license CC BY 2.0.)

Bossou chimpanzees younger than 3.5 years do not crack nuts with the ***hammer–anvil tool*** but frequently manipulate nuts and stones (Inoue-Nakamura & Matsuzawa, 1997). Since the hammer–anvil practice generally develops in a social setting, it is widely believed that social learning plays a major role in its acquisition (Figure 7.10). Six-month-old chimpanzees do not engage in any type of prerequisite behavior in isolation but only when accompanied by adult members of the group. Mothers are an important source of information for the young, but the skill usually develops even in infants whose mothers do not crack nuts. This suggests that other group members can provide information about this practice.

Five basic individual actions have been identified in the hammer–anvil skill, and their integration into a single repertoire occurs gradually during the first 3.5 years of age. The individual acts are "take or pick," "put," "hold," "hit," and "eat." A 2.5-year-old would often put a nut on a stone, hit it with its hand, and then turn toward its mother and eat a kernel from a nut she had cracked before. At this age, then, the behavioral components are present, but they are not organized into a functional sequence. Figure 7.11 depicts the developmental progression of the hammer–anvil practice in terms of transitions between these five basic behaviors. Not only do certain transitions change in strength (represented by arrow thickness), but also some emerge with experience. At 3.5 years of age, these actions are interconnected in a reciprocal manner.

In addition to chimpanzees, there is evidence for tool use that has been trained or has been spontaneously observed in the wild in bottlenose dolphins, corvids (rooks, ravens, and crows), elephants, and some marine invertebrates (e.g., *Amphioctopus marginatus)*. Tool use, combined with other habitat specializations, has led to populations with characteristic genetic

Figure 7.10 **Learning the use of a tool.** A young chimpanzee cracking an oil palm nut at Bossou, Guinea, by using the hammer–anvil stone tool. (From Matsuzawa et al., 2011; Photo courtesy of Tetsuro Matsuzawa.)

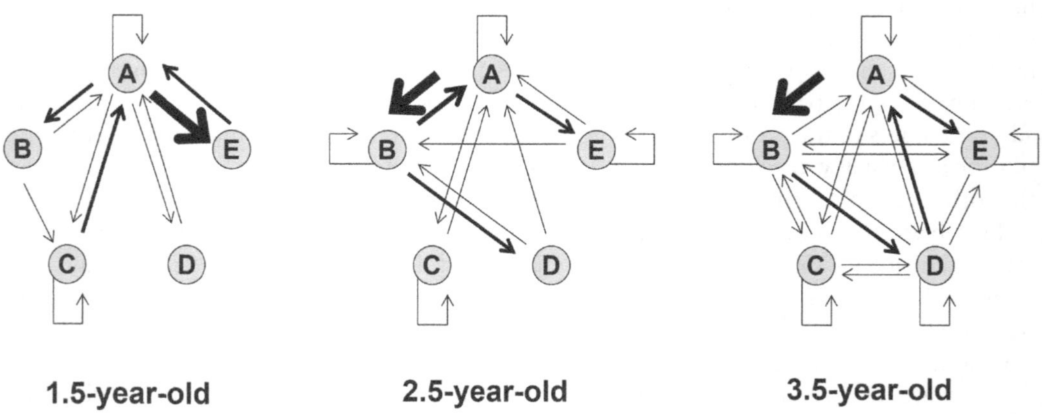

Figure 7.11 **Development of hammer–anvil tool use in young chimpanzees**. Five basic behaviors are plotted in these diagrams: (A) "take or pick," (B) "put," (C) "hold," (D) "hit," (E) "eat." Arrows represent the tendency for one act to be followed by the other or by itself, whereas the thickness of the arrow represents the statistical strength of that sequential tendency. Notice that at 1.5 years of age all the basic behaviors required for the use of this stone tool are present, but certain transitions do not occur. At 3.5 years of age, all the transitions occur, and the behavior emerges in the animal's repertoire. (From Inoue-Nakamura & Matsuzawa, 1997; reproduced by permission from the American Psychological Association).

structures (e.g., in terms of mitochondrial DNA) within bottlenose dolphins in western Shark Bay, Australia (Kopps et al., 2014). Some of these dolphins use a particular foraging strategy involving sponges as tools in deep water.

In addition to cases that match well the definition of tool use given here, it is worth noting other cases that are less clear. For example, a chimpanzee that spits water into a tube to displace a nut to a reachable height is likely using the water as a tool. However, is the same true for archer fish that spit water to dislodge prey from a nearby twig or leaf? Bonobos have been observed to throw rocks at predators, which could be referred to as a form of tool use. However, ant lions throw sand at potential prey to increase the likelihood of capture. Both examples of less well-defined tool use involve a reflex component, but that should not entirely preclude their inclusion as tool users. Rooks have been reported to spontaneously bend and use twigs to retrieve hidden food (Bird & Emery, 2009; Seed et al., 2009), yet their behavior is frequently referred to as tool use. If species-typical behaviors are not precluded from being classified as tool use, then there is evidence for cultural transmission in nesting behavior (Tello-Ramos et al., 2024). These cases highlight the fact that examples of tool use are not always as clear-cut as one would expect.

How does an infant learn to use a tool? The development of tool use has also been studied in human infants (Connolly & Dalgleish, 1989). For example, in the emergence of spoon use practices in 11- and 17-month-old infants, prerequisite actions such as "put spoon in dish and remove it" or "put spoon in mouth and remove it" are initially functionally inefficient. While one hand may be engaged in these actions, the other may be used to pick up food from the dish. Only later do these two actions become integrated in a larger sequence. Additional practice is required before correction loops are incorporated into this sequence (e.g., check to see if there is enough food in the spoon before putting it into the mouth).

7.6 Teaching

Learning the sequence of actions required to use a tool is remarkably similar in human children and infant chimpanzees, but there are some interesting differences. For example, human mothers play a more active teaching role than do chimpanzee mothers, providing verbal instructions, molding the infant's behavior, and reinforcing appropriate responses with social praise. By contrast, infant chimpanzees are provided no obvious source of feedback for their actions by their mother or other adults. Observations like this led some to argue that teaching behavior was unique to humans. But this view has been challenged by evidence suggesting the presence of teaching behavior in some nonhuman animals.

In *teaching behavior*, an experienced individual actively facilitates the learning of new information or a new skill by a naïve individual. In teaching interactions, the teacher may incur some cost, even if small, whereas the benefit to the learner should be greater than the benefit it would accrue by acquiring the information or skill by its own experience (Caro & Hauser, 1992).

There is some evidence of teaching in primates. For example, in some primates, mothers actively encourage infants to learn motor skills, such as independent locomotion (Maestripieri, 1995). In Goulougo, Republic of Congo, in Central Africa, chimpanzees have been observed to actively encourage young chimpanzees to learn to pick up termites by using twigs. Teachers have been observed to provide learners with twigs prepared for collecting termites from their nests. Learners use these twigs in the presence of teachers. These interactions reduce the feeding of teachers, who therefore incur a cost for teaching, but they greatly benefit learners by leading to significant improvement of their feeding behavior (Musgrave et al., 2016).

Teaching may be encouraged by the relatively complex behavior of termite gathering in these chimpanzees. Only twigs from certain plants are selected for use, and they are actively modified to adapt them for collecting termites in nests that are either above ground or subterranean. Experienced chimpanzees would use special twigs to open the entrance to termite nests but herbaceous twigs to pick up termites deep in the nest. Typically, these teaching events occur between a mother and her infant offspring. Teaching behavior between two adults is rarely observed in these chimpanzees.

Evidence consistent with active teaching behavior is not restricted to primates. An interesting example is provided by meerkats (*Suricata suricatta*), a carnivore mammal. Mothers provide their infants with opportunities to handle scorpions, a typical prey for meerkats, but their prey-provisioning method changes as the infants acquire the skill (Thornton & McAuliffe, 2006). The mother may remove the sting from a scorpion or even provide a dead prey to the infant, but prey would be more likely to be provided live and intact for older infants. Following prey provision, the mother will remain observing the infant's handling of the prey for a longer period if the prey was moving or large (Thornton, 2008).

Although several proposed examples of teaching behavior in nonhuman animals have been published involving ants, birds, and primates, there is still controversy about the definition of teaching and the interpretation of these results. Some claim that none of the examples reviewed previously meet the criteria advanced by Caro and Hauser (1992) and that a more integrative framework is needed to understand the evolution of teaching behavior in both human and nonhuman animals (Kline, 2015).

Glossary

Alarm reaction Defensive behavior induced by substances (e.g., pheromones) released by damaged tissue.

Attachment Mother–infant bond involving individual recognition, a preference for the attached organism, and an aversive response to separation.

Blind imitation An observer copying a response without reference to the consequences of the response.

Classical conditioning theory of imprinting A theory of imprinting based on the principles of classical or Pavlovian conditioning. The CS are static features of the imprinting object and the US are salient features, such as movement.

Contact comfort Touch among animals, particularly in primates, that provides an important source of information for the development of attachments.

Corticosteroid hormones A class of hormones secreted by the adrenal gland during exposure to emotionally stressful events.

Counterconditioning Pavlovian procedure involving the pairing of two stimuli with opposite hedonic value (e.g., shock→food). If successful, the first stimulus comes to evoke a response different from the unconditioned response originally elicited (e.g., shock comes to evoke salivation).

Cross-fostering design Some infants in a litter are moved to a foster litter while others are left in the original litter. A design aiming at detecting the contributions of maternal behavior to the development of a specific behavior in the infant.

Culture The spread of a behavior in a group via social learning. As defined here, culture is not dependent upon human language.

Distress vocalizations Vocalizations induced by aversive stimuli, particularly in young animals.

Dithering behavior Directing courtship and social behaviors to members of more than one species.

Embryonic experience Events that affect the animal and that occur during embryonic development.

Emulation Similar to imitation, except that the demonstrator's and the observer's responses do not match precisely, but they both lead to the same outcome.

Following response In filial imprinting, the behavior of the imprinted chick of following the maternal object, whether its biological parent or an artificial substitute.

Hammer–anvil tool This tool is used by some chimpanzees to crack hard nuts and feed on the kernel. A stone or stick is used as a hammer and another stone or wood is used as an anvil.
Hypothalamic-pituitary-adrenal axis Structures linked through the action of hormones that participate in the organism's response to emotionally arousing situations.
Imitation The observer copies a response emitted by the demonstrator more or less precisely.
Imprinting, chemical The establishment of a preference for the place where an organism spent the early period of its development based on chemical cues present in that location.
Imprinting, double sexual Sexual imprinting to more than one species.
Imprinting, filial A learning process wherein a young bird learns to recognize its mother.
Imprinting, geomagnetic Acquiring the magnetic signature of the early environment that can later be used to locate that place during a breeding season.
Imprinting, maternal A mother that develops a bond with her newborn.
Imprinting, secondary Development of a second attachment.
Imprinting, sexual In some species, early social experience that affects species recognition in the adult.
Individual recognition The ability to distinguish a particular animal from other conspecifics.
Intermediate-medial mesopallium (IMM) An area of the avian telencephalon involved in learning (formerly known as IMHV).
Kin recognition Ability to identify close relatives.
Latent learning Acquired information that remains unexpressed during a temporal gap between the acquisition of information and its behavioral expression.
Local enhancement Observing a salient stimulus led the observer to pay special attention to the setting.
Long-term potentiation A neural phenomenon involving the strengthening of specific synapses resulting from high-frequency stimulation.
Master–yoked design A design that equates the number and frequency of reinforcements across two groups, allowing one of the groups (master) to have behavioral control over the occurrence of the reinforcer while the other (yoked) has no such control.
Mobbing Antipredator behavior displayed by a group of potential prey that tends to discourage the predator from attempting an attack.
NMDA receptors A type of excitatory glutamate receptor. When associated with AMPA receptors in the same synapses, NMDA receptors respond to glutamate only when the neuron is also activated. The activation of NMDA receptors initiates a cellular cascade that can lead to the synthesis of new AMPA receptors, thus facilitating synaptic transmission. This process is involved in conditioning.
Omission training A training procedure in which the occurrence of the response prevents the presentation of a reinforcer. The reinforcer is presented provided that a response has not occurred during a stipulated interval.
Perceptual learning Acquisition of information by mere exposure.
Predator recognition Learning to recognize a potential predator by experience.
Sensitive (or critical) period The classic notion of "critical period" was replaced by sensitive period. It refers to a period during early development when some brain circuits are especially susceptible to experience.
Social facilitation The mere presence of an animal attracts the observer to the location.
Social learning Interactions between organisms (usually of the same species) that produce changes in behavior in at least one of them.
Social reinforcement Behavior influenced by the response of conspecifics. Examples include verbal praise in humans or attention of an offspring in distress by a mammalian mother.
Teaching behavior A situation in which an experienced animal (teacher) facilitates the acquisition of information or a skill in a naïve animal (pupil).
Tool-use behavior Behavior of using an object selected to facilitate access to a resource that is otherwise inaccessible.
Two-action method A procedure used to study imitation in which different groups of observers are exposed to demonstrators that achieve an outcome by performing responses that differed in topography, such as pressing a lever to obtain food by either stepping or pecking at it. Ideally, the observers will imitate the response topography they had observed.
Ventral tegmental area (VTA) A brainstem nucleus that originates the dopaminergic reward system of the brain. VTA neurons project to several regions, especially the nucleus accumbens and the prefrontal cortex.

Vicarious reinforcement An observer acquires a new response after observing a demonstrator obtain an outcome for performing a specific response.
Within-compound associations Associations among the elements of a compound stimulus.

References

Ainsworth, M. D. S. (1972). Attachment and dependency: A comparison. In J. L. Gewirtz (Ed.), *Attachment and dependency* (pp. 97–137). Winston & Sons.

Alem, S., Perry, C. J., Zhu, X., Loukola, O. J., Ingraham, T., Søvik, E., & Chittka, L. (2016). Associative mechanisms allow for social learning and cultural transmission of string pulling in an insect. *PLoS Biology*, *14*, e1002564. https://doi.org/10.1371/journal.pbio.1002564

Bailey, M. T., & Coe, C. L. (1999). Maternal separation disrupts the integrity of the intestinal microflora in infant rhesus monkeys. *Developmental Psychobiology*, *35*, 146–155. https://doi.org/10.1002/(SICI)1098-2302(199909)35:2<146::AID-DEV7>3.0.CO;2-G

Bandura, A., & Walters, R. H. (1963). *Social learning and personality development*. Holt, Rinehart, & Winston.

Bird, C. D., & Emery, N. J. (2009). Insightful problem solving and creative tool modification by captive nontool-using rooks. *Proceedings of the National Academy of Sciences, USA*, *106*(25), 10370–10375. https://doi.org/10.1073/pnas.0901008106

Bischof, H. J., Geißler, E., & Rollenhagen, A. (2002). Limitations of the sensitive period for sexual imprinting: Neuroanatomical and behavioral experiments in the zebra finch (*Taeniopygia guttata*). *Behavioural Brain Research*, *133*, 317–322. https://doi.org/10.1016/s0166-4328(02)00016-5

Blumberg, M. S., Efimova, I. V., & Alberts, J. R. (1992). Ultrasonic vocalizations by rat pups: The primary importance of ambient temperature and the thermal significance of contact comfort. *Developmental Psychobiology*, *25*, 229–250. https://doi.org/10.1002/dev.420250402

Boakes, R. A., & Panter, D. (1985). Secondary imprinting in the domestic chick blocked by previous exposure to a live hen. *Animal Behaviour*, *33*, 353–365. https://doi.org/10.1016/S0003-3472(85)80059-2

Boesch, C., Kalan, A. K., Mundry, R., Arandjelovic, M., Pika, S., Dieguez, P., Ayimisin, E. A., Barciela, A., Coupland, C., Egbe, V. E., Eno-Nku, M., Fay, M. J., Fine, D., Hernandez-Aguilar, A. R., Hermans, V., Kadam, P., Kambi, M., Llana, M., Maretti, G., . . . Kühl, H. S. (2020). Chimpanzee ethnography reveals unexpected cultural diversity. *Nature Human Behavior*, *4*(9), 910–916. https://doi.org/10.1038/s41562-020-0890-1

Bolhuis, J. J., & Honey, R. C. (1994). Within-event learning during filial imprinting. *Journal of Experimental Psychology: Animal Behavior Processes*, *20*, 240–248. https://doi.org/10.1037/0097-7403.20.3.240

Bolhuis, J. J., Johnson, M., Horn, G., & Bateson, P. P. G. (1989). Long-lasting effects of IMHV lesions on social preferences in domestic fowl. *Behavioral Neuroscience*, *103*, 438–441. https://doi.org/10.1037/0735-7044.103.2.438

Boysen, S. T., & Berntson, G. G. (1989). Conspecific recognition in the chimpanzee (*Pan troglodytes*): Cardiac responses to significant others. *Journal of Comparative Psychology*, *103*, 215–220. https://doi.org/10.1037/0735-7036.103.3.215

Brock, J., Wolf, A., & Braun, K. (1996). Influence of the N-methyl-D-aspartate receptor antagonist DL-2-amino-5-phosphonovaleric acid on auditory filial imprinting in the domestic chick. *Neurobiology of Learning and Memory*, *65*, 177–188. https://doi.org/10.1006/nlme.1996.0019

Brown, S. D., & Dooling, R. J. (1992). Perception of conspecific faces by budgerigars (*Melopsittacus undulatus*): I. Natural faces. *Journal of Comparative Psychology*, *106*, 203–216. https://doi.org/10.1037/0735-7036.106.3.203

Brown, S. D., & Dooling, R. J. (1993). Perception of conspecific faces by budgerigars (Melopsittacus undulatus): II. Synthetic models. Journal of Comparative Psychology, *107*(1), 48–60. https://doi.org/10.1037/0735-7036.107.1.48

Capitanio, J. P. (1985). Early experience and social processes in rhesus macaques (*Macaca mulatta*): II. Complex social interaction. *Journal of Comparative Psychology*, *99*, 133–144. https://doi.org/10.1037/0735-7036.99.2.133

Caro, T. M., & Hauser, M. D. (1992). Is there teaching in nonhuman animals? *Quarterly Review of Biology*, *67*, 151–174. https://doi.org/10. 1086/417553

Coe, C. L., Mendoza, S. P., Smotherman, W. P., & Levine, S. (1978). Mother-infant attachment in the squirrel monkey: Adrenal response to separation. *Behavioral Biology*, *22*, 256–263. https://doi.org/10.1016/S0091-6773(78)92305-2

Connolly, K., & Dalgleish, M. (1989). The emergence of a tool-using skill in infancy. *Developmental Psychology*, *25*(6), 894–912. https://doi.org/10.1037/0012-1649.25.6.894

Curio, E., Ernest, U., & Vieth, W. (1978). Cultural transmission of enemy recognition: One function of mobbing. *Science*, *202*, 899–901. https://doi.org/10.1126/science.202.4370.899

Curry, R. L., & Grant, P. R. (1990). Galapagos mockingbirds: Territorial cooperative breeding in a climatically variable environment. In P. B. Stacey & W. D. Koenig (Eds.), *Cooperative breeding in birds: Long-term studies of ecology and behavior* (pp. 291–331). Cambridge University Press.

DePaulo, P., & Hoffman, H. S. (1981). Reinforcement by an imprinting stimulus versus water on simple schedules in ducklings. *Journal of the Experimental Analysis of Behavior*, *36*, 151–169. https://doi.org/10.1901/jeab.1981.36-151

Domjan, M., Blesbois, E., & Williams, J. (1998). The adaptive significance of sexual conditioning: Pavlovian control of sperm release. *Psychological Science*, *9*, 411–415. https://doi.org/10.1111/1467-9280.00077

Eiserer, L. A. (1980a). Development of filial attachment to static visual features of an imprinting object. *Animal Learning and Behavior*, *8*, 159–166. https://doi.org/10.3758/BF03209744

Eiserer, L. A. (1980b). Long-term potential for imprinting in ducks and chickens. *Journal of the Experimental Analysis of Behavior*, *33*, 383–395. https://doi.org/10.1901/jeab.1980.33-383

Eiserer, L. A., & Swope, R. L. (1980). Acquisition of behavioral control by static visual features of an imprinting object: Species generality. *Animal Learning and Behavior*, *8*, 481–484. https://doi.org/10.3758/BF03199637

Galef, B. G., Jr., Dudley, K. E., & Whiskin, E. E. (2008). Social learning of food preferences in "dissatisfied" and "uncertain" Norway rats. *Animal Behaviour*, *7*, 631–637. https://doi.org/10.1016/j.anbehav.2007.06.024

Galef, B. G., Jr., Iliffe, C. P., & Whiskin, E. E. (1994). Social influences on rats' (*Rattus norvegicus*) preferences for flavored foods, scented nest materials, and odors associated with harborage sites: Are flavored foods special? *Journal of Comparative Psychology*, *108*, 266–273. https://doi.org/10.1037/0735-7036.108.3.266

Gottlieb, G. (1978). Development of species identification in ducklings. IV. Change in species-specific perception caused by auditory deprivation. *Journal of Comparative and Physiological Psychology*, *92*, 375–387. https://doi.org/10.1037/h0077473

Griffin, A. S. (2004). Social learning about predators: A review and prospectus. *Learning and Behavior*, *32*, 131–140. https://doi.org/10.3758/BF03196014

Gubernick, D. J. (1980). Maternal "imprinting" or maternal "labelling" in goats? *Animal Behaviour*, *28*, 124–129. https://doi.org/10.1016/S0003-3472(80)80016-9

Gubernick, D. J., Jones, K. C., & Klopfer, P. H. (1979). Maternal "imprinting" in goats? *Animal Behaviour*, *27*, 314–315. https://doi.org/10.1016/0003-3472(79)90157-X

Gutiérrez, G., & Domjan, M. (1996). Learning and male-male sexual competition in Japanese quail (*Coturnix japonica*). *Journal of Comparative Psychology*, *110*, 170–175. https://doi.org/10.1037/0735-7036.110.2.170

Harlow, H. F. (1971). *Learning to love*. Albion Press.

Harlow, H. F., & Suomi, S. J. (1971). Social recovery by isolation-reared monkeys. *Proceedings of the National Academy of Sciences, USA*, *68*, 1534–1538. https://doi.org/10.1073/pnas.68.7.1534

Harlow, H. F., & Zimmerman, R. R. (1959). Affectional responses in the infant monkey. *Science*, *130*, 421–432. https://doi.org/10.1126/science.130.3373.421

Hikami, K., Hasegawa, Y., & Matsuzawa, T. (1990). Social transmission of food preferences in Japanese monkeys (*Macaca fuscata*) after mere exposure or aversion training. *Journal of Comparative Psychology*, *104*, 233–237. https://doi.org/10.1037/0735-7036.104.3.233

Hoffman, H. S. (1987). Imprinting and the critical period for social attachments: Some laboratory investigations. In M. H. Bornstein (Ed.), *Sensitive periods in development* (pp. 99–121). Erlbaum.

Hoffman, H. S., Eiserer, L. A., & Singer, D. (1972). Acquisition of behavioral control by a stationary imprinting stimulus. *Psychonomic Science*, *26*, 146–148. https://doi.org/10.3758/BF03335462

Hoffman, H. S., & Ratner, A. M. (1973). A reinforcement model of imprinting: Implications for socialization in monkeys and men. *Psychological Review*, *80*, 527–544. https://doi.org/10.1037/h0035533

Hoffman, H. S., Schiff, D., Adams, J., & Searle, J. (1966). Enhanced distress vocalization through selective reinforcement. *Science*, *151*, 352–354. https://www.jstor.org/stable/1717223
Hoffman, H. S., Stratton, J. W., & Newby, V. (1969a). Punishment by response-contingent withdrawal of an imprinting stimulus. *Science*, *163*, 702–704. https://doi.org/10.1126/science.163.3868.702
Hoffman, H. S., Stratton, J. W., & Newby, V. (1969b). The control of feeding behavior by an imprinted stimulus. *Journal of the Experimental Analysis of Behavior*, *12*, 847–860. https://doi.org/10.1901/jeab.1969.12-847
Hollis, K. L. (1982). Pavlovian conditioning of signal-centered action patterns and autonomic behavior: A biological analysis of function. *Advances in the Study of Behavior*, *12*, 1–64. https://doi.org/10.1016/S0065-3454(08)60045-5
Hollis, K. L., Dumas, M. J., Singh, P., & Fackelman, P. (1995). Pavlovian conditioning of aggressive behavior in blue gourami fish (*Trichogaster trichopterus*): Winners become winners and losers stay losers. *Journal of Comparative Psychology*, *109*, 123–133. https://doi.org/10.1037/0735-7036.109.2.123
Hollis, K. L., Pharr, V. L., Dumas, M. J., Britton, G. B., & Field, J. (1997). Classical conditioning provides paternity advantage for territorial male blue gouramis (*Trichogaster trichopterus*). *Journal of Comparative Psychology*, *111*, 219–225. https://doi.org/10.1037/0735-7036.111.3.219
Horn, G. (1991). Cerebral function and behaviour investigated through a study of filial imprinting. In P. Bateson (Ed.), *The development and integration of behaviour: Essays in honour of Robert Hinde* (pp. 121–148). Cambridge University Press.
Horn, G., Bradley, P., & McCabe, B. J. (1985). Changes in the structure of synapses associated with learning. *Journal of Neuroscience*, *5*, 3161–3168. https://doi.org/10.1523/JNEUROSCI.05-12-03161.1985
Immelmann, K. (1972). Sexual and other long-term aspects of imprinting in birds and other species. *Advances in the Study of Behavior*, *4*, 147–174. https://doi.org/10.1016/S0065-3454(08)60009-1
Inoue-Nakamura, N., & Matsuzawa, T. (1997). Development of stone tool use by wild chimpanzees (*Pan troglodytes*). *Journal of Comparative Psychology*, *111*(2), 159–173. https://doi.org/10.1037/0735-7036.111.2.159
Johnson, M. H., & Horn, G. (1988). Development of filial preferences in dark-reared chicks. *Animal Behaviour*, *36*, 675–683. https://doi.org/10.1016/S0003-3472(88)80150-7
Junco, F. (1988). Filial imprinting in an altricial bird: The blackbird (*Turdus merula*). *Behaviour*, *106*, 25–42. https://doi.org/10.1163/156853988X00070
Junco, F. (1993). Acquisition of a filial preference in an altricial bird without food reinforcement. *Animal Behaviour*, *46*, 1237–1239. https://doi.org/10.1006/anbe.1993.1318
Kaplan, J., & Russell, M. (1974). Olfactory recognition in the infant squirrel monkey. *Developmental Psychobiology*, *7*, 15–19. https://doi.org/10.1002/dev.420070104
Kendrick, K. M., Levy, F., & Keverne, E. G. (1992). Changes in the sensory processing of olfactory signals induced by birth in sheep. *Science*, *256*, 833–836. https://doi.org/10.1126/science.1589766
Kline, M. A. (2015). How to learn about teaching: An evolutionary framework for the study of teaching behavior in humans and other animals. *Behavioral and Brain Sciences*, *38*, e31. https://doi.org/10.1017/S0140525X14000090
Kling, A., Lloyd, R., Tachiki, K., Prince, H., Klimenko, V., & Korneva, E. (1992). Effects of social separation on immune function and brain neurotransmitters in cebus monkey (*C. apella*). *Annals of the New York Academy of Sciences*, *650*, 257–261. https://doi.org/10.1111/j.1749-6632.1992.tb49133.x
Kopps, A. M., Ackermann, C. Y., Sherwin, W. B., Allen, S. J., Bejder, L., & Krützen, M. (2014). Cultural transmission of tool use combined with habitat specializations leads to fine-scale genetic structure in bottlenose dolphins. *Proceedings of the Royal Society: Biological Sciences*, *281*(1782), 20133245. https://doi.org/10.1098/rspb.2013.3245
Leon, M. (1975). Dietary control of maternal pheromone in the lactating rat. *Physiology and Behavior*, *14*, 311–319. https://doi.org/10.1016/0031-9384(75)90039-6
Livingstone, M. S. (2022). Triggers for mother love. *Proceedings of the National Academy of Science USA*, *119*, e2212224119. https://doi.org/10.1073/pnas.2212224119
Lohmann, K. J., Putman, N. F., & Lohmann, C. M. F. (2008). Geomagnetic imprinting: A unifying hypothesis of long-distance natal homing in salmon and sea turtles. *Proceedings of the National Academy of Sciences USA*, *105*, 19096–19101. https://doi.org/10.1073/pnas.0801859105
Maestripieri, D. (1995). Maternal encouragement in nonhuman primates and the question of animal teaching. *Human Nature*, *6*, 361–378. https://doi.org/10.1007/BF02734206

Mateo, J. M. (2017). The ontogeny of kin-recognition mechanisms in Belding's ground squirrels. *Physiology and Behavior, 173*, 279–284. https://doi.org/10.1016/j.physbeh.2017.02.024
Matsuzawa, T., Humle, T., & Sugiyama, Y. (Eds.). (2011). *The chimpanzees of Bossou and Nimba*. Springer Science + Business Media. https://doi.org/10.1007/978-4-431-53921-6
McCabe, B. J. (2019). Visual imprinting in birds: Behavior, models, and neural mechanisms. *Frontiers in Physiology, 10*, 658. https://doi.org/10.3389/fphys.2019.00658
McCabe, B. J., Cipolla-Neto, J., Horn, G., & Bateson, P. P. G. (1982). Amnesic effects of bilateral lesions placed in the hyperstriatum ventral of the chick after imprinting. *Experimental Brain Research, 48*, 13–21. https://doi.org/10.1007/BF00239568
McCabe, B. J., & Horn, G. (1988). Learning and memory: Regional changes in N-methyl-D-aspartate receptors in the chick brain after imprinting. *Proceedings of the National Academy of Sciences, USA, 85*, 2849–2853. https://doi.org/10.1073/pnas.85.8.2849
McCabe, B. J., Horn, G., & Bateson, P. P. G. (1981). Effects of restricted lesions of the chick forebrain on the acquisition of filial preferences during imprinting. *Brain Research, 205*, 29–37. https://doi.org/10.1016/0006-8993(81)90717-4
McGregor, A., Saggerson, A., Pearce, J., & Heyes, C. (2006). Blind imitation in pigeons, *Columba livia. Animal Behaviour, 72*, 287–296. https://doi.org/10.1016/j.anbehav.2005.10.026
McGrew, W. C. (1992). *Chimpanzee material culture: Implications for human evolution*. Cambridge University Press.
Michel, G. F., & Tyler, A. N. (2005). Critical period: A history of the transition from questions of when, to what, to how. *Developmental Psychobiology, 46*, 156–162. https://doi.org/10.1002/dev.20058
Moriceau, S., & Sullivan, R. M. (2005). Neurobiology of infant attachment. *Developmental Psychobiology, 47*, 230–242. https://doi.org/10.1002/dev.20093
Moriceau, S., Wilson, D. A., Levine, S., & Sullivan, R. M. (2006). Dual circuitry for odor-shock conditioning during infancy: Corticosterone switches between fear and attraction via amygdala. *Journal of Neuroscience, 26*, 6737–6748. https://doi.org/10.1523/JNEUROSCI.0499-06.2006
Morin, P.-P., Dodson, J. J., & Doré, F. Y. (1989). Cardiac responses to a natural odorant as evidence of a sensitive period for olfactory imprinting in young Atlantic salmon, *Salmo salar. Canadian Journal of Fisheries and Aquatic Sciences, 46*, 122–130. https://doi.org/10.1139/F89-016
Musgrave, S., Morgan, D., Lonsdorf, E., Mundry, R., & Sanz, C. (2016). Tool transfers are a form of teaching among chimpanzees. *Scientific Reports, 6*, 34783. https://doi.org/10.1038/srep34783
Nakamori, T., Maekawa, F., Sato, K., Tanaka, K., & Ohki-Hamazaki, H. (2013). Neural basis of imprinting behavior in chicks. *Development, Growth, and Differentiation, 55*, 198–206. https://doi.org/10.1111/dgd.12028
Nakamori, T., Sato, K., Atoji, Y., Kanamatsu, T., Tanaka, K., & Ohki-Hamazaki, H. (2010). Demonstration of a neural circuit critical for imprinting behavior in chicks. *Journal of Neuroscience, 30*, 4467–4480. https://doi.org/10.1523/JNEUROSCI.3532-09.2010
Panksepp, J., Vilberg, T., Bean, N. J., Coh, D. H., & Kastin, A. J. (1978). Reduction of distress vocalizations in chicks by opiate-like peptides. *Brain Research Bulletin, 3*, 663–667. https://doi.org/10.1016/0361-9230(78)90014-x
Papini, M. R. (2021). *Comparative psychology: Evolution and development of brain and behavior* (3rd ed.). Taylor & Francis.
Parr, L. A., Winslow, J. T., Hopkins, W. D., & de Waal, F. B. (2000). Recognizing facial cues: Individual discrimination by chimpanzees (*Pan troglodytes*) and rhesus monkeys (*Macaca mulatta*). *Journal of Comparative Psychology, 114*, 47–60. https://doi.org/10.1037/0735-7036.114.1.47
Parsons, C. H., & Rogers, L. J. (1997). Pharmacological extension of the sensitive period for imprinting in *Gallus domesticus. Physiology and Behavior, 62*, 1303–1310. https://doi.org/10.1016/S0031-9384(97)00342-9
Pavlov, I. P. (1927). *Conditioned reflexes*. Oxford University Press.
Peterson, N. (1960). Control of behavior by presentation of an imprinted stimulus. *Science, 132*, 1395–1396. https://doi.org/10.1126/science.132.3437.1395
Petrinovich, L. (1974). Individual recognition of pup vocalization by northern elephant seal mothers. *Zeitschrift für Tierpsychologie, 34*, 308–312. https://doi.org/10.1111/j.1439-0310.1974.tb01803.x
Pryce, C. R., Döbeli, M., & Martin, R. D. (1993). Effects of sex steroids on maternal motivation in the common marmoset (*Callithrix jacchus*): Development and application of an operant system with maternal reinforcement. *Journal of Comparative Psychology, 107*, 99–115. https://doi.org/10.1037/0735-7036.107.1.99

Ratner, A. M. (1976). Modification of duckling's filial behavior by aversive stimulation. *Journal of Experimental Psychology: Animal Behavior Processes, 2*, 266–284. https://doi.org/10.1037/0097-7403.2.3.266

Robinson, S. R., & Smotherman, W. P. (1991). Fetal learning: Implications for the development of kin recognition. In P. G. Hepper (Ed.), *Kin recognition* (pp. 308–334). Cambridge University Press.

Rosa-Salva, O., Hernik, M., Broseghini, A., & Vallortigara, G. (2018). Visually-naïve chicks prefer agents that move as if constrained by a bilateral body-plan. *Cognition, 173*, 106–114. https://doi.org/10.1016/j.cognition.2018.01.004

Rosenblum, L. A. (1968). Some aspects of female reproductive physiology in the squirrel monkey. In L. A. Rosenblum & R. W. Cooper (Eds.), *The squirrel monkey* (pp. 147–169). Academic Press.

Salzen, E. A., & Meyer, C. C. (1968). Reversibility of imprinting. *Journal of Comparative and Physiological Psychology, 66*, 269–275. https://doi.org/10.1037/h0026349

Seed, A., Emery, N., & Clayton, N. (2009). Intelligence in corvids and apes: A case of convergent evolution? *Ethology, 115*(5), 401–420. https://doi.org/10.1111/j.1439-0310.2009.01644.x

Skinner, B. F. (1986). The evolution of verbal behavior. *Journal of the Experimental Analysis of Behavior, 45*(1), 115–122. https://doi.org/10.1901/jeab.1986.45-115

Smotherman, W. P., Wiener, S. G., Mendoza, S. P., & Levine, S. (1977). Maternal pituitary-adrenal responsiveness as a function of differential treatment of rat pups. *Developmental Psychobiology, 10*, 113–122. https://doi.org/10.1002/dev.420100204

Solié, C., Girard, B., Righetti, B., Tapparel, M., & Bellone, C. (2022). VTA dopamine neuron activity encodes social interaction and promotes reinforcement learning through social prediction error. *Nature Neuroscience, 25*, 86–97. https://doi.org/10.1038/s41593-021-00972-9

Suboski, M. D., Bain, S., Carty, A. E., McQuoid, L. M., Seelen, M. I., & Seifert, M. (1990). Alarm reaction in acquisition and social transmission of simulated-predator recognition by zebra danio fish (*Brachydanio rerio*). *Journal of Comparative Psychology, 104*, 101–112. https://doi.org/10.1037/0735-7036.104.1.101

Tello-Ramos, M. C., Harper, L., Tortora-Brayda, I., Guillette, L. M., Capilla-Lasheras, P., Harrison, X. A., Young, A. J., & Healy, S. D. (2024). Architectural traditions in the structures built by cooperative weaver birds. *Science, 385*(6712), 1004–1009. https://doi.org/10.1126/science.adn2573

ten Cate, C. (1986). Sexual preferences in zebra finch (*Taeniopygia guttata*) males raised by two species (*Lonchura striata* and *Taeniopygia guttata*): I A case of double imprinting. *Journal of Comparative Psychology, 100*, 3, 248–252. https://doi.org/10.1037/0735-7036.100.3.248

Thornton, A. (2008). Variation in contributions to teaching by meerkats. *Proceedings of the Royal Society, Biological Sciences, 275*(1644), 1745–1751. https://doi.org/10.1098/rspb.2008.0268

Thornton, A., & McAuliffe, K. (2006). Teaching in wild meerkats. *Science, 313*, 227–229. https://doi.org/10.1126/science.1128727

Tomasello, M., Davis-DaSilva, M., Camak, L., & Bard, K. (1987). Observational learning of tool-use by young chimpanzees. *Human Evolution, 2*, 175–183. https://doi.org/10.1007/BF02436405

Ueda, H. (2016). Physiological mechanisms of imprinting and homing migration of Pacific salmon. *Aqua-BioScience Monographs, 9*, 1–27. https://doi.org/10.5047/absm.2016.00901.0001

Vidal, J.-M. (1980). The relations between filial and sexual imprinting in the domestic fowl: Effects of age and social experience. *Animal Behaviour, 28*, 880–891. https://doi.org/10.1016/S0003-3472(80)80148-5

Whiten, A., Horner, V., & De Waal, F. B. (2005). Conformity to cultural norms of tool use in chimpanzees. *Nature, 437*(7059), 737–740. https://doi.org/10.1038/nature04047

Yoerg, S. I. (1991). Social feeding reverses learned flavor aversions in spotted hyenas (*Crocuta crocuta*). *Journal of Comparative Psychology, 105*, 185–189. https://doi.org/10.1037/0735-7036.105.2.185

Zentall, T. R., Sutton, J. E., & Sherburne, L. M. (1996). True imitative learning in pigeons. *Psychological Science, 7*, 343–346. https://doi.org/10.1111/j.1467-9280.1996.tb00386.x

Part III

Cognition

8 Timing behavior

8.1 Introduction: cognition

Cognition has been broadly defined as any mental activity involved in thinking, or in comparative psychology, as the stages of information processing (Beran, 2023). Both definitions are problematic and raise many questions. For example, what is mental activity, what is thinking, what is information, and is information in the world or in us? The latter definition, though having fewer of these problems, does need unpacking. The stages of information processing most commonly referred to are encoding, storage, and retrieval. They are often understood by using a computer metaphor with encoding akin to typing words into a computer via the keyboard, storage to clicking to save the document, and retrieval to opening a saved file. When referring to organisms, these stages require biological and behavioral correlates; however, it is worth noting that some researchers question the notion of distinct processing stages altogether (Jonides et al., 2008; Öztekin et al., 2010).

One popular approach is to connect each stage with distinct circuits or processing pathways. Encoding refers to the circuits or pathways that are more active when a stimulus in the environment is detected (i.e., a biochemical cascade that starts at a receptor) than at other times. A stimulus in the environment must be detected by specialized receptors and transduced into cellular activity. This process is also referred to as *sensation*. *Perception* refers to the convergence of cellular activity from other receptors during detection, including those receptive to other kinds of sensations, as well as any reactivations of cells previously active in the presence of the same or related stimuli.

Animals differ in the kinds of physical stimuli they can detect (e.g., odors vs. light), but they can also differ in the degree to which they can detect the same kind of physical stimulus (e.g., the spectrum of frequencies an organism can hear or wavelengths of light they can see). Encoding provides the opportunity for storage, which refers to the neurobiological processes that occur in cells downstream from the receptor and lead to short-term or long-term changes in and between those cells. Retrieval refers to cue-initiated reactivation of a subset of the cells and synaptic connections that were active during encoding and storage.

Another approach, more in line with the methodology of behaviorism, is to refer to these different stages in terms of what is happening outside of the organism. Encoding refers to the presentation of stimuli, storage refers to a period of time after the presentation of stimuli (during which the stimulus is absent), and retrieval refers to observable changes in behavior when the same or a similar stimulus is delivered after a previous exposure.

This chapter focuses more than previous chapters on changes inside the organism but always with an emphasis on the external events which produce those changes. No matter what definition is used, cognition is directly or indirectly the product of interactions of the

DOI: 10.4324/9781003401957-11

organism with its environment. We have to be careful to use cognitive terms only as labels to aid in how we organize findings, make predictions, and communicate with one another. They should not be used to create hypothetical constructs that replace interactions with the environment as the cause of behavior. For example, the search behavior of rats has been said to result from the formation of a *cognitive map*, a mental representation of space formed as the rats explored their environment. If we accept the cognitive map as the cause of behavior, then we will have learned very little. What are the conditions that lead to a cognitive map? In what ways do rats behave as if they have a map?

Alternatively, Tolman's (1938) concept of the cognitive map as an *intervening variable* was wholly reducible to the empirical relationships that it embraced; outside of these relationships, the intervening variable had no surplus meaning or independent status. It proposes no additional entities or processes that exist inside the animal. If we apply this terminology to Tolman's cognitive map, then the map was purely theoretical in character; it was in his brain but not necessarily in the rat's. We can contrast Tolman's cognitive map with Church's (1978) description of an internal clock that controlled the timing of many learned behaviors in animals. Church's hypothetical construct (*internal clock*) was in his head and in the rat's. Wasserman (1981) emphasized that labeling an intervening variable (i.e., a cognitive map) can be a useful tool for the comparative study of learning and cognition (see Figure 8.1) but cautioned against the use of hypothetical constructs.

The term *learning* is an intervening variable. It doesn't explain behavior, but rather, it describes functional relationships between exposure to external stimuli (e.g., CS and US) and observable changes in behavior (e.g., CR). Cognition refers to stages of information processing, whereas learning refers to functional relationships. These represent different levels of analysis, with cognition looking for causes of behavior inside organisms and learning looking for causes in the interactions between the organism and events outside of organisms.

Given this distinction, you might think it is a bit odd to have a separate set of chapters under the title of "Cognition" in a textbook that has so far concentrated mostly on learning. When we discuss findings in this and in the following chapters that claim a particular behavior is the result of cognition, perhaps the best way to interpret this claim is that behavior has been observed that is not well predicted by the functional relationships between external stimuli and changes in behavior discussed so far (see the psychological mechanistic level in Figure 3.1). When this happens, researchers will often look inside the organism to determine

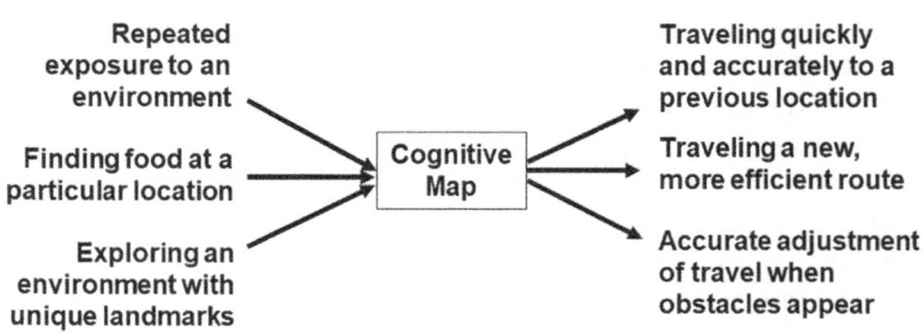

Figure 8.1 **Intervening variables.** An example of a hypothetical construct or intervening variable that organizes the conditions under which certain behaviors are expected. If the cognitive map is a hypothesized entity or process inside the animal, then it represents a hypothetical construct; however, if the term supports investigation of the relations between groupings of empirical observations of conditions and behaviors without adding anything, then it represents an intervening variable.

whether the behavior can be better predicted if we consider differences in how a stimulus is processed (e.g., encoded, stored, and retrieved) within the organism or by stimuli inside the organism (internal) that operate somewhat independently of external events (e.g., a circadian clock).

Many behaviors described in what follows reflect the influence of stimuli that are not immediately obvious to researchers. It is important to remember that for behavior to reflect stimulus control, the probability of its occurrence must vary as a function of the stimuli that are present. This requires that external stimuli be discriminable (e.g., a light paired with a food and a tone paired with nothing), but the same is true for internal stimuli (e.g., the phase of a biological rhythm). A reliance on the use of observable, external stimuli has practical advantages for psychological science; most obviously, external audiovisual stimuli can be precisely controlled (e.g., onset, termination, and intensity) and objectively measured. However, there are instances in which behavior indicates a functional role for cellular activity that is correlated with external events, referred to hereafter as an ***internal stimulus***.

In the present chapter, we will discuss behavior that is controlled not directly by the rise and fall of the sun but by biological rhythms that are synced to this pattern.

For example, humans and other organisms exhibit ***circadian timing***, which consists of behavioral patterns that occur at the same time across an approximately 24-h circadian period (circa, Latin for about, and diem, Latin for a day). Take a moment to think about which of your behaviors occur around the same time every day. How about when you get out of bed, brush your teeth, eat, socialize, exercise, relax, and sleep? You may be thinking, but these behaviors are controlled by a clock, an external stimulus, not some stimulus inside of me.

In the laboratory, we can remove the influence of external stimuli (e.g., clocks) to determine whether these behavioral patterns continue in their absence. Behaviors can be organized around a circadian period, but they often occur based on an estimated interval of time between events. For example, you might need to leave 30 min after your alarm clock wakes you up. This kind of timing behavior operating over a seconds-to-minutes range from the onset of a stimulus is referred to as ***interval timing***. Lastly, it may be that your behavior has to occur in a particular sequence, such as needing to take out the trash before you go to bed. ***Ordinal timing*** refers to behavior that occurs based on the sequence, or order, of events within a time period (Thorpe & Wilkie, 2006).

8.2 Circadian timing

8.2.1 Behavioral evidence

Researchers have asked two main questions with respect to behavior that occurs around the same time every day. Would organisms benefit from circadian behavior? And what conditions would result in control by an internal stimulus like ***circadian rhythms***?

Answering the first question in the affirmative requires little effort. For example, diurnal species would be more likely to locate food and encounter a mate at one time of day than another (e.g., noon rather than at midnight). There are also advantages when biological processes, such as body temperature, hormone release, and gene expression, occur at specific times of the day that anticipate important environmental changes (e.g., the sunrise, Figure 8.2). In fact, Yan et al. (2008) reported that nearly half of all mammalian genes are rhythmically expressed. The rhythmic activity in cells throughout the same tissue (an organ) are more resistant to disruption when they are synchronized to the same phase of a circadian period.

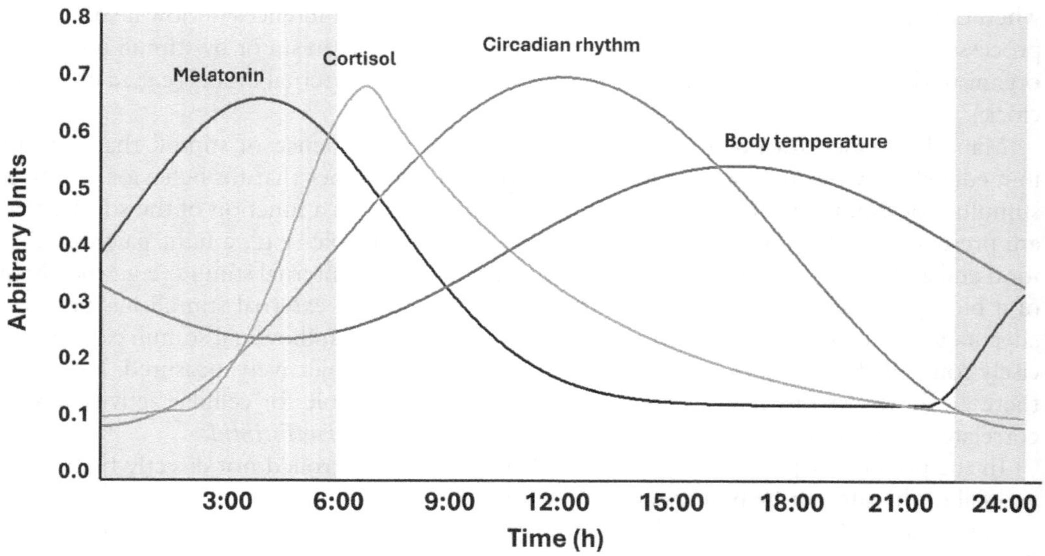

Figure 8.2 **Biological rhythms.** Example circadian rhythms for melatonin, cortisol, and body temperature. In mammals, the timing of these rhythms is synced to a master circadian rhythm. The Y-axis represents arbitrary units of relative activity level.

Furthermore, when a consistent rhythm occurs in each region throughout the central and peripheral nervous systems, then synchronized activity across the entire nervous system is possible. Disruptions in the synchronization of circadian rhythms strongly correlate with the increased incidence of mood disorders in humans and results in depressive-like behaviors in rodents with acute light exposure and anxiety-like behaviors with chronic exposure (Walker et al., 2020). In mammals and birds, a region of the brain that receives input from specialized light-sensitive cells in the retina, called the ***suprachiasmatic nucleus*** (*SCN*), transmits its rhythmic information to cells in other regions. If you are familiar with the movie *Lord of the Rings*, then it might be helpful to remember that the SCN is the "one clock to rule them all."

Regarding the conditions for the development of circadian behaviors, consistency is key. Regularities in the environment permit synchronization of behavior to optimize the probability of success (e.g., finding food). An environmental stimulus that has had a very regular pattern throughout history is the rise and fall of the sun (i.e., a 12-h light and 12-h dark cycle) produced by the rotation of the Earth. By altering variables like light, heat, and humidity, the sun's position has influenced fluctuations in molecular and cellular activity inside organisms, as well as overt behavior, throughout the evolution of organisms. These fluctuations are, in a sense, a representation of the position of the sun. In other words, one could predict the time of day by measuring the activity level of a nocturnal animal (i.e., an increase in overall activity means it is dusk). Similarly, many flowers open and close their leaves or petals at different times of day. This led the Swedish biologist Carolus Linnaeus to design a clock with each hour signaled by a flower that opened and closed at that same time every day, regardless of weather or season (see Figure 8.3; Silver & Rainbow, 2013).

Given the persistent and regular position of the sun, it is no surprise that circadian rhythms have been found in almost all organisms, including fungi, plants, insects, and mammals (Brady et al., 2021), as well as in unicellular organisms (Mergenhagen, 1980) and isolated cells in a

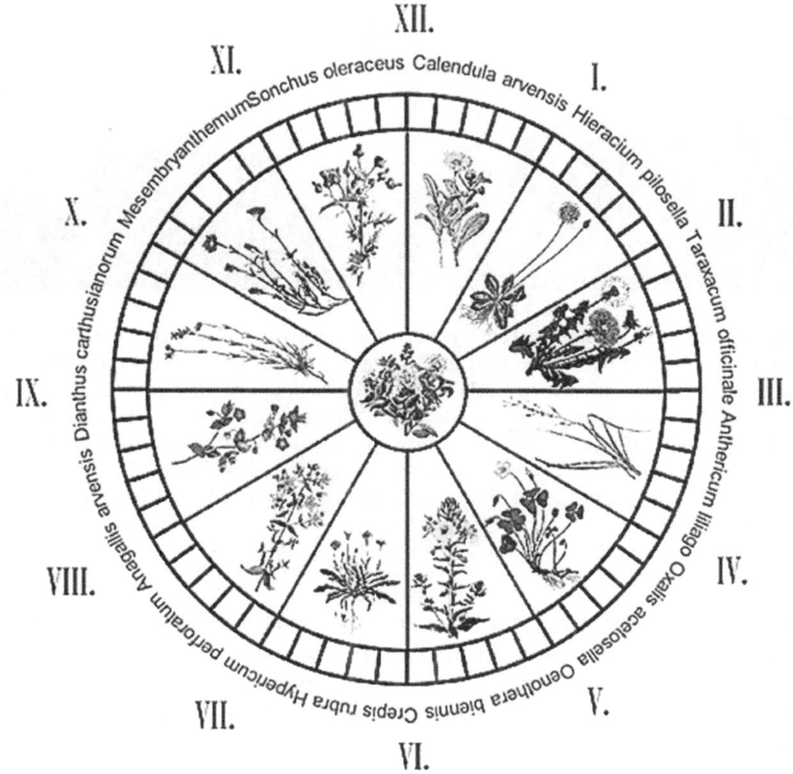

Figure 8.3 **Linnaeus' flower clock.** A representation of a living clock, inspired by Linnaeus' observation that certain flowers open and close their petals at different times of day. (From Creative Commons, www.creativecommons.org, "Linnaeus's flower clock 2" by Kiss Veronika is licensed under CC BY-SA 4.0.)

Petri dish (Welsh et al., 1995). In insects, there is evidence for circadian behavioral rhythms controlling egg hatching, larval feeding, flight, mating, and migration. Regarding foraging, disrupting the circadian rhythm in honeybees alters the direction they fly to find a previously learned-about food source (Gallistel, 1990; Figure 8.4). Honeybees determine the direction of their flight to a previously visited food source relative to the position of the sun, adjusted for the current time of day (i.e., the position of the sun is in constant motion). Their circadian rhythm signals the position of the sun, which is the cue most responsible for their spatial orientation. While the ubiquity of circadian rhythms in organisms might not be surprising, the early development of the SCN and its oscillations in utero in primates might well be. In utero, the neonate's circadian rhythm is synchronized to the mother's SCN (Rivkees, 2007)! After birth, cells in the infant's SCN are not immediately able to synchronize to light. As new parents are well aware, infant behaviors, such as sleep, do not exhibit circadian patterns until about 1 month of age.

One fundamental characteristic of a circadian rhythm is that it occurs with a period close to 24 h in the absence of external cues, known as the free-running period. We say "close to" because free-running circadian rhythms, or those operating in the absence of *zeitgebers*, or external timing cues, occur with a period shorter than 24 h. When zeitgebers are available, such as a consistent light–dark cycle, then the circadian rhythm will synchronize to them

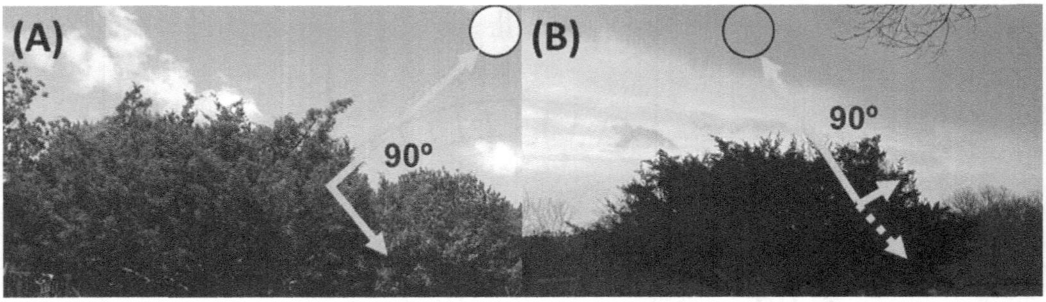

Figure 8.4 **Flight direction compensated by circadian rhythm. (A)** A bee that finds a food source at 10 a.m. will return to the nest and signal the direction of the food relative to the angle between the hive and the sun. **(B)** If the receiver bees are delayed and do not leave the nest for several hours, then traveling the flight direction communicated to them earlier (solid arrow) would provide an erroneous bearing. Even when the sun is obscured and polarized light is scattered, the bees compensate for the current position of the sun based on an internal circadian clock and travel along the adjusted bearing toward the actual location of food (dashed arrow).

through a process called *entrainment*. Rats fed at the same time every day in a consistent light–dark environment will exhibit an increase in activity level an hour or two before the feeding period (Bolles & Moot, 1973). However, it may be that rats are using the onset of light and dark as external cues to search for food. These alternatives must be ruled out.

Remembering back to tests of Pavlovian conditioning (see Chapters 3 and 4), control by a CS can best be assessed on trials that omit the US (i.e., a probe test) after one or more pairings of the CS and US. Similarly, if light onset is directly controlling behavior and not the circadian rhythm, then animals must be tested in conditions in which the light is omitted or is constantly present (e.g., 24 h dark or 24 h light environment). When organisms are tested under these conditions, conditioned behaviors occurring at particular times within a 24-h period continue their pattern with little disruption.

For example, Biebach et al. (1991) trained garden warblers to retrieve food from four grain dispensers located in different rooms, with each dispenser providing food at different times throughout a day but at the same time across days (e.g., Dispenser 1 provided food at 8 a.m. and Dispenser 2 provided food at 11 a.m. every day). Visits to each dispenser continued to occur most often at the appropriate time when the lighting remained constant for 24 h, as opposed to the usual 12-h light–dark cycle.

In addition to cycles of light onset and offset, a zeitgeber can be a consistent time of day you eat, socialize, or exercise. The cycles can occur on a longer time scale, such as circalunar (about 29.5 days) or circannual (about 12 months; Merrow et al., 2005). One concern raised by researchers is that geophysical zeitgebers caused by the Earth's rotation may continue even under constant-lighting laboratory conditions. Experiments conducted with the National Aeronautics and Space Administration (NASA) have revealed that circadian rhythms continued in a fungus tested in space (Sulzman et al., 1984). We can conclude that circadian rhythms can operate as independent internal CSs capable of setting the occasion for conditioned (e.g., foraging) and operant (e.g., lever pressing in rats) responses trained to occur at a particular time of day.

For behavior to occur at the same time of day (i.e., a 24-h period), circadian rhythms require zeitgebers. Biebach et al. (1991) continued to test the garden warblers in constant dim light for several days and found a 1-h shift advance in search times each day (23-h period). A zeitgeber that occurs out of phase (e.g., light that turns on early) will cause an adjustment in the circadian rhythm, but it does not reset it. A 6-h delay in the onset of light caused only a 0.5-h adjustment in the golden warbler's circadian rhythm.

You may be wondering about the effect of other external stimuli, such as an alarm clock, on circadian rhythms. For example, suppose you set your alarm 2 h earlier than usual for an entire week (6 a.m. instead of 8 a.m.), how much will that change your circadian rhythms? Less than you might think; researchers distinguish between rhythms driven endogenously and those driven exogenously. Much of our behavior is entrained to exogenous CSs, like the alarm clock, rather than our endogenous circadian rhythms. This would become most obvious when your schedule returns to normal (along with your alarm clock wake time), and you wake up the next morning around 8 a.m., revealing little effect of the weeklong change in wake time on your endogenous circadian rhythm.

Although feeding behavior has been shown to be synchronized to a circadian clock in many animals, including cockroaches, honeybees, rats, and fruit flies, there are limitations to its accuracy. Crystal (2001) trained hungry rats to retrieve food by breaking a photo beam at the entrance to a feeder. Food was available for different groups of rats at different intervals of time, ranging from every 14 to 24 h with a typical light–dark cycle (Figure 8.5). By plotting the frequency of head entries at the feeder when rats were subsequently tested in constant darkness, Crystal identified that rats were most sensitive to food that was delivered every 24 h, which he referred to as the local maximum in sensitivity. These data indicate that behaviors that occur at a consistent point within a circadian rhythm are most likely to become well synchronized. Imagine again the various behaviors you do throughout the day. If food were to be delivered every morning (24 h) while you were brushing your teeth, you would

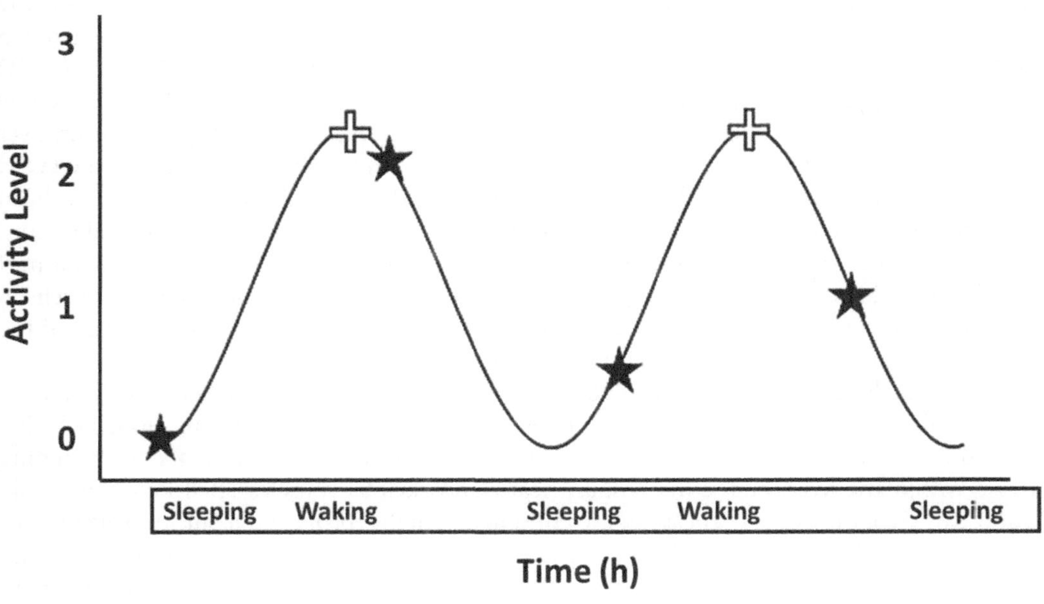

Figure 8.5 **An example of food delivered consistently every 14 (stars) or 24 (plus) h.** The line represents a hypothetical circadian rhythm with a 24-h period. In the 14-h condition, food is delivered at the 0, 14, 28, and 44th h. In the 24-h condition, food is delivered at the 12 and 36th h.

likely start preparing for the delivery of food when you began to brush your teeth. However, if food was to be delivered every 14 h, then it would be delivered while brushing your teeth (9 a.m.) and while sleeping (11 p.m.) on one day, and while attending class (1 p.m.) and sleeping (3 a.m.) the next day.

As Figure 8.5 indicates, with no consistency in the 14-h delivery-of-food condition, there is no chance for conditioning. Each food delivery occurs at a different point in the circadian period. It could be interesting to think about what you would do if food were delivered on this schedule. Can you imagine how you might adjust? Would you come to expect food at any moment throughout the day, or would you try to estimate how long it has been since your last delivery of food? Responding based on the time since another event elapsed is a different way of synchronizing behavior. In fact, researchers have proposed at least three different timing systems: circadian, interval, and ordinal systems. Each system is functionally incompatible with the others.

8.2.2 *Neurobiology of circadian rhythms*

Circadian molecular activity is evident in many organisms, including bacteria (e.g., *Synechococcus elongatus*), fungi (e.g., *Neurospora crassa*), insects (e.g., *Drosophila melanogaster*), amphibians, reptiles, birds, and mammals. The process by which rhythmicity of molecular activity within a cell is achieved is conserved, resulting in at least two common properties across organisms. The first is a combination of positive and negative elements that support autoregulatory transcription–translation feedback loops, and the second is entrainment by environmental zeitgebers. Within a cell, the positive elements activate the transcription of so-called clock genes, whereas the negative elements inhibit them.

Perhaps not surprisingly, the feedback loops take about 24 h to complete a full molecular cycle. In mammals, the primary feedback loop begins with the clock genes and protein products of "circadian locomotor output cycles kaput," or CLOCK, and "brain and muscle ARNT-like." or BMAL1, activating transcription of the negative elements. By midcircadian cycle, the buildup of the negative elements, the genes and protein products of period (PER) and cryptochrome (CRY), then inhibit the transcription of CLOCK and BMAL1, thereby suppressing their own transcription. If this continued, the cycle would stop. However, over time, the negative elements degrade, which allow the positive elements to restart the cycle. There are at least two other feedback loops, and hundreds of clock modifiers have been identified (Bell-Pedersen et al., 2005). Though the core clock genes are remarkably conserved (evidence of the evolutionary patterns described in Chapter 1), the coordination of the rhythmicity of other molecular processes within the same cell, as well as in other cells in the same tissue and throughout the organism, differs greatly across species (evidence of the evolutionary processes also described in Chapter 1).

In mammals, autoregulated molecular activity exists in most cells throughout the central and peripheral nervous systems. However, there is a hierarchy of synchronization, such that a central oscillator, the SCN, synchronizes the rhythmicity of downstream cells, including those within the liver, endocrine tissues, heart, and skeletal muscles (Bell-Pedersen et al., 2005). In vivo, only cells in the SCN are entrained by light (projected from specialized photoreceptors in the retina) and have been shown to coordinate the rhythmicity of other cells. Evidence for these properties come from findings that peripheral oscillations synchronize to light entrainment of the SCN with a delay of 4 to 12 hours (Zylka et al., 1998). This appears to be the time it takes for the signal from SCN to reach cells in the peripheral nervous system.

Furthermore, an entrained SCN transplanted from a donor to an SCN-lesioned host can restore rhythmicity in the host that matches that of the donor's SCN, whereas non-SCN cell types cannot (Earnest et al., 1999). An isolated SCN can remain rhythmic with little change in amplitude for over a year, whereas cells in the periphery decrease in amplitude when isolated. Although the SCN is the central oscillator within a hierarchical structure in mammals, other species demonstrate wide variations. For example, in the unicellular eukaryote *Lingulodinium polyedrum* (formerly known as *G. polyedra*), independent oscillators exist for controlling bioluminescence and phototaxis (the directional movement toward or away from light described in Chapter 2; Morse et al., 1994), and a similar distinction is found in fruit flies for circadian locomotion and rhythmic olfactory responses (Krishnan et al., 1999).

Interestingly, birds also possess two primary oscillators, but in contrast to unicellular organisms and fruit flies, these central oscillators synchronize downstream rhythmic activity, and there is evidence that they regulate one another. The regulation of melatonin (Figure 8.2), which is synchronized to the SCN in mammals, is coordinated by a central oscillator in the pineal gland of many birds. Birds also possess an SCN, which regulates hypothalamic functions and autonomic nervous system activity (Bell-Pedersen et al., 2005).

In addition to differences between birds and mammals in the negative elements, the positive elements BMAL1 and CLOCK are expressed rhythmically in the pineal gland, but only BMAL1 is rhythmically expressed in the retina of birds. Despite homologies between avian and mammalian clock genes, divergence may be the result of the nocturnal nature of early mammals (see Chapter 1). Birds have extraocular photoreceptors in the pineal gland and other brain areas that respond to changes in light throughout the day, whereas early nocturnal mammals primarily encountered low levels of light during sunset and sunrise. Consequently, mammals have lost these extraocular receptors, which likely supported selection of the SCN as the central oscillator of all downstream rhythmic synchronization (Bell-Pedersen et al., 2005).

8.3 Interval timing

Interval timing occurs when responding is based on the time between events in the seconds-to-minutes range. The first formal report of timed conditioned behavior was observed in dogs after delivering food 30 s after the onset of the CS (Pavlov, 1927). After a single trial, the dogs began to salivate during the 30-s CS. However, after only a few additional trials, salivation began to disappear. If the CS was then extended to 35 s, salivation reappeared during the last 5 s of the CS. It was as if the initial 30 s of the CS had acquired inhibitory value that suppressed responding, but the remaining 5 s were free to acquire excitatory value and thus elicited conditioned responding. Of course, this meant that the dogs must be discriminating the first 30 s of the CS from the last 5 s.

In another experiment, dogs were trained with a 120-s flashing light CS that terminated with food delivery (Figure 8.6). Over sessions, the onset of salivation was gradually delayed, until the dogs did not reliably salivate for 75 s after the onset of the CS. After many such experiments, Pavlov reported that the duration of the delay in salivation was proportional to the duration of the CS–US interval. These observations again suggest that animals are responding differently to the same CS after one interval of time than another (e.g., 5 s vs. 75 s).

In operant conditioning, Ferster and Skinner (1957) reported that pigeons gradually increased their rate of pecking toward the end of an interval that determined when a response would be reinforced (i.e., a fixed-interval schedule of reinforcement; see Chapter 4). Most models of learning do not predict that a CR or operant will occur at a particular time relative to the onset of a stimulus but rather merely predict the magnitude or probability of the response and assume responding occurs with uniform excitatory or inhibitory value throughout a stimulus. Given the importance and prevalence of learned behavior occurring at specific times, researchers have developed theoretical models to predict this behavior.

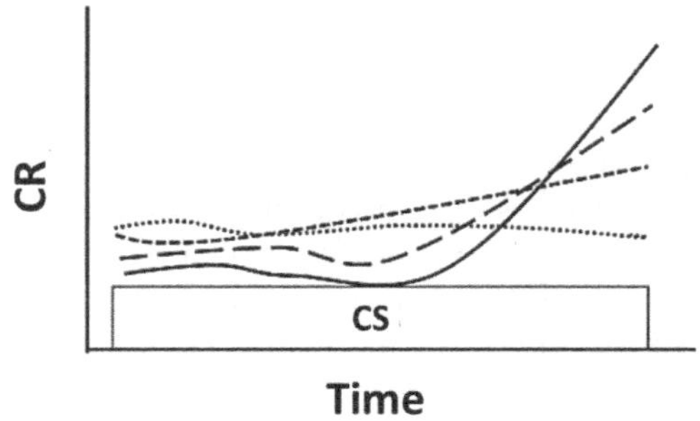

Figure 8.6 **Interval timing in dogs.** A representation of the pattern of responding during Pavlov's (1927) long delay CS (120 s) that terminated with food. The lines indicate hypothetical levels of salivation (higher equals more salivation) during the CS from early trials (smallest dashes) to later trials (solid line).

8.3.1 Scalar timing theory

The most influential model of timing, *scalar timing theory*, uses an information-processing approach that involves encoding, storage, and retrieval (Gibbon & Church, 1984; Gibbon et al., 1984). When exposed to an interval of time, organisms need some way of measuring the elapsed time. Scalar timing theory proposes that organisms have an internal pacemaker that generates pulses at a consistent rate. It is worth noting that individual differences in the rate of pulses are expected and accounted for in the model. Perception and encoding involve temporary storage of the accumulation of pulses during exposure to a stimulus or the interval between stimuli in *working memory*. After exposure, a representation of the accumulated pulses is stored in a more permanent form, known as *reference memory*. The reference memory for the timed interval is scalar, such that the variability in the memory of the duration is proportional to the duration of the to-be-remembered interval (i.e., more variability for longer durations). When the stimulus is subsequently encountered, the number of pulses that have accumulated in working memory is compared to a sample from reference memory, which determines whether a response occurs.

One of the most important assumptions of scalar timing theory is a linear psychological scale for time, which means that for every unit of increase in physical time (e.g., a second), there is a unit of increase in the psychological measurement of time passed. This assumption leads to many testable hypotheses regarding timing behavior. We will consider the predictions of symmetry and superposition in two common timing tasks. Studies of timing can be broken down into time-production and time-perception tasks. In *time-production tasks*, the animal is expected to learn to respond at a particular time relative to some other event (e.g., the onset of a light), whereas in *time-perception tasks*, the animal responds based on the duration of an event (e.g., the duration of a light). Support for *symmetry* and *superposition* in timing tasks comes primarily from time-production tasks.

8.3.1.1 Time-production tasks

The most commonly used time-production task is the *peak procedure* (Catania, 1970; Roberts, 1981). In this task, animals are trained on a fixed-interval (FI) schedule of reinforcement, such that the first response after a specified interval is reinforced. For example, Roberts (1981) trained rats to press a lever 20 s after the onset of one stimulus (e.g., a Light) to obtain a reinforcer (a FI 20-s schedule), but the first press after 40 s delivered a reinforcer when a different stimulus was presented (FI 40-s schedule). After many such trials, responding took the form of the familiar *scallop* shape, with an increase in response rate toward the end of the fixed interval (20 or 40 s) for each stimulus (see Figure 8.7-A).

A complete record of timing should include not just changes in the rate of responding as the fixed interval (20th second) approached but also changes in the rate of responding in the seconds following the fixed interval. In the peak procedure, probe trials in which reinforcement is withheld and the trial duration is extended are intermixed with baseline trials that include the delivery of the reinforcer. Consistent with other studies, Roberts (1981) observed that the response rate was highest (i.e., peak) near the interval defining the fixed-interval schedule (either 20 s or 40 s). To observe the decrease in response rate after the fixed interval, thus revealing peak responding, the animal needs to receive extensive exposure to probe trials ending in nonreinforcement (Papini & Hollingsworth, 1998). Importantly, a psychological scale of time predicts that the response rate after the fixed interval expires should also correspond to physical time. On a FI 20-s schedule, this means that the rate of responding at the 19th second should correspond to the rate of responding at the 21st second because they are both one unit of time removed from the interval defining reinforcement. This prediction of symmetrical search around the fixed interval can be seen in Figure 8.7 and has been supported in nearly every case (Cheng & Roberts, 1991). When the probability of the reinforcer on baseline trials was reduced from 80% to 20%, the peak response time and symmetry remained, but the height of the peak was reduced (Figure 8.7-B).

The second prediction, superposition, refers to the similarity in the rate of responding with longer and shorter intervals. A typical experiment with shorter (FI 20-s) and longer (FI 40–s) probe trials will reveal two main differences. One difference is that the shorter FI will

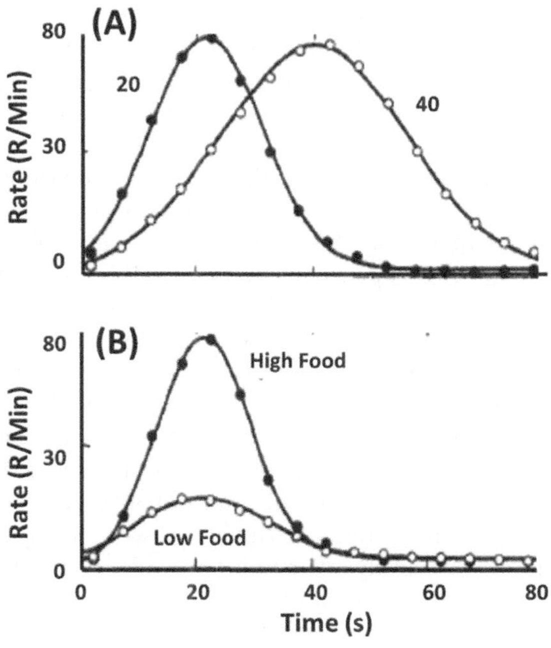

Figure 8.7 **Operant responding in fixed-interval schedules. (A)** The rate of responding for rats in a FI 20-s schedule in the presence of one stimulus and on an FI 40-s schedule in the presence of a second stimulus. **(B)** Data from an FI 20-s schedule when the probability of a reinforcer on baseline trials was decreased from 80% to 20%. (From Roberts, 1981; reproduced with permission from the American Psychological Association.)

have a higher peak; the other is that the shorter FI will exhibit a narrower spread of the distribution around the peak, having a higher positive (before the peak) and negative (after the peak) slope. To account for these differences, we can think of the discriminability of moments of time. In what ways can one second be discriminated from another? From one second to the next, you may have moved, objects around you may have moved, and the phase of your biological rhythms may have advanced. The closer two points are in time, the less likely it is that the movements of objects and phases of biological rhythms can be discriminated.

One approach to interpreting the discrimination of time is by using principles from signal detection theory (Green & Swets, 1966). If the acquisition of appropriate stimulus control of behavior is a problem of learning to respond to some stimuli (target signal) and not to others, then we must consider the influence of nontarget signals (nontarget noise) on the probability of making a response. It might be helpful here to think of trying to hear your friend (target signal) in a room with one other conversation taking place simultaneously (i.e., low nontarget noise) versus many other simultaneous conversations (i.e., high nontarget noise). In fact, many researchers (Mackintosh, 1976) interpret the overshadowing effect as a kind of nontarget signal problem in which the more salient signal, CS1, prevents the acquisition of responding to the less salient signal, CS2 (see overshadowing in Chapter 5). Nontarget noise includes all neural activity occurring at or near the time of the target signal, which includes a discrete stimulus presented independent of the target (e.g., a Light when the target signal is a Tone), changes in contextual stimuli (e.g., presenting the Tone in a new location), cue-dependent neural activity (e.g., if the Tone was previously paired with a Light), as well as any portions of a stimulus in which a response is not reinforced (e.g., the first 14 s of a Tone reinforced on a FI 15-s schedule).

On FI schedules, the stimulus at one point in time (e.g., at exactly 20 s) should influence the probability of responding differently than the same stimulus at any other point in time. A longer stimulus includes more points in time during which responding will not result in reinforcement (nontarget noise), which should make it more difficult to discriminate the target signal and respond at exactly the right moment in time. Consequently, we must consider sensitivity to the difference between the nontarget noise and signal within the context of the overall intensity of the nontarget noise.

Let us continue with our example in which the number of responses that occurred during each second of trials with an FI 20-s schedule has been measured. In this example, nontarget noise includes the 19 nontarget intervals (seconds 1–19). The difference between the nontarget noise and signal (i.e., the change to be discriminated) is 1 s (from second 19 to second 20). According to *Weber's Law*, to maintain the same level of timing discrimination performance observed during an FI 20-s schedule (1 out of 20 s = 0.05, which is the probability constant, or *Weber's fraction*) on an FI 40-s schedule, the duration of time to be discriminated must be increased by multiplying the total FI period by probability constant (40 s × 0.05 = 2 s). If the measure of discrimination remains 1 s, then timing accuracy will decrease. Poor timing accuracy would appear as a lower peak at 40 s and shallower slope (i.e., wider peak) of responding during an FI 40-s schedule than the peak and distribution on an FI 20-s schedule.

It may be easier to consider the common example of discriminating a change in the volume of sound when the volume is relatively low and increased by 5 dB (from 10 to 15 dB). The change is 5 dB when the background intensity is 15 dB (5/15 = 0.33). When the volume is much higher (60 dB) and the same change occurs (5 dB), it is much more likely to go unnoticed (5/60 = 0.08). If the same level of discrimination performance was needed, how much would a 60-dB stimulus need to be increased by? You could find this by multiplying 60 by the probability constant obtained with 15 dB (60 × 0.33 = 20 dB change). We will return to Weber's law when discussing spatial search (Chapter 9) and numerical competence (Chapter 10).

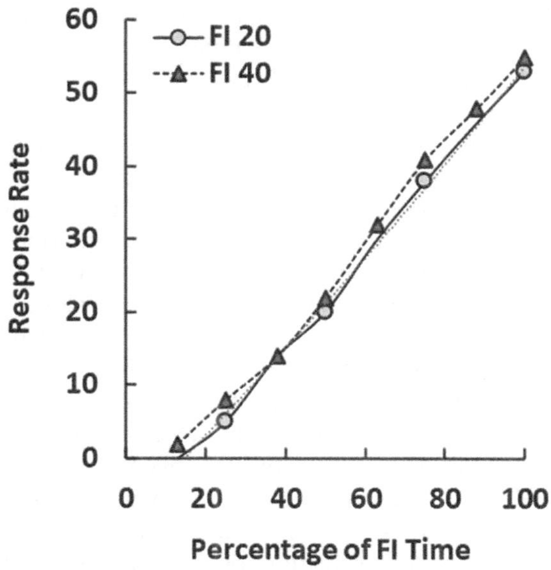

Figure 8.8 **Responding in FI schedules plotted in relative time**. Temporal distributions of response rate during two FI schedules (20 and 40 s) with the X-axis adjusted for FI duration. A polynomial trend line was added to the FI 20-s data. (From Roberts, 1981; reproduced with permission from the American Psychological Association.)

Do distributions obtained under different FI schedules superimpose (overlap) when the probability constant is considered? Yes, the response distributions for different FI schedules are nearly identical when the duration being measured is accounted for (Cheng & Roberts, 1991). Despite large differences in slope when Roberts (1981) plotted response rate as a function of absolute time (see Figure 8.7), the distributions superimpose when plotted as a function of relative time during the FI (Figure 8.8). Findings of peak symmetry and superposition support the proposition that under many conditions, the psychological scale for time is linear. Thinking of timing behavior as a discrimination problem provides a unifying theme throughout this textbook.

8.3.1.2 Time-perception tasks

Another way to investigate timing is using time-perception tasks. The most common of these is the *temporal-bisection procedure* (Church & Deluty, 1977). Subjects are exposed to different durations of a stimulus, and a correct response is associated with each. The advantage of time-perception tasks is that they reduce the influence of contextual variables associated with the response itself (e.g., how fast the animal can respond, how quickly it fatigues, etc.). The temporal-bisection procedure has been used with nonhumans and humans, including children as young as 3 years old (Droit-Volet & Wearden, 2002) and clinical samples (Melgire et al., 2005). In early time-perception experiments with rats, the duration of physical restraint (10 vs. 30 s) predicted which of two alleys at the end of the maze contained a reinforcer (e.g., Alley A after 10 s vs. Alley B after 30 s; Cowles & Finan, 1941). In another version of a time-perception procedure (switching), pigeons were reinforced for pecking one colored key early in the session (Stubbs, 1976). After a certain amount of time had passed (switch interval), pecks to key A were no longer reinforced. The pigeons were required to peck a separate switch key (X) to gain access to a different colored key (B) to earn additional reinforcers. More accurate timing would be reflected in how close to the switch interval they pecked the switch key.

The most common temporal bisection procedure consists of training on two anchor durations; one response (e.g., a left lever press) is reinforced after a short-duration stimulus (2 s), but another response (e.g., a right lever press) is reinforced after a long-duration stimulus (8 s). After training, reinforced trials of the anchor durations are intermixed with nonreinforced trials of durations intermediate to the anchors (Figure 8.9). In other words, the researcher is asking the animal, given only two response options (short or long), was that a short- or a long-duration stimulus? The resulting data are displayed as the probability with which a given duration is classified as long or short (Meck & Church, 1983).

These data can be analyzed in three ways. Firstly, by calculating the steepness of the psychometric response function of intermediate values, which reveals the degree to which intermediate durations are discriminated as short or long. Secondly, the *bisection point*, or *point of subjective equality* (PSE), is the stimulus duration with an equal probability of being classified as short or long. Thirdly, the steepness of the function could be divided by the bisection point, to produce a kind of Weber fraction, or ratio, that would predict similar patterns of timing behavior if the duration of the anchor points changed but the ratio remained consistent.

Are the data from time-perception procedures consistent with the linear psychological scale for time observed in time-production procedures? Research with human and nonhuman animals has shown that the response functions from the intermediate values of time

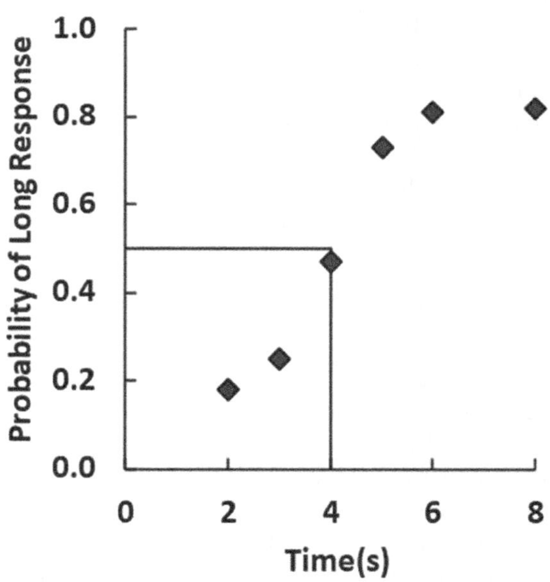

Figure 8.9 **Data from a temporal bisection procedure.** Short- (2 s) and long-duration stimuli (8 s) were associated with different responses during training. After training, intermediate values were tested along with both the short- and long-duration stimuli and the two response options present. Lines mark the bisection point. (From Meck & Church, 1983; reproduced with permission from the American Psychological Association.)

bisection procedures with different anchor durations, but the same Weber fraction, do superimpose (Gibbon, 1981; Penney et al., 2000). However, the bisection point was at a position in time best described by the geometric mean (multiplying the numbers in the sample and then calculating the *n*th root, where "*n*" is the sample size) rather than the arithmetic mean (the average), as predicted by a linear scale for time. Careful analysis by Gibbon (1981) indicated that subjective time may still be linear if the processes controlling the response are influenced by the similarity of the current time to the remembered time (i.e., generalization).

This point raises some interesting questions. If you were asked to time a 23-s interval without counting or using a timer, how accurate would you be? Have you ever timed a 23-s interval before? If not, how would you know when 23 s had elapsed? The answer is likely to be that you would generalize from other intervals that you have experienced. If you have not timed a 23-s interval, have you timed a 30-s interval? Maybe in school, you have had experience with teachers saying, "I'll give you 30 s to find a partner." If past experience with different intervals influenced your perception of time, then the anchor values used during training should influence performance in time-perception procedures. Indeed, there is evidence in nonhuman animals (Raslear, 1983, 1985) and humans (Wearden, 1991) that groups trained with anchor pairs with different Weber fractions have different bisection points.

Additionally, consistent with the description of factors influencing stimulus control in Chapter 2, timing accuracy is better after training with anchor pairs that are more difficult to discriminate (e.g., 8 vs. 10 s compared to 3 vs. 10 s). Both pieces of evidence suggest that an interval of time is not a simple stimulus that is innately discriminable, but rather, past performance influences what constitutes an interval of time and how distinct it is from other intervals.

8.3.2 Oscillators and nonlinear timing

It is worth noting that timekeeping has always relied on the movement of objects. Of course, space and time are intricately linked, but it was not the distance traveled, per se, that was critical for measuring time but the regularity of the cycle period, or *oscillation*. A grandfather clock relies on a system of weights and pulleys to produce the iconic oscillation of a pendulum, and consequently, the movement of the various hands on the clock face. Many clocks have a single pendulum, and its movement results in the movement of a gear that turns the second hand but also advances the minute hand after so many turns. Simultaneous biological rhythms can occur with different rhythmicity in animals; some oscillate quickly (i.e., a short period) and would be more useful for short intervals, whereas others have longer oscillations (Figure 8.10).

Much like the behavior of the hands on the clock face, once a behavior occurs at a particular point in a cycle, the behavior itself, not just the biological rhythm, can now become part of the timing process. For example, if you tap your hand once per second for 15 s, you will be using a biological rhythm to try to time 1-s intervals, and then you will use the noise or sight of each tap as the stimulus to be counted.

There is another potential implication of a timing process based on oscillators with different periods. If oscillators have different periods, then it may be the case that timing behavior is more precise when the interval to be timed more closely aligns with the cycle period of a set of oscillators, referred to above as the local maximum in sensitivity.

Errors in timing behavior based on oscillators will be systematic, with the fewest errors occurring at intervals that align with the period of the oscillator. Notice that it is not that a particular phase of the oscillation is more discriminable than another phase but rather that

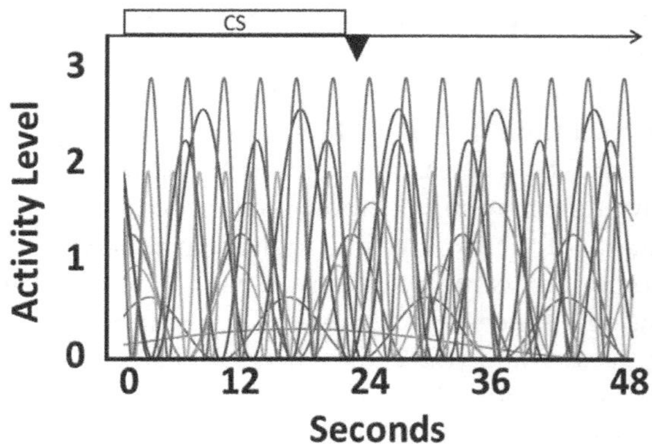

Figure 8.10 **Variation in the period of biological oscillations.** Biological oscillations with periods occurring in the range of seconds. Timing accuracy is hypothesized to improve the closer an interval is to an oscillator with a period that aligns the interval with the same phase. A hypothetical 20-s CS terminates in the delivery of a US (black inverted triangle).

the same phase occurs consistently at the time the behavior should occur. We earlier reviewed data supporting this prediction for circadian behaviors, such that a circadian timer was more accurate for food delivered every 24 h, as opposed to every 14 h (Crystal, 2001). This prediction contradicts a linear psychological scale for timing, which assumes that errors in timing behavior will be random.

Using a ramp procedure, in which the FI begins at a particular value and increases or decreases across trials with a constant step size (e.g., 2 s), Crystal et al. (1997) have shown a systematic trend in the timing accuracy of rats pressing a lever to earn reinforcers (range = 10–140 s). These data were first plotted as the mean time to start pressing at each fixed interval. Then the residuals (observed minus expected start times) were plotted and the resulting distribution indicated fewer errors (better timing) at specific intervals that were uncorrelated with a prediction based on Weber's Law (i.e., the rats did not decrease in accuracy simply as a function of increasing FI duration). Similarly, time-perception procedures utilizing many closely spaced interval conditions have found several peaks in sensitivity to time in the 0- to 30-s range, which suggest the use of several oscillators with different periods (Crystal, 1999, 2001).

The possibility of a unified theory of timing based on oscillators with periods ranging from milliseconds to about 24 h is parsimonious. A full evaluation of the theory and its predictions will require the use of other procedures common in the interval and circadian timing literature. For example, Gibbon et al. (1997) trained rats with a FI 100-s schedule, followed by a phase advance in the form of an early, free food pellet. Timing theories based on oscillators (e.g., circadian) predict a slow adjustment in timing as a result of the phase shift, whereas pacemaker theories predict rapid adjustment due to a quick reset of the timer (Church, 1978). The data indicated slow adjustment following the phase shift. Studies such as these will elucidate whether the multiple oscillator theory of timing will replace or complement pacemaker theories of timing.

8.3.3 Time as a stimulus property

We have reviewed ways to conceive of time as well as evidence for stimulus control of behavior by time. Remember, *stimulus control* means that the probability of a behavior varies as a function of the presence or absence of some stimulus. Previous chapters highlighted many procedures for revealing stimulus control by various properties of external stimuli, such as the color of an object or the frequency of a tone. If time is a property of a stimulus, like color or shape, then the same effects of stimulus control should be observed when the physical properties of external stimuli are held constant and the time of an event is manipulated.

8.3.3.1 Acquisition

Much of the research described in previous chapters presented a simplified view of stimuli as unitary and static. Of course, stimuli are made of many different properties, and those that support adaptive behavior are most likely to control behavior. That is, slight variations in the frequency of a tone may be critical for determining when a response will be reinforced, but slight variations in the volume of the tone may be irrelevant. Similarly, time after the onset of a stimulus may be critical, whereas the location of the stimulus may be irrelevant.

It has been proposed that the time and location of objects are learned about even in the absence of directed attention (Myers, 2013). This suggests that the time of the delivery of a US relative to a CS will be learned about automatically as part of the conditioning process. However, there are many other properties of the stimulus present during conditioning, and consequently, the proximity and stability of the time of the US will determine whether the temporal property of a stimulus comes to control behavior. Proximity is a pure measure of the temporal distance between the onset (or termination) of the CS and the onset of the US. When the onset of the US is too far removed from the onset of the CS, then timing, and indeed conditioned responding, can be eliminated. Stability is defined as variability in the timing of the US relative to CS onset. If the US is delivered at an unpredictable time within a 30-s CS, then responding will occur at a relatively constant rate throughout the duration of the CS. In this sense, time may still be controlling behavior, but equally throughout the CS because the US was delivered at several times within the duration of the CS.

When Pavlov's (1927) dogs were trained with a 120-s flashing Light CS that terminated with food delivery, the onset of salivation was delayed. In this procedure, the temporal proximity of the CS relative to US delivery was sufficient to result in conditioned responding, and trial-to-trial stability in the delivery time of the US was high. This result of delayed CR, also known as inhibition of delay, has been found with many different conditioning preparations and with different CS–US intervals (Drew et al., 2004). Some early theories of conditioning included a notion that the emergence of the CR was controlled by one process, which preceded response timing via a second process (Gibbon & Balsam, 1981). The first process controlled the emergence of the CR based on a difference in the rate of reinforcement during the CS versus during the ITI (intertrial interval), whereas the second process is scalar timing theory.

Several subsequent studies have found that the CS–US interval influences the timing of the CR from the moment the CR is detected (Balsam et al., 2002; Holder & Roberts, 1985; Kirkpatrick & Church, 2000). Furthermore, as the CR increases in strength across acquisition, there is no significant change in the timing (peak and spread) of the response (Balsam et al., 2002). These results support the hypothesis that one process determines both the emergence and timing of the CR.

Further support for this hypothesis comes from Ohyama and Mauk (2001), who trained ring doves in a conditioned eyeblink preparation with pairings of a Tone and Shock at a 750-ms interstimulus interval (ISI) during Phase 1 (Table 8.1). Training with this ISI was terminated before a CR was detected during the CS. The subjects were then trained with a

Table 8.1 A test of latent timing

Group	*Phase 1* (~4 sessions)	*Phase 2* (~5 sessions)	*Test* (1 session)
Paired (PP)	Tone→750 ms→Shock	Tone→250 ms→Shock	Tone? (1,250 ms)
Unpaired (UP)	Tone, Shock	Tone→250 ms→Shock	Tone? (1,250 ms)
Not Paired (NP)	Box exposure	Tone→250 ms→Shock	Tone? (1,250 ms)

Note. Based on Ohyama and Mauk (2001). The ISI is the time from the onset of the CS to the delivery of the US. Group Unpaired received both Tone and Shock, but separated in time. Group Not Paired was placed in the conditioning box during Phase 1, but no Tones or Shocks were delivered. Phase 2 and the Test were the same for the three groups.

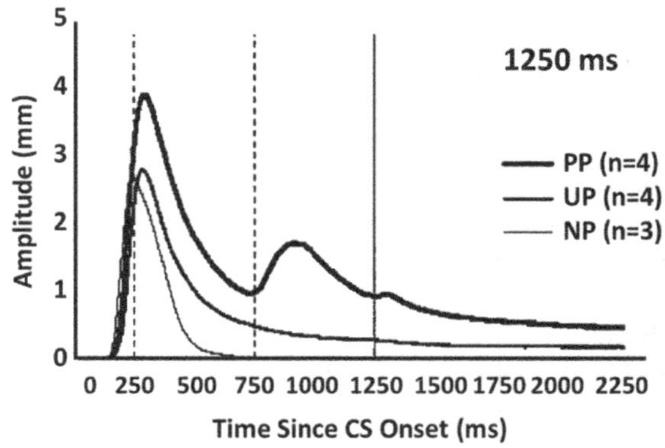

Figure 8.11 **Latent timing.** Data from a peak trial following differences in training in Phase 1 and consistent training with pairings of Tone and Shock with a 250 ms ISI (first dashed vertical line). At test, all animals were tested with a 1,250-ms Tone (terminated at the solid vertical line), which encompasses the 750-ms ISI (second dashed vertical line) originally trained in Group Paired. Response amplitude is displayed as millimeters (mm) of eyelid closure. (From Ohyama & Mauk, 2001; reproduced with permission from the Society for Neuroscience.)

250-ms Tone to Shock ISI until a large CR was observed in Phase 2. Peak-interval trials were then delivered at a duration of 1,250 ms. Under these Test conditions, CRs were observed at both the 250-ms interval (trained in Phase 2) and 750-ms intervals (trained in Phase 1; Figure 8.11).

8.3.3.2 Extinction

Extinction is most often measured by the number of responses that occurred during the CS across trials of the CS presented without the US. However, extinction of timing should include a measure of how much conditioned responding occurs at the interval during which the US is expected compared to other intervals. Ohyama et al. (1999) trained ring doves with an 8-s CS–US interval in an autoshaping preparation until responding was stable, after which extinction trials were delivered with a 48-s CS duration. The speed at which the pigeons were pecking decreased gradually over trials, but the timing of conditioned key pecking remained stable across extinction trials. This is consistent with evidence for the stability of timing after other manipulations, such as decreasing the probability of reinforcer delivery (see Figure 8.7-B). These findings, combined with the emergence of timed pecking even when a consistent CR was not initially observed (Ohyama & Mauk, 2001), suggest that timing will be evident throughout extinction until the CR is completely eliminated.

Another method for evaluating whether time is learned as part of the conditioning process is to manipulate CS–US interval by varying the CS duration across acquisition and extinction. That is, animals could be trained with one CS–US interval during acquisition (e.g., 16-s CS terminating in the US) and then subsequently extinguished with a different CS duration (e.g., 4 s CS alone). If time is a part of the stimulus controlling the CR, then subsequent tests with the originally trained CS duration (e.g., 16 s) would likely reveal reduced CRs during the initial 4-s CS (as in extinction) but little to no reduction of the CR at the originally trained CS–US interval (16 s) within the CS. However, if exposure to the CS during extinction is all that is required for extinction to occur, then changing the CS–US interval across phases should have no effects on the CR.

Drew et al. (2004) autoshaped ring doves on a fixed CS–US interval followed by extinction with the same or different CS duration. The rate of extinction of the CR and the degree of transfer of extinction to the originally trained CS–US interval was dependent on the similarity of the CS–US interval encountered during training and the CS duration during extinction.

8.3.3.3 *Postextinction relapse of the CR*

Many extinction procedures result in a recovery of the original response, including spontaneous recovery and renewal (see Chapter 5). *Spontaneous recovery* of behavior after extinction occurs when a resting period (a period without CS presentations) is inserted between extinction and subsequent testing, whereas *renewal* occurs when the properties of the conditioning context change across acquisition, extinction, and testing. Though the procedures appear quite different, there is evidence that the effects are dependent on similar properties of stimulus control. In a typical procedure testing for renewal of a CR, all rats receive Tone→Shock pairings in a conditioning chamber, A, with distinct sensory features (i.e., the way it looks, smells, and feels). This acquisition phase (A: Tone→Shock) is followed by an extinction phase in a chamber with a different set of distinct features (B: Tone-only). Finally, these animals are tested with the Tone in the original context (A: Tone-only). The control group is tested with the Tone in the same context experienced in extinction (B).

In terms of the contexts, renewal involves a comparison between ABA vs. ABB conditions. In another variation, testing occurs in yet a third context (ABC renewal). Renewal is observed in both the ABA and ABC designs, more than in the ABB design. This has led to the prediction that the initial learning is less susceptible to interference by contextual changes. This prediction has been supported by results from a variety of procedures, including those in which an inhibitory stimulus is trained prior to extinction (Fiori et al., 1994; Sissons & Miller, 2009). A procedure for spontaneous recovery has acquisition, extinction, and testing occurring in the same context (AAA design). What causes the relapse of the CR in spontaneous recovery?

One interpretation is that time (e.g., the internal state of the organism) is part of the features that form the context in which conditioning occurs (Bouton et al., 2021). Consequently, we could interpret the animal as acquiring the CR at one point in time (temporal context A) and extinguishing the response at a different time (temporal context B). If testing occurs immediately after extinction, then the procedure takes the form of ABB, but if testing is delayed by a certain amount of time, then it would take place in a different temporal context (ABC), and some amount of renewal would be expected. Indeed, animals tested in a spontaneous recovery procedure and those tested in an ABC renewal procedure with manipulation of the physical context demonstrate significant relapse of the CR.

8.3.3.4 Cue competition and integration based on timing

Time is a kind of stimulus property, and consequently, control by the temporal property of a CS may compete with control by other properties of the CS (e.g., the frequency of a tone) or other aspects of the conditioning situation (e.g., the US–US interval). Gibbon et al. (1997) trained pigeons in a task in which food was signaled by both a 30-min CS–US interval (Keylight→Food) and by the Time of Day. When the CS was displaced in time relative to the time of day, neither the CS nor the Time of Day perfectly controlled the timing of the response.

The *midsession reversal task* represents a similar opportunity for competition, but within a single session (Zentall, 2020). In this task, two stimuli are presented throughout a session; responses to one stimulus are reinforced during the first half of the session, whereas responses to the other stimulus are reinforced during the second half of the session (Figure 8.12). Behavior could come under the control of local reinforcement, such that responses to one stimulus should continue until a reinforcer is omitted, and then the animal should switch to the other stimulus. This strategy would result in few errors. However,

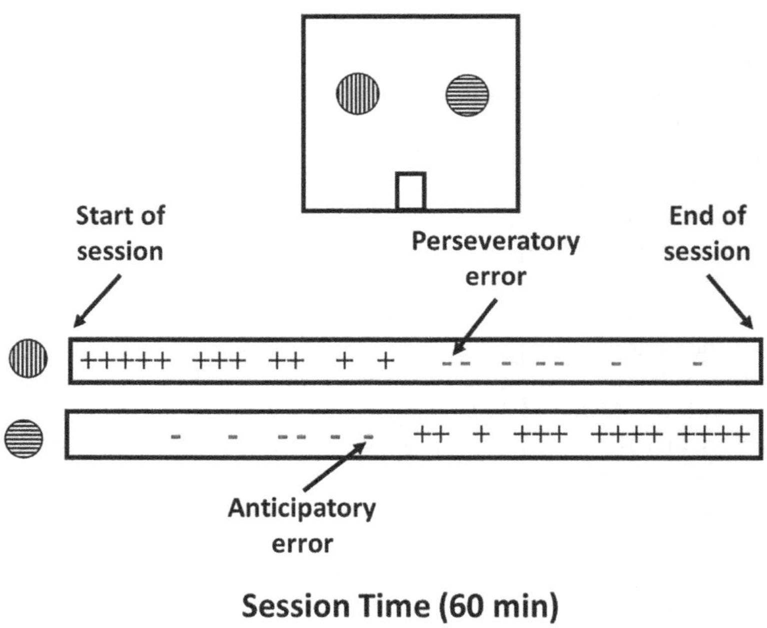

Figure 8.12 **Midsession reversal procedure.** Hypothetical data from a touchscreen-based midsession reversal task with two visual stimuli displayed on the monitor throughout a 60-min session. Responses to one stimulus (vertical stripes) are reinforced (+) during the first half of the session and responses to another stimulus (horizontal stripes) are reinforced (+) during the second half. Anticipatory errors are nonreinforced (-) responses that occur to the incorrect stimulus (horizontal) prior to the midpoint of the session, whereas perseveration errors occur to the incorrect stimulus after the midpoint (vertical).

because the midpoint of the session occurs relative to the start of the session, the interval of time from the start of the session to the midpoint could be the controlling stimulus. Due to errors in timing accuracy, this strategy would result in many anticipatory (switching to peck the other stimulus too soon) and perseveratory errors (switching to peck the other stimulus too late).

Pigeons demonstrate a pattern of errors consistent with timing, producing anticipatory and perseveration errors. However, when a cue signaling the first half (early) or second half (late) of the session was inserted immediately before the opportunity to peck, pigeons reduced their errors (Rayburn-Reeves et al., 2017). If, on occasional test trials, a late cue was inserted at the beginning of the session, pigeons largely ignored it and continued to respond based on time in the session (early). However, if a late cue was inserted just before the midpoint of the session, pigeons responded largely based on the cue and not the time in session. This makes good sense, as the middle of the session is neither "early" nor "late" in a session and thus is the most ambiguous. Interestingly, rats show more control by local reinforcement (Zentall, 2020). It is not surprising that sensitivity to time would vary across species and, even more important for successful adaptation, by task.

A simple way to evaluate the temporal property of a CS would be to compare how two CSs with similar or different CS–US intervals overshadow one another (see ***overshadowing*** in Chapter 5). If the CS–US intervals are not part of the stimulus controlling learning, then all other things being equal, there should be no difference in the degree of overshadowing when the CS–US intervals differ. Blaisdell et al. (1998) paired two CSs (Light and Tone) with an aversive US (Shock) but varied the timing of the CSs relative to the US across groups. In one group (Overshadowing), both CSs were forward paired with the US (LightTone→Shock). In another group, the Tone was forward paired the US, which occurred simultaneously with the Light (Tone→LightShock). The critical test was whether any excitatory strength was conditioned to the Tone as a result of the presence of the Light. Overshadowing effects were maximal when the temporal relations between two CSs and USs were the same (e.g., Blaisdell et al., 1998; Miller et al., 1992).

Better control by the temporal property of a more proximal CS would be expected due to greater accuracy in timing the US compared to more distal CSs. Consequently, a CS presented closer in time to the US would be more likely to overshadow a more distal CS. Mackintosh and Reese (1979) tested this hypothesis using one-trial fear conditioning in rats (Table 8.2). In the control group, rats were shocked 30 s after the termination of a 15-s Tone (Tone→Shock). In Group Simultaneous, the Tone and Light were presented simultaneously for 15 s and followed 30 s later by Shock (ToneLight→Shock). In Group Overshadowing, the Tone terminated with the onset of a 15-s Light, which was followed 15 s later by Shock (Tone→Light→Shock). All subjects were tested on the Tone.

Table 8.2 Timing and overshadowing

Group	*Training*	*Test*	*Results*
Overshadowing	Tone→Light→15 s→Shock	Tone?	Low fear
Simultaneous	ToneLight→30 s→Shock	Tone?	High fear
Control	Tone→30 s→Shock	Tone?	High fear

Note. All CSs were 15 s long. Thus, in Group Overshadowing, the Tone was separated from the Shock by 30 s (15 s of Light duration plus a 15-s interval from the end of the Light to the Shock). In all groups, the Shock occurred 30 s after the end of the Tone.

Overshadowing of the Tone, in the form of attenuated fear elicited by the Tone, was found in Group Overshadowing relative to Groups Simultaneous and Control. Similarly, Fairhurst et al. (2003) trained pigeons in an appetitive procedure to predict the US based on the serial compound of a Short CS embedded near the end of a Long CS. The distribution of responses on compound trials of both the Long and Short CS more closely resembled that of another group given trials of the Short cue alone than the distribution of a group given the Long cue alone. When the Short CS was displaced (e.g., embedded in the early or middle part of the Long CS) relative to the Long CS, responding was found to follow shifts in the position of the Short CS and showed no evidence of timing the US based on the Long CS. Timed behavior based on a CS is affected by the relative temporal proximity of that stimulus to the US in many cases, though some studies have reported overshadowing that is insensitive to temporal proximity (Jennings et al., 2007).

Another procedure in which cues are said to compete for stimulus control is blocking (see blocking in Chapter 5). The ***blocking*** effect is observed when the magnitude of conditioned responding to a CS (B) paired with another CS (A) and the US (AB→US) is reduced by prior training of A and the US (A→US). Barnet et al. (1993) tested rats in a fear conditioning procedure to determine whether the temporal property of a stimulus (CS–US interval) can influence the degree of stimulus control by a CS subsequently paired with the same US (Table 8.3). A larger blocking effect was observed when a CS (A) was forward paired with the US in Phase 1 and subsequently paired with another CS (B) in the same temporal relationship (forward) to the US during Phase 2 (Group Forward-Forward) than when the same CSs were simultaneously paired with the US during Phase 1 (Group Simultaneous-Forward). Blocking was maximal when the temporal relationship between A and B was consistent throughout both phases.

In addition to competition between cues presented with the same temporal relationship to the outcome during training, temporal integration has been observed with higher-order conditioning procedures in rats (Barnet et al., 1997; Leising et al., 2007) and humans (Molet et al., 2010). Leising et al. (2007) trained rats in a ***sensory preconditioning*** procedure. In Phase 1, rats were given presentations of a short CS (10-s Short X) embedded within the duration of a longer CS (60-s Long A). In Group Early, Short X was embedded 10 s after the onset of the Long A, whereas in Group Late, Short X was presented 40 s after the onset Long A. Phase 2 consisted of trials with Short X paired simultaneously with the US for both groups. At Test, Long A was presented alone, and the timing of approaches to the US delivery location was recorded. Despite no pairings of Long A with the US, Figure 8.13 shows that the conditioned approach responses were consistently higher during the early portion of Long A for Group Early and consistently higher during the later portion of Long A for Group Late. These data suggest that the presentation of Long A in each group retrieved the prior experience of Short X occurring at a particular time within Long A (early or late) and

Table 8.3 Temporal determinants of blocking

Group	*Phase 1*	*Phase 2*	*Test*	*Results*
Forward-Forward	A→US/YUS	AB→US	B?	Low CR
Simultaneous-Forward	X→US/AUS	AB→US	B?	High CR

Note. Based on Barnet et al. (1993). A, B, X, and Y are CSs. An "→" indicates a forward CS→US pairing (e.g., A→US). A contiguous CS and US (e.g., YUS) indicates the two are presented simultaneously.

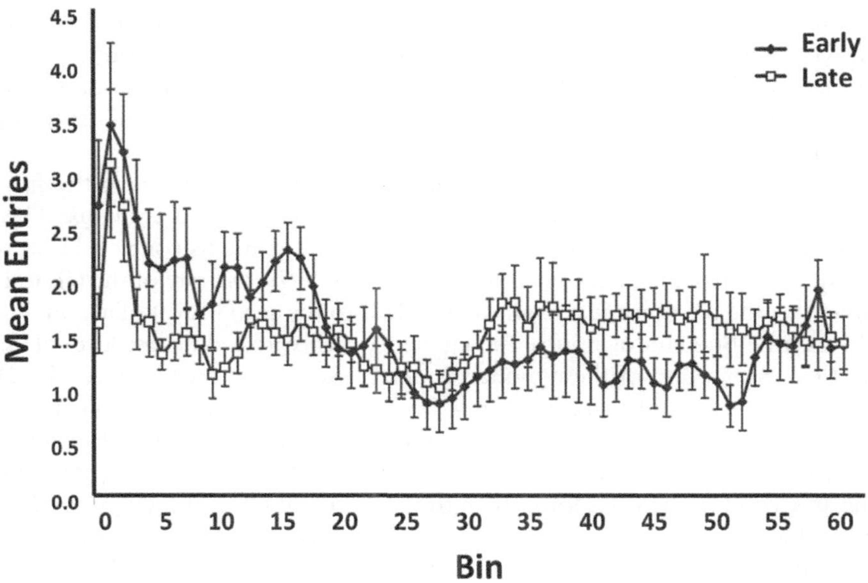

Figure 8.13 **Timing of the CR in sensory preconditioning.** Rats were trained in a sensory preconditioning procedure in which a short-duration CS (X) was embedded either early or late within a long-duration CS, A, during Phase 1. CS X was paired with the US during Phase 2, followed by testing with CS A. The figure displays search behavior for the US as mean entries during each second of the 60 CS A. (From Leising et al., 2007; reproduced with permission from The Psychonomic Society).

that the value of the retrieved experience of Short X was excitatory as a result of recent pairings of Short X with the US during Phase 2.

8.4 Where is timing in models of conditioning?

Most models of conditioning were developed to predict how the associative strength of a stimulus changed across trials of a conditioning procedure, but they are unable to predict even the simplest of timed behavior. The most influential of these models was proposed by Rescorla and Wagner (1972). The *Rescorla-Wagner model* estimates changes in associative strength using two terms. The first term represents the salience, or noticeability, of all of the cues present during conditioning (i.e., salience of the CS and US), and the second is an error-correction term made up of the difference between the value of the US received on that trial and the associative strength accrued to all the CSs present in that trial and acquired during all previous trials.

There is no term for the CS–US interval, which has been shown to influence the rate of learning as well as the magnitude of the CR. There are also no terms for specifying whether the US occurred immediately before, during, immediately after, or long after the CS. In fairness, the salience terms and the value of the US could be adjusted to account for some of these effects, but clearly, the model was not developed with the intent to represent the temporal properties of the conditioning procedure. Furthermore, even if the terms were estimated to account for the temporal properties, the model is still unable to predict the timed conditioned responding found in Pavlov's (1927) original studies or the majority of studies reviewed throughout this chapter.

Real-time theories of conditioning (Klopf, 1988; Moore & Desmond, 1992; Sutton & Barto, 1981, 1990; Tessauro, 1986) model changes in learning throughout the CS and ITI. Most of these are hybrid models because the underlying error-correction process that produces a CR is integrated with the process for timed behavior. The most influential of these is a class referred to as temporal difference models.

Perhaps the easiest way to understand these models is to elaborate on the finding that animals can respond differently to the early and late portions of a stimulus. This finding suggests that these portions can exhibit different levels of stimulus control. However, if we look closely at data from the peak procedure (see Figure 8.7), the rate of the CR differs from one moment to the next, not just from the first half to the second half of a stimulus. A 40-s CS could then be broken down into 1-s segments, each with a different level of associative strength. One assumption of these models is delay discounting (see Chapter 5). *Delay discounting* captures the familiar feeling that a US delivered in 5 s is more valuable (and thus likely to influence behavior right now) than the same reinforcer delivered in 5 days. If we apply this concept to our 40-s CS that terminates in the US, then the discounted value of the US in the 1st second of the CS is lower than the value of the US at the 40th second of the CS.

Where is the difference within these temporal-difference models? An error-correction term like that of the Rescorla-Wagner model (1972), which was discussed in Chapters 4 and 5, is applied to every segment in time rather than once across the whole stimulus (Figure 8.14). Assuming an acquisition procedure, the predicted value of the US at each segment of the CS at the start of conditioning will be zero, which will then be updated in every segment after each CS-US pairing. The value of the US in each segment of the CS is the sum of the actual (i.e., not estimated) US experienced in the next segment of time plus a prediction of the discounted value of the US in the remaining segments of the CS. This is equivalent to lambda (i.e., what you get) in the Rescorla-Wagner model.

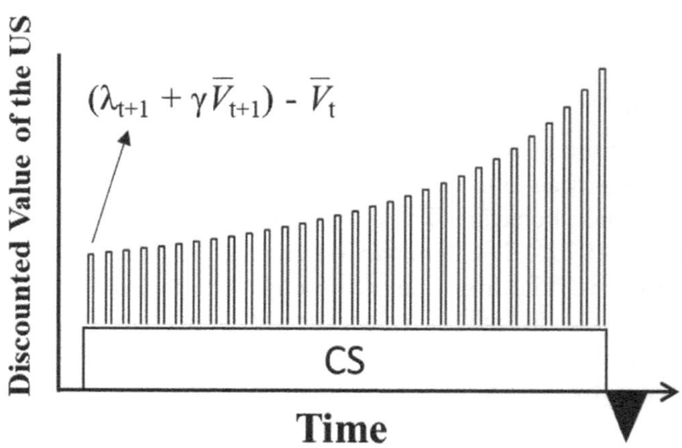

Figure 8.14 **Delay discounting of the US value.** This figure represents the predictions of the discounted US value at each time step during a CS based on a hyperbolic discounting equation. The total value of the US is distributed across the CS. The magnitude of the CR is predicted by the value at each time step. Error correction adjusts the value at each time segment based on the experienced value of the US in the next time segment (λ_{t+1}) plus the predicted discounted value of the US at all remaining time segments (γV_{t+1}) minus the previous estimate of the expected discounted future value of the US at all remaining time segments (V_t).

In temporal difference models, the predicted value of the US at the current time segment (i.e., what you expect) is the result of the previous error correction for the value of the US in all of the remaining time segments. Recall that the size of error correction in the Rescorla-Wagner model, which drives learning, results from the subtraction of an estimate of the US value (i.e., what you expect) from lambda (i.e., what you get; actual US minus expected US). The same is true in temporal difference models, but the subtraction occurs for every segment of the CS. In other words, no CR in the 31st second of a 40-s CS that terminates in a US would require error correction; the CR should be based on the discounted value of the experienced US during that segment of time. Error correction leads to timed behavior, as segments early in the 40-s CS will acquire little-to-no predicted US value, while segments closer to the end of the CS will acquire more value.

Other assumptions that make up temporal difference models include eligibility traces, a kind of memory trace, and a learning rate parameter. Sutton and Barto (1990) have shown that a temporal difference model is able to simulate the results of a variety of conditioning procedures, from timed behavior with varying CS–US intervals to blocking and second-order conditioning. Additionally, these models predict that overshadowing and blocking are dependent on the temporal properties of the CSs (see the previous section on **Cue competition and integration based on timing**).

8.5 Can nonhuman animals time travel?

It has been said that humans can mentally travel into the past and future (Roberts, 2002; Suddendof & Corballis, 2007). What does *mental time travel* mean? Some examples might be retelling the story of a painful breakup months after the moment has passed or packing items into a suitcase weeks before a planned vacation. A critical aspect of both examples is that the current motivational state differs from that of the past or future moment, which means the moment is seemingly not reflexively triggered. These criteria would eliminate examples like nest building and other evolved predispositions. Additionally, Suddendof and Corballis (2007) emphasized that mental time travel to the past or future involves more than just knowledge from regularities in the environment of what did or will happen but rather reconstructions or constructions of the particularities of past or future events. This does not eliminate associative learning procedures as a means to study mental time travel, but it suggests caution when evaluating examples with many trials. Many associative learning procedures can be conducted in one trial, but others may require many trials of pretraining and test in a novel apparatus. However, analyzing only the first trial in the novel apparatus does not eliminate the potential effects of pretraining.

What examples are there of mental time travel in a nonhuman animal? Mahoney and Ayres (1976) trained water-deprived rats to drink from a sipper tube for 4 days. On the 5th day, the bottle was removed, and one group (Paired) received one pairing of a Noise followed by Shock, and another group (Control) was given the same Shock, but the Noise was omitted. The next day, the bottle was returned, and rats were allowed to drink from the sipper tube for a few seconds before the Noise was presented. Time to complete another 10 licks in the presence of the Noise was measured. Rats in the paired group took an average of 71 s longer than the control group to complete 10 additional licks. In other words, a rat in an operant chamber drinking water (i.e., motivational state of thirst) suddenly freezes when a Noise previously paired with Shock is presented.

The only difference between this example and other examples of conditioning discussed is that the rats only experienced a single trial of fear conditioning. Is the rat mentally time traveling into the past when the Noise was paired with Shock? Perhaps. Is it mentally traveling to the future, when the Shock will be presented following the Noise? Perhaps. We can evaluate the example based on the criteria listed earlier: Does the current motivational state differ from that of the past or future moment? Assuming the animal is calm when the noise is presented, then its motivation state differs from that of the past moment when the shock occurred.

Is the time travel reflexively triggered? Given that the rat did not reflexively freeze to the Noise during the first trial, the time travel was not reflexive.

An additional criterion may be that mental time travel must be under the rat's control. We could ask the same question of the individual retelling the story of a painful breakup when asked or packing items into a suitcase the night before travel. What we do know is that rats hearing a Noise previously paired once with Shock will exhibit behavior that reflects their past history with the Noise and is consistent with a specific future threat.

With respect to the particularities of remembered events, when rats drink plain water while a Tone previously paired with Sucrose is played, they exhibit consummatory behaviors similar to when they drink sucrose (Delamater et al., 1986). It is as if the animals' specific past experience with a sucrose solution is being reexperienced (i.e., they are time traveling to the past) while drinking normal water. Is this an example of reconstruction, as the current experience of the rat is influenced by past experience?

Roberts (2002) proposed that memory for time must include how long ago an event occurred, the location of an event within a time scale, or the order of events with respect to other events occurring over time. One of the most common examples of possible mental time travel in nonhuman animals was provided by an experiment with scrub jays. Scrub jays display *food-storing behavior* that is retrieved at a later time. In nature, scrub jays cache perishable food items, such as mealworms, at a lower rate and retrieve them more quickly, whereas other food items remain viable long after they are cached.

Clayton et al. (2001) allowed scrub jays to cache various foods and retrieve them 4, 28, or 100 h later (Table 8.4). On each trial, half of an ice tray was covered and the other half was open for the scrub jays to cache either mealworms or crickets in sand. Then the other half was made available for caching peanuts. In one group (Degrade), the researchers removed

Table 8.4 Food-storing memory in scrub jays for what, when, and where

Group		*4 h*	*28 h*	*100 h*
Degrade	Side 1	Mealworms-P	Mealworms-D	Mealworms-D
		Crickets-P	Crickets-P	Crickets-D
	Side 2	Peanuts-P	Peanuts-P	Peanuts-P
	Recovery preference	*Mealworms or crickets*	*Crickets*	*Peanuts*
Replenish	Side 1	Mealworms-P	Mealworms-P	Mealworms-P
		Crickets-P	Crickets-P	Crickets-P
	Side 2	Peanuts-P	Peanuts-P	Peanuts-P
	Recovery preference	*Mealworms or crickets*	*Mealworms or crickets*	*Mealworms or crickets*

Note. Based on Clayton et al. (2001). P: a palatable food. D: a degraded or unpalatable food. The time intervals refer to the duration in between a caching event and retrieval. Caching in the side that was not peanuts alternated between mealworms and crickets. Recovery preference identifies what the scrub jays should prefer to retrieve if they can remember what, when, and where they stored the different food types.

the mealworms before the 28-h retrieval time and replaced them with degraded mealworms; removed crickets before the 100-h retrieval time and replaced them with degraded crickets; peanuts, however, were viable at all intervals. In another group (Replenish), all food types were replaced by the experimenters so they would be fresh at all intervals. In Group Degrade, this should lead to a preference for mealworms and crickets over peanuts at 4 h, a preference

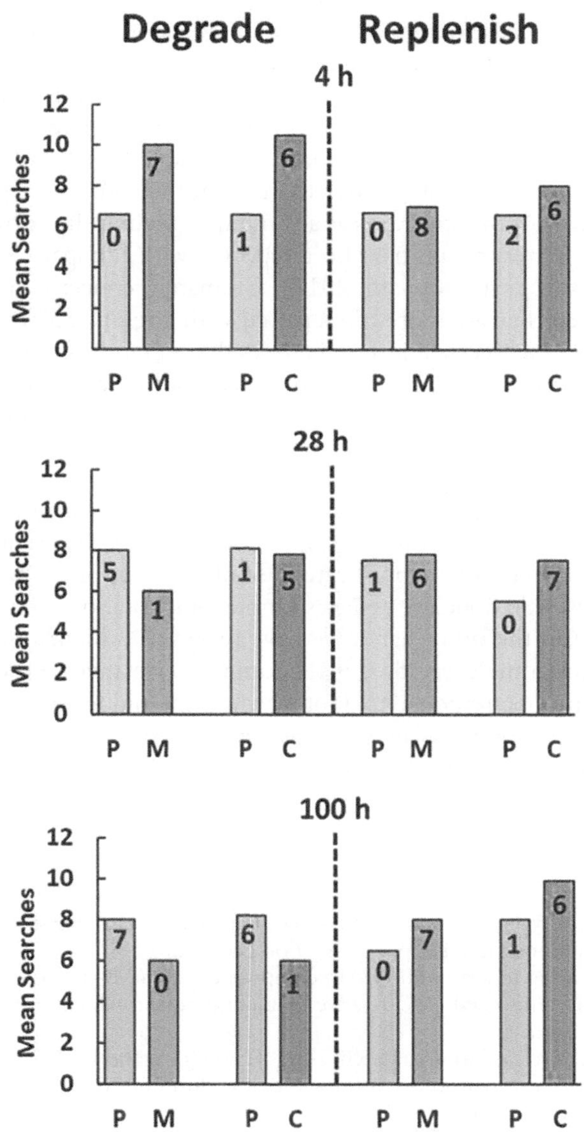

Figure 8.15 **Time-traveling scrub jays.** These data were obtained from tests with scrub jays that were trained that certain cached food items degrade or replenish at specific intervals (4, 28, or 100 h). The numbers inside the bar indicate the number of birds that searched each location first. C: Crickets. M: Mealworms. P: Peanuts. (From Clayton et al., 2001; reproduced with permission from the American Psychological Association.)

for peanuts or crickets at 28 h, and a preference for peanuts only at 100 h. In Group Replenish, a preference for mealworms or crickets should be observed at all intervals.

At test, all items were removed after caching so that retrieval behavior was determined only by memory and not by local cues. The results matched the predictions expected if the scrub jays remembered what, where, and how long ago they cached an item (Figure 8.15). As we have noted, memory traces likely play a role in timed behavior, though they do not permit the kind of mental time travel observed in this experiment. Furthermore, scrub jays in nature cache before they retrieve, and thus, there is a predisposition toward this behavior that involves memory, but because of its reflexive nature, it is not considered mental time travel.

An area of research investigating future planning that involves instrumental behaviors is *tool use*. Mulcahy and Call (2006) tested whether orangutans and bonobos would select a functional tool over distractor tools to take into another room for an hour and then bring the tool back into the test room. Subjects transported a suitable tool out of the test room in 40% of the trials, which was significantly better than chance (25%). Subsequent tests addressed concerns about the role of the apparatus as a stimulus signaling the correct tool and the role of motivational state. Similar results have been reported with chimpanzees (Osvath & Osvath, 2008) and corvids (Kabadayi & Osvath, 2017). Ultimately, concerns about the higher value of suitable tools (given they are more often paired with a reinforcer than less suitable tools) have prevented widespread recognition of these results as demonstrations of future planning. Boeckle et al. (2020) addressed this limitation by varying the scenario that matched the suitable tool, such that all tools were of similar value, but only one was appropriate for the current scenario. Crows still chose the tool that was appropriate for the future task.

Mental time travel is often discussed as entirely dependent on verbal behavior, which allows unique retrieval cues to be attached to events as they occur in time. The same verbal behavior can then be used later to think about or communicate the event with others. On the one hand, other animals lack our sophisticated use of language and external sources of time-keeping, which leaves little hope for demonstrations of mental time travel if verbal behavior plays a central role. On the other hand, we have reviewed evidence that animals can learn to respond at the same time every day, at the same time relative to the start of a stimulus, to switch from making one response to another after the midpoint of the session, to search a location based on how long ago an item was stored there, and to select a suitable tool to complete a future task. So the possibility of mental time travel in nonhuman animals remains viable.

Glossary

Bisection point The stimulus duration with an equal probability of being classified as either of the two anchor points trained in a temporal bisection procedure.

Blocking Less responding to a stimulus (B) in compound trials (AB+) when the accompanying stimulus was previously reinforced (A+) relative to a condition in which the accompanying stimulus was not trained before.

Circadian rhythms A cycle of approximately 24 h of biological and behavioral changes.

Circadian timing Behavior that occurs at the same time during a cycle of approximately 24 h.

Cognition Mental activity involved in thinking. The stages of information processing.

Cognitive map A mental representation of space formed as the animal explored the environment.

Delay discounting The value of an experience is reduced as a function of distance until the onset of that experience.

Entrainment The process by which a circadian rhythm synchronizes to external timing cues.

Food-storing behavior Some animals store food during the summer months and later retrieve it during the winter months.

Internal clock A brain circuit that measures time.
Internal stimulus Cellular activity correlated with external events.
Interval timing Behavior that occurs after an estimated time between events lasting in the order of seconds to minutes.
Intervening variable A variable postulated to explain functional relationships among stimuli and responses.
Learning An intervening variable postulated to describe functional relationships between stimuli and behavior.
Mental time travel The ability to mentally experience a past event or a predicted future event.
Midsession reversal task Reinforcing one stimulus in the first half of a session but another stimulus in the second half of the session.
Ordinal timing Behavior that occurs based on the sequence or order of events within a time period.
Oscillation Degree of regularity in a temporal cycles.
Overshadowing Less responding to a less salient stimulus when reinforced in the presence of a more salient stimulus relative to the training of the weak stimulus on its own.
Peak procedure a procedure for determining the time of maximum response rate by intermixing nonreinforced probe trials that are at least twice the duration of the fixed interval with baseline trials of a reinforced fixed-interval schedule.
Perception The process by which prior experience and other factors (e.g., motivational state) influence the cognitive or behavioral effects of a sensation.
Point of subjective equality (PSE) The stimulus duration with an equal probability of being classified as either of the two anchor points trained in a temporal bisection procedure.
Real-time theories of conditioning Theories that attempt to predict the results of conditioning (the CR) continuously, on a moment-by-moment basis.
Reference memory A more permanent memory storage of information than working memory.
Renewal Acquisition in one context (A) and extinction in a different context (B) lead to a relapse of the CR if the CS is tested in the acquisition context (ABA renewal) or in a new context (ABC renewal).
Rescorla-Wagner model A model of Pavlovian conditioning that describes changes in the associative strength (predictive value) of a CS on a trial-by-trial basis. Changes in associative strength are a direct function of the salience of the CS and US multiplied by the size of the discrepancy between the actual US and the strength of the anticipated US. The latter is usually referred to as "error correction."
Scalar timing theory A model of timing based on an information-processing approach involving encoding, storage, and retrieval.
Scallop A pattern of responding developing after extensive training in FI schedules consisting of a gradual increase in responding until the time when a reinforcer was presented during training.
Sensation The process by which specialized receptors transduce physical energy into cellular activity.
Sensory preconditioning Pairing of two neutral stimuli (A→B), followed by reinforced presentations of one of them (B→US), allowing the first stimulus (A) to control responding in a subsequent test.
Spontaneous recovery After extinction of an acquired response, a resting period in which no stimuli are presented results in the relapse of the response during the next presentation of the training stimulus.
Stimulus control The probability of a behavior varies with the presence vs. absence of a stimulus.
Superposition Temporal response distributions from probe trials of different fixed-interval durations will overlay with one another when each unit of time is proportioned equally (divided by the fixed interval).
Suprachiasmatic nucleus (SCN) A region of the hypothalamus receiving inputs from cells in the retina of the eye that is involved in circadian timing processes.
Symmetry Matching response rates during a probe trial in the half before and after a fixed interval expires.
Temporal-bisection procedure Training on different responses for two anchor stimulus durations (short and long duration) followed by tests with nonreinforced trials of durations intermediate to the anchors.
Time-perception tasks Training to respond based on the duration of an event.
Time-production tasks Training to respond at a particular time relative to some stimulus onset.

Tool use Utilizing some object to procure access to a resource that is otherwise inaccessible.
Weber's fraction The result of dividing a change in the intensity of a stimulus by the overall intensity of the stimulus.
Weber's Law Sensitivity to a perceived stimulus change is proportional to the magnitude or intensity of the original stimulus.
Working memory A temporary memory storage of information.
Zeitgebers External timing cues to which circadian rhythms will synchronize.

References

Balsam, P. D., Drew, M. R., & Yang, C. (2002). Timing at the start of associative learning. *Learning and Motivation*, *33*, 141–155. https://doi.org/10.1006/lmot.2001.1104

Barnet, R. C., Cole, R. P., & Miller, R. R. (1997). Temporal integration in second-order conditioning and sensory preconditioning. *Animal Learning & Behavior*, *25*(2), 221–233. https://doi.org/10.3758/BF03199061

Barnet, R. C., Grahame, N. J., & Miller, R. R. (1993). Temporal encoding as a determinant of blocking. *Journal of Experimental Psychology: Animal Behavior Processes*, *19*(4), 327–341. https://doi.org/10.1037/0097-7403.19.4.327

Bell-Pedersen, D., Cassone, V. M., Earnest, D. J., Golden, S. S., Hardin, P. E., Thomas, T. L., & Zoran, M. J. (2005). Circadian rhythms from multiple oscillators: Lessons from diverse organisms. *Nature Reviews Genetics*, *6*(7), 544–556. https://doi.org/10.1038/nrg1633

Beran, M. J. (2023). Congratulations to animal cognition on its 50th birthday! Some thoughts on the last 50 years of animal cognition research. *Animal Cognition*, *26*(1), 13–23. https://doi.org/10.1007/s10071-022-01706-5

Biebach, H., Falk, H., & Krebs, J. R. (1991). The effects of constant light and phase shifts on a learned time-place association in garden warblers (*Sylvia borin*): Hourglass or circadian clock? *Journal of Biological Rhythms*, *6*, 353–365. https://doi.org/10.1177/074873049100600406

Blaisdell, A. P., Denniston, J. C., & Miller, R. R. (1998). Temporal encoding as a determinant of overshadowing. *Journal of Experimental Psychology: Animal Behavior Processes*, *24*(1), 72–83. https://doi.org/10.1037/0097-7403.24.1.72

Boeckle, M., Schiestl, M., Frohnwieser, A., Gruber, R., Miller, R., Suddendorf, T., Gray, R. D., Taylor, R. D., & Clayton, N. S. (2020). New Caledonian crows plan for specific future tool use. *Proceedings of the Royal Society B*, *287*(1938), 20201490. https://doi.org/10.1098/rspb.2020.1490

Bolles, R. C., & Moot, S. A. (1973). The rat's anticipation of two meals a day. *Journal of Comparative and Physiological Psychology*, *83*(3), 510–514. https://doi.org/10.1037/h0034666

Bouton, M. E., Maren, S., & McNally, G. P. (2021). Behavioral and neurobiological mechanisms of Pavlovian and instrumental extinction learning. *Physiological Review*, *101*, 611–681. https://doi.org/10.1152/physrev.00016.2020

Brady, D., Saviane, A., Cappellozza, S., & Sandrelli, F. (2021). The circadian clock in Lepidoptera. *Frontiers in Physiology*, *12*, 776826. https://doi.org/10.3389/fphys.2021.776826

Catania, A. C. (1970). Reinforcement schedules and psychophysical judgments: A study of some temporal properties of behavior. In W. N. Schoenfeld (Ed.), *The theory of reinforcement schedules*. Appleton-Century-Crofts.

Cheng, K., & Roberts, W. A. (1991). Three psychophysical principles of timing in pigeons. *Learning and Motivation*, *22*(1–2), 112–128. https://doi.org/10.1016/0023-9690(91)90019-5

Church, R. (1978). The internal clock. In S. H. Hulse, H. Fowler, & W. K. Honig (Eds.), *Cognitive processes in animal behavior*. Erlbaum.

Church, R. M., & Deluty, M. Z. (1977). Bisection of temporal intervals. *Journal of Experimental Psychology: Animal Behavior Processes*, *3*(3), 216–228. https://doi.org/10.1037/0097-7403.3.3.216

Clayton, N. S., Yu, K. S., & Dickinson, A. (2001). Scrub jays (*Aphelocoma coerulescens*) form integrated memories of the multiple features of caching episodes. *Journal of Experimental Psychology: Animal Behavior Processes*, *27*(1), 17–29. https://doi.org/10.1098/rstb.2001.0947

Cowles, J. T., & Finan, J. L. (1941). An improved method for establishing temporal discrimination in white rats. *Journal of Psychology: Interdisciplinary and Applied*, *11*, 335–342. https://doi.org/10.1080/00223980.1941.9917040

Crystal, J. D. (1999). Systematic nonlinearities in the perception of temporal intervals. *Journal of Experimental Psychology: Animal Behavior Processes*, *25*(1), 3–17. https://doi.org/10.1037/0097-7403.25.1.3

Crystal, J. D. (2001). Circadian time perception. *Journal of Experimental Psychology: Animal Behavior Processes*, *27*(1), 68–78. https://doi.org/10.1037/0097-7403.27.1.68
Crystal, J. D., Church, R. M., & Broadbent, H. A. (1997). Systematic nonlinearities in the memory representation of time. *Journal of Experimental Psychology: Animal Behavior Processes*, *23*(3), 267–282. https://doi.org/10.1037/0097-7403.23.3.267
Delamater, A. R., LoLordo, V. M., & Berridge, K. C. (1986). Control of fluid palatability by exteroceptive Pavlovian signals. *Journal of Experimental Psychology: Animal Behavior Processes*, *12*(2), 143. https://doi.org/10.1037/0097-7403.12.2.143
Drew, M. R., Yang, C., Ohyama, T., & Balsam, P. D. (2004). Temporal specificity of extinction in autoshaping. *Journal of Experimental Psychology: Animal Behavior Processes*, *30*(3), 163. https://doi.org/10.1037/0097-7403.30.3.163
Droit-Volet, S., & Wearden, J. (2002). Speeding up an internal clock in children? Effects of visual flicker on subjective duration. *Quarterly Journal of Experimental Psychology: Section B*, *55*(3), 193–211. https://doi.org/10.1080/02724990143000252
Earnest, D. J., Liang, F.-Q., Ratcliff, M., & Cassone, V. M. (1999). Immortal time: Circadian clock properties of rat suprachiasmatic cell lines. *Science*, *283*(5402), 693–695. https://doi.org/10.1126/science.283.5402.693
Fairhurst, S., Gallistel, C. R., & Gibbon, J. (2003). Temporal landmarks: Proximity prevails. *Animal Cognition*, *6*, 113–120. https://doi.org/10.1007/s10071-003-0169-8
Ferster, C. B., & Skinner, B. F. (1957). *Schedules of reinforcement*. Appleton-Century-Crofts. https://doi.org/10.1037/10627-000
Fiori, L. M., Barnet, R. C., & Miller, R. R. (1994). Renewal of Pavlovian conditioned inhibition. *Animal Learning & Behavior*, *22*(1), 47–52. https://doi.org/10.3758/BF03199955
Gallistel, C. R. (1990). *The organization of learning*. Bradford Books, MIT Press.
Gibbon, J. (1981). On the form and location of the psychometric bisection function for time. *Journal of Mathematical Psychology*, *24*(1), 58–87. https://doi.org/10.1016/0022-2496(81)90035-3
Gibbon, J., & Balsam, P. (1981). Spreading associations in time. In C. M. Locurto, H. S. Terrace, & J. Gibbon (Eds.), *Autoshaping and conditioning theory* (pp. 219–253). Academic Press.
Gibbon, J., & Church, R. M. (1984). Sources of variance in an information processing theory of timing. In H. L. Roitblat, T. G. Bever, & H. S. Terrace (Eds.), *Animal cognition* (pp. 465–488). Erlbaum.
Gibbon, J., Church, R. M., & Meck, W. H. (1984). Scalar timing in memory. *Annals of the New York Academy of Sciences*, *423*, 52–77. https://doi.org/10.1111/j.1749-6632.1984.tb23417.x
Gibbon, J., Fairhurst, S., & Goldberg, B. (1997). Cooperation, conflict and compromise between circadian and interval clocks in pigeons. In *Advances in psychology* (Vol. 120, pp. 329–384). North-Holland.
Green, D. M., & Swets, J. A. (1966). *Signal detection theory and psychophysics*. Wiley.
Holder, M. D., & Roberts, S. (1985). Comparison of timing and classical conditioning. *Journal of Experimental Psychology: Animal Behavior Processes*, *11*(2), 172. https://doi.org/10.1037/0097-7403.11.2.172
Jennings, D. J., Bonardi, C., & Kirkpatrick, K. (2007). Overshadowing and stimulus duration. *Journal of Experimental Psychology: Animal Behavior Processes*, *33*(4), 464. https://doi.org/10.1037/0097-7403.33.4.464
Jonides, J., Lewis, R. L., Nee, D. E., Lustig, C. A., Berman, M. G., & Moore, K. S. (2008). The mind and brain of short-term memory. *Annual Review of Psychology*, *59*(1), 193–224. https://doi.org/10.1146/annurev.psych.59.103006.093615
Kabadayi, C., & Osvath, M. (2017). Ravens parallel great apes in flexible planning for tool-use and bartering. *Science*, *357*(6347), 202–204. https://doi.org/10.1126/science.aam8138
Kirkpatrick, K., & Church, R. M. (2000). Independent effects of stimulus and cycle duration in conditioning: The role of timing processes. *Animal Learning & Behavior*, *28*(4), 373–388. https://doi.org/10.3758/BF03200271
Klopf, A. H. (1988). A neuronal model of classical conditioning. *Psychobiology*, *16*, 85–125.
Krishnan, B., Dryer, S. E., & Hardin, P. E. (1999). Circadian rhythms in olfactory responses of Drosophila melanogaster. *Nature*, *400*(6742), 375–378. https://doi.org/10.1038/22566
Leising, K. J., Sawa, K., & Blaisdell, A. P. (2007). Temporal integration in Pavlovian appetitive conditioning in rats. *Animal Learning & Behavior*, *35*(1), 11–18. https://doi.org/10.3758/BF03196069
Mackintosh, N. J. (1976). Overshadowing and stimulus intensity. *Animal Learning & Behavior*, *4*(2), 186–192. https://doi.org/10.3758/BF03214033
Mackintosh, N. J., & Reese, B. (1979). One-trial overshadowing. *Quarterly Journal of Experimental Psychology*, *31*(3), 519–526. https://doi.org/10.1080/14640747908400743

Mahoney, W. J., & Ayres, J. J. (1976). One-trial simultaneous and backward fear conditioning as reflected in conditioned suppression of licking in rats. *Animal Learning & Behavior*, *4*(4), 357–362. https://doi.org/10.3758/BF03214421
Meck, W. H., & Church, R. M. (1983). A mode control model of counting and timing processes. *Journal of Experimental Psychology: Animal Behavior Processes*, *9*(3), 320–334. https://doi.org/10.1037/0097-7403.9.3.320
Melgire, M., Ragot, R., Samson, S., Penney, T. B., Meck, W. H., & Pouthas, V. (2005). Auditory/visual duration bisection in patients with left or right medial-temporal lobe resection. *Brain and Cognition*, *58*(1), 119–124. https://doi.org/10.1016/j.bandc.2004.09.013
Mergenhagen, D. (1980). Circadian rhythms in unicellular organisms. *Current Topics in Microbiology and Immunology*, *90*, 123–147. https://doi.org/10.1007/978-3-642-67717-5_6
Merrow, M., Spoelstra, K., & Roenneberg, T. (2005). The circadian cycle: Daily rhythms from behaviour to genes. *EMBO Reports*, *6*(10), 930–935. https://doi.org/10.1038/sj.embor.7400541
Miller, R. R., Esposito, J. J., & Grahame, N. J. (1992). Overshadowing-like effects between potential comparator stimuli: Covariation in comparator roles of context and punctate excitor used in inhibitory training as a function of excitor salience. *Learning and Motivation*, *23*(1), 1–26. https://doi.org/10.1016/0023-9690(92p)90020-M
Molet, M., Jozefowiez, J., & Miller, R. R. (2010). Integration of spatial relationships and temporal relationships in humans. *Learning & Behavior*, *38*(1), 27–34. https://doi.org/10.3758/LB.38.1.27
Moore, J. W., & Desmond, J. E. (1992). A cerebellar neural network implementation of a temporally adaptive conditioned response. In I. Gormezano & E. A. Wasserman (Eds.), *Learning and memory: The behavioral and biological substrates* (pp. 347–368). Erlbaum.
Morse, D., Hastings, J. W., & Roenneberg, T. (1994). Different phase responses of the two circadian oscillators in *Gonyaulax*. *Journal of Biological Rhythms*, *9*(3–4), 263–274. https://doi.org/10.1177/074873049400900307
Mulcahy, N. J., & Call, J. (2006). Apes save tools for future use. *Science*, *312*(5776), 1038–1040. https://doi.org/10.1126/science.1125456
Myers, D. G. (2013). *Psychology* (10th ed.). Worth.
Ohyama, T., Gibbon, J., Deich, J. D., & Balsam, E. D. (1999). Temporal control during maintenance and extinction of conditioned keypecking in ring doves. *Animal Learning & Behavior*, *27*, 89–98. https://doi.org/10.3758/BF03199434
Ohyama, T., & Mauk, M. D. (2001). Latent acquisition of timed responses in cerebellar cortex. *Journal of Neuroscience*, *21*(2), 682–690. https://doi.org/10.1523/JNEUROSCI.21-02-00682.2001
Osvath, M., & Osvath, H. (2008). Chimpanzee (Pan troglodytes) and orangutan (Pongo abelii) forethought: Self-control and pre-experience in the face of future tool use. *Animal Cognition*, *11*, 661–674. https://doi.org/10.1007/s10071-008-0157-0
Öztekin, I., Davachi, L., & McElree, B. (2010). Are representations in working memory distinct from representations in long-term memory? Neural evidence in support of a single store. *Psychological Science*, *21*(8), 1123–1133. https://doi.org/10.1177/0956797610376651
Papini, M. R., & Hollingsworth, P. R. (1998). Role of nonreinforcement in the fixed-interval performance of pigeons. *Psychonomic Bulletin & Review*, *5*(1), 84–90. https://doi.org/10.3758/BF03209460
Pavlov, I. P. (1927). *Conditioned reflexes: An investigation of the physiological activity of the cerebral cortex*. Oxford University Press.
Penney, T. B., Gibbon, J., & Meck, W. H. (2000). Differential effects of auditory and visual signals on clock speed and temporal memory. *Journal of Experimental Psychology: Human Perception and Performance*, *26*(6), 1770–1787. https://doi.org/10.1037/0096-1523.26.6.1770
Raslear, T. G. (1983). A test of the Pfanzagl bisection model in rats. *Journal of Experimental Psychology: Animal Behavior Processes*, *9*(1), 49. https://doi.org/10.1037/0097-7403.9.1.49
Raslear, T. G. (1985). Perceptual bias and response bias in temporal bisection. *Perception & Psychophysics*, *38*(3), 261–268. https://doi.org/10.3758/BF03207153
Rayburn-Reeves, R. M., Qadri, M. A., Brooks, D. I., Keller, A. M., & Cook, R. G. (2017). Dynamic cue use in pigeon mid-session reversal. *Behavioural processes*, *137*, 53–63. https://doi.org/10.1016/j.beproc.2016.09.002
Rivkees, S. A. (2007). The development of circadian rhythms: From animals to humans. *Sleep Medicine Clinics*, *2*(3), 331–341. https://doi.org/10.1016/j.jsmc.2007.05.010

Roberts, S. (1981). Isolation of an internal clock. *Journal of Experimental Psychology: Animal Behavior Processes*, *7*(3), 242–268. https://doi.org/10.1037/0097-7403.7.3.242

Roberts, W. A. (2002). Are animals stuck in time? *Psychological Bulletin*, *128*(3), 473–489. https://doi.org/10.1037/0033-2909.128.3.473

Silver, R., & Rainbow, M. (2013). The suprachiasmatic nucleus and the circadian timekeeping system of the body. In D. W. Pfaff (Ed.), *Neuroscience in the 21st century*. Springer. https://doi.org/10.1007/978-1-4614-1997-6_66

Sissons, H. T., & Miller, R. R. (2009). Spontaneous recovery of excitation and inhibition. *Journal of Experimental Psychology: Animal Behavior Processes*, *35*(3), 419–426. https://doi.org/10.1037/a0014815

Stubbs, D. A. (1976). Scaling of stimulus duration by pigeons. *Journal of the Experimental Analysis of Behavior*, *26*(1), 15–25. https://doi.org/10.1901/jeab.1976.26-15

Suddendorf, T., & Corballis, M. C. (2007). The evolution of foresight: What is mental time travel, and is it unique to humans? *Behavioral and Brain Sciences*, *30*(3), 299–313. https://doi.org/10.1017/S0140525X07001975

Sulzman, F. M., Ellman, D., Fuller, C. A., Moore-Ede, M. C., & Wassmer, G. (1984). Neurospora circadian rhythms in space: A reexamination of the endogenous-exogenous question. *Science*, *225*(4658), 232–234. https://doi.org/10.1126/science.11540800

Sutton, R. S., & Barto, A. G. (1981). Toward a modern theory of adaptive networks: Expectation and prediction. *Psychological Review*, *88*, 135–171. https://doi.org/10.1037/0033-295X.88.2.135

Sutton, R. S., & Barto, A. G. (1990). Time-derivative models of Pavlovian reinforcement. In M. Gabriel & J. Moore (Eds.), *Learning and computational neuroscience: Foundations of adaptive networks* (pp. 497–537). MIT Press.

Tessauro, G. (1986). Simple neural models of classical conditioning. *Biological Cybernetics*, *55*, 187–200. https://doi.org/10.1007/BF00341933

Thorpe, C. M., & Wilkie, D. M. (2006). Properties of time-place learning. In E. A. Wasserman & T. R. Zentall (Eds.), *Comparative cognition: Experimental explorations of animal intelligence* (pp. 229–245). Oxford University Press.

Tolman, E. C. (1938). The determiners of behavior at a choice point. *Psychological Review*, *45*(1), 1–41. https://doi.org/10.1037/h0062733

Walker, W. H., Walton, J. C., DeVries, A. C., & Nelson, R. J. (2020). Circadian rhythm disruption and mental health. *Translational Psychiatry*, *10*, 28. https://doi.org/10.1038/s41398-020-0694-0

Wasserman, E. A. (1981). Comparative psychology returns: A review of Hulse, Fowler, and Honig's cognitive processes in animal behavior. *Journal of the Experimental Analysis of Behavior*, *35*, 243–257. https://doi.org/10.1901/jeab.1981.35-243

Wearden, J. H. (1991). Human performance on an analogue of an interval bisection task. *Quarterly Journal of Experimental Psychology Section B*, *43*(1b), 59–81.

Welsh, D. K., Logothetis, D. E., Meister, M., & Reppert, S. M. (1995). Individual neurons dissociated from rat suprachiasmatic nucleus express independently phased circadian firing rhythms. *Neuron*, *14*, 697–706. https://doi.org/10.1016/0896-6273(95)90214-7

Yan, J., Wang, H., Liu, Y., & Shao, C. (2008). Analysis of gene regulatory networks in the mammalian circadian rhythm. *PLoS Computational Biology*, *4*(10), e1000193. https://doi.org/10.1371/journal.pcbi.1000193

Zentall, T. R. (2020). The midsession reversal task: A theoretical analysis. *Learning & Behavior*, *48*(2), 195–207. https://doi.org/10.3758/s13420-020-00423-8

Zylka, M. J., Shearman, L. P., Weaver, D. R., & Reppert, S. M. (1998). Three period homologs in mammals: Differential light responses in the suprachiasmatic circadian clock and oscillating transcripts outside of brain. *Neuron*, *20*(6), 1103–1110. https://doi.org/10.1016/s0896-6273(00)80492-4

9 Spatial behavior

9.1 Introduction: spatial behavior

Navigating to a particular location in space is a discrimination problem, just as it is for responding to a particular point in time. The position of a target location must be discriminated with a degree of accuracy sufficient to support successful navigation. In some cases, success may require discriminating one point in space from another on the order of centimeters (e.g., buried seeds) or meters (e.g., an ant's nest in the desert), but in other cases, kilometers may do (e.g., breeding grounds). Thinking of spatial behavior as a discrimination problem provides a unifying theme across many chapters of this book.

Navigating to a particular location requires the use of cues in the environment, such as a mountain ridge in the distance or an odor near a destination. The cues most useful to accurate spatial behavior differ depending on the current distance from the goal and the availability of cues in the environment. Most of us have navigated both within and between cities. You may have noticed that successful orientation within a city was supported by a set of cues that differed from those of an intercity trip. The majority of cities are filled with lots of unique visual, auditory, and even olfactory cues, but the landscape between cities tends to involve less diversity. Consequently, you may have received directions from a friend to a destination within the city in the form of a route, or a series of spatial responses (e.g., turn right at the museum and left at the park) controlled by unique cues. Alternatively, when receiving directions between cities, a simple heading may have sufficed (e.g., head east).

Similarly, nonhuman animals typically depend on different cues for long-distance and small-scale navigation. Furthermore, within long-distance migration, the journey can be broken down into a long-distance phase, a narrowing-in or homing phase, and a pin-pointing the goal phase (Mouritsen, 2018). In each phase, different environmental cues may be utilized (Figure 9.1).

When animals are exposed to similar conditions but rely on different cues for navigation, researchers often look inside the organism (i.e., *cognition*) to determine whether behavior can be better predicted if we consider how the cues are processed (e.g., perception, encoding, storage, and retrieval). It is critical that the investigation does not stop there but rather continues to the next question of what conditions led to processing differences across animals. There remains a healthy debate between those that propose that an internal *representation* of the external world supports many forms of spatial behavior (Nadel, 2013) and those that deny any involvement of a structured spatial representation of the world (e.g., Reid & Staddon, 1998). Both groups agree that reflexes, Pavlovian conditioning, and operant conditioning play a crucial role in successful small- and large-scale spatial behavior.

DOI: 10.4324/9781003401957-12

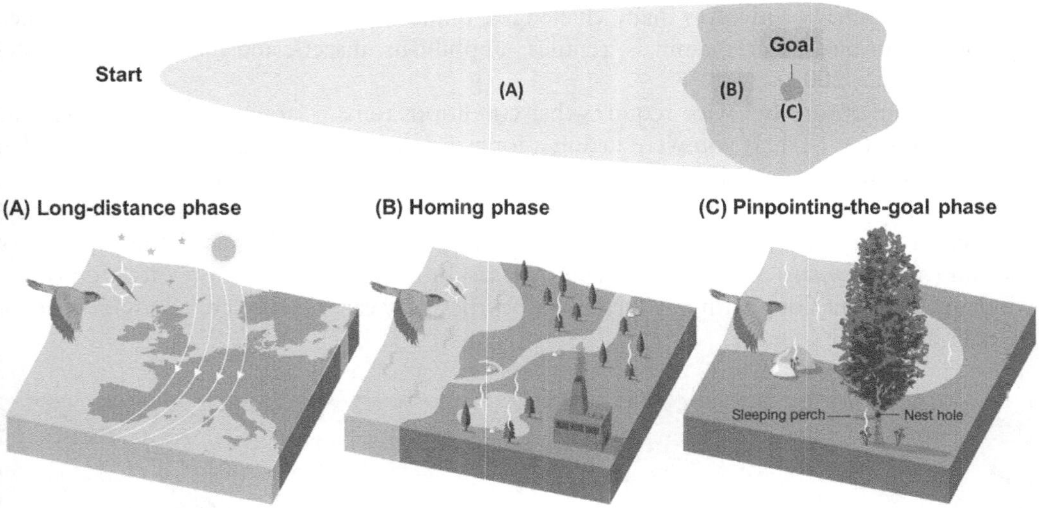

Figure 9.1 **Three different phases of a long-distance navigation.** **(A)** During the long-distance phase, celestial and magnetic compass and map cues are very important, and landmarks such as coastlines can function as physical constraints. **(B)** During the homing phase, compasses are usually still important, and regional map cues such as olfactory and visual landmarks, olfactory gradients, strong magnetic anomalies, and soundscapes become important. **(C)** During the pinpointing-the-goal phase, specific within-habitat cues such as a cave entrance, a specific tree, or a smelly lake are needed to locate, for example, a nest hole or sleeping perch. (From Mouritsen, 2018; reproduced with permission from Nature.)

9.2 Migration and large-scale spatial behavior

It is fascinating to think about how some animals, from flying insects to terrestrial mammals, can travel distances of over 5,000 kilometers to arrive at a destination that can be as small as an 8-kilometer target island (Alerstam et al., 2003). *Migration* can be defined according to the type of behavior that occurs and the cues that influence it. For example, migration has been defined as persistent, straightened-out movements that are undistracted by the cues that would stop other types of movements (Dingle, 2014; Dingle & Drake, 2007). Others define migration with respect to the consequences of the movements, reserving the term "migration" for round-trip movements between breeding and nonbreeding grounds, and use dispersion to refer to other long-range trips.

It is also important to think about the selective pressures that support the evolution of migratory behavior. The most frequently identified selective pressure relates to seasonal peaks in the abundance of resources needed for survival and breeding. For example, the clutch size (the number of eggs) of many birds is, in part, determined by the degree of seasonal fluctuation in resources, such as food and nesting areas (Ashmole, 1963; Ricklefs, 1980). Many habitats have an abundance of the kind of resources optimal for survival, but those same habitats may have suboptimal resources for breeding. Consequently, a migratory species is able to exploit the resources for survival in one location and those for breeding in another location. Successful migration is likely to correlate with changes in certain anatomical features, such as size, mass, shape, and metabolic rate (Alerstam et al., 2003). The benefits of migration must outweigh the costs, which include increased energy requirements, as well as potential increases in exposure to predators, parasites, and pathogens. Although the evolution of migratory behavior involves many challenges, migration has evolved independently (i.e., homoplasy) in birds, fish, mammals, reptiles, amphibians, insects, and marine invertebrates (Alerstam et al., 2003).

Evolved migratory behavior requires that conditions remain largely consistent from one generation to the next. If you were taking a long-distance trip without a smartphone, what types of cues would be available to you, as well as several generations of humans after you, to determine your heading and to correct for any error that accumulates along your journey? You might think of the brave open-water mariners of antiquity that used the position of the sun (*solar compass*) and stars (*celestial compass*) in the sky, as well as the direction of the wind and currents along with any reliable odors they may carry. These are all useful cues for humans and other animals.

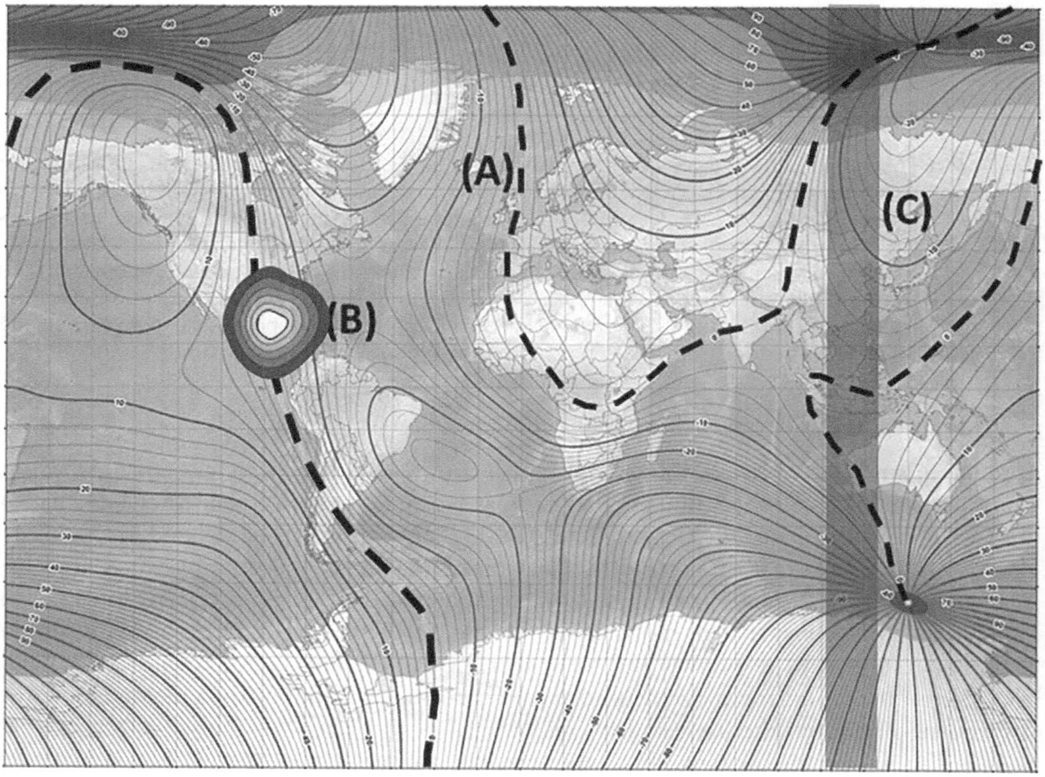

Figure 9.2 **Visualizations of contour maps created by magnetic fields, infrasound, and polarized light. (A)** The various solid lines indicate deviations in the Earth's magnetic field from true north across the world. Dashed lines indicate where magnetic north and true north are equal. Sensitivity to a target location (e.g., a loft) relative to these deviations could be used to adjust a heading during large-scale spatial behavior, or a particular deviation line could be followed. **(B)** The circles in the southern U.S. and northern part of Mexico represent a contour map of infrasound, with brighter colors indicating higher sound pressure levels. **(C)** The rectangular band running north to south over a portion of the eastern hemisphere is a representation of the appearance of polarized light. Before sunlight reaches the Earth's surface, it is scattered by molecules in Earth's atmosphere, which polarize the light waves. Polarized sunlight would appear to insects, even on a cloudy day, as a band of light that is always at an angle of 90° from the sun. (Adapted from NONOAA NCEI Geomagnetic Modeling Team; British Geological Survey, 2024: World Magnetic Model.)

Other cues are beyond human sensory thresholds but enable accurate movements for other animals. These include the distribution of geomagnetic gradients across the earth that enable a ***geomagnetic compass***, the distribution of low-frequency sound that enables an ***infrasound compass***, and the polarization of sunlight as it passes through the Earth's atmosphere (Figure 9.2). Although learning may influence migration in species that make annual movements, its role is limited in the first migration or in species that complete only one portion of the migration in their lifetime. Spatial behavior under these conditions must largely be under the control of genetics and imprinting or learned prior to their first departure.

Although the conditions in which migratory behavior evolved must have remained *largely* consistent across generations, slow environmental change, such as the drifting of the continents, may result in a migratory phenomenon that parallels shaping by successive approximations (see Chapter 4). ***Shaping by successive approximations*** describes a process in which behaviors are reinforced in steps, with each next step more closely resembling the terminal, or target behavior, than the last. Skinner (1975) reviewed several instances of migration in which a sort of ***phylogenetic shaping*** may have played a role.

Let us start with the terminal behavior. Adult green turtles of Brazil utilize geomagnetic and olfactory cues to make a thousand-mile journey across the Atlantic Ocean to return to their natal beaches (i.e., where they hatched) on Ascension Island for breeding. Such a feat seems highly unlikely to have arisen via saltation (e.g., mutation) or a single jump from one generation to the next. If these migratory behaviors did not simply appear but were shaped by successive approximations, then the baseline behavior and successive steps could be reconstructed. One hypothesis is that journeys such as these occurred between two locations that were originally much shorter in distance (baseline) but have drifted apart over tens of millions of years (Carr & Coleman, 1974). As the South American and African continents drifted apart (~1.5 cm per year), the next generation of navigators would have to compensate for trivial increases in distance traveled (successive approximations, Figure 9.3). If the original breeding grounds have the optimal resources for breeding, then the green turtles that successfully completed the trip would outreproduce the others.

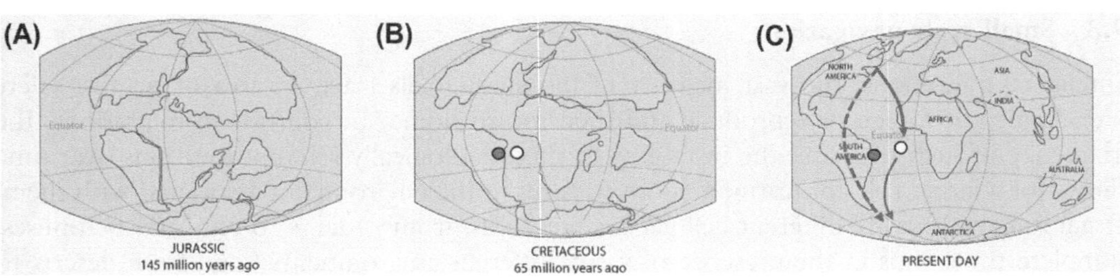

Figure 9.3 **Shaping of migration by successive approximations. (A)** South America and Africa were closer during the Jurassic period. **(B)** The map displays estimated continental drift over years encompassing the evolutionary history of turtles. The red (dark) dot indicates a common feeding location for the green turtle on the coast of Brazil, and the yellow (clear) dot indicates its breeding grounds at Ascension Island, which represents a distance of over 1000 miles. **(C)** This map adds the shortest route (dashed arrow, following the curvature of the Earth) for an arctic tern that breeds in the North-Eastern Atlantic coast of North America and feeds in the Antarctic and a common path (continuous arrows). The actual path maximizes access to the coastline but adds miles of additional travel. (Adapted from U.S. Geological Survey. This dynamic Earth: The story of plate tectonics. U.S. Department of the Interior. https://pubs.usgs.gov/gip/dynamic/)

Once natal homing across long distances evolved, it could support the development of new colonies that might start as a result of many turtles blown off course during storms or other natural events. Two additional parallels between evolved behavior and migration can be made.

First, just as turtles imbued with natal homing can exhibit the same behavior under new conditions (i.e., inhabit new territory), once a new operant behavior has been established (e.g., manipulating metal to make weapons and improve the likelihood of success in battle), its effectiveness may spread beyond the original conditions (e.g., manipulating metal to make jewelry to improve the likelihood of success in mating).

Second, as is often the case with acquired behavior, remnants of earlier steps can be detected in the form of the target behavior. One such example might be the path of the Arctic tern that breeds in the northeastern Atlantic coast of North America. The shortest route from the coast of North America to its breeding grounds in the Antarctic is due south. However, the tern travels southeast toward the coastline of west Africa, adding hundreds of miles to the journey. This seemingly maladaptive behavior makes sense in the context of continental drift (Figure 9.3-B–C). Coastlines provide more cues for navigation and resources than open water. Millions of years ago, the coastline of Africa would have coincided with the shortest route from Arctic to Antarctic. Over time, however, the coastline has drifted, but the Arctic terns in this area continue to follow it. One could consider this a kind of evolutionary mismatch, much like the continued mass consumption of high-fat, high-calorie foods by humans in modern times that may have evolved to support survival in times when such food sources were scarce.

As migration transitions from a long-distance phase to a narrowing-in and pinpointing-the-goal phase, new stimuli come to control behavior (Mouritsen, 2018). Although the green turtle of Brazil uses a geomagnetic compass for orientation throughout most of its journey, its spatial behavior comes under the control of olfactory stimuli as it nears Ascension Island. This same progression occurs for ocean navigators as well, who may use one type of cue (celestial compass) on the open sea and other cues as their destination nears (e.g., a lighthouse or familiar features of a coastline).

9.3 Small-scale navigation

Similar to migrations, the vast majority of mobile animals leave an area of relative safety (i.e., home) to forage or reproduce and then return home. In contrast to migrations, the frequency of such trips and the instability of these biologically relevant locations over time allows for a larger role for learning about features in the environment associated with them. Organisms with vastly different cellular architectures, from rodents to ants and octopuses, complete these trips in the presence of vastly different environments (e.g., from deserts to rainforests and ocean floors) and features (e.g., visual, olfactory, and auditory). It is not surprising, then, that there are many forms of spatial behavior that enable organisms to navigate to a familiar location.

However, the types of cues that provide accurate spatial information are less variable, such that we can expect some consistency in the principles that guide spatial behavior across animals. For example, cues that are more stable should have a greater influence on search behavior than cues that are more likely to be moved by wind, water, or sunlight. This is likely why many animals, including mollusks, ants, caterpillars, and rats, can follow a trail of olfactory cues emitted from their own bodies while foraging (Biegler, 2006). However, olfactory cues are subject to degradation by wind and water, and they are often an inefficient means for returning to the start location. Evaluating potential stimulus control of spatial behavior based on factors such as *salience* and *contiguity* should remind you of Chapter 2. In Chapter 2, these factors determined how strongly different stimuli conditioned. With respect to spatial behavior, the probability and location of a response are measured.

9.3.1 Path integration

An organism may evolve in an environment with few unique cues near the target area, as is the case for the desert ant (*Cataglyphis fortis*). Consequently, it must rely on *idiothetic feedback* (self-motion) from its own movement to determine distance traveled and distal cues (e.g., celestial compass or a landscape silhouette) to determine direction traveled. Due to the hypothesized integration of these two types of information, this form of spatial behavior is commonly referred to as *path integration* (or *dead reckoning*) and was first described by Darwin (1873). With respect to distance traveled, common idiothetic cues include how quickly objects are passing by the navigator (optic flow), how tired they are (energy use), or how many steps they have taken (pedometer).

Wittlinger et al. (2006) allowed ants to complete 10-m trips from a nest to a feeding site within a channel (eliminating the need to determine direction) over the course of a day. After training, ants were caught at the feeding site, and their legs were either intact (control), shortened, or lengthened. The ants were then released at a test site parallel to the original channel to complete their return journey. Ants with longer legs traveled farther (15.30 m) than the originally trained distance before transitioning from their straight-run to nest-searching behavior, whereas those with shortened legs transitioned at a location (5.75 m) well before the trained distance. Path integration is consistent with a kind of *working memory* for the distance and direction of the current trip that updates, or is replaced, by a new trip to minimize spatial errors due to interference. Consistent with this hypothesis, when the ants with manipulated legs (long and short) were subsequently allowed to complete a new outbound trip to the feeder, their return trip in a parallel test channel was marked by a relatively accurate transition to search in both groups (10.38 m). Under some conditions, information from a path-integration trip can be stored in *long-term memory* (Etienne et al., 1998).

Regarding cues for direction, insects require allothetic cues (i.e., external cues), whereas mammals are able to maintain a sense of direction based solely on internal cues (Klatzky et al., 1990; McNaughton et al., 1996; Mittelstaedt & Mittelstaedt, 1982; Wehner et al., 1996). Ants track direction relative to a variety of cues provided by the sun, such as its height in the sky, as well as the spectral and polarized pattern of light created by its position. If the ant is displaced in a dark box from a trained path, these cues would remain, and the ant should continue in a direction consistent with its location prior to displacement. When local features are eliminated, this is exactly the behavior observed (Wehner et al., 1996).

Similarly, Maaswinkel and Whishaw (1999) trained rats to leave an entrance hole (i.e., shelter) to forage in an open area for large pellets of food. Once a pellet was found, the rats naturally returned to the shelter to consume it. Much like the foraging ants, Maaswinkel and Whishaw displaced the rats and started them from a novel location relative to the normal entrance. If the rats used allothetic cues, they would return to the normal entrance after finding food. If the rats used idiothetic cues, they would return to the novel location. Unrestricted rats used local visual cues to return to the normal entrance, and blindfolded rats used olfactory cues to do the same. However, when both cues were removed, rats used path integration to return to the novel entrance.

Beyond its utility in landmark-barren environments, path integration produces accurate navigation in an unfamiliar area, and it appears to play a vital role in binding allothetic cues (i.e., external) to coordinates within the environment. Path integration does not require a US or reinforcer to change the probability of behavior. An organism's path integrator is continuously and automatically active and tuned to return to a home location. Of course, once food is consumed or reproduction occurs at a location, the features surrounding it can become associated with those outcomes and the coordinates of the path integrator. Doing so increases the accuracy of subsequent path integration (Etienne & Jeffery, 2004).

9.3.2 Beacon homing

In the best possible scenario for a mobile organism, a salient cue (beacon) exists at the target area. For example, churches often include a tall spire or tower that can be used to assist with navigation to their location from a distance. In *beacon homing*, simple Pavlovian conditioning should result in approach to the goal. A beacon (CS) at the target area is associated with some biologically relevant outcome (US), such as a nest or burrow, and approach (CR) to the CS is elicited when the animal is searching for that outcome. Animals can travel farther from the CS and return to safety if the beacon becomes associated with other cues through *higher-order conditioning*. By contrast, other cues in the same area may fail to influence spatial behavior (e.g., a *blocking* or *overshadowing* effect) if a beacon, a highly salient and proximal stimulus, is at the target area.

As in other Pavlovian conditioning procedures, testing the influence of the CS on spatial behavior involves a presentation of the CS by itself. This can be accomplished by moving the CS from its original location so that the US is no longer present (e.g., entrance to a burrow, Figure 9.4), or training the behavior in a laboratory environment that allows the researcher to maintain the location of the CS but simply remove the US (i.e., withhold food at the target area). The path of the animal (e.g., latency to arrive at the location of the US on previous trials and the time spent in the area of the US on previous trials) and the distribution of search behaviors (e.g., percentage of searches at the location of the previous US compared to other areas and number of return visits to the previous location of the US) within the environment are two common measures of spatial behavior (Figure 9.5).

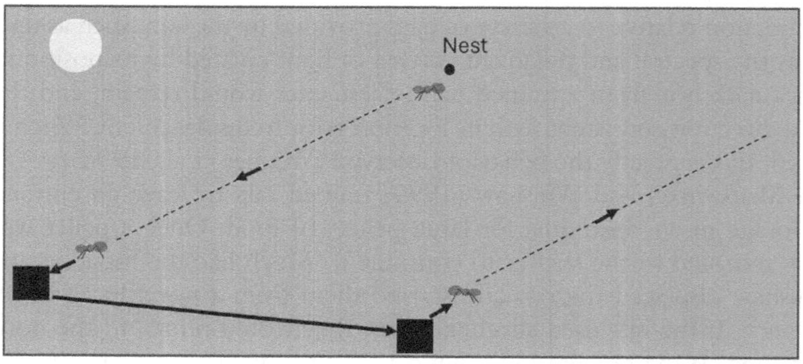

Figure 9.4 **Spatial orientation in ants.** Ants picked up on an outbound journey and transported in darkness to a new location will return along the same bearing using allothetic cues.

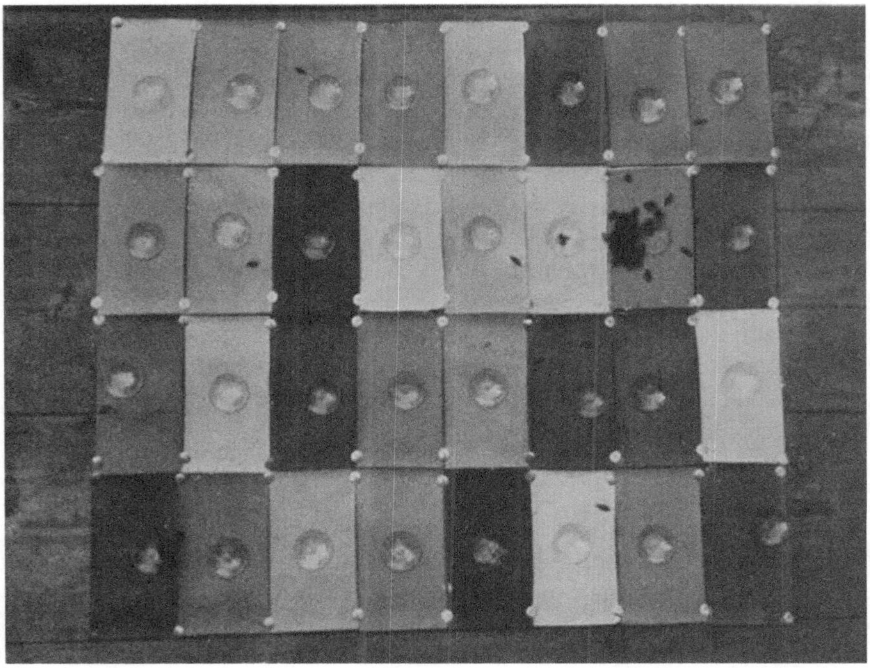

Figure 9.5 **Honeybee spatial orientation.** The apparatus used by von Frisch (1914) to train honeybees to approach a location marked by a particular color (blue) and food (sugar water). The dark spots are bee bodies. Von Frisch initially placed honey out on a table filled with a matrix of papers of varying degrees of gray and one colored paper. Within 1 to 2 h, many bees were regularly returning to and from their nests. Cups were then placed on all of the papers, and the honey, initially placed on the colored paper, is replaced with sugar water in the cup. (From von Frisch (1914); public domain; retrieved from https://www.biodiversitylibrary.org/bibliography/48429.)

One characteristic of beacon homing is that search behaviors are typically distributed somewhat randomly around the beacon. In other words, the beacon signals the US is near (i.e., proximity or distance to US) and elicits approach, but it does not signal the direction of the US.

One of the most influential observations of spatial behavior was that honeybees orient toward and approach a point in space marked by a particular color and food (Tinbergen, 1951; Turner, 1908; von Frisch, 1914; Figure 9.5). Tinbergen utilized this technique by surrounding the ground burrow of a digger wasp with a particular pattern: a circle of pine cones. Digger wasps lay eggs in several burrows made in the ground, and they navigate to and from these burrows to supply their larvae with honeybees that have been captured and paralyzed. The wasps perform a learning flight after leaving the burrow by turning to face the burrow and rising in the air gradually in a zig-zag flight pattern (Collett & Collett, 2007). After a digger wasp left its burrow, Tinbergen would move the pine cones and dig a mock burrow a short distance from the original (~30 cm away). When the wasps returned, both areas (the original burrow and the mock burrow) were present, but the wasps predominately searched at the location marked by the pine cones, not the original location. Tinbergen found that other cues, such as scents or a different pattern of pine cones, did not have the same effect on search behavior.

The pine cones, however, may be functioning as more than beacons. Search behavior occurred predominately toward the inside of the circle of pine cones rather than equally often inside and outside of the circle. This is because the pine cones were not suspended directly above the entrance to the burrow, but were at some distance and direction from it.

The small-scale spatial behavior reviewed thus far involved the animal learning about a cue located at (von Frisch, 1914) or very close to (Tinbergen, 1951) the target area. However, in nature, successful foraging is rarely the result of approaching one stimulus. The destination is often imperceptible from the start location, and salient landmarks are frequently at some distance from the destination. Variations of the beacon homing procedure require the animal to approach a sequence of target areas (e.g., approach three choice points as the animal progresses through a small maze) and require a spatially specific response (e.g., turn right) at each target area. Similar to beacon homing, animals in these tasks must first approach the choice point, but then they cannot simply search around the choice point. A spatial response is required at each choice point.

9.3.3 Route behavior

Animals navigating to and from the same locations within an area are likely to encounter obstacles that require deviation from a straight path (e.g., if a tree is located between the nest and feeding site). Recording the frequency of making the correct spatial response at these deviation points reveals how spatial behavior changes over time. When animals learn to make a spatial operant response (R, e.g., turn left) at a choice point (S), it is often referred to as S→R, or *response learning*. In a situation with many choice points, an animal can learn a *route* consisting of S→R chains (a sequence of responses at each choice point), such as turn left at the first tree encountered and then right at the tall grass, in the same manner as a human might learn to turn left at the first gas station and then right at the grocery store. As the route is repeated, fewer errors would be expected, and the rate of travel should increase, and both would result in a shorter latency to reach the target area from the start location. Repeated travel in an area also creates the conditions for other cues to control behavior as well, such as olfactory scent cues, which do not require learning and must be controlled.

Around the same time Pavlov (1927) was training dogs to salivate and Thorndike (1898) was training cats to press a pedal to exit a puzzle box, Small (1901) built a spatial apparatus modeled after the *Hampton Court maze* (Figure 9.6) to study how rats solved "real-life" learning tasks. The maze consisted of a complex series of connected alleys with raised opaque walls to prevent jumping or shortcutting, but the top of the maze was open. Rats navigated from a start box to a goal box, where they found food.

The conditions of the maze were quite impoverished compared to the rats' natural environment. Scent was controlled for across trials and the color of the walls was monochrome; the most salient stimuli available to the rat were the geometric features of the maze itself (e.g., a short wall on the left and long wall on the right) and any visual stimuli above the maze as well as the sequence of movements required at each choice point to reach the target area. Small (1901, p. 218) made a number of observations regarding the behavior of rats in these experiments, including "the gradually increasing certainty of knowledge," "the clear indication of centrally excited sensations (images) of some kind; memory," and "the almost automatic character of the movements in the later experiments." Despite his references to memory and cognition, the latter comment regarding the automatic nature of learning in the maze received the most immediate attention (Carr & Watson, 1908; Dashiell, 1930; Dennis, 1932; Gengerelli, 1929; Watson, 1907).

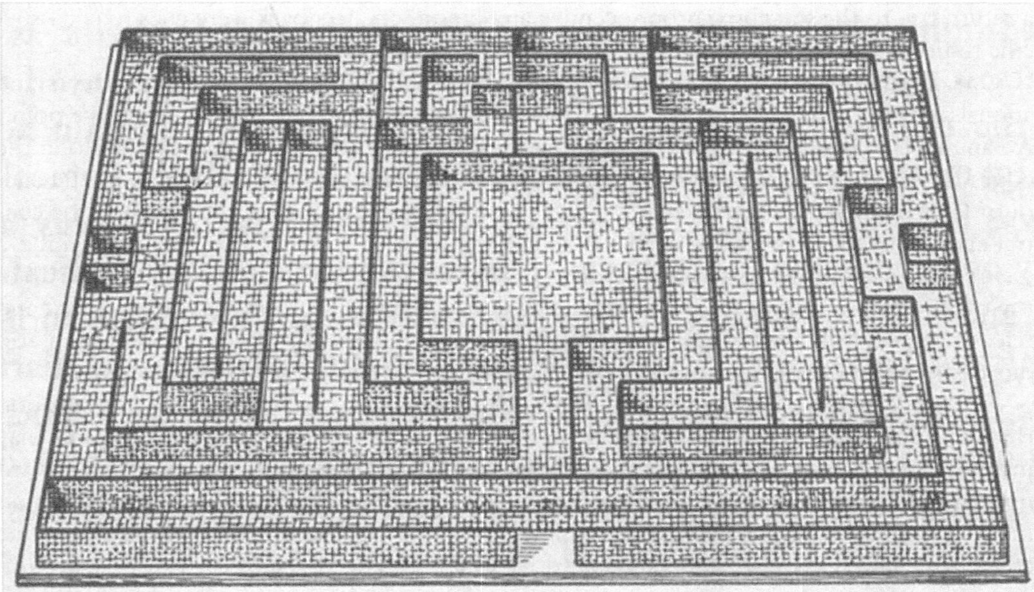

Figure 9.6 **Hampton Court maze.** Illustration of a maze used to train rats in a spatial learning task. (From Small, 1901; public domain.)

Small's (1901) task was well suited to rats because they travel along tunnels in natural settings. In one remarkable study of rat ecology, Calhoun (1963) introduced rats into a 0.25-acre enclosed grassy area with internal barriers added to imitate a typical city block. At the center of the enclosure, food and water were made continuously and abundantly available. Additionally, 36 wooden boxes were buried in the ground to serve as burrows.

Five pairs of rats were introduced to the area, and observations of behavior were made in the two years that followed. During this time, the rats established two main burrows with tunnels radiating out from each burrow toward significant areas of the enclosure, such as food or a nearby buried wooden box. Rats exhibited two types of navigation. The first was to use the shortest or most efficient route between two places, characteristic of response learning, while the second involved longer, windier, and less efficient travel, characteristic of investigatory and exploratory behavior. Remarkably, rats were able to accurately navigate between burrows and food through tunnels below 15 inches of snow, which eliminated the availability of above-ground landmarks.

Calhoun's (1963) observations of efficient, seemingly automatic navigation were consistent with Watson's (1907) laboratory tests with rats in a Hampton Court maze. Watson believed that spatial behavior was entirely supported by S→R chains established as a result of the frequency of pairing a particular stimulus (e.g., a start box) with a response (e.g., forward movement) that ultimately led to a reinforcer (e.g., food). The S→R chain was thought to be initiated by stimuli located at the start box and continued by kinesthetic sensation and muscle movements until the rat reached the reinforcer at the destination.

Watson (1907) supported his theory by demonstrating that even rats surgically deprived of sight, hearing, smell, touch, or their combination could navigate the Hampton Court maze as well as control rats. Unlike path integration, in which idiothetic cues would support a return trip to the start box, proprioceptive and kinesthetic feedback were cues to elicit specific responses needed to navigate away from the start box toward a target area.

One apparatus that has been used extensively to study spatial behavior in rodents and animals is the T-maze (Figure 9.7-A), which creates a simple route with one choice point. An animal is released at the base of an elevated table in a T-shape with short walls along the edges. The top of the T-maze is typically open to allow the animal access to allothetic cues outside of the maze (extramaze cues). After being released, the animal travels along the central alley to a left–right choice point. If no food is located in either arm, rats will exhibit a *spontaneous alternation* pattern, choosing the side opposite to the last choice in about 80% of the trials. That is, if they explore the right arm during the first trial and they are removed and released again at the base of the T-maze, then 8 out of 10 times, they will explore the left arm during the second trial. This has also been described as a loose-shift strategy.

For some species, this may represent an ecologically valid scenario in which a location is visited and food is not found, such that return visits would waste resources and may increase the risk of predation. In other species, for related reasons, it may be a bias toward novelty (Richman et al., 1986). Given its potential impact on fitness, it is not surprising that many species show spontaneous alternation, including opossums, cats, pill bugs, marine crabs, fruit flies, zebrafish, and humans (d'Isa et al., 2021). A reinforcer can be placed in either the left or right arm of the maze, and spontaneous alternation will still be observed. This has been described as a win-shift strategy. In this case, food consumed at one location should encourage exploration and investigation of locations not yet visited. However, if food is always placed in one arm of the maze (e.g., the right), then over trials, rats will

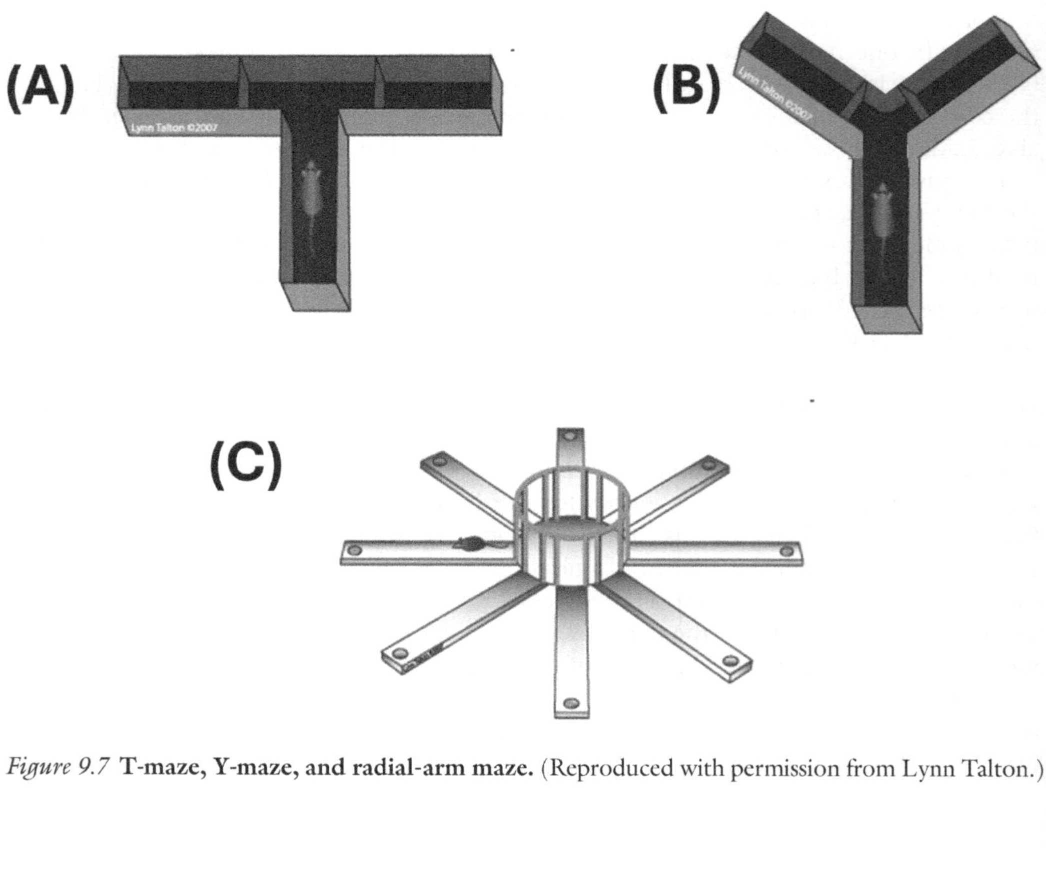

Figure 9.7 **T-maze, Y-maze, and radial-arm maze.** (Reproduced with permission from Lynn Talton.)

come to consistently make a right turn at the choice point. Given a single choice point in the T-maze, repeating a recently reinforced behavior (i.e., the "R") could be elicited by the rat's own movements (distance traveled down the alley) or approaching the wall marking the choice point.

Is learning a route in a T-maze distinctly different from learning other kinds of operant discriminations? In an experiment comparing spatial behavior in a T-maze to brightness discrimination, Wolfe (1934) evaluated how a delay between the response at the choice point and consumption of a reinforcer (food) would alter learning.

You may remember from Chapter 2 that *contiguity* is critical for Pavlovian and operant conditioning; in general, increasing the *delay* between the correct response and consumption of the reinforcer should disrupt acquisition. Wolfe hypothesized that the effect of a delay in a nonspatial discrimination should be similar to that of a spatial discrimination task. Rats were tested in a T-maze that included sliding doors to trap the rat after a left or right response was made. After a correct response, a delay (from 0 to 20 min) was imposed in the delay compartment before the rat could continue on to consume food at the end of the arm.

In the nonspatial task, a rat approached a choice point with two boxes, one marked with a white plastic card and the other a dark card. If it entered the box with the card associated with reward, it proceeded into a delay compartment, followed by food.

The spatial and nonspatial tasks revealed the same functional relationship between delay and accuracy, indicating that both tasks were a kind of discrimination problem in which stimuli associated with a correct response must be learned about. Evidence for learning in both tasks was found at all delays up to but not including 20 min. This is surprising, given that acquisition of lever pressing is eliminated by a 1-min delay (Perin, 1943). Hull (1943) and others speculated that secondary reinforcement may have played a role in supporting acquisition across longer delays in the T-maze and other discrimination tasks, which was then confirmed by Grice (1948; see Figure 4.11).

Does route behavior provide evidence of an *allocentric representation* (e.g., viewer independent) of the search space? By itself, it does not. The *snapshot model* describes how memory for the *egocentric representation* of stimuli near a target area can be used to control route behavior. Organisms are hypothesized to actively adjust their search bearing to match their current view of an environment with a previous view (snapshot or local view) associated with a biologically significant outcome (Cartwright & Collett, 1982).

There are many ways in which a snapshot model may be instantiated in an animal (Biegler, 2006). In the simplest version, during training, an organism associates the view of the target area (e.g., a beacon) with an outcome (e.g., food). From the current view, a continuously updating algorithm determines a bearing that takes the organism closer to the remembered view of the target area. There is good evidence for this kind of spatial behavior in cockroaches, fruit flies, and honeybees (Cheng & Graham, 2013); snapshots in insects include the size of objects, edge orientation, color, and vertical center of gravity.

In another version of the snapshot model, a measure of the discrepancy of the current view and snapshot can determine whether an organism keeps going in the same direction (if the discrepancy is being reduced) or changes direction. Single snapshot models have been expanded to include multiple snapshots. In one version, the current view could serve as a retrieval cue for all of the snapshots of the target area. The adjacent place most closely matching the snapshot is pursued. In another version, the current view retrieves both the appropriate response and a view of the outcome associated with it. If these retrieved views are chained together, an animal could adjust its behavior at the start of a sequence of responses to avoid a location with a devalued reinforcer (e.g., Kosaki et al., 2018). It is worth noting that none

Table 9.1 Landmark-based spatial behavior

Type	*Conditions*	*Representation*
Beacon-homing or guidance	Single object marking the exact goal	Egocentric or None
Response or S-R	Object marking a single choice point, impoverished environment	Egocentric or None
Route or S-R chains	A sequence of choice points, distinct cues at choice points	Egocentric or None
Directional or piloting	Impoverished environment, prominent distal cues	Allocentric
Place or map-like or S-S	Several distinct cues, environment too large for a single view, common elements across views	Allocentric

Note. S: stimulus. R: response. None: indicates that a representation is not required.

of the snapshot models discussed requires a mental representation of the distance and direction between objects.

In the experiments reviewed thus far, spatial behavior was studied in relatively impoverished stimulus conditions (e.g., monochrome walls) that constrict behavioral flexibility (e.g., a single left or right choice point). It is unsurprising, then, that the resulting spatial behavior would be controlled by a small set of relevant cues. Beacon homing and route behavior consist of spatial responses to stimuli that are dependent on the navigator's perspective. Consistent with the snapshot model, this kind of learning is very effective when the current conditions match the conditions during training.

Other experiments have evaluated how animals learn to navigate environments with more stimuli available and a greater breadth of response options, which could lead to spatial behavior reflecting an ***allocentric representation***. Spatial behavior supported by an allocentric representation of the environment, of which the spatial relations are accessible independent of any particular view of the stimuli, would allow an animal placed anywhere within the environment to navigate to any location. This type of map-like spatial behavior is associated with flexible navigation, such that removal of a cue or some other manipulation of one aspect of the environment should result in little to no disruption of spatial behavior.

9.3.4 Map-like spatial behavior

There is strong evidence that animals can learn to make specific spatial responses when a particular stimulus is encountered within a maze, but other evidence indicates that animals can also learn about the spatial relationships between landmarks. Though investigations of the distinction between learning specific spatial responses and learning about spatial relationships have utilized multiple approaches, the common theme is the need for the animal to make a different response within some configuration of the landmarks encountered in training.

For example, Macfarlane (1930) trained rats to swim through a maze and reported no disruption in performance when the rats later ran through the same maze drained to a depth of 1 inch. Rats trained in the reverse order transferred equally well. Macfarlane found that even with disparate responses, animals transferred what they had learned about a maze from one response to another (Ruch, 1930). Tolman (1948) proposed that ***stimulus–stimulus associations*** (S→S) were formed between stimuli within and around the maze during training sessions, which led to an expectancy of the outcome at a particular place. For a time, many researchers attempted to claim that one kind of spatial behavior (S→R or S→S) was simpler and more dominant in rats.

Tolman et al. (1946) trained rats in a Plus maze such that different groups of rats reliably found food by making the same response (S→R response learning) or navigating to the same place in the maze (S→S map-like behavior). The rats in both groups started from the north or south end of the Plus maze, alternating across days. Rats in the response group would always be required to make a right turn to find food (i.e., food varied from east to west based on start position), whereas rats in the place group would need to make a different response to arrive at the same geographical location to find food (i.e., food was always located in the east location irrespective of start position).

Rats in the map group acquired the correct strategy in fewer trials and were faster to make a correct decision. However, Restle (1957) reviewed findings from the Plus maze and other tasks and concluded that that both types of behavior are evident in most spatial tasks; any dominance of one or the other was best predicted by the conditions of the methodology, including the organism's current or perceived orientation, the shape or design of the spatial environment, the availability of distinct visual cues, motivational factors (e.g., food deprivation vs. predation avoidance), and the amount of training given in the environment.

In addition to response learning, two types of map-like behavior can occur in the T and Plus mazes: directional and place behavior. ***Directional learning*** occurs when a heading is determined based on familiarity with discrete objects around (extramaze cues) the search area or a reference frame (e.g., geometry or contour of an extended surface). The second, ***place learning***, occurs when vectors between multiple ***intramaze*** and ***extramaze cues*** in the environment are used to orient and continuously update current location and heading with respect to a target area (i.e., a place).

Both can explain the transfer of spatial learning from swimming to running by Macfarlane (1930). Place behavior is hypothesized to be more resistant to stimulus degradation and stimulus displacement, as current position and the predicted position of the target area are continuously updated using a variety of intramaze and extramaze cues. Tests of these two types of learning typically involve shifting the apparatus across trials, such that the direction and place of the target area are in conflict (Figure 9.8).

Blodgett et al. (1949) used a T-maze to conduct the first systematic evaluation of the two search strategies (direction and place) and reported that rats trained to search in a particular direction made fewer errors than those trained to navigate to a place in space (Figure 9.8-A). They also reported that directional and place responding were mutually exclusive, such that responding consistent with one search strategy impeded a rat's ability to develop the other. Skinner et al. (2003) replicated both effects with rats trained to navigate to one corner of an open field, which was repositioned across trials to encourage responding in a particular direction or location in the room.

Arguably the most systematic and comprehensive evaluation of directional and place responding has been conducted by Hamilton et al. (2009) with rats in the Morris water maze. The Morris water maze was developed to study spatial behavior (Morris, 1981). In this procedure, a circular pool was filled with opaque-colored water (Figure 9.8-B). A small platform was located just below the surface of the water and anchored to the floor of the pool. A rat was released into the pool at various points along the circumference of the pool. As natural swimmers, the rats initially searched in a seemingly random manner until they found the platform. Across trials, rats quickly learned to swim directly towards the hidden platform.

The spatial demands of the task are reflected in the search for a location that cannot be seen, heard, or smelled; it can only be found through the use of distal visual cues serving an

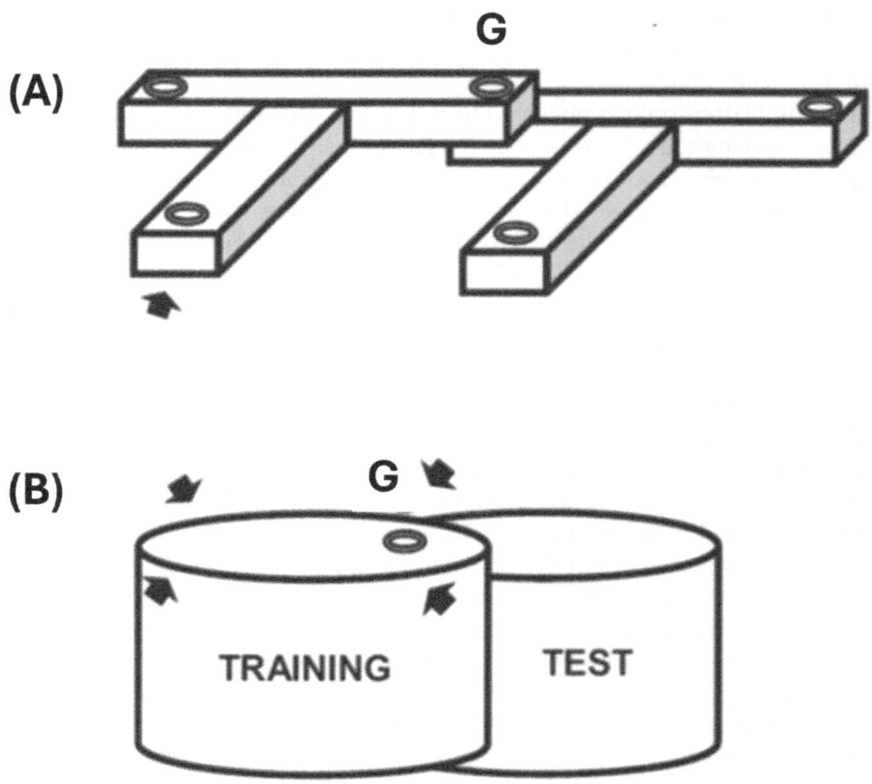

Figure 9.8 **Evaluation of search strategies. (A)** The T-maze apparatus is trained with one location (left), such that the rat must traverse the alley from the starting location (near the black arrow) and turn right at the choice point to obtain a hidden reinforcer at the end of the right arm. At test, the apparatus is shifted within the room to a new location (all other cues in the room remain in their original position), with the location of the target area before the shift now overlapping with the left arm of the T-maze. Rats using a directional strategy will turn right, the direction relative to an external frame of reference that was trained before the test. Rats using a place strategy will turn left, returning to the location of the target area based on the combination of extramaze cues marking the original position. **(B)** A similar procedure can be utilized with a Morris water maze, with the exception that rats are generally released from four different locations (near the black arrows) during training, and they are swimming to find a hidden platform rather than food. Following the shift test, the sector of the pool on the left now overlaps with the previous location of the target area, which was located in the right sector prior to the shift. G: goal.

orientation and directionality function (Morris, 1981; Morris et al., 1986). Beacon homing is observed when an object is suspended directly above the platform or the platform is visible, whereas map-like behavior is observed with a hidden platform and extramaze landmarks (Morris et al., 1982; Rodrigo et al., 1997; Sutherland et al., 1983). As in the T-maze, Hamilton et al. found that place responding in the Morris water task was more likely to occur earlier in training than directional responding.

Other studies have utilized landmarks placed within the search space (i.e., intramaze). Behavior in these conditions often reflects the geometric properties (distances, angles, and directions) between the landmark and target area as well as between two or more landmarks.

For example, after training pigeons to find a hidden target area relative to a block of wood against the wall, Cheng (1988) found that changes in the size of the wood did not alter search. A snapshot, or retinal matching, model would predict the search distance from the wood landmark would change proportional to the size of the wood. Furthermore, when the landmark was displaced relative to the rest of the box (apparatus and room), then the pigeons adjusted their search to a location consistent with a weighted average of the vectors (distance and direction from the landmark to the goal and from self to landmark) learned during training and the current location of the displaced landmark.

Similar results were found with pigeons, but not with rats or corvids, when a configuration of landmarks was used (Figure 9.9-A). Pigeons trained to search in the middle of a configuration of landmarks exhibited a displacement in search consistent with weighted vector averaging of the displaced landmark in a touchscreen (Spetch & Mondloch, 1993) and open

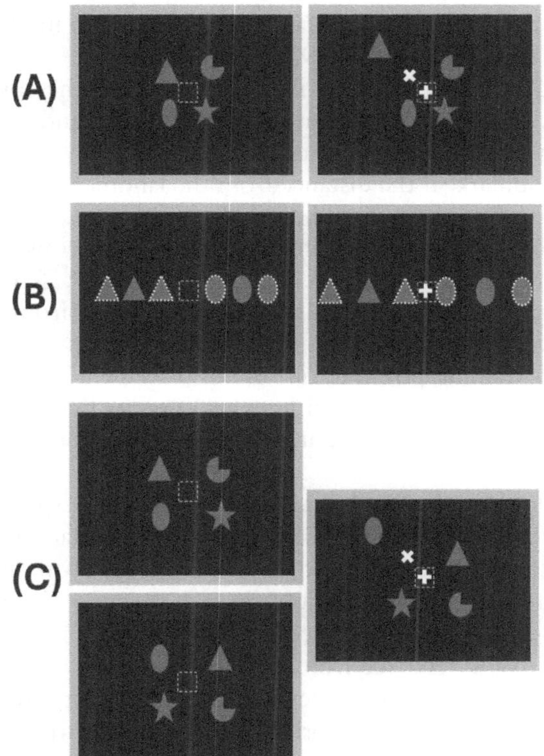

Figure 9.9 **Procedures for studying landmark learning. (A)** An example of a touchscreen-equipped training stimulus set. Four landmarks are displayed with a target area in the center. Pecks to the target area are reinforced. The target area was not marked during the task. The right display demonstrates a test situation in which one of the landmarks has been displaced. Animals could continue to respond in the middle of the remaining landmarks (marked by the plus sign) or peck at a weighted average of the center of all four landmarks (marked by the X-shaped symbol). **(B)** A similar test, but with only two landmarks trained in several positions. A sample location is displayed, as well as dashed lines to indicate other possible locations. Tests included novel distances that were shorter, longer, and in between those used during training. **(C)** Training of a configuration of four landmarks, but the landmarks change across trials of training.

arena (Spetch et al., 1997). These findings were touted as indicating a fundamental difference between animals that learned to search relative to a geometric shape (i.e., rodents, corvids, and humans) versus those that learn to search at a particular distance and direction from the landmarks (pigeons).

For example, Clark's nutcrackers, a food-storing corvid, were found to search at the middle of two landmarks even when the distance between the two landmarks was extended at test (Kamil & Jones, 1997; Figure 9.9-B). These birds did not follow a weighted average based on the displaced landmark or search at the correct location based on a single landmark, but rather, they searched at the midpoint of the configuration of the two landmarks. The difference in sensitivity to the midpoint between pigeons and Clark's nutcrackers could have resulted from species differences (e.g., food storing) or methodological differences.

Jones et al. (2002) tested both pigeons and Clark's nutcrackers using a similar methodology and found they both searched in the middle of a configuration of two landmarks during tests with novel distances. Importantly, Jones et al. trained with multiple interlandmark distances during training (Kamil & Jones, 1997; Figure 9.9-B).

These results remind us that animals will often default to the computationally simplest solution to a problem. If a target area lies at the same distance and direction from two landmarks, then it may be found using extramaze cues to establish a frame of reference and a vector from a single landmark. If the distance from the landmarks to the target area changes across trials, then the configuration should control search.

In another test of this hypothesis, Sutton (2002) trained pigeons to locate a different target area within two configurations of the same four landmarks (A, B, C, and D) positioned in a small open arena (Figure 9.9-C). With this training, the vector from one landmark (e.g., A) would be unstable across the two configurations. During subsequent tests, one landmark was displaced relative to its training position, but the displacement of search was minimal. The spatial search of pigeons, rats, corvids, and humans suggests that animals can learn about a target area relative to a geometrical configuration of landmarks, such that no single landmark controls search behavior.

The local features defining the geometric shape of the search space itself can be a feature that signals a target area (Pearce, 2009). Cheng (1986) and Margules and Gallistel (1988) placed rats within a rectangular search space that was decorated with distinct features, such as high-contrast stripes on the walls or small lights in each corner of the arena. Food was placed in one of the corners of the arena, and the rat was allowed to search and consume a small amount of food before being removed from the arena.

During the interval, the test area was replaced with an exact replica (i.e., free from any odors) and rotated at random to a new orientation relative to the room. Rats searched in the area predicted by the features defining the shape of the environment (e.g., long wall on the left and short wall on the right) and the placement of food in training, which included a correct corner (based on shape and the environmental features located in each corner) and the geometrically opposite corner (based on shape alone). Searches at both the correct and opposite corners were at the appropriate distance and direction from the corner, based on training. Searches at the incorrect corner indicate a failure to use the unique individual features marking each corner.

This result has been replicated in several species, including pigeons, fish, and humans (Cheng & Newcombe, 2005). In some experiments, however, learning about these geometric features was facilitated by the presence of local landmarks (Pearce, 2009). Perhaps the best way to think of the shape of an environment is simply as providing another kind of landmark

(Miller & Shettleworth, 2007), which, depending on the conditions, may compete or integrate with other landmarks to support accurate search in an environment.

It is worth noting that the title of this section is "Map-like spatial behavior." Despite many early claims of human and nonhuman animals forming global allocentric representations (i.e., a ***cognitive map***) of a spatial environment, the accumulated data are more consistent with animals learning about a subset of S-S relations and snapshots, along with path integration, which can then be expressed as flexible spatial behavior (e.g., shortcutting). In general, it is difficult to experimentally rule out the effects of these simpler forms of spatial behavior (Pritchard & Healy, 2017). How to reconcile these behavioral findings with the findings that place cells in the mammalian brain have similar properties to a map is still a matter of debate (see what follows: **Neurobiology of small-scale navigation**).

9.4 Location as a stimulus property

All events occur at a given time and location. The spatial distance and temporal interval separating one event from another are positively correlated, such that the farther apart two objects are in space, the longer the time it would take to travel between them. Researchers have used similar methodologies to study both timing and spatial behavior and have accumulated evidence from pigeons, rats, humans, and in some cases, bees for several general principles. These principles were first discussed in Chapter 8 for timing behavior, but they also apply to spatial behavior.

When rats and pigeons are required to search for a particular location, the peak of search reflects a linear relationship between psychological and physical scales of distance measurement, that is, the search error is proportional to the distance measured (*Weber's law*), and search is influenced by multiple sources (Cheng, 2007). According to a linear measurement scale for spatial search, for every unit of increase in physical space (e.g., a cm), there is an increase in the psychological measurement of space. This principle predicts the symmetrical distribution of searches typically observed around a hidden target area signaled by a landmark when the number of searches is plotted as a function of distance (Cheng, 1990; Figure 9.10).

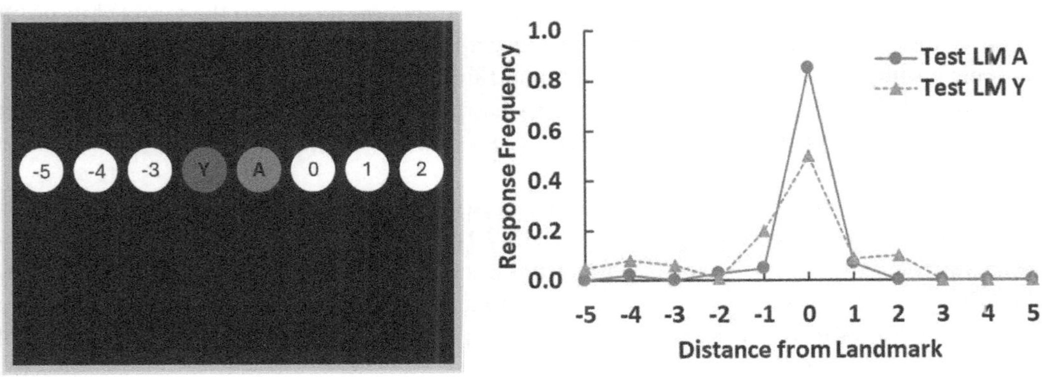

Figure 9.10 **Data from a landmark-based task using a touchscreen-equipped monitor with pigeons.** Pigeons were trained on separate trials to peck at a target area (0) that was one (LM A) or two (LM Y) locations removed from a landmark. On the test, each landmark was presented in the absence of reinforcer delivery (i.e., a peak trial). (From Leising et al., 2011; reproduced with permission from American Psychological Association.)

In this same distribution of searches, if most pecks are occurring at the goal and few responses around it, then the distribution would be said to have a narrow peak and a small standard deviation. The standard deviation is the average distance of a search from the mean (peak) distance, and it can be thought of in spatial behavior as a measure of ***location uncertainty***. A narrow peak, or small standard deviation, indicates low location uncertainty. When the distribution of search for landmarks at different distances from a target area are compared, consistent with Weber's law, the standard deviation is proportional to the distance measured. This represents a functional relationship, such that the absolute value of the distance to a goal may be different between animals (e.g., 5 m for ants, 10 m for rodents), but the effect of distance on standard deviation is constant.

One could think of the target area as the standard and the space around the target as the region to be discriminated from the standard. Your location uncertainty regarding where you parked your car would be lower (narrow peak) if you were parked in a grocery store parking lot compared to a spot in the parking lot of a large amusement park. Thankfully, many of these establishments recognize the challenge and place regular markers in their parking lots (e.g., "Row Z").

The last principle is that animals often integrate multiple sources when searching. For example, there is evidence of interactions between map-like learning and path integration. Additionally, as discussed, when multiple landmarks are trained and one is subsequently displaced, under some conditions, pigeons will search at a location that represents a weighted average of each of the landmark-to-goal vectors.

Of course, there are important distinctions between time and space that could result in behavioral differences. First, the contextual features that allow organisms to determine a point in time are typically less salient than those defining a location in space. For example, in most situations, the visible features defining the location of a target contrast with the visible contextual features surrounding the target (i.e., there is an edge created where the object ends and the features surrounding it begin), whereas the time before the onset of a stimulus cannot be perceived following its onset. However, a kind of edge is created with the onset and termination of an event, and research has found that these edges carry disproportional influence on timing behavior similar to that of visual edges (e.g., Sutton & Barto, 1990).

Second, the stability of a cue relative to a reinforcer can be dissociated in space and time. That is, a cue may be spatially unstable (i.e., change direction relative to the target) but occur at the same time (and distance) relative to a target event.

Third, different brain areas support interval timing and map-like spatial behavior. Phasic dopamine activity in the midbrain of rodents has been implicated in timing (e.g., Petter et al., 2018), whereas map-like spatial behavior relies primarily on the hippocampus, entorhinal cortex, and subiculum (Jeffery, 2010).

Most cues can be spatially informative with respect to the location of a reinforcer (e.g., a mate, food source, or predator). Leising et al. (2015) extended previous discussions on factors controlling spatial behavior (e.g., Nardini et al., 2008; Ratliff & Newcombe, 2008) by identifying three orthogonal properties that influence the degree to which a cue (i.e., as a landmark) comes to control spatial behavior: (1) proximity, (2) stability, and (3) validity of the cue in relation to the goal.

First, proximity was defined as a pure measure of the spatial distance between a landmark and a goal. When bees estimated the distance to fly down a tunnel to reach a food source, landmarks more proximal to the source exerted better control on behavior (Collett et al., 2002; Srinivasan et al., 2024). Furthermore, Clark's nutcrackers will store food near conspicuous landmarks or beacons unless other cache-stealing birds or rodents are nearby (Vander

Wall & Balda, 1981). The influence of proximity on the utility of a spatial cue may vary as a function of the distance of the organism to the target area. Hamilton et al. (2007) reported evidence with rodents in a Morris water maze that the initial heading (i.e., direction) during search is determined by distal cues and search distance is driven by proximal cues. Similarly, results with Clark's nutcrackers revealed that increasing the distance of landmarks to the goal resulted in larger errors in the distance compared to the direction of search (Kamil & Jones, 1997).

Second, stability was defined as the variance of a landmark's vector (distance and direction) to the goal across trials. Accuracy during the presentation of any one landmark, for instance, varies as a function of whether the distance and direction of the landmark were more or less stable across trials (e.g., Biegler & Morris, 1993).

Third, validity was defined as the probability that food will be encountered in the presence of a landmark, irrespective of its proximity or stability, compared to the likelihood of encountering food in the absence of the landmark. This dimension is inherently nonspatial and reflects the contingencies encountered during training.

Consistent with Chapters 2 and 4, salience is another factor that should be considered. Salience predicts how likely a stimulus is to become associated with an outcome. Salience is determined by many factors, including the physical magnitude of the stimulus (e.g., size, brightness) and its biological relevance. With respect to spatial behavior, two of the three factors mentioned, proximity and stability, are known to influence salience.

9.4.1 Acquisition and extinction

Acquisition of spatial behavior is most commonly measured as the latency to make a response at a target area. The target area may mark hidden food or the location of escape from an aversive stimulus (e.g., cool water or a bright light). These tasks may take place in an open arena (e.g., open field, Morris water maze, Barnes maze), an area defined by a particular geometric shape (e.g., square, rectangle, or triangle), or on a touchscreen-equipped monitor. Other measures involve some variation of response rate at the target area, such as time spent in the area or number of searches/visits at the target area on probe trials in which the outcome or escape response is eliminated. A wide variety of organisms have demonstrated the ability to decrease the latency to return to the target area, including vertebrates and invertebrates and even slime (see Chapter 3). Of course, the mere acquisition of spatially accurate behavior tells us little of the mechanism.

If conditions change and a location no longer offers the same outcome, then visits should become less frequent and eventually extinguish altogether. If associative learning is involved in spatial behavior, then spontaneous recovery should be observed.

Prados et al. (2003) trained rats to search for a hidden platform in a Morris water maze with four landmarks suspended above the edge of the pool. In a test conducted immediately after extinction, the amount of time spent in the platform quadrant indicated no preference, but a group tested 4 days later spent significantly more time in the platform quadrant, thereby demonstrating spontaneous recovery.

Leising et al. (2015) investigated extinction and spontaneous recovery of spatial behavior using a landmark-based search task in a touchscreen preparation with pigeons (Figure 9.11). Four visual landmarks (A, B, C, and D) signaled a location that resulted in reinforcement when pecked a few cm below (A and C) or above (B and D) each landmark. After conditioning, A and B were extinguished. As was the case for the timing of key pecking in pigeons (Ohyama et al., 1999), throughout extinction and testing, the overall response rate and peak

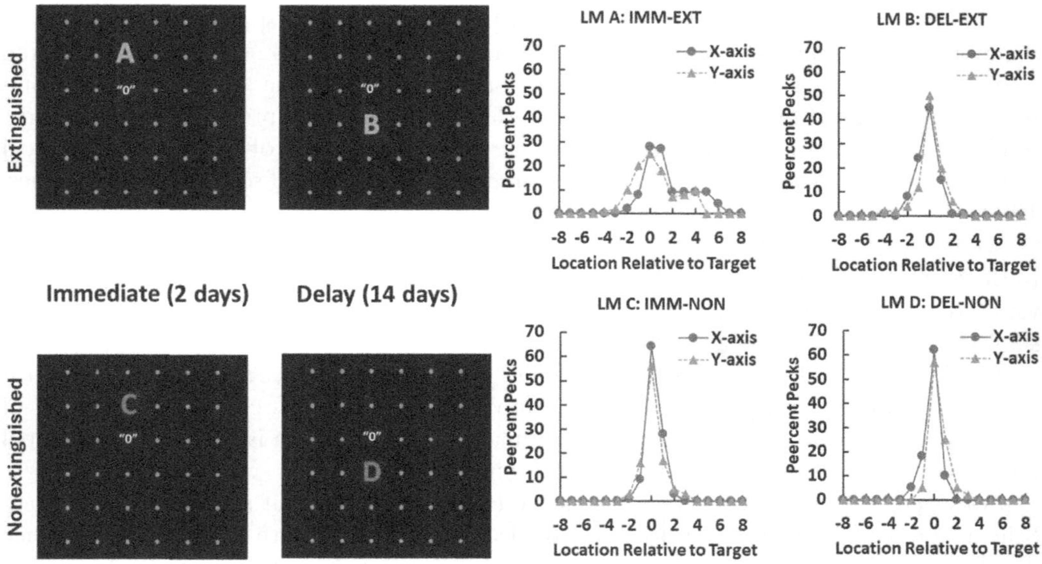

Figure 9.11 **Extinction and spontaneous recovery data from a landmark-based task with pigeons.** Pigeons were trained on separate trials to peck at a target area (0), that was one location below (LMs A and C) or above (LMs B and D) a landmark. After acquisition, two landmarks were presented and nonreinforced (LMs A and B) for several sessions. Landmarks A and C were tested 2 days after the final extinction session, whereas LMs B and D were tested 14 days later. (From Leising et al., 2015; reproduced with permission from the American Psychological Association.)

rate at the target area were reduced, but the peak location of pecking remained at the target area (LM A in Figure 9.11). Spontaneous recovery to A was assessed 2 two days following extinction, whereas B was tested 14 days after extinction. Spontaneous recovery of the peak of responding at the target area was observed 14 days but not 2 days after extinction. Landmarks C and D were controls for forgetting (i.e., testing occurred 14 days later for one landmark) and indicated high spatial accuracy at 2- and 14-day delays.

9.4.2 Generalization and discrimination

Perhaps the clearest method for testing stimulus control is the *stimulus generalization-gradient procedure*. Recall that an animal is trained with one type of stimulus (e.g., an orange light) and then tested with variations of that stimulus (e.g., other colored lights selected from the visible spectrum). In timing behavior, Russell and Kirkpatrick (2007) trained rats to respond to a lever following a 20-s light, followed by tests of the light ranging in duration from 2 to 80 s. Rats responded correctly most often when the light was presented for 20 s and progressively worse with longer and shorter durations.

Rodrigo et al. (2006) trained rats to swim to a hidden platform in a Morris water maze in the presence of a beacon that was above the hidden platform, followed by tests in which the beacon was displaced relative to training. Rats spent more time swimming near the beacon when it was closer to the trained position.

Cheng et al. (1997) found the same result after training pigeons in a touchscreen-equipped operant box with a beacon located at a particular position within an array of response options followed by tests of the beacon at other locations.

The distribution of responses in time or space has also revealed a *peak-shift effect* when trials with an S- were included during training (Cheng et al., 1997; Russell & Kirkpatrick, 2007). The pattern of generalization and discrimination around a single response peak has been found with rats (Cheng, 1986), pigeons (Cheng, 1988), and bees (Cartwright & Collett, 1982).

9.4.3 Cue competition

An environment may include many stimuli with a consistent spatial relationship to a target area. Consequently, after training, there is an opportunity to assess whether stimulus control is evident in the presence of each of the stimulus elements. Factors such as stimulus proximity, stability, validity, and salience are likely to influence the acquisition of stimulus control in spatial tasks in a manner similar to what has been observed in nonspatial tasks. Although we have discussed several types of spatial behavior independently, it is likely that these forms of spatial behavior develop in parallel, as opposed to one system inhibiting the other (Shettleworth & Sutton, 2005).

Redundancy would be particularly important when survival depends on returning to a nest or finding previously buried food, and the types of cues available may change throughout the day or season. For example, Clark's nutcrackers bury seeds in the summer and fall and retrieve them in the winter, often in snow-covered environments. Successful retrieval likely depends on a combination of spatial strategies. However, given the expansive literature on cue competition in nonspatial tasks, it is informative to evaluate whether cue competition effects (e.g., blocking and overshadowing) are evident in spatial tasks.

In a conventional *blocking* procedure, CS (A) is first paired with a US in Phase 1 (A→US), and then a compound of CS A and a second CS (X) is paired with the US in Phase 2 (AX→US). Responding to X on a subsequent test is diminished relative to responding to X in a control group lacking the Phase 1 A→US pairings (Kamin, 1969). Within the spatial domain, landmarks play the role of a signal for the location of a hidden goal. For example, subjects may learn to navigate to a hidden goal (e.g., the hidden platform in a Morris pool) in the presence of landmark A (a spatial cue located outside of the perimeter of the pool) in Phase 1 (A→Platform), followed by training to find the goal in the presence of landmarks A and X in Phase 2 (AX→Platform). A final test with X alone can reveal whether spatial control by X was blocked (i.e., weakened) by the presence of the previously trained A. Associative accounts of spatial learning predict that spatial control by landmark X should be blocked by previous training of landmark A.

Rodrigo et al. (1997) used a Morris pool with landmarks suspended above the edge of the pool. Rats in the blocking group were placed on the platform with landmarks A, B, and C (Table 9.2). Rats in the control group received trials with landmarks A, B, C, and X (Experiment 2) or a separate set of landmarks (e.g., A', B', and C'; Experiment 3). In Phase 2, all groups received additional placement trials with landmarks A, B, C, and X. Rats were tested with two subsets of the landmarks on separate trials: ABC and ABX. On ABC trials, both groups performed equally well, but on ABX trials the blocking group showed a significant deficit in locating the quadrant of the hidden platform.

Similar blocking effects have been observed in humans trained to navigate a computerized version of the task (Hamilton & Sutherland, 1999), pigeons trained in a touchscreen

Table 9.2 Spatial cue competition and integration procedures

Procedure	*Phase 1*	*Phase 2*	*Test*	*Results*
Blocking				
Blocking	ABC:Goal	ABCX:Goal	ABC? ABX?	ABC > ABX
Control	ABCX:Goal	ABCX:Goal	ABC? ABX?	ABC = ABX
Overshadowing				
Overshadowing	ABCDX:Goal	--	ABC?ACD?ACX	ACD = ACX < ABC
Control	ABCD:Goal	--	ABC?ACD?	ACD = ABC
Integration				
Integration	ABC:Goal CEF:Goal	--	AB?AE?	AB = AE
Control	ABC:Goal DEF:Goal	--	AB?AE?	AB > AD

Note. Procedures for studying cue competition and integration in landmark-based spatial tasks. A, B, C, D, E, F, X, and Y: stimuli.?: indicates a nonreinforced probe test. *C:* indicates a common element in the integration procedure.

procedure and an automated open field (Leising et al., 2014), and rats in a conventional open field (Biegler & Morris, 1999; Stahlman & Blaisdell, 2009) and a radial-arm maze (Figure 9.7-C; Diez-Chamizo et al., 1985). Another effect, ***unblocking***, was found when landmark X was introduced in Phase 2 after training with A, B, and C if the location of the hidden platform relative to the landmarks was changed before Phase 2. Given that all of the landmarks continued to signal the presence of a platform, this finding suggests that the landmarks signaled if the platform was present and where it was located.

The presence of multiple stimuli (e.g., landmarks A and X, and food) during training may result in a disruption in spatial control by one of the stimuli (e.g., X) relative to a control group in which the same stimulus was trained by itself (e.g., landmark X and food). There is overwhelming evidence for landmark-based ***overshadowing*** effects in a variety of vertebrate species, including rodents, pigeons, and humans (Chamizo, 2003).

Sanchez-Moreno et al. (1999) investigated overshadowing of landmarks in a spatial search task in a Morris pool with rats (Table 9.2). Subjects in the control group were trained to swim to a platform hidden in a pool of water relative to four visual landmarks (A, B, C, and D). In the overshadowing group, a noise (X) emanated from the location of landmark D (DX→Platform). When subsequently tested with three subsets of the stimuli (ABC, ACD, and ACX), rats in the overshadowing group, but not in the control group, performed worse on ACD than ABC. In other words, the presence of two stimuli at one location (D and X) during training reduced stimulus control by both stimuli (i.e., reciprocal overshadowing).

Increasing the physical salience of a stimulus or reducing its temporal proximity to the outcome can result in more overshadowing of the less salient or less proximal stimulus (Mackintosh, 1976). Chamizo et al. (2006a) trained rats in a Morris water maze with interspersed trials of two pairs of landmarks (AB or BC) suspended above the perimeter of the pool. In the overshadowing group, landmark B was positioned closer to the hidden platform than in the control group. At test, spatial control by a configuration of landmarks AC was worse in the overshadowing group relative to the control group. A similar result was reported in pigeons searching for grain in a substrate (Cheng, 1989), using an automated open field (Leising et al., 2011), or interacting with a touchscreen-equipped monitor (Spetch, 1995). Proximity has also been found to influence overshadowing in insects (Cheng et al., 1987) and humans (Hamilton et al., 2002).

In addition to blocking and overshadowing between landmarks, cue competition has been reported between beacons or other intramaze cues and extramaze cues (Diez-Chamizo et al., 1985; Redhead et al., 1997; Roberts & Pearce, 1999). Diez-Chamizo et al. (1985) trained rats with an intramaze cue (e.g., a floor of one texture) that signaled the correct arm of a maze regardless of the spatial position or an extramaze cue that was located at a fixed position relative to the correct arm. The spatial behavior of rats in the presence of the extramaze cue was disrupted when they were pretrained with an intramaze cue, and the reverse was also true. Although intramaze and extramaze cues engage different kinds of spatial behavior, there is strong evidence for blocking and overshadowing between these two types of cues (e.g., March et al., 1992; Roberts & Pearce, 1999). In addition to proximity, the stability of the spatial relationship between the cues and the target area influences the degree of cue competition. Roberts and Pearce (1998) found greater overshadowing of extramaze cues in the Morris water maze with rats when the target area moved across sessions but remained in a consistent spatial relationship to an intramaze cue.

Interestingly, cue competition between geometric cues provided by the shape of a test arena and landmarks is not always observed (Pearce, 2009). Pearce et al. (2001) trained one group (Blocking) of rats in a circular Morris water maze to locate a hidden platform with a beacon located at the platform, followed by training with the same beacon in a triangular-shaped water maze. Group Control received no initial training with the beacon. If blocking occurred, then a subsequent test with the beacon removed would reveal poor stimulus control by the shape of the pool on spatial search in the Blocking compared to the Control. *Potentiation*, not blocking, was found; pretraining with the beacon improved stimulus control of spatial search by the shape of the pool in the blocking group (i.e., potentiated in Phase 2) relative to the control.

The absence of cue competition between proximal cues and geometric shape has been found in a number of species and procedures (Cheng & Newcombe, 2005). Gallistel (1990) formalized the claim that the global geometric shape of an environment was immune to cue competition from other stimuli. Subsequent research, however, has revealed that whether or not cue competition can be found is dependent on a number of factors, including the sex of the animals (McGregor, 2020). For example, previous research reported that male rats rely more heavily on extramaze cues (i.e., higher salience) than females in small-scale navigation, but the reverse was found with female rats (Williams et al., 1990). A similar sex difference was also reported in humans (Saucier et al., 2002).

Male rats with a bias toward extramaze cues would be expected to learn about geometry at the expense of landmarks but not the reverse; and female rats should learn about landmarks at the expense of geometry. Rodríguez et al. (2011) reported just that: Spatial control by geometry was immune to overshadowing by landmarks in male rats but not the other way around; spatial control by geometry was strongly overshadowed by landmarks in females, but the reverse was not found.

In addition to competition or immunity due to evolutionary predispositions, direct manipulation of the salience of geometry or landmarks produced parallel results (McGregor, 2020). In humans, Learmonth et al. (2001) found that changing the size of the search space influenced whether or not overshadowing occurs, with geometry overshadowing landmarks in smaller environments where geometry is likely more salient. Taken together, these data have chipped away at the claim that learning about geometry occurs independently from learning about other cues.

Lastly, there is strong evidence that geometric shape is not learned globally or even extracted as a principal axis in rodents but rather can be reduced to local, relevant geometric

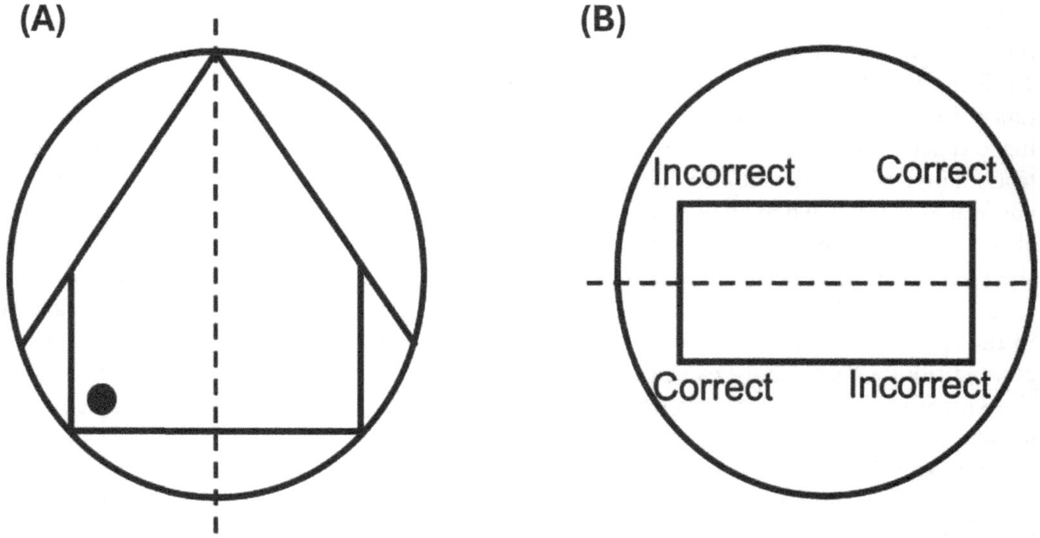

Figure 9.12 **Principal axis versus local features. (A)** Rats trained in a Morris water pool with walls inserted to create a pentagon shape with a principal axis running top to bottom (dashed lines) and a hidden platform in a target area (black dot in the bottom left). **(B)** After training, walls are inserted to create a rectangular shape with a principal axis running in at 90° from the original. Rats following the principal axis from training will primarily search at the top-left corner labeled incorrect in the rectangular test arena. Rats learning about the local features during training (long left, short right) will search at the correct corner in the test arena. (From McGregor et al., 2006; reproduced with permission from the American Psychological Association.)

features of the shape. For example, McGregor et al. (2006) trained rats to find a hidden platform in a Morris water maze at a particular location (e.g., bottom left) within a geometric shape (e.g., house). The principal axis is an imaginary line that divides a shape along its length into equal halves. At test, the rats were tested in a different shape (e.g., rectangle) with a different principal axis than in training but preserving the geometric features most proximal to the platform during training. Spatial behavior based on global shape at test would be predicted to be random or biased toward a new location consistent with the test shape's principal axis. However, search was found to be consistent with the local geometric features shared between the training and test shapes (Figure 9.12).

9.5 Spatial integration

In many situations, animals only have access to one portion of the environment at a time. For example, I may leave my house and go south during one trip and then leave my house and go north on another. The features encountered during these trips did not overlap, but my house served as a common landmark to locations south and north. Consequently, if I find myself to the south of my house and in need of traveling somewhere to the north, then I can determine a bearing based on the common element of my house.

Chamizo et al. (2006b) found evidence for spatial integration among configurations of landmarks suspended above the edge of a Morris water maze (Table 9.2). Rats in the integration group received alternating trials of a three-landmark configuration (A, B, C, and C, E, F) with C as the common element in both configurations. Rats in the control group were given similar sets of configurations (A, B, C and D, E, F) but with no common element between them. Rats were tested on novel configurations of two and three landmarks without the common element, C. The integration group showed better spatial control by novel two- and three-landmark configurations than the control group. These findings support the critical role of a common element to integrate spatial control by stimuli encountered during independent conditioning trials.

Sawa et al. (2005) reported a similar effect in pigeons but in a sensory preconditioning procedure in which two landmarks were preexposed in Phase 1 with no reinforcer. In Phase 1, pigeons received presentations of landmarks A and X on some trials and of B and Y on other trials (Figure 9.13). The landmark in each pair maintained a stable spatial relationship to the other, but the screen location of the compounds varied across trials. In Phase 2, pigeons learned to peck at a hidden target area for a reinforcer in the presence of A and B. The target area was always located relative to A, but B was randomly positioned on the screen. At test, pigeons received tests of X and Y on separate trials. Pigeons could respond based on the A–X spatial relationship in Phase 1 and the A–Goal relationship in Phase 2 based on the common element A or simply generalize between some subset of landmarks. The search pattern at test indicated integration, consistent with other findings of integration from rats (Chamizo et al., 2006b) and humans (Bouchekioua et al, 2013; Molet et al., 2010; Prados, 2011)

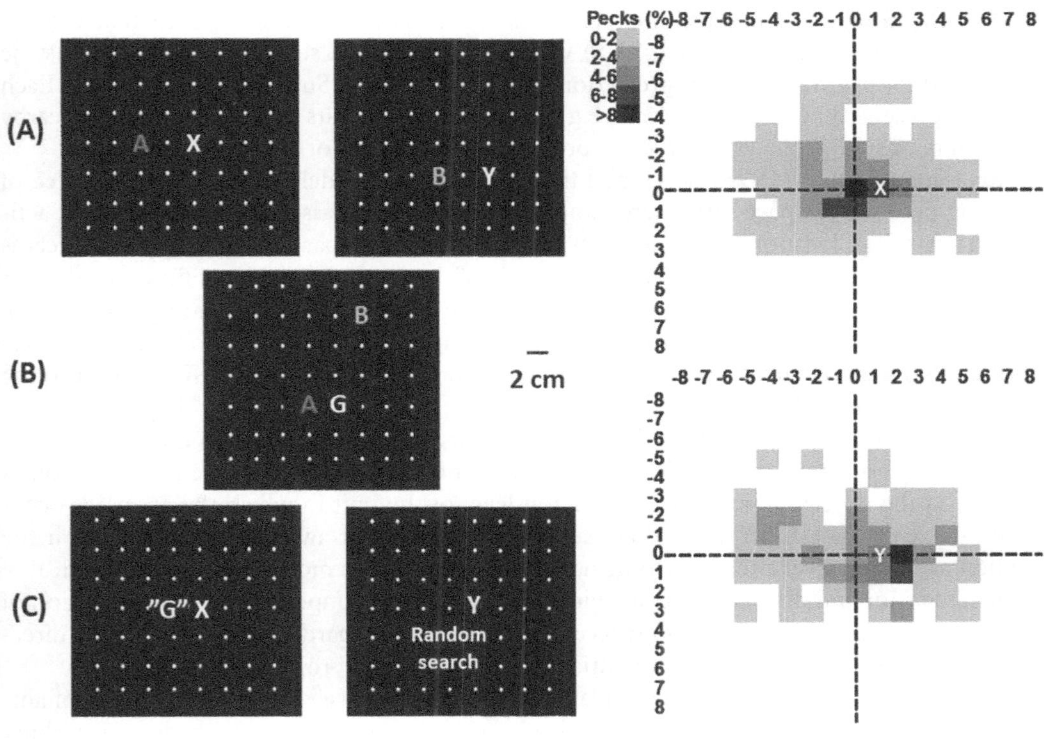

Figure 9.13 **Data from a landmark-based task using a touchscreen-equipped monitor with pigeons. (A)** Pigeons were given nonreinforced trials with two sets of landmarks, AX and BY. **(B)** Pigeons were trained to peck at a target area (G) that was in a consistent spatial relationship to one landmark, A, but unstable relative to another, B. **(C)** On the test, pigeons were given separate nonreinforced trials of X and Y. (Adapted from Leising et al., 2009; reproduced with permission from the Comparative Cognition Society.)

9.6 Where is location in models of conditioning?

As a reminder, many models of learning are based on an *error-correction rule*. That is, if the outcome of a stimulus or a response is not well predicted by past experience, then the degree of error (the discrepancy between what was obtained and what was expected) drives an update to the prediction to better capture the predictive value of any stimuli or responses present during the outcome. The CR of an animal after receiving a CS→US pairing is correlated with the strength of the prediction.

According to these models, after an animal has received many pairings of a Light and Shock, the presence of the Light would generate a prediction of Shock, and the strength of the CR would correlate with the strength of the prediction. There is no parameter that directly incorporates the spatial or temporal contiguity, or proximity, between the CS and US into the development of this prediction. However, there is strong evidence that spatial and temporal proximity is a critical factor determining the effectiveness of a conditioning procedure.

One way to incorporate proximity into these models would be to include spatial and temporal proximity as an influence on the salience of a stimulus, which is a factor common to error-correction learning models. That is, a stimulus that is presented closer in space and time to the US is more likely to be noticed and, thus, more easily conditioned. However, proximity changes not just the rate of conditioning but also the temporal and spatial location of the response, which cannot be accounted for by differences in salience.

Temporal difference models, discussed in more detail in Chapter 8, apply an error-correction rule to the concept of microstimuli (e.g., 1-s segments of a stimulus), such that error is adjusted in each unit of time (e.g., 1 s) within or following a stimulus, and error must be accounted for based on the sum prediction of all microstimuli (Sutton & Barto, 1990). Each unit is represented by a basis function (e.g., Gaussian) that results in generalization to nearby time units. A similar concept has been applied to spatial behavior (Foster et al., 2000).

Reid and Staddon (1998) developed their route-finder model based on a similar idea of dividing up a search space into microstimuli and the diffusing associative strength (i.e., activation) from one location to nearby units of space. A unit of space containing a reinforcer is set to an activation level related to the magnitude of the reinforcer, which diffuses to adjacent locations at a particular rate in a manner analogous to stimulus generalization (Figure 9.14). This diffusion creates a matrix of interconnected units, each with an activation level corresponding to the average of its neighbors (unless it contains the reinforcer; then it is set to the maximum activation level).

The decision rule for action in the matrix of units is simply to move to the adjacent unit with the highest activation level. With that movement, the next set of adjacent units becomes active and the process repeats. The activation level of the unit in which the animal is occupying decreases as a function of time, supporting movement away from the unit with the highest activation level after some time has passed. This simple model predicts a good deal of spatial behavior and does so using an animal with a relatively impoverished representation of the environment. The animal has no access to information regarding the distance and direction of an outcome and thus cannot anticipate future required responses.

Impressively, without any map, simulations approximated well the search behavior of ants when captured 20 m from their nest and released to return, European badgers searching for peanuts in an open field, dogs taking a shortcut to a food location, as well as rats in tasks that require navigation around a barrier. The degree of learning is not governed by an error-correction rule per se, as diffusion spreads evenly across adjacent locations.

Miller and Shettleworth (2007) proposed a model of small-scale spatial learning that utilizes an error-correction rule for assigning associative strength to locations. Similar to Reid

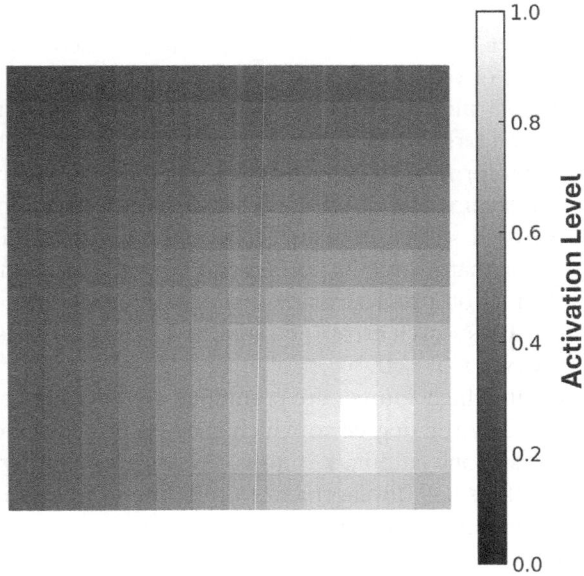

Figure 9.14 **An approximation of activation levels in a search space.** This space is divided into a 12 × 12 grid with a target area (white square) and diffusion spreading from this location to nearby areas. No matter where an animal is dropped in the search space, by approaching the nearby square with the highest relative activation level (i.e., brighter), the animal will reach the target area. A grid structure was chosen for simplicity, to discretize what is otherwise a continuous search space.

and Staddon (1998), locations have an activation level, or associative strength. However, in Miller and Shettleworth's model, it is the features, not locations, that acquire associative strength. Any feature of an environment, including a local feature of geometry, acquires associative strength when it is encountered in the presence of an outcome (e.g., the platform in a Morris water maze). The associative strength of each location in an environment is calculated as the sum of the associative strength of all of the features at that location.

Critically, features may acquire or lose associative strength if they are encountered at more than one location in an environment. The probability of approaching a particular location is determined by the associative strength of that location divided by the sum of the associative strength of all other locations. This model is particularly effective at predicting interactions (e.g., potentiation and cue competition) between learning about local features of an environment's geometry and other features, but it is equally relevant for predicting spatial behavior in environments lacking a distinct geometry. We have mentioned how models of conditioning may incorporate different types of cues used by navigating animals, but we have ignored the fact that animals use cues for different kinds of spatial behavior (e.g., path integration and map-like behavior).

Cheng (2007) suggested a different kind of spatial model based on Bayesian principles. Cheng applied Bayes's (1763) theorem, which describes how to determine the probability of something after you have observed some new information about the world, to the problem of navigating through an environment when multiple sources of spatial information are available within and across different forms of spatial behavior. Using Bayes's theorem, multiple sources are combined as a function of their proportional variance. In other words, while navigating through an environment, the animal accumulates an average estimate of the variance of the location of an outcome from different features of the environment (traveling somewhat farther or shorter from a landmark to the outcome across trials due to errors or movement of the landmark or outcome).

As described earlier, this model treats spatial navigation as a discrimination problem. Searching an open area for a target area with no intramaze features will lead to lots of errors. Adding a source of spatial information, such as path integration (distance and direction traveled), will facilitate the discrimination of the target area, as would adding a beacon or landmark. The weighting of each source of spatial information is determined by dividing the estimate of the variance for that source by the estimate of variance from other sources. The weighting of spatial information predicts many spatial learning effects, such as control by a more proximal landmark. Less search error (i.e., smaller variance) occurs in the presence of a more proximal landmark (see Figure 9.10).

Furthermore, the way in which sources are combined to influence spatial behavior is also determined, in some cases, by the degree to which they point to the same location. As discussed, in displacement tests, one landmark is moved relative to another and relative to their location during training. If a small displacement occurs, then the location of search is likely to be a function of the weightings established during training for the stable landmarks and displaced landmark (in its new location). However, if there is a large displacement, most animals will revert to the use of a single source of spatial information.

For example, Shettleworth and Sutton (2005) trained rats in a well-lit arena to leave a start box and forage for food at different locations. When the rats found the food, they returned to the start box to consume it. The location of the start box and the food moved across trials, and the location of the start box was hidden once the rat entered the arena. In this environment, the rats could only use path integration to return to the start box.

In another group, a distinctive black panel served as a beacon to mark the door to the start box. Rats with the beacon performed no better than rats in the group without it and navigated just as accurately when the beacon was removed; indicating that path integration was operating automatically in the background and was just as effective as the beacon. A 45° displacement of the beacon resulted in most rats ignoring path integration as a source of spatial information and approaching the beacon, whereas a 90° displacement resulted in a greater influence of path integration.

Lastly, as indicated by spatial integration in the landmark-based spatial task used by Sawa et al. (2005) and the potentiation results of Pearce et al. (2001), within-compound associations can be learned about. This kind of learning can follow a *contiguity* rule, such that two objects that occur in close proximity together will acquire some ability for one to generate an expectation of the other. This kind of learning, which is well documented in nonspatial tasks, is not well integrated into most models of spatial behavior. There is some suggestion that it could form the basis for a version of map-like behavior that resembles that of a cognitive map (Leising & Blaisdell, 2009; McGregor, 2020). Though the evidence for rich cognitive maps controlling spatial behavior is weak, there is little doubt that animals can learn about S→S associations.

9.7 Neurobiology of spatial behavior

9.7.1 Insects

We have covered three main types of spatial behavior: path integration, beacon homing, and map-like landmark use. Path integration requires allothetic (e.g., a celestial compass and optic flow) or idiothetic cues (e.g., nonvisual angular movement and a step counter) to determine direction and distance traveled from a place of origin.

Insects and mammals display path integration, suggesting this primitive form of spatial behavior can successfully generate many important movements in an environment (e.g., foraging). In insects, the central complex (CX), which is well conserved across insect species, has been implicated based on the known sensory inputs (allothetic and idiothetic) to this area and its involvement in controlling movement (Honkanen et al., 2019). In fruit flies and cockroaches, CX neurons have been found to respond to visual motion (e.g., optic flow). Using a form of neuroimaging that records the influx of calcium into a cell during neuronal activity, Seelig and Jayaraman (2015) found a population of neurons in the CX that tracks the fruit fly's current direction as it walked on a trackball, even in the darkness. With regard to the control of spatial behavior, lesioning the CX results in disrupted orientation in both fruit flies and cockroaches (Webb &Wystrach, 2016).

The CX has also been implicated in processing navigation-relevant sensory cues in three of the most well-studied long distance insect migrators: monarch butterfly, bogong moth, and the desert locust. Interestingly, slight differences in connectivity in the CX among different insects correspond to differences in the demands of movement, such as those required for migration versus dynamic small-scale navigation (Le Moël & Wystrach, 2020).

Although there is good evidence for insects' continuous and automatic updating of direction and distance of travel, they have also been known to use visual landmarks. In particular, we reviewed the snapshot or local-views hypothesis, which states that views along the route and at the target area are stored and later compared to the current view when subsequently navigating to that area.

In insects, a separate brain area, the mushroom bodies (MB), has been implicated in this type of search. As does the CX, the MB receives input from many different sensory pathways, including proprioceptive. The circuitry in the MB that receives olfactory input from the antennae has been shown to support olfactory Pavlovian conditioning, providing the necessary function of linking sensory input to valence to alter subsequent behavior (Webb & Wystrach, 2016). Although historically associated with olfactory discrimination and learning, Farris and Schulmeister (2011) have suggested that the need to search for targets in a dynamic environment drove the evolution of this structure in some insects. Consistent with a role for the MB in landmark-based search behavior, visual inputs to the MB are more extensive in those insects that rely more heavily on vision for foraging.

In certain aquatic species with underdeveloped antennal lobes, the typical olfactory input to the MB is reduced or absent. In fact, in an aquatic beetle that lives on the water, this input to the MB is exclusively supplied by visual information from compound eyes that face up toward the sky (Lin & Strausfeld, 2012). The visual input into the MB, for some species, along with the suitability of the circuitry of this area for Pavlovian conditioning, led Ardin et al. (2016) to adapt a model of olfactory conditioning to associate a pattern of visual input (i.e., a snapshot) with a value of whether or not the pattern was paired with a reward or punisher. This model of the function of the MB provides a plausible means of beacon homing, route behavior, and some map-like spatial behavior in insects.

9.7.2 Mammals

After studying the spatial behavior of rats, Tolman (1948) described in vague terms the kind of processing underlying their performance. He referenced that our nervous systems are bombarded with the sensory information of features in the environment. Complicated and patterned brain processes then connect the features selected from the bombardment into an elaborate *cognitive-like map* of the environment. Tolman distinguished these comprehensive cognitive-like maps from narrow strip maps. A *strip map* is capable of generating a correct response but is less flexible when presented with variations in the features of the area. Tolman described the formation of a strip map as induced by a damaged brain, an inadequate array of environmental cues, overtraining, and/or extreme motivating or frustrating conditions. Many years later, these two types of maps were more fully described by O'Keefe and Nadel (1978) in a book summarizing the extant literature on the neurobiology of small-scale spatial behavior and proposing an organizational framework for future investigations.

O'Keefe and Nadel (1978) suggested that two systems, the locale and taxon systems, generate the primary behavioral strategies of navigation. The *locale system* supports the cognitive-like map that Tolman (1948) hypothesized. In mammals, regions of space within each distinctive environment are represented by individual *place cells* in the hippocampal formation (Nyberg et al., 2022). The *mammalian hippocampal formation* includes the hippocampus proper, the subicular complex, the parasubiculum, and the entorhinal cortex (Figure 1.19).

Place cells increase their frequency of action potentials only when the animal is present in a specific area, referred to as the cell's place field (Hough & Bingman, 2004; O'Keefe & Dostrovsky, 1971). Place cells in rats have also shown sensitivity to the shape and size of the environment, as well as to the presence of landmarks or salient features (Gothard et al., 1996; Hetherington & Shapiro, 1997; Muller & Kubie, 1987; O'Keefe & Burgess, 1996; O'Keefe & Conway, 1978; O'Keefe & Nadel, 1978; O'Keefe & Speakman, 1987). Documentation of these place fields provided the first empirical evidence for a neuron's spatial selectivity, which could be integrated with surrounding place cells to provide the organism with a rudimentary spatial representation of the environment.

Other spatially tuned neurons have since been discovered, including head-direction cells, grid cells, and boundary cells. Each of these is consistent with an *allocentric representation* of space, such that head direction cells preferentially fire when the animal is facing an allocentric direction (e.g., north) relative to extramaze cues and updated by idiothetic cues, and boundary cells preferentially fire when the animal is at a particular distance and direction from cues defining the boundaries of environmental, irrespective of head direction (Nyberg et al., 2022). The properties of *head-direction cells* in the subiculum and entorhinal cortex resemble those of CX cells in insects, though this is almost certainly a homoplasy.

Though place cells fire preferentially in different areas, they lack the consistent scale and organization needed to estimate the distance from one place field to another. *Grid cells* have been proposed to provide a consistent metric due to their organization in a regular lattice of equilateral triangles. Grid-cell reliability depends first on path integration and then on continued input from place cells (Parra-Barrero et al., 2023).

Interestingly, during development, head direction cells are present from postnatal day 16 in the rat, followed by place cell activity and then grid cells. Not surprisingly, map-like spatial behavior in the rat does not appear until postnatal day 21. This same progression is evident in humans, with toddlers exhibiting beacon homing and route behavior prior to map-like behavior, which begins to emerge after 21 months (Nadel, 2013).

The second, the *taxon system*, attaches valence to a stimulus and encodes S-R associations that lead the subject from one place to another. The taxon system controls behavior when a beacon at the goal is available, when there are few behavioral options, or when there are few to no cues present. O'Keefe and Nadel (1978) reviewed studies of maze learning and found deficits in animals with damage to the hippocampus in 26 of 28 studies. O'Keefe and Nadel suggested the deficits were attributable to the absence of place information (e.g., a cognitive map), usually provided by an intact hippocampus and necessary for spatial behavior in the absence of a guidance cue (e.g., beacon). Furthermore, another brain area, the caudate nucleus, seemed to be responsible for learning the correct response in nonspatial tasks, such as a tactile discrimination (Colombo et al., 1989), as well as in taxon-supported tasks in which the correct spatial response is cued (e.g., approaching a lit versus dark arm of a maze).

An experiment described in detail in Chapter 4 (see Figure 4.10) investigated the effects of hippocampal vs. caudate nucleus inactivation and limited vs. extensive maze training on spatial learning (Packard & McGaugh, 1996). After limited training in a T-maze, rats with saline injections were more likely to exhibit map-like behavior (place learning) than those tested after extensive training. However, rats with hippocampal inactivation showed deficits after limited training but not after extensive training, whereas rats with caudate nucleus inactivation showed deficits after extensive training but not after limited training. In Chapter 4, the emphasis was on the role of the caudate nucleus in habit formation (taxon responding), but here, the emphasis is on the role of the hippocampus on map-like behavior (locale responding). These results suggest that after overtraining, route responding (i.e., taxon responding, according to O'Keefe & Nadel, 1978) suppresses the expression of place responding (i.e., locale responding, according to O'Keefe & Nadel, 1978). The caudate seems to function more like the MB in insects than the hippocampus.

The hippocampus has also been implicated in successful homing in pigeons, caching behavior in Clark's nutcrackers, and taxi driving by humans. The basic idea follows the *principle of proper mass* introduced in Chapter 1, which states that there is a positive correlation between the size of a brain area and the amount of information processed by that area. This principle also applies to insects, with the size of MB in red ants positively correlated with foraging efficiency in a maze and the size of MB in species of butterflies positively correlated with the complexity of their foraging behavior (Webb & Wystrach, 2016).

Research with rodents has focused more on the neuroanatomy underlying spatial memory, whereas a good deal of research with birds has investigated spatial memory as a function of natural history, including foraging strategy. Birds possess a hippocampus that is homologous to that of mammals (Colombo & Broadbent, 2000), which means the hippocampus includes divergent features due to approximately 300 million years of independent evolution, but a primitive version of the hippocampus was present in the last shared ancestor (see Figure 1.19).

Disruption of spatial behavior in birds has been found when the avian hippocampus is lesioned or temporarily deactivated (Bingman et al., 2005; Hampton & Shettleworth, 1996; Shiflett et al., 2003). Additionally, birds that cache (store) extra food when food is abundant and return days, weeks, or even months later to retrieve or relocate the food outperform those that cache less on spatial (Balda & Kamil, 1989; Clayton & Krebs, 1994; Olson et al., 1995) but not on other tasks (Olson et al., 1995). The relative volume of the hippocampus has been reported to be positively correlated with spatial memory and scatter hoarding (Healy & Krebs, 1992).

However, caution is recommended here for a variety of reasons. First, greater efficiency in neuronal connectivity, which may decrease volume, can support improved performance. Second, other studies have found inconsistent results when investigating the correlation between hippocampal volume and food caching (Gould et al., 2013). There is some evidence that the relative number of hippocampal neurons may better correlate with spatial memory. Third, a forced dichotomy approach (i.e., some animals have spatial memory and others do not) is misguided, generally, and specifically when studying spatial memory in animals. Rather, a comparative approach should investigate the abilities that support spatial memory in the context in which it operates, including differences in visual acuity and visual processing, as well as the resolution, capacity and duration of spatial memory (Smulders et al., 2010).

Given that there is good evidence that the activity of place cells correlates with accurate spatial behavior in some landmark-based tasks and that path integration is continuously and automatically operating, could these systems interact? Path integration is less dependent upon prior experience or a rich set of cues in the environment than map-like behavior. Consequently, path integration appears to support map-like behavior by anchoring objects to various locations and refining the precision and reliability of place fields. The dependence of path integration, at least initially, on idiothetic and distal cues leads to the accumulation of error in the system that scales with the distance traveled.

Consistent with this interpretation, place field firing is often less robust during the first 10 min of exploration, when path integration would be based primarily on idiothetic cues (Wilson & McNaughton, 1993). As place fields become more reliable, error in path integration is reduced, and spatial behavior based on this system improves. Further highlighting the importance of the interaction between the two systems, place fields established in the light are maintained in the dark (i.e., supported by path integration) but become less reliable over time as idiothetic cues are again the only input into the path integrator (McNaughton et al., 1996).

This view of the neural systems underlying spatial behavior is not without challenges. First, the emergence of route and map-like spatial behavior in a T-maze has been found to occur in the opposite direction when the maze is placed in water and the rats are aversively motivated to seek a submerged platform in one of the two arms. Second, performance in a spatial task requiring a sequence of responses (i.e., route behavior) is disrupted by lesions to the hippocampus and striatum. These findings suggest that the role of the hippocampus might be to synchronize behavior, generally (i.e., in time or space) with respect to cues in the environment.

Consistent with this interpretation, recordings of the activity of neurons across the hippocampus, called local field potentials, exhibit a particular rhythmic pattern of firing referred to as theta waves (7 Hz) during navigation, attentive behavior, and REM sleep. Sensory input (e.g., views, sounds, and smells) from the environment into the hippocampus is thought to be synched with place field firing based on the phase of the theta wave. This should remind you of the association of objects and events at particular times of day to the phase of the circadian rhythm discussed in Chapter 8. When recording from a particular place cell, the cell fires late in the theta cycle as the animal enters the boundary of a cell's place field and progressively earlier in the cycle as the animal progresses into the field, syncing with the peak of the cycle at the center of the place field and then later in the cycle as the animal moves toward the opposite edge of the place field. In this way, the phase procession of a sequence of place cells could represent a route (e.g., a sequence of locations) or a sequence of items in a list (e.g., the order of steps in a recipe; Redish & Ekstrom, 2013).

Additionally, two input pathways converge on the hippocampus; one pathway brings information related to the position of objects in space (e.g., from the parietal cortex), and the other brings contextual and object property information. The convergence of these inputs in the hippocampus could support a snapshot model of spatial behavior and its role in route behavior. Third, rats navigating to a beacon continue to perform well following lesions of the hippocampus and striatum. This suggests additional brain areas, such as posterior parietal cortex, may also be involved in some forms of spatial behavior.

Finally, consistent with Packard and McGaugh (1996), rats and humans with bilateral hippocampal lesions have been found to navigate complex environments to remembered locations (e.g., a London taxicab driver) as long as the environment was learned about prior to the lesion, which indicates a larger role for areas outside of the hippocampus in the expression of map-like behavior (Winocur & Moscovitch, 2011).

Glossary

Allocentric representation Cellular activity that encodes the spatial relations between objects in the environment independent of the perspective from which they were initially perceived.

Beacon homing Approach to a target area is supported by a single object marking the exact area.

Blocking Training first with a CS (A+) followed by training with a compound stimulus (AB+) and ending with a test of the other CS (B?). In the test, B elicits less responding than a control stimulus not subjected to the A+ training.

Celestial compass The positions of the objects in the night sky are used to orient and maintain directional movement.

Cognition Psychological processes involving perception, learning, memory, decision-making, action selection, thinking, and (in humans) language.

Cognitive map Traditional notion of a mental map of a search space that includes an allocentric representation of space, which includes the spatial relations within and between intramaze and extramaze objects.

Cognitive-like map Tolman's notion of a cognitive map that results from the complicated and patterned brain processes that connect features of the environment.

Contiguity or proximity The degree to which events occupy the same space and time.

Directional learning Occurs when discrete objects around (extramaze cues) the search area or a reference frame (e.g., geometry or contour of an extended surface) are used to determine a heading.

Egocentric representation Cellular activity that encodes the spatial relations between objects in the environment from the perspective of the viewer.

Error-correction rule A formula that states how a prediction should be updated based on the difference between the predicted value of the US and the actual experienced value of the US.

Extramaze cues Discrete objects outside of the search space, including the geometry or contour of extended surfaces that define the search space.

Grid cells These cells activate when an animal occupies specific locations in its environment, but they are also organized in a hexagonal lattice, which provides a metric framework for allocentric representations.

Hampton Court maze An apparatus used to study spatial learning that consists of tunnels and dead ends connecting a start location to an end location.

Head-direction cells Cells that preferentially fire when the animal is facing an allocentric direction (e.g., North) relative to extramaze cues and updated by idiothetic cues.

Higher-order conditioning A neutral stimulus becomes a conditioned stimulus (CS) by being paired with an already established CS.

Hippocampal formation Includes the hippocampus proper, the subicular complex, parasubiculum, and the entorhinal cortex.

Idiothetic feedback Cues generated from an organism's own movement that can be used to determine distance traveled.

Infrasound compass Low-frequency sound waves generated by natural (e.g., ocean surf, wind over mountains) or manmade phenomena that are used to orient and maintain directional movement.

Intramaze cues Discrete objects or features in the search space.

Locale system The cognitive processes and neurological structures that enable allocentric representations of a search space.

Location uncertainty Refers to the degree of error regarding the position of a target area that results from an inability to discriminate the target area from nearby areas due to poor spatial information (e.g., landmark instability) or other factors (Weber's law).

Long-term memory Morphological changes in cell structures that are essential for expression of learned behaviors over extended periods, ranging from hours to a lifetime.

Migration Persistent, straightened-out movements that are undistracted by the cues that would stop other types of movements.

Overshadowing In compound conditioning, reinforcing a compound (AB+) usually leaves one of the elements less capable of inducing responding in a test (B?) compared to a situation in which that element was trained by itself (B+).

Path integration or dead reckoning The use of idiothetic and allothetic motion cues to continuously update current position relative to a starting point.

Peak-shift effect Phenomenon in which discrimination training with S+ and S- stimuli along a single dimension finds maximal responding not to the S+ but at a location shifted away from the S-.

Phylogenetic shaping Analogous to operant shaping by successive approximations, except behavior tendencies are selected for across generations with gradual shifts toward the current behavior.

Place cells Cells that increase their frequency of action potentials only when the animal is present in a specific area.

Place learning Occurs when discrete objects in (intramaze) and around (extramaze cues) the search area are used to continuously update current position and determine distance and direction to a target area.

Potentiation The presence of one stimulus enhances the conditioning, or the expression of a conditioned response, to another stimulus when the two are presented together.

Principle of proper mass Describes a positive correlation between the size of a brain area and the amount of information processed by that area.

Representation A neural record equivalent to an external event (stimulus) or a response performed by the organism.

Response learning When animals learn to make a spatial operant response at a choice point (S) or based on proprioceptive and kinesthetic feedback from a particular movement (S, e.g., distance traveled).

Route When animals learn to make a series of spatial operant responses at choice points (S) or based on proprioceptive and kinesthetic feedback from particular movements (S, e.g., a right then left turn).

Salience Concept referring to the relative noticeability of stimuli and the rate at which they may feature into learning.

Shaping by successive approximations The process by which behaviors are reinforced in steps, with each next step more closely resembling the terminal, or target behavior, than the last.

Snapshot model or local view hypothesis A model of spatial learning that hypothesizes navigation is accomplished by actively adjusting a search bearing to match the current view of an environment with a previous view associated with a biologically significant outcome.

Solar compass The position of the sun is used to orient and maintain directional movement.

Spontaneous alternation or win-shift A response pattern in which the next spatial response leads to a different location from the previous response.

Stimulus generalization-gradient procedure A function by which behavior changes in the presence of a stimulus as its similarity deviates from a trained stimulus.

Stimulus–stimulus associations Pavlovian conditioning that is dependent on the relationship (e.g., contiguity) between two stimuli (e.g., CSs).

Strip map Tolman's notion of spatial behavior that results from learning about only a portion of the features in an environment.

Taxon system Attaches valence to a stimulus and encodes S→R associations that lead the subject from one place to another.

Unblocking After training with a blocking procedure, one group received extinction treatment with the blocking stimulus (CS A-) followed by testing with the other CS (B?). In the test, B elicits more responding after extinction of A than in a control group lacking the extinction treatment or with extinction of a different stimulus (C).

Weber's law States that sensitivity to a change in the intensity of a stimulus is proportional to the overall magnitude of that stimulus.

Working memory Task-relevant neural activity that persists after the removal of a stimulus for a brief time (seconds) or, under some conditions, until the task is complete.

References

Alerstam, T., Hedenström, A., & Åkesson, S. (2003). Long-distance migration: Evolution and determinants. *Oikos*, *103*(2), 247–260. https://doi.org/10.1034/j.1600-0706.2003.12559.x

Ardin, P., Peng, F., Mangan, M., Lagogiannis, K., & Webb, B. (2016). Using an insect mushroom body circuit to encode route memory in complex natural environments. *PLoS Computational Biology*, *12*(2), e1004683. https://doi.org/10.1371/journal.pcbi.1004683

Ashmole, N. P. (1963). The regulation of numbers of tropical oceanic birds. *Ibis, 103b*(3), 458–473. https://doi.org/10.1111/j.1474-919X.1963.tb06766.x
Balda, R. P., & Kamil, A. C. (1989). A comparative study of cache recovery by three corvid species. *Animal Behaviour, 38*(3), 486–495. https://doi.org/10.1016/S0003-3472(89)80041-7
Bayes, T. (1763). Essays towards solving a problem in the doctrine of chances. *Philosophical Transactions of the Royal Society, 53,* 370–418.
Biegler, R. (2006). Functional considerations in animal navigation: How do you use what you know? In M. F. Brown & R. G. Cook (Eds.), *Animal spatial cognition: Comparative, neural, and computational approaches.* [On-line]. https://pigeon.psy.tufts.edu/asc/biegler/
Biegler, R., & Morris, R. G. M. (1993). Landmark stability is a prerequisite for spatial but not discrimination learning. *Nature (London), 361*(6413), 631–633. https://doi.org/10.1038/361631a0
Biegler, R., & Morris, R. G. M. (1999). Blocking in the spatial domain with arrays of discrete landmarks. *Journal of Experimental Psychology: Animal Behavior Processes, 25*(3), 334–351. https://doi.org/10.1037/0097-7403.25.3.334
Bingman, V. P., Gagliardo, A., Hough, G. E., Ioalé, P., Kahn, M. C., & Siegel, J. J. (2005). The avian hippocampus, homing in pigeons and the memory representation of large-scale space. *Integrative and Comparative Biology, 45*(3), 555–564. https://doi.org/10.1093/icb/45.3.555
Blodgett, H. C., McCutchan, K., & Mathews, R. (1949). Spatial learning in the T-maze: The influence of direction, turn, and food location. *Journal of Experimental Psychology, 39*(6), 800–809. https://doi.org/10.1037/h0058978
Bouchekioua, Y., Miller, H. C., Craddock, P., Blaisdell, A. P., & Molet, M. (2013). Spatial integration of boundaries in a 3D virtual environment. *Acta Psychologica, 144*(2), 316–323. https://doi.org/10.1016/j.actpsy.2013.06.015
Calhoun, J. B. (1963). *The ecology and sociology of the Norway rat.* U.S. Dept. of Health, Education, and Welfare, Public Health Service.
Carr, A., & Coleman, P. J. (1974). Seafloor spreading theory and the odyssey of the green turtle. *Nature (London), 249*(5453), 128–130. https://doi.org/10.1038/249128a0
Carr, H., & Watson, J. B. (1908). Orientation in the white rat. *Journal of Comparative Neurology and Psychology, 18*(1), 27–44. https://doi.org/10.1002/cne.920180103
Cartwright, B. A., & Collett, T. S. (1982). How honeybees use landmarks to guide their return to a food source. *Nature (London), 295*(5850), 560–564. https://doi.org/10.1038/295560a0
Chamizo, V. D. (2003). Acquisition of knowledge about spatial location: Assessing the generality of the mechanism of learning. *Quarterly Journal of Experimental Psychology. B, Comparative and Physiological Psychology, 56*(1), 102–113. https://doi.org/10.1080/02724990244000205
Chamizo, V. D., Manteiga, R. D., Rodrigo, T., & Mackintosh, N. J. (2006a). Competition between landmarks in spatial learning: The role of proximity to the goal. *Behavioural Processes, 71*(1), 59–65. https://doi.org/10.1016/j.beproc.2005.11.003
Chamizo, V. D., Rodrigo, T., & Mackintosh, N. J. (2006b). Spatial integration with rats. *Learning & Behavior, 34*(4), 348–354. https://doi.org/10.3758/BF03193198
Cheng, K. (1986). A purely geometric module in the rat's spatial representation. *Cognition, 23*(2), 149–178. https://doi.org/10.1016/0010-0277(86)90041-7
Cheng, K. (1988). Some psychophysics of the pigeon's use of landmarks. *Journal of Comparative Physiology, A, 162*(6), 815–826. https://doi.org/10.1007/BF00610970
Cheng, K. (1989). The vector sum model of pigeon landmark use. *Journal of Experimental Psychology: Animal Behavior Processes, 15*(4), 366–375. https://doi.org/10.1037/0097-7403.15.4.366
Cheng, K. (1990). More psychophysics of the pigeon's use of landmarks. *Journal of Comparative Physiology, A, 166*(3), 857–863.
Cheng, K., Collett, T. S., Pickhard, A., & Wehner, R. (1987). The use of visual landmarks by honeybees: Bees weight landmarks according to their distance from the goal. *Journal of Comparative Physiology, A, 161*(3), 469–475. https://doi.org/10.1007/BF00603972
Cheng, K., & Graham, P. (2013). Spatial memory: Place learning, piloting, and route knowledge. In *Handbook of spatial cognition* (pp. 137–154). American Psychological Association. https://doi.org/10.2307/j.ctv1chs7vk.12
Cheng, K., & Newcombe, N. S. (2005). Is there a geometric module for spatial orientation? squaring theory and evidence. *Psychonomic Bulletin & Review, 12*(1), 1–23. https://doi.org/10.3758/BF03196346
Cheng, K., Shettleworth, S. J., Huttenlocher, J., & Rieser, J. J. (2007). Bayesian integration of spatial information. *Psychological Bulletin, 133*(4), 625–637. https://doi.org/10.1037/0033-2909.133.4.625

Cheng, K., Spetch, M. L., & Johnston, M. (1997). Spatial peak shift and generalization in pigeons. *Journal of Experimental Psychology: Animal Behavior Processes, 23*(4), 469–481. https://doi.org/10.1037/0097-7403.23.4.469

Clayton, N. S., & Krebs, J. R. (1994). Memory for spatial and object-specific cues in food-storing and non-storing birds. *Journal of Comparative Physiology A, 174*(3), 371–379. https://doi.org/10.1007/bf00240218

Collett, M., & Collett, T. S. (2007). Spatial aspects of foraging in ants and bees. In G. North & R. J. Greenspan (Eds.), *Invertebrate neurobiology*. Cold Spring Harbor Laboratory Press.

Collett, M., Harland, D., & Collett, T. S. (2002). The use of landmarks and panoramic context in the performance of local vectors by navigating honeybees. *Journal of Experimental Biology, 205*(6), 807–814. https://doi.org/10.1242/jeb.205.6.807

Colombo, M., & Broadbent, N. (2000). Is the avian hippocampus a functional homologue of the mammalian hippocampus? *Neuroscience & Biobehavioral Reviews, 24*(4), 465–484. https://doi.org/10.1016/S0149-7634(00)00016-6

Colombo, P. J., Davis, H. P., & Volpe, B. T. (1989). Allocentric spatial and tactile memory impairments in rats with dorsal caudate lesions are affected by preoperative behavioral training. *Behavioral Neuroscience, 103*(6), 1242–1250. https://doi.org/10.1037/0735-7044.103.6.1242

Darwin, C. (1873). Origin of certain instincts. *Nature, 7*(179), 417–418. https://doi.org/10.1038/007417a0

Dashiell, J, F. (1930). Direction orientation in maze running by the white rat. *Comparative Psychology Monographs, 7*, No. 32.

Dennis, W. (1932). Multiple visual discrimination in the block elevated maze. *Journal of Comparative Psychology, 13*(3), 391–396. https://doi.org/10.1037/h0073485

Diez-Chamizo, V., Sterio, D., & Mackintosh, N. J. (1985). Blocking and overshadowing between intramaze and extramaze cues: A test of the independence of locale and guidance learning. *Quarterly Journal of Experimental Psychology Section B, 37*(3b), 235–253. https://doi.org/10.1080/14640748508402098

Dingle, H. (2014). *Migration: The biology of life on the move* (2nd ed.). Oxford University Pres. https://doi.org/10.1093/acprof:oso/9780199640386.001.0001

Dingle, H., & Drake, V. A. (2007). What is migration? *Bioscience, 57*(2), 113–121. https://doi.org/10.1641/B570206

d'Isa, R., Comi, G., & Leocani, L. (2021). Apparatus design and behavioural testing protocol for the evaluation of spatial working memory in mice through the spontaneous alternation T-maze. *Scientific Reports, 11*(1), 21177–21177. https://doi.org/10.1038/s41598-021-00402-7

Etienne, A. S., & Jeffery, K. J. (2004). Path integration in mammals. *Hippocampus, 14*(2), 180–192. https://doi.org/10.1002/hipo.10173

Etienne, A. S., Maurer, R., Berlie, J., Reverdin, B., Rowe, T., Georgakopoulos, J., & Séguinot, V. (1998). Navigation through vector addition. *Nature, 396*(6707), 161–164. https://doi.org/10.1038/24151

Farris, S. M., & Schulmeister, S. (2011). Parasitoidism, not sociality, is associated with the evolution of elaborate mushroom bodies in the brains of hymenopteran insects. *Proceedings of the Royal Society. B, Biological Sciences, 278*(1707), 940–951. https://doi.org/10.1098/rspb.2010.2161

Foster, D. J., Morris, R. G. M., & Dayan, P. (2000). A model of hippocampally dependent navigation, using the temporal difference learning rule. *Hippocampus, 10*(1), 1–16. https://doi.org/10.1002/(SICI)1098-1063(2000)10:1<1::AID-HIPO1>3.0.CO;2-1

Gallistel, C. R. (1990). *The organization of learning*. MIT Press.

Gengerelli, J. A. (1929). Preliminary experiments on the causal factors in animal learning. *Journal of Comparative Psychology, 9*(4), 245–274. https://doi.org/10.1037/h0073956

Gothard, K., Skaggs, W., Moore, K., & McNaughton, B. (1996). Binding of hippocampal CA1 neural activity to multiple reference frames in a landmark-based navigation task. *Journal of Neuroscience, 16*(2), 823–835. https://doi.org/10.1523/jneurosci.16-02-00823.1996

Gould, K. L., Gilbertson, K. E., Hrvol, A. J., Nelson, J. C., Seyfer, A. L., Brantner, R. M., & Kamil, A. C. (2013). Differences in relative hippocampus volume and number of hippocampus neurons among five corvid species. *Brain, Behavior and Evolution, 81*(1), 56–70. https://doi.org/10.1159/000345560

Grice, G. R. (1948). The relation of secondary reinforcement to delayed reward in visual discrimination learning. *Journal of Experimental Psychology, 38*(1), 1–16. https://doi.org/10.1037/h0061016

Hamilton, D. A., Akers, K. G., Weisend, M. P., & Sutherland, R. J. (2007). How do room and apparatus cues control navigation in the Morris water task? Evidence for distinct contributions to a movement

vector. *Journal of Experimental Psychology: Animal Behavior Processes*, *33*(2), 100–114. https://doi.org/10.1037/0097-7403.33.2.100
Hamilton, D. A., Driscoll, I., & Sutherland, R. J. (2002). Human place learning in a virtual Morris water task: Some important constraints on the flexibility of place navigation. *Behavioural Brain Research*, *129*(1), 159–170. https://doi.org/10.1016/S0166-4328(01)00343-6
Hamilton, D. A., Johnson, T. E., Redhead, E. S., & Verney, S. P. (2009). Control of rodent and human spatial navigation by room and apparatus cues. *Behavioural Processes*, *81*(2), 154–169. https://doi.org/10.1016/j.beproc.2008.12.003
Hamilton, D. A., & Sutherland, R. J. (1999). Blocking in human place learning: Evidence from virtual navigation. *Psychobiology*, *27*(4), 453–461. https://doi.org/10.3758/bf03332140
Hampton, R. R., & Shettleworth, S. J. (1996). Hippocampal lesions impair memory for location but not color in passerine birds. *Behavioral Neuroscience*, *110*(4), 831–835. https://doi.org/10.1037/0735-7044.110.4.831
Healy, S. D., & Krebs, J. R. (1992). Food storing and the hippocampus in corvids amount and volume are correlated. *Proceedings of the Royal Society. B, Biological Sciences*, *248*(1323), 241–245. https://doi.org/10.1098/rspb.1992.0068
Hetherington, P. A., & Shapiro, M. L. (1997). Hippocampal place fields are altered by the removal of single visual cues in a distance-dependent manner. *Behavioral Neuroscience*, *111*(1), 20–34. https://doi.org/10.1037/0735-7044.111.1.20
Honkanen, A., Adden, A., da Silva Freitas, J., & Heinze, S. (2019). The insect central complex and the neural basis of navigational strategies. *Journal of Experimental Biology*, *222*, jeb188854. https://doi.org/10.1242/jeb.188854
Hough, G. E., & Bingman, V. P. (2004). Spatial response properties of homing pigeon hippocampal neurons: Correlations with goal locations, movement between goals, and environmental context in a radial-arm arena. *Journal of Comparative Physiology A*, *190*(12), 1047–1062. https://doi.org/10.1007/s00359-004-0562-z
Hull, C. L. (1943). *Principles of behavior: An introduction to behavior theory*. Appleton-Century-Crofts.
Jeffery, K. J. (2010). Theoretical accounts of spatial learning: A neurobiological view (commentary on Pearce, 2009). *Quarterly Journal of Experimental Psychology (2006)*, *63*(9), 1683–1699. https://doi.org/10.1080/17470210903540771
Jones, J. E., Antoniadis, E., Shettleworth, S. J., & Kamil, A. C. (2002). A comparative study of geometric rule learning by nutcrackers (*Nucifraga columbiana*), pigeons (*Columba livia*), and jackdaws (*Corvus monedula*). *Journal of Comparative Psychology (1983)*, *116*(4), 350–356. https://doi.org/10.1037/0735-7036.116.4.350
Kamil, A. C., & Jones, J. E. (1997). The seed-storing corvid Clark's nutcracker learns geometric relationships among landmarks. *Nature*, *390*(6657), 276–279. https://doi.org/10.1038/36840
Kamin, L. J. (1969). Predictability, surprise, attention, and conditioning. In B. A. Campbell & R. M. Church (Eds.), *Punishment and aversive behavior* (pp. 279–296). Appleton-Century-Crofts.
Klatzky, R. L., Loomis, J. M., Golledge, R. G., Cicinelli, J. G., Doherty, S., & Pellegrino, J. W. (1990). Acquisition of route and survey knowledge in the absence of vision. *Journal of Motor Behavior*, *22*(1), 19–43. https://doi.org/10.1080/00222895.1990.10735500
Kosaki, Y., Pearce, J. M., & McGregor, A. (2018). The response strategy and the place strategy in a plus-maze have different sensitivities to devaluation of expected outcome. *Hippocampus*, *28*(7), 484–496. https://doi.org/10.1002/hipo.22847
Le Moël, F., & Wystrach, A. (2020). Towards a multi-level understanding in insect navigation. *Current Opinion in Insect Science*, *42*, 110–117. https://doi.org/10.1016/j.cois.2020.10.006
Learmonth, A. E., Newcombe, N. S., & Huttenlocher, J. (2001). Toddlers' use of metric information and landmarks to reorient. *Journal of Experimental Child Psychology*, *80*(3), 225–244. https://doi.org/10.1006/jecp.2001.2635
Leising, K. J., & Blaisdell, A. P. (2009). Associative basis of landmark learning and integration in vertebrates. *Comparative Cognition & Behavior Reviews*, *4*, 80–102. https://doi.org/10.3819/ccbr.2009.40010
Leising, K. J., Garlick, D., & Blaisdell, A. P. (2011). Overshadowing between landmarks on the touchscreen and in ARENA with pigeons. *Journal of Experimental Psychology: Animal Behavior Processes*, *37*(4), 488–494. https://doi.org/10.1037/a0023914
Leising, K. J., Wong, J., & Blaisdell, A. P. (2015). Extinction and spontaneous recovery of spatial behavior in pigeons. *Journal of Experimental Psychology: Animal Learning and Cognition*, *41*(4), 371–377. https://doi.org/10.1037/xan0000076

Leising, K. J., Wong, J., Ruprecht, C. M., & Blaisdell, A. P. (2014). Blocking between landmarks during 2-D (touchscreen) and 3-D (ARENA) search tasks with pigeons. *Learning & Behavior*, *42*(4), 357–364. https://doi.org/10.3758/s13420-014-0153-y

Lin, C., & Strausfeld, N. J. (2012). Visual inputs to the mushroom body calyces of the whirligig beetle *Dineutus sublineatus*: Modality switching in an insect. *Journal of Comparative Neurology*, *520*(12), 2562–2574. https://doi.org/10.1002/cne.23092

Maaswinkel, H., & Whishaw, I. Q. (1999). Homing with locale, taxon, and dead reckoning strategies by foraging rats: Sensory hierarchy in spatial navigation. *Behavioural Brain Research*, *99*(2), 143–152. https://doi.org/10.1016/S0166-4328(98)00100-4

Macfarlane, D. A. (1930). *The role of kinesthesis in maze learning*. University of California Press.

Mackintosh, N. J. (1976). Overshadowing and stimulus intensity. *Animal Learning & Behavior*, *4*(2), 186–192. https://doi.org/10.3758/BF03214033

March, J., Chamizo, V. D., & Mackintosh, N. J. (1992). Reciprocal overshadowing between intramaze and extramaze cues. *Quarterly Journal of Experimental Psychology. B, Comparative and Physiological Psychology*, *45*(1), 49–63. https://doi.org/10.1080/14640749208401024

Margules, J., & Gallistel, C. R. (1988). Heading in the rat: Determination by environmental shape. *Animal Learning & Behavior*, *16*(4), 404–410. https://doi.org/10.3758/BF03209379

McGregor, A. (2020). What can we learn about navigation from associative learning? *Comparative Cognition & Behavior Reviews*, *15*, 163–186. https://doi.org/10.3819/CCBR.2020.150001

McGregor, A., Jones, P. M., Good, M. A., & Pearce, J. M. (2006). Further evidence that rats rely on local rather than global spatial information to locate a hidden goal: Reply to Cheng and Gallistel (2005). *Journal of Experimental Psychology: Animal Behavior Processes*, *32*(3), 314–321. https://doi.org/10.1037/0097-7403.32.3.314

McNaughton, B., Barnes, C., Gerrard, J., Gothard, K., Jung, M., Knierim, J., Kudrimoti, H., Qin, Y., Skaggs, W., Suster, M., & Weaver, K. (1996). Deciphering the hippocampal polyglot: The hippocampus as a path integration system. *Journal of Experimental Biology*, *199*(1), 173–185. https://doi.org/10.1242/jeb.199.1.173

Miller, N. Y., & Shettleworth, S. J. (2007). Learning about environmental geometry: An associative model. *Journal of Experimental Psychology: Animal Behavior Processes*, *33*(3), 191–212. https://doi.org/10.1037/0097-7403.33.3.191

Mittelstaedt, H., & Mittelstaedt, M. L. (1982). Homing by path integration. In *Avian navigation: International symposium on avian navigation (ISAN) held at Tirrenia (Pisa), September 11–14, 1981* (pp. 290–297). Springer.

Molet, M., Jozefowiez, J., & Miller, R. R. (2010). Integration of spatial relationships and temporal relationships in humans. *Learning & Behavior*, *38*(1), 27–34. https://doi.org/10.3758/LB.38.1.27

Morris, R. G. M. (1981). Spatial localization does not require the presence of local cues. *Learning and Motivation*, *12*(2), 239–260. https://doi.org/10.1016/0023-9690(81)90020-5

Morris, R. G. M., Garrud, P., Rawlins, J. N. P., & O'Keefe, J. (1982). Place navigation impaired in rats with hippocampal lesions. *Nature*, *297*(5868), 681–683. https://doi.org/10.1038/297681a0

Morris, R. G. M., Hagan, J. J., & Rawlins, J. N. P. (1986). Allocentric spatial learning by hippocampectomised rats: A further test of the "spatial mapping" and "working memory" theories of hippocampal function. *Quarterly Journal of Experimental Psychology. B, Comparative and Physiological Psychology*, *38*(4), 365–395. https://doi.org/10.1080/14640748608402242

Mouritsen, H. (2018). Long-distance navigation and magnetoreception in migratory animals. *Nature*, *558*(7708), 50–59. https://doi.org/10.1038/s41586-018-0176-1

Muller, R., & Kubie, J. (1987). The effects of changes in the environment on the spatial firing of hippocampal complex-spike cells. *Journal of Neuroscience*, *7*(7), 1951–1968. https://doi.org/10.1523/jneurosci.07-07-01951.1987

Nadel, L. (2013). Cognitive maps. In *Handbook of spatial cognition* (pp. 155–172). American Psychological Association. https://doi.org/10.2307/j.ctv1chs7vk.12

Nardini, M., Jones, P., Bedford, R., & Braddick, O. (2008). Development of cue integration in human navigation. *Current Biology*, *18*(9), 689–693. https://doi.org/10.1016/j.cub.2008.04.021

Nyberg, N., Duvelle, É., Barry, C., & Spiers, H. J. (2022). Spatial goal coding in the hippocampal formation. *Neuron*, *110*(3), 394–422. https://doi.org/10.1016/j.neuron.2021.12.012

Ohyama, T., Gibbon, J., Deich, J. D., & Balsam, E. D. (1999). Temporal control during maintenance and extinction of conditioned key pecking in ring doves. *Animal Learning & Behavior, 27,* 89–98.

O'Keefe, J., & Burgess, N. (1996). Geometric determinants of the place fields of hippocampal neurons. *Nature*, *381*(6581), 425–428. https://doi.org/10.1038/381425a0

O'Keefe, J., & Conway, D. H. (1978). Hippocampal place units in the freely moving rat: Why they fire where they fire. *Experimental Brain Research*, *31*(4), 573–590. https://doi.org/10.1007/BF00239865
O'Keefe, J., & Dostrovsky, J. (1971). The hippocampus as a spatial map: Preliminary evidence from unit activity in the freely-moving rat. *Brain Research*, *34*(1), 171–175. https://doi.org/10.1016/0006-8993(71)90358-1
O'Keefe, J., & Nadel, L. (1978). *The hippocampus as a cognitive map*. Oxford University Press.
O'Keefe, J., & Speakman, A. (1987). Single unit activity in the rat hippocampus during a spatial memory task. *Experimental Brain Research*, *68*(1), 1–27. https://doi.org/10.1007/BF00255230
Olson, D. J., Kamil, A. C., Balda, R. P., & Nims, P. J. (1995). Performance of four seed-caching corvid species in operant tests of nonspatial and spatial memory. *Journal of Comparative Psychology*, *109*(2), 173–181. https://doi.org/10.1037/0735-7036.109.2.173
Packard, M. G., & McGaugh, J. L. (1996). Inactivation of hippocampus or caudate nucleus with lidocaine differentially affects expression of place and response learning. *Neurobiology of Learning and Memory*, *65*, 65–72. https://doi.org/10.1006/nlme.1996.0007
Parra-Barrero, E., Vijayabaskaran, S., Seabrook, E., Wiskott, L., & Cheng, S. (2023). A map of spatial navigation for neuroscience. *Neuroscience and Biobehavioral Reviews*, *152*, 105200–105200. https://doi.org/10.1016/j.neubiorev.2023.105200
Pavlov, I. P. (1927). *Conditioned reflexes: An investigation of the physiological activity of the cerebral cortex*. Oxford University Press.
Pearce, J. M. (2009). The 36th Sir Frederick Bartlett lecture: An associative analysis of spatial learning. *Quarterly Journal of Experimental Psychology*, *62*(9), 1665–1684. https://doi.org/10.1080/17470210902805589
Pearce, J. M., Ward-Robinson, J., Good, M., Fussell, C., & Aydin, A. (2001). Influence of a beacon on spatial learning based on the shape of the test environment. *Journal of Experimental Psychology: Animal Behavior Processes*, *27*(4), 329–344. https://doi.org/10.1037/0097-7403.27.4.329
Perin, C. T. (1943). The effect of delayed reinforcement upon the differentiation of bar responses in white rats. *Journal of Experimental Psychology*, *32*(2), 95–109. https://doi.org/10.1037/h0057249
Petter, E. A., Gershman, S. J., & Meck, W. H. (2018). Integrating models of interval timing and reinforcement learning. *Trends in Cognitive Sciences*, *22*(10), 911–922. https://doi.org/10.1016/j.tics.2018.08.004
Prados, J. (2011). Blocking and overshadowing in human geometry learning. *Journal of Experimental Psychology: Animal Behavior Processes*, *37*(1), 121–126. https://doi.org/10.1037/a0020715
Prados, J., Manteiga, R. D., & Sansa, J. (2003). Recovery effects after extinction in the Morris swimming pool navigation task. *Learning & Behavior*, *31*(3), 299–304. https://doi.org/10.3758/BF03195991
Pritchard, D. J., & Healy, S. D. (2017). Homing and navigation. In J. Call, G. M. Burghardt, I. M. Pepperberg, C. T. Snowdon, & T. Zentall (Eds.), *APA handbook of comparative psychology: Perception, learning, and cognition* (pp. 485–508). American Psychological Association. https://doi.org/10.1037/0000012-022
Ratliff, K. R., & Newcombe, N. S. (2008). Reorienting when cues conflict: Evidence for an adaptive-combination view. *Psychological Science*, *19*(12), 1301–1307. https://doi.org/10.1111/j.1467-9280.2008.02239.x
Redhead, E. S., Roberts, A., Good, M., & Pearce, J. M. (1997). Interaction between piloting and beacon homing by rats in a swimming pool. *Journal of Experimental Psychology: Animal Behavior Processes*, *23*(3), 340–350. https://doi.org/10.1037/0097-7403.23.3.340
Redish, A. D., & Ekstrom, A. (2013). Hippocampus and related areas: What the place cell literature tells us about cognitive maps in rats and humans. In D. Waller & L. Nadel (Eds.), *Handbook of spatial cognition* (pp. 15–34). American Psychological Association. https://doi.org/10.1037/13936-002
Reid, A. K., & Staddon, J. E. R. (1998). A dynamic route finder for the cognitive map. *Psychological Review*, *105*(3), 585–601. https://doi.org/10.1037/0033-295X.105.3.585
Restle, F. (1957). Discrimination of cues in mazes: A resolution of the "place-vs.-response" question. *Psychological Review*, *64*, 217–228.
Richman, C. L., Dember, W. N., & Kim, P. (1986). Spontaneous alternation behavior in animals: A review. *Current Psychology*, *5*(4), 358–391. https://doi.org/10.1007/BF02686603
Ricklefs, R. E. (1980). Geographical variation in clutch size among passerine birds: Ashmole's hypothesis. *Auk*, *97*(1), 38–49.
Roberts, A. D. L., & Pearce, J. M. (1998). Control of spatial behavior by an unstable landmark. *Journal of Experimental Psychology: Animal Behavior Processes*, *24*(2), 172–184. https //doi.org/10.1037/0097-7403.24.2.172

Roberts, A. D. L., & Pearce, J. M. (1999). Blocking in the Morris swimming pool. *Journal of Experimental Psychology: Animal Behavior Processes*, *25*(2), 225–235. https://doi.org/10.1037/0097-7403.25.2.225

Rodrigo, T., Chamizo, V. D., McLaren, I. P. L., & Mackintosh, N. J. (1997). Blocking in the Spatial Domain. *Journal of Experimental Psychology: Animal Behavior Processes*, *23*(1), 110–118. https://doi.org/10.1037/0097-7403.23.1.110

Rodrigo, T., Sansa, J., Baradad, P., & Chamizo, V. D. (2006). Generalization gradients in a navigation task with rats. *Learning and Motivation*, 37(3), 247–268. https://doi.org/10.1016/j.lmot.2005.08.001

Rodríguez, C. A., Chamizo, V. D., & Mackintosh, N. J. (2011). Overshadowing and blocking between landmark learning and shape learning: The importance of sex differences. *Learning & Behavior*, *39*(4), 324–335. https://doi.org/10.3758/s13420-011-0027-5

Ruch, F. L. (1930). Food-reward vs. escape-from-water as conditions motivating learning in the white rat. *Journal of Genetic Psychology*, *38*, 127–145.

Russell, R., & Kirkpatrick, K. (2007). The role of temporal generalization in a temporal discrimination task. *Behavioural Processes*, *74*(2), 115–125. https://doi.org/10.1016/j.beproc.2006.08.004

Sánchez-Moreno, J., Rodrigo, T., Chamizo, V. D., & Mackintosh, N. J. (1999). Overshadowing in the spatial domain. *Animal Learning and Behavior*, *27*, 391.

Saucier, D., Green, S., Leason, J., MacFadden, A., Bell, S., & Elias, L. (2002). Are sex differences in navigation caused by sexually dimorphic strategies or by differences in the ability to use the strategies? *Behavioral Neuroscience*, *116*(3), 403–410. https://doi.org/10.1037//0735-7044.116.3.403

Sawa, K., Leising, K. J., & Blaisdell, A. P. (2005). Sensory preconditioning in spatial learning using a touch screen task in pigeons. *Journal of Experimental Psychology: Animal Behavior Processes*, *31*, 368–375.

Seelig, J. D., & Jayaraman, V. (2015). Neural dynamics for landmark orientation and angular path integration. *Nature*, *521*(7551), 186–191. https://doi.org/10.1038/nature14446

Shettleworth, S. J., & Sutton, J. E. (2005). Multiple systems for spatial learning: Dead reckoning and beacon homing in rats. *Journal of Experimental Psychology: Animal Behavior Processes*, *31*(2), 125–141. https://doi.org/10.1037/0097-7403.31.2.125

Shiflett, M. W., Smulders, T. V., Benedict, L., & DeVoogd, T. J. (2003). Reversible inactivation of the hippocampal formation in food-storing black-capped chickadees (*Poecile atricapillus*). *Hippocampus*, *13*(4), 437–444. https://doi.org/10.1002/hipo.10065

Skinner, B. F. (1975). The shaping of phylogenic behavior. *Journal of the Experimental Analysis of Behavior*, *24*(1), 117–120. https://doi.org/10.1901/jeab.1975.24-117

Skinner, D. M., Etchegary, C. M., Ekert-Maret, E. C., Baker, C. J., Harley, C. W., Evans, J. H., & Martin, G. M. (2003). An analysis of response, direction, and place learning in an open field and T-maze. *Journal of Experimental Psychology: Animal Behavior Processes*, *29*(1), 3–13. https://doi.org/10.1037/0097-7403.29.1.3

Small, W. S. (1901). Experimental study of the mental processes of the rat. II. *American Journal of Psychology*, *12*, 206–239.

Smulders, T. V., Gould, K. L., & Leaver, L. A. (2010). Using ecology to guide the study of cognitive and neural mechanisms of different aspects of spatial memory in food-hoarding animals. *Philosophical Transactions of the Royal Society B: Biological Sciences*, *365*(1542), 883–900. https://doi.org/10.1098/rstb.2009.0211

Spetch, M. L. (1995). Overshadowing in landmark learning: Touch-screen studies with pigeons and humans. *Journal of Experimental Psychology: Animal Behavior Processes*, *21*(2), 166–181. https://doi.org/10.1037/0097-7403.21.2.166

Spetch, M. L., Cheng, K., MacDonald, S. E., Linkenhoker, B. A., Kelly, D. M., & Doerkson, S. R. (1997). Use of landmark configuration in pigeons and humans: II. Generality across search tasks. *Journal of Comparative Psychology*, *111*(1), 14–24. https://doi.org/10.1037/0735-7036.111.1.14

Spetch, M. L., & Mondloch, M. V. (1993). Control of pigeons' spatial search by graphic landmarks in a touch-screen task. *Journal of Experimental Psychology: Animal Behavior Processes*, *19*(4), 353–372. https://doi.org/10.1037/0097-7403.19.4.353

Srinivasan, M. V., Zhang, S. W., & Bidwell, N. J. (2024). Visually mediated odometry in honeybees. *Journal of Experimental Biology*, *227*(12). https://doi.org/10.1242/jeb.248085

Stahlman, W. D., & Blaisdell, A. P. (2009). Blocking of spatial control by landmarks in rats. *Behavioural Processes*, *81*(1), 114–118. https://doi.org/10.1016/j.beproc.2009.02.007

Sutherland, R. J., Whishaw, I. Q., & Kolb, B. (1983). A behavioural analysis of spatial localization following electrolytic, kainate- or colchicine-induced damage to the hippocampal formation in the rat. *Behavioural Brain Research*, *7*(2), 133–153. https://doi.org/10.1016/0166-4328(83)90188-2

Sutton, J. E. (2002). Multiple-landmark piloting in pigeons (*Columba livia*): Landmark configuration as a discriminative cue. *Journal of Comparative Psychology (1983)*, *116*(4), 391–403. https://doi.org/10.1037/0735-7036.116.4.391

Sutton, R. S., & Barto, A. G. (1990). Time-derivative models of Pavlovian reinforcement. In M. Gabriel & J. Moore (Eds.), *Learning and computational neuroscience: Foundations of adaptive networks* (pp. 497–537). MIT Press.

Thorndike, E. (1898). Some experiments on animal intelligence. *Science*, *7*(181), 818–824. https://doi.org/10.1126/science.7.181.818

Tinbergen, N. (1951). *The study of instinct*. Clarendon Press.

Tolman, E. C. (1948). Cognitive maps in rats and men. *Psychological Review*, *55*, 189–208.

Tolman, E. C., Ritchie, B. F., & Kalish, D. (1946). Studies in spatial learning: II. Place learning versus response learning. *Journal of Experimental Psychology*, *36*, 221–229.

Turner, C. H. (1908). The homing of the burrowing-bees (Anthophoridae). *Biological Bulletin*, *15*(6), 247–258.

Vander Wall, S. B., & Balda, R. P. (1981). Ecology and evolution of food-storage behavior in conifer-seed-caching corvids. *Zeitschrift Für Tierpsychologie*, *56*(3), 217–242. https://doi.org/10.1111/j.1439-0310.1981.tb01298.x

von Frisch, K. (1914). Der Farbensinn und Formensinn der Biene. *Zoologische Jahrbücher Abteilung für allgemeine Zoologie und Physiologie*, *37*(1), 1–187.

Watson, J. B. (1907). Kinaesthetic and organic sensations: Their role in the reactions of the white rat to the maze. *Psychological Review Monograph Supplement*, *8*, No. 33.

Webb, B., & Wystrach, A. (2016). Neural mechanisms of insect navigation. *Current Opinion in Insect Science*, *15*, 27–39. https://doi.org/10.1016/j.cois.2016.02.011

Wehner, R., Michel, B., & Antonsen, P. (1996). Visual navigation in insects: Coupling of egocentric and geocentric information. *Journal of Experimental Biology*, *199*(1), 129–140. https://doi.org/10.1242/jeb.199.1.129

Williams, C. L., Barnett, A. M., & Meck, W. H. (1990). Organizational effects of early gonadal secretions on sexual differentiation in spatial memory. *Behavioral Neuroscience*, *104*(1), 84–97. https://doi.org/10.1037/0735-7044.104.1.84

Wilson, M., & McNaughton, B. (1993). Dynamics of the hippocampal ensemble code for space. *Science*, *261*(5124), 1055–1058. https://doi.org/10.1126/science.8351520

Winocur, G., & Moscovitch, M. (2011). Memory transformation and systems consolidation. *Journal of the International Neuropsychological Society*, *17*(5), 766–780. https://doi.org/10.1017/S1355617711000683

Wittlinger, M., Wehner, R., & Wolf, H. (2006). Ant odometer: Stepping on stilts and stumps. *Science*, *312*(5782), 1965–1967. https://doi.org/10.1126/science.1126912

Wolfe, J. B. (1934). The effect of delayed reward upon learning in the white rat. *Journal of Comparative Psychology*, *17*(1), 1–21. https://doi.org/10.1037/h0070755

10 Categories, concepts, and numerical competence

10.1 Conceptual behavior

At this point, you are familiar with the themes of stimulus control and discrimination learning that run throughout this book. *Stimulus control* is present when the probability of a behavior varies based on the presence or absence of a stimulus. We could train a rat that lever presses will be followed by a reinforcer if they occur when a particular English vowel sound (e.g., "e") is playing through a speaker but presses in the absence of the sounds will not. To train a discrimination more like that faced by students learning English, the same rat could also receive trials in which lever presses in the presence of a different sound, an English consonant (e.g., "k"), are never reinforced. Finally, similar to the student, we could train the rat to distinguish all vowel sounds (paired with a reinforced lever press) from an equal number of consonant sounds (never paired with a reinforcer). In this example, vowels and consonants are *categories*, or groups of stimuli that share one or more physical features or functions. The mental representation of a category is commonly referred to as a *concept*.

Conceptual behavior, or *categorization*, occurs when a class of stimuli is responded to similarly (e.g., a lever press for a rat or a raised hand for a human) on the basis of perceptual, associative, or relational similarity. For example, if a skeptical website programmer requires you to prove that you are human by demonstrating that you have a concept of a tree, then they may ask you to respond similarly to (i.e., to click) pictures of trees that vary in their size, shape, color, and location and make a different response to (i.e., to not click) pictures that contain anything but trees. In this and other tests, concept learning can be inferred from behavioral results that indicate generalization within a category (perceptual, associative, or relational) and discrimination across categories (Keller & Schoenfeld, 1950).

This approach has revealed that a variety of species are capable of concept learning on the basis of the perceptual similarity between two stimuli or by association of the stimuli with each other, with a common response (e.g., approach), or with a common outcome (e.g., food). So much so that successfully clicking all of the trees would not distinguish you from a well-trained pigeon or monkey (but fortunately for the programmer and for society at large, pigeons and monkeys are unlikely to access the internet). The evidence for relational concept learning in nonhuman animals is more limited.

Changes in conceptual behavior require corresponding changes in neural processing; various theories of concept learning are considered later in this chapter to assess the nature and the neurobiology of the mental representation of categories.

The utility of conceptual behavior in addressing discrimination problems in the natural world cannot be overstated. Imagine that an animal's survival depended on approaching fruit trees versus other kinds of trees. A fruit tree must, by definition, grow flowers that mature as

DOI: 10.4324/9781003401957-13

Figure 10.1 **Family resemblance in fruit trees.** Peach (left) and fig (right) share many perceptual features, but the fruit tree category is structured by family resemblance, such that both trees share one or more attributes but neither tree has all of the attributes of the category.

fruit. However, all fruit trees do not appear the same, and they share many features with trees that do not bear fruit. The category of fruit tree is structured by *family resemblance*, such that all fruit trees share one or more attributes, but there is no one fruit tree that has all of these attributes. Of course, even with trees bearing the same fruit, there is a great deal of variety in appearance (e.g., height, canopy width and density; Figure 10.1).

At one extreme, the animal could learn to approach a tree depending on *item-specific learning*, which relies on direct experience with each tree. This would be a slow but highly accurate solution that maximizes correct approaches but at the expense of missing many fruit trees that look dissimilar to trees directly experienced.

At the other extreme, if after a visit to a tree, the animal abstracted some of the essential attributes of that type of tree, then it could approach new fruit trees in the future with a fairly high degree of accuracy, minimizing the likelihood of missing a fruit tree at the expense of approaching some nonfruit trees. It seems unlikely that animals would only respond based on item-specific learning (i.e., that animals would not generalize from previous experience with the attributes of one fruit tree to other fruit trees), but it seems equally unlikely that an animal could extract the most important attributes of a category given experience with only a single member.

In this same scenario, if two trees with differing amounts of fruit are present, approaching the tree with more fruit is likely to provide a direct fitness advantage. The efficiency and, consequently, adaptive value of learning about categories provides the basis for an assumption that many animals will exhibit some degree of conceptual behavior. The goal of this chapter is to describe different levels of conceptual behavior based on the category attributes that are used to generalize within and discriminate between them. This problem has been most extensively studied in birds and mammals.

10.2 Generalization and discrimination revisited

Generalization and discrimination are central to learning. In Chapter 2, you were introduced to generalization gradients and discrimination training. For example, in an experiment with visual stimuli, Hanson (1959) trained pigeons to peck a key that was illuminated with a light that humans see as Green (550 nm) for access to mixed grain (G+ trials). Some pigeons also received trials of a key with another wavelength of light, 590 nm, which to humans will look more Orange-Yellow (Y); pecks to this key were never reinforced (a G+/Y- discrimination). After training, the birds were tested with a variety of wavelengths in the visible spectrum (400–700 nm) to obtain a generalization gradient. For birds that had received only G+ trials (and not Y- trials), the distribution of pecks was centered at 550 nm, with decreased peck rates as the distance from this wavelength increased. For example, the pigeons were likely to peck vigorously to Yellow (590 nm) and to colder Greens (e.g., Cyan, 530 nm) but to respond little to deep Violet (400 nm) and Red (700 nm). Pecking at Cyan is an example of primary generalization, as the birds were not trained to peck this color but did so as a result of overlapping perceptual and neural activity with the wavelength that was reinforced (550 nm).

Comparable generalization gradients are found with stimuli differing in sound frequency as well as the size or shape of a stimulus, which suggests primary generalization has been subject to natural selection rather than being a mere side effect of neural processing. The philosopher Quine (1969, p. 13) suggested, "If people's innate spacing of qualities is a gene-linked trait, then the spacing that has made for the most successful inductions will have tended to predominate through natural selection." In other words, it may provide a fitness advantage to treat similarly objects that look similar in size, shape, or color (Miller & Dollard, 1941). In particular, taxa near the specificity level of the genus have been characterized by clusters of salient, correlated attributes (Smith, 2014). As the saying goes, if it looks like a duck and sounds like a duck, then it is probably a duck.

Returning to Hanson's (1959) study with pigeons, what about birds that were trained in the G+/Y- problem? In these animals, the peak of responding was seen not at the wavelength of the reinforced stimulus (G, 550 nm) but shifted away from the nonreinforced stimulus (Y, 590 nm). The most vigorous pecking was observed at approximately 540 nm, closer to Blue than Green, and the entire distribution was skewed toward the G+. This phenomenon is called *peak shift*.

Three conclusions relevant for concept learning follow from Hanson's (1959) data. First, generalization gradients may reveal the natural sensory and perceptual boundaries of a category. For example, consider a scenario in which a toddler has learned to touch an index card when the parent emits the verbal label ("green") and the wavelength of the colored circle on the index card corresponds to green (no other colors were trained; Figure 10.2). The toddler could then be tested in the same way as the pigeons; show the toddler a series of index

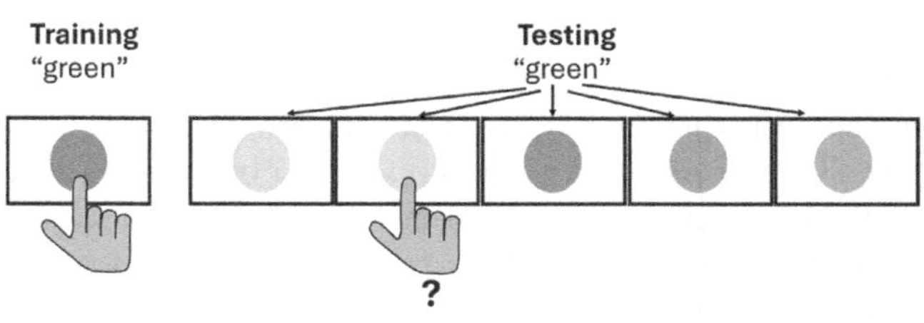

Figure 10.2 **Testing the natural boundaries of color perception.** A toddler is trained to touch a notecard with a green colored circle when a parent says "green." After training, notecards with other colored circles could be presented one at a time along with "green." Calculating response probability along with response latency, one could determine the color boundaries extending from training with the original circle. This could be used to evaluate the toddler for abnormal color perception when compared with the average boundaries of age-matched toddlers.

cards with a circle of a different color each time and say "green." The generalization gradient of the toddler's touches to the cards of different colors would reveal the natural boundaries of the visual system (i.e., a sensitivity function within a continuous dimension). Test enough toddlers and you would get an averaged lower and upper bound for what a toddler "sees" as green. A New Zealand tribal society, the Dani, used only the words "lighter" and "darker" to refer to colors, yet when tested on a wide range of colors, they demonstrated category boundaries that corresponded closely to those of English speakers (Rosch, 1973).

Second, generalization gradients can be sharpened through training. If conceptual behavior is defined by generalization within a category, then category boundaries can be narrowed through discrimination training. Lashley and Wade (1946) considered generalization to result from insufficient training. Pavlov (1927, p. 117) evaluated whether more trials of the trained stimulus were sufficient to reduce generalization:

> we were inclined to think that this effect could be obtained by two different methods: the first method consisted in repeating the definite conditioned stimulus a great number of times always accompanied by reinforcement, and the second method consisted in contrasting the single definite conditioned stimulus, which was always accompanied by reinforcement, with different neighbouring stimuli which were never reinforced. At present, however, we are more inclined to regard this second method as more probably the only efficacious one, since it was observed that no absolute differentiation was ever obtained by the use of the first method, even though the stimulus was repeated with reinforcement over a thousand times. On the other hand, it was found that contrast by even a single unreinforced application of an allied stimulus, or by a number of single unreinforced applications of different members of a series of allied stimuli at infrequent intervals of days or weeks, led to a rapid development of differentiation.

Training the toddler to touch the index card when the parent says "green" but not "yellow" would sharpen the original category boundaries. Narrowing the distribution of stimuli that affords a response through discrimination training corresponds well to the developmental trajectory of categorization in humans (Mandler, 2000; Warrington, 1975). The three levels of categorization are superordinate, basic, and subordinate, ordered by least restrictive for category membership to the most restrictive. *Basic-level* categories share the most perceptual similarity with other members and fewest similarity with members across the category (Lazareva & Wasserman, 2008). *Subordinate-level* categories contain high within-category perceptual similarity but also high between-category perceptual similarity. At the *superordinate level*, generalization occurs across several basic-level categories that share low within-category perceptual similarity. Humans are said to learn categories beginning with basic levels (e.g., "duck"), or in some cases superordinate levels (e.g., "animal"), followed by increasingly more narrow subordinate levels (e.g., "Mallard").

Third, peak shift suggests that training an S- can do more than simply reduce responding at the S-; it also has the unintended consequence of shifting the category boundary for the S+. Peak shift can be accounted for by inferring that explicit reinforcement and nonreinforcement each produce characteristic, antagonistic functions (i.e., excitatory and inhibitory) that interact to produce behavior (Spence, 1937). Reinforcement of a target stimulus may create an excitatory generalization gradient peaking at the target stimulus, and nonreinforcement (or extinction) of a different stimulus may create an inhibitory generalization gradient around that stimulus (Figure 10.3). An inhibitory generalization gradient would be reflected in a distribution of stimuli to which an organism is less likely to respond than during baseline

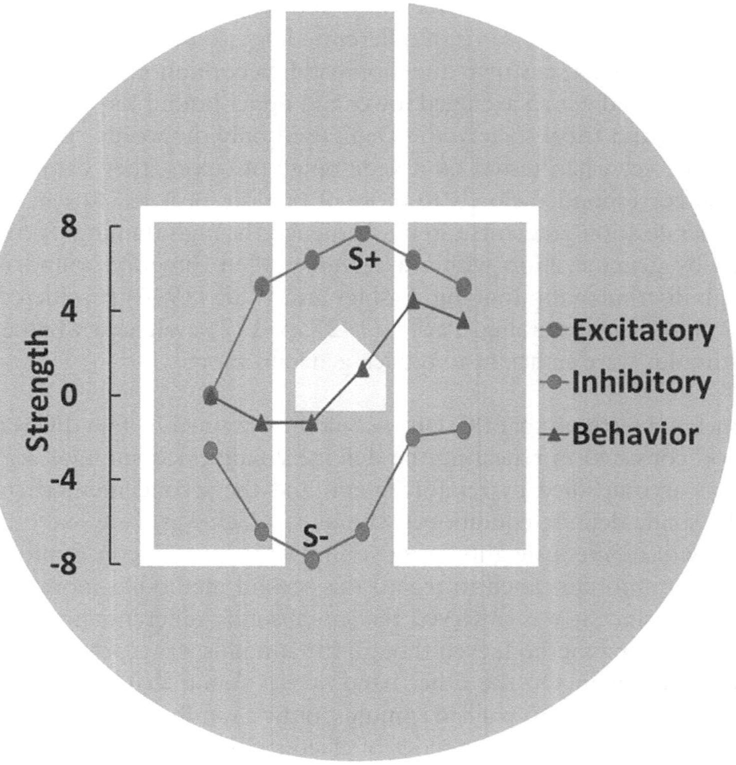

Figure 10.3 **Home plate.** Hypothetical excitatory and inhibitory gradients overlayed on home plate (white pentagon) within a baseball field. The gradients reveal the pitcher's recent success (i.e., strikes) on the right side of home plate (S+), whereas the left side of the plate reveals more failures (i.e., hits, S-). The combination of the excitatory and inhibitory gradients is likely to shift the peak of actual pitches (behavior) thrown by this pitcher to the right of the peak (in the direction away from the S-).

conditions. Under conditions in which these gradients are close to one another—as in our example with a G+/Y- color discrimination in pigeons—the conjoint control exerted by the separate gradients has the net effect of pushing the peak of responding away from the apex of the inhibitory gradient and thus away from the value of the target stimulus.

Early studies did not directly reveal the inhibitory gradient that supposedly was integral to the peak shift phenomenon. Directly measuring the nature of an inhibitory gradient would go a long way to confirming its role (Honig et al., 1963). For one group of pigeons, pecks to a lit key with a Vertical line were reinforced with Grain, and a lit key without a line was nonreinforced (V+/NL- problem); for a second group, pecks to a lit key with no line were reinforced, and pecks to one with a Vertical line were nonreinforced (NL+/V- problem). Following initial training, test trials were performed in which single lines were presented at various orientations (Figure 10.4). As you might expect, in V+/NL- pigeons, deviations from the target stimulus reduced pecking to the key. For example, a line presented at 30° from vertical produced less pecking than a vertical line (90°) but more than one presented at 0° from vertical. This maps onto previous examples of discrimination that were discussed.

But what about NL+/V- pigeons? For these birds, an otherwise blank lit key was the target stimulus, but V was the nonreinforced stimulus. In this case, increased deviations from

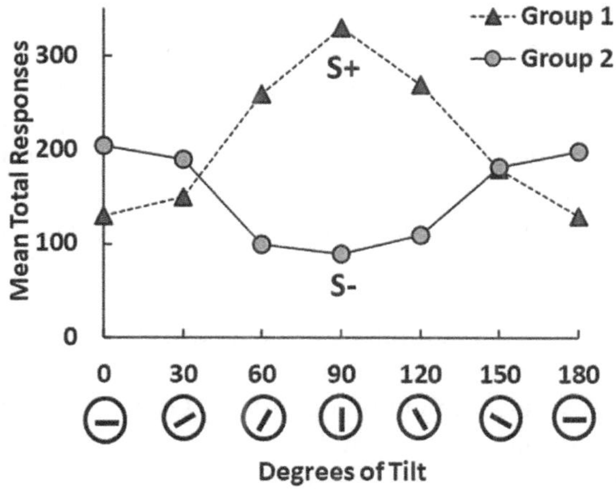

Figure 10.4 **Stimulus-dependent gradients.** Generalization gradients for two groups of birds trained to peck stimuli under different conditions. For one group (Group 1: V+/NL-), pecks to the key with a vertical bar (S+) resulted in reinforcers, whereas pecks to a key without a bar (S-) were not reinforced. For another group (Group 2: NL+, V-), pecks to a key with no bar (S+) resulted in reinforcers, whereas pecks to a key with a vertical bar (S-) were nonreinforced. On the test, responses to keys with various bar orientations were recorded to obtain generalization gradients. The same stimulus (e.g., a vertical bar) elicited the most (S+) or the fewest (S-) pecks depending on the group. (From Honig et al., 1963; reproduced with permission from the American Psychological Association.)

V increased pecking. The fewest pecks happened in the presence of the Vertical line and the most in the presence of a Horizontal line. This effect supports the explanation of peak shift as being the interaction of excitatory and inhibitory gradients, centered around the stimulus values corresponding to the reinforced and nonreinforced stimuli, respectively. Relating this back to our example of pitching (Figure 10.3), a pitcher will have unique excitatory and inhibitory gradients for high-profile hitters that incorporate their past experience with that hitter. The peak-shift effect can also result from an asymmetric range of nonreinforced trials used in the generalization testing procedure (e.g., Thomas, 1993; Thomas et al., 1991), so the number of probe stimuli on either side of the S+ must be equated.

In human categorization, the peak shift would manifest as a certain pattern of data, such as identifying a member of a category, dog, faster that is more dog-like than the average dog after S+ and S- training with a dog and cat, respectively. Peak shift is also responsible for one kind of conceptual behavior in nonhuman animals: ***transposition***. If a pigeon is trained to peck the larger of two circles (small and large) and is subsequently tested with two novel circles (medium and extra-large), then it will peck the larger of the novel circles (Lazareva et al., 2005). Consistent with these experiments, it has been argued that primary generalization is the root of conceptual behavior (Wasserman, 2016).

10.3 Acquired distinctiveness and equivalence

10.3.1 Procedures

Primary generalization refers to the perceptual categories revealed after bringing a response under the control of a stimulus and subsequently testing with variations along some dimension of that stimulus (e.g., color). A response to one stimulus is trained, and generalization occurs to perceptually similar stimuli without being directly trained (i.e., "for free"). Narrowing of the perceptual boundary around the S+ can occur during discrimination training with a S- because different responses are required or different outcomes occur if the same response is made (Table 10.1). For example, in the case of clicking pictures of trees to access a website, the task requires different responses to similar stimuli (e.g., click a tree but not a stalk of celery) and results in different outcomes if the same response is made (e.g., progressing to the website if a tree is clicked or receiving a new set of pictures if the celery stalk is clicked). Different responses leading to different outcomes is also true for a pigeon pecking a green key light and not an orange key light.

An intermediate case would be if the same response is elicited (Pavlovian) or emitted (operant) in the presence of two stimuli associated with different outcomes. For example, Delamater (1998) trained rats in a Pavlovian procedure to approach and retrieve USs delivered in the same feeder within a conditioning box. In Group Distinctiveness, one outcome was consistently delivered following one auditory stimulus (CSA-US1) and a different outcome following a second auditory stimulus (CSB-US2), whereas Group Same received the same outcome after both CSs. None of the rats were required to discriminate one CS from the other. However, the mere delivery of different outcomes in Group Distinctiveness may have resulted in acquired distinctiveness. This was tested in a second phase, in which the US was delivered after CSA (CSA+) but not CSB (CSB-). This discrimination was facilitated in

Table 10.1 Procedures for acquired distinctiveness and equivalence

Type	*Conditioning*	*Training*	*Retrain or test*
Acquired Distinctiveness			
Different Outcome	Pavlovian	A→Food B→Sucrose	A→Food B
	Operant	A→LP→Food B→CP→Food	A→LP→Food B→CP→NoFood
Different Response, Same Outcome (Functional distinctiveness)	Operant	A→LP→Food B→CP→Food	A→LP→Food B→CP→No Food
Both Different (Differential outcomes)	Operant	A→LP→Food B→CP→Sucrose	A→LP→Food B→CP→No Food
Acquired Equivalence			
Same Outcome	Pavlovian	A→Food B→Food	A→Food B→No Food
Same Response, Different Outcome (Functional equivalence)	Operant	A→LP→Food B→LP→Sucrose	A→LP→Food B→LP→No Food
Both Same	Operant	A→LP→Food B→LP→Food	A→LP→Food B→LP→No Food
Many to one/Arbitrary MTS	Operant	Red→H→Food Green→H→Food Blue→V→Food Yellow→V→Food	Retrain: Red→B→Food Blue→W→Food Test: Green→B vs. W? Yellow→B vs. W?

Note. A, B, C, D: an audiovisual stimulus (e.g., Tone, Light) serving as a CS or discriminative stimulus; LP: lever press; CP chain pull; Red, Green, Blue, Yellow: conditional visual dues signaling which discriminative stimulus will be reinforced; H, V: discriminative visual stimuli with a horizontal or vertical line across the middle; B, W: discriminative visual stimuli filled black or white; "→": serially paired; MTS: match-to-sample. Transfer of control tests only shown for Many-to-One training for brevity.

Group Distinctiveness compared to Group Same. Acquired distinctiveness effects may result from learning about the association between each CS and the outcome or between the CS and the response to the outcome as well as from changes in the way the nervous system represents each CS (Delamater, 1998).

It is not hard to imagine, as shown in Chapter 2, the other side of discrimination or, in this case, the other side of acquired distinctiveness, that is, ***acquired equivalence***. Acquired equivalence should develop if the same response and outcome occur in the presence of different stimuli. This is also known as ***secondary generalization***, as the animal is explicitly trained to generalize a response between two stimuli that appear different (e.g., to treat two different stimuli equally). The results of this training are said to enable conceptual behavior that is associative (i.e., it is the result of associative learning with a common response or outcome). This training is typically present as the control group in an acquired distinctiveness study. In Delamater (1998), different outcomes followed CSs in Group Distinctiveness compared to the same outcome after both CSs in Group Same.

Another way to interpret these results is to hypothesize that training with the same outcome resulted in a ***functional equivalence class*** that contained both CSs. Functional equivalence classes can be tested by taking one of the two stimuli in the class and pairing it with a new outcome (i.e., transfer of control). The researchers are testing the hypothesis that what is true for one member of a class should be true for the remaining members. This is the case in human classes. For example, if you recently had an allergic reaction to almonds, you are likely to generalize your avoidance to all nuts.

Johns and William (1998) trained rats in Group Consistent that the same outcome (food) followed CSs A and B but not C. In Group Alternating, the outcome sometimes preceded and at other times followed CSs A and B. After training, B was counterconditioned in both groups by pairing it with shock. The rats in Group Consistent exhibited more freezing when tested with A relative to C than those in Group Alternating. This suggests that new learning about B→Shock generalized better to A when A and B shared a common outcome (Food) during training. Pigeons demonstrate evidence of acquired equivalence even when the common outcome that followed a stimulus was another stimulus. Bonardi et al. (1993) reported equivalence when key lights A and B were followed by the same key light, X (A→X, B→X). Astley and Wasserman (1999) found that equivalence classes can be formed between stimuli when they have a common delay to a reinforcer, or when they terminate in a reinforcer with a common probability or with a common magnitude.

A functional equivalence class can also be established by pairing distinct stimuli with a common response (Table 10.1). The most common procedure for this is ***match to sample*** (***MTS***). In the MTS procedure, a sample stimulus is presented (e.g., a Red circle) and then followed by the opportunity to select from two or more comparisons (e.g., Red and Green circles). The correct comparison may match the sample in its perceptual features (identity MTS) or in a manner determined entirely by the experimenter (arbitrary or symbolic; Urcuioli & DeMarse, 1994).

Functional equivalence classes formed during ***arbitrary MTS*** are most similar to superordinate categories. If you think of several members of the superordinate category of tools (e.g., a hammer, drill press, and pliers), then you will note that they do not have a common perceptual feature, but they are handled (common response) by a person and assist in the goal of building or creating (common outcome).

In an arbitrary MTS, a reinforcer would be delivered for selecting one line orientation (e.g., Horizontal) following one set of colored circles (e.g., Red and Green), whereas a response to the other orientation (e.g., Vertical) would be reinforced following a different set of stimuli (e.g., Blue and Yellow). Note that Red and Green are separated by Yellow on the color spectrum, so it is not the case that Red and Green share more color similarity than Blue and Yellow.

A transfer-of-control test would involve training a new response (e.g., Black or White circle) in the presence of one colored circle from each set, followed by test trials of the other circle in each set with the new response options (i.e., comparison stimuli). If previous training with the same response led to an equivalence class that included both colors from the set, then training the new response should generalize better to all members of that class than to members of the other class.

Urcuioli et al. (1989) found this result with pigeons, but in their experiment, the transfer-of-control test involved training some pigeons (Group Congruent) to peck the new response option (e.g., Black circle) consistent with the retrained member of the class (e.g., Black circle) for a reinforcer and training other pigeons (Group Incongruent) to peck the response option (e.g., White circle) inconsistent with the retrained member of the class (e.g., Black circle) for a reinforcer. The pigeons in Group Incongruent pecked the consistent response option more often than those in Group Congruent. Data from rats, pigeons, and humans have all indicated an ability to form equivalence classes based on many-to-one mapping (Zentall et al., 2014).

10.3.2 Stimulus equivalence and emergent relations

A related phenomenon, *stimulus equivalence*, has been more challenging to document in nonhuman animals (Sidman & Tailby, 1982; Galizio & Bruce, 2018; Lionello-DeNolf, 2021; Zentall et al., 2014). When a pigeon views a sample (A, e.g., a Green-colored circle) and pecks a comparison (B, e.g., an Orange-colored circle) in an arbitrary MTS procedure, it may be as though the pigeon is learning that A and B are equal. Sidman (1971) demonstrated the spontaneous emergence of three equivalence relations (reflexivity: A = A, symmetry: A→B = B→A, and transitivity: A = C) after training a child with severe disability to match the sound of a word for an object to the picture of the object on some trials (A→B) and to match the sound of a word for an object to the written word for that object on other trials (A→C).

Pigeons could be trained to peck an Orange-colored key (B) after viewing a Green-colored sample key (A) to receive Food (A→B; Figure 10.5), to peck a Blue key (C) after viewing an Orange sample to receive Food (B→C), and a Black key (E) after a White key (D) to be reinforced with Food (D→E). After this training, *reflexivity* would be revealed by the selection of A from among other options (A vs. D) after exposure to A as the sample (A→A). *Symmetry* would involve selection of A after viewing B as the sample (B→A).

Lastly, *transitivity* (A = B, B = C, and thus A = C) would be demonstrated by selection of C more often than E following A as the sample (A→C). Not surprisingly, the conditions in which the behavior is trained influence what features of the task animals tend to learn about. The timing and location of A and B on the screen should play no role in what an animal learns (e.g., it is typically the case that A is presented before B, and A and B are presented in different parts of the screen), but there is good evidence that rats, pigeons, and monkeys do learn about these attributes (the timing and location of the stimuli) during equivalence training (Urcuioli, 2008).

Equivalence relations form the basis for many of the complexities of human verbal (e.g., novel sentence construction) and mathematical (e.g., novel sequences of mathematical operations) behavior (Chen & Mo, 2004; Lipkens et al., 1993). There is continued debate regarding whether nonhuman animals are capable of the kind of stimulus equivalence demonstrated in humans. One major factor, which we will discuss in the upcoming section on

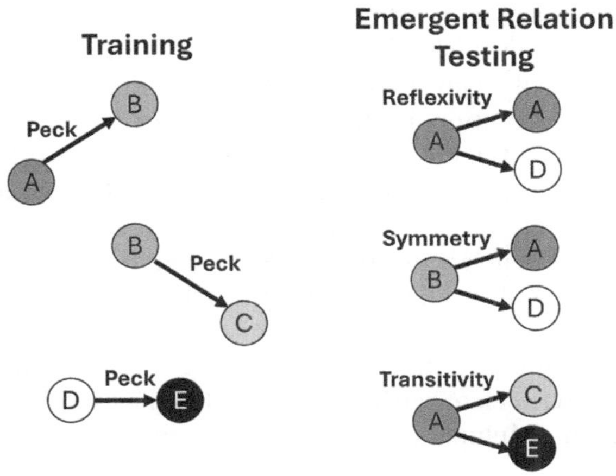

Figure 10.5 **An example of stimulus equivalence training and testing.** The initial links A→B (pecking B following A is reinforced) and B→C (pecking C following B is reinforced) are trained, along with a separate pair of stimuli (D→E; pecking E following D is reinforced). Examples of reflexivity, symmetry, and transitivity tests are shown. More complex designs would control for familiarity during testing.

multiple-exemplar training, is the significant difference between past experience with equivalence relations in humans vs. other animals. Although the evidence that nonhuman animals exhibit spontaneous emergence of all three equivalence relations is controversial, there is overwhelming evidence that they do form functional equivalence classes that transcend primary generalization (Zentall et al., 2014).

10.3.3 Real-world applications

Evidence for acquired distinctiveness and equivalence in rats, pigeons, monkeys, dogs, apes, and humans suggests that these effects do not require a recently evolved neocortex, that they are adaptive, and that for most birds and mammals, they *will* emerge under the right training conditions (Zentall et al., 2014). Differential-response and differential-outcome training leads to distinctiveness and discrimination, whereas common-response and common-outcome training leads to equivalence and generalization. Acquired and functional equivalence have additional adaptive value when an animal is attacked by more than one type of predator. For example, vervet monkeys may be attacked from the air by eagles or from the ground by leopards and snakes (see referential calls in Chapter 11). There may be a direct fitness advantage to responding similarly to predators that do not look exactly alike and transferring new learning about one predator to others in the same equivalence class (i.e., transfer of control).

The consequences of acquired distinctiveness and equivalence are evident in many real-world examples. In the landmark Supreme Court case (*Brown v. Board of Education of Topeka*, 1954) that led to public school integration in the United States of America, the court ruled unanimously that "separate education facilities are inherently unequal (347 U.S. 483)." This is consistent with the results of acquired distinctiveness training procedures (Table 10.1), such that requiring individuals that share a common feature (e.g., body type) to make a different response in the presence of the same stimulus (e.g., a water fountain) will facilitate acquired distinctiveness (i.e., a narrowing of the category of body type by skin color) and the formation of different classes of individuals. The same is true when the same response is followed by different outcomes for different groups of people, which is the case when, all other things being equal, individuals of different sexes, ethnicities, or countries of citizenship are paid different amounts of compensation for the same work.

An additional point of caution is that once a separate equivalence class is formed, transfer-of-control experiments indicate that new properties (e.g., work ethic) found to apply to one member of the class will generalize to other members. Consequently, the media must be careful to report on sensational acts of kindness in addition to those of concern (e.g., violent crimes). Fortunately, the reverse is also true: Requiring the same responses and providing the same outcomes to those that differ on some attribute will facilitate inclusive equivalence classes.

In many scenarios, acquired distinctiveness is the goal of training. Ph.D. students are expected to be able to discriminate between topics within their specialties beyond the level of an undergraduate student. Multiple-choice exam questions assess whether students can discriminate several distractor comparisons from the correct answer. In conversations with students, they often study (i.e., discrimination training) sufficiently to distinguish between the less relevant options, narrowing their choice down to the two most relevant answer choices. At this point, additional studying is required to distinguish between them. More discrimination training will result in greater acquired distinctiveness and higher grades on exams. Similarly, pilots and others that interact with instrument boards with many switches and response options must learn to flip some switches but not others under certain conditions. Their training will support acquired distinctiveness and, consequently, your successful flight.

10.4 Multiple-exemplar training

The preceding section provided a detailed account of how generalization and discrimination may be modified by experience to account for some conceptual behavior. We discussed studies with single discriminations (S+, S-) and others with four stimuli divided into two equivalence classes. Here, we review the evidence for conceptual behavior within experiments that involve perceptual categories and relational categories with many, sometimes hundreds, of members per class. The role of multiple exemplars in supporting stimulus control by a relationship between stimuli (e.g., responding on the basis of the size of an object) rather than the features of individual stimuli was noted as far back as Skinner (1953). The convenience of presenting multiple exemplars within human-defined categories (e.g., tree) has led to the use of standard laboratory animals with highly developed visual systems (e.g., pigeons, monkeys, apes, and humans) for the majority of this research.

10.4.1 Perceptual categories

10.4.1.1 Basic level

Perceptual categories are defined as a group of natural or artificial objects that share one or more physical features (e.g., color, shape, or some combination). The category "tree" is one that has been frequently used in the animal cognition literature. What is the defining feature of a tree? Is it the presence of a thick brown trunk, a broad canopy of green leaves, or perhaps the presence of branches that emerge from a central trunk? The diversity of features found in trees, shrubs, and other plants has resulted in no particular feature that is necessary and sufficient to identify a tree. However, all trees do share many features (e.g., they have a trunk and some form of branches and canopy).

Basic-level categories share more perceptual similarities within the category than across categories (Lazareva & Wasserman, 2008). Many perceptual categories are best represented by the basic level. Primary generalization should facilitate the acquisition of basic-level categories.

Can pigeons learn to discriminate basic-level categories? Herrnstein et al. (1976) tested pigeons in daily sessions that included 40 pictures of settings that contained trees (S+) and 40 photographs of settings without trees (S-) selected from a pool of more than 900 individual instances, or exemplars, of each class. The S+ pictures were taken from different angles and perspectives and contained a portion of, or all of, at least one tree. The same was true for the S-, except pictures with trees, bushes, or shrubs were omitted. Within 700 trials, the pigeons readily sorted Tree and No-tree pictures. Any given session included some photographs from previous sessions as well as never-before-seen (novel) photographs.

Take a moment to think about why testing novel photographs would be important to determine whether the pigeons are demonstrating conceptual behavior. If you are not sure, then consider that research has shown that pigeons can correctly respond to more than 800 pictures that do not share any specific perceptual resemblance (Cook et al., 2005). Pigeons could be learning to make the correct response to each picture that includes a tree—referred to as *item-specific learning*. Including novel pictures eliminates the influence of item-specific learning. In a sense, novel pictures assess the formation of concepts similarly to the transfer-of-control tests used to evaluate acquired equivalence classes, except that the class of stimuli being tested is hypothesized to exist due to perceptual similarity rather than functional similarity (i.e., common outcome or common response training).

For this reason, Herrnstein et al. (1976) also included sessions of only novel pictures; the novel pictures were discriminated with the same or better accuracy than pictures that were previously encountered. Similar conceptual behavior was observed in separate groups of pigeons that discriminated pictures with or without water, or with or without a specific person. The issue of whether and how much exposure to exemplar variation is needed for conceptual behavior to develop remains controversial (Galizio & Bruce, 2018).

Wasserman and colleagues (Bhatt, 1988; Wasserman & Bhatt, 1992) investigated the role of exemplar variation but also sought to address criticisms that previous demonstrations of conceptual behavior were restricted to dichotomous classes (tree or no tree), which are qualitatively different than the flexible and indeterminate number of classes (e.g., deciduous or conifer tree) used by humans. Bhatt (1988) trained pigeons in a four-alternative forced-choice task with visual stimuli (pictures) from four basic-level categories (cats, flowers, cars, and chairs, Figure 10.6).

Recall that basic-level categories have high within-category perceptual similarity and low between-category perceptual similarity. The procedure was modeled after the "name game," in which a parent might hold up a flashcard with a picture of an animal and ask their toddler, "What is it?" Each category of stimuli (e.g., cats) was assigned to one of four key lights positioned in the corners of the operant box. During each session, all pigeons received 48 daily trials of the equivalent of the name game ("What is it?"). Different groups of pigeons received sessions that consisted of a different number of exemplars for each class (Figure 10.6). Group 1 received the same exemplar for each class, Group 4 received 4 different exemplars for each class, and Group 12 received 12 different exemplars for each class.

Not surprisingly, the pigeons in Group 1 reached an accuracy of equal to or greater than 70% after only 2 sessions of training, whereas pigeons in Group 4 required 11 sessions and those in Group 12 required 22 sessions. However, transfer accuracy in the presence of novel exemplars from each category was a function of the number of exemplars during training,

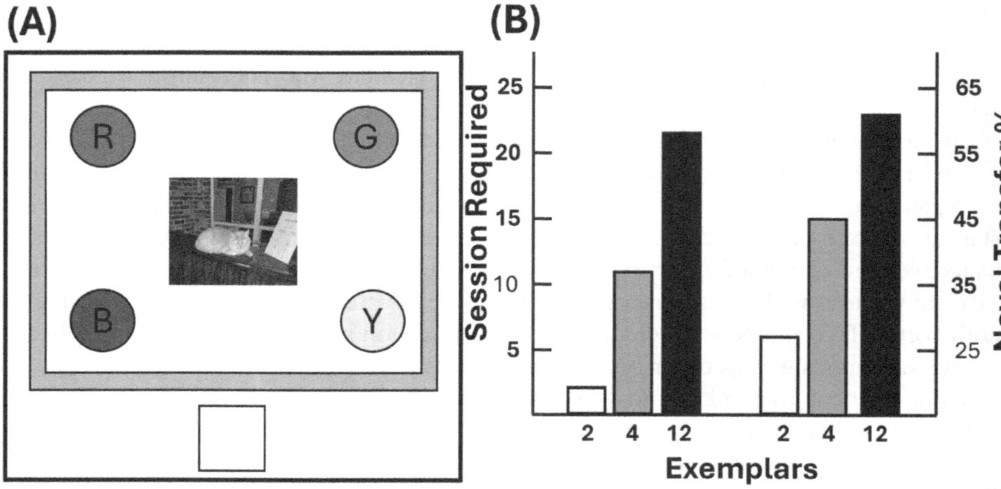

Figure 10.6 **Four-alternative forced-choice task. (A)** A touchscreen-equipped display with four colored circles and a photograph sample shown. Each colored circle would be assigned to a particular category (e.g., cats, flowers, cars, and chairs). The food hopper is located below the computer monitor (square). R, G, B, Y: letters identifying the color of each circle were added for illustration purposes only. **(B)** Data plotted with one Y-axis displaying the number of sessions required to reach 70% accuracy and the other Y-axis displaying choice accuracy during novel transfer trials. (From Bhatt, 1988, unpublished doctoral dissertation.)

with transfer performance improving from 27% correct in Group 1 to 45% in Group 4 and to 62.5% in Group 12. The need for the variation provided by multiple exemplars to improve transfer performance has also been observed in humans (Chen & Mo, 2004; Homa et al., 1981).

The results with pigeons are similar in kind to those of desirable-difficulty experiments with humans (Bjork & Bjork, 2020). *Desirable difficulties* are study strategies that lower initial success with the material encountered while studying but provide more robust success in other metrics, such as transfer to new items. One of the three most well-studied desirable difficulties is the interleaving vs. blocking of trials of different topics while studying (Carvalho & Goldstone, 2014; Rohrer, 2012). In Bhatte (1988), the use of multiple exemplars with pigeons disrupted acquisition via the fast and accurate item-specific learning strategy but improved transfer to novel exemplars.

The formation of functional equivalence classes with perceptually dissimilar stimuli in the previous section of this chapter indicates that pigeons can exhibit secondary generalization (i.e., transfer) within a class of perceptually similar stimuli without learning about their shared features. In other words, common response (e.g., peck top-left key when any picture of a cat is present) training would create a functional equivalence class containing all pictures of cats, and differential response training (e.g., peck top-right when any picture of a flower is present) would create a different functional equivalence class that contains all flowers.

Wasserman et al. (1988) tested whether the pigeons were utilizing the perceptual similarity of the objects in a category by training one group (True) with the original stimuli sorted into the usual categories of cats, flowers, cars, and chairs task, and training another group

(Pseudo) with the same pictures sorted into four arbitrary categories (a mixture of pictures of cats, flowers, cars, and chairs in each category). After over a month of training, Group True was responding correctly 35% more often than Group Pseudo. This suggests a functional role for the perceptual similarity between objects at the basic level of categorization.

Using a slightly different procedure, split-category discrimination, to confirm this result, Wasserman et al. (1988) trained a new group of pigeons to respond to one key (e.g., top-left key) when 10 pictures of one category (e.g., cats) were present and a different key (e.g., bottom-right key) when the remaining 10 pictures from that category were present. They trained another category (e.g., flowers) in the same manner (e.g., top-right and bottom-left keys). If the perceptual similarity within a category were ignored, then mistakes in the presence of a picture of a cat would be equally distributed across the three incorrect response options. However, a pattern of errors that includes more responses at the other key associated with that category would be additional evidence of a functional role for perceptual similarity. This is exactly what Wasserman et al. (1988) observed.

A similar pattern of errors was observed with rhesus monkeys (Sands et al., 1982). The monkeys were trained to push a lever in one direction if the same picture (a human face, monkey face, tree, flower, or fruit) was shown in succession but in the other direction if the two pictures differed. The monkeys more often treated pictures of faces (human or rhesus monkey) as more similar than a face followed by a picture from another category. This result was also found with pictures of different types of fruit. Perceptual similarity facilitates demonstrations of conceptual behavior of basic-level categories and leads to confusion errors at the superordinate level when basic-level categories are combined.

Subsequent research by Wasserman et al. (2015) established accurate conceptual behavior in pigeons with 16 categories of objects, each assigned to a unique picture in a *pexigram* (named after the lexigrams used by the bonobo Kanzi; see Chapter 11). The accumulation of evidence led Wasserman (2016, p. 8) to claim that "conceptual behavior and its underlying processes are generally similar in humans and many other animals."

10.4.1.2 *Subordinate level*

Subordinate-level categories contain high within-category perceptual similarity as well as high between-category perceptual similarity. Given the overlap in perceptual similarity, it was predicted that conceptual behavior at the subordinate level should be slower to learn than the basic level. That is, dogs share many features with one another as well as with many other pets (e.g., four legs). Pigeons, monkeys, and apes have been shown to learn classes at the subordinate level (Lazareva & Wasserman, 2008), including classes of leaves (e.g., oak leaves), species of birds (e.g., kingfisher from nonkingfisher), as well as human facial expressions (Parr et al., 1998) or gender (Koba & Izumi, 2006) and conspecifics (Poole & Lander, 1971; Yoshikubo, 1985).

10.4.1.3 *Superordinate level*

Herrnstein and de Villiers (1980) suggested that evolution may imbue species with an ability to learn about ecologically relevant categories (e.g., elements that are part of a pigeon's natural environment). We have already reviewed evidence against this hypothesis in the form of pigeons learning about the artificial categories of cars and chairs. Additional indications that pigeons are not bound by evolutionarily predisposed categories come from evidence of learning superordinate categories. Superordinate categorization is a form of associative conceptual behavior that generalizes across several basic-level categories that share low within-category perceptual similarity. Once again, pigeons and monkeys have been shown to demonstrate superordinate classes of bodies of water, furniture, mammals, animals, and man-made or living objects (Lazareva & Wasserman, 2008).

Classifying a group with disparate features is impressive, but humans can classify the same object at different levels of categorization, including those categories (subordinate) with subgroups of members within a basic-level category and those categories (superordinate level) that combine members across a basic-level category (i.e., that share little perceptual similarity). For example, imagine a website filter that requires the user to first identify all of the pictures that contain an animal (e.g., from among pictures of a worm, Dog 1, Dog 2, Dog 3, a bird, a light post, a computer mouse, and a car) followed by a prompt to select from those pictures, only the ones that contain dogs (e.g., three dog pictures) and, lastly, a prompt to select from those only a specific breed (e.g., Irish Setters). This kind of flexibility in classifying objects is a hallmark of human conceptual behavior (Markman, 1989).

Lazareva et al. (2004) demonstrated that pigeons can flexibly classify a stimulus at the basic level or superordinate level (Table 10.2). They trained pigeons with eight exemplars of each of the categories cat, flower, car, or chair in the four-choice forced-alternative procedure. Additionally, the two basic-level categories were combined to create natural (flowers and people) and artificial (cars and chairs) superordinate categories with two other choice keys in a two-choice forced-alternative procedure. On half of the trials, a picture was presented along with four keys and conceptual behavior based on the basic-level categories was reinforced. On the other half of trials, the other two keys were present, and responses based on superordinate categories were reinforced.

Consistent with some human research, the pigeons acquired conceptual behavior based on the basic-level categories faster than the superordinate categories. After approximately 2 months of training, the mean accuracy on the training trials was an impressive 89.5% on the basic-level trials and 92.3% on the superordinate-level trials. Additionally, transfer to eight novel stimuli in each basic-level category was successful at both levels of categorization. An analysis of errors indicated that objects in the basic-level (natural) category shared more similarities than those in the superordinate category. Hughes and Barnes-Holmes (2014) have questioned whether nonhuman animals will be able to demonstrate the breadth of conceptual behavior based on superordinate categories like opposition, comparison, and deictics. These categories present difficulties for comparative studies.

Superordinate categories and stimulus-equivalence classes are both based on associative similarity, but equivalence classes must demonstrate receptivity, symmetry, and transitivity (Figure 10.5). Of these, symmetry has been the most difficult to document in nonhuman

Table 10.2 Flexible basic-level and super-ordinate level categorization

Basic level	*Super-ordinate level*	*Results*
"Person"→R1→Food	"Person"→R5→Food	Basic: 89.5% (chance level = 25%)
"Flower"→R2→Food	"Flower"→R5→Food	
"Chair"→R3→Food	"Chair"→R6→Food	Superordinate: 92.3% (chance level = 50%)
"Car"→R4→Food	"Car"→R6→Food	

Note. Each word in quotes denotes a class of numerous stimuli presented in different trials. R1-R6 are six different responses. All pigeons received these training and testing trials in a within-subject design. In each case, choosing the wrong response led to nonreinforcement (e.g., "Person"→R2→No Food), but these sequences are not represented for simplicity.

animals. Recall that symmetry is evident when initial training to choose B (from among other options) following A leads to untrained, accurate selection of A (from other options) following the presentation of B. Given the strong evidence for conceptual behavior with multiple exemplars, researchers have evaluated multiple-exemplar training of symmetry in nonhuman animals.

In humans, multiple-exemplar training is present even during the first year of life, and thus, testing in the laboratory may involve nothing more than testing novel exemplars (rather than training). However, if equivalence fails, then the role of multiple exemplars may be evaluated as subsequent training that builds from the initial training (i.e., multiple-exemplar training). Luciano et al. (2007) reported symmetry in a toddler (16 months, 25 days) but only after two rounds of testing and 10 new objects. Better control over previous history with multiple exemplars can be obtained in nonhuman animal experiments.

The strongest evidence for the role of multiple-exemplar training comes from a sea lion, Rio, who, much like the toddlers, had an extensive prior history of discrimination training (Schusterman & Kastak, 1993). After training on 30 AB relations, Rio failed tests for BA symmetry. Multiple-exemplar training of symmetry was given with the initial 30 AB relations. That is, Rio was directly trained to select B following A (AB) and to select A following B (BA). Rio was then given BC training and successfully demonstrated CB symmetry, as well as AC transitivity. A procedure with pigeons given varying amounts of multiple-exemplar training of symmetry showed either no evidence of transfer of symmetry to novel items (Bujedo et al., 2014; Lionello-DeNolf & Urcuioli, 2002) or only partial evidence (Velasco et al., 2010). The results with monkeys and chimpanzees have also produced mixed results (Dugdale & Lowe, 2000; Yamamoto & Asano, 1995). Overall, the evidence in favor of complete stimulus equivalence following multiple-exemplar training remains controversial.

10.4.2 Relational categories

In previous sections, the categories were defined by perceptual or associative similarity (e.g., common response and common outcome). Relational categories are defined by the relationship (e.g., same, different, above, below) between or among stimuli. Early attempts to determine whether pigeons could evaluate the relationship between two pictures involved simultaneous or successive presentations of the same or different stimuli. For example, Zentall and Hogan (1975) used a go/no-go procedure that involved reinforcer delivery for one group of pigeons (Same) when they pecked a key illuminated with the same color on both halves of a key (red/red and green/green) and no reinforcer delivery for pecks that occurred when the halves did not match (green/red and green/red), whereas a different group of pigeons (Different) received the opposite training (Figure 10.7-A). Following training, pigeons were retrained with two new colors (blue and yellow), and the relationship trained was either congruent (e.g., peck if same during training and peck if same during retraining) or incongruent (e.g., peck if same during training but peck if different during retraining) with initial training.

If pigeons are merely learning to peck or not in the presence of each stimulus configuration, then the congruence should not disrupt acquisition of retraining. However, if the pigeons attended to the relationship between stimuli, then acquisition should be much slower when retraining was incongruent. Although all pigeons exhibited poor performance on Session 1, but the pigeons retrained in the congruent condition acquired the discrimination significantly faster than those trained in the incongruent condition.

In a procedural variation in which the stimuli were presented successively, Greene (1983) trained pigeons to peck a picture if it were only presented once (i.e., novel) in a session but to withhold pecking if the picture was shown more than once (i.e., familiar). She reported strong evidence for item-specific memory along with some evidence for concept learning. Early findings that included control by item-specific features led some to claim that true concept behavior (i.e., transfer performance based only on the relation must be equal to performance on the training items) would not be found in nonverbal animals. However, subsequent research suggests early failures were likely due to procedural limitations, including, in many cases, the use of very few exemplars.

Another common procedure for evaluating relational learning involves the presentation of one stimulus as the sample followed by the presentation of one or more comparison stimuli (Figure 10.7-B). Prichard et al. (2015) trained rats in a go/no-go procedure with odors (e.g., vanilla) as the sample and comparison stimuli. Rats were required to poke their nose into a recessed port in the middle of the operant chamber, which initiated the release of a scent into the port. After another nose-poke response, the port was closed for 1 s and a vacuum pump removed the scent, followed by the release of the same or a different scent. Rats were reinforced for another nose-poke response only if the scents were the same.

Following training, the rats were tested with nonreinforced trials of four novel odors. Transfer performance, even on the first trial, indicated matching based on the "same" relation. Despite the use of few exemplars, other studies using the go/no-go procedure have also found good transfer (Cook et al., 2003; Urcuioli & Swisher, 2012). For example, Giurfa et al. (2001) trained honeybees to fly into a chamber with a comparison (visual or odor) that matched or did not match (i.e., oddity) a sample encountered in an earlier chamber. After training with only two exemplars, in both cases, the honeybees transferred to novel exemplars. In one experiment, honeybees learned to match with two odor stimuli and transferred the matching concept to visual patterns! These results suggest that matching may be a capacity shared with some invertebrates and, in some cases, does not require multiple-exemplars.

In contrast to go/no-go procedures, much of the literature has utilized procedures that reinforce one response in the presence of a "same" relation and a different response in the presence of a "different" relation (Figure 10.7-C-D). This procedure takes advantage of the role of different responses in facilitating discrimination learning discussed earlier in the chapter.

Wright and Katz (2006) reviewed evidence for concept behavior in pigeons, capuchin monkeys, and rhesus monkeys trained to respond in a functionally identical same–different procedure. All animals were presented with a real-world picture including one or more objects, along with (1) a comparison picture placed below the sample that was the same or different and (2) a white rectangle positioned adjacent to the comparison picture (Figure 10.7-D). A response (touch or peck) to the comparison picture was followed by a reinforcer if it was the same as the sample picture, and a response to the white rectangle was followed by a reinforcer if the comparison picture was different.

All subjects were initially trained with eight pictures, which resulted in eight possible trials of the same picture and 56 possible combinations of different pictures. Each session included 50 same trials and 50 different trials, selected from the possible combinations with replacement. After an animal reached a criterion of greater than 80% correct on same and different trials, then 30 novel same and different displays were presented and reinforced as in training. Analyzing only the first test trial with each display, they reported that no species transferred at a level above chance. This indicates that in their same–different procedure, eight exemplars resulted in item-specific learning of the correct response to specific pairs of stimuli rather than control by the same–different relation (Figure 10.8).

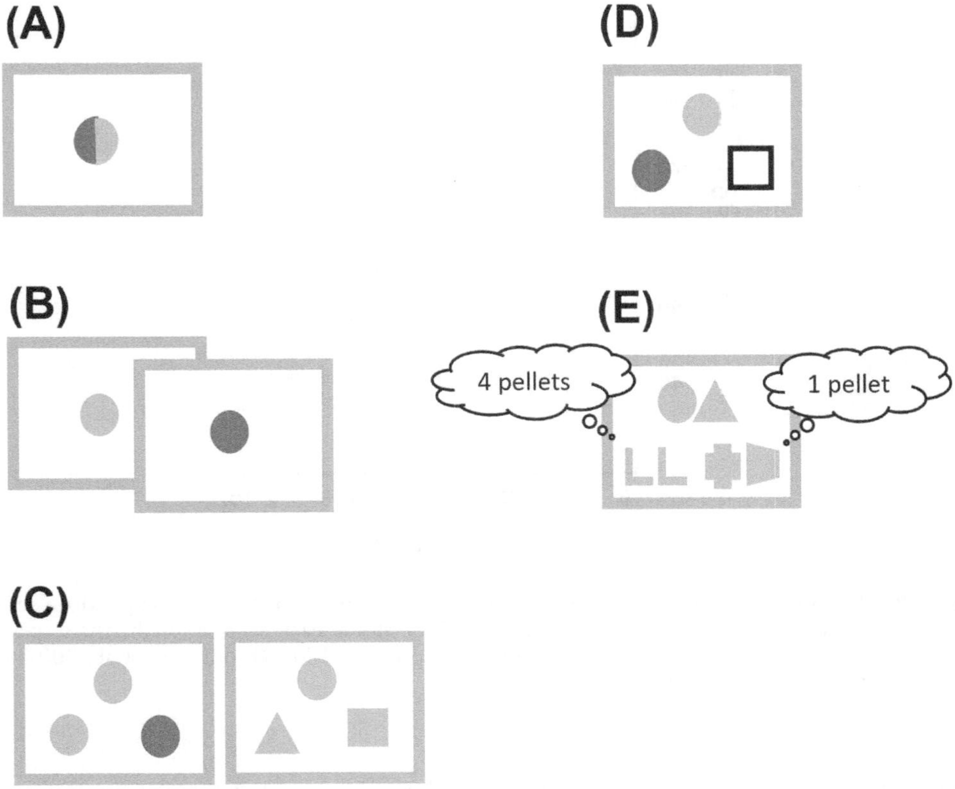

Figure 10.7 **Variations of relational learning tasks on a touchscreen-equipped display. (A)** A split-half colored circle procedure. In the matching condition, reinforcers are delivered for responses to ("go") the stimulus when both halves match but not when they are nonmatching (displayed). **(B)** A successive MTS procedure. In the matching condition, reinforcers are delivered for responses to ("go") the second stimulus when it matches the first but not when they are nonmatching (displayed). The delay between the presentations of stimuli can be lengthened to increase the difficulty. **(C)** A traditional MTS procedure is displayed on the left. In the matching task, reinforcers are delivered for responses to the stimulus in the bottom row (comparison stimuli) that matches the sample (top) but not for responses to the nonmatch. On the right, a symbolic MTS procedure is displayed. In this procedure, the matching stimulus shares no features with the sample, but rather, the "match" is determined by the experimenter. A delay can be inserted in between the presentation of the sample and comparison stimuli along with the absence of the sample to increase difficulty (delayed MTS). **(D)** A same–different procedure. Reinforcers are delivered for responses to the comparison stimulus (bottom left) if it matches the sample (top), or to the stimulus (bottom right) next to comparison stimuli when they do not match. **(E)** A relation-between-relations procedure. On a matching trial, the sample stimuli (top) would be presented as matches or nonmatches (shown), and reinforcers would be delivered for responding to pairs of stimuli exhibiting the same relation. The idea bubbles with the words "1 pellet" are meant to illustrate that the reinforcer quantity associated with each relation (1 pellet for different and 4 pellets for same) could be used as a kind of label, similar to the use of the verbal labels "same" and "different" for humans, to identify the matching relation.

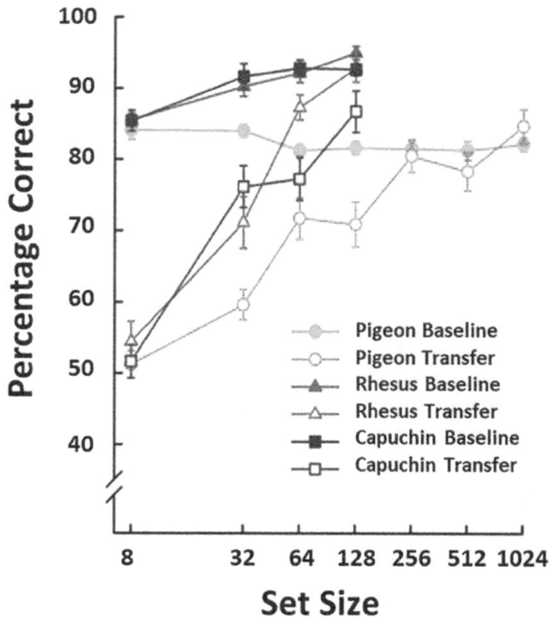

Figure 10.8 **Baseline and transfer across items for pigeons and monkeys with expanding set size.** Mean percentage correct for baseline and transfer at each set size for the three species in the same–different procedure. Error bars represent SEMs. (From Katz et al., 2007; Creative Commons Attribution 4.0 License.)

The set size was expanded to include 16 and then 32 items, but on average, only partial transfer was observed in each species (Wright & Katz, 2006). This means that transfer to novel exemplars was above chance level (50%) but not equal to the accuracy of trials with the training stimuli. Full concept learning was demonstrated during novel transfer trials by monkeys but not by pigeons following training with 128 exemplars of the same–different relation. Pigeons required 256 exemplars to demonstrate full concept learning. These results suggest that learning the same–different relation was not required for acquisition of the task (remember that past research indicated that pigeons can learn the correct response to hundreds of pictures), but it is more likely to occur with larger sets of exemplars. In other words, as the correct response based on each pair of items becomes harder to learn, the correct response based on the relation (same or different) between any two items becomes easier to learn.

A similar result has been found in MTS identity matching and nonmatching procedures, in which a sample stimulus is presented along with one or more comparison stimuli and the correct response is to the matching (Bodily et al., 2008) or nonmatching (i.e., oddity; Lombardi et al., 1984) comparison stimulus. Tests with other species of birds, Clark's nutcrackers and black-billed magpies (Wright et al., 2016, 2017), in the MTS procedure have revealed transfer after eight exemplars, which is similar to monkeys tested in the same MTS procedure. Cook (2002) extended the concept of same–different to include training and transfer to novel displays that differed in terms of texture, feature, or geometry. Wright and Katz (2006) hypothesized the same functional relationship between the number of exemplars and full concept learning in chimpanzees and humans, but these species would be expected to require fewer exemplars.

Other concept-learning tasks have provided multiple exemplars of the same or different relation in the same display. Young et al. (1997) trained pigeons to peck one key below a display that contained 16 matching cartoon icons and another key below the display when it contained 16 icons that differed. With a limited set size of only 32 total icons (16 for same and 16 for different trials), pigeons learned the task within four sessions. The pigeons were then tested for transfer to displays containing fewer than 16 of the familiar icons (2, 4, 8, and 12). If the pigeons learned about the same–different relation among the items, then they should perform equally well on a test in which the display contained 2 items exemplifying the same or different relation as with those with 16 items.

Pigeons demonstrated a gradual decrement in performance as a function of the number of icons in the display. Pigeons were equally likely to respond to an eight-item different display as same or different, but more than 90% of the time they responded to a two-item different display as same. Young et al. concluded that pigeons learned about the amount of variability, or entropy, in the display, and generalized this to displays with fewer items. Consequently, performance in the presence of the 2-item display generalized better to a same display with no entropy than to the 16-different-items display with maximal entropy (Figure 10.9).

A version of a same–different task has also been used in a long series of studies with a single subject: an African grey parrot called Alex (*Psittacus erithacus*). Alex had received previous training on the use of English vocalizations to identify, request, refuse, or comment on as

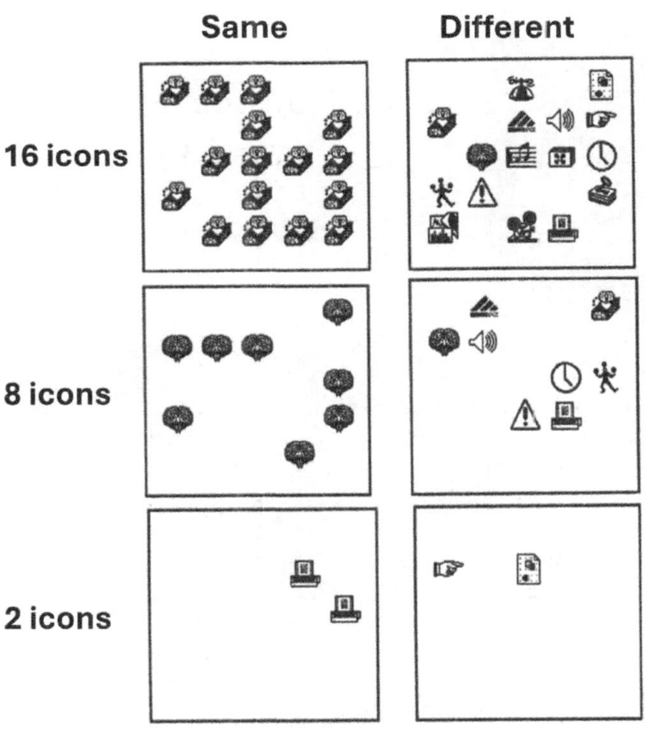

Figure 10.9 **Entropy of displays with decreasing items.** A subset of the displays presented to pigeons. "Same" displays are shown in the left column, whereas "different" displays are shown in the right column. (From Young et al., 1997; reproduced by permission from the American Psychological Association.)

many as 80 different objects. During training trials, Alex was presented with two objects while the trainer verbally asked either "What's same?" or "What's different?" (Pepperberg, 1987). The objects could differ in terms of color (red, green, blue), shape (triangle, square), or matter (rawhide, wood). The correct response was to name the dimension on which the objects were the same or different but not the actual stimulus. For example, when confronted with a Red Wooden triangle and a Blue Wooden triangle, and asked "What's different?" the correct response was "Color." The rewards for a correct response were praise from the trainer and an opportunity to interact with the object.

Correct responses were recorded by an observer who could hear Alex but could not see the stimuli. To avoid cueing effects, the trainer presenting the stimuli was not familiar with the same–different task. Tests on the same–different task were interspersed with training trials related to other problems, and they involved both familiar and novel objects. Alex was correct on 75% or more of the test trials, even with new stimuli.

In yet other tests, Alex faced two objects that were equal in two of the three attributes and was asked to judge sameness or difference when two of the three alternatives were correct. For example, Alex faced a "Yellow Wooden Triangle" and a "Blue Wooden Triangle," and was asked "What's same?" Notice that if Alex was responding to the physical attributes of the

Figure 10.10 **Same–different task with Alex.** An African grey parrot called Alex was presented with a number of wooden blocks that differ in color. Alex could answer many questions about which blocks belong to a particular category (e.g., Red). (Photo courtesy of Irene Pepperberg.)

stimuli rather than the verbal question, its prior training would have prompted the incorrect response "Color." This is because color is the only attribute that differs and all training trials involved pairs of stimuli differing in only one attribute. But the question made it such that there were two correct answers in probe trials; in this example, giving the question "What's same?" both "Matter" and "Shape" are correct. In addition, the ambiguity in the correct response for these probe trials tended to further dilute any cueing effects from the trainers. Overall, Alex was correct on 90% of the trials. The performance was similarly high for same and different questions and for color, shape, and matter problems.

10.4.3 Relation between relations

In the tasks described, objects were presented either successively or simultaneously, and animals selected the correct response for the category of the item (e.g , a chair) or based on the relationship between items (e.g., same). Additionally, novel objects were then presented so that some category features (e.g., same picture) remained, but the exact features encountered during training could not control behavior. Successful transfer required the animal to learn about the features that best represent the category (e.g., a chair or same relation).

A further step removed from control by a single or small configuration of features is to require the animal to choose a relation that matches the sample (i.e., a *second-order relationship*) in a situation in which there are no matching perceptual features (Figure 10.7-E). In other words, a sample that contains a pair of items that are either the same (AA) or different (BC) is followed by a comparison display with two pairs of novel items (DD and EF), and the correct pair (results in a reinforcer when touched) is the one that matches the sample display in terms of the relation between items.

This relation-between-relations matching task may sound easy if you recall the use of entropy in the experiment by Young et al. (1997) discussed earlier. When a display contained 16 items that were all the same or different, the complexity of the displays controlled responding. In a relation-between-relations task, if the animals are simply matching the visual complexity of the sample items or symmetry between items in the sample to the visual complexity of the comparison items, then monkeys and pigeons will have little trouble.

However, recall that Young et al. (1997) trained with 16 items in the display, but when the number of items was reduced to 2, then pigeons, baboons, and even some humans performed at chance level (Wasserman et al., 2001; Young & Wasserman, 2002). The relation-between-relations task involves only two items in the sample display, which indicates a simple solution like entropy is unlikely (Figure 10.7-E).

The relation-between-relations task is thought to better approximate the kind of analogical reasoning characteristic of humans (Flemming et al., 2011). Support for this claim comes from some previous failures by chimpanzees (Oden et al., 1988, 1990) and monkeys (Thompson & Oden, 2000) to learn the task. There are many possible explanations for previous failures of animals to learn the task.

First, the two items in the sample must be perceived as separate. If an animal perceives the two items in the sample display as a single configuration, then there is no same or different relation present and thus nothing to match in the comparison display made up of novel configurations. However, some previous studies have used 3D objects, which makes this explanation unlikely to explain all previous failures.

Second, the two items have to be perceived as related to one another. Flemming et al. (2011) referenced prior findings that monkeys are more likely than chimpanzees and humans to focus on the local properties of stimuli grouped together. This suggests perception may fail at the other extreme from a single configuration, such that the two objects are perceived as so distinct that they have no relation (i.e., they are neither same nor different). Consistent with this suggestion, Fagot and Parron (2010) found that baboons could solve the relation-between-relations matching task when the two items (color patches) were adjoined during initial trials and then later separated by incrementally larger gaps.

Third, learning about the relation between relations may require the use of a symbol, or tag, attached to the relation, thereby reducing the problem to one of matching the symbols. In humans, this may be as simple as the word "same" elicited when viewing the sample followed by matching to the comparison pair that also elicits "same." In nonhuman animals, this could be accomplished by associating a matching pair of items with a specific tag (e.g., an object) and a pair of different items with a different tag.

As suggested by Premack (1990) and Thompson et al. (1997), the tag would serve a retrieval function for each relation in the same manner as does a word for humans. Thompson et al. tested chimpanzees that were previously trained to select one token as a tag (e.g., heart shape) when viewing a pair of the same items and a different token (e.g., diagonal shape) in the presence of a pair of different items. Two chimpanzees performed at above-chance level on the relation-between-relations matching task in the first session, and 4 of the 5 did so within four sessions. Accuracy on the last two sessions for the four chimpanzees was 84.4%. Given the extensive history of token use, it was not possible to remove the tokens to evaluate how reliant the chimpanzees were on the use of the tokens as tags.

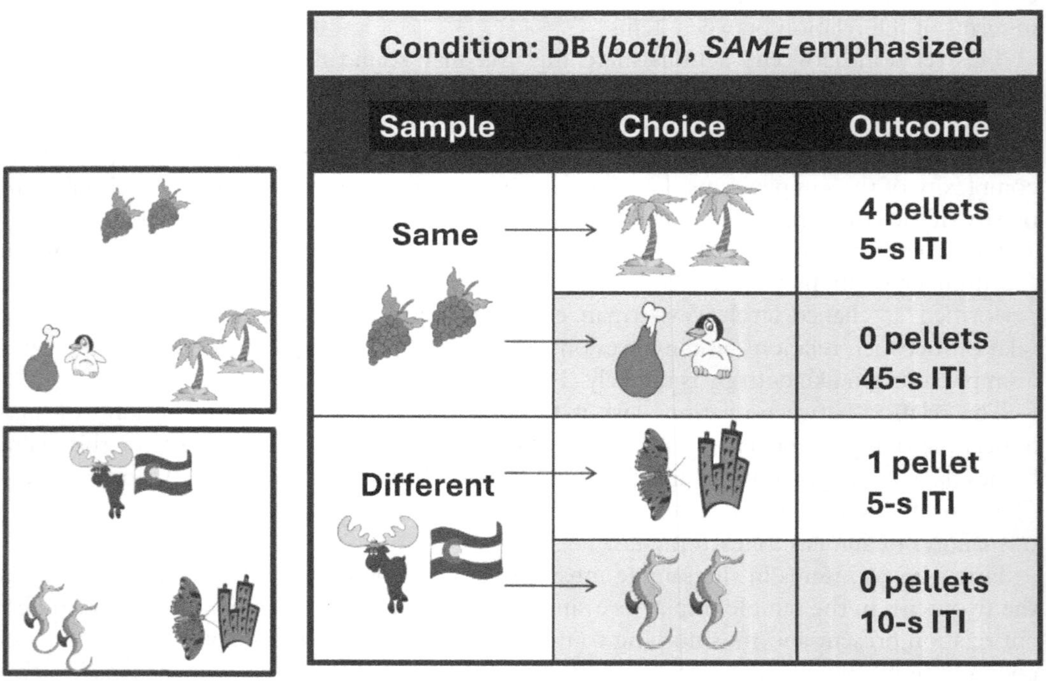

Figure 10.11 **Relation-between-relations matching task.** A sample of all of the stimuli in the positions used in a same and different trial are shown on the left-side of the figure, along with a flowchart indicating the outcomes of various responses (choices) during each type of trial. DB: differential both. ITI: intertrial interval. (From Flemming et al., 2011; reproduced with permission from the American Psychological Association.)

Table 10.3 Relation-between-relations matching task

Group	*Trial*	*Outcomes*	*Results (%)*
Diff Both (DB)	AA→DD or EF	DD: Correct: 4 pellets EF: Incorrect: 40-s timeout	85%
	BC→DD or EF	EF: Correct: 1 pellet DD: Incorrect: 5-s timeout	
Diff Reward-only (DR)	AA→DD or EF	DD: Correct: 4 pellets EF: Incorrect: 0-s timeout	49%
	BC→DD or EF	EF: Correct: 1 pellet DD: Incorrect: 0-s timeout	
Diff Punish-only (DP)	AA→DD or EF	DD: Correct: 1 pellet EF: Incorrect: 40-s timeout	53%
	BC→DD or EF	EF: Correct: 1 pellet DD: Incorrect: 5-s timeout	

Note. All stimuli (e.g., "A") were digital images presented on a touchscreen-equipped monitor with rhesus monkeys. Results are estimated from data in Flemming et al. (2011). Results are presented as percent correct across all trial types. One monkey found to have a side bias was not included in the results for Group DP.

Flemming et al. (2011) used a differential outcomes procedure with monkeys trained on the relation-between-relations matching task (Figure 10.11, Table 10.3). Rather than have the monkeys associate same or different relations with tokens, they paired each relation with differential reinforcement (DR) as a kind of tag (e.g., one pellet after matching same pairs and four pellets after matching different pairs) for some monkeys. In this way, when the monkey was looking at a pair of matching items on a sample display, it might be as if the monkey is eating one pellet (i.e., an expectation of one pellet); it could then select the pair in the comparison display that elicits the same expectation (Figure 10.7-E).

In the same manner, some monkeys (the two monkeys in Groups DP and DB) received differential outcomes following incorrect responses (e.g., a 45-s time-out when "different" was selected after viewing a sample pair of the same items and a 10-s time-out when "same" was selected after viewing a sample pair of different items). Only the two monkeys in Group DB received differential outcomes following correct and incorrect responses. During training, Group DB was the only group in which both monkeys learned to respond correctly on both trial types (a mean of 85% correct compared to 56% in the other groups).

When these same monkeys were then given nondifferential outcomes, their performance fell to chance level (50%) but recovered when differential outcomes were reinstated. These two monkeys were then assigned to receive either DR or DP treatment, and performance again fell to chance. However, when one monkey from Group DP was given training equivalent to that of Group DB, their accuracy rose from 51% to 82% correct. These results suggest the tags (i.e., different reinforcer and punisher values) were required to acquire and maintain performance. Differential outcomes have also been found to support judgments of relations in humans (Estévez et al., 2007).

10.5 Theories and models of conceptual behavior

This section reviews theories and models that identify some of the stimuli controlling conceptual behavior with family resemblance categories, in which it is unlikely that there is a single necessary or sufficient feature that defines the category. The theories reviewed in what follows include learning about features according to an error-correction rule, generalizing from whole objects previously encountered, the development of a representation corresponding to the central tendency (i.e., averaged) of a category, and a neural network approach that combines error-correction with representations.

10.5.1 Linear feature models

Application of the model proposed by Rescorla and Wagner (1972), discussed in Chapter 4, to conceptual behavior utilizes an *error-correction rule* to identify which features of a stimulus would excite a response (i.e., indicative of a member of the category), inhibit a response (i.e., indicative of a nonmember), or have no effect on behavior (i.e., neither excite nor inhibit). Animals may learn about many separate features, and the sum of the value of all features may determine whether or not a response occurs. For example, every time a picture of a tree with green color (A), a thick trunk (B), branches (C), and a canopy (D) is followed by a reinforced peck, then each feature acquires some excitatory strength.

The strength of the response to a feature (e.g., color) is determined by the associative strength of all of the available stimuli. If the stimuli continue to be followed by food, then the associative strength of the feature will increase in proportion to the difference between the actual value of the food and the current associative value of all of the available stimuli (i.e., an error-correction rule). On the other hand, when green is present on a picture (e.g., of a green car) without a tree (i.e., S-, nonreinforced), then that feature would lose excitatory strength proportional to the error. The feature most often present on S+ trials and not on S- trials will gain the most excitatory strength. The strength or frequency of the response will be a function of the summation of the strength of all the available features.

Some of the strongest evidence for this *linear feature model* comes from studies of artificial categories. In these studies, artificial categories are defined by the *m* out of *n* rule, such that *m* of *n* features must be present for category membership. Huber and Lenz (1993) trained pigeons with line drawings of Brunswick faces that varied along four dimensions: eye height (EH), eye separation (ES), nose length (NL), and mouth height (MH; Figure 10.12). Each dimension could take one of three discrete values (+1, 0, or –1) for 81 total combinations. The summed value of the four dimensions must be greater than 0 for pecks to the face to be reinforced. Consequently, no single dimension or feature is necessary and sufficient for the delivery of a reinforcer, which simulates natural categories. The results confirmed that response rate was a function of the sum of feature values.

Subsequently, Aust and Huber (2002) trained pigeons to discriminate scenes with and without a person, followed by tests with probe stimuli that depicted parts of the human body or patches of human skin. Overall, these results indicated that some features carried more weight (e.g., hands) than others (e.g., feet) but that classification as a person was largely predicted by the summation of category-relevant features.

Another approach used to evaluate the features used by nonhuman animals is to present the images blurred, scrambled, or with a portion of the screen covered (e.g., a partial mask). Aust and Huber (2001) trained pigeons to discriminate pictures with and without a person. After training, they divided the screen into different numbers of squares, or pixels, and scrambled them (i.e., mosaic processing). The greater the number of pixels, the fewer combinations of features are present in each pixel.

If pigeons are discriminating people from nonpeople based on a human having feet, legs, a trunk, arms, and all other necessary features, then any amount of pixilation should disrupt conceptual behavior. However, if the pigeons are relying on one feature or a small configuration of features, then those features are likely to be preserved in all but the smallest pixels.

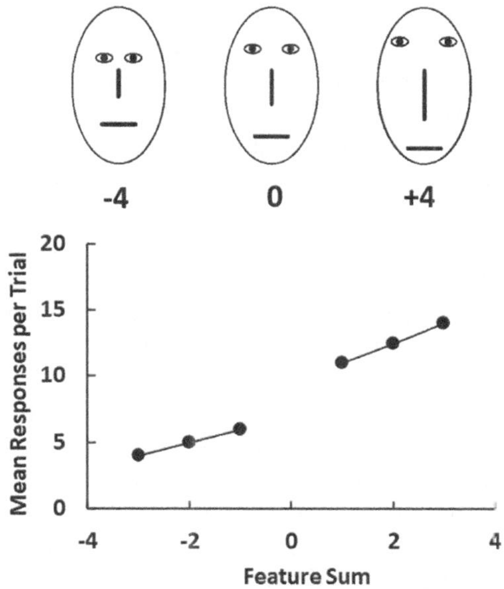

Figure 10.12 **Artificial categories.** Faces were made up of characteristics that could vary along four dimensions: eye height, eye separation, nose length, and mouth height. Each dimension could take one of three discrete values (+1, 0, or −1) for 81 total combinations. The faces shown illustrate the highest negative (left, −4) or positive value (right, +4), as well as a neutral face (middle, 0). A reinforcer was delivered for a response to a stimulus with a summed value greater than 0. The results from test trials with novel faces are shown. (From Pearce, 2008; reproduced with permission from Taylor & Francis.)

Figure 10.13 **Imaging scrambling.** This image was reformatted to occupy 128 × 128 pixels at a resolution of 1,024 × 768 pixels. The image is progressively scrambled from none to maximum (from left to right: unscrambled, degree 1, degree 3, degree 6). Though performance declined as the degree of scrambling increased, significant discrimination of familiar images was reported for all pigeons from degree 1 to 5, and two pigeons continued to discriminate at degree 6. (Photo by K. J. Leising.)

Their results indicated that pigeons continued to discriminate well with large pixels but failed at the smallest degree of pixilation. This result suggests that pigeons were "seeing" not people but small configurations of features that were consistently part of a person.

In another study, Watanabe (2010) taught pigeons to discriminate between "good" or "bad" paintings (watercolor and pastel) drawn by children (ages 9–11) and rated by adults. Pigeons learned the discrimination and transferred to novel stimuli. Discrimination accuracy was unaffected by a reduction in the size of the paintings or large pixel scrambling but was significantly disrupted by removal of color and small pixel scrambling. This suggests that small patches of color were critical for pigeons to identify a painting as "good"; an aesthetic quality any art connoisseur would be hard-pressed to dispute.

Interestingly, a similar pattern of results was found when a separate group of pigeons was trained to discriminate the same pictures but on the basis of the painting method (watercolor versus pastel paintings). This suggests that the same mechanism (i.e., low-level features) produced accurate discrimination of good from bad paintings as well as watercolor from pastel paintings. Watanabe (2001) has also trained humans and pigeons to discriminate painting by Van Gogh and Chagall. Both species transferred without disruption to novel paintings and demonstrated similar patterns of discrimination when scrambling was applied to the image; these results revealed that the discrimination was based on the integration of several different cues.

Results such as these have led some to highlight that linear feature models are insufficient to account for conceptual behavior with complex visual stimuli (Neumann, 1974). Linear feature models are limited by how many separable features can be processed simultaneously (e.g., color, shape, pattern, brightness, orientation, etc.) and may not capture well the independent associative value of configurations of features (e.g., the value of a red diagonal line as opposed to independent values for red patches of color and diagonal lines).

10.5.2 Exemplar theory

A model of conceptual behavior that captures the whole configuration of an item, or exemplar, rather than specific features is *exemplar theory* (or context theory; Medin & Schaffer, 1978). If a picture of a tree is followed by a reinforcer, then the whole configuration of features in the picture becomes associated with a particular response (i.e., category). When a new item is encountered, generalization from previous exemplars (i.e., previous configurations) determines the probability of responding to the new item as part of the category or not. Consistent with the assumptions of this theory, Vaughan and Greene (1984) speculated that memorization of particular slides, along with generalization from certain physical dimensions, could account for the data from categorization tasks that appear to implicate the abstraction of a concept.

Natural categories typically exhibit continuous variation along their dimensions, which result in feature distributions that are symmetrical and unimodal around a central tendency (e.g., most birds have a wingspan close to the average wingspan of all birds). This suggests that if you randomly sample from a group of category members, then exemplars with characteristics more representative of the group are more likely to be sampled, and these members will be weighted more heavily in the generalizations that are used to evaluate new members.

An overrepresentation of certain members, particularly those with features representing the central tendencies of the category, will result in a *typicality effect*, which is faster and more accurate recognition of members that are most representative (i.e., typical) of that category (Jitsumori, 2006). A penguin is likely not well represented in your exemplar space, and consequently, your latency to say "a bird" when asked "What is that?" will be longer in the presence of a penguin than a robin (Rosch, 1973). However, if you have just returned from a trip to the Antarctic on which you encountered many penguins, then you will likely be faster and more accurate in labeling a penguin as a bird than someone who lacked that experience.

Exemplar theory should predict performance particularly well when experience with members of a category is limited and when some of those members are exceptions to the central tendency. In other words, it would be beneficial to remember specific exemplars (e.g., penguins) rather than the central tendency (e.g., average wing length), if you are likely to need to respond to those members again in the future. However, several tasks have revealed that conceptual behavior in these scenarios is not well predicted by experience with specific exemplars in pigeons (Aydin & Pearce, 1994; Jitsumori, 1993), monkeys (Smith et al., 2008), and humans (Smith & Minda, 2002). The results of these studies are consistent with another approach, prototype theory, that relies exclusively on animals learning about the central tendencies of members of a category.

10.5.3 Prototype theory

According to another theory of conceptual behavior, a most typical member need not exist but rather can be an abstraction of the central tendencies of a category derived from past experience. *Prototype theory* (Reed, 1972; Smith & Minda, 2002) suggests that exemplar experience is averaged into an idealized representation, or prototype, of the category. The membership of a new item will be determined by generalization from the prototype to the item. My prototype of a bird need not be a robin or a penguin but rather the central tendency of all of my experience with birds.

Smith (2014) argued that there is a fitness advantage to averaging experience with exemplars into a prototype, so much so that prototype abstraction was likely selected for over the last hundreds of millions of years. Similar to other evaluations of conceptual behavior in this chapter, prototype models are often tested using a family-resemblance task in which pairs of members will share some but not all features, and the shared features will change from one pair to the next.

Smith (2014) compared exemplar and prototype models predictions in an eight-dimensional family-resemblance task. The models used 500 exemplars generated from the prototype (i.e., the central tendency of each of the eight dimensions) for each category. Across several experimental variations, including one that limited the number of exemplars to favor exemplar theory, there remained a performance advantage for the prototype model.

Other experiments with humans (Cook & Smith, 2006), rhesus monkeys (Smith et al., 2010), and pigeons (Cook & Smith, 2006) have used the prototype-exception task, which established two categories (A and B) defined by several typical members of each category, along with a couple of exception exemplars (those appearing more typical of the other category). In this task, responding to each individual exemplar (i.e., as exemplar theory would predict) rather than responding based on a prototype would result in relatively quick acquisition of the correct response to the exception exemplars. Despite all three species quickly learning to make the correct response to typical members (greater than 75% of trials), they consistently (about 15,000 trials for the monkeys) responded incorrectly to the exception exemplars (less than 40% correct; i.e., as if they were a member of the other category) until much later in training.

The processes discussed thus far that lead to conceptual behavior are by no means mutually exclusive. When salient, separable features predict category boundaries, then linear features would likely support behavior. By contrast, when experience with a few exemplars that include multiple features poorly correlated with one another (i.e., a sparse category), then an exemplar process may predict behavior. In many conditions with natural categories, a prototype process will be most effective. Of course, all of the processes may be active under most conditions, with conceptual behavior reflecting some combination of them.

10.5.4 Neurobiology and neural networks

The neurobiology of the mammalian brain suggests contributions from two processes involved in conceptual behavior. An implicit process, which is reliant on associative learning, enables animals to make the correct response in the presence of individual items, and an explicit process, which supports abstract rule-based categorical distinctions. With the implicit process, individual items are encoded holistically, and the learner is unaware of its operation. You may recall our earlier discussions (Chapters 4 and 9) of stimulus–response learning subserved by the basal ganglia and dopamine-strengthening synapses in the midbrain dopaminergic brain systems. This network is also hypothesized to support linear feature- and exemplar-based category learning (Shohamy et al., 2008).

Antzoulatos and Miller (2011) trained monkeys to make a left or right response to exemplars that defined new categories of dot patterns (A and B) each day. After learning the correct response to one set of exemplars, new exemplars of the categories were added across eight blocks of training each day. Early in training (the first two blocks), the salient features of each exemplar were expected to guide performance (i.e., press left in the presence of Dot Pattern 1). During this period of training, activity in the striatum predicted whether the animals would make a left or right response. Activity in the hippocampus, generally associated with explicit memories, was shown to precede activity in the basal ganglia when learning about the value of individual items as well as during transfer of conceptual behavior to new items (Myers et al., 2003; Poldrack et al., 2001; Shohamy & Wagner 2008).

The basal ganglia, which may drive learning via an implicit process, are highly connected through various loops to other regions of the brain, including the prefrontal cortex (Figure 10.14). The explicit process supporting rule-based categorical distinctions relies on activity in a network of regions, including the prefrontal cortex, the anterior cingulate cortex, the head of the caudate nucleus, and the medial temporal lobe (Seger & Miller, 2010). Antzoulatos and Miller (2011) also analyzed the category performance of the monkeys trained with the dot patterns each day during the middle and last blocks of training.

During these blocks, activity in the prefrontal cortex came to predict category responding more strongly and earlier in the trial than striatum. Prefrontal activity is more robust for category members, even with significant within-category variation. Freedman et al. (2001) found that differential activity in the prefrontal cortex persisted for images of different-looking members from the same category but not for similar-looking members from different categories. Similar results were found in monkeys trained to apply a same–different rule to pairs of pictures (Wallis et al., 2001). Smith et al. (2016) suggested that the implicit process is responsible for the continuity in findings of conceptual behavior across vertebrates, whereas the explicit process may separate primates from other animals.

Researchers have used a neural network approach to better understand how different brain areas cooperate during category learning (Zhang et al., 2022). *Neural network models* have three main attributes. The first is a structure with at least three layers. An input layer is made of nodes (simulated neurons) that can be activated to a particular level (e.g., 1) when a stimulus is presented. The hidden unit layer is composed of nodes activated by the input layer. This layer may contain multiple sub layers or even receive input from parallel networks of nodes in the same layer. The last layer is the output layer. Activity in this layer determines the model's behavior.

For example, if one were attempting to develop a neural network model to identify letters of the English alphabet displayed on a 10 × 10 matrix of pixels (Figure 10.15), then the model would need each layer. The input layer could be composed of 100 nodes (one

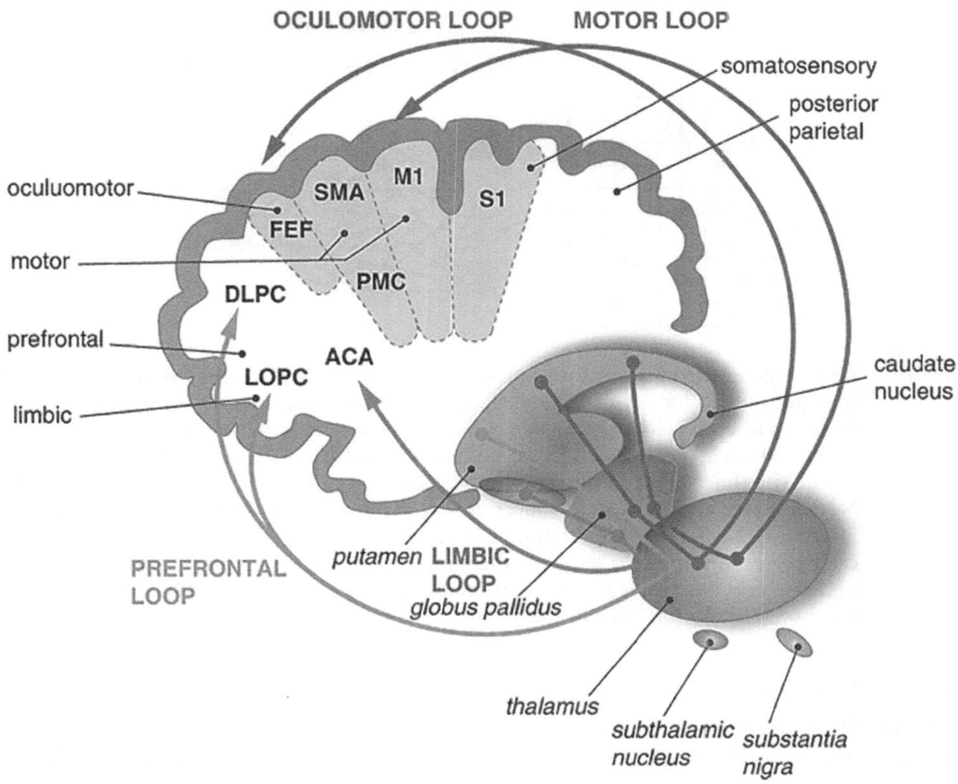

Figure 10.14 **Cortico-striatal loops.** The basal ganglia are highly interconnected with the rest of the brain in the form of four loops with outputs to largely the same cortical areas that gave rise to the initial input. Most relevant for concept learning are the limbic or motivational loop and the prefrontal or executive loop. ACA: anterior cerebral artery, which supplies blood to parts of both the prefrontal cortex and cingulate gyrus. DLPC: dorsolateral prefrontal cortex. FEF: frontal eye fields. LOPC: lateral orbital prefrontal cortex. M1: primary motor area. PMC: premotor cortex. S1: primary sensory area. SMA: supplementary motor area. (From Miall, 2022; reproduced with permission from Springer-Nature.)

corresponding to each pixel), or it could average across some number of pixels to reduce the total nodes. The number of nodes in the hidden unit layer typically scales with the complexity of the task. There are specific rules for determining the identity of letters. Thus, we could start with 50 nodes in the hidden unit layer and scale up or down depending on the model's performance. The output layer is fixed to the 26 letters of the alphabet. The model could then be trained with a particular input, the letter B, and given some output (e.g., the model says "B") the connections between nodes would be modified.

The second attribute of neural network models is weighted connections. The initial connections between nodes in different layers may be drawn from a normal distribution, may be uniform, or may use more complicated initializations. Most neural networks models use some kind of error-correction rule to modify the weights between nodes in different layers. The weights between nodes are modified based on the difference between what it obtained (e.g., it was shown the letter "A") and what it expected (e.g., it answered that it was shown

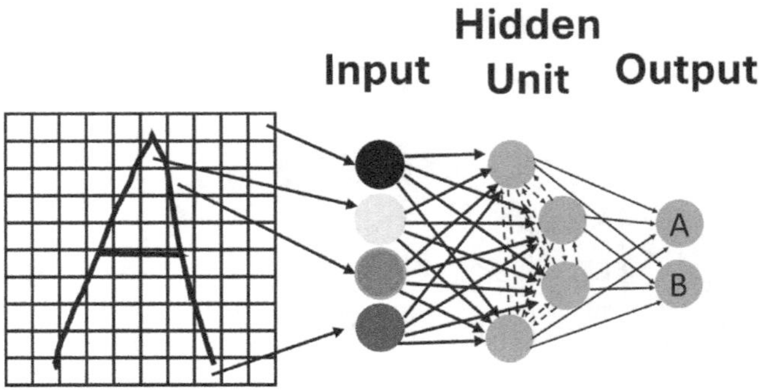

Figure 10.15 **Letter-recognition neural network model.** An example of a neural network model for recognition of a letter of the English alphabet. The input is broken down into a 10 × 10 matrix, and each cell of the matrix corresponds to a node in the input layer. The amount of the cell occupied by an edge is translated into activity with a corresponding node of the input layer. Each node in the input node is connected to nodes within a hidden unit layer. Nodes within the hidden unit layer are interconnected, providing lateral excitation and inhibition. Nodes in the hidden unit layer are connected to 26 nodes in the output layer, each corresponding to a letter of the alphabet. The weight of the connections between nodes in and between each layer are modifiable with experience. Only a subset of nodes are displayed in each layer for simplicity.

the letter "B"). Connections may be strengthened (i.e., excitatory) or weakened (i.e., inhibitory) throughout training of the model.

Similar to the Rescorla-Wagner (1972) model, larger errors result in greater weight adjustments. These connections enable the third attribute of neural network models: spreading activation. Activity in one or more nodes will spread to other nodes. ***Spreading activation*** is responsible for pattern completion (priming, generalization, and transfer effects in category learning). It also enables ***graceful degradation***, which is continued function (e.g., classification) even if a portion of the system is damaged (e.g., a loss of a few hundred neurons).

Zhang et al. (2022) developed a neural network model to learn the same category-learning task that was previously given to monkeys while recording from their prefrontal cortex (Pan et al., 2008). Zhang reported that the nodes in the hidden-unit layer of the model could be divided into those that were involved in representing the individual stimuli and those that were representing the category in a manner similar to neurons in the prefrontal cortex of the monkey. These results, and the success of neural network models generally (ChatGPT, Google AI, Tesla self-driving systems, etc.), indicate the broad implications of studies targeting the factors (e.g., error correction) that influence associative learning. Beyond neural networks, similar error-correction learning algorithms have been used in the development of hearing- and sight-assisting devices for humans.

10.6 Numerical competence

It should not come as a surprise that the behavior of most organisms exhibits stimulus control based on the presence and absence of a stimulus but also the magnitude (e.g., quantity) of a stimulus. A response (e.g., approach) that varies in probability, strength, timing, and location as a function of the number of food items, mates, predators, and competitors should provide a reproductive advantage. Perhaps this is why there is evidence for numerical competence across the animal kingdom, including vertebrate and invertebrate species (Gatto et al., 2022).

If we apply an associative learning lens to numerical competence, then we would expect that more identical stimuli in an environment would increase the overall magnitude, or salience, of that stimulus, making it more likely to overshadow learning about other stimuli present at the same time. The separate stimuli could be perceived as one large configural stimulus or as many separate stimuli. If we apply what we learned from Chapters 8 and 9, animals can learn to respond to segments of the same stimulus that occupy different locations in time (e.g., 5th vs. 30th second of a CS) or space (e.g., the right or left side of a landmark).

Consistent with this interpretation of stimuli, animals are sensitive to the total number of separate items in each of two arrays, even when the overall magnitude (i.e., area) of the stimuli in each array is held constant. Not surprisingly, response distributions from number discriminations conform to *Weber's law*, that is, more items lead to more errors (Figure 10.16).

Given the consistency with which Weber's law accounts for errors when estimating intervals of time, space, and number, we could have easily transitioned to numerical competence following our review of any of these topics. Why, then, is numerical competence across species so interesting, and why is it covered alongside conceptual behavior in this book? It is interesting, in part, because one form of numerical competence, arithmetic (e.g., addition), was assumed by many to be uniquely human (Dehaene, 1992) and can be applied to quantities of

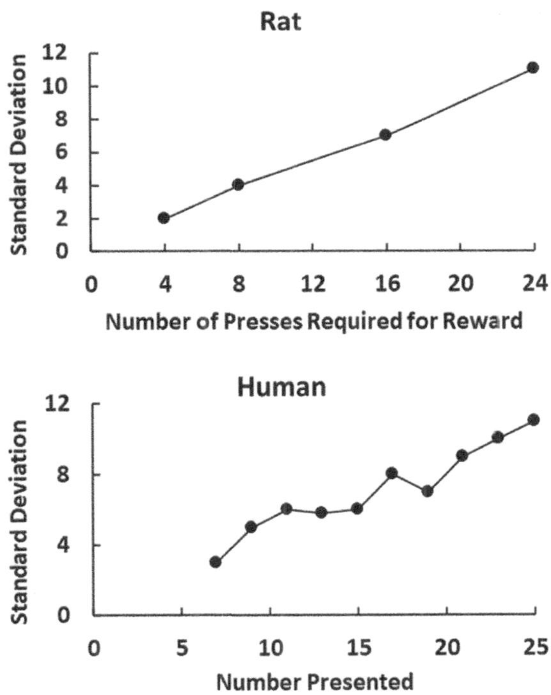

Figure 10.16 **Numerical production in rats and humans.** Rats and humans were trained to press a lever in an operant chamber or press a key on a keyboard a certain number of times. Weber's law predicts more uncertainty resulting in more errors as the number of required responses increases. Degree of error is indicated by the value of the standard deviations. There was a positive correlation between the mean number of required responses and the standard deviations in rats and humans. (From Shettleworth, 2010; reproduced with permission from Oxford University Press.)

nearly anything (e.g., rocks, stars, and atoms). Numerical competence transcends the identity of the individual items and persists even when nonnumerical factors (e.g., total area of the items) are controlled.

Methodological approaches to the study of numerical competence include two main variations: numerical perception and production. *Numerical perception* tasks ask the subject to make a different response (e.g., touch, look at, or gesture toward) based on the number of items. The response may be based on an ordinal rule (e.g., select the array with more or fewer items than the array beside it), may involve two or more arrays (e.g., select the smallest to largest), may involve sequentially presented items (i.e., counting), or may involve an arbitrary correspondence between the number of items and a symbol representing the total number of items (e.g., the Arabic numeral or the left lever in an operant box).

As a result of the structure of these tasks, the response is treated categorically (e.g., a response corresponds to a particular number or relationship). By contrast, *numerical-production* tasks require the animal to produce a particular number of the same response based on a number presented as the sample or a discriminative stimulus associated with a particular schedule of reinforcement (e.g., a FR 9 schedule). The response is treated as a continuous rather than categorical variable.

Another distinction in methodologies involves the number of items presented; many studies utilize four or fewer items, whereas other studies utilize quantities greater than four. One of the greatest challenges in the study of *numerosity* has been to control for nonnumerical continuous variables that correlate with quantity. In other words, as the number of items in an area increases, so too do many nonnumerical variables (e.g., the total surface area, total contour length, item density; Figure 10.17). Lastly, numerical competence has

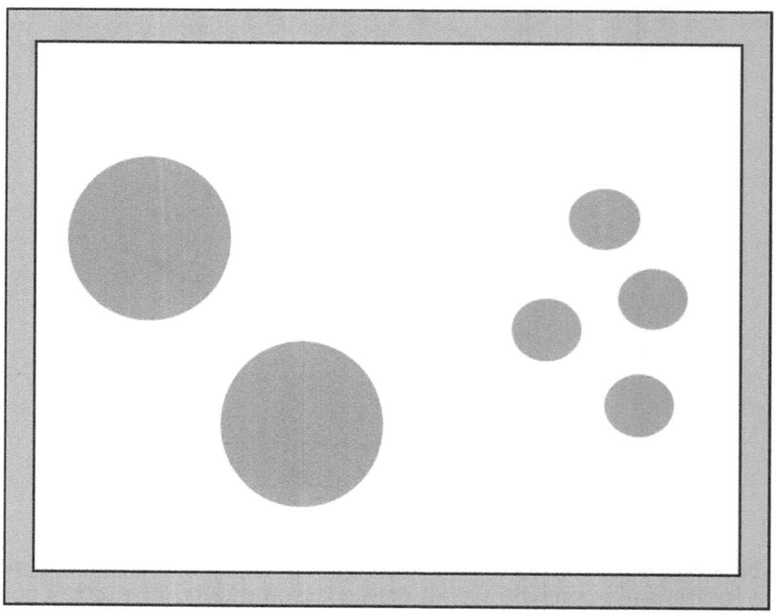

Figure 10.17 **Nonnumerical considerations.** In the study of numerical competence, factors such as overall area, density, and contour length must be controlled for. In the figure, the two items on the left occupy more area than the four items on the right, but other nonnumerical factors remain. Variation across displays ensures that nonnumerical factors are unreliable cues for discrimination of numerosity.

been investigated in laboratory and field studies, with the former allowing better control of nonnumerical variables.

10.6.1 Approximate numerical magnitude

There is overwhelming evidence from many species for stimulus control by the approximate numerical magnitude of the item. Perception of the approximate numerical magnitude of items allows for discrimination and ordering of quantities presented in any modality and is independent of control by nonnumerical variables.

In hindsight, the failure of early studies to find evidence for this competence is not surprising. For example, Greene (1983) trained pigeons to discriminate between hand-drawn displays of one or two squiggles. After training, the pigeons did not transfer their discrimination to new squiggles that were drawn by a second person. This study failed to train with multiple exemplars and failed to control for nonnumerical variables. Scarf et al. (2011) trained pigeons to peck in ascending order sets of one, two, or three items displayed on the screen.

The authors created 35 lists of sets, with the items in each list varying in a nonnumerical dimension. For example, sometimes a set with three items occupied less total area than a set with two items in the same list. Pigeons achieved 80% accuracy with these displays (baseline), and were then tested with sets of one to nine items (familiar and novel quantities). Transfer to sets that contained a familiar quantity (sets with one, two, or three items) were at the same level as baseline, and trials with only novel quantities (sets with four or more items) were well above chance level. Additionally, pigeons exhibited two effects, distance and magnitude, that are characteristic of results from other species, including monkeys and humans (Cantlon & Brannon, 2006).

Both effects are an instantiation of Weber's law, which predicts better accuracy as a function of the ratio of the smaller to the larger number of items. Distance effects refer to higher accuracy and faster response times with greater absolute distances between the numbers being discriminated on a number line (e.g., 2 vs. 7 compared to 4 vs. 5). Magnitude effects predict lower accuracies for the same absolute distances when the discrimination involves more items (e.g., 1 vs. 3 compared to 7 vs. 9).

These effects have also been found when the number to be estimated is a colored light flashed sequentially (three Red lights) and compared with a different number of flashes of another color of light (two Blue lights; Alsop & Honig, 1991). There is also evidence that approximate numerical magnitude is cross-modal. Rats that were trained to discriminate different numbers of bursts of auditory stimuli transferred (i.e., without training) to discriminate different numbers of cutaneous shocks (Meck & Church, 1983). Sensitivity to number with both types of stimuli was consistent with the use of visual items in previous research with pigeons and monkeys.

Finally, approximate numerical magnitude can also support estimation of elementary arithmetic (i.e., addition or subtraction) in pigeons (Brannon et al., 2001) and monkeys (Flombaum et al., 2005) as well as infant (Wynn, 1992) and adult humans (Barth et al., 2003).

In the field, these discriminations take on greater ecological validity. The controlled conditions in the laboratory cannot be recreated in the field, but the laboratory can only approximate the ecological challenges of animals in the wild. The combination of both types of studies is critical for evaluating the prevalence and importance of numerical competence in animals. McComb et al. (1994) studied the likelihood that lions living in the Serengeti National Park in Tanzania would approach previously recorded roars of single females compared to roars of groups of three females. The sound was played at 116 dB when subjects were 200 m away and in the center of their territory. If the lions were sensitive to the number of different females in the intruder playback, they should be more likely to approach the speaker when the playback contained a single lion. Additionally, approach should be a function of the ratio of the number of lions in their group to the number of intruder lions in the playback; they should only approach the speaker when the likelihood of winning any contest with the intruder lions was high.

The approach data were consistent with both predictions. A lion was more likely to approach a speaker when there was only one lion in the intruder playback and their group contained three (~75%) lions versus them alone (~16%), which was similar to the likelihood of approaching the speaker when both group size and intruder size contained three lions (~18%). Field studies allow for the evaluation of other relevant variables, such as the presence of cubs, which decreased the difference ratio required for females to investigate (i.e., they were more likely to investigate even if they lacked an otherwise acceptable ratio of group size to intruder size). Similar effects have been reported with chimpanzees, hyenas, fish, and ants (Agrillo, 2015).

In a study bridging the gap between laboratory and field research, Dacke and Srinivasan (2008) trained honeybees outdoors with a tunnel containing five landmarks spaced at regular intervals and the entrance of the tunnel positioned 7 m from the hive. After training one group of bees to find food at the third landmark, the bees continued to search for sucrose at the third landmark even when the interlandmark distance was irregular, when the total area of the landmarks was changed, and when a baffle prevented a view of subsequent landmarks. The results of these studies are consistent with those collected in laboratory tasks and suggest additional methods and conditions that can be used in the study of numerical competence.

The honeybees tested by Dacke and Srinivasan (2008) flew past a specific number of landmarks in the tunnel, such that their behavior reflected more than an arbitrary response to a number of landmarks. In addition to associating an approximate or exact number with a particular categorical response (e.g., choose more), nonhuman animals show similar patterns to humans in time-production tasks when producing a particular number of responses under conditions that prevent the use of language.

Rats trained to press a lever a particular number of times (i.e., a fixed-ratio schedule of reinforcement) and humans told to press a computer key as fast as they could without counting demonstrated a similar pattern of results that matched the predictions of approximate magnitude estimation (rats, Platt & Johnson, 1971; humans, Whalen et al., 1999). Namely, the standard deviation, or error, of the number of responses for different numbers, or error, was proportional to the total number of responses required (Figure 10.16). Similar results were obtained in a task with chimpanzees (Rumbaugh et al., 1993) when an Arabic numeral (e.g., 2) displayed on each trial specified how many items in a subsequent screen were to be removed by clicking them with a computer joystick (e.g., remove 2 objects).

All of the studies reviewed thus far are consistent with approximate magnitude estimation, which suggests that animals are discriminating between something like the accumulation of neural magnitudes based on the frequency of items. True counting, however, should not exhibit this same pattern of results.

10.6.2 Counting

True counting requires a one-to-one assignment of a unique tag (e.g., "1") to each item in an array (Gelman & Gallistel, 1978). The order in which the unique tags are assigned is always the same (e.g., "1" and then "2"), and the final tag is the representative of the numerosity of the set. The tags do not necessarily need to be verbal. One could conclude that with unique and ordered tags applied to objects, the error for estimates of large numbers should be reduced. All that is required is that the animal remembers the most recent tag and then assigns the next tag to the next item. This should be as difficult for the second item as it is for the ninth item. Indeed, when humans count with language, distance and numerosity effects are eliminated (Whalen et al., 1999).

However, this may be too optimistic for nonhuman animals. If tags are used without language, then more items could be expected to increase the likelihood of erroneously assigning a new tag to an already tagged item or assigning an incorrect tag based on interference from previously assigned tags. This view is consistent with recordings from the prefrontal cortex while monkeys performed a numerosity matching task, in which a third of prefrontal neurons fired selectively after the visual presentation of a certain numerosity of dots (Nieder et al., 2002), indicating a kind of neural tag for each numerosity, but the width of the tuning curves for each numerosity scaled with the number of items.

Though approximate magnitude estimation can support addition, identifying the correct symbol (e.g., the Arabic numeral 6) following exposure to subsets (3 + 3 or 8 − 2) would

Figure 10.18 **Addition in the chimpanzee Sheba.** The setting included three locations that Sheba was trained to search before choosing a card. In the initial tests, two of the three locations had different numbers of oranges, and the correct response was to point to the Arabic number that equaled the sum of oranges. In the situation represented in this figure, plastic cards with Arabic numbers replaced the oranges, and Sheba was asked to add the numbers and point to the appropriate card. Sheba performed above chance in both tasks from the first session. (From Boysen & Berntson, 1989; reproduced with permission from the American Psychological Association.)

demonstrate a higher level of numerical competence. Intriguing evidence of addition was reported in Alex, the African gray parrot mentioned earlier (Pepperberg, 2012). Alex could name digits up to eight by using English words, and in a series of tests, when shown two numerals and asked "How many total?" he added two Arabic numerals correctly in 9 out of 12 trials (75% correct). Moreover, when shown three Arabic numerals, he correctly added them in 8 out of 10 trials (80% correct). Alex could also flexibly combine category information with addition when asked, "How many green?" (Figure 10.10).

Chimpanzees trained to count objects by assigning Arabic numerals can perform addition in a rudimentary form. In one experiment (Boysen & Berntson, 1989), a chimpanzee named Sheba was trained to move through three different locations in the lab, as shown in Figure 10.18. In a first task, Sheba found oranges hidden in two of the three locations and was asked to point to the number representing the total (up to 4). She performed above chance from the first session, but her performance could reflect counting rather than addition. However, when oranges were substituted by plastic cards with Arabic numbers between 0 and 4 in two of the three locations, Sheba performed above chance from the first session. Performance was also above chance independently of whether the correct sum equaled 1, 2, 3, or 4. Overall, Sheba was correct in 81% of the trials. To avoid cueing, the experimenter scoring Sheba's performance stayed behind her, and numbers were placed in each site by a different experimenter.

There is also evidence that under some conditions, animals can respond to small numbers of objects quickly and with little error, consistent with true counting, but also consistent with a purely perceptual mechanism that recognizes and distinguishes between small numbers of items (Feigenson et al., 2004). As a result, we are left with strong evidence that many animals estimate numerical magnitude, independent of nonnumerical variables, but additional research is needed to evaluate what aspects of true counting are evident in nonhuman animals.

Glossary

Acquired equivalence or secondary generalization Generalization, which may establish a functional equivalence class, is facilitated between disparate stimuli as a result of pairings of the stimuli with a common outcome, common response, or both.

Arbitrary MTS A behavioral procedure in which a sample stimulus is presented and a reinforcer is delivered for selecting a matching comparison stimulus from two or more alternatives. The matching stimulus is assigned by the experimenter, making any perceptual resemblance between the sample and matching stimulus irrelevant to learning the correct response.

Basic level Intermediate level of categorization, with the most perceptual similarity between members in the same category and least similarity with members across the category.

Categories Groups of stimuli that share one or more physical features or functions.

Concept The mental representation of a category.

Conceptual behavior or categorization Occurs when a category of stimuli is responded to similarly on the basis of perceptual, associative, or relational similarity.

Desirable difficulties Study strategies that lower initial success with the material encountered while studying but provide more robust success in other metrics, such as transfer to new items.

Error-correction rule A formula that states how a prediction should be updated based on the difference between the predicted value of US and the actual experienced value of the US.

Exemplar theory or context theory A model of conceptual behavior that captures the whole configuration of an item, or exemplar, rather than specific features. When a new item is encountered, generalization from previous exemplars (i.e., previous configurations) determines the probability of responding to the new item as part of the category.

Family resemblance All members of a category share one or more attributes, but no member has all of the attributes.

Functional equivalence class A group of distinct stimuli that come to be treated similarly, exhibiting generalization within the group and discrimination from other groups due to shared associations with a common response or common outcome. This is most commonly tested by changing the response to one member and evaluating generalization to the others or interchanging members within the same group.

Graceful degradation A property of neural network models that allows the network to continue to function even when a portion of the network is destroyed or the input is incomplete.

Item-specific learning The process by which an organism responds to a stimulus based on prior experience with the properties of specific stimuli (e.g., their appearance, location, or context).

Linear feature model States that the response to a stimulus will be based on a weighted combination of the associative value of the individual features of the stimulus, with each feature contributing additively.

Match to sample (MTS) A behavioral procedure in which a sample stimulus is presented and a reinforcer is delivered for selecting a matching comparison stimulus from two or more alternatives.

Neural network models Inspired by the properties of neural processing, these models consist of interconnected units organized in at least three layers, where each connection has a weight that adjusts based on experience, allowing the system to simulate learning and produce complex behavior.

Numerical perception Tasks that require the subject to make a different response (e.g., touch, look at, or gesture toward) based on how many items are present.

Numerosity Perception of the number of discrete items in a set, independent of other nonnumerical factors such as overall area, density, or total contour length.

Peak shift Phenomenon in which discrimination training with S+ and S- stimuli along a single dimension finds maximal responding not to the S+ but at a location shifted away from the nonreinforced stimulus.

Pexigram An array of visual symbols, each associated with the delivery of a reinforcer if pecked in the presence of a specific category of items. Importantly, the assignment of symbol to category is arbitrary.

Prototype theory An idealized representation is abstracted from past experience. The membership of a new item will be determined by generalization from the representation to the item.

Reflexivity A response that demonstrates that a stimulus is equivalent to itself. Often tested in an MTS task with the same stimulus being presented as the sample and one of the comparison stimuli.

Second-order relationship A relation between relationships, such as matching (i.e., a relation) based on whether two sample items are the same (i.e., their relationship).

Spreading activation A property of neural network models in which the activity in one node spreads to nearby nodes based on weighted connections that adjust with experience.

Stimulus control The degree to which the probability of behavior varies in the presence of external physical events.

Stimulus equivalence The spontaneous emergence of reflexivity, symmetry, and transitivity among a set of stimuli after training of one of the relations.

Subordinate level Lowest level of categorization, with high within-category perceptual similarity but also high between-category perceptual similarity.

Superordinate level Highest and most abstract level of categorization, with generalization occurring across several basic-level categories that share low within-category perceptual similarity.

Symmetry A response that demonstrates the reversal of a learned relationship. Often tested in an MTS task with the role of a sample and correct comparison stimulus reversed.

Transitivity A response that demonstrates the relationship between two stimuli never paired directly but sharing prior training with a common element.

Transposition Transfer of a learned relational rule from one set of stimuli to another.

Typicality effect Faster and more accurate recognition of members that are most representative (i.e., typical) of a category.

Weber's law States that sensitivity to a change in the intensity of a stimulus is proportional to the overall magnitude of that stimulus.

References

Agrillo, C. (2015). Numerical and arithmetic abilities in non-primate species. In R. C. Kadosh & A. Dowker (Eds.), *The Oxford handbook of numerical cognition* (pp. 214–236). Oxford University Press.

Alsop, B., & Honig, W. K. (1991). Sequential stimuli and relative numerosity discriminations in pigeons. *Journal of Experimental Psychology: Animal Behavior Processes*, *17*(4), 386–395. https://doi.org/10.1037/0097-7403.17.4.386

Antzoulatos, E. G., & Miller, E. K. (2011). Differences between neural activity in prefrontal cortex and striatum during learning of novel abstract categories. *Neuron*, *71*(2), 243–249. https://doi.org/10.1016/j.neuron.2011.05.040

Astley, S. L., & Wasserman, E. A. (1999). Superordinate category formation in pigeons: Association with a common delay or probability of food reinforcement makes perceptually dissimilar stimuli functionally equivalent. *Journal of Experimental Psychology: Animal Behavior Processes*, *25*(4), 415–432. https://doi.org/10.1037/0097-7403.25.4.415

Aust, U., & Huber, L. (2001). The role of item- and category-specific information in the discrimination of people versus nonpeople images by pigeons. *Learning & Behavior*, *29*(2), 107–119.

Aust, U., & Huber, L. (2002). A comparative approach to pigeons' categorization of human faces. *Journal of Comparative Psychology*, *116*(3), 259–261. https://doi.org/10.1037/0735-7036.116.3.259

Aydin, A., & Pearce, J. M. (1994). Prototype effects in categorization by pigeons. *Journal of Experimental Psychology: Animal Behavior Processes*, *20*(3), 264–277. https://doi.org/10.1037/0097-7403.20.3.264

Barth, H., Kanwisher, N., & Spelke, E. (2003). The construction of large number representations in adults. *Cognition*, *86*(3), 201–221. https://doi.org/10.1016/S0010-0277(02)00178–6

Bhatt, R. S. (1988). *Categorization in pigeons: Effects of category size, congruity with human categories, selective attention, and secondary generalization* (Unpublished Doctoral dissertation). University of Iowa.

Bjork, R. A., & Bjork, E. L. (2020). Desirable difficulties in theory and practice. *Journal of Applied research in Memory and Cognition*, *9*(4), 475–479.

Bodily, K. D., Katz, J. S., & Wright, A. A. (2008). Matching-to-sample abstract-concept learning by pigeons. *Journal of Experimental Psychology: Animal Behavior Processes*, *34*(1), 178–184. https://doi.org/10.1037/0097-7403.34.1.178

Bonardi, C., Rey, V., Richmond, M., & Hall, G. (1993). Acquired equivalence of cues in pigeon autoshaping: Effects of training with common consequences and with common antecedents. *Animal Learning & Behavior*, *21*(4), 369–376. https://doi.org/10.3758/BF03198003

Boysen, S. T., & Berntson, G. G. (1989). Numerical competence in a chimpanzee (Pan troglodytes). *Journal of Comparative Psychology*, *103*(1), 23.

Brannon, E. M., Wusthoff, C. J., Gallistel, C. R., & Gibbon, J. (2001). Numerical subtraction in the pigeon: Evidence for a linear subjective number scale. *Psychological Science*, *12*(3), 238–243. https://doi.org/10.1111/1467-9280.00342

Brown v. Board of Education, 347 U.S. 483 (1954).

Bujedo, J. G., Garcia, A. G., & Fernandez, V. P. (2014). Failure to find symmetry in pigeons after multiple-exemplar training. *Psicothema*, *4*(26), 435–441. https://doi.org/10.7334/psicothema2013.352

Cantlon, J. F., & Brannon, E. M. (2006). Shared system for ordering small and large numbers in monkeys and humans. *Psychological Science*, *17*(5), 401–406. https://doi.org/10.1111/j.1467-9280.2006.01719.x

Carvalho, P. F., & Goldstone, R. L. (2014). Putting category learning in order: Category structure and temporal arrangement affect the benefit of interleaved over blocked study. *Memory & Cognition*, *42*, 481–495.

Chen, Z., & Mo, L. (2004). Schema induction in problem solving: A multidimensional analysis. *Journal of Experimental Psychology: Learning, Memory, and Cognition*, *30*(3), 583–600. https://doi.org/10.1037/0278-7393.30.3.583

Cook, R. G. (2002). The structure of pigeon multiple-class same-different learning. *Journal of the Experimental Analysis of Behavior*, *78*(3), 345–364. https://doi.org/10.1901/jeab.2002.78-345 c

Cook, R. G., Kelly, D. M., & Katz, J. S. (2003). Successive two-item same-different discrimination and concept learning by pigeons. *Behavioural Processes*, *62*(1), 125–144. https://doi.org/10.1016/S0376-6357(03)00022–6

Cook, R. G., Levison, D. G., Gillett, S. R., & Blaisdell, A. P. (2005). Capacity and limits of associative memory in pigeons. *Psychonomic Bulletin & Review*, *12*(2), 350–358. https://doi.org/10.3758/bf03196384

Cook, R. G., & Smith, J. D. (2006). Stages of abstraction and exemplar memorization in pigeon category learning. *Psychological Science*, *17*(12), 1059–1067. https://doi.org/10.1111/j.1467-9280.2006.01833.x

Dacke, M., & Srinivasan, M. V. (2008). Evidence for counting in insects. *Animal Cognition*, *11*(4), 683–689. https://doi.org/10.1007/s10071-008-0159-y

Dehaene, S. (1992). Varieties of numerical abilities. *Cognition, 44*(1), 1–42. https://doi.org/10.1016/0010-0277(92)90049-N

Delamater, A. R. (1998). Associative mediational processes in the acquired equivalence and distinctiveness of cues. *Journal of Experimental Psychology: Animal Behavior Processes, 24*(4), 467–482. https://doi.org/10.1037/0097-7403.24.4.467

Dugdale, N., & Lowe, C. F. (2000). Testing for symmetry in the conditional discriminations of language-trained chimpanzees. *Journal of the Experimental Analysis of Behavior, 73*(1), 5–22. https://doi.org/10.1901/jeab.2000.73-5

Estévez, A. F., Vivas, A. B., Alonso, D., Marí-Beffa, P., Fuentes, L. J., & Bruce Overmier, J. (2007). Enhancing challenged students' recognition of mathematical relations through differential outcomes training. *Quarterly Journal of Experimental Psychology (2006), 60*(4), 571–580. https://doi.org/10.1080/17470210600820039

Fagot, J., & Parron, C. (2010). Relational matching in baboons (*Papio papio*) with reduced grouping requirements. *Journal of Experimental Psychology: Animal Behavior Processes, 36*(2), 184–193. https://doi.org/10.1037/a0017169

Feigenson, L., Dehaene, S., & Spelke, E. (2004). Core systems of number. *Trends in Cognitive Sciences, 8*(7), 307–314. https://doi.org/10.1016/j.tics.2004.05.002

Flemming, T. M., Thompson, R. K. R., Beran, M. J., & Washburn, D. A. (2011). Analogical reasoning and the differential outcome effect: Transitory bridging of the conceptual gap for rhesus monkeys (*Macaca mulatta*). *Journal of Experimental Psychology: Animal Behavior Processes, 37*(3), 353–360. https://doi.org/10.1037/a0022142

Flombaum, J. I., Junge, J. A., & Hauser, M. D. (2005). Rhesus monkeys (*Macaca mulatta*) spontaneously compute addition operations over large numbers. *Cognition, 97*(3), 315–325. https://doi.org/10.1016/j.cognition.2004.09.004

Freedman, D. J., Riesenhuber, M., Poggio, T., & Miller, E. K. (2001). Categorical representation of visual stimuli in the primate prefrontal cortex. *Science, 291*(5502), 312–316. https://doi.org/10.1126/science.291.5502.312

Galizio, M., & Bruce, K. E. (2018). Abstraction, multiple exemplar training and the search for derived stimulus relations in animals. *Perspectives on Behavior Science, 41*(1), 45–67. https://doi.org/10.1007/s40614-017-0112-y

Gatto, E., Loukola, O. J., & Agrillo, C. (2022). Quantitative abilities of invertebrates: A methodological review. *Animal Cognition, 25*(1), 5–19. https://doi.org/10.1007/s10071-021-01529-w

Gelman, R., & Gallistel, C. R. (1978). *The child's understanding of number* (1st ed.). Harvard University Press. https://doi.org/10.4159/9780674037533

Greene, S. L. (1983). Feature memorization in pigeon concept formation. In M. L. Commons, R. J. Herrnstein, & A. R. Wagner (Eds.), *Quantitative analyses of behavior: Discrimination processes* (Vol. 4, pp. 209–229). Ballinger.

Giurfa, M., Zhang, S., Jenett, A., Menzel, R., & Srinivasan, M. V. (2001). The concepts of 'sameness' and 'difference' in an insect. *Nature, 410*(6831), 930–933. https://doi.org/10.1038/35073582

Hanson, H. M. (1959). Effects of discrimination training on stimulus generalization. *Journal of Experimental Psychology, 58*(5), 321–334. https://doi.org/10.1037/h0042606

Herrnstein, R. J., Loveland, D. H., & Cable, C. (1976). Natural concepts in pigeons. *Journal of Experimental Psychology: Animal Behavior Processes, 2*(4), 285.

Herrnstein, R. T., & de Villiers, P. A. (1980). Fish as a natural category for people and pigeons. In *Psychology of learning and motivation* (Vol. 14, pp. 59–95). Academic Press.

Homa, D., Sterling, S., & Trepel, L. (1981). Limitations of exemplar-based generalization and the abstraction of categorical information. *Journal of Experimental Psychology: Human Learning and Memory, 7*(6), 418–439. https://doi.org/10.1037/0278-7393.7.6.418

Honig, W. K., Boneau, C. A., Burstein, K. R., & Pennypacker, H. S. (1963). Positive and negative generalization gradients obtained after equivalent training conditions. *Journal of Comparative and Physiological Psychology, 56*(1), 111–116. https://doi.org/10.1037/h0041747

Huber, L., & Lenz, R. (1993). A test of the linear feature model of polymorphous concept discrimination with pigeons. *Quarterly Journal of Experimental Psychology. B, Comparative and Physiological Psychology, 46*(1), 1–18. https://doi.org/10.1080/14640749308401092

Hughes, S., & Barnes-Holmes, D. (2014). Associative concept learning, stimulus equivalence, and relational frame theory: Working out the similarities and differences between human and nonhuman behavior. *Journal of the Experimental Analysis of Behavior, 101*(1), 156–160.

Jitsumori, M. (1993). Category discrimination of artificial polymorphous stimuli based on feature learning. *Journal of Experimental Psychology: Animal Behavior Processes*, *19*(3), 244–254. https://doi.org/10.1037/0097-7403.19.3.244
Jitsumori, M. (2006). Category structure and typicality effects. In E. A. Wasserman & T. R. Zentall (Eds.), *Comparative cognition* (pp 343–362). Oxford University Press.
Johns, K. W., & Williams, D. A. (1998). Acquired equivalence learning with antecedent and consequent unconditioned stimuli. *Journal of Experimental Psychology: Animal Behavior Processes*, *24*(1), 3–14. https://doi.org/10.1037/0097-7403.24.1.292
Katz, J. S., Wright, A. A., & Bodily, K. D. (2007). Issues in the comparative cognition of abstract-concept learning. *Comparative Cognition & Behavior Reviews*, *2*, 79–92. https://doi.org/10.3819/ccbr.2007.20006
Keller, F. S., & Schoenfeld, W. N. (1950). *Principles of psychology: A systematic text in the science of behavior*. Appleton-Century-Crofts.
Koba, R., & Izumi, A. (2006). Sex categorization of conspecific pictures in Japanese monkeys (*Macaca fuscata*). *Animal Cognition*, *9*(3), 183–191. https://doi.org/10.1007/s10071-006-0020-0
Lashley, K. S., & Wade, M. (1946). The Pavlovian theory of generalization. *Psychological Review*, *53*(2), 72–87. https://doi.org/10.1037/h0059999
Lazareva, O. F., Freiburger, K. L., & Wasserman, E. A. (2004). Pigeons concurrently categorize photographs at both basic and superordinate levels. *Psychonomic Bulletin & Review*, *11*(6), 1111–1117. https://doi.org/10.3758/BF03196745
Lazareva, O. F., & Wasserman, E. A. (2008). Categories and concepts in animals. In R. Menzel (Ed.), *Learning and memory: A comprehensive reference* (Vol. 1, pp. 197–226). Elsevier.
Lazareva, O. F., Wasserman, E. A., & Young, M. E. (2005). Transposition in pigeons: Reassessing spence (1937) with multiple discrimination training. *Learning & Behavior*, *33*(1), 22–46. https://doi.org/10.3758/BF03196048
Lionello-DeNolf, K. M. (2021). An update on the search for symmetry in nonhumans. *Journal of the Experimental Analysis of Behavior*, *115*(1), 309–325. https://doi.org/10.1002/jeab.647
Lionello-DeNolf, K. M., & Urcuioli, P. J. (2002). Stimulus control topographies and tests of symmetry in pigeons. *Journal of the Experimental Analysis of Behavior*, *78*(3), 467–495. https://doi.org/10.1901/jeab.2002.78-467
Lipkens, R., Hayes, S. C., & Hayes, L. J. (1993). Longitudinal study of the development of derived relations in an Infant. *Journal of Experimental Child Psychology*, *56*(2), 201–239. https://doi.org/10.1006/jecp.1993.1032
Lombardi, C. M., Fachinelli, C. C., & Delius, J. D. (1984). Oddity of visual patterns conceptualized by pigeons. *Animal Learning & Behavior*, *12*(1), 2–6. https://doi.org/10.3758/BF03199807
Luciano, C., Becerra, I. G., & Valverde, M. R. (2007). The role of multiple-exemplar training and naming in establishing derived equivalence in an infant. *Journal of the Experimental Analysis of Behavior*, *87*(3), 349–365. https://doi.org/10.1901/jeab.2007.08-06
Mandler, J. M. (2000). Perceptual and conceptual processes in infancy. *Journal of Cognition and Development*, *1*(1), 3–36. https://doi.org/10.1207/S15327647JCD0101N_2
Markman, E. M. (1989). *Categorization and naming in children: Problems of induction*. MIT Press.
McComb, K., Packer, C., & Pusey, A. (1994). Roaring and numerical assessment in contests between groups of female lions, Panthera leo. *Animal Behaviour*, *47*(2), 379–387. https://doi.org/10.1006/anbe.1994.1052
Meck, W. H., & Church, R. M. (1983). A mode control model of counting and timing processes. *Journal of Experimental Psychology: Animal Behavior Processes*, *9*(3), 320–334. https://doi.org/10.1037/0097-7403.9.3.320
Medin, D. L., & Schaffer, M. M. (1978). Context theory of classification learning. *Psychological Review*, *85*(3), 207–238. https://doi.org/10.1037/0033-295X.85.3.207
Miall, R. C. (2022). Basal ganglia: Basic principles. In D. W. Pfaff, N. D. Volkow, & J. L. Rubenstein (Eds.), *Neuroscience in the 21st century*. Springer. https://doi.org/10.1007/978-3-030-88832-9_37
Miller, N. E., & Dollard, J. (1941). *Social learning and imitation*. Yale University Press.
Myers, C. E., Shohamy, D., Gluck, M. A., Grossman, S., Kluger, A., Ferris, S., Golomb, J., Schnirman, G., & Schwartz, R. (2003). Dissociating hippocampal versus basal ganglia contributions to learning and transfer. *Journal of Cognitive Neuroscience*, *15*(2), 185–193. https://doi.org/10.1162/089892903321208123
Neumann, P. G. (1974). Effects of directional and neutral category labels in bidimensional rule-learning problems. *Memory & Cognition*, *2*(4), 695–699. https://doi.org/10.3758/BF03198142

Nieder, A., Freedman, D. J., & Miller, E. K. (2002). Representation of the quantity of visual items in the primate prefrontal cortex. *Science, 297*(5587), 1708–1711. https://doi.org/10.1126/science.1072493

Oden, D. L., Thompson, R. K. R., & Premack, D. (1988). Spontaneous transfer of matching by infant chimpanzees (*Pan troglodytes*). *Journal of Experimental Psychology: Animal Behavior Processes, 14*(2), 140–145. https://doi.org/10.1037/0097-7403.14.2.140

Oden, D. L., Thompson, R. K. R., & Premack, D. (1990). Infant chimpanzees spontaneously perceive both concrete and abstract same/different relations. *Child Development, 61*(3), 621–631. https://doi.org/10.2307/1130949

Pan, X., Sawa, K., Tsuda, I., Tsukada, M., & Sakagami, M. (2008). Reward prediction based on stimulus categorization in primate lateral prefrontal cortex. *Nature Neuroscience, 11*(6), 703–712. https://doi.org/10.1038/nn.2128

Parr, L. A., Dove, T., & Hopkins, W. D. (1998). Why faces may be special: Evidence of the inversion effect in chimpanzees. *Journal of Cognitive Neuroscience, 10*(5), 615–622. https://doi.org/10.1162/089892998563013

Pavlov, I. P. (1927). *Conditioned reflexes: An investigation of the physiological activity of the cerebral cortex.* Oxford University Press.

Pearce, J. M. (2008). *Animal learning & cognition: An introduction* (3rd ed.). Psychology Press. https://doi.org/10.4324/9781315782911

Pepperberg, I. M. (1987). Acquisition of the same/different concept by an African grey parrot (*Psittacus erithacus*): Learning with respect to categories of color, shape, and material. *Animal Learning & Behavior, 15*(4), 423–432. https://doi.org/10.3758/BF03205051

Pepperberg, I. M. (2012). Further evidence for addition and numerical competence by a grey parrot (*Psittacus erithacus*). *Animal Cognition, 15*(4), 711–717. https://doi.org/10.1007/s10071-012-0470-5

Platt, J. R., & Johnson, D. M. (1971). Localization of position within a homogeneous behavior chain: Effects of error contingencies. *Learning and Motivation, 2*(4), 386–414. https://doi.org/10.1016/0023-9690(71)90020-8

Poldrack, R. A., Clark, J., Paré-Blagoev, E. J., Shohamy, D., Creso Moyano, J., Myers, C., & Gluck, M. A. (2001). Interactive memory systems in the human brain. *Nature, 414*(6863), 546–550. https //doi.org/10.1038/35107080

Poole, J., & Lander, D. G. (1971). The pigeon's concept of pigeon. *Psychonomic Science, 25*(3), 157–158.

Premack, D. (1990). Words: What are they, and do animals have them? *Cognition, 37*(3), 197–212. https://doi.org/10.1016/0010-0277(90)90045-L

Prichard, A., Panoz-Brown, D., Bruce, K., & Galizio, M. (2015). Emergent identity but not symmetry following successive olfactory discrimination training in rats. *Journal of the Experimental Analysis of Behavior, 104*(2), 133–145. https://doi.org/10.1002/jeab.169

Quine, W. V. (1969). Natural kinds. In N. Rescher (Ed.), *Essays in honor of Carl G. Hempel.* Synthese Library, Vol. 24. Springer. https://doi.org/10.1007/978-94-017-1466-2_2

Reed, S. K. (1972). Pattern recognition and categorization. *Cognitive Psychology, 3*(3), 382–407. https://doi.org/10.1016/0010-0285(72)90014-X

Rescorla, R. A., & Wagner, A. R. (1972). A theory of Pavlovian conditioning: Variations in the effectiveness of reinforcement and nonreinforcement. In A. H. Black & W. F. Prokasy (Eds.), *Classical conditioning II: Current research and theory* (pp. 64–99). Appleton Century Crofts.

Rohrer, D. (2012). Interleaving helps students distinguish among similar concepts. *Educational Psychology Review, 24*(3), 355–367. https://doi.org/10.1007/s10648-012-9201-3

Rosch, E. H. (1973). Natural categories. *Cognitive Psychology, 4*(3), 328–350. https://doi.org/10.1016/0010-0285(73)90017-0

Rumbaugh, D. M., Washburn, D. A., Capaldi, E. J., & Boysen, S. T. (1993). Counting by chimpanzees and ordinality judgments by macaques in video-formatted tasks. In *The Development of Numerical Competence* (1st ed., pp. 87–106). Psychology Press. https://doi.org/10.4324/9781315807393-5

Sands, S. F., Lincoln, C. E., & Wright, A. A. (1982). Pictorial similarity judgments and the organization of visual memory in the rhesus monkey. *Journal of Experimental Psychology. General, 111*(4), 369–389. https://doi.org/10.1037/0096-3445.111.4.369

Scarf, D., Hayne, H., & Colombo, M. (2011). Pigeons on par with primates in numerical competence. *Science, 334*(6063), 1664–1664. https://doi.org/10.1126/science.1213357

Schusterman, R. J., & Kastak, D. (1993). A California sea lion (*Zalophus californianus*) is capable of forming equivalence relations. *Psychological Record*, *43*(4), 823–839. https://doi.org/10.1007/bf03395915
Seger, C. A., & Miller, E. K. (2010). Category learning in the brain. *Annual Review of Neuroscience*, *33*(1), 203–219. https://doi.org/10.1146/annurev.neuro.051508.135546
Shettleworth, S. J. (2010). *Cognition, evolution, and behavior* (2nd ed.). Oxford University Press.
Shohamy, D., Myers, C. E., Kalanithi, J., & Gluck, M. A. (2008). Basal ganglia and dopamine contributions to probabilistic category learning. *Neuroscience and Biobehavioral Reviews*, *32*(2), 219–236. https://doi.org/10.1016/j.neubiorev.2007.07.008
Shohamy, D., & Wagner, A. D. (2008). Integrating memories in the human brain: Hippocampal-midbrain encoding of overlapping events. *Neuron*, *60*(2), 378–389. https://doi.org/10.1016/j.neuron.2008.09.023
Sidman, M. (1971). Reading and auditory-visual equivalences. *Journal of Speech and Hearing Research*, *14*(1), 5–13. https://doi.org/0.1044/jshr.1401.05
Sidman, M., & Tailby, W. (1982). Conditional discrimination vs. matching to sample: An expansion of the testing paradigm. *Journal of the Experimental Analysis of Behavior*, *37*(1), 5–22. https://doi.org/10.1901/jeab.1982.37-5
Skinner, B. F. (1953). *Science and human behavior*. MacMillan.
Smith, J. D. (2014). Prototypes, exemplars, and the natural history of categorization. *Psychonomic Bulletin & Review*, *21*(2), 312–331. https://doi.org/10.3758/s13423-013-0506-0
Smith, J. D., Chapman, W. P., & Redford, J. S. (2010). Stages of category learning in monkeys (*Macaca mulatta*) and humans (*Homo sapiens*). *Journal of Experimental Psychology: Animal Behavior Processes*, *36*(1), 39–53. https://doi.org/10.1037/a0016573
Smith, J. D., & Minda, J. P. (2002). Distinguishing prototype-based and exemplar-based processes in dot-pattern category learning. *Journal of Experimental Psychology. Learning, Memory, and Cognition*, *28*(4), 800–811. https://doi.org/10.1037/0278-7393.28.4.800
Smith, J. D., Redford, J. S., & Haas, S. M. (2008). Prototype abstraction by monkeys (*Macaca mulatta*). *Journal of Experimental Psychology: General*, *137*(2), 390–401. https://doi.org/10.1037/0096-3445.137.2.390
Smith, J., Zakrzewski, A., Johnson, J., Valleau, J., & Church, B. (2016). Categorization: The view from animal cognition. *Behavioral Sciences*, *6*(2), 12. https://doi.org/10.3390/bs6020012
Spence, K. W. (1937). The differential response in animals to stimuli varying within a single dimension. *Psychological Review*, *44*(5), 430–444. https://doi.org/10.1037/h0062885
Thomas, D. R. (1993). A model for adaptation-level effects on stimulus generalization. *Psychological Review*, *100*(4), 658–673. https://doi.org/10.1037/0033-295X.100.4.658
Thomas, D. R., Mood, K., Morrison, S., & Wiertelak, E. (1991). Peak Shift Revisited: A Test of Alternative Interpretations. *Journal of Experimental Psychology: Animal Behavior Processes*, *17*(2), 130–140. https://doi.org/10.1037/0097-7403.17.2.130
Thompson, R. K. R., & Oden, D. L. (2000). Categorical perception and conceptual judgments by nonhuman primates: The paleological monkey and the analogical ape. *Cognitive Science*, *24*(3), 363–396. https://doi.org/10.1207/s15516709cog2403_2
Thompson, R. K. R., Oden, D. L., & Boysen, S. T. (1997). Language-naive chimpanzees (*Pan troglodytes*) judge relations between relations in a conceptual matching-to-sample task. *Journal of Experimental Psychology: Animal Behavior Processes*, *23*(1), 31–43. https://doi.org/10.1037/0097-7403.23.1.31
Urcuioli, P. J. (2008). Associative symmetry, antisymmetry, and a theory of pigeons' equivalence-class formation. *Journal of the Experimental Analysis of Behavior*, *90*(3), 257–282. https://doi.org/10.1901/jeab.2008.90-257
Urcuioli, P. J., & DeMarse, T. (1994). On the relationship between differential outcomes and differential sample responding in matching-to-sample. *Journal of Experimental Psychology: Animal Behavior Processes*, *20*(3), 249–263. https://doi.org/10.1037/0097-7403.20.3.249
Urcuioli, P. J., & Swisher, M. (2012). Emergent identity matching after successive matching training. II: Reflexivity or transitivity? *Journal of the Experimental Analysis of Behavior*, *97*(1), 5–27. https://doi.org/10.1901/jeab.2012.97-5
Urcuioli, P. J., Zentall, T. R., Jackson-Smith, P., & Steirn, J. N. (1989). Evidence for common coding in many-to-one matching: Retention, intertrial interference, and transfer. *Journal of Experimental Psychology: Animal Behavior Processes*, *15*(3), 264–273. https://doi.org/10.1037/0097-7403.15.3.264

Vaughan, W., & Greene, S. L. (1984). Pigeon visual memory capacity. *Journal of Experimental Psychology: Animal Behavior Processes, 10*(2), 256–271. https://doi.org/10.1037/0097-7403.10.2.256

Velasco, S. M., Huziwara, E. M., Machado, A., & Tomanari, G. Y. (2010). Associative symmetry by pigeons after few-exemplar training. *Journal of the Experimental Analysis of Behavior, 94*(3), 283–295. https://doi.org/10.1901/jeab.2010.94-283

Wallis, J. D., Anderson, K. C., & Miller, E. K. (2001). Single neurons in prefrontal cortex encode abstract rules. *Nature, 411*(6840), 953–956. https://doi.org/10.1038/35082081

Warrington, E. K. (1975). The selective impairment of semantic memory. *Quarterly journal of experimental psychology, 27*(4), 635–657.

Wasserman, E. A. (2016). Conceptualization in pigeons: The evolution of a paradigm. *Behavioural Processes, 123*, 4–14. https://doi.org/10.1016/j.beproc.2015.09.010

Wasserman, E. A., Bhatt, R. S. (1992). Conceptualization of natural and artificial stimuli by pigeons. In W. K. Honig & J. G. Fetterman (Eds.), *Cognitive aspects of stimulus control* (pp. 203–223). Erlbaum.

Wasserman, E. A., Brooks, D. I., & McMurray, B. (2015). Pigeons acquire multiple categories in parallel via associative learning: A parallel to human word learning? *Cognition, 136*, 99–122. https://doi.org/10.1016/j.cognition.2014.11.020

Wasserman, E. A., Kiedinger, R. E., Bhatt, R. S., (1988). Conceptual behavior in pigeons: Categories, subcategories, and pseudocategories. *Journal of Experimental Psychology, 14*, 235–246.

Wasserman, E. A., Young, M. E., & Fagot, J. (2001). Effects of number of items on the baboon's discrimination of same from different visual displays. *Animal Cognition, 4*(3), 163–170. https://doi.org/10.1007/s100710100095

Watanabe, S. (2001). Van Gogh, Chagall and pigeons: Picture discrimination in pigeons and humans. *Animal Cognition, 4*(3), 147–151. https://doi.org/10.1007/s100710100112

Watanabe, S. (2010). Pigeons can discriminate "good" and "bad" paintings by children. *Animal Cognition, 13*, 75–85. https://doi.org/10.1007/s10071-009-0246-8

Whalen, J., Gallistel, C. R., & Gelman, R. (1999). Nonverbal counting in humans: The psychophysics of number representation. *Psychological Science, 10*(2), 130–137. https://doi.org/10.1111/1467-9280.00120

Wright, A. A., & Katz, J. S. (2006). Mechanisms of same/different concept learning in primates and avians. *Behavioural Processes, 72*(3), 234–254. https://doi.org/10.1016/j.beproc.2006.03.009

Wright, A. A., Magnotti, J. F., Katz, J. S., Leonard, K., & Kelly, D. M. (2016). Concept learning set-size functions for Clark's nutcrackers. *Journal of the Experimental Analysis of Behavior, 105*, 76–84. https://doi.org/10.1002/jeab.174.

Wright, A. A., Magnotti, J. F., Katz, J. S., Leonard, K., Vernouillet, A., & Kelly, D. M. (2017). Corvids outperform pigeons and primates in learning a basic concept. *Psychological Science, 28*, 437–444.

Wynn, K. (1992). Addition and subtraction by human infants. *Nature, 358*(6389), 749–750. https://doi.org/10.1038/358749a0

Yamamoto, J., & Asano, T. (1995). Stimulus equivalence in a chimpanzee (*Pan troglodytes*). *Psychological Record, 45*(1), 3–21.

Yoshikubo, S. (1985). Species discrimination and concept formation by rhesus monkeys (*Macaca mulatta*). *Primates, 26*(3), 285–299. https://doi.org/10.1007/BF02382403

Young, M. E., & Wasserman, E. A. (1997). Entropy detection by pigeons: Response to mixed visual displays after same-different discrimination training. *Journal of Experimental Psychology: Animal Behavior Processes, 23*(2), 157–170. https://doi.org/10.1037/0097-7403.23.2.157

Young, M. E., & Wasserman, E. A. (2002). Detecting variety: What's so special about uniformity? *Journal of Experimental Psychology. General, 131*(1), 131–143. https://doi.org/10.1037/0096-3445.131.1.131

Zentall, T. R., & Hogan, D. E. (1975). Concept learning in the pigeon: Transfer to new matching and nonmatching stimuli. *American Journal of Psychology, 88*(2), 233–244. https://doi.org/10.2307/1421593

Zentall, T. R., Wasserman, E. A., & Urcuioli, P. J. (2014). Associative concept learning in animals. *Journal of the Experimental Analysis of Behavior, 101*(1), 130–151. https://doi.org/10.1002/jeab.55

Zhang, Y., Pan, X., & Wang, Y. (2022). Category learning in a recurrent neural network with reinforcement learning. *Frontiers in Psychiatry, 13*, 1008011. https://doi.org/10.3389/fpsyt.2022.1008011

11 Communication and language

11.1 Animal signals

Contemporary research in animal learning and cognition has examined the informational value of signals (e.g., visual, auditory, olfactory, etc.) in the context of social interactions. This research has led to a much greater appreciation for how organisms communicate as well as a better understanding of the basic processes underlying language. Many instances of animal signals seem to originate in relatively stereotypical behaviors or even morphological traits (e.g., antlers) and convey information to a recipient.

Many examples arise in the context of predator–prey interactions. Some butterflies display what appears to be a pair of eyes when they open their wings; this visual signal may deter potential predators from approaching the butterfly. Other insects look like sticks in a plant—a camouflage that makes them less detectable by predators. Red salamanders, *Pseudotriton ruber*, are edible, but by evolving an external appearance similar to that of venomous newts, *Taricha torosa*, they benefit from the experience of predators that had an aversive encounter with the newts and therefore tend to avoid attacking potential preys with that appearance.

Experiments with scrub jays, *Aphelocoma californica*, show that they are more hesitant to attack edible salamanders with the external appearance of toxic newts than salamanders with different visual appearance (Kuchta et al., 2008). This is called *Batesian mimicry*. In other cases, equally toxic species tend to evolve similar external appearance, which presumably potentiates learning to avoid them by predators. For example, several species of toxic, cyanide-generating millipedes have evolved similar visual appearance although they are not closely related (Marek & Bond, 2009). The convergence of these signals potentiates their avoidance by predators and circumvents the evolutionary cost of evolving a novel appearance. This is called *Müllerian mimicry*.

These are well-validated studies of the effects of natural selection on the evolution of traits that have a direct effect on survival. In a way, the animal bearing the trait (*sender*) conveys a *message* that influences the behavior of another animal (*receiver*). The process of communication illustrated by these examples of mimicry reveal its components clearly, but there is little room for learning to play a significant role. Yet there are many instances in which the system involving sender, message, and receiver becomes assembled during ontogeny as a result of individual experience. These learning-dependent examples of communication are the focus of Chapter 11. We start with vocal learning in birds.

11.2 Avian vocal learning

Birds have evolved developmental programs that produce *vocal behavior* of various levels of complexity and beauty that have attracted human interest for centuries. The canary, *Serinus*

DOI: 10.4324/9781003401957-14

canaria, originally from the Azores, Madeira, and Canary Islands in the Atlantic, was domesticated in the 17th century because of the beauty of its song and plumage. Songbirds like the canary attracted scientific interest because their beautiful songs were also complex and exhibit some interesting features during development. Other birds were known by enthusiast bird-watchers to have large song repertoires, and still others were observed to imitate the songs of other species. The first attempts at describing the development of songs revealed a number of surprising features that captured scientific attention.

Thorpe (1961) was among the first to record bird songs in natural habitats using a sound spectrograph, an instrument that provided a visual representation of the temporal and spectral properties of the song. He focused on the songs of chaffinches (*Fringilla coelebs*). *Sonograms* show the components of a song, the range of frequencies modulated during singing, and the temporal structure of the song (Figure 11.1).

Thorpe also used the *isolation experiment* to study the development of avian songs. Chaffinch chicks were brought from their nests to the laboratory, where they were hand-reared

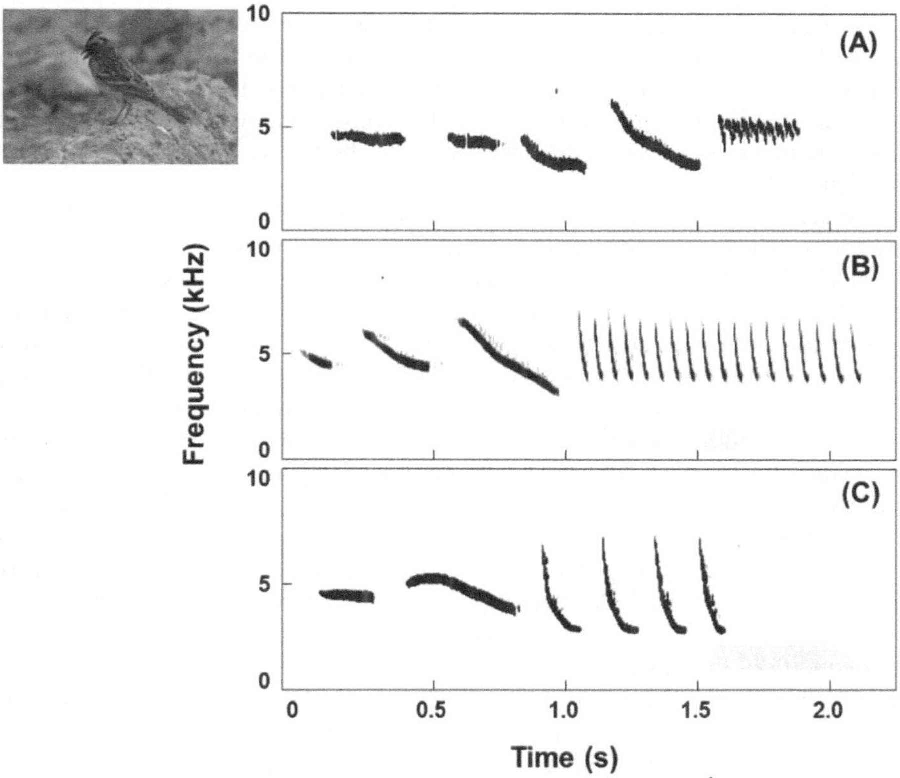

Figure 11.1 **Song sonograms of the rufous-collared sparrow (*Zonotrichia capensis*).** The initial part of the song includes two to four relatively long elements in these samples and is called the theme. The ending portion of the song includes a variable number of fast notes and is called the trill. These sonograms were recorded in different regions of Argentina: **(A)** and **(C)** were recorded in forested habitats, southwest of the Pampas region, whereas **(B)** comes from a male living in the highland grasslands of Cordoba, in central Argentina. Differences in trill structure reflect geographic variations in the song, called dialects (sonograms courtesy of Pablo Tubaro; photo from Creative Commons https://search.creativecommons.org, by Arthur Chapman, license CC BY-NC 2.0).

in acoustic isolation. That research led to the discovery of extensive species differences in developmental profiles that highlighted the complex interactions between ecological factors, genetics, early experience, and social influences. The calls and songs produced by birds function in several contexts, including parent–offspring interactions, reproductive activities, and flocking behavior. Vocalizations allow birds to communicate information about aversive internal states, food availability, predatory danger, territoriality, and reproductive readiness, among others. Depending on the species, a song can identify the species, the region of origin (dialect), or the particular individual singing.

11.2.1 Calls

Calls are vocalizations considered simple, stereotypical, largely independent of vocal experience for their development, and usually produced by both males and females during the entire year. Calls tend to be unimpaired by deafening after hatching, suggesting that they develop normally even in the absence of auditory feedback (Konishi, 1963). However, research also shows that the context in which some of these calls occur depends on experience. For example, chickens emit ***alarm calls*** advertising the presence of a predator in the vicinity, but the frequency of these alarm calls depends on the type of audience. Male chickens (*Gallus gallus*) emitted more alarm calls when surrounded by conspecifics than by bobwhite quail (*Colinus virginianus*), whether the conspecifics were mates, other females, or chicks. The frequency of calls was also very low when the animals were alone in the test arena (Karakashian et al., 1988).

In some *precocial species*, different calls are elicited by different food items. For example, the *food calls* of chickens (*Gallus gallus*) convey information about the quality of the food (Marler et al., 1986). A hen's food call attracts her chicks to food sources, and a cock's food call attracts hens to his vicinity, increasing courtship opportunities. In the laboratory, high-quality food calls can be released by providing a mealworm, whereas the low-quality calls can be induced by providing regular laboratory food. The two calls involve the same note, but the note is repeated at a higher frequency in the high-quality call.

In some species, food calls can control behavior even before they are associated with high- or low-quality food items. Calls are therefore said to be ***prefunctionally organized*** (Moffatt & Hogan, 1992). In one experiment, two groups of Burmese red junglefowl chicks (*Gallus gallus spadiceus*) received instrumental training in a runway, where they were exposed to two kinds of trials in a random order. In one group, running when the high-quality food call (signal) was being played back through a speaker was reinforced with a mealworm (reward), whereas running when the low-quality food call was being presented was nonreinforced.

In this condition, the signal matched the quality of the reward, and chicks rapidly learned to run faster in the presence of the high-quality food call. In the reverse condition, the low-quality food call was the signal for a mealworm reward, whereas the high-quality call was paired with nonreinforcement. The speed of running was initially higher for the high-quality call than for the low-quality call, but as training progressed, chicks ran faster in the presence of the low-quality call signaling a mealworm. While chicks tend to respond faster to the high-quality food call, this tendency can be reversed by experience.

Maternal calls are also attractive to chicks of several precocial species soon after hatching. These vocalizations are referred to as *assembly calls* because the young birds respond by approaching the source of acoustic stimulation. Experiments with Peking ducks (*Anas platyrhynchos*) have uncovered the importance of auditory embryonic experience in the development of such preference (Gottlieb, 1981). To exhibit preference for the distinctive maternal call, duckling embryos must be exposed to their own vocalizations and those of their brood mates during prehatching development in the nest. The calls emitted by one embryo can be heard by that embryo inside the egg as well as by other embryos in adjacent eggs.

The importance of these sources of experience was demonstrated by a combination of devocalization, deafening, and individual incubation. When embryonic acoustic experience is prevented, ducklings respond to the maternal calls of several species. Interestingly, the embryonic calls that are so important in this process bear little overall resemblance to the assembly call emitted by the hen, containing only isolated features in common (e.g., the range of frequencies, or notes per second, is similar). Moreover, this experience must occur before hatching to be effective, suggesting the presence of a *sensitive period* (Gottlieb, 1985).

Calls can be simple and stereotypical, but they are quite malleable. Calls can control behavior acting as discriminative stimuli and require prehatching experience to develop their species-typical form.

11.2.2 Vocal learning

Vocal learning is demonstrated when the adult vocalization requires auditory experience for normal development. Such demonstrations require convergent evidence from a variety of procedures, including devocalization, deafening, and rearing in isolation. Vocal learning has been observed in three avian orders: parrots and budgerigars (Order Psittaciformes), hummingbirds (Order Trochiliformes), and songbirds (Order Passeriformes). This phylogenetic distribution suggests that the mechanisms underlying vocal learning in birds have evolved independently more than once.

Little is known about the contribution of learning to the development of vocal behavior in budgerigars and hummingbirds. Experiments in which nestling budgerigars (*Melopsittacus undulatus*) are deafened a few days after hatching indicate that auditory feedback is important in the development of complex food-begging calls (Heaton & Brauth, 1999) and contact calls (Dooling et al., 1987). For example, deaf budgerigars emit significantly longer and less variable food-begging calls than those of control animals. The deleterious effects of posthatching deafening in budgerigars are analogous to the effects of deafening in songbirds discussed in what follows, and they contrast with the invulnerability of stereotypical calls to similar manipulations noted previously. Various aspects of contact calls of budgerigars can be modified by instrumental training with food reinforcement, including the intensity, accuracy, and response latency, although learned calls were not observed outside of the conditioning chamber (Manabe et al., 2008).

The vocalizations of songbirds are called songs. The difference between a call and a song is somewhat arbitrary. *Songs* are melodious vocalizations usually (but not always) produced by males in the context of reproductive behavior (e.g., songs advertise the occupation of a territory by a male and attract females).

There are two major taxonomic groups of songbirds: the oscines (e.g., mockingbirds, sparrows, finches, etc.) and suboscines (e.g., manakins, woodcreepers, ovenbirds, etc.). Vocal learning has been extensively studied in oscine species. Based on molecular phylogenetic analyses, suboscine species are thought to be relatively more basal (Sibley & Ahlquist, 1990). Their vocalizations are less sensitive to sensory restrictions, implying that learning plays a minor role in song production (Kroodsma, 1984). These groups were established on the basis of anatomical differences in the syrinx (avian vocal organ) and middle ear ossicles (important for sensory detection). In these traits, suboscines exhibit less complexity than oscines.

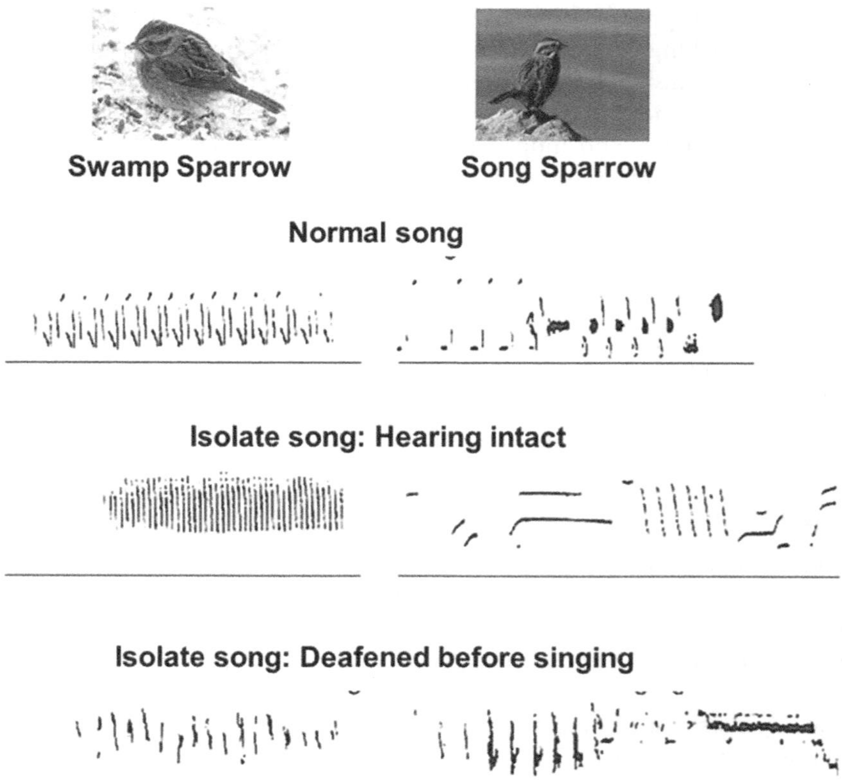

Figure 11.2 **Isolation experiment.** Effects of early isolation on song development in sparrows (Marler & Sherman, 1983; reproduced with permission from the *Society for Neuroscience*). Social isolation (lack of an opportunity to hear a model singing) and deafening (lack of an opportunity to hear their own singing) drastically affect the final song of both swamp and song sparrows. However, the song of isolate song sparrows preserves a considerable degree of internal structure and elicits social behavior from conspecifics, suggesting that these two species differ in the processes underlying song development. (Photos from Creative Commons https://search.creativecommons.org; *M. georgiana* by erryoldenettel, license CC BY-NC-SA 2.0; *M. melodia* by Mathesont, license CC BY-NC 2.0.)

Auditory feedback is vital to song development, but its importance varies across species. Deafening impaired song structure in white-crown sparrows (*Zonotrichia leucophrys*) but had minor effects in juncos (*Junco* sp.; Konishi, 1964, 1965). Similarly, in most species, early social isolation leads to abnormal vocalizations in adults, but there is a range of developmental effects. As shown in Figure 11.2, acoustic isolation eliminates most features of the song in swamp sparrows (*Melospiza georgiana*), but song sparrows (*M. melodia*) retain a considerable amount of structure in the song (Marler & Sherman, 1983). Moreover, the songs of song sparrows reared in acoustic isolation elicit some amount of behavior from conspecifics, certainly much more than the song of deaf animals (although less than the song of normally reared animals). Thus, in some cases, the communicative function of song is partially spared.

11.2.3 Age-dependent plasticity

Age-dependent plasticity occurs in species that acquire the song during early development. The bird will produce the final song for the rest of its life. The best-studied species in this

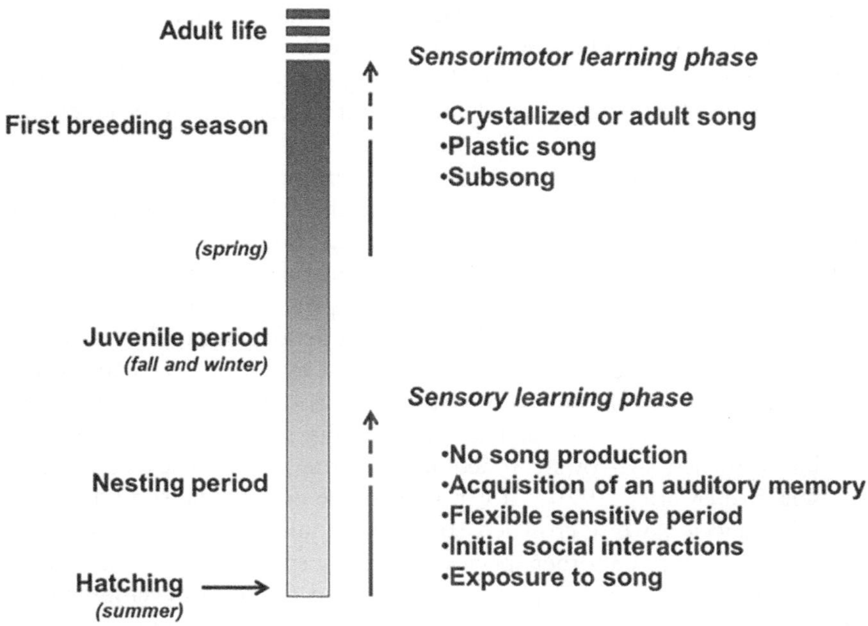

Figure 11.3 **Development of vocal behavior.** The early development of vocal behavior in species exhibiting age-dependent plasticity. In the sensory learning phase, nestlings learn the father's song by mere exposure but do not produce a song. In the following spring, juveniles start singing and pass through a series of periods known as subsong, plastic song, and crystallized song (the sensorimotor learning phase). (Modified from Papini, 2021; reproduced with permission from Taylor & Francis.)

group is the white-crowned sparrow (*Zonotrichia leucophrys*), but other species in which the adult song also depends on exposure to a singing adult model exhibit a similar developmental profile (Figure 11.3).

Age-dependent song learning passes through two phases. Song acquisition occurs in an initial *sensory learning phase* during which the young bird does not vocalize. As in imprinting and latent learning, acquisition occurs by exposure to the model, and it can be accomplished in the laboratory if the real model is replaced by a tape recorder that plays back the song to the nestling (Marler, 1970). Such experiments show that adults sing normally only if exposed to the songs during a sensitive period ranging between 10 and 50 days after hatching but not if exposed to the songs before 10 days of age or after 50 days of age. Interestingly, the type of experience determines the temporal boundaries of the sensitive period. For example, white-crowned sparrows exposed to live tutors acquire the normal song beyond 50 days of age (Baptista & Petrinovich, 1984). In zebra finches (*Taeniopygia guttata*), the sensitive period spans from 25 to 65 days after hatching, but in the absence of auditory input, birds can acquire a template beyond 65 days of age (Gobes et al., 2019).

The white-crowned sparrow starts emitting vocalizations in its first spring, during the *sensorimotor learning phase*. The song undergoes a series of changes that have been described in terms of three successive transitions in development (Marler, 1991):

- **Subsong.** Initially, the song lacks general structure. The subsong period establishes the basic motor skills involved in singing and the ability to modulate sound based on auditory feedback.

- **Plastic song.** Eventual production of syllables usually sung in rapid succession. Some syllables are discarded, while others become part of the final repertoire.
- **Crystallized song.** The song the animal will sing for the rest of its life is stable in the number of syllables, frequency range, duration, and rhythm of song production.

Several factors determine the transition from subsong to crystallized song in the white-crowned sparrow. Deafening before or during the subsong period leads to an abnormal adult song, suggesting that sensorimotor learning involves a process of matching the current song to a *template*—memory of the song learned during the sensory learning phase (Konishi, 1965). Final matching of the song to the template requires hormonal contribution. Castrated males exhibit both subsong and plastic song periods but do not develop a crystallized song unless testosterone, the hormone eliminated by castration, is administered. This crystallized song remains viable so long as testosterone is kept above a certain level.

Age-dependent plasticity in vocal learning exhibits some additional properties. For example, white-crowned sparrows can acquire the song played back by a tape, but this learning is selective (Marler, 1970). If exposed to the conspecific song as well as to the song of another species, white-crowned sparrows acquire only the conspecific song. If exposed only to the song of another species (e.g., song sparrow), the final song resembles that of neither species. Whereas experience is required for song development, the effective input has precise limits. In some species, imitation of an *allospecific song* is possible if exposed to a live tutor. For example, white-crowned sparrows acquire the song of a song sparrow provided exposure is extensive and social interactions are possible (Baptista & Petrinovich, 1984).

11.2.4 Dialects

Vocal learning creates the conditions for the evolution of song *dialects*—regional differences in the song among populations of the same species. Like human dialects, avian dialects are cultural traits transmitted by social learning (Marler & Tamura, 1964). Two species that exhibit song dialects are the rufous-collared sparrow (*Zonotrichia capensis*) from Argentina (Figure 11.1; Kopuchian et al., 2004) and the white-crown sparrow (*Z. leucophrys*) from the western United States (Figure 11.4; Marler, 1970). In both species, the song can be divided into two components: theme and trill. The theme, the initial part, is composed of one to a few notes. The trill, the ending part, usually involves a rapid succession of short notes. The sonograms in Figure 11.4 show greater consistency in trill structure within each area than across areas.

In the rufous-collared sparrow, dialects are defined by the rate of trill notes. In the Argentinean Pampas, a vast herbaceous steppe, trills vary little, with intervals separating successive notes averaging about 60 ms (Nottebohm, 1969). Dialect transitions occur over short distances when the habitat changes abruptly. For example, rufous-collared sparrows inhabiting a 1-km-wide stripe of woodland parallel to the De La Plata River and adjacent to the steppe display a slower trill, with intervals averaging 80 ms in some locations (Tubaro et al., 1993). Similar transitions occur in adjacent habitats that differ in altitude.

Marler's (1970) isolation and play-back experiments demonstrated that white-crowned sparrows learn the dialect they hear during the sensitive period. Therefore, dialects are maintained by early social learning. There appears to be no selectivity to learn dialect variations in this species. Because the song is a major component of courtship behavior, dialects would encourage mating among individuals from the same area. Such selective mating also requires that females, which do not sing, prefer males that sing the dialect that females heard as nestlings.

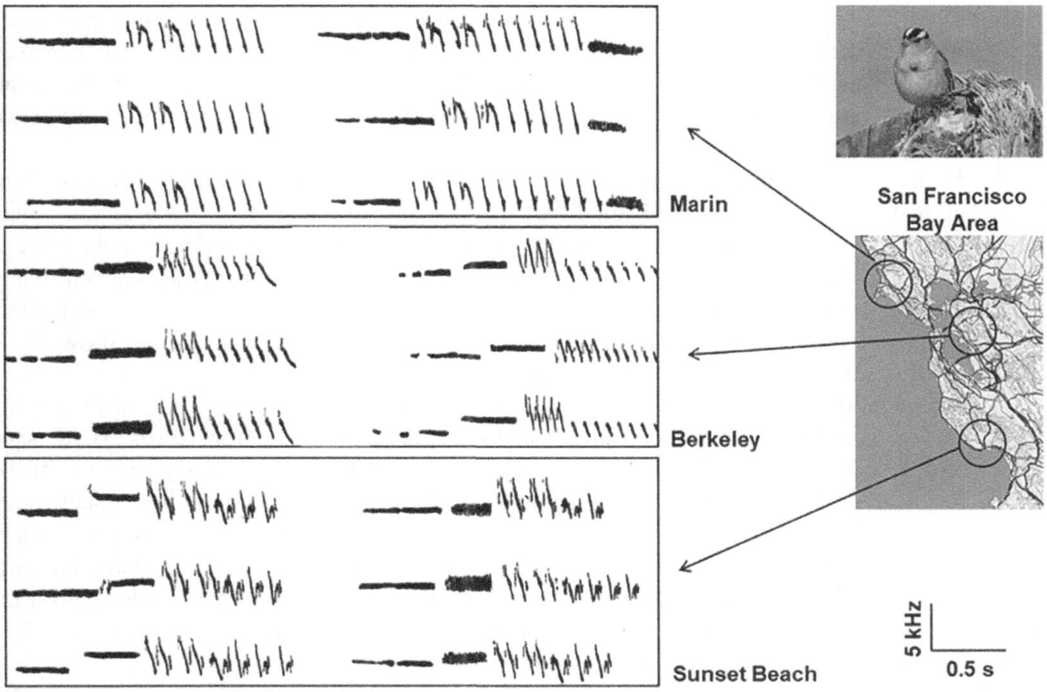

Figure 11.4 **Dialects.** Dialects of white-crowned sparrows from different areas near San Francisco Bay, California (Marler, 1970; reproduced with permission from the American Psychological Association). Notice that there is more consistency within than across areas. (Photo from Creative Commons https://search.creativecommons.org; *Zonotrichia leucophrys* by Upupa4me, license CC BY-SA 2.0.)

Several populations of white-crowned sparrows in the western United States were studied in terms of the response of females to dialect playbacks from different populations and their genetic distance. Evidence showed that some features of the dialect, including the length of the song's first note, were reliable predictors of the genetic distance between individuals (Lipshutz et al., 2016). Similarly, female white-crown sparrows showed preference for males from the same dialectal area (Danner et al., 2011). Female choice based on preference for the home dialect is a sexual selection mechanism that can potentially yield speciation based on a cultural trait.

Dialects are open to learning errors that could promote random changes in song structure across generations, a process called ***cultural mutation***. However, cultural mutation does not seem to be a major factor in the stability of songs. In swamp sparrows (*Melospiza georgiana*), for example, the rate of cultural mutation (the probability that a new song will be generated during development) has been estimated to be on the order of 2% (Lachlan et al., 2018). Such a low error rate can lead to cultural traditions in songbirds lasting many generations.

11.2.5 Age-independent plasticity

In species that practice ***brood parasitism*** (laying eggs in the nest of other species) the young bird is not exposed to the conspecific song as a nestling but to the song of a foster parent. Song development in cowbirds (*Molothrus ater*), a brood parasite, is interesting because these animals are raised by a variety of hosts and exposed to different types of early experience. Yet they must recognize conspecifics to engage in reproductive activities. Although learning probably plays a small role in the development of the species-typical song in cowbirds, social learning contributes to the vocal behavior of adult cowbird males and, vice versa, singing also affects social behavior.

Birds taken from their nest at 2 days of age and maintained in social and acoustic isolation until the first breeding season confirmed that naive males produce effective songs and naive females respond with the appropriate copulatory posture to a male's song (West et al., 1981). In fact, social isolation actually improves the efficiency of the song, making males about twice as effective in eliciting the female copulatory posture compared to normally reared males. This is true for both laboratory-reared and wild-caught females. Acoustic analysis shows that the song of isolated males is more potent than that of group-reared males.

To understand the source of this *isolate song effect*, males were raised under four conditions during their first year of life: audio-visual isolation, visual isolation (birds could hear other birds), social isolation (birds could see and hear other birds), and group rearing (birds could see, hear, and interact with other birds). When the songs produced by these males were played back to females, visually isolated males elicited about twice as many female copulatory responses as did the songs of males that could see other cowbirds interacting in an adjacent cage or interact directly with conspecifics. Interestingly, the effectiveness of males reared in isolation and later transferred to a group was reduced, whereas the effectiveness of males reared in a group and later placed in isolation was increased.

The modifiability of the adult cowbird's song is an example of *age-independent plasticity*. Juvenile cowbirds flock together and learn the song from other males during social interactions. Such social interactions adjust the potency of the song and singing frequency. When males reared in isolation are introduced into an established colony, their potent singing elicits aggressive behavior from resident males. By contrast, socially reared males introduced into a colony sing little, at lower intensity, and are rarely attacked by residents. Within a few days after being introduced into the colony, isolated males decrease the frequency of vocal behavior, thus eliciting little aggression.

Resident males can kill introduced isolated males with their aggressive attacks. In one experiment, 9 of 21 isolated males that sang a potent song were killed by resident males. Importantly, whereas isolated males sing in the presence or absence of resident males, socially reared males sing mostly when the resident males are absent. Moreover, isolated males can adjust the potency of their song to a level that elicits few attacks by resident males.

Additional evidence of instrumental modulation comes from experiments in which males from North Carolina are housed with females from Texas, each population with its own dialect (King & West, 1983). Males tended to produce a song that resembled the dialect of the female's area of origin, indicating that adult males can modify their vocal behavior as a function of the female's response. In the natural environment, the songs of juvenile males are shaped during the winter, when they associate closely with females. Females respond to a male singing a particular song by moving their wings, and the same songs that elicit wing movements during the winter also elicit copulatory response during the breeding season (West & King, 1988). The potency and type of male song is thus shaped by a complex combination of appetitive (the female's copulatory responses and wing movements) and aversive factors (aggressive behavior from other males).

In turn, the way males sing affects the social fabric of the group (Maguire et al., 2013). As shown in what follows, a brain area known as *HVC* controls vocal behavior in birds. Female cowbirds with HVC lesions lose selectivity, responding vigorously to playbacks of male songs that are differentially effective when tested in normal females. Females with HVC lesions chatter nonselectively, which tends to attract males, whereas regular females chatter mostly to their pair mate. When these females are released in a social group, their receptive behavior affects the way males and other females interact. Not surprisingly given the instrumental sensitivity of males to female responsiveness, males increase song production directed at females, which had two social consequences: increased competition for females among males and increased chattering in normal females. This further illustrates plasticity for song learning in adult cowbirds.

11.2.6 Brain mechanisms of avian song learning

11.2.6.1 Brain circuit

Female white-crowned sparrows, which do not normally sing, can be induced to sing by the administration of testosterone, which acts on receptors located in neurons distributed over several telencephalic regions. In oscine species, androgen and estrogen receptors are found in brain nuclei that control vocal behavior, implying that these hormones exert control over singing. Some components of the neural circuit underlying vocal behavior are shared across species that exhibit age-dependent plasticity (e.g., zebra finches) or age-independent plasticity (e.g., canaries).

A simplified version of the vocal behavior network of songbirds is presented in Figure 11.5. Afferent information from the inner ear enters the nucleus ovoidalis of the thalamus (Ov) and then into the HVC. Axons from HVC neurons generate two parallel circuits. The first circuit involves connections from the HVC to the robust nucleus of the arcopallium (RA) and then to the motor control of syrinx muscles, mediated by the tracheosyringeal branch of the hypoglossal nerve (cranial nerve XII). The second circuit involves connections from the HVC to Area X, to the medial part of the dorsolateral nucleus of the thalamus (DLM), to the lateral part of the magnocellular nucleus of the anterior nidopallium (LMAN), and to RA, from which the motor output is controlled. Both of these circuits participate in vocal behavior in different ways. The study of this circuit led to some surprising discoveries (Nottebohm & Liu, 2010).

The size of some of these nuclei and the amount of song production are related. In species in which only the male sings, such as zebra finches, the song-control nuclei HVC and RA can be five times larger in males than in females. Sexual dimorphism is not so evident in the canary, a species in which females are known to occasionally sing, and is greatly reduced or even eliminated in songbird species in which both male and female engage in singing behavior. The HVC and RA nuclei of male canaries are larger during the spring, when singing is at its peak, than during the fall, when singing declines.

Several factors contribute to the enlargement of these nuclei, including the number of neurons, their size, and the extent of their dendritic arborizations. Interestingly, this annual cycle of shrinking and enlargement of the canary brain involves *neurogenesis*—the production of new neurons in the area adjacent to the cerebral ventricles that migrate into areas of the vocal circuit. Neurogenesis contributes to size changes in the HVC, but RA volume depends on changes in soma and dendritic arborization size. These changes are controlled by the expression of different genes (Thompson et al., 2012).

Neurogenesis occurs at a high rate in species that acquire new songs throughout their lives (i.e., age-independent plasticity, as in the canary) and during the time of the year when new songs are acquired. The discovery of neurogenesis in the adult canary brain (an earlier report

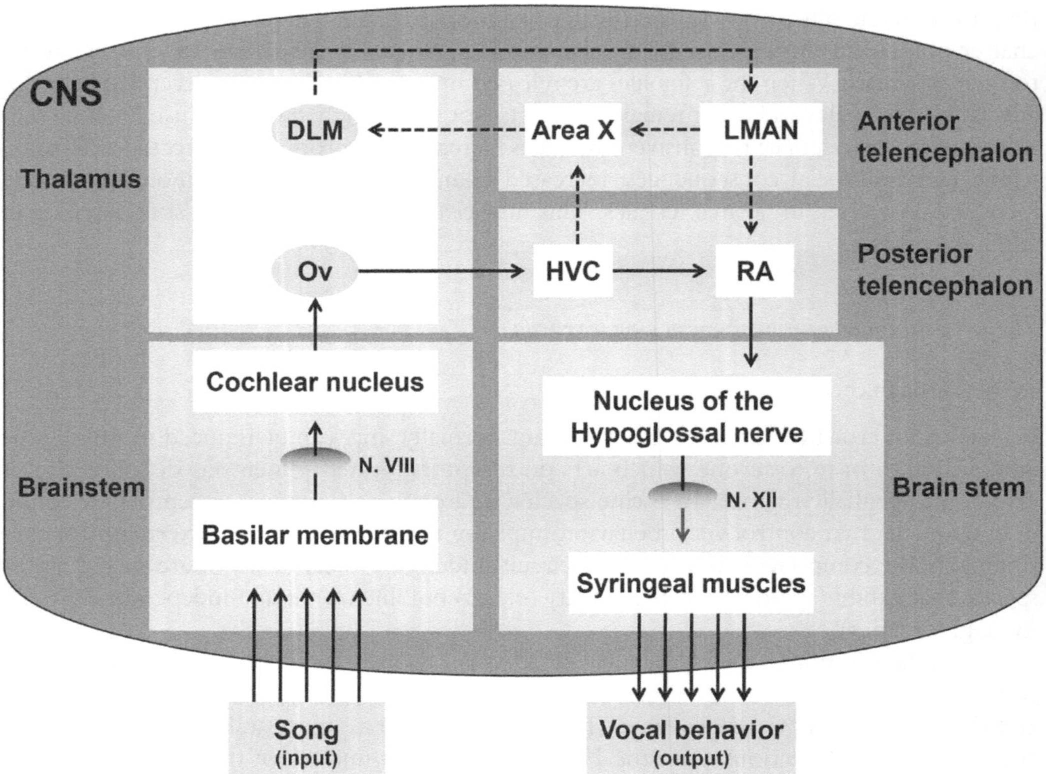

Figure 11.5 **Neurobiology of song learning.** A schematic representation of the brain circuitry underlying vocal learning in songbirds. Notice two processing circuits running in parallel. The circuit in the posterior telencephalon is related to song production (continuous arrows), whereas that of the anterior telencephalon and thalamus is involved in the acquisition process (dashed arrows). The auditory input has some additional details not represented in this figure. Ov projects to the nucleus interfacialis of the nidopallium (NIF), which, in turn, projects to HVC. As for the output, it is the tracheosyringeal portion of the hypoglossal nucleus that projects to the syrinx. DLM: medial part of the dorso-lateral nucleus of the thalamus. LMAN: lateral part of the magnocellular nucleus of the anterior nidopallium. Ov: nucleus ovoidalis of the thalamus. N. VIII: auditory cranial nerve. N. XII: hypoglossal cranial nerve. RA: robust nucleus of the arcopallium. (Modified from Papini, 2021; reproduced with permission from Taylor & Francis.)

in rats had gone unnoticed; Altman, 1962) forced a change in the then-prevailing view that new neurons are not produced in adult brains (Goldman & Nottebohm, 1983). Since then, neurogenesis has been reported in several species and brain areas, including in human brains, but the issue remains contentious (e.g., Lipp & Bonfanti, 2016).

Additional evidence supports the hypothesis that some of the components of the circuit described in Figure 11.5 are critical in the production of vocal behavior. Lesions of the HVC nucleus cause severe deficits in song production. Moreover, neuronal activity in HVC and RA correlates with ongoing singing behavior. In zebra finches, lesions of Area X and LMAN disrupt song learning but do not affect song production when lesions are administered after song crystallization (Bottjer et al., 1984). These results have encouraged the view that the HVC-RA circuit of the posterior telencephalon is relevant to song production, whereas the Area X-LMAN circuit of the anterior telencephalon is important for song acquisition.

11.2.6.2 Patterns of gene expression

Brain areas that become more active when the bird is acquiring a song can also be assessed by measuring the degree of activation of ***transcription factors*** that regulate gene expression. One such gene, *ZENK*, produces a protein that regulates the transcription of other genes and is a marker for synaptic plasticity. In zebra finches, ZENK induction increases during singing in HVC, RA, and Area X. However, when songs are played back to a bird, ZENK induction is elevated in auditory telencephalic areas such as the caudomedial nidopallium, which projects to both HVC and Area X (Jin & Clayton, 1997). ZENK induction in the caudomedial nidopallium is high during the sensitive period for song acquisition, but levels decay in adult animals after song crystallization. In the canary, ZENK induction is also high in the caudomedial nidopallium when males are hearing a new song (Mello et al., 1992).

The induction of ZENK transcription in RA is particularly interesting because of the convergence of inputs to this area from LMAN (involved in song plasticity) and HVC (involved in song production). This convergent neural architecture evokes the coincidence detectors in the amygdala that play a key role in fear conditioning (see Chapter 4). A similar role is suggested by the fact that ZENK levels peak during the plastic song phase, when zebra finches are engaged in singing behavior eventually leading to the crystallization of the adult song. One implication of these findings is that RA functions as the site where associations are established between two different inputs, one (from HVC) involving motor information derived from song production, and the other (from LMAN) carrying information about the match between the auditory feedback from singing and the song template stored in memory from the sensory learning phase (Johnson & Whitney, 2005).

Are vocal learning mechanisms in birds and mammals related in any way? Expression patterns of a gene called ***parvalbumin*** (*PV*) were assessed in vocal learners (budgerigars, hummingbirds, zebra finches, humans) and nonlearners (doves, quail, macaques). Although the brain circuit involves different areas, there are some common features, including a direct connection from the telencephalon to the nuclei controlling vocal production—the nucleus for the XIIth cranial nerve controlling the syrinx in birds and the nucleus ambiguous innervating the larynx in humans, each controlling sound modulation.

These nuclei are also present in species that have limited ability for sound modulation, but direct connections from the telencephalon are minor or absent. PV was reported to be selectively upregulated in vocal learners relative to nonlearners (Hara et al., 2012). PV's functions involve neural protection against excessive excitation and synaptic plasticity, two functions that might explain the repeated recruitment of this gene in lineages that exhibit vocal learning. Thus, the evolution of vocal learning involves homologous cell-molecular mechanisms active in neural circuits that have evolved independently, suggesting a type of parallel evolution already encountered in the realm of conditioning (see Figure 3.20).

11.2.7 From proximate to ultimate causation

Poor nutrition and high stress levels influence the size of brain areas involved in vocal behavior (Nowicki et al., 2002). Early nutrition and adult feeding affect the size of the vocal repertoire of adult songbirds and, by implication, the size of the brain areas involved in vocal plasticity. Poor early nutrition is related to small singing repertoires, reduction in singing behavior, and small brain areas in the vocal circuit. In addition, high stress levels induced by corticosterone administration also reduce the size in these brain areas.

The ***proximate mechanism*** underlying this reduction in singing behavior is related to the link between lipid metabolism and endogenous cannabinoids. Birds exposed to poor

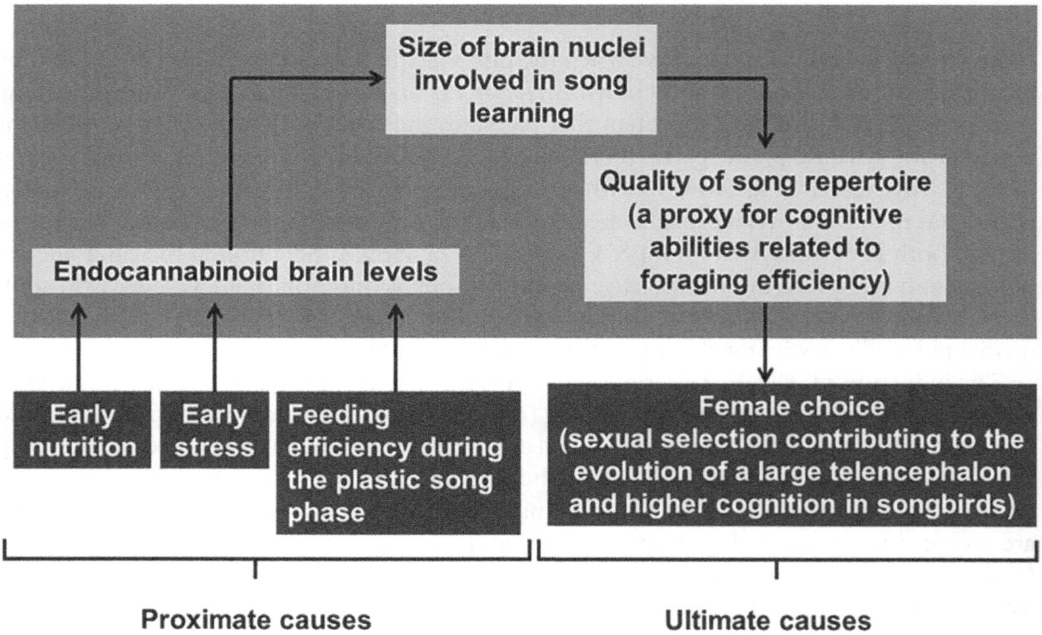

Figure 11.6 **Proximate and ultimate causes.** An integration of proximate and ultimate causes in the analysis of song learning in passerine birds.

nutrition are forced to switch from carbohydrates to lipids as a source of energy, a change that raises telencephalic levels of *cannabinoids*—a family of neurotransmitters related to the processing of pain signals. Brain areas involved in vocal learning expressed high densities of cannabinoid receptors; blocking such receptors in food-restricted birds restores normal levels of singing behavior (Johnson & Whitney, 2005). Therefore, the quality of the vocal repertoire of an adult male is a proxy for its ability to forage for food as well as for its early nestling environment.

Female songbirds of several species have been shown to prefer males with larger song repertoires. In turn, large song repertoires are related to higher reproductive success, longevity, increased parental care, and holding large territories longer than males with smaller song repertoires (Figure 11.6). To the extent that the female's reproductive receptivity is influenced by the male's singing behavior, sexual selection, an *ultimate cause*, based on the male's vocal repertoire may indirectly determine the evolution of brain mechanisms that control the vocal behavior and other cognitive abilities, including those involved in foraging behavior (Peters et al., 2014).

11.3 Referential calls in mammals

The examples of mimicry described in the introduction to this chapter were based on morphological traits, such as external coloration. In other cases, the message is transmitted behaviorally. Belding's ground squirrels (*Spermophilus beldingi*), meerkats (*Suricata suricatta*), Diana monkeys (*Cercopithecus diana*), ringtailed lemurs (*Lemur catta*), and vervet monkeys (*Cercopithecus aethiops*) emit calls with different acoustic properties depending on the type of predator they detected. Such *referential calls*, like human spoken words, have specific meaning. Vervets have distinctive calls for leopards, eagles, and snakes, common predators in the Amboseli National Park of Kenya, where this behavior has been studied using call playbacks (Figure 11.7). Monkeys tended to move up a tree when hearing a playback of a "Leopard Call" but move down a tree when hearing an "Eagle Call." A "Snake Call" induced a looking-down behavior and, if vervets were on the ground, they would adopt a bipedal posture while looking around them (Price et al., 2015).

Behavior is shaped by so many factors that its use to convey messages guarantees greater flexibility than that afforded by morphology. Flexible communication is associated with complex social behavior by animals living in stable social groups and having evolved the capacity for social reinforcement. For example, chimpanzees engage in social interactions when solving problems and, at least in some locations, hunt colobus monkeys in groups. The degree of coordination required for effective ***group hunting*** suggests the presence of complex sets of signals.

Human language differs from these examples of communication in the assembling of series of symbols within specific grammatical constraints. A person sending the same message that a vervet monkey produces with a single alarm call would say something like "There is a snake on your left!" Moreover, human language is less constrained by the situation in which it is used. In addition to alerting a friend about the snake, a similar interaction could occur later, when the two friends remember the episode. Such flexibility appears to be unique to human language. Rather than ask whether nonhuman animals have language, it is more

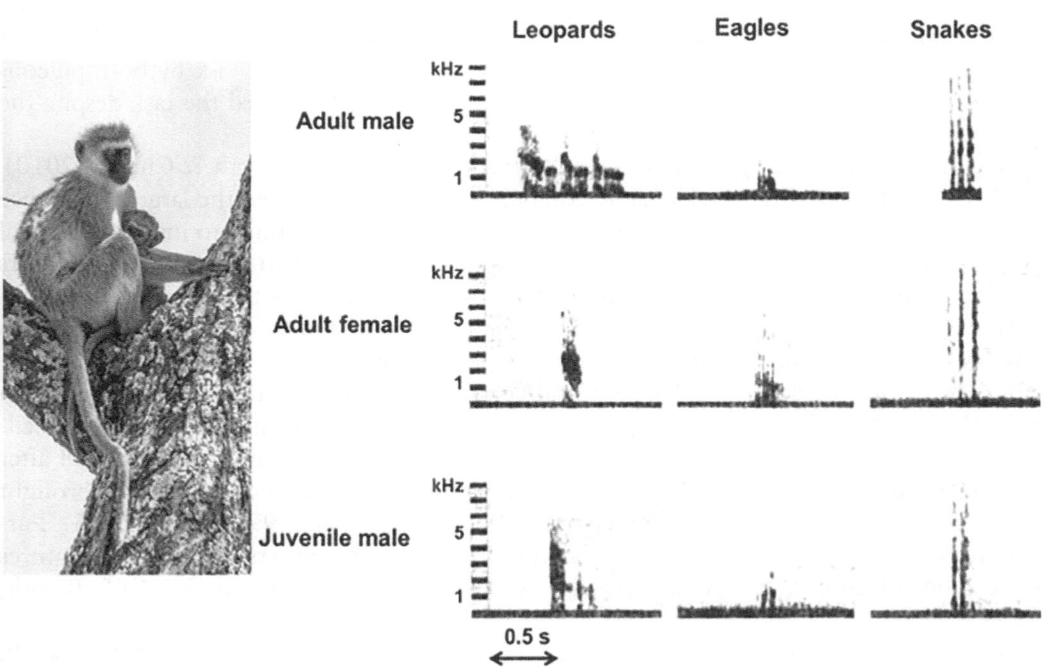

Figure 11.7 **Referential calls.** Calls emitted by vervet monkeys in the presence of different predators (from Seyfarth et al., 1980; reproduced with permission from Elsevier). The behavior of other monkeys is appropriate to the type of predator advertised by the call. (Photo from Creative Commons https://search.creativecommons.org, by richardrichard, license CC BY-ND 2.0.)

productive to ask what abilities are part of language and what is the evidence for these abilities in other animals.

11.4 Human language

11.4.1 Properties

Human language is said to be arbitrary, flexible, displaced, and regular. It is arbitrary, in that, save a few words (onomatopoeia, e.g., "ring" in reference to a phone call), there is no resemblance between the pattern of letters (symbols) that make up a word or the sound of the word and the referent; "rock" looks and sounds no more like a rock than does "paper." Nonhuman animal vocalizations also exhibit this property. The acoustic structure of a bird's song does not correspond to the physical features of the bird (e.g., a higher frequency earlier in a song does not reveal how much blue color is on its wings). The call of a vervet monkey for an aerial predator does not resemble an aerial predator any more than it does a ground predator.

There are other cases of species utilizing symbols as referents. In one example (Epstein et al., 1980), a pigeon looked behind a curtain in an operant box to view the color of an illuminated key light hidden there. After viewing the color, the pigeon had to peck a separate key light with the symbol ("R", "G", or "Y") that corresponded to the color of the light. You may say, but the "R" stands for red, so the symbol is not arbitrary. Of course, the visual features of the letters forming "red" have no innate correspondence to the wavelength of light they represent, and even if they did, the pigeon does not have the required history of equivalence between "R," red, and the color red. Additionally, an observer pigeon, watching the first pigeon peck "R," was required to convert this symbol back to the wavelength of light corresponding to red and peck the red key light. Completion of the task by both pigeons was reinforced with food to both of them. The pigeons readily learned the task despite the arbitrary correspondence between the color and symbol.

Flexibility can refer to production, usage, or comprehension (Seyfarth & Cheney, 2010). If we consider each of these as separate components of language, then the largest difference between humans and other animals is in production. Humans continue to invent individual words and combinations of words to express new ideas and to refer to new objects. As fathers and professors, the authors of this textbook understand that some of the words we are familiar with from our youth no longer signal the same referent, and we frequently hear words uttered that, given our experience in the world, have no referent.

There is some evidence for flexibility and voluntary control of production in nonhuman animals. For example, baboons (*Papio hamadryas ursinus*) may or may not give a reconciliatory grunt after a threat, capuchin monkeys (*Cebus capucinus*) may or may not call after finding food, and in the laboratory, the timing, duration, and rate of calling may be brought under operant control (Cheney & Seyfarth, 1990; Cheney et al., 1995; Pierce, 1985). Furthermore, when wild chimpanzees are hooting in chorus with others, the acoustic features of two individuals calling together several times will become more similar (Mitani & Brandt, 1994).

Evidence of call combination is limited in nonhuman animals (Crockford & Boesch, 2003). Though these examples indicate some degree of flexibility, it is minimal in comparison to that of humans. Evidence for moderate to high degree of flexible production has only been reported in three orders of birds, cetaceans, harbor seals, and humans (Janik & Slater, 1997). More flexibility is found in the usage of acoustic vocalizations in nonhuman animals, but for most animals, specific vocalizations are used in a limited range of contexts.

Animals do not seem constrained in their ability to learn new ways to respond to vocalizations in the wild or in the lab. It was mentioned in Chapter 2 that rats can be trained to discriminate English vowel sounds. Seyfarth and Cheney (2010, p. 95) put it this way: "A tone that informs a rat about the imminence of a shock, an alarm call that informs a vervet about the presence of an eagle, or a scream that informs a baboon that her offspring is involved in a fight all have the potential to provide a listener with precise information." Given the importance of this kind of information for direct and indirect fitness, it is not surprising that most animals show a high degree of flexible comprehension of vocalizations.

Displacement is a property of language that refers to vocalizations that are removed from the referent. As already indicated, animals are largely limited to vocal production when the referent (e.g., a predator) is present or likely to be present, whereas humans are able to speak and write about things far removed from the present. Lastly, human language is regular, in that it is governed by a system of rules, or *syntax*, for how symbols (e.g., vocalizations) can be combined to create meaning. We expand later on the evidence for syntax in nonhuman animals, but suffice to say, it is limited.

Human language exhibits many properties, only some of which are reviewed here. On the one hand, language and nonhuman animal vocalizations are both arbitrary and exhibit a large degree of flexibility in how the listener responds to the signal (comprehension). On the other hand, there is little evidence currently that nonhuman animals can exhibit anywhere near the same degree of flexibility and regularity in the production and use of signals for communication as is the case with human language.

11.4.2 Basic functions

At a social event, a professor in the psychology department expressed dismay that another colleague in the department approached the study of language as a learning phenomenon. The reply to their comment was one of equal dismay: How could you study language without considering it a learning phenomenon? Spoken and written words are both stimuli and responses. If a professor asked the entire class to "raise your hand if you are awake," the sound waves traveling through the air would have the effect of spurring many students to raise their hands and, in doing so, distinguish between those listening or not (or those with the requisite anatomy and prior experience to correctly respond to such a question, if say, an international student is unfamiliar with this phrase in English). The professor could have written the words on a whiteboard to the same effect. Another familiar example to students is a multiple-choice exam question that requires the student to choose the written words in the answer choice that are an appropriate response to the written words in the question.

These examples highlight a functional approach to language. A functional approach to language is less concerned with properties and structure and more focused on how the behavior of speakers is shaped by its effects on listeners and how the behavior of listeners is shaped by its effects on speakers. This approach refers to any behavior involving words, regardless of modality, as *verbal behavior*. Catania (2017, p. 205) wrote, "But our taxonomy must be functional, not structural. A grammatical classification of words in a sentence doesn't tell us how it was produced or what consequences it had for the one who produced it." Skinner (1953) remarked that asking for salt in French with proper grammatical structure will get you an "A" in a French class and the salt in France. The verbal community in which the behavior occurs is crucial to predicting its form, probability, and effects.

We have all participated in verbal behavior of various lengths, with strangers and family, at home and on vacation, in kindness and in anger; in every case, the verbal behavior of the speaker had some effect on the listener, and most likely, the roles of speaker and listener were reversed one or more times. Verbal behavior is maintained by our verbal communities. Even the verbal behavior of asking for the salt in France would be met with some response by the listener. Ideally, the salt was passed, but perhaps instead, the listener responded with "The salt is there"; if the latter, then the original speaker has become the listener and may respond with "Thank you," followed by another reversal to listener of "You are welcome." The verbal behavior "Thank you" is both a response to the speaker and a stimulus for the speaker-turned-listener to respond.

Imagine that your request to pass the salt was met with silence. Would you ask again? How many times would you ask before you conclude that your verbal behavior is powerless to move the listener. Like other forms of learned behavior, verbal behavior need not be reinforced by the listener every time, but verbal behavior in the context of a specific listener may extinguish over time. The listener of the salt request may shape future interactions by responding with, "Only if you say please first," which highlights the role of the verbal community in shaping and maintaining verbal behavior.

11.4.3 Verbal operants

Verbal behavior refers to any behavior involving words, whether they are spoken or heard, written, or read. The correspondence between *classes* of words that are seen or heard (as stimuli) and those classes of words spoken or written (as responses), reflect how verbal stimuli and verbal responses in different modalities (a word spoken or written) produce similar effects in the verbal community. In other words, they are *verbal operants*. Verbal behavior depends on consistent, reinforced correspondences that allow people to move between modalities while maintaining correspondence (e.g., from a vocal lecture to written notes). Though gestures (i.e., in sign language) and textures (i.e., in Braille) can qualify as verbal, only four correspondences between spoken and written classes are covered here: echoic, transcription, textual, and dictation-taking. Each correspondence identifies a controlling variable, an antecedent (i.e., the circumstances leading to verbal behavior), for an instance of verbal behavior (e.g., seeing the word "fish" increases the probability that a speaker will say "fish"). Different forms of verbal operants are identified by reference to their controlling conditions.

An *echoic* refers to correspondence between verbal behavior heard and spoken, such that the probability of saying a particular word is controlled by whether the word was just heard. The unit of an echoic ranges from single *phonemes* to sentences. Phonemes are the smallest units of functional sound in a language. Examples include exchanges between a mother and an infant (e.g., say "da-da"), when an actor repeats lines spoken by a prompter, or when repeating the name of a new acquaintance (Catania, 2017).

Importantly, variation in the acoustic features of the response is expected, but the verbal units (e.g., phonemes) prompted by the spoken phonemes must have functional value within a larger verbal community. This disqualifies a parrot that simply matches the acoustic properties of what it heard. Parrots are just as likely to reproduce other nonverbal sounds they have recently heard, and they do so in the presence and absence of an observer. *Partial echoics* are those that include only a portion of what was heard in the speaker, as in: "You say, *life is like chocolates*, but do you really believe it?" This reinforces the friend's storytelling and may in turn be quickly reinforced by the other person's verbal behavior ("Yes, I do!").

Transcription is the correspondence between an antecedent written word and a response of the same written word. However, the response does not have to be written using the same medium; it can be typed or entered on a smartphone by dragging your finger from one letter to the next. What is critical is that the verbal properties are recreated and the

Table 11.1 Correspondences between spoken and written classes

		Response	
		Spoken	**Written**
Stimulus	**Spoken**	Echoic	Dictation
	Written	Textual	Transcription

Note. Correspondence is critical for establishing and maintaining verbal behavior. Each correspondence contains both an antecedent and a consequence, both of which should have similar effects on the verbal community. That is, the word "fire" should have similar effects on the listener whether it is read or written. In the case of the written word, it may occasion the spoken word and vice versa.

written word is the controlling variable. For example, if you needed access to a digital copy of notes that you previously printed, but the file has since been corrupted, then you could retype the notes directly from the printed copy. You might type so quickly that you did not read the notes so much as simply recreate the movements required to produce the words—this is pure transcription. If you had read or understood what you typed, then forms of verbal behavior other than transcription would have been involved. Echoic behavior will ordinally develop in children without instruction, but transcription must be taught (Catania, 2017).

Textual behavior is the correspondence between a written word and a spoken word. These correspondences are so familiar, it is worth taking a moment to appreciate how strange they are. As we discussed, words are arbitrary. How a word looks gives no indication as to how it should sound (at least in English) or its functional value in a verbal community (i.e., what response it will likely have in a listener). For example, there is no innate relationship between the visual properties of the letter "R" and the sound we produce when we see it. Consequently, textual behavior must be taught.

Reading involves textual behavior and more, but instances of pure textual behavior (i.e., without understanding) appear like reading. For example, when very sleepy parents speak the words written in a bedtime story to their children, they often do so with no understanding of what is being read. The vocal response to written words diminishes with age and experience, but textual behavior persists in the absence of vocal sounds. Consequently, a very sleepy person silently reading a book in bed is also engaged in a form of textual behavior.

Lastly, *dictation-taking* refers to the correspondence between a spoken stimulus and a written one. The classic example is taking notes during a lecture. The written response can include letters, words, or sentences and may take the form of shorthand, script, and typing. The controlling variable is the lecture being listened to, the response is notetaking, and the behavior is maintained by a verbal community.

These are only a few verbal operants, neatly constrained by the classes of spoken or written verbal behavior with a one-to-one correspondence between verbal units (Table 11.1).

11.4.3.1 Intraverbals, mands, and tacts

The four verbal operants reviewed earlier are identified by a strict correspondence between the verbal units constituting the controlling variable and those constituting the verbal response. For example, if students hear a professor say "Know the four correspondences for the exam," they might dictate in their notes the exact same sequence of words. The probability of writing that sequence was controlled by exposure to hearing the words emitted by the professor. However, in everyday discourse, correspondences are rarely one-to-one.

In many cases, the probability of verbal behavior is determined by how frequently two words occur in proximity to one another. If so, this is an *intraverbal* operant. For example, when it was mentioned that a "rock" looks and sounds no more like a rock than does "paper," did you think "scissors?" Doing so is an example of an intraverbal, the result of the fact that these three words are vocalized in proximity prior to competing in the rock-paper-scissors hand game popular in school hallways and classrooms. This *intraverbal chain* is maintained by the response of the listener continuing to play the game. The chain will become an *intraverbal chunk* with extended practice, such that the individual verbal units ("rock") no longer function independently.

Intraverbals are frequently taught in educational settings, for example, when mastering multiplication tables (e.g., 5 × 5 = ?). Intraverbals also describe what is referred to as *semantic priming* in the literature on memory and cognition. For example, after seeing a grand piano at a concert, I might be more likely to vocalize "piano" rather than "keyboard" when asked what the word is for a digital instrument with a series of levers that can produce the sounds of various instruments when touched. Intraverbal responding is in some ways more impressive than other forms—a speaker who can present on a complex topic, and do so while interweaving relevant historical comparisons, jokes, and connected information, is likely to be viewed more positively than one who is reading the text directly from a notecard or from the presentation slides (as in textual behavior).

Another correspondence, a *tact*, is the first to illustrate contact with actual environmental events, rather than other verbal behavior. A tact occurs when the probability of verbal behavior is controlled by the presence of an object in the environment, such as saying the word "piano" in the presence of a piano. This correspondence is maintained by the verbal community and can be thought of as an individual learning that people respond positively to saying "piano" in the presence of a piano. Tacting is similar to naming, but tacting can only occur in the presence or very recent presence of the tacted stimulus (Catania, 2017).

This form of behavior is not limited to humans, as it is simply an extension to verbal behavior of the stimulus control already described for many nonhuman animals. In fact, the experiment in which Epstein et al. (1980) taught pigeons to peck a key corresponding to the color of the key light recently viewed qualifies as the pigeon tacting red, green, and yellow. In a toddler, tact training might go like this: A toddler is playing with blocks with a caregiver and picks up a red cube; he then says, "Blue!" To which a caregiver may offer light admonishment and tact the color: "No, that's red." Often, this will be followed by a question: "Can you say red?" The toddler thus prompted may well then say, "Red!" To which the caregiver is likely to respond with social reinforcers—smiling, cheering, clapping, and hugging. On a subsequent occasion, with a different red object, the toddler may be more likely to say the word "red." A similar process occurs when a laboratory instructor brings college students into contact with new stimuli, such as during the dissection of an animal; a biology student gestures to an organ and says the word "liver," to which—if the organ is indeed the liver—the instructor may say: "Correct!"

Tacts can refer to specific or general features of the environment, with general features corresponding more to the superordinate level of categorization discussed in Chapter 10, like saying "sports" in the presence of a web page advertising equipment for golf, soccer, and baseball. A tact can also reveal factors inside the speaker. This property is illustrated by the phrase, "one person's trash is another person's treasure." The same object in the environment increases the probability of different verbal responses (e.g., saying "trash" or "treasure") depending on the person. An individual can also tact the relation between events, such as "same," "different," "above," "below," "long," or "short."

There are many opportunities for tacts to be extended to encompass novel circumstances. Novel metaphors are examples of extended tacts in which some common and often abstracted property of two objects, events, or people are identified. If one were to say that a child is as lively as a supernova, then they identify a common property of the child and an exploding star, namely that they are both high energy.

Verbal behavior may also be controlled by a state of deprivation or aversive stimulation. In other words, speaking the word "food" becomes more likely when one is hungry. A ***mand***, short for "command" and "demand," is verbal behavior that specifies its own reinforcer. Simply put, "words are ways to get people to do things" (Catania, 2017, p. 221), and a mand is an effective means to get people to assist with access to a specific reinforcer. When we are given what is asked for, the verbal behavior of the speaker is reinforced by the listener. If no students raise their hand when asked to by the professor, then the professor may begin speaking more softly or cease speaking altogether. Asking for food is an ***object-mand***, whereas asking students to raise their hand is an ***action-mand***.

Mands are ubiquitous, and the consequences are vast and varied. Verbal behavior is as subject to the antecedent and prevailing conditions as any other behavior. One may ask for steak in one context (e.g., a restaurant), for a copy of a quarterly report in another (e.g., an executive office), and for someone to turn the volume down on loud music in still another (e.g., at home). In most cases, the verbal response is reinforced by the appropriate, specified outcome. However, in some cases, humans mand when no reinforcer could possibly be forthcoming. Watching a horror movie, we might shout at an imperiled character to run out the front door rather than up the stairs. A child holding a tea party for stuffed animals might ask one of them to pass the sugar. These forms of mands, in which the verbal response cannot possibly have a consequence, may be interpreted as a form of generalization (see Chapter 2) from other verbal episodes with persons that have reinforced similar mands.

Instances of verbal behavior are not usually neatly categorized as a pure example of any one of the aforementioned verbal operants but instead reflect multiple causation in which numerous factors combine. In natural speech, it is sometimes difficult to know the class to which any particular response belongs. For example, did the child say "milk" because she saw the carton on the breakfast table (i.e., tacted the milk), or was she requesting a glass of milk (i.e., manding), or did she say it because someone else just said it (i.e., echoic)? A careful analysis demonstrates the validity of the various verbal operants, but it might not necessarily say much regarding their relative importance in any given verbal instance. Overall, the evidence supports the efficacy of utilizing this kind of analysis to develop interventions to improve the verbal behavior of children with developmental disabilities (Fuller & Kaiser, 2020; Lovaas, 1987).

11.5 Teaching language to nonhuman animals

11.5.1 Brief history

Scholars have entertained the possibility of teaching language to nonhuman animals for centuries. Julien De La Mettrie [1709–1751] speculated that properly educated chimpanzees might be able to learn to speak. He based this idea on the similarity in the brains of chimpanzees and humans and suggested that gestures could be used as a medium for communication (Fouts & Rigby, 1980). Robert M. Yerkes [1876–1956] attempted, with limited success, to teach chimpanzees and orangutans to speak during the 1910s. An orangutan was reported capable of producing a few recognizable words, including "cup" and "Papa." Impressed by the rich repertoire of gestures exhibited by apes, Yerkes (1916) suggested that perhaps chimpanzees could be taught to use their fingers to communicate, much as do hearing-impaired people, as had been suggested by La Mettrie on purely theoretical grounds.

Two additional projects following similar approaches provided some additional evidence of the speech limitations of chimpanzees (Fouts & Rigby, 1980). Luella and Winthrop Kellogg housed a chimpanzee named Gua in their home for about a year in 1931–32, where he was raised together with their son. Gua understood spoken words and followed commands but never spoke. Keith and Cathy Hayes also raised a chimpanzee called Viki in their home during the 1940s. Vicky produced only a few words.

These early efforts suggested that the anatomy of the vocal tract makes it difficult for apes to modulate sound as required by speech. Whereas spoken language has been ruled out for apes, new generations of comparative psychologists developed novel approaches to the study of language acquisition in nonhuman animals. One premise of modern studies is the hypothesis that the linguistic skills of apes can be studied independently of sound modulation.

11.5.2 Language production

11.5.2.1 Hand gestures

Several procedures were developed to teach linguistic skills to chimpanzees (*Pan troglodytes*), bonobos (*Pan paniscus*), gorillas (*Gorilla gorilla*), orangutans (*Pongo pygmaeus*), dolphins (*Tursiops truncatus*), sea lions (*Zalophus californianus*), and Alex, the African gray parrot (*Psittacus erithacus*) already mentioned. Communication was mediated by the English language, gestures, plastic tokens, or computer-controlled symbols manipulated from a specially designed keyboard. In some studies, the emphasis has been on *language production*, that is, the creation of syntactically appropriate strings of symbols (whether words or arbitrary geometric symbols called lexigrams). Research on *language comprehension* (described in the following section) concerns the extent to which animals can follow commands presented in a symbolic manner, whether with spoken words, gestures, or lexigrams (Corballis, 2017).

Following Yerkes (1916), language production based on hand gestures was studied in two chimpanzees, Washoe (Gardner & Gardner, 1969) and Nim (Terrace, 1979); a gorilla named Koko (Patterson, 1990); and an orangutan named Chantek (Miles, 1990). These animals acquired a repertoire of signs that referred to objects (e.g., apple, ball) and actions (e.g., tickle, give). Sequential structure is important because it suggests the presence of *syntax*, a major feature of human language. In English, for example, sentences in which adjectives precede nouns are syntactically correct ("Beautiful day"), but the opposite sequence is incorrect ("Day beautiful"). Syntactic rules vary across languages, but all languages contain sequential constraints. In addition, word order has meaning. For example, "Romulus killed Remus" and "Remus killed Romulus" have the same words but opposite meaning. Signing apes reportedly exhibited some consistency in their sequential use of gestures, suggesting that they had acquired the rudiments of language.

Terrace et al. (1979) suggested that apes trained to use hand gestures were not using language but simply performing actions to obtain rewards, much like animals do in instrumental conditioning tasks. Their argument was based on data they collected from their own chimpanzee, Nim, which had received strict instrumental training, and on a reanalysis of videotape evidence from Washoe's training sessions, which were less structured and often involved no food reinforcement for correct actions. Many of the signs produced by these chimpanzees matched similar signs produced by their trainers shortly before, a fact suggesting imitation.

Chimpanzees often produced long strings involving a pointless repetition of signs. For example, an answer to a question such as, "Do you want to eat an apple?" could take the form, "Apple eat eat apple eat apple hurry apple hurry hurry."

Alternative interpretations for a number of striking examples of apparent linguistic proficiency were also available. For example, Washoe was reported to articulate the signs for "water" and "bird" upon seeing a duck swimming on a lake. Lacking a sign for "duck," this was originally interpreted as evidence of creativity—a property of language that allows us to combine known words to refer to new objects (e.g., "flying saucer"). Rather, Washoe could have been simply signing two familiar objects, water and a bird. No creativity needed to be assumed. A reanalysis of sign use by other chimpanzees from 1992 to 1999 produced results that supported those of Terrace, revealing mostly requests for objects and actions, a large degree of experimenter imitation, repetition in longer combinations, and little evidence of syntax (Rivas, 2005).

The Nim project led to controversy (Pepperberg, 2017) but also to an improvement in the testing conditions for animals trained to communicate with hand gestures (American Sign Language). Four additional chimpanzees received training in the same style used with Washoe, that is, in close contact with human trainers and in a context of two-way communication, but at an earlier age. These chimpanzees were tested under controlled conditions for their ability to sign specific objects (e.g., shoes, trees, cars) and under observation by two experimenters who could not see each other. Their task was to interpret the sign made by the chimpanzee. The interobserver agreement ranged between 70% and 95%, suggesting that these five chimpanzees produced signs that carried the appropriate meaning (Gardner & Gardner, 1984).

In another study (Jensvold & Gardner, 2000), a human interlocutor waited for one of four chimpanzees trained in American Sign Language to make a request and then the interlocutor made a sign. The question of interest was to determine whether the chimpanzees would respond in a way appropriate to the interlocutor's request. For example, Washoe signed for "give me" and the interlocutor questioned the expression; then Washoe specified signing the equivalent for "give me food." Another chimpanzee, Moja, signed for "flower" and the interlocutor asked "what?" to which Moja signed "flower" again. Examples like these suggest that the responses to the interlocutor's request were appropriate.

11.5.2.2 Symbols

Premack's (1976) alternative method was based on plastic tokens that his chimpanzees could manipulate and place on a magnetic board. This procedure had two advantages over the sign language method. First, a sentence of tokens could be easily recorded and analyzed objectively. Second, since the tokens were under the animal's continuous view, sentence formation placed a light burden on short-term memory.

Using this token procedure, chimpanzees were trained in progressively more complex tasks. With a repertoire of about 130 tokens, the vocabulary of a chimpanzee named Sarah allowed for the design of a variety of problems including naming, interrogation, and object classification. Chimpanzees were trained to comprehend commands involving two-, three-, and four-word sentences. For example, when shown a piece of apple, they were required to place the tokens for "Give apple" in the board; subsequently, the chimpanzee had to correctly choose the token corresponding to its name from two different names and place it at the end of the string ("Give apple Sarah"); and finally, a token corresponding to a trainer's name was added so as to form a request of the form "Debbie give apple Sarah." Test performance was above 90% correct when sentences involved two words. However, correct responses dropped below 75% correct immediately after a shift to four-word strings. Errors included choosing the wrong token and placing the tokens in an incorrect sequence (e.g., "Give Debbie apple Sarah"). With sufficient training, performance in four-word sentences exhibited some improvement but, curiously, the chimpanzees refused to continue with the training.

A somewhat more elaborate procedure involved *lexigrams*—arbitrary geometric patterns symbolizing objects and actions. Lexigrams were presented as keys in a keyboard; chimpanzees were trained to press the keys to form strings that could be roughly translated into English phrases such as "Please machine give piece of apple." In one study combining language comprehension and production, chimpanzees Sherman and Austin were first trained to share food (e.g., apple) and instruments (e.g., wrench) and subsequently exposed to situations that required their cooperation to obtain a particular reward. For example, one chimpanzee learned to request a tool from the other to obtain food by using the correct tool and food lexigrams. Once obtained, the food was shared (Savage-Rumbaugh et al., 1978).

Notice that the procedure used by Premack (1976) aimed mainly at the resolution of problems based on tokens, but symbols were not used for communication, thus lacking an important feature of language. It is not surprising that the performance of these chimpanzees, impressive as it is, can still be understood in nonlinguistic terms. Sign-language training procedures had communicative properties, but their results were difficult to evaluate and the possibility of experimenter cueing difficult to eliminate.

The lexigram procedure, which had none of these drawbacks, has also been applied to dogs with some success (Rossi & Ades, 2008). A dog named Sofia received training from an early age to use symbols displayed in a keyboard to request objects. Initially, the lexigrams were placed closed to the object they represented, but eventually, the distance was increased until the lexigrams appeared only as part of a keyboard. Sofia was required to paw a particular symbol when requesting specific objects. Sofia showed some evidence of categorization by using a given symbol to request access to a variety of related objects (e.g., toys). Sofia did not use the keyboard when alone but only when in the presence of humans, a fact suggesting a communicative function of the lexigrams.

11.5.3 Language comprehension

The lexigram procedure used with Sherman and Austin was applied to other apes. In one such project with bonobos, there was an unexpected consequence. The first bonobo trained with the lexigram procedure, Matata, was a wild-caught female that showed little progress in learning to use symbols during 4 years of training. Matata's training took place in the presence of her infant, a male named Kanzi, born in 1980 (Kanzi was 44 years old when he died in 2025). Whereas Kanzi was not specifically trained to manipulate lexigrams, he soon showed an ability to use symbols in the appropriate manner (Figure 11.8). Most interestingly, Kanzi demonstrated an understanding of spoken English that parallels that of human infants during the first stages of language acquisition, thus becoming the focus of intensive study (Segerdahl et al., 2005; Savage-Rumbaugh et al., 1993).

Kanzi's training was different from previous projects in that it was informal, spontaneous, and started at an early age. A similar informal setting was used with three young animals, two bonobos and a chimpanzee, all of which showed progress in language comprehension comparable to Kanzi's. Such level of proficiency is considered higher than that achieved by chimpanzees whose training started at a later age. It is possible that early exposure is beneficial

Figure 11.8 **Kanzi.** Kanzi using the lexigram system with researcher Sue Savage-Rumbaugh. (Photo by William H. Calvin; from https://commons.wikimedia.org/w/index.php?curid=49108225.)

because of greater neural plasticity in the developing brain or because of the presence of a sensitive period for learning related to communicative functions.

Kanzi showed the first signs of comprehension of spoken English at about 2 years of age. After Kanzi was separated from his mother (2.5 years old), he began to spontaneously use lexigrams for communication. As with human infants, language comprehension was evident before Kanzi became proficient with the use of lexigrams (i.e., comprehension precedes production). Moreover, comprehension of a particular word usually occurred before the acquisition of the lexigram that corresponded to that word. Kanzi's day consisted of a daily walk through a 50-acre area surrounding the laboratory where different types of foods and objects could be found at predictable locations. Caretakers accompanied Kanzi during these trips and provided informal training by talking, pointing to lexigrams when that was possible, and interacting with others as the opportunities arose. Activities were organized around Kanzi's interests to keep him motivated to interact.

At 8 to 8.5 years of age, Kanzi's performance in a series of language comprehension tests was compared to that of Alia, a human female infant who was then 1.5 to 2 years of age. The trainer who provided the stimulus (a sentence in spoken English) was separated from the subject by a one-way mirror that prevented visual cueing. When the task involved a third participant (e.g., subjects were asked to give an object to a person), this participant was equipped with headphones through which loud music masked the verbal requests, making the participant unaware of what the subject was required to do. Trainers testing Kanzi and Alia were unaware of the results obtained in analogous tests by the other trainer. Approximately 400 blind trials were administered to each subject.

The general procedure consisted of giving the subjects a verbal request and recording whether the subject carried out the requested action correctly or not. Neither Kanzi nor Alia was reinforced for correct responses, although food, toys, and other objects were available in the testing room. The types of sentences and results are shown in Table 11.2. The performance of Kanzi and Alia was generally quite accurate and similar. On this basis, it is tempting to conclude that Kanzi's English comprehension skills were similar to those of a 2-year-old human infant—a remarkable conclusion. Some of Kanzi's correct responses indicate an accurate use of word order within a sentence. For example, Kanzi performed well in contrasting sentences such as "Place object X in object Y" vs. "Place object Y in object X," indicating that he was not responding to the words used in the sentence but to their order. When accuracy differed substantially across subjects (e.g., by 20% or greater), as in four sentence types (2B, 5B, 5C, and 7), Kanzi generally outperformed Alia.

A major difference was in the extent to which Kanzi and Alia engaged in a conversation. For example, in the announcement sentences (type 4), Alia often added some verbal comments during the test. If the sentence was "Alia is going to chase mommy" then Alia responded "chase me, chase me," indicating a degree of communicative engagement that was

Table 11.2 Sentence types and results of language comprehension tests of Kanzi and Alia

Type	*Description* *"example"*	*% Correct (blind trials only)*	
		Kanzi	*Alia*
1A	Put object X in/on transportable object Y "Put the ball on the pine needles"	63	73
1B	Put object X in nontransportable object Y "Put the ice water in the potty"	77	71
2A	Give (or show) object X to animate A "Give the lighter to Rose"	78	84
2B	Give object X and object Y to animate A "Give the peas and the sweet potatoes to Kelly"	37	57
2C	Do action A on animate A "Give Rose a hug"	91	91
2D	Do action A on animate A with object X "Get Rose the snake"	76	61
3	Do action A on object X with object Y "Knife the sweet potato"	82	63
4	Announce information "The surprise is hiding in the dish washer"	67	83
5A	Take object X to location Y "Take the snake outdoors"	78	71
5B	Go to location Y and get object X "Go to the refrigerator and get a banana"	82	45
5C	Go get object X that is in location Y "Go get the carrot that's in the microwave"	77	52
6	Make pretend animate A do action A on recipient Y "Make the doggie bite the snake"	67	56
7	All other sentence types	78	33

Note. Examples and results from Savage-Rumbaugh et al. (1993).

not observed in Kanzi. Would this be a unique property of human language? Whatever the case, these results show that apes can acquire some aspects of language.

11.5.4 Language training in nonprimate species

A degree of language comprehension has also been observed in several nonprimate species. Using a small set of gestures that allowed for a large number of sentences, language comprehension has also been demonstrated with dolphins (Herman et al., 1993). Trained dolphins show understanding of the sequential properties of sentences, performing correctly when asked, for example, "Take the frisbee on your *left* to the hoop on your *right*" and also when asked the complementary sentence "Take the frisbee on your *right* to the hoop on your *left*." Notice that these sentences involve the same words in different order. Similarly, trained dolphins correctly executed actions that resulted from interchanging "frisbee" and "hoop" in the sentence. In some trials, dolphins are reported to rearrange their environment in order to be able to execute a specific request. For example, a dolphin asked to swim through a hoop was observed to lift a hoop that was lying on the bottom of the tank and subsequently swam through it as requested. Analogous performance was reported in California sea lions also trained to respond to instructions based on gestures by performing a variety of actions (Schusterman & Krieger, 1984). In these tests, animals received a fish reward for correct responses.

Dogs (*Canis familiaris*) show impressive learning and cognitive skills, especially in connection to social interactions (Bensky et al., 2013). This is not surprising given the extensive process of artificial selection based upon human–dog interactions during the process of domestication. Dogs show a variety of attention-grabbing responses directed at humans, especially in situations involving unsolvable problems. Dogs also show understanding of human words and the ability to acquire new words by exclusion (Kaminski et al., 2004). For example, a dog that has learned the words for a series of objects would rapidly acquire a novel word for the only novel object among a string of familiar objects. This ability is referred to as *fast mapping*.

Alex, the African grey parrot who had demonstrated the acquisition of abstract concepts, is especially interesting because he provided evidence of both comprehension and production of spoken English (see Figure 10.10). Alex began vocal training at 13 months of age, in 1977, and eventually acquired the English words for a wide variety of colors ("green," "rose," "blue," etc.), shapes ("two-cornered" in reference to a football-shaped object, "three-cornered" for triangle, etc.), materials ("cork," "wood," "rock," etc.), a variety of objects ("key," "cup," "truck," etc.), and labels for abstract categories such as "color," "shape," and "material." Alex's vocabulary reached approximately a hundred words. In one experiment (Pepperberg, 1993), two to seven objects (in different trials) were placed in a tray, and one of four possible questions was asked to Alex. Two of the questions concerned the color attribute of objects: "What color is X?" and "What object is color A?" The other two questions concerned the shape of objects: "What shape is X?" and "What object is shape B?" Precautions were taken to avoid Clever Hans effects. Alex's overall effectiveness was 80% for the color questions and 89% for the shape questions.

Does the seemingly linguistic performance exhibited by these animals reflect the operation of complex yet nonlinguistic cognitive processes? This question sparks substantial controversy. Despite the similarity in training procedures, there are important distinctions in the experimental protocols used in these projects and in the role played by language in the lives of these animals. Savage-Rumbaugh et al. (1993) pointed out some differences, including the relatively rich variety of consequences that linguistic interactions had for Kanzi, unlike the food reward used with dolphins and sea lions. Perhaps even greater cognitive capacities could be revealed if these marine mammals could be trained under conditions more analogous to those used with apes.

In addition, the performance of sea lions in tests involving sentences with anomalous syntax suggests that sentence comprehension can be accounted for in nonlinguistic terms as the acquisition of conditional discriminations (Gisiner & Schusterman, 1992). In this gesture language, signs referring to objects (O) and actions (A) were exclusively combined in O→A sequences. Different responses were required when given O and A signs. For example, the sign for an object (say "bottle") typically induced visual scan of the pool while remaining close to the trainer, but a sign for an action (say "fetch") would require the animal to remain in position, facing the trainer, until the sentence was concluded—signaled by dropping one foot in the water. When given anomalous sentences that contained enough information to induce responses, sea lions tended to remain close to the trainer, showing little evidence of transfer across stimulus conditions. Whether accounts such as this one can be usefully extended to other linguistically trained animals remains controversial.

Glossary

Age-dependent plasticity The type of song learning that occurs in species that acquire the song during early development, during a sensitive period.

Age-independent plasticity Song learning unconstrained by sensitive periods.

Alarm calls Vocalizations that induce antipredator defensive behavior in the recipient.

Allospecific song Imitating the song of another species.

Assembly calls Maternal vocalizations that induce approach behavior in the offspring.

Batesian mimicry Edible species evolve the external appearance of toxic species and benefit from predators avoiding toxic species.

Brood parasitism In several species of birds, females lay eggs in the nests of other species. These eggs are thus incubated by foster parents that also eventually care for the chicks.

Calls Relatively simple vocalizations.

Cannabinoids A class of neurotransmitters involved in the modulation of physical pain.

Classes A group of distinct stimuli that come to be treated similarly, exhibiting generalization within the group and discrimination from other groups, due to shared associations with a common response or common outcome.

Cultural mutations Inaccurate learning, improvisation, and similar selectively neutral factors that lead to the development of new songs in birds.

Dialect Geographical variations in song (birds) or language (humans), maintained by social learning.

Dictation-taking A correspondence between written and spoken classes, such that an increase in the probability of writing a particular word is controlled by whether the word was just heard.

Echoic A correspondence between spoken classes, such that an increase in the probability of saying a particular word is controlled by whether the word was just heard.

Fast mapping The ability to connect a new word with its meaning after a single exposure. Fast mapping is common in children and in some experiments with nonhuman animals (e.g., dogs).

Food calls Vocalizations that convey information about the quality of a food source.

Group hunting Coordinated attack on a prey by a group of predators.

HVC An area of the avian telencephalon involved in vocal learning. Originally an acronym for hyperstriatum ventralis pars caudalis; now simply called HVC after the new nomenclature for the avian brain (https://www.avianbrain.org).

Intraverbal A flexible correspondence, such that an increase in the probability of a particular instance of verbal behavior is controlled by the proximity of verbal behavior recently heard or seen to other verbal behaviors in the individual's personal history.

Intraverbal chain When independent instances of verbal behavior control the probability of the next instance of verbal behavior.

Intraverbal chunk When separate units of verbal behavior are integrated into a single unit of verbal behavior, such that the occurrence of instance results in the occurrence of the entire unit.
Isolate song effect A greater-than-normal efficacy of the song of male cowbirds reared in social isolation.
Isolation experiment A developing organism is reared under conditions that prevent the influence of a certain type of stimulation to determine whether that source of experience is necessary for the emergence of a specific behavior.
Language comprehension Understanding linguistic messages received.
Language production Responding to linguistic messages received.
Lexigrams Arbitrary geometric symbols that refer to objects or actions. Lexigrams are used in language studies.
Mand A correspondence between a deprivation state or aversive state of the individual and verbal behavior, such that the probability of verbal behavior that specifies its own reinforcer is controlled by deprivation or aversion. Object-mand: request for a thing; action-mand: request for an action.
Message In terms of communication, the information moving from sender to receiver.
Müllerian mimicry Unrelated toxic species evolving similar external appearance independently (i e., convergent evolution).
Neurogenesis The production of new neurons.
Partial echoics. Echoics that include only a portion of what was heard.
Parvalbumin (PV) A gene involved in vocal learning.
Phonemes The smallest unit of sound with meaning. With reference to a functional account, it can be defined as the smallest unit of sound with functional value (i.e., it will have an effect on the behavior of the listener).
Precocial species Species that hatch or are born in a relatively mature state of development, including sensory and motor functions.
Prefunctional organization Behavioral patterns that appear in the appropriate context (e.g., feeding) even in the absence of specific experience.
Proximate cause Causes of behavior related to internal processes (motivation, neural activity, physiology), to external stimuli (rewards, stimuli), or to developmental factors (early learning).
Receiver In terms of communication, the organism receiving the message.
Referential calls Vocalizations unique to a specific predator.
Sender In terms of communication, the organism transmitting a message, whether in terms of morphology or behavior.
Sensitive period The classic notion of "critical period" was replaced by sensitive period. It refers to a period during early development when some brain circuits are especially susceptible to experience.
Sensorimotor learning phase A phase in the vocal learning process of birds during which the animal starts emitting vocalizations. The song develops through a series of phases known as subsong, plastic song, and crystallized song.
Sensory learning phase A phase in the vocal learning process of birds during which the chick acquires the species-typical song. No singing occurs in this phase.
Songs Vocal output produced by songbirds.
Sonogram A graphic record of a vocalization.
Syntax Sequential constraints in communication, especially characteristic of language.
Tact A correspondence between an object in the environment and verbal behavior, such that the probability of verbal behavior is controlled by the presence of an object in the environment.
Template Auditory memory of the adult song acquired by the bird during the sensory learning phase, early in its life.
Textual behavior A correspondence between written and spoken classes, such that an increase in the probability of saying a particular word is controlled by whether the word was just seen.
Transcription A correspondence between written classes, such that an increase in the probability of writing a particular word is controlled by whether the word was just seen.
Transcription factors A family of regulatory genes that modulates the transcription of other genes.
Ultimate cause Causes of behavior found in evolutionary history or adaptive function.
Vocal behavior Communication based on the emission of vocalizations.
Vocal learning Vocal behavior dependent on specific acoustic learning.
ZENK A transcription factor. A gene that regulates the expression of other genes involved in synaptic plasticity.

References

Altman, J. (1962). Are new neurons formed in the brains of adult mammals? *Science*, *135*, 1127–1128. https://doi.org/10.1126/science.135.3509.1127

Baptista, L. F., & Petrinovich, L. (1984). Social interaction, sensitive phases, and the song template hypothesis in the white-crowned sparrow. *Animal Behaviour*, *32*, 172–181. https://doi.org/10.1016/S0003-3472(84)80335-8

Bensky, M. K., Gosling, S. D., & Sinn, D. L. (2013). The world from a dog's point of view: A review and synthesis of dog cognition research. *Advances in the Study of Behavior*, *45*, 209–406. https://doi.org/10.1016/B978-0-12-407186-5.00005-7

Bottjer, S. W., Miesner, E. A., & Arnold, A. P. (1984). Forebrain lesions disrupt development but not maintenance of song in passerine birds. *Science*, *224*, 901–903. https://doi.org/10.1126/science.6719123

Catania, A. C. (2017). *The ABCs of behavior analysis*. Sloan Publishing.

Cheney, D. L., & Seyfarth, R. M. (1990). *How monkeys see the world*. University of Chicago Press.

Cheney, D. L., Seyfarth, R. M., & Silk, J. B. (1995). The responses of female baboons to anomalous social interactions: Evidence for causal reasoning? *Journal of Comparative Psychology*, *109*, 134–141.

Corballis, M. C. (2017). The evolution of language. In J. Call (Ed.), *APA handbook of comparative psychology. Vol. 1. Basic concepts, methods, neural substrate, and behavior* (pp. 273–297). American Psychological Association.

Crockford, C., & Boesch, C. (2003). Context-specific calls in wild chimpanzees (*Pan troglodytes verus*): Analysis of barks. *Animal Behaviour*, *66*, 115–125.

Danner, J. E., Danner, R. M., Bonier, F., Martin, P. R., Small, T. W., & Moore, I. T. (2011). Female, but not male, tropical sparrows respond more strongly to the local song dialect: Implications for population divergence. *American Naturalist*, *178*, 53–63. https://doi.org/10.1086/660283

Dooling, R. J., Gephart, B. F., Price, P. H., McHale, C., & Brauth, S. E. (1987). Effects of deafening on the contact call of the budgerigar (*Melopsittacus undulatus*). *Animal Behaviour*, *35*, 1264–1266. https://doi.org/10.1007/BF02350105

Epstein, R., Lanza, R. P., & Skinner, B. F. (1980). Symbolic communication between two pigeons (*Columba livia*). *Science*, *207*(4430), 543–545. https://doi.org/10.1126/science.207.4430.543

Fouts, R. S., & Rigby, R. L. (1980). Man-chimpanzee communication. In T. A. Sebeok & J. Umiker-Sebeok (Eds.), *Speaking of apes. Topics in contemporary semiotics*. Springer. https://doi.org/10.1007/978-1-4613-3012-7_15

Fuller, E. A., & Kaiser, A. P. (2020). The effects of early intervention on social communication outcomes for children with autism spectrum disorder: A meta-analysis. *Journal of Autism and Developmental Disorders*, *50*(5), 1683–1700. https://doi.org/10.1007/s10803-019-03927-z

Gardner, R. A., & Gardner, B. T. (1969). Teaching sign language to a chimpanzee. *Science*, *165*, 664–672. https://doi.org/10.1126/science.165.3894.664

Gardner, R. A., & Gardner, B. T. (1984). A vocabulary test for chimpanzees (*Pan troglodytes*). *Journal of Comparative Psychology*, *98*, 381–404. https://doi.org/10.1037/0735-7036.98.4.381

Gisiner, R., & Schusterman, R. J. (1992). Sequence, syntax, and semantics: Responses of a language-trained sea lion (*Zalophus californianus*) to novel sign combinations. *Journal of Comparative Psychology*, *106*, 78–91. https://doi.org/10.1037/0735-7036.106.1.78

Gobes, S. M. H., Jennings, R. B., & Maeda, R. K. (2019). The sensitive period for auditory-vocal learning in the zebra finch: Consequences of limited-model availability and multiple-tutor paradigms on song imitation. *Behavioural Processes*, *163*, 5–12. https://doi.org/10.1016/j.beproc.2017.07.007

Goldman, S. A., & Nottebohm, F. (1983). Neuronal production, migration, and differentiation in a vocal control nucleus of the adult female canary brain. *Proceedings of the National Academy of Sciences, USA*, *80*, 2390–2394. https://doi.org/10.1073/pnas.80.8.2390

Gottlieb, G. (1981). Roles of early experience in species-specific perceptual development. In R. N. Aslin, J. R. Alberts, & M. R. Petersen (Eds.), *Development of perception* (Vol. 1, pp. 5–44). Academic Press.

Gottlieb, G. (1985). Development of species identification in ducklings: XI. Embryonic critical period for species-typical perception in the hatchling. *Animal Behaviour*, *33*, 225–233. https://doi.org/10.1016/S0003-3472(85)80136#x2013;6

Hara, E., Rivas, M. V., Ward, J. M., Okanoya, K., & Jarvis, E. D. (2012). Convergent differential regulation of parvalbumin in the brains of vocal learners. *PLoS ONE*, *7*, e29457. https://doi.org/10.1371/journal.pone.0029457

Heaton, J. T., & Brauth, S. E. (1999). Effects of deafening on the development of nestling and juvenile vocalizations in budgerigars (*Melopsittacus undulatus*). *Journal of Comparative Psychology, 113*, 314–320. https://doi.org/10.1037/0735-7036.113.3.314

Herman, L. M., Pack, A. A., & Morrel-Samuels, P. (1993). Representational and conceptual skills of dolphins. In H. L. Roitblat, L. M. Herman, & P. E. Nachtigall (Eds.), *Language and communication: Comparative perspectives* (pp. 403–442). Erlbaum.

Janik, V. W., & Slater, P. J. B. (1997). Vocal learning in mammals. *Advances in the Study of Behavior, 26*, 59–99.

Jensvold, M. L. A., & Gardner, R. A. (2000). Interactive use of sign language by cross-fostered chimpanzees (*Pan troglodytes*). *Journal of Comparative Psychology, 114*, 335–346. https://doi.org/10.1037/0735-7036.114.4.335

Jin, H., & Clayton, D. F. (1997). Localized changes in immediate-early gene regulation during sensory and motor learning in zebra finches. *Neuron, 19*, 1049–1059. https://doi.org/10.1016/s0896-6273(00)80396-7

Johnson, F., & Whitney, O. (2005). Singing-driven gene expression in the developing songbird brain. *Physiology and Behavior, 86*, 390–398. https://doi.org/10.1016/j.physbeh.2005.08.009

Kaminski, J., Call, J., & Fischer, J. (2004). Word learning in a domestic dog: Evidence for "fast mapping". *Science, 304*, 1682–1683. https://doi.org/10.1126/science.1097859

Karakashian, S. J., Gyger, M., & Marler, P. (1988). Audience effects on alarm calling in chickens (*Gallus gallus*). *Journal of Comparative Psychology, 107*, 129–135. https://doi.org/10.1037/0735-7036.102.2.129

King, A. P., & West, M. J. (1983). Epigenesis of cowbird song: A joint endeavor of males and females. *Nature, 305*, 704–706. https://doi.org/10.1038/305704a0

Konishi, M. (1963). The role of auditory feedback in the vocal behaviour of the domestic fowl. *Zeitschrift für Tierpsychologie, 20*, 349–367. https://doi.org/10.1111/j.1439-0310.1963.tb01156.x

Konishi, M. (1964). Effects of deafening on song development in two species of juncos. *Condor, 66*, 85–102. https://doi.org/10.2307/1365388

Konishi, M. (1965). The role of auditory feedback in the control of vocalization in the white-crowned sparrow. *Zeitschrift für Tierpsychologie, 22*, 770–783. https://doi.org/10.1111/j.1439-0310.1965.tb01688.x

Kopuchian, C., Lijtmaer, D. A., Tubaro, P. L., & Handford, P. (2004). Temporal stability and change in a microgeographical pattern of song variation in the rufous-collared sparrow. *Animal Behaviour, 68*, 551–559. https://doi.org/10.1016/j.anbehav.2003.10.025

Kroodsma, D. E. (1984). Songs of the alder flycatcher (*Empidonax alnorum*) and willow flycatcher (*Empidonax traillii*) are innate. *Auk, 101*, 13–24. https://doi.org/10.1093/auk/101.1.13

Kuchta, S. R., Krakauer, A. H., & Sinervo, B. (2008). Why does the yellow-eyed Ensatina have yellow eyes? Batesian mimicry of Pacific newts (genus *Taricha*) by the salamander *Ensatina eschscholtzii xanthoptica*. *Evolution, 62*(4), 984–990. https://doi.org/10.1111/j.1558-5646.2008.00338.x

Lachlan, R. F., Ratmann, O., & Nowicki, S. (2018). Cultural conformity generates extremely stable traditions in bird song. *Nature Communications, 9*, 2417. https://doi.org/10.1038/s41467-018-04728-1

Lipp, H. P., & Bonfanti, L. (2016). Adult neurogenesis in mammals: Variations and confusions. *Brain, Behavior and Evolution, 87*(3), 205–221. https://doi.org/10.1159/000446905

Lipshutz, S. E., Overcast, I. A., Hickerson, M. J., Brumfield, R. T., & Derryberry, E. P. (2016). Behavioural response to song and genetic divergence in two subspecies of white-crowned sparrows (*Zonotrichia leucophrys*). *Molecular Ecology, 26*, 3011–3027. https://doi.org/10.1111/mec.14002

Lovaas, O. I. (1987). Behavioral treatment and normal educational and intellectual functioning in young autistic children. *Journal of Consulting & Clinical Psychology, 55*, 3–9.

Maguire, S. E., Schmidt, M. F., & White, D. J. (2013). Social brains in context: Lesions targeted to the song control system in female cowbirds affect their social network. *PLoS One, 8*, e63239. https://doi.org/10.1371/journal.pone.0063239

Manabe, K., Dooling, R. J., & Brittan-Powell, E. F. (2008). Vocal learning in Budgerigars (*Melopsittacus undulatus*): Effects of an acoustic reference on vocal matching. *Journal of the Acoustical Society of America, 123*, 1729–1736. https://doi.org/10.1121/1.2835440

Marek, P. E., & Bond, J. E. (2009). A Müllerian mimicry ring in Appalachian millipedes. *Proceedings of the National Academy of Sciences, U.S.A., 106*(24), 9755–9760. https://doi.org/10.1073/pnas.0810408106

Marler, P. (1970). A comparative approach to vocal learning: Song development in white-crowned sparrows. *Journal of Comparative and Physiological Psychology Monograph*, *71*(No. 2, Part 2), 1–25. https://doi.org/10.1037/h0029144
Marler, P. (1991). Differences in behavioural development in closely related species: Birdsong. In P. Bateson (Ed.), *The development and integration of behaviour. Essays in honour of Robert Hinde* (pp. 41–70). Cambridge University Press.
Marler, P., Dufty, A., & Pickert, R. (1986). Vocal communication in the domestic chicken: I. Does a sender communicate information about the quality of a food referent to a receiver? *Animal Behaviour*, *34*, 188–193. https://doi.org/10.1016/0003-3472(86)90022–9
Marler, P., & Sherman, V. (1983). Song structure without auditory feedback: Emendations of the auditory template hypothesis. *Journal of Neuroscience*, *3*, 517–531. https://doi.org/10.1016/1044-5765(92)90050-C
Marler, P., & Tamura, M. (1964). Culturally transmitted patterns of vocal behavior in sparrows. *Science*, *146*, 1483–1486. https://doi.org/10.1126/science.146.3650.1483
Mello, C. V., Vicario, D. S., & Clayton, D. F. (1992). Song presentation induces gene expression in the songbird forebrain. *Proceedings of the National Academy of Sciences, U.S.A.*, *89*, 6818–6822. https://doi.org/10.1073/pnas.89.15.6818
Miles, H. L. W. (1990). The cognitive foundations for reference in a signing orangutan. In S. T. Parker & K. R. Gibson (Eds.), *Language and intelligence in monkeys and apes: Comparative developmental perspectives* (pp. 511–539). Cambridge University Press.
Mitani, J. C., & Brandt, K. L. (1994). Social factors influence the acoustic variability in the long-distance calls of male chimpanzees. *Ethology*, *96*, 233–252.
Moffatt, C. A., & Hogan, J. A. (1992). Ontogeny of chick responses to maternal food calls in the Burmese red junglefowl (*Gallus gallus spadiceus*). *Journal of Comparative Psychology*, *106*, 92–96. https://doi.org/10.1037/0735-7036.106.1.92
Nottebohm, F. (1969). The song of the chingolo, *Zonotrichia capensis*, in Argentina: Description and evaluation of a system of dialects. *Condor*, *71*, 299–315. https://doi.org/10.2307/1366306
Nottebohm, F., & Liu, W. C. (2010). The origins of vocal learning: New sounds, new circuits, new cells. *Brain and Language*, *115*, 3–17. https://doi.org/10.1016/j.bandl.2010.05.002
Nowicki, S., Searcy, W. A., & Peters, S. (2002). Brain development, song learning, and mate choice in birds: A review and experimental test of the "nutritional stress hypothesis." *Journal of Comparative Physiology A*, *188*, 1003–1014. https://doi.org/10.1007/s00359-002-0361-3
Papini, M. R. (2021). *Comparative psychology. Evolution and development of brain and behavior*. Taylor & Francis.
Patterson, F. L. (1990). Language acquisition by a lowland gorilla: Koko's first ten years of vocabulary development. *Word*, *41*, 97–143. https://doi.org/10.1080/00437956.1990.11435816
Pierce, J. (1985). A review of attempts to condition operantly alloprimate vocalizations. *Primates*, *26*, 202–213.
Pepperberg, I. M. (1993). Cognition and communication in an African Grey parrot (Psittacus erithacus): Studies on a nonhuman, nonprimate, nonmammalian subject. In H. L. Roitblat, L. M. Herman, & P. E. Nachtigall (Eds.), *Language and communication: Comparative perspectives* (pp. 221–248). Erlbaum.
Pepperberg, I. M. (2017). Animal language studies: What happened? *Psychonomic Bulletin and Review*, *24*, 181–185. https://doi.org/10.3758/s13423-016-1101-y
Peters, S., Searcy, W. A., & Nowicki, S. (2014). Developmental stress, song-learning, and cognition. *Integrative and Comparative Biology*, *54*, 555–567. https://doi.org/10.1093/icb/icu020
Premack, D. (1976). *Intelligence in ape and man*. Erlbaum.
Price, T., Wadewitz, P., Cheney, D., Seyfarth, R., Hammerschmidt, K., & Fischer, J. (2015). Vervets revisited: A quantitative analysis of alarm call structure and context specificity. *Science Reports*, *5*, 13220. https://doi.org/10.1038/srep13220
Rivas, E. (2005). Recent use of signs by chimpanzees (Pan troglodytes) in interactions with humans. *Journal of Comparative Psychology*, *119*(4), 404–417. https://doi.org/10.1037/0735-7036.119.4.404
Rossi, A. P., & Ades, C. (2008). A dog at the keyboard: Using arbitrary signs to communicate requests. *Animal Cognition*, *11*, 329–338. https://doi.org/10.1007/s10071-007-0122-3
Savage-Rumbaugh, E. S., Murphy, J., Sevcik, R. A., Brakke, K. E., Williams, S. L., & Rumbaugh, D. M. (1993). Language comprehension in ape and child. *Monographs of the Society for Research in Child Development*, *58*(3–4), No. 233.

Savage-Rumbaugh, E. S., Rumbaugh, D. M., & Boysen, S. (1978). Symbolic communication between two chimpanzees (*Pan troglodytes*). *Science*, *201*, 641–644. https://doi.org/10.1126/science.675251
Schusterman, R. J., & Krieger, K. (1984). California sea lions are capable of semantic comprehension. *Psychological Record*, *34*, 3–23. https://doi.org/10.1007/BF03394849
Segerdahl, P., Fields, W., & Savage-Rumbaugh, S. (2005). *Kanzi's primal language. The cultural initiation of primates into language*. Palgrave Macmillan.
Seyfarth, R. M., & Cheney, D. L. (2010). Production, usage, and comprehension in animal vocalizations. *Brain and Language*, *115*(1), 92–100. https://doi.org/10.1016/j.bandl.2009.10.003
Seyfarth, R. M., Cheney, D. L., & Marler, P. (1980). Vervet monkeys alarm calls: Semantic communication in a free-ranging primate. *Animal Behaviour*, *28*, 1070–1094. https://doi.org/10.1016/S0003-3472(80)80097-2
Sibley, C. G., & Ahlquist, J. E. (1990). *Phylogeny and classification of birds. A study in molecular evolution*. Yale University Press.
Skinner, B. F. (1953). *Science and human behavior*. MacMillan.
Terrace, H. S. (1979). *Nim*. Knopf.
Terrace, H. S., Petitto, L. A., Sanders, R. J., & Bever, T. G. (1979). Can an ape create a sentence? *Science*, *206*, 891–902. https://doi.org/10.1126/science.504995
Thompson, C. K., Meitzen, J., Replogle, K., Drnevich, J., Lent, K. L., Wissman, A. M., Farin, F. M., Bammler, T. K., Beyer, R. P., Clayton, D. F., Perkel, D. J., & Brenowitz, E. A. (2012). Seasonal changes in patterns of gene expression in avian song control brain regions. *PLoS One*, *7*, e35119. https://doi.org/10.1371/journal.pone.0035119
Thorpe, W. H. (1961). *Bird song*. Cambridge University Press.
Tubaro, P. L., Segura, E. T., & Handford, P. (1993). Geographic variation in the song of the rufous-collared sparrow in eastern Argentina. *Condor*, *95*, 588–595. https://doi.org/10.2307/1369603
West, M. J., & King, A. P. (1988). Female visual displays affect the development of male song in the cowbird. *Nature*, *334*, 244–246. https://doi.org/10.1038/334244a0
West, M. J., King, A. P., & Eastzer, D. H. (1981). The cowbird: Reflections on development from an unlikely source. *American Scientist*, *69*, 56–66.
Yerkes, R. M. (1916). *The mental life of monkeys and apes*. Holt.

Name index

Note: Page numbers in *italics* indicate a figure on the corresponding page.

Subject index

Note: Page numbers in *italics* indicate a figure and page numbers in **bold** indicate a table on the corresponding page.

For Product Safety Concerns and Information please contact our EU representative GPSR@taylorandfrancis.com Taylor & Francis Verlag GmbH, Kaufingerstraße 24, 80331 München, Germany